STALIN AND HIS HANGMEN

THE TYRANT AND THOSE WHO KILLED FOR HIM

STA

RANDOM HOUSE - NEW YORK

LIN

AND HIS HANGMEN

DONALD RAYFIELD

LIBRARY OF CONGRESS CATALOGING-IN-PUBLICATION DATA

This work was originally published in Great Britain by Viking,
a division of Penguin UK, in 2004.

Rayfield, Donald.
Stalin and his hangmen : the tyrant and those who killed for him/Donald Rayfield.
p.   cm.
Includes bibliographical references and index.
ISBN 0-375-50632-2
1. Soviet Union—Politics and government—1917–1936.   2. Soviet Union—Politics and
government—1936–1953.   3. Stalin, Joseph, 1879–1953.   4. Kommunisticheskaëi partiëi
Sovetskogo Soiuza—Purges—History.   5. Soviet Union. Narodnyæ komissariat vnutrennikh
del—History.   6. Political atrocities—Soviet Union.   I. Title.

DK268.4.R39 2004
947.084'092'2—dc22   2004042833

Allen Knechtschaffenen
An alle Himmel schreib ich's an,
die diesen Ball umspannen:
Nicht der Tyrann ist ein schimpflicher Mann,
aber der Knecht des Tyrannen.

To All the Enslaved
I write it all over the heavens
That encompass our earthly sphere:
It's not the tyrant we should abuse,
But the serf who works for the tyrant.

Christian Morgenstern

PREFACE

Everything might have come right in the course of time.
Russian life could have been pulled into order. . . . What
bitch woke up Lenin? Who couldn't bear the child sleeping?

There is no precise answer to this question. . . .

Anyway, he himself probably didn't know, although his
supply of vengeance never dried up. . . . And spiteful in his
failure, he immediately started a revolution for all, so that
nobody escaped punishment.

And our fathers followed him to Golgothas with banners
and songs. . . .

In Russia you mustn't wake anybody.

Naum Korzhavin

I have tried, rather than write a new biography of Stalin or another history of the USSR, to examine Stalin's path to total power and the means—and the men—which enabled him to hold on to it. The careers and personalities of Stalin's henchmen occupy the foreground, especially the five who headed the security forces and secret police which we call by a sequence of different names: the Cheka (Extraordinary Commission), GPU and OGPU ([United] State Political Directorate), NKVD (People's Commissariat of Internal Affairs), MVD (Ministry of Internal Affairs), and MGB (Ministry of State Security). After Stalin, the latter became known as the KGB and is today the Russian FSB.

Of these five—Feliks Dzierżyński, Viacheslav Menzhinsky, Genrikh Iagoda, Nikolai Ezhov, and Lavrenti Beria—the last two were appointed by Stalin, while the first three were induced to do his bidding. They were the instruments of a mind more malevolent than theirs. They looked after the means, while Stalin looked after the end. A study of their motivations and actions sheds a strong light on Stalin's tyranny.

The Nuremberg trials established the principle that obeying orders is no defense against charges of crimes against humanity. There is a moral, not just a legal and tactical, aspect to obeying orders, even if disobedience is fatal. What Stalin's and Hitler's henchmen lacked was a social or moral structure firm enough to induce them to disobey. Goldhagen's *Hitler's Willing Executioners,* a much criticized but important book, established (a) that the murder of the Jews was known to most Germans and (b) that involvement was not required on pain of death, at least for most who participated in this genocide. Goldhagen's thesis needs revision if we apply it to Stalin's Soviet Union. Abstaining from the witch hunt for enemies, real or imaginary—bourgeois, Trotskyists, Bukharinites, saboteurs, fascists, Zionists—would have classed the dissenter as an enemy. But there were situations and spheres of activity in which a moral choice was offered, particularly for intellectuals, who were, admittedly, the state's dependents and servants, but who had been brought up to follow professional and ethical codes, and who knew or guessed what was happening. As in Nazi Germany, a few individuals stood their ground against threats, privations, torture, and death. But why so few, and why did Stalin, supported by a group of fanatics, cynics, sadists, and moral cowards, never encounter serious resistance?

Stalin valued in his underlings the ability to choose managers and executives; he himself excelled at personnel management. As well as the heads of the secret police, others in Stalin's close circle—after 1930, when he no longer compromised with other politicians—were as impenetrably callous as Dzierżyński and his successors. We must delve deeply into the activities of Viacheslav Molotov, Lazar Kaganovich, and Klim Voroshilov, who signed death warrants by the thousand, for without their spellbound submission Stalin could not have done what he did.

Parallel study of Stalin and Hitler often misleads. The differences are as striking as the similarities. The Nazis had a symbiotic relationship with German business and the German army, and their murderous aggression was directed at others, whether Slav or Jew, homosexual or communist. An ordinary German citizen wearing large blinkers could, making allowances for the horrors of total war, live much as he or she had under other regimes. Stalin's aggression turned on his own kind: loath to make war on his neighbors, he would murder his own generals, his professional elite, even his own family—people on whom his economic and political lifeblood depended. However revolting, there is consistency, even logic, in Adolf Hitler's gamble: genocide and blitzkrieg united a people and gave it goals. Stalin's policies dragged others deep into his paranoia. An amoral intellect like Albert Speer's could throw in his lot with Hitler; mere calculation was not enough for throwing in your lot with Stalin it needed extreme fear, sadism, moral idiocy, or delusion as well.

Every country has a heritage which its heirs cannot easily renounce, but Russia's fate in the twentieth century cannot be dismissed as that of a barbarous, semifeudal country erupting into primeval violence. Russia in the 1900s and 1910s lagged behind the rest of Europe economically; its political institutions had grave flaws. But the culture that gave the world novelists like Fiodor Dostoevsky and Leo Tolstoi also had historians, newspaper magnates, philosophers, lawyers, doctors, and politicians the equal of any in the world. It had a small, highly motivated middle and professional class, as well as a gentry and merchant class that had not lost its social coherence. Nineteenth-century Russia was more brutal, corrupt, and ignorant than England or France, but not by many orders of magnitude.

What was done to innocent victims in the USSR is not unique to totalitarian regimes; the difference is that it was done at home, to those of the same national group. The British committed atrocities on the other side of the world: they founded concentration camps in the Transvaal, the Andaman Islands, and Kenya, and mined African tin with forced labor. King Leopold II of Belgium killed and maimed as large a proportion of the Congolese as Stalin did of the Russians. Absolute power corrupts absolutely, and when the fabric of a complex society is torn to shreds by world war, famine, and emigration, absolute power falls into the hands of whoever grabs it.

Historians must learn from zoology: nothing is more violent than a large group of chimpanzees or baboons when short of food or territory under the leadership of an alpha male. Life is "solitary, poor, nasty, brutish, and short," to quote Thomas Hobbes, when a society loses the complex play of forces—judiciary, army, executive, public opinion, religion, culture—that keep each other in check, and both anarchy and

tyranny at bay. Russia and Germany were unlucky in that evil geniuses—
Vladimir Ilyich Lenin and Hitler—seized power when world war and
pariah status in the postwar world had left their countries shattered.
And even in a society protected by a balance of authorities, enough people can be found in a small town to staff Auschwitz, as the American
psychologist Stanley Milgram proved. In the 1960s Milgram had no
trouble inducing two thirds of volunteers from the public to obey men in
white overalls and administer what they were told were lethal electric
shocks to actors pretending to be inadequate pupils in a game of
"teacher and pupil."

In Germany, "Holocaust deniers" have no credibility outside a lunatic fringe. The last articulate writer to deny Hitler's Holocaust, David
Irving, does however serve one useful purpose: he forces historians to
marshal their facts again and tell the story more cogently than before, in
order to silence him. But people still deny by assertion or implication,
and not only in Russia, Stalin's holocaust.

The Nuremberg trials, however many criminals escaped judgment,
began a process of rehabilitation for Germany. In the USSR, neither the
shooting of a dozen of Beria's men, nor Nikita Khrushchiov's twentieth
Communist Party congress speech of 1956 brought the Soviet population face-to-face with the realities of the past. The guilty were, by and
large, not brought to account nor even removed from power. Despite all
the revelations in ten years of perestroika, Stalinism remains a deep-
seated infection in Russia's body politic, liable to flare up at any crisis.
Vladimir Putin's Russia has rejoined the world community but it does
not so much deny as set aside Stalin's holocaust, by celebrating Stalin instead as the architect of victory and the KGB as Russia's samurai. The
mayor of Moscow has proposed reerecting the statue of Dzierżyński opposite the Lubianka. In 2002, without comment abroad or at home, the
Russian post office issued a set of stamps, "The 80th Anniversary of Soviet Counterintelligence": the stamps show Artur Artuzov né Frautschi,
one of the most dreaded OGPU leaders in the early 1920s; Sergei Puzit-
sky, who organized the killing of half a million Cossacks in 1931;
Vladimir Styrne, who slaughtered thousands of Uzbeks in the 1920s;
Vsevolod Balitsky, who purged the Ukraine and enslaved the Soviet
peasantry. Imagine the uproar if Germany issued stamps commemorat-

ing Reinhard Heydrich, Heinrich Himmler, and Adolf Eichmann. Nobody in Germany smokes "Auschwitz" cigarettes but Belomorkanal cigarettes, commemorating a camp where 100,000 were exterminated, are still sold in Russia. The city of Dzerzhinsk, appropriately the most polluted township in the world, still commemorates Feliks Dzierżyński. (Admittedly, there is a sprinkling of rues Robespierres in France—another case of pride in the atrocities of the past.) How can Stalin and his hangmen be exorcised if we fail to take heed when George W. Bush and Tony Blair drink beer with Putin and the Russian army carries on Beria's genocidal work in Chechnya?

A new focus is one reason for writing this book; a second is the flood of material. Like the Nazis, the Stalinists left a trail of paper behind their most shameful crimes. In 1989 the Soviet archives, themselves under the control of the KGB, opened their doors to researchers, foreign and Soviet. In the early 1990s both the Presidential Archive and even the KGB's offered access. For most researchers, the State Archive of Social-Political History (formerly the Communist Party Archives, then the Russian Center for the Preservation and Study of Documents of Modern History) and the State Archive of the Russian Federation have been the richest resources. Recently the Presidential Archive has declassified less and less, and restricted access, while the new FSB opens its archives only to the families of the repressed or to its former employees.

I have relied on my own research in these archives and others (the Georgian Central State Archive, the Russian State Archive of Literature and Art) and a few private holdings, notably the surviving Nestor Lakoba Archive (now acquired by the Hoover Institute). There is enough material for seven maids with seven mops for seven thousand years, and much remains unexplored, particularly since archival catalogues give only the vaguest indication of what anything may hold.

Fortunately, several dozen dedicated and ill-rewarded Russian historians have published in the last decade some 200 important monographs and many hundreds of articles, and these I have drawn on, in some cases heavily. The most important are compilations of formerly inaccessible documents—unedited records of Central Committee meetings and Politburo discussions, telegrams, telephone calls, and letters from and to Stalin (particularly to his inner circle), NKVD indictments, interrogations, and sentences, biographical records of hundreds of NKVD men, correspondence of intellectuals, economists, and scientists, diaries, OGPU and NKVD reports of public and private opinion, and so on.

In using articles and monographs, one must bear in mind the bias and background of the writer, and Russian and Western historians fall into several categories. The rarest and most valuable group gives a presentation as objective as possible of the material, and suggests rather than imposes an interpretation of the relative weight to be attached to, or the reasons behind, events. These include, above all, Oleg Khlevniuk and A. I. Kokurin; Aleksandr Ostrovsky, the author of a pioneering study of the early Stalin, *Kto stoial za spinoi Stalina* (*Who Backed Stalin?*); K. A. Zalessky, who compiled a biographical encyclopedia, *Imperia Stalina: biograficheskii èntsiklopedicheskii slovar* (*Stalin's Empire*); the biographers of Ezhov, Marc Janson, and Nikita Petrov; the latter, with Skorkin, co-author of the biographical reference work *Kto rukovodil NKVD 1934–1941 spravochnik* (*Who Ran the NKVD 1934–1941*); and Michael Parrish, who followed up Robert Conquest with his *The Lesser Terror.*

A valuable group arranges original material to make a good story: Leonid Mlechin, Kirill Stoliarov, Arkadi Vaksberg, Vitali Shentalinsky, Boris Sokolov, the late Dmitri Volkogonov.

Another useful group comprises those who were personally involved, either as victims or relatives of the victims, or oppressors or their children. They have information and sometimes access denied to others; they have axes, some good, to grind. Former KGB operatives have access to otherwise closed archives, but a lifetime devoted to disinformation imposes caution on the reader.

To be used with great reserve are historians with an ideological position. Some of the most prolific and cogent, such as the late Vadim Rogovin, believe that Stalin has to be understood as a betrayer of Leninism-Trotskyism. Others, such as Valeri Shambarov, believe the West to bear responsibility for destroying Russia in 1917, 1941, and 1991.

Western historians naturally lag behind but have written a number of peerless works. Forty years later, Robert Conquest's *The Great Terror* remains a classic. Though his sources were a tiny fraction of today's in quantity, Conquest got it right. Catherine Merridale's chronicle of death and mourning, *Night of Stones,* and Simon Sebag-Montefiore's *Stalin:*

The Court of the Red Tsar show that non-Russian writers can provide insights as deep as any native historian or sociologist.

The only useless works are those that justify Stalin's ways. The majority (both in titles and print runs) of works in Russian bookshops today belong to this category. Some authors, like Iuri Mukhin, even assert that the Katyn forest massacres were carried out by the Nazis.

Documents can lie, and rumors can tell the truth. A number of issues, such as Stalin's part in the deaths of Mikhail Frunze, Sergei Kirov, and Sergo Orjonikidze, the degree of initiative shown by henchmen such as Ezhov, and the motivation for Beria's sea change in March 1953, need a juror's intuition as much as a judge's trained logic to resolve. I have tried to indicate degrees of certainty in a legalistic way. First comes "beyond reasonable doubt," in other words, sufficient to secure conviction in a criminal court. An example is Stalin and Viktor Abakumov's murder of Solomon Mikhoels. Second comes the "balance of probabilities" sufficient to decide a civil case (for instance, the poisoning of Nestor Lakoba by Beria). Third are cases in which there is sufficient evidence to begin a prosecution (Stalin's plans to deport the Jews en masse) but not to reach a conclusion. Fourth, as in the murder of Kirov, the evidence suffices to begin an investigation but not to prosecute. Fifth is *se non è vero, è ben trovato,* in which, with or without regret, our suspicions have to be discarded (for example, Molotov's assertion that a real military coup was planned by Marshal Mikhail Tukhachevsky).

The bibliography, as well as remarks in the text and notes, shows not just sources, but the degree of my reliance on, and trust in, them. Sources have been referenced to original language sources, printed or archival. In some cases, where the source is readily identifiable, I have not always given detailed references: for instance, a letter from Stalin to Lazar Kaganovich or Molotov on a specific date will be found quickly in editions of Stalin's correspondence with these associates.

Russian names are presented in a slightly simplified readable version of the standard Anglo-American system; Polish spellings are used for Poles, and Georgian names are transliterated directly from Georgian. Thus we have Dzierżyński, not Dzerzhinsky, Jughashvili, not Dzhugashvili. All translations are my own, unless otherwise indicated.

ACKNOWLEDGMENTS

I have many people to thank for their assistance: among them Mikhail Voroshilov in the Russian State Archive of Social-Political History, Natalia Volkova in the Russian State Archive of Literature and Art, and Rezo Kverenchkhiladze of the Georgian Union of Writers. The staff of the Memorial Society in Moscow, as well as the manuscript department of the Russian State Library, and the Russian National Library in St. Petersburg who compiled the *Leningrad Martyrology,* have been very helpful, as has Memed Jikhashvili of Batum. Olga Makarova, Vika Musvik, and other friends located ephemeral periodical material I would have missed otherwise. Boris Ravdin helped me with texts in Latvian, as well as with certain sources. Anna Pilkington lent me help, linguistic and ideological, with hundreds of bits of text, not to mention an objective critical eye.

CONTENTS

Contents

LIST OF ILLUSTRATIONS

Section One

1. "Koba" Stalin, police photograph, Baku, 1910
2. Suren Spandaryan and Koba, c. 1911
3. Stalin with fellow exiles, Monastyrskoe (Siberia), July 1915
4. Dzierżyński, Peterss, and senior *chekisty*, 1918
5. Dzicrżyński's funeral, 1926
6. Menzhinsky with his first wife, Iulia; his two daughters; and his son, Rudolf, Iaroslavl, 1904
7. Menzhinsky in the Cheka, c. 1919
8. American Relief Agency clinic, Volga famine, 1921
9. Stalin, Rykov, Zinoviev, and Bukharin at dacha, 1924
10. Sergei Kirov and Sergo Orjonikidze, north Caucasus, 1920
11. Trotsky, Kamenev, and Zinoviev, mid-1920s
12. Delivering prisoners to the Lubianka, 1928
13. Boris Savinkov, 1922
14. Menzhinsky, 1925
15. Menzhinsky's funeral, 1934
16. Stalin relaxing at dacha, c. 1930
17. Mayakovsky shortly after his suicide, 1930
18. Pavel Dybenko and Aleksandra Kollontai with Dybenko's sister and parents, 1918

Section Two

19. Genrikh Iagoda and Maxim Gorky, 1934
20. Famine, Kharkov province, 1932
21. Stalin and Voroshilov fishing, Abkhazia, 1933
22. Stalin and his second wife, Nadezhda Allilueva-Stalina, c. 1928
23. Stalin, his daughter, Svetlana, and second son, Vasili, 1936

Section Three

Illustration Acknowledgments

Except where indicated in the following list, all the photographs are reproduced courtesy of the David King Archive, London.

3. from Ostrovsky, Aleksandr, *Kto stoial za spinoi Stalina,* St. Petersburg, Neva, 2002
13. from Litvin, A. L. et al. (eds.), *Boris Savinkov na Lubianke. Dokumenty*
18. from Kollontai, A. M., *Diplomaticheskie dnevniki,* Moscow, Academia, 2001
21, 24, 44, 45, 46. from Lakoba Archive, Hoover Institute, Stanford, California, courtesy of Memed Jikhashvili
25. from Chuev, Feliks, *Molotov: poluderzhavnyi vlastelin,* Moscow, Olma, 2002
26, 27, 28. from Kirilina, Alla, *Neizvestnyi Kirov,* St. Petersburg, Neva, 2001

CHRONOLOGY

Date	Russian and Soviet History	Stalin and His Hangmen
1874		Menzhinsky born
1877	Russo-Turkish war	Dzierżyński born
1878		Stalin born
1881	Tsar Alexander II murdered	Voroshilov born
1887		Lenin's brother hanged
1889		Mekhlis born
1890		Molotov born
1891	Volga famine begins	Iagoda born
1893	Franco-Russian entente	Lazar Kaganovich born
1895		Nikolai Ezhov born
1896	Tsar Nicolas II crowned	Dzierżyński's mother dies
1897		Lenin sent to Siberia
1899		Beria born; Stalin expelled from seminary
1900		Lenin leaves for Europe
1903	Bolsheviks split from socialists	
1904	Russo-Japanese war begins	
1905	Uprisings in Russia; constitution	
1906		Menzhinsky leaves for exile
1907	Second and third Dumas convened	Stalin's first wife dies
1908		Stalin in prison with Vyshinsky
1909		Stalin's father dies
1911	Prime Minister Stolypin murdered	Peterss acquitted of murders
1912	Fourth Duma convened	Lenin founds *Pravda;* Stalin co-opted to Central Committee

1913	Strikes in major Russian cities	Stalin sent to Siberia
1914	First World War begins	
1916		Iagoda's brother shot
1917	Tsar abdicates March; Bolsheviks overthrow provisional government November	Stalin in Politburo; Dzierżyński heads Cheka
1918	Treaty of Brest-Litovsk signed; Bliumkin kills Count Mirbach	Lenin fired on
1919	Petrograd defended from Whites	Stalin and Dzierżyński in Perm
1920	War with Poland; Bolsheviks win civil war	
1921	Georgia invaded; Kronstadt rebellion; Volga famine	Iagoda deputy to Menzhinsky; Nikolai Ezhov's first party job
1922	New Economic Plan begins; Rapallo Treaty	Stalin general secretary; Menzhinsky crushes Church and deports academics
1923	Warsaw citadel blown up	Lenin incapacitated
1924	"Socialism in one country"	Lenin dies; USSR founded
1925	Bukharin tells peasants, "Get rich!"	Savinkov falls to his death
1926		Dzierżyński dies; Zinoviev ousted
1927	Communists in Shanghai killed	Trotsky expelled from party
1928	Shakhty trial	Trotsky exiled
1929	Collectivization begins; first five-year plan implemented	Trotsky deported from USSR; Bukharin ousted
1930	After pause, elimination of kulaks	Menzhinsky "tries" Prompartiia
1932	Second five-year plan	Stalin's second wife kills herself
1933	Famine in Volga, Ukraine, Kuban	
1934	USSR joins League of Nations; Union of Writers meets	Menzhinsky dies; Kirov murdered

1935	Rationing ends	Iagoda general secretary of NKVD
1936	Soviet constitution promulgated; Gorky dies	Kamenev, Zinoviev shot; Ezhov takes over NKVD; Lakoba killed
1937	USSR intervenes in Spanish civil war; February–March plenum starts purges	Army purged; Great Terror starts; Orjonikidze dies
1938	Czechoslovakia invaded; Mandelstam dies in camp	Bukharin, Iagoda shot; Beria takes over NKVD
1939	Molotov–Ribbentrop pact; Hitler and Stalin invade Poland	
1940	Baltic states invaded; Finland attacked	Ezhov shot; Trotsky murdered; Katyn forest massacres; Babel, Mikhail Koltsov shot
1941	Hitler attacks USSR	Merkulov runs MGB
1942	Battle of Stalingrad	
1943	Kursk victory; Comintern abolished	Abakumov runs SMERSH
1944	Warsaw uprising; Baltic states reoccupied	Deportations of Tatars, Kalmyks, Chechens, Karachai, etc.
1945	Berlin falls	Stalin takes first holiday in nine years
1946	Nuremberg trials; Fulton speech	Abakumov takes over MGB; Zhdanov attacks poets
1947	Communist coups in east Europe; Death penalty suspended	Malenkov sent to Kazakhstan
1948	USSR quarrels with Yugoslavia	Mikhoels murdered; Zhdanov dies
1949	Soviet atomic test; NATO born; Vyshinsky foreign minister	Leningrad party purged
1950	Korean War; Death penalty returns	

1951		Riumin arrests Abakumov; Rukhadze arrests Beria's men
1952	Czech communists hanged	Kremlin doctors arrested
1953		Stalin dies March 5; Beria arrested June, shot December
1954		Riumin and Abakumov shot
1955	Malenkov ousted by Bulganin	Rukhadze shot
1956	Khrushchiov's "de-Stalinization"	Rodos, last Beria man, shot

ONE

THE LONG ROAD TO POWER

O muse, today sing of Jughashvili, the son of
a bitch,
He has artfully combined the donkey's
stubbornness and the fox's cunning,
By cutting a million nooses he has made his
way to power.

Pavel Vasiliev [1]

Childhood and Family

Instead of saying something like "X was raised by croco-
diles in a septic tank in Kuala Lumpur," they tell you about
a mother, a father . . .

Martin Amis, Koba the Dread

IN THE RUSSIAN EMPIRE, especially Georgia, 1878 was not a bad year to
bring a child into the world. True, Georgians of all classes seethed with
resentment. Their Russian overlords, into whose hands the last Georgian
kings had surrendered their shattered realm at the beginning of the nineteenth century, ruled the country through a bureaucracy that was often
callous, corrupt, and ignorant, while those Georgian children who went
to school were instructed in Russian. The Russian viceroy in Tbilisi,
however humane and liberal, was determined to keep things as they
were: Armenians ran commerce, foreign capitalists controlled industry,
while Georgian aristocrats and peasants, upstaged in their own capital
city, led a more or less tolerable life in the fertile countryside.

Georgians had some reasons to be grateful for Russian rule. For
nearly a century Georgia had been free of the invasions and raids by its
neighbors that had devastated and periodically nearly annihilated the
nation since the thirteenth century. Russians might impose punitive
taxes, Siberian exile, and cultural humiliation, but, unlike the Turks, they
did not decapitate the entire male population of villages and, unlike the
Persians, they did not drive away the survivors of massacres to be cas-
trated, enslaved, and forcibly converted to Islam. Under Russian rule
towns had been rebuilt and railways linked the capital to the Black Sea,
and thus the outside world. The capital city, Tbilisi, had newspapers and
an opera house (even if it had no university). A new generation of Georgians, forced to become fluent in Russian, realized the dreams of their
ancestors: they were now treated as Europeans, they could study in Eu-

ropean universities and become doctors, lawyers, diplomats—and revolutionaries. Many Georgians dreamed of regaining independent statehood; so far, few believed that they should work toward this by violence. Most Georgians in the 1870s grudgingly accepted Russian domination as the price of exchanging their Asiatic history for a European culture.

For the inhabitants of the empire's metropolis, St. Petersburg, 1878 was a year that threatened to totter into anarchy. The terrorists who would kill Tsar Alexander II in 1881 were already tasting blood: the honeymoon between the Russian government and its intellectuals and new professional classes was over. The seeds of revolution found fertile ground not in the impoverished peasantry nor in the slums that housed the cities' factory workers, but among the frustrated educated children of the gentry and the clergy who were not content to demand just human rights and a constitution. They went further and were plotting the violent overthrow of the Russian state. Such extremism might be fanatical but was not unrealistic. A rigid state is easier to destroy than to reform, and the Russian state was so constructed that a well-placed batch of dynamite or a well-aimed revolver, by eliminating a handful of grand dukes and ministers, could bring it down. The weakness of the Russian empire lay in its impoverished social fabric: the state was held together by a vertical hierarchy, from Tsar to gendarme. In Britain or France society was held together by the warp and weft of institutions—judiciary, legislature, Church, local government. In Russia, where these institutions were only vestigial or embryonic, the fabric was single-ply.

The killers of Tsar Alexander II, the generation of Russian revolutionaries that preceded Lenin, saw this weakness but they had no popular support and no prospect of achieving mass rebellion. Russia in the 1880s and 1890s was generally perceived as stagnant, retrograde, even heartless and cynical—but stable. Episodes of famine, epidemics, and anti-Jewish progroms rightly gave Russia a bad international name in the 1880s. The 1860s and 1870s had been a period of reform, hope, and, above all, creativity: Fiodor Dostoevsky, Ivan Turgenev, Leo Tolstoi, and Nikolai Leskov were writing their greatest novels. But the zest was gone: only the music of Piotr Tchaikovsky and the chemistry of Dmitri Mendeleev testified to Russian civilization. Nevertheless, there was tranquillity in stagnation. This was the Russian empire's longest recorded period of peace. Between Russia's victory over Turkey in 1877 and its defeat by Japan in 1905, half a human lifetime would elapse.

Around the time Ioseb Jughashvili was born on December 6, 1878, in the flourishing town of Gori, forty miles west of Tbilisi, the atmosphere among the town's artisans, merchants, and intellectuals was quietly buoyant. A boy whose parents had a modest income could secure an education that would make a gentleman of him anywhere in the Russian empire. Few observers had cause to agree with the prophecies of Dostoevsky and the philosopher Vladimir Soloviov: that within forty years a Russian tyranny so violent and bloody would be unleashed that Genghis Khan's or Nadir Shah's invasions would pale into insignificance by comparison. Even less did anyone sense that Ioseb Jughashvili, as Joseph Stalin, would be instrumental in establishing this tyranny over the Russian empire and would then take sole control of it.

★ ★ ★ The family that begot Ioseb (Soso) Jughashvili had no more reason than other Georgians to fear the future. The cobbler Besarion Jughashvili was in 1878 twenty-eight years old, a skilled and successful artisan working for himself; he had been married six years to Katerine (Keke), who was now twenty-two. She was a peasant girl with strong aspirations, well brought up, and had even been taught to read and write by her grandfather. Their first two sons had died in infancy; this third son, by Georgian (and Russian) tradition, was a gift from God, to be offered back to God. Katerine Meladze's father had died before she was born, and she was brought up by her uncle, Petre Khomuridze. In the 1850s the Khomuridzes had been serfs from the village of Mejrokhe near Gori but in 1861 Tsar Alexander II made them, like all serfs, freemen. Petre Khomuridze, once freed, proved an enterprising patriarch: he raised his own child and the children of his widowed sister. Katerine's brothers Sandro and Gio became a potter and a tile-maker respectively; when Katerine became a cobbler's wife, all the Meladze siblings had succeeded in rising from peasant to artisan status.

The family of Stalin's father Besarion seemed to be on the same upward course. Stalin's paternal great-grandfather, Zaza Jughashvili, had also lived near Gori, in a largely Osetian village.[2] Zaza was also a serf. He took part in an anti-Russian rebellion in the 1800s, escaped retribution and was resettled, thanks to a charitable feudal prince, in a hovel in the windswept and semi-deserted village of Didi Lilo, ten miles north of Tbilisi. Here Zaza's son Vano moved up the social ladder: he owned a vineyard. Zaza's two grandchildren Giorgi and Besarion seemed destined to climb further. After Vano's death, Giorgi became an innkeeper but their rise to prosperity was brutally interrupted: Stalin's uncle Giorgi was killed by robbers, and his younger brother Besarion, destitute, left for Tbilisi to be a cobbler. By 1870 the Jughashvilis had resumed their climb: working for an Armenian bootmaker, Besarion acquired not only his craft, but learned to speak some Russian, Armenian, and Azeri Turkish, as well as Georgian. Unlike most Georgian artisans at that time, Besarion was literate.

One in three great dictators, artists, or writers witness before adolescence the death, bankruptcy, or disabling of their fathers. Stalin, like Napoleon, Dickens, Ibsen, and Chekhov, was the son of a man who climbed halfway up the social ladder and then fell off. Why did Besarion Jughashvili fail, when everything seemed to favor a man of his origins and skills? Contemporaries recall little of Besarion. One remembers that the Jughashvilis never had to pawn or sell anything. Another remembers: "When Soso's father Besarion came home, we avoided playing in the room. Besarion was a very odd person. He was of middling height, swarthy, with big black mustaches and long eyebrows, his expression was severe and he walked about looking gloomy."[3] Whatever the reasons, in 1884, when Stalin was six, Besarion's affairs went sharply downhill. The family moved house—nine times in ten years. The cobbler's workshop lost customers; Beso took to drink.

Early in 1890 the marriage of Stalin's parents broke up. This was the last year the young Stalin had any contact with his father: the twelve-year-old boy was run over by a carriage and his father and mother took him to Tbilisi for an operation. Besarion stayed in the capital, finding work at a shoe factory. When the boy recovered, Besarion gave him an ultimatum: either become an apprentice cobbler in Tbilisi or return to Gori, follow his mother's ambitions, train to be a priest, and be disowned by his father. Soso went back to school in Gori in autumn 1890. Besarion, after visits to Gori to beg Katerine to take him back, vanished.

(Stalin later stated in official depositions that his father had abandoned the family.) Besarion Jughashvili became an alcoholic tramp. On August 12, 1909, taken to the hospital from a Tbilisi rooming house, he died of liver cirrhosis. He was buried in an unmarked grave, mourned only by one fellow cobbler.[4]

Some Georgians found it hard to believe that Stalin could have such lowly origins: they speculated that Stalin was illegitimate, which would explain Besarion deserting his "unfaithful" wife and her offspring. Legend puts forward two putative fathers for Stalin: Nikolai Przhevalsky, explorer of central Asia, and a Prince Egnatashvili. It is true that Stalin physically resembled Przhevalsky but the latter was a misogynistic homosexual, camped on the Chinese border when Stalin was begotten. In Soviet times two Egnatashvili brothers, related to the priest who married both Stalin and Stalin's parents, and to the Prince Egnatashvili for whom Katerine allegedly did housework, led remarkably charmed lives. Stalin was frequently called a bastard and whoreson, but the abuse was figurative. Adultery in a small Georgian town was rare: Keke was a conventional, if strong-willed, wife and mother, and Ioseb was undoubtedly Besarion's son.

Stalin discouraged prying into his origins and was most evasive about his father; only in 1906 did he give him the most cursory acknowledgment when he briefly adopted a new pseudonym for his journalism: Besoshvili (son of Besarion). Katerine exerted a more prolonged influence on her son. She bequeathed her obstinacy in pursuing goals. Ruined then deserted, constantly moving house, demoted from artisan's wife to drudge, she nevertheless scraped together the money and cajoled the authorities to get her son off the streets and into school. By several accounts she beat Ioseb as often as Besarion did, but for nobler reasons. Religious piety and instinct told her that education, preferably directed at the priesthood, provided the only way in which her son could make his way in the world. Katerine was nothing if not single-minded; religion and her son were her only interests. Her sole surviving letter to Stalin, from the 1920s, shows how much she had in common with him: "My dear child Ioseb first of all I greet you with great love and wish you a long life and good health together with your good family. Child, I ask nature to give you complete victory and the annihilation of the enemy. . . . Be victorious!"[5]

If Stalin avoided speaking of his father, he was conventionally, if casually, fond of his mother. He sent her short letters and sporadic gifts of money. In the 1930s Katerine could be seen, an austere widow in black, carrying her basket to Tbilisi's collective-farm market accompanied by a squad of smart NKVD guards—at the fawning initiative of Lavrenti Beria, not at her son's behest. Stalin visited his mother twice in the 1920s and once in 1935. He just sent a wreath to her funeral.

All who came across Stalin in power were struck by his self-sufficiency and solitude. Perhaps Stalin's solitary habits came from being the only son of an impoverished and lonely woman, but was his childhood the solitary hell that would produce a psychopath? What we can glean of Ioseb's childhood does not bear this out. The Jughashvilis lived on amicable terms with their neighbors, who were cosmopolitan, upwardly mobile artisans. Nearby lived Katerine's extended family—craftsmen and innkeepers, with connections to merchants and even aristocrats. Like Beso's first two short-lived sons (Mikhail 1875, Giorgi 1876) Ioseb Jughashvili had prominent godfathers on whom the family could also count for support. The young Stalin had for company a foster brother (apprenticed to Besarion) a year younger than himself, Vano Khutsishvili. Vano had no complaints when in 1939 he recalled their apparently happy childhood in a letter to Stalin.[6] Even after Besarion parted from his wife and son, Katerine and Ioseb kept up contact with that side of the family. Besarion's sister was married to a Iakob Gveseliani, and although they lived near Tbilisi their offspring, Ioseb's cousins, often visited Gori. As for Katerine, she and her children were part of an extended family in Gori, including her cousin Mariam Mamulashvili, who had seven children. Not until his twenties could Stalin have known involuntary solitude.

Stalin's cousins—particularly Pepo (Euphemia) Gveseliani on his father's side and Vano Mamulashvili on his mother's side—kept in touch with him until his death. They sent letters—ingratiating, begging, sometimes affectionate. They came to Moscow and on two occasions threatened to commit suicide if Stalin refused to see them. His cousins were the only family category for whom Stalin never sanctioned arrests (Stalin's in-laws, the Svanidzes and Alliluevs, suffered the same near-extermination as did other "old Bolsheviks"). Admittedly, Stalin did his blood relatives few favors—they endured the same hardships all Georgia's peasantry and artisans underwent after the revolution—but they were the only human beings with whom Stalin sustained a semblance of normal relations. In his old age he would send them and some schoolmates parcels of cash (his earnings as a Supreme Soviet deputy). In 1951, General Nikolai Vlasik, the commandant at Stalin's dacha, drew up a list of Stalin's surviving relatives and schoolmates for a bus trip to a reunion in Georgia. Vlasik would not have dared to do so had Stalin not shown some last flicker of human affection.

The most telling events in Stalin's childhood are his brushes with death: his years in Georgia were marked by crippling illnesses and ghastly traffic accidents. All his life Stalin was rarely free of physical pain—which must have stimulated his sadism and irritability—and most of his pain, mental as well as physical, was a residue of childhood. He survived all the childhood illnesses—from measles to scarlet fever—that had carried off his infant brothers but in 1884 caught smallpox and was left badly scarred, earning the nickname Chopura (Poxy). Soon afterward he was run over by a carriage, and the subsequent blood poisoning apparently withered his left shoulder and arm. In early 1890 in another street accident his legs were run over by a carriage and Ioseb acquired another nickname, Geza (Crooked). His injuries left him with a waddling, strutting walk and a decade later he would plead leg injuries to mitigate his prison sentences. Illnesses, psychological and physical, hold one key to Stalin's pathological personality; the other is his pursuit of information. From a very early age he understood that ruthless aggression was useless unless he was armed with knowledge: he had to know his enemy and everything that his enemy knew. Very early in his life Stalin became an autodidact, and even in his senility he gathered and tried to retain all the information he could.

Not until her child was eight, a street urchin and, by some accounts, a violent brawler, did Katerine succeed in placing him in school. In 1886 the Jughashvilis had moved to the upper story of a house owned by a priest, Kristopore Charkviani. Keke begged Charkviani to teach Ioseb to read and write Russian so that he could win a place in Gori's clerical college, where instruction was mostly in Russian. In summer 1888, still only nine, Soso was accepted into the two-year preparatory class of the college; he learned Russian so quickly that he graduated to the main school in one year.

Gori clerical college formed the young Stalin. Some of its teachers, particularly the Georgians, were radical intellectuals with considerable talents: one, Giorgi Sadzghelashvili, would become catholicos of the newly autocephalous Georgian Church in 1917; another, Zakare Davitashvili, belonged to literary and revolutionary circles. Davitashvili had Keke's thanks for "singling out my son Soso . . . you helped him grow to love learning and because of you he knows the Russian language well." Even before puberty, Stalin combined the conformist's desire to study with the radical's instinct to rebel. At Gori he was influenced by classmates with older brothers, such as the Ketskhovelis, one of whom had been expelled from Tbilisi seminary for radicalism.

Kinship and friendship also linked twelve- and thirteen-year-old boys with their teachers, and thus with Georgia's radical intelligentsia as well as its merchants and officials. Georgia differed from Russia in that all educated men, regardless of their social origins and political alignments, were united in their resentment of Russian domination. Wealthy middle-aged capitalists would shelter impoverished radical schoolboys simply because they were fellow Georgians and fellow victims of the empire. That they were, to use Maupassant's simile, like corn merchants protecting rats, apparently never occurred to these patrons of dissidence.

If Ioseb Jughashvili was disliked by his classmates for his surliness, he was favored by teachers for his willingness to be class monitor, for his absorption in books and homework. Even the most hated teacher (as usual in Georgian schools, the Russian language teacher), Vladimir Lavrov, known as the gendarme, put his trust in Ioseb Jughashvili. Just as well, for when Katerine became a pauper, the school waived the twenty-five-ruble annual fee and gave the boy a scholarship of three, later seven, rubles a month for "exemplary" performance. He came top in every subject and was an outstanding choirboy and reader in the college's liturgical services.

When in 1894 Jughashvili graduated from Gori, he had acquired enough patronage to have a choice of further education. Tbilisi had no university, but it had two tertiary institutions: a pedagogical institute, where the Gori college singing teacher was moving and where he offered to take Jughashvili; and a theological seminary where, with help from his former teachers, Ioseb would be equally sure of placement. With examination results of "excellent" in Bible studies, Church Slavonic, and Russian, catechism, Greek, Georgian, geography, calligraphy, church singing, and Georgian (only in arithmetic did he gain just "very good"), Ioseb Jughashvili actually needed little patronage. Whatever his mother wished, and regardless of his own religious beliefs, the turbulent student life of the Tbilisi seminary would have lured any boy with a desire to make an impact on the world to choose a priest's, rather than a pedagogue's, path.

The seminary gave by far the best education in Tbilisi. It was a strange institution where obscurantist Orthodox monk-teachers (mostly Russians appointed by the viceroy of the Caucasus) fought the mainly Georgian liberals among staff and students. Disruption in the seminary was a perennial topic in the Georgian press for the last thirty years of the nineteenth century. In the early 1890s, the heavy hand of Tsar Alexander III's bureaucracy began to lose its grip. The new generation of students was more radical and the ferment such that one rector, Kersky, was demoted by the government to monkhood, and another, Chudetsky, was murdered by a former student. The writer Iakob Gogebashvili, like many Georgian luminaries a former teacher there, declared that any student, Russian or Georgian, not gripped by egotistical fear would rebel against the seminary authorities.[7] In 1893, the year before Jughashvili entered, the students' protests and demonstrations frightened the seminary's hierarchs to such a degree that tuition was suspended and troublemakers expelled.

Despite antagonism between Russian staff and Georgian students, there were some Russian teachers whom Stalin and his classmates later recalled with respect, even reluctant affection. Some reactionaries on the staff were men of character: the deputy rector in the mid-1890s, Father Germogen, later became bishop of Tobolsk and a member of the Holy Synod. In 1914, he was dismissed for denouncing Grigori Rasputin and in 1918 he tried to rescue Tsar Nicholas II from captivity.

Although he had no clerical background, Jughashvili impressed the seminary enough to be awarded a half-scholarship. The withdrawn, introverted surliness that repelled his fellow students seemed to his teachers the seriousness of a dedicated scholar. It took time for Jughashvili's religious conformism to collapse under the influence of the radicals in the seminary. Even in 1939, in the USSR, it was admitted in print: "Ioseb in his first years of study was very much a believer, going to all the services, singing in the church choir . . . he not only observed all religious rites but always reminded us to carry them out."[8]

Stalin's career at the seminary falls into two periods. Until 1896, when he was seventeen, he was an exemplary student. He acquired the rudiments of classical and modern languages and had begun to read widely in secular Russian and European literature as well as in sacred texts. He had a basic knowledge of world history. His reports show him as fifth in his class with top marks for behavior, Georgian, church singing, mathematics and "very good" for Greek. He rebelled in earnest in 1897, his third year. The previous year, when a crowd had been trampled to death at the coronation of Tsar Nicholas II in Moscow, Russian public opinion had turned hostile to the new Tsar, his ministers, and the imperial establishment. Jughashvili's conformism was swept away in this tide of radical anger. His faith collapsed; his term reports became deplorable. By 1898 Jughashvili had fallen to twentieth in the class, he had failed scripture, and was due to retake his annual examinations.

The reading prescribed at Tbilisi seminary was theological, and the lives of the Church fathers were the perfect preparation for reading the classics of Marxism. Ten years of ecclesiastical reading turned Stalin into that chimerical creature: the diehard atheist with a profound knowledge and love of religious texts and music. In his sixties Stalin sought out others who had had a seminary education—Marshal Aleksandr Vasilevsky, the opera bass Maksim Mikhailov. To them he remarked, "One thing priests teach you is to understand what people think."

Stalin's transition to atheism was neither abrupt nor complete. His atheism was a rebellion against God rather than a disavowal of the deity. The transition from Orthodoxy to Marxism, from the discipline of the Church to that of the party, was easy. Stalin went only halfway. Marxists declare man to be naturally good; all evil stems from social injustice. Stalin knew all human beings to be sinners in need of punishment and expiation. He took with him into power the deeply held conviction that the duty of the ruler was not to make his subjects happy but to prepare their souls for the next world.

At the seminary Stalin's intellectual interests veered toward forbidden authors and topics. He was now boarding in the same house as the young philosopher Seit Devdariani and illicitly subscribing to the Georgian Society for the Spreading of Literacy, which had a cheap lending library. The cluster of acolytes around Seit and Jughashvili still regarded themselves as trainee priests; the aim that bonded them was to broaden their education through reading political and scientific literature. The books, if found, were confiscated by their teachers, and persistent disobedience of the seminary rules led to imprisonment in a cell on a diet of bread and water.

Seit Devdariani was too mild a philosopher for Jughashvili, and in any case was off to Estonia to study at Tartu (Iuriev) University. In 1897 Jughashvili came under the spell of a more charismatic activist, Lado Ketskhoveli, who had just returned to Tbilisi from Kiev University after being expelled for reading forbidden literature. Ketskhoveli managed an underground printshop and was Stalin's first contact with the world of revolutionary propaganda. Under Ketskhoveli's tutelage Jughashvili now read exegeses of Marxism, not of the Bible. By 1898 he was engaged outside the seminary in propaganda work among Tbilisi's largest proletarian group, the Caucasian railway workers. He earned money by coaching a boy for entry to the seminary. That autumn the seminary considered expelling Jughashvili; he suffered reprimands, searches, and detentions, but he was more preoccupied with fomenting a strike of railway engineers in December 1898.

On May 29, 1899, the seminary announced: "I. V. Jughashvili is expelled from the seminary for failing for unknown reasons to appear for examinations." These "unknown reasons" might have been propagating Marxism, not paying seminary fees after his scholarship was withdrawn, or, as Katerine (who came to take him home) maintained, incipient TB. There may have been another reason. To judge by a semiliterate letter that Stalin hid in his private archive in April 1938 he had become in 1899 the father of a baby girl. All we know of her, apart from her later disappearance, was that she bore an extraordinary resemblance to Stalin, that she was called Pasha (Praskovia Georgievna Mikhailovskaia), and that Stalin's mother at some point took care of her.[9]

The seminary was generous to its wayward student: the marks in

Jughashvili's leaving certificate reflect his exemplary early years. But the seminary fined him seventeen rubles for unreturned library books—all his life Stalin hung on to books he had borrowed—and they demanded 630 rubles—two years' salary from Stalin's first employment—to repay his scholarship, since he had dishonored his undertaking to repay his education by becoming a priest or schoolteacher.

Being Georgian

WHEN IN 1937 writers were commissioned to write about Stalin's childhood some took as their model the childhood of Jesus Christ—a risky but tempting choice. Jesus and Stalin both had an artisan father who very soon played no role in the family, an austere mother, and an abrupt end, at the age of twelve, to any semblance of family life. Such adolescents may show tremendous self-sufficiency to the point of never trusting another human being, as well as intellectual precocity and vehement intolerance of others' views, but countless thousands of them do not rise to tyrannize the world. The qualities that determined Stalin's rise—first, a sense, a conviction, of his mission to rule; second, an acute sense of timing; and third, a deep insight into others' motivation and a hypnotist's skill in manipulating them—were yet to manifest themselves.

What we know of Stalin's formative years—a traumatic home life, a brilliant school career, a crippled body, a vigorous intellect—are clichés in the biographies of many men and women. Being a provincial or a member of an ethnic minority is also a virtual prerequisite for any tyrant, but how did being Georgian shape Stalin's destiny? Being Georgian gave Stalin far more than the provincial's inferiority complex, the need to prove himself to a metropolitan world. His Georgian heritage was a source of superiority: it justified his adopting an outlook more cruel and ruthless than those humanistic clichés of nineteenth-century Europe which other Russian revolutionaries had to overcome in order to destroy the existing order and impose their own.

In later life, Stalin's ethnic ties seemed as weak as his family bonds. In 1950 a group of Georgian historians was summoned to the Kremlin to hear Stalin's pontifications on their work. They were puzzled by Stalin's use of pronouns: "They, the Russians, don't appreciate . . . You, the Georgians, have failed to mention . . . " If the Russians were "they" and the Georgians "you," then what nationality was "I" or "we"? Like many non-Russian Bolsheviks—Jews, Armenians, Poles, Latvians, or Georgians—Stalin had discarded one ethnos without acquiring another: should not citizenship of a socialist society transcend ethnic affiliation? But Stalin remained Georgian more deeply than Feliks Dzierżyński remained Polish, or Leon Trotsky Jewish, and to penetrate his motivations we must ponder his Georgian upbringing and heritage.

Victims and enemies of Stalin naturally ascribed his vindictiveness, his rage at any slight to his dignity, to his Georgian culture. Stalin's younger son Vasili yelled, when drunk, "In our family we never forgive an offense." For Russians and Turks the cliché that no Caucasian can leave an insult unavenged is a self-evident truth. Stalin possessed, however, deeper traits of the Caucasian male: emotions, with the exception of anger and indignation, are in the Caucasus not to be revealed outside the family home. Georgian social life was as ritualized as English Victorian behavior. Such ritualization taught Stalin to act in public and with outsiders in ways that completely belied his real motives and feelings. Likewise, the liberal sexual morals of the revolutionary only overlaid the rigid puritanism of the Caucasian. Stalin studiously annotated his copy of Friedrich Engels's *The Origin of the Family* as if he shared the author's egalitarian views, but privately he insisted, like a Caucasian patriarch, on the subordination of women and children to the adult male.

Two things reminded Stalin's immediate circle that he was an alien: his Georgian accent (more pronounced in public speaking than in private) and a preference for red wine over vodka. After 1917 he spoke Georgian to his fellow Georgians Orjonikidze and Beria only in a few asides or outbursts. To his elder son, Iakov, who did not speak a word of Russian until he was seventeen years old, Stalin never spoke Georgian. The one Georgian male trait Stalin ostentatiously preserved was the preparation of meat: in the mid-1930s with his own knife Stalin would slaughter a lamb, cut up the meat, and grill kebabs.

After 1917, apart from a very few notes to his mother and marginal scribbles in his books, Stalin wrote exclusively in Russian. Writing Russian, Stalin made typically Georgian mistakes—for instance, he believed that "macaroni" was a singular noun, and in phrases like "put in the coffin" or "crucify on the cross" he would sometimes confuse the accusative and prepositional cases for the noun—but very few. Stalin never lost an intense interest in the Georgian language or Georgian history. We know of his interest from the impassioned scribbles he made in Georgian books, to his arguments with Georgian scholars and party bosses, and his involvement in the great eight-volume *Explanatory Dictionary of the Georgian Language.*

Stalin was a poet in Georgian. True, he stopped composing verse in the language at sixteen, but right into old age he continued to read Georgian and made brutal underlinings and exclamations in red or blue pencil in the margins of his books. He read like a very competent and unforgiving copy editor: he corrected Georgian grammar or style, and questioned obscure words with an angry, "What's that?" in Russian. He even improved an author's translation from Greek into Georgian. Where a phrase stung Stalin, he responded in Russian or Georgian. For instance, Konstantine Gamsakhurdia, in the afterword to his historical novel *Davit Aghmashenebeli* (*David the Builder*), remarks: "If brought up by the path of historical patriotism, we can make a Napoleon out of any bandit." Stalin retorts in the margin "Stupidity!" and to Gamsakhurdia's assertion that "Hegel and Balzac considered the novel to be the highest peak of poetry," Stalin reacts with "Ha, ha. Nonsense!"[10]

More important, Stalin shared with Georgia's luminaries, medieval and modern, a messianic view of their country. Obsessed with Georgia's mythical greatness in prehistory and its real grandeur in the twelfth century, Georgians to this day suspect themselves to be a people chosen to lead humanity. That conviction lay deep in Stalin's mentality. In the margins of Ivane Javakhishvili's *History of Georgia* of 1943 Stalin asks indignantly, "Why does the author fail to mention that Mithridates and the Pontic Empire were a Georgian ruler and a Georgian state?" In the collected writings of Nikolai Marr, a prodigiously learned Scottish-Georgian charlatan who invented a class theory of language and for a time persuaded Stalin of its validity, he approvingly underlined a particularly lunatic passage in *The Abkhaz and Abkhazology* where Marr asserts that the Russians evolved from the "Japhetic" peoples of the

Caucasus, thus making Georgia the ancestral hearth of Russian culture. Stalin never doubted that he was the scion of an elect nation.

In real not mythical terms, Georgia's turbulent history is a font of historical and political wisdom. What the seminary taught Stalin of Georgia's medieval past provided him with strategies for gaining and holding power, and with an ideal of absolute monarchy. The Georgian Bagratid kings of the twelfth century, among them David the Builder, or of the sixteenth, such as Teimuraz I, whether they built empires like David or lost them like Teimuraz, were ruthless autocrats who eliminated all rivals, even those who fought for their cause. (No wonder Stalin annotated so heavily his copy of *David the Builder.*) The stoicism of medieval Georgian kings amounted to psychopathic callousness. They set the needs of the state high above those of their people, even those of their families. They defended their ideology, Orthodox Christianity, by the most devious ruses including temporary conversion to Islam but, as good Christian kings, they loathed themselves with religious zeal. King David the Builder's *Songs of Repentance* and King Teimuraz I's *Passion on the Death of St. Ketevan* (his mother) portray the king-poets as figures sunk in sin, losing their souls to save the kingdom. And in that self-loathing, that deep conviction of man's spiritual filth, lie the most poisonous aspects of Stalin's godless, but nevertheless religious, outlook.

Not just historically but culturally, Georgia illuminates Stalin's actions. The ideal ruler, for Georgian kings, was a universal genius— a scholar and an artist as well as a strategist. Virtually all the Bagratids, the dynasty that ruled Georgia for nearly a thousand years, were poets. Some were men of serious learning: in the 1570s the exiled King David XI of Kartli wrote one of the greatest handbooks of medieval medicine; in the 1780s Prince Vakhushti was his country's first and best geographer. Stalin's obsession with literature and writers, with science and scientists, and his personal jealousies in these fields, mirror Georgian kings such as Teimuraz I, who, like Nero, envied his rivals as much in poetry as in politics. Few dictators since the Italian Renaissance have manipulated the poets among their subjects so assiduously as Stalin.

The six poems that Stalin wrote in Georgian and published when he was a mere sixteen years old are unguarded utterances (a rare thing for Stalin, in speech or in writing) and they shed some light on his personality. Psychiatrists of several schools would be struck by the recurrent symbolism: moonlight is one obsession. One poem concludes: "I shall undo my vest and thrust out my chest to the moon, / With outstretched arms I shall revere / The spreader of light upon the earth!" Another begins: "When the luminary full moon / Drifts across the vault of the sky," making this an allegory of restored political faith, but concludes with suspicion: "I find my soul rejoicing, my heart beats peacefully; / But is this hope genuine / That has been sent to me at these times?" The solitude of a moon worshipper culminates in mistrust and suspicion.

Another poem depicts a despised and rejected bard:

> Wherever the harp was plucked,
> The mob set before the outcast
> A vessel filled with poison [. . .]
> And they said to him: "Drink this, o accursed,
> This is your appointed lot! We do not want your truth
> Nor these heavenly tunes of yours!"

Ingratitude and poison were to loom large in Stalin's dealings with his rivals and subordinates: he was fearful of being betrayed, even killed, by those who owed most to him, and in preemptive strikes he would smite, even literally poison, those who most expected his gratitude and trust. The verbs that the young poet uses show a predilection for violent action—hang, strike, snatch, clutch. Stalin's lyrics have a strange vertical perspective from "moon . . . glaciers" through "outstretched arms" to "troughs," which represents the swing from mania to depression. It is no wonder that in later life Stalin discouraged sycophants who commissioned Russian translations of his adolescent poetry, just as he forbade portraits or statues of himself with pockmarks, and dismissed actors who portrayed him with a limp and a Georgian accent.

Stalin modeled himself on fictional characters, too. He was enthralled by the first novelists in Georgian literature. His revolutionary nom de guerre Koba came from a melodramatic tale by Aleksandre Qazbegi, *The Parricide*.[11] Qazbegi's Koba is a wild highlander, a chivalrous outlaw; he reunites the unhappy lovers of the story (including the supposedly parricidal heroine) and finally avenges them by shooting the local lords who have, in connivance with the Russian conquerors, brought about their deaths. Koba the avenger is the only character still alive at the end of Qazbegi's story; his success in outliving both his enemies and his friends made Stalin especially fond of this pseudonym (he had a dozen others) and it remained his nickname among close associates even in the 1930s.

In the summers of the 1890s, when the seminary was on holiday, Stalin did not go home but spent his days near Tbilisi with other seminary students. He and they were fired by sophisticated Georgian students back from the universities of Warsaw, Kharkov, Moscow, and St. Petersburg. Each successive generation of Georgian rebels was more radical: Stalin's adolescence coincided with the Marxism of Mesame Dasi, a loose group that endorsed violent overthrow of the state and disowned nationalism so as to collaborate with all the subject peoples of the Russian empire. Radicalism in Georgia was more widespread, even among merchants and aristocrats, than in Russia. Georgia's struggle for self-determination made them overlook the differences between parliamentary liberals and revolutionary socialists. Thus the League for Freedom in Georgia embraced constitutional socialists such as Noe Zhordania, who was to lead the Georgian republic of 1917–21, and internationalist Marxists like Pilipe Makharadze, who were Stalin's first mentors. Tbilisi was still a sleepy provincial city but in 1895 Georgian intellectuals scattered across Russia and Europe by exile or university study established a small group of Marxists there. The scarcity of proletarians (the city was dominated by Armenian traders and Russian administrators) made it less suitable than the Caucasus's major industrial city Baku or its main port Batumi for preaching socialism.

Stalin as a Thinker

THE EXISTENCE OF GOD vexed Stalin all his life. Around 1926, reading a Russian translation of Anatole France's *Sous la rose,* Stalin was most intrigued by the story of Charles Baudelaire visiting Théophile Gautier, examining a grotesque African carved idol and wondering, "Suppose God is really like that!" Stalin exclaims in the margin: "Hah!! Sort that one out!" He seems distressed by France's comment that, "God is the point of intersection for all human contradictions," and scrawls: "Reason—feeling, is that really also ⊕?!'"

If Stalin lost faith in God, he kept his Calvinist beliefs on sin, the fall, grace, and damnation. He even retained his belief in the supremacy of love. Much has been plundered from Stalin's library but his copy of Dostoevsky's *The Brothers Karamazov* still exists. The chapters that Stalin underlined most heavily have nothing to do with murdering one's father or the right of the individual to do what he wants once God is shown to be dead; what held Stalin's attention was the philosophy of Dostoevsky's monks. Father Zosima's musings on the nature of "active love" for one's fellow human beings are underlined by Stalin: "active love, compared with dreaming love, is a cruel and terrifying business."[12]

Stalin could accept Anatole France's declaration that God was dead; as a Dostoevskian superman, Stalin felt he could supplant God with his own self. What distressed him was his own mortality. Reading France on old age, he underlined the remark that some persons would prefer hell to not existing at all. Even as an adolescent, Stalin worried about old age and death. His best (and last) Georgian poem anticipates the lonely impotence of his last years:

> Our Ninika has grown old,
> His hero's shoulders have failed him
> [. . .]
> How did this desolate gray hair break an iron strength?
> [. . .]
> But now he can no longer move his knees,
> Scythed down by old age,
> He lies down, or he dreams, or he tells
> His children's children of the past . . .

In his last years Stalin could conjure up from the mob whenever he wanted the acclaim and gratitude that his romantic poet persona fails to win, but if he recalled this poem in his debilitated senility, it must have seemed a bitter prophesy.[13]

Dostoevsky's vision of the Church's cruel love was attractive; Tolstoi's more Quakerish Christianity, with its leanings toward self-reliance and sentiment, irritated him. Stalin energetically marked up his (and his daughter's) copies of Tolstoi's work: one passage that provoked his mockery ("Ha-ha-ha" he scrawled in red) runs, "The sole, undoubted means of salvation from the evil people suffer from is that they should admit themselves to be guilty before God and therefore incapable of punishing or correcting other people."[14]

The most common mistake of Stalin's opponents was to underestimate how exceptionally well read he was. That he was erudite we now know from the remnants of his library of 20,000 volumes, from the slips of paper and letters in which he asked for books, and from the recollections of those who knew him in his early years. What the seminary did not make its pupils read, it banned them from reading, thus stimulating the trainee priests to read even more. In 1910 the Tsarist secret police observed the exiled Stalin visiting the library in Vologda seventeen times in 107 days. By the time Stalin was thirty he had read quantities of classical, Western, and Russian literature, philosophy, and political theory. In four years' exile, from 1913 to 1917, in the Siberian wilderness—unsociable, uncommunicative—Stalin read whatever he could scrounge from fellow exiles. Even in the chaos of revolution and the pursuit of power, he read. He read all Russian émigré periodicals from the 1920s to his death.

Once he had an office and an apartment in the Kremlin, as well as dachas around Moscow and on the Black Sea, Stalin built up his library. Some books he ordered, some he purloined from the state library; most came from the publisher or the author. Reading up to 500 pages a day, making notes in the margins and, despite his frequent laments about memory lapses, able to recall innumerable phrases and arguments years later, Stalin was a phenomenal, and dangerous, reader. As he got older, he quickly lost patience—typically he heavily annotated a book for around the first hundred pages. But if ever a devil could quote scripture to his purpose, it was Stalin.

A complete list of the books that a poet reads, Osip Mandelstam wrote, is his biography. Stalin liked books that gave an overview of European history, literature, linguistics. He was attached to books by authoritarian figures: Niccolò Machiavelli's *The Prince,* Hitler's *Mein Kampf,* Carl von Clausewitz's *On War,* Otto von Bismarck's memoirs. In the mid-1920s, when the bulk of Stalin's books were in the Kremlin, Nadezhda Allilueva-Stalina, his second wife, took a lead from Sergei Kirov, Stalin's satrap in Leningrad and fellow bibliophile. She had a librarian classify and reshelve them. Stalin was furious. He jotted down his own classification of books and had his secretary Aleksandr Poskriobyshev rearrange them accordingly.

All that hampered Stalin were his linguistic limitations: only in Georgian and Russian could he cope without a dictionary. Yet here too Stalin was underestimated by his opponents. In the seminary he had learned a lot of Greek (visitors were amazed to find Stalin in his Kremlin office perusing Plato in the original) and afterward a little French and German. For a while, in Siberian exile, he even toyed with Esperanto.[15] Stalin's interest in Marxism and his first prolonged stay in Berlin impelled him to struggle with German periodicals.

People wrote to Stalin not only in Russian and Georgian, but also, from Baku, in Azeri Turkish (then written in Arabic script). When on the run from the police, Stalin sometimes went under the name Zakhariants or Melikiants; either would have been foolish without a smattering of colloquial Armenian. In 1926 during the British General Strike, and afterward, Stalin perused the British press. His letters to his wife from Sochi express annoyance at her forgetting to send him his copy of *A Model Complete Teach-Yourself English Course.*[16] In languages, as in many other subjects, Stalin's tactics were to conceal, not display, his knowledge.

Stalin had an intimidatingly detailed recall of what he read and heard. He showed an uncanny instinct for inconsistencies and things left unsaid, although his evaluations of what he believed a writer had meant are often naive, even weird. Stalin's throwaway remarks and angry scrawls in red pencil give us insight into his motives at points in his endless war on opposition and dissent.

Some books which Stalin read in his formative years sketch out his future actions. One work is credibly rumored to have authenticated for Stalin the principles of revolutionary dictatorship: Dostoevsky's *The*

Devils. The well-informed Georgian novelist Grigol Robakidze asserts in his novel *The Murdered Soul* that the Tbilisi seminary library copy of *The Devils* was heavily marked up by Stalin. The most vociferously anti-revolutionary novel in Russian literature, it was approved by the seminary authorities. Dostoevsky's plot, in which a cynical provocateur uses a self-destructive aristocrat and a nihilist philosopher to create a violent uprising in a provincial town, must have given Stalin ideas for how to organize a revolution. One of Dostoevsky's characters, a theorist who demands that a hundred million heads roll to make future generations eternally happy, did not seem to Stalin as ghoulish as he did to the author.

Like Dostoevsky's heroes, Stalin sought in philosophy a license to transgress human and divine law. The most significant statement that Stalin ever made is a note he made in red pencil on the back flyleaf of the 1939 edition of Lenin's theoretical work *Materialism and Empirocriticism* (a treatise on the existence of the real world outside our perception). Stalin's comment gives a Machiavellian gloss to the credo of a Dostoevskian satanic antihero and is an epigraph to his whole career:

> 1) Weakness, 2) Idleness, 3) Stupidity. These are the only
> things that can be called <u>vices</u>. Everything else, in the absence
> of the aforementioned, is undoubtedly <u>virtue</u>.
> NB! If a man is 1) strong (spiritually), 2) active, 3) clever (or
> capable), then he is good, regardless of any other "vices"!
> 1) and 3) make 2)[17]

It is not surprising to learn that in 1915, when both were in Siberian exile, Lev Kamenev (shot by Stalin twenty years later but then Stalin's mentor) gave him a copy of Machiavelli. Kamenev's praise of Machiavelli reflects the political theorist's enthusiasm for a precocious precursor; Stalin's reading shows the pragmatist's appreciation of a writer who authorizes what he has long been thinking and doing. Marxism provided Stalin (and Lenin) with the end—the terminology and justification for action; Machiavelli provided the means—the political tactics and amorality. Stalin was a Marxist in the same sense that Machiavelli was a Christian: both saw the retention of power as the sole task for a ruler

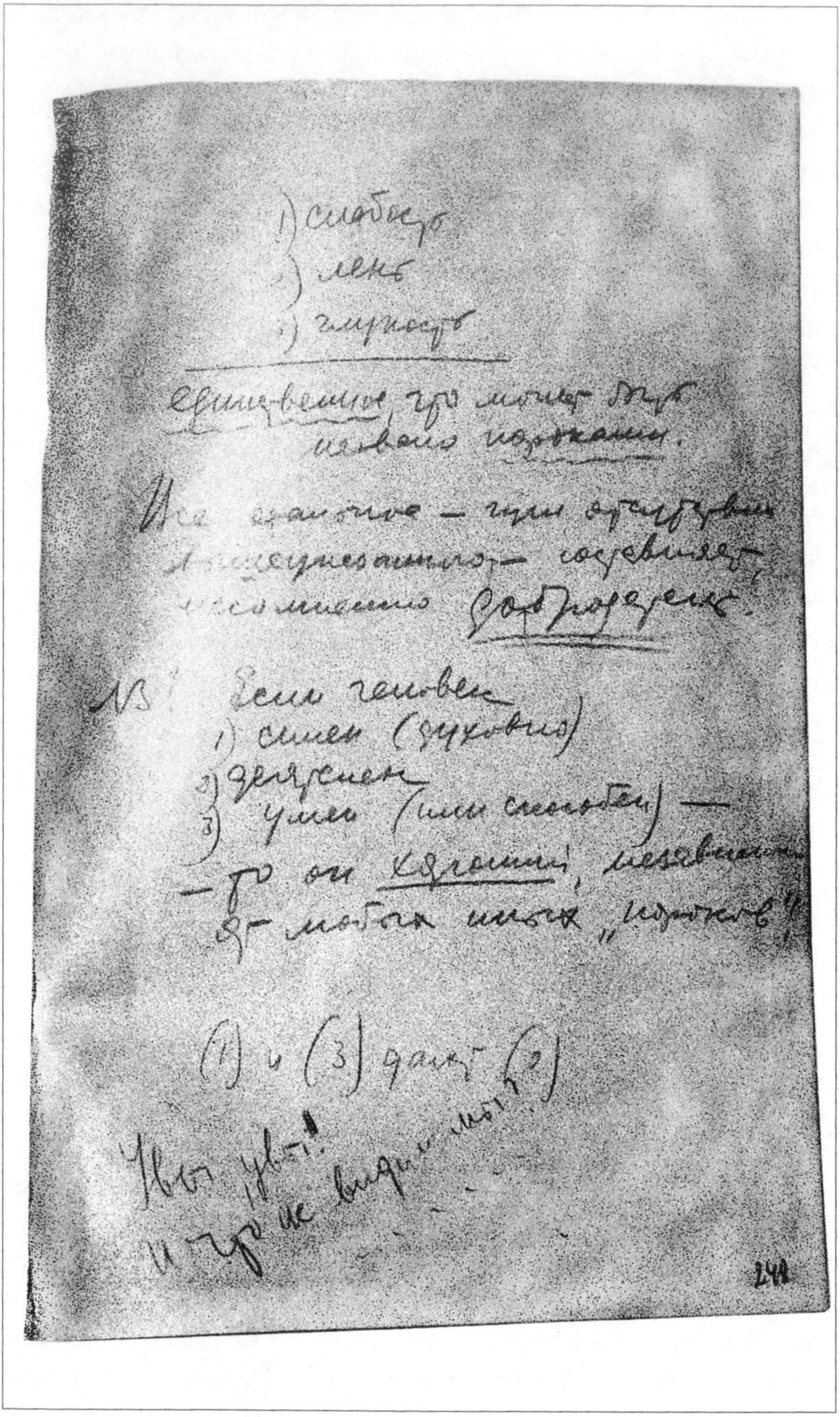
1) слабость
2) лень
3) глупость

Единственное, что может быть названо пороками.

Все остальное — при отсутствии вышеуказанного — составляет, несомненно, добродетель!

NB! Если человек
1) силен (духовно)
2) деятелен
3) умен (или способен) —
— то он хороший, независимо от любых иных „пороков"!

(1) и (3) дают (2)

241

and examined all the means by which power, once acquired, could be retained, regarding the ideology in whose name the ruler ruled as a mere rallying flag.

Stalin's marginal doodling is sometimes mystifying: elaborate patterns of triangles and circles.[18] Occasionally we come across two initial letters scrawled in the margin of a book: T and U. One can infer that T stands for Tbilisi and its seminary, and the psychological insights that Stalin had gained from a Christian education. U stands for *uchitel'*—teacher. Possibly, the teacher is Lenin, or perhaps it is Stalin's view of himself.

Political Initiation

AFTER LEAVING THE SEMINARY in 1898 Stalin did not go back to Gori with his disappointed mother; he hid from the police in a village near Tbilisi. In autumn he was helped by his friend Lado Ketskhoveli's younger brother Vano to secure an undemanding job as one of six observers at the Tbilisi meteorological station for twenty rubles a month. One might reasonably have predicted that the promising boy was now doomed to be a marginal, semi-educated clerk.

What saved Stalin was a chance to foment trouble for the authorities. In January 1900, with Lado Ketskhoveli, Jughashvili helped organize a strike of tram workers. The strike was soon broken. Lado fled to Baku, Vano was forced to leave the meteorological station, and Jughashvili was caught and imprisoned but, after his mother intervened, released.

Isolated from his friends, the young Stalin had to seek support from Russian socialists whom the authorities had rashly exiled to Tbilisi from St. Petersburg. Thus in 1900 Stalin began his network. His first significant contact was a Russian exile working in the railway workshops, Mikhail Kalinin. Stalin would later maintain Kalinin for twenty-eight years as his front man, the puppet head of the Soviet state from 1918 to 1946. Kalinin, all his life a dog in search of a master, would prove an archetypical Stalinist employee, but in 1900 another Russian contact, Dr. Viktor Kurnatovsky, seemed more useful to Stalin. Kurnatovsky was an educated Marxist, the friend of another Caucasian Bolshevik, Sergei Alliluev, and the lover of his wife: Kurnatovsky thus introduced Stalin to the Marxist underground and to his future father-in-law.

Within a year Jughashvili, an obscure clerk, was again a wanted man. Of twenty-nine Russian "social democratic revolutionary party" members listed by the Tbilisi gendarmerie in early 1901, Viktor Kurnatovsky, Pilipe Makharadze, and Ioseb Jughashvili were singled out as dangerous. Jughashvili was noted as "an intellectual who leads a group of railway workers . . . behaving very cautiously, always looks around when walking . . ."

In 1901 Stalin began sixteen formative years of life on the run, in prison, or in exile. He had no address he could call home, and no serious expectations of settling down, let alone achieving power. He visited Gori only when the gendarmes made Tbilisi too hot for him. He organized demonstrations and set up an illegal printshop.

Even in his early twenties Stalin attached himself to two sorts of men. One sort, like Kalinin and Kurnatovsky—doctrinaire, self-educated Marxists—would constitute his inner circle. The other sort were killers. In 1901, Stalin took up with the first of the many criminals that he was to use and employ: a half-Georgian, half-Armenian youth, Simon (Kamo) Ter-Petrosiants. Stalin had known Kamo since childhood; the Ter-Petrosiants and Jughashvili families were neighbors. Kamo would soon be the Caucasus's most notorious bandit: his bloody "expropriations" of millions of rubles from mail coaches and post offices funded the Bolsheviks' arms and propaganda and alienated "legal" Marxists from their violent Bolshevik fellow travelers. In 1901 Kamo was only nineteen. Expelled from school for professing atheism, he now sought expertise in explosives and arms by applying to enter Tbilisi's military academy.

At the end of 1901 Jughashvili took cover in Batumi from the gendarmes. Batumi was then, as today, Georgia's second city, a lawless port influenced as much by Turkey and Islam as by Russia. Here the oil terminals, the Rothschild factory, and the port had built up a critical mass of disaffected proletarians. This was no provincial exile for Stalin but a chance to make his mark. For the first time he encountered an urban proletariat. That he, a stranger from Tbilisi, made an impact in an industrial area where many workers spoke little Georgian, says something for the force of his personality. Within two months he was making furtive trips to Tbilisi to fetch machinery for printing leaflets in Georgian and Armenian. He was helped by a twenty-year-old Armenian, Suren Spandaryan, the editor of *Nor Dar* (*New Century*) and son of a typesetter. Spandaryan was, until his death in 1916, one of the few people Stalin might have called a friend and whose death he, if perfunctorily, mourned.

In early 1902 Tbilisi's social democrat revolutionaries were crushed by the police. In Batumi, however, the strikes that Stalin had helped foment were victorious. By April 1902, though, Jughashvili was arrested for "incitement to disorder and insubordination against higher authority." He was cursorily examined by a doctor, Grigol Eliava, who gave the first objective description of Stalin: "height 1.64, long, swarthy, pockmarked face, second and third toes on left foot joined . . . missing one front, right lower molar tooth . . . mole on left ear."[19]

Stalin was no prison hero. In autumn he implored Prince Golitsyn, the viceroy of the Caucasus: "An increasingly choking cough and the helpless position of my elderly mother, abandoned by her husband twelve years ago and seeing me as her sole support in life, forces me to address the commander-in-chief's chancellery for the second time and humbly request release under police supervision. . . ." A major of Tbilisi's gendarmerie warned against clemency (making the young Stalin sound like an asset to the police force): "at the head of the Batumi organization is Ioseb Jughashvili, under special police supervision, Jughashvili's despotism has enraged many people and the organization [in Batumi] has split. . . ."

In spring 1903 Stalin roused prisoners to protest against a visit by the exarch of the Georgian Church. He was moved a hundred miles east, to Kutaisi, where he was described by the social democrat Grigol Urutadze: "a beard, long hair combed back. An insinuating gait, in little steps. He never laughed with an open mouth. . . . He was absolutely imperturbable." The gendarmerie proposed exiling him to eastern Siberia for six years.

It took the bureaucracy until the winter of 1903–04 to send Jughashvili, with two dozen other social democrats, in summer clothing, across the Black Sea and the Urals to Siberia, to a village forty miles from the railway. After two months Jughashvili persuaded a peasant (who was flogged for complicity) to drive him to the railhead from where he escaped back to the Caucasus. He was sheltered in Tbilisi by a fellow student of Suren Spandaryan, an engineer's son who would become a key figure in Lenin's entourage, Lev Kamenev (Rosenfeld). For some days, before he himself fled north to St. Petersburg, Kamenev protected Jughashvili, a comradely gesture which he must have bitterly regretted twenty years later. Few people suffered such scorpionlike ingratitude as Kamenev had from Stalin.

Not for the last time Stalin was suspected of being a police collaborator, a provocateur. So fast a return from Siberia unsettled Jughashvili's associates. How had he gotten the hundred rubles for the fare from Siberia? Jughashvili said that he had forged a certificate that he was a police agent. But where had he found forms and stamps in the Siberian swamps? He went to Baku but was ostracized. He flitted to Tbilisi and back again. On May Day 1904 he was beaten up. He hid with a maternal uncle in Gori for two months. Only in August was he rehabilitated by the party, which was too short of educated activists to persist with its suspicions.

Using the name Koba, Stalin climbed ranks thinned by arrests and soon came to dominate the Caucasian Social Democrats. After the split between moderate Mensheviks and intransigent Bolsheviks at the second Social Democrat Party congress in 1903, the Bolsheviks felt free to act violently. In Geneva, Lenin, his spouse Krupskaia, Rozalia Zemliachka, and other extremists called for a new congress to endorse revolutionary action. At last Stalin had a policy he could impose on his Caucasian colleagues with enthusiasm. With Lado Ketskhoveli dead, nobody had more charisma and authority than Koba among the Georgian Bolsheviks. Intermittently, he received moral and financial support from the Russian Bolsheviks: Kamenev returned to Tbilisi in September 1904; Lenin's emissary Tsetsilia Zelikson came from Switzerland; Kamo Ter-Petrosiants escaped from Batumi prison and joined him. That year Stalin was always on the move across Transcaucasia. His contacts among the railway workers served him well: he was hidden in train cars for his journeys.

From 1900 discontent swept the urban workers of the Russian empire. Whenever the Tsar's government gave an inch, the workers (as the reactionaries rightly warned) tried to take a yard. In 1900 a tram workers' depot was all that Stalin could shut down; in 1904, when the country was not only rapidly industrializing but also preparing for war with Japan, Koba's Armenian and Azeri colleagues led a strike that paralyzed the oil fields of Baku and, for the first time in Russian history, forced employers to yield to workers. The gendarmes and Okhranka (security service) arrested so many Bolsheviks that Tbilisi's more law-abiding Mensheviks temporarily took over the Social Democrat Party.

Russia's defeat by Japan, and the promised reforms wrung from the Tsar after unarmed workers were gunned down in St. Peterburg's notorious "Bloody Sunday" of January 1905, gave revolutionaries a sense of power. In summer 1905 they roused the Baku workers to burn down half the oil wells of the city. Koba traveled thousands of miles, attending meetings, delegating work to new and old recruits. When nothing was demanded of him Koba was quarrelsome and surly, buried in books for months on end, and yet, in crises, he organized the feckless, persuaded the irresolute, and conciliated the fractious, barely sleeping at all and rarely in the same place for more than a few days. Comrades overlooked his repellent personal manner, given his organizational genius.

At the age of twenty-five Stalin made the first of his few close attachments. He was hidden by his friend Mikhail Monaselidze, who had married into the Svanidze family. The three Svanidze sisters were dressmakers to the wives of army and gendarmerie officers; they lived close to the barracks and their house was the last place the police would search. Here Koba felt safe and here he courted Monaselidze's sister-in-law Kato. Koba's relationship with Kato Svanidze was as near as he came to commitment to another person.

In 1905 Stalin finally met the only man he ever recognized as his leader, Lenin. Koba went, under the name of Ivanovich, as one of three delegates from the Caucasus to a clandestine congress of the Russian Social Democrat Party, held at Tampere in Finland which, though in the Russian empire, offered some protection against arrest. In Tampere Koba met, most for the first time, forty other delegates of the Russian Social Democrat Party. He became known to some who would lead the Bolshevik uprising twelve years later: Lenin, Iakov

Sverdlov, Leonid Krasin. Koba won praise from Lenin for his report on the Caucasus and for his hard-line stance. Back in Tbilisi early in 1906, Koba could proclaim himself as "the Lenin of the Caucasus." He finally had authority.

The first murder in which Stalin was implicated occurred on January 16, 1906. General Griaznov, who had smashed down the barricades erected during the workers' insurrection in Tbilisi the previous month, was "sentenced to death" by the party and killed. Koba had fallen off a tram and was lying up with head injuries when the police searched for him. Despite being a wanted escaped prisoner, Koba had had an extraordinarily easy journey to Finland and back. Understandably, other party members wondered if Koba was a police agent. He subsequently claimed to have been arrested early in April 1906 but his name is missing from Tbilisi's Metekhi prison register.[20] Soon Koba was again off north, under the name of Vissarionovich, this time to Stockholm to the fourth Social Democrat Party congress while the gendarmes, uncannily tipped off, were raiding the socialist printing presses in Tbilisi.

Stockholm attracted many more delegates than Tampere. Here Stalin saw the doyen of Russian Marxism, Giorgi Plekhanov, as well as familiar Tbilisi faces such as Mikhail Kalinin. He also first encountered two men who would be instrumental in his struggle for total power: the first head of the Soviet secret police, Feliks Dzierżyński, and Klim Voroshilov, future commissar for defense and eventual butcher of the Red Army. Koba shared a hotel room in Stockholm with Voroshilov (an uneducated metalworker endowed with the voice of an opera singer). Koba and Klim bonded, master and servant, for life. As for those who would be killed by Stalin after they attained power, Koba first met in Stockholm Andrei Bubnov, Aleksandr Smirnov, and Aleksei Rykov. In Stockholm Koba briefly acquired a suit, a tie, a hat, and a pipe (the latter the only one of these bourgeois accessories he retained).

Back in Tbilisi, when Kato Svanidze realized she was pregnant, Koba married her, at one in the morning. They enjoyed little conjugal life: Koba was off to Baku, and the gendarmes arrested Kato for sheltering revolutionaries on the run. It took six weeks to free Kato: her sister, Aleksandra Monaselidze-Svanidze, went to see the wife of a gendarme colonel whose dresses she made. The colonel secured for Kato visits from Koba (allegedly her cousin) and then release, and at the same time a reprieve for Kato's real cousin, who was to be hanged.

Stalin took up writing again, not lyrical poetry but political prose. He compiled in Georgian treatises on socialism and anarchism which were published in the periodicals *Akhali droeba* (*New Times*) and *Chveni tskhovreba* (*Our Life*). The birth of a son, Iakov, on March 18, 1907, did not distract him. A month later, the sole Bolshevik at liberty to travel from Transcaucasia to the fifth Social Democrat congress, Koba was in Copenhagen. The Danish government succumbed to Russian protests and the congress moved to London. On his way Stalin apparently visited Lenin in Berlin, where they agreed to authorize a bank robbery by Kamo Ter-Petrosiants to fund their activities—against party policy, for the fifth congress was about to vote for the ballot box and against the gun.

Koba returned to Georgia via Paris on a dead Georgian's passport; his first exploit was to organize a spectacular robbery, carried out by Kamo on June 13, 1907, in the middle of Tbilisi. Koba put Kamo in touch with an old school friend who worked in the posts and telegraph at Gori, and he provided information on the transportation of bank-notes. The robbery netted a quarter of a million rubles, unfortunately in 500-ruble notes the numbers of which were circulated throughout Europe. Kamo's hand grenades killed and maimed about fifty people, mostly bystanders, and Koba was expelled from the Caucasian Social Democrat Party for terrorism.

With his wife and infant son, Koba retreated east to Baku where he could rely on Bolshevik supporters among the oil workers. A new ally and eventual victim, Sergo Orjonikidze, joined Koba's circle. Stalin's authority derived from his unofficial mandate from Lenin; it is likely that he made two more journeys to see Lenin—in August 1907 to Stuttgart and to Switzerland in January 1908.

Koba was soon free of family ties. On November 22, 1907, Kato died, perhaps of TB. Koba handed his baby son Iakov over to his sister-in-law and did not ask after the child for fourteen years. On March 25, 1908, the Baku gendarmerie rounded up Baku's Bolsheviks, including Koba, now known as Kaioz Nizheradze. Incompetence and perhaps corruption blinded them to the fact that Koba was a leading Bolshevik organizer on the run from Siberia. Besides, times had changed in Russia: the Tsar's government had conceded a parliament and political prisoners were amnestied. Koba claimed he had been abroad all 1904 and 1905 and thus qualified for the 1905 amnesty. Even when the truth emerged, he was dealt with leniently: three years' exile in northern Russia, in Vologda province.

★ ★ ★ Why did the Russian state treat with such leniency those it knew were trying to overthrow it by organizing assassinations, armed robberies, sabotage, and strikes? In 1908 in France, Koba and Kamo would have gone to the guillotine, in Britain to the gallows, in America to the electric chair. True, revolutionaries in Russia were often tried by military tribunals, convicted on flimsy evidence, and hanged; but this happened mostly in the west of Russia, in Vilnius, Kiev, or Odessa, where governors-general ruled and where the revolutionaries were more often than not reviled Poles or Jews. Piotr Stolypin, the most effective prime minister that Tsarist Russia ever had, for all his pragmatic liberalism was so willing to hang those who threatened the state that the hangman's rope became known as the Stolypin necktie.

Nevertheless, Stalin and his kind—Sverdlov, Kalinin, Kamenev— could get away with a few months in prison followed by an amnesty. In prison their secondary education entitled them to be treated as gentlemen—to receive visitors, good food, medical treatment, and polite warders. When they were sent to Siberia, they were given a living allowance that provided ample heating, food, even a servant and a cow. They lived among a friendly population; even the gendarmes who guarded them usually looked kindly on them, and when they were bored with each other's company or the long Siberian winter, they could easily escape. In Britain, Switzerland, France, or America, they found a sympathetic reception. Nobody in western Europe believed that intellectual socialist revolutionary refugees from Russia posed a danger to anybody, and tolerating them provided some leverage on the Russian state, should it threaten the colonial empires of Britain or France in the Far East.

Tolerance apart, the Russian state had two fatal flaws in the second decade of the twentieth century. First, it spoke with a forked tongue. One fork was the Tsar, Nicholas II, a constitutional, not an absolute monarch after 1905, he still had enormous power. Under the influence of his wife, a woman far more willful than he and just as stupid, he would dismiss any minister who seemed to diminish his authority. The other fork was the new parliament, the Duma, which talked up radical reform. Each successive Duma had a more restricted electorate and thus became less radical, but despite the presence of a monarchist right wing, its liberals and socialists demanded human rights and economic reforms. Between the Tsar and the Duma stood the ministers. The Russian state was sustained by a series of wise, energetic self-sacrificing ministers—Count Sergei Witte, who made the Russian ruble one of Europe's strongest currencies; Piotr Stolypin, who for five brief years truly liberated the Russian peasant; Piotr Sviatopolk-Mirsky, who brought about the liberal spring of 1904. But the uncomprehending conservatism of the Tsar and the irresponsibility of the Duma nullified their efforts.

The economic boom that gathered strength in 1908 deceived most observers. They underestimated the weakness of Russia's political structures and discounted the threat posed by the revolutionary left. Even the Ministry of the Interior and the gendarmerie had a liberal view of their educated opponents. Russian public opinion generally adopted a Christian attitude toward criminals, particularly politically motivated ones. When the anarchist Giashvili was sentenced to death for exploding a bomb that killed a senior government official, nobody in Tbilisi would act as his executioner. He was reprieved—laudable in a Christian or humanistic culture, but disastrous for a state whose weaknesses were being probed by embittered fanatics.

Because these fanatics were split into factions, the consensus was that they were too weak to cause serious damage. The Social Revolutionaries, whose incoherent mysticism made them spectacular assassins, aroused most alarm, while the Bolshevik Social Democrats, who used violence selectively and who seemed in thrall to obscure German political ideas, were belittled despite their nearly overturning the state with their workers' and soldiers' soviets in the 1905 uprising.

Corruption, endemic in the bureaucracy at all but the highest levels, undermined the Russian state. Bribery and infiltration crippled the Tsar's gendarmerie—even if, by the standards of today's Russian militia (which a cynic might call the uniformed branch of the mafia), the gendarmerie was an efficient and dedicated force.

In 1908 the prophets of doom—and their voice was loud among Russia's newspaper tycoons, philosophers, theologians, and poets—sensed that Russia's Armageddon would come from a world war into which its alliance with Britain, France, and Serbia, and the myopia of the Tsar's family, would drag it. There was no good reason for Russia to be drawn into a quarrel with the Kaiser's Germany or Habsburg Austria-Hungary; Russia had no seas whose waves they needed to rule, no colonies to expand at the expense of other empires. The rush toward 1914 was that of Gadarene swine.

The Bolsheviks attacked the Russian state not because it was oppressive but because it was weak. The Russia of 1908 did nearly as much for its citizens as the states of western Europe did for theirs. Trial by jury, equality before the law, enlightened treatment of ethnic minorities, religious tolerance, cheap credits for farmers, an efficient postal and railway service, a free press, flourishing universities with leading scientists, doctors, and scholars, universal (if impoverished) primary education and primary medical care, the most powerful outburst of creativity in all the arts that Europe had known since the Italian Renaissance—all this outweighed for many observers the endemic alcoholism and syphilis, the idleness and bribery, the foul roads, the idle bureaucrats, the general poverty. Russia's ills seemed curable by economic progress.

Lenin's followers had a clever motto: "The worse, the better." They actively encouraged (if only by not assassinating them) brutal governors-general, stupid gendarmerie colonels, exploitative factory owners, because these men might create a resentful proletariat who would follow the social democrats.

When Stalin went to prison and into exile, he was not isolated or disadvantaged. He could educate himself further, meet other revolutionary socialists from all over the Russian empire and, when he left this incubation stage, emerge all the more effective and dangerous a pestilence.

Prison and Exile

. . . from the forest a rifle fired, it shot Diambeg dead . . . and wounded next to him Giorgola, who heard a voice: "I am Koba! I have avenged my friend Iago!"

Aleksandre Qazbegi, The Parricide

AWAITING DEPORTATION in cell No. 3 of Baku's Bailov prison, Koba was visited by his mother and a girl, a neighbor from Gori. He valued his fellow inmates more than visitors, forging bonds with two in particular: Sergo Orjonikidze, a Transcaucasian bandit and party organizer, and Andrei Vyshinsky, a well-educated Menshevik lawyer from Kiev. Orjonikidze was emotional if brutal, and loyal. Vyshinsky was the most calculating and cynical of all Stalin's associates; for twenty years he would provide the oratory and the legal framework to send hundreds of thousands to their death. Even in prison Vyshinsky found a comfortable niche: he was cell monitor and worked in the prison kitchens.

Koba made two escape attempts, but by early 1909, delayed en route by typhus, he was in exile in the north of Russia, at Solvychegodsk, fifteen miles over a frozen river from the railhead at Kotlas. Little detained Koba there; as exiles remarked, only those who couldn't be bothered to escape stayed. Koba fled first to St. Petersburg, where his future father-in-law Sergei Alliluev found him a safe house owned by a concierge. (Concierges in Russia as in France, trusted by the police, provided the safest refuge for criminals on the run.)

That summer Koba was hiding in Baku, printing newssheets. He saw neither his mother nor his son. Another woman entered Koba's life: Stefaniia Petrovskaia, who had left her Odessa home when her father remarried and entered into a common-law marriage with a political exile in Solvychegodsk, but fell in love with Koba and followed him to Baku.

In March 1910, Koba pronounced his first death sentence on a party member. When the typesetters refused to continue working at the Bolshevik underground printworks, Koba believed that the party had been infiltrated by half a dozen informers and demanded that one, Nikolai

Leontiev, be summoned to a meeting and killed. Leontiev, however, fought back and demanded a "trial," agreeing to die if found guilty. Support for a kangaroo court evaporated and Leontiev lived. Shortly afterward, Koba was again arrested.

Under interrogation, Koba disavowed all his activities; he claimed again his rights to the 1905 amnesty; he even denied that he was living with Stefaniia Petrovskaia, who had admitted that she was his common-law wife. The gendarmerie at Kutaisi, Tbilisi, and Baku took so long to make sense of the evidence that he was aiming to overthrow the state that he was spared lifelong exile to Siberia. (Corruption may have helped; at least one Baku gendarme, Major Zaitsev, was in the pay of the local revolutionaries.) Koba also obtained phlegm from a prisoner with advanced tuberculosis, bribed the prison doctor to certify him as seriously ill, and asked to be allowed to marry Stefaniia. Koba's sentence was again lenient: he was banned from the Caucasus for five years and handed back to the Vologda authorities as "a person harmful to public peace." Consent for Koba and Stefaniia to marry came through too late, on the day he was dispatched northward. In Solvychegodsk Koba knew no one; ironically his most faithful henchman in the future, Viacheslav Molotov, had just left the town for Vologda, the provincial capital where they met a few months later.

Having proved himself capable of robbing, killing, resisting interrogation, and withstanding prison and exile, Koba was now important enough to the party in Europe to be worth rescuing: he was in 1910 picked out for the Central Committee, in case any members should risk working in Russia. Koba began writing to Lenin, pointing out that the workers, even if they preferred Lenin's line to the law-abiding approach of Leon Trotsky, had no respect for a party which cowered in Paris cafés and Zurich libraries: "Let them climb up the wall as much as they feel like, but we think that those who value the movement's interest just get on with it."[21]

Koba was visited by the gendarmerie twice a day. Consolation in Solvychegodsk came from his landlady, Maria Kuzakova, who in late 1911 gave birth to a son, perhaps Koba's, Konstantin. On July 6, 1911, Koba was allowed to move to live under police supervision in Vologda, where there was a public library, a theater, a left-wing newspaper, and easy communications with the rest of Russia and with Bolsheviks abroad. In Vologda Koba met another exile, Piotr Chizhikov, who, while in exile further north in Totma had become engaged to a schoolgirl, Pelageiia (Polina) Georgievna Onufrieva. She followed him to Vologda and, with Chizhikov out all day, whiled away the hours with Koba.

Koba often mentioned his dead wife to Polina: "You can't imagine what beautiful dresses she used to make!"[22] Koba inscribed books "to clever, nasty Polina from Oddball Iosif" and wrote affectionate postcards: "I kiss you in turn, but I don't kiss in an ordinary way, but arrrrrdently (it's not worth just plain kissing). Iosif." Stalin showed characteristic pedantry: he told her how important was William Shakespeare's *The Tempest* (as one might expect from someone who was a Caliban impersonating Prospero). He described to Polina the paintings of the Louvre. After they parted she gave him the cross she wore, and Iosif, instead of a photograph of himself, sent her pictures of bare-breasted nymphs and half-undressed kissing couples. On his secret trip to Petersburg in August he used a passport in the name of her fiancé who, although an exile, was not a wanted man.

The Okhranka now took a closer look at Koba: they decided at first not to rearrest him, but to use him as a tracer to lead them to other Bolsheviks. They let Koba reach St. Petersburg, where Orjonikidze gave him a message from Lenin. In October 1911 he left again; this time, he hoped, for good. He was followed closely, arrested, and so well interrogated that he gave, for almost the only time, his real date of birth. Even so, the Okhranka failed to translate the Georgian and German entries in Koba's notebooks, and gave him a railway pass to Vologda and permission to live anywhere except St. Petersburg and Moscow. The gendarmerie had so vague a description of Koba—omitting his pockmarks and crippled arm—that he could not be recaptured easily.

In Baku or Tbilisi such leniency indicated corruption. Administrative sanctions against revolutionaries were determined at the highest level—by the minister of the interior, even the Tsar—but on the basis of reports compiled by lowly captains or majors. The gendarmes and prison wardens in the provinces had their tariff, from fifty rubles for letting someone impersonate a prisoner, to 800 rubles for sending the prisoner to a tolerable part of European Russia, not Siberia. In Petersburg, however, such laxity occurred for serious reasons: either the Okhranka had made its prisoner a police informer or the Okhranka wanted other revolutionaries to suspect that its prisoner was an informer.

There were even more sophisticated motives: at the Ministry of the Interior, the head of police Sergei Zubatov was infiltrating the Social Democrat and Social Revolutionary movements. Merely to bribe or blackmail revolutionaries into being police informers was futile; an effective informer such as Roman Malinovsky—soon to be a member of the Bolshevik Central Committee and the leader of the Social Democrat faction in the Duma—would be either found out or paralyzed every time his information was acted on. More Mephistophelean were plans to encourage, even subsidize, extreme and fractious revolutionaries to splinter the left into feuding factions.

If Koba collaborated with the Okhranka, this is a tribute to his equally Mephistophelean recognition of the common interests that bound the Tsar's Ministry of the Interior with the Social Democrat movement. Certain murders—of the Georgian Christian liberal writer and politician Prince (now Saint) Ilia Chavchavadze in 1907, of Russian Prime Minister Piotr Stolypin in 1911—were the joint work of the establishment's right wing and the revolution's left wing, united against the parliamentary liberals who thwarted them both. Arrests and exiles of Social Democrats still took place, but only if the revolutionaries were no use to the police as informers or allies.

Koba stayed in Vologda until February 1912, cementing his relationship with Viacheslav Molotov in St. Petersburg by an exchange of letters. He closeted himself studying German verbs. He missed the Prague party conference, but wrote a letter which showed, as Krupskaia expostulated, that, "He is terribly cut off from everything as if he has come from another planet." In February 1912 Koba left for Moscow, his every move reported to the police by agents, among them Roman Malinovsky whom Koba treated as a bosom friend. In Petersburg Koba learned that the Prague conference had co-opted him onto the Central Committee and made him, with Elena Stasova, Orjonikidze, and Malinovsky, a member of the Russian Bureau that would implement within the country decisions taken abroad.

In April 1912 Koba was instrumental in setting up the Bolsheviks' legal newspaper, *Pravda,* in St. Petersburg. In May, Molotov took over as editor, so that even in Stalin's absence the paper would remain Stalinist.

The authorities, informed about the Prague congress, rounded up all the Central Committee members on Russian territory, with the exception of their own spy Malinovsky and, for show, Grigori Petrovsky.[23] The Bolshevik fraction suddenly became a party in exile. This time the security services worked professionally: Koba was properly described and a dossier of over 1,000 pages (the charge sheet amounted to sixty pages) was compiled.[24] The sentence was not, however, harsh. Koba was exiled to Narym, a village of a few hundred persons on the river Ob in Siberia, north of the railhead in Tomsk. Ernest Ozoliņš, a Latvian socialist, accompanied Stalin and other political prisoners on the very uncomfortable train journey. To Ozoliņš, Stalin stood out with his mocking, ironical sense of superiority, his aggressiveness, and self-confidence.[25] In September 1912, after a few months' languishing, Koba took a boat and, near Tomsk, found a friendly railwayman to smuggle him onto a passenger train back to Europe.

The authorities took two months to put him on the wanted list. By then, Koba was organizing the Bolshevik campaign for the fourth Duma elections. Koba made his way to the Caucasus, probably to help Kamo Ter-Petrosiants stage a mail robbery. By October he was back in Petersburg, where he helped ensure the Okhranka's coup: their spy Roman Malinovsky was elected to the Duma to represent both Bolsheviks and the secret police. Soon Malinovsky had reported Koba's arrival and both were on their way to Kraków to see Lenin. Here Koba met one more key associate: Grigori Zinoviev, a dairy farmer's son who had spent most of the last decade in Switzerland, studying and lecturing in socialist politics.

No sooner had Malinovsky and Koba recrossed the Austrian-Russian frontier to get to St. Petersburg for the opening of the Duma than Lenin, Zinoviev, and Krupskaia, sensing a trap, urgently called Koba back: "Rush him out as soon as possible, otherwise we can't save him and he's needed and has already done the essentials." Stalin nevertheless returned to Russia and there was no reason to panic. Malinovsky, now Bolshevik spokesman in the Duma, had taken such a soft line that many of his colleagues began to believe he was a police agent.

At the Duma's Christmas break, Koba left for Kraków via Finland and Germany—his longest and his last journey abroad for thirty years. He stayed in apartments in Kraków and Vienna. His energy pleased Lenin—"the wondrous Georgian writing an article on the nationalities question" wrote his first substantial treatise, "Marxism and the Nationality Question," laboriously plowing through German sources. Koba thus gained enough status as a Marxist theoretician to ensure that he would be minister for nationalities in the first Soviet government. On this journey he made two more acquaintances, Trotsky and Nikolai Bukharin.

By 1913 he had made an impression, positive or negative, on virtually everyone who would participate in the October 1917 revolution. Above all, like Dzierżyński, he had won Lenin's trust: here was a comrade who could and would do anything the party asked and, unlike Trotsky, Zinoviev, Kamenev, or Bukharin, would not argue policy, tactics, or morals but would stay contentedly in the background. The secret of Stalin's charm was that the deeper their acquaintance with him, the more his admirers wondered at the mixture of ruthless activity and well-hidden intellect. He still struck them as a coarse, monoglot barbarian, but they would at some point be stunned by his mastery of information, human character, and his ability to orientate himself in any group.

Another ten years would pass before Stalin, as general secretary of the Communist Party, could exercise his own judgment in choosing, not whom to flatter or court, but whom to appoint, whom to dismiss. But long before the revolution, by 1913, he had met most of those who would play a part in his rise to power—whom he would follow, patronize, or kill. Of those he would need most, he had gotten to know Mikhail Kalinin, his puppet head of state, in 1900 and Emelian Iaroslavsky, his most effective propagandist, in 1905. In 1906 Stalin met Dzierżyński, who would swing Lenin's secret police behind him, and Klim Voroshilov, who would subordinate the army to Stalin's will and then supervise the slaughter of every possible dissident senior officer. In 1907 he acquired a loyal ally in Sergo Orjonikidze, and in 1908 the unprincipled lawyer Vyshinsky, who would organize the parody of legal process by which terror could be instituted. In 1910 Stalin won over the most devoted of his subordinates, Viacheslav Molotov. Lazar Kaganovich was the only figure close to Stalin during the revolution whom he had not met in the revolutionary underground.

Likewise, by 1913 Stalin had met, and taken a dislike to, the party's theoreticians, the rivals whom he would exterminate. He met Kamenev in 1904, Rykov in 1906, Trotsky and Zinoviev in 1912, and Bukharin in 1913. They would pay for their condescension to Koba decades later.

Trotsky disliked Stalin at first sight: "The door was flung open, without a preliminary knock, an unknown person appeared on the threshold—squat, with swarthy face and traces of smallpox." Koba poured himself tea and without a word walked out. Bukharin, a daily visitor to the apartment where Koba stayed, reacted to him with a mix of admiration, affection, fear, and horror. To judge from Koba's letters intercepted by the Russian secret service, he felt unhappy in the bourgeois luxury of Vienna and, despite Lenin's admiration, Russian intellectuals in exile irritated him. "There's nobody to let my hair down with. Nobody to have a heart-to-heart," he complained to an unknown girlfriend. Koba's recent encounter with three persons in Lenin's entourage—Zinoviev, Trotsky, and Bukharin—was a blow to his self-esteem which gave him no peace until he had killed all three.

Nineteen thirteen, the year the Romanov dynasty celebrated its three hundredth anniversary, seemed to doom Koba to ignominy and obscurity. He fell into a depression that lasted four years. First, Malinovsky was denounced as a police agent in a calculated blow to the left wing by Vladimir Dzhunkovsky, the head of the gendarmerie. Lenin would not believe it. The Bolsheviks now looked like a farcical band of deluded intellectuals, its Central Committee a handful of Okhranka puppets. Second, the police rounded up virtually every important Bolshevik activist at large in Russia. Third, the Romanov tercentenary, Russia's economic boom, and liberal legislation had dulled the proletarian grievances that fueled Bolshevik popularity. Fourth, as Europe headed for war, as in Germany so in Russia the Social Democrats collapsed as an internationalist party: its members put nation first and socialism second. The revolution was indefinitely postponed.

Koba wrote to the Bolsheviks in exile abroad to complain of the bacchanalia of arrests and hinted to Lenin that Malinovsky was putting a wrench in the works and was a police spy. In February Iakov Sverdlov (who would be first head of the Soviet state), then Koba, were arrested. This time it was decided not just to make Koba finish his exile but to pack him off for four years to farthest Siberia, to Turukhansk on the river Enisei where it crosses the Arctic Circle.

Despondent despite money offered by the party, Koba made no escape attempt, although he now signed himself K. (for Koba) Stalin (man of steel).[26] From Turukhansk, Koba was sent still farther north to the tiny settlement of Miroedikha. Here Koba's behavior made him hated. The exile who had preceded him, Iosif Dubrovinsky, had drowned in the river Enisei that May. Stalin violated revolutionary etiquette by appropriating Dubrovinsky's library. He was transferred ninety miles south to the village of Kostino, and then north again to a hamlet, Monastyrskoe. Koba was, one guesses, more miserable than ever before or afterward. From here he wrote to Zinoviev asking for books. He asked a woman friend to send his underwear. He wrote to, of all people, Roman Malinovsky, asking for sixty rubles, complaining of poverty—no bread, meat, or paraffin in an area where the only food an exile could have for free was fish—of emaciation and an ominous cough. Then, on September 27, 1913, he moved in with Iakov Sverdlov ten miles away. Money arrived, but it was meant only for Sverdlov's escape. The gendarmerie, who read all letters, deducted the money from Stalin's and Sverdlov's board allowances and deported them, with a gendarme, Laletin, a hundred miles farther north to an even more desolate outpost, Kureika. Again Stalin begged Malinovsky for money, as if he did not know that Malinovsky had resigned after being exposed as a spy.

Sverdlov found Stalin bad company. He wrote to his wife: " . . . you know my dear what foul conditions I lived in at Kureika. The comrade [Stalin] we were with turned out on a personal level to be such that we didn't speak or see each other." By Easter 1914, Stalin had forced Sverdlov out and moved in with a family of seven orphans, the Pereprygins. He scandalized both Sverdlov and Ivan Laletin by seducing the thirteen-year-old Lidia Pereprygina. Bolsheviks had tolerant sexual mores, but sleeping with a pubescent girl was for them typical of the hated feudal gentry. Koba was now beyond the pale. Laletin caught Stalin in flagrante and had to fight off Koba's fists with his saber. (Stalin then promised to marry Lidia Pereprygina when she came of age.) At

Stalin's insistence, the Turukhansk chief of police, the Osetian Ivan Kibirov, replaced the indignant Laletin—who nearly drowned on his return upriver—with a more compliant gendarme.[27] Lidia became pregnant; in 1916, after the baby died, she conceived again.[28]

Cohabitation with an adolescent girl gave Stalin no joy. He read, he tried to master languages. He wrote very little—to Zinoviev to ask for English newspapers, to the Alliluevs to ask for postcards with pictures of pleasant scenery. He made one visit 120 miles upstream to Monastyrskoe, where his Armenian friend Suren Spandaryan, now dying of TB, had been transferred. When the ice melted in spring 1915, five Bolshevik Duma deputies, all "anti-patriotic defeatists," arrived, exiled to Monastyrskoe, and with them one familiar face from Tbilisi, Lev Kamenev. Here the exiles conferred, but Stalin could never endure more than a day or two of these gatherings, even though the news of Russia's catastrophic defeats by the Germans must have rekindled hopes of revolution. Dispossessed radicals, cut off from their ideological leaders by war and 7,000 miles of Asia and Europe, seemed to Koba "a little bit like wet chickens. Ha, there's 'eagles' for you."[29]

The company soon dispersed: the Duma deputies and Kamenev were allowed south to the town of Eniseisk. The remaining exiles were demoralized and began to accuse each other of crimes: Sverdlov had been teaching a policeman German; Spandaryan had helped loot the local stores. Stalin voted that Sverdlov be ostracized. Another exile was beaten up; after the brawl Spandaryan had a hemorrhage which led to his death in September, despite the Tsar freeing him on compassionate grounds. Nobody saw Stalin in his last months in Siberia; perhaps he fled to Eniseisk, from hostility toward him at Kureika when Lidia Pereprygina became pregnant again.

By autumn 1916 the Russian army's losses in the war were so horrendous that the authorities began calling up political exiles: even Stalin, aged thirty-seven and with a withered arm, was summoned to the recruiting office in Krasnoyarsk. In February 1917 he was rejected as unfit for service. The Tsar's regime was collapsing; political exiles were effectively released. Stalin was allowed to settle, with Kamenev, in the town of Achinsk on the Trans-Siberian railway. On March 2 the Tsar abdicated, a provisional parliamentary government took power in Petrograd, as St.

Petersburg had been renamed in 1915, and the old regime was dismantled. Peasants, burghers, and officials celebrated. At a meeting Lev
Kamenev proposed a congratulatory telegram to the Tsar's brother for
refusing the throne—a conciliatory message that Stalin would never let
him forget. On March 12 Stalin, Kamenev, and other exiles arrived in
Petrograd to begin months of conspiratorial work to prepare for the return of Lenin and the seizure of power. First, Stalin and Kamenev took
control of *Pravda* and typeset their own articles. All Koba's rudeness,
perversity, and surliness were set aside by his colleagues in the interests
of the struggle.

The Lone Sadist

Thought unrevealed can do no ill
But words past out turn not again.
Be careful aye for to invent
The way to get thine own intent.

King James VI of Scotland

UNTIL 1913, Stalin in the Caucasus and Vologda was not outstandingly
different from other revolutionaries in behavior, thought, and morality.
In 1917, an embittered recluse after his journey to Kraków and Vienna
and four years in Siberia, he was now an outsider. He now brooked no
equals and recognized only one superior, Lenin. He was on intimate
terms with fellow revolutionaries, such as Kamenev, but they could pre-
sume no intimacy. After the deaths of Kato Svanidze and Suren
Spandaryan, both women and men deluded themselves if they thought
they had a personal relationship with Stalin.

Stalin had for some time been complicit in murders—assassinations
or retributions possibly including the betrayal of comrades. But he could
not, on his euphoric return from exile in Siberia to the threshold of
power in Petrograd, have contemplated the killing of enemies and the
manipulation of comrades on the scale that was to come. The maelstrom

of revolution, the temptations of power, the character of his comrades and underlings, as much as his unscrupulous personality, determined this escalation.

Cynical about everything else, Stalin nevertheless professed one constant ideal: Leninism. From his first encounters with Lenin in 1906 and 1907 to the point when he became Lenin's manager, caretaker, and interpreter, Stalin looked up to him as a disciple looked to Jesus Christ. We may see Stalin as Saint Paul, Saint Peter, Saint Thomas, or Judas, but Lenin's writings were for Stalin holy writ.

Stalin's sincerity is most evident in his correspondence with the Bolshevik poetaster Demian Bedny.[30] Before Stalin outgrew, or suppressed, his need for permanent friends, Demian Bedny was one of very few correspondents who could write to Stalin freely and coarsely, and receive a reply in the same vein. The letters of 1924 between Stalin and Demian, the latter at the time in the Caucasian resort of Essentuki, like Stalin's scrawls in the margins of books, are unguarded words, which give us some insight into Stalin's personality:[31]

Stalin to Demian July 15: Our Philosophy is not "cosmic grief," our philosophy was rather neatly put by the American Whitman: "We are alive. Our scarlet blood boils with the fire of unused strength."

Demian to Stalin July 29: I can't boast that I know you "inside out." And anyway that would be unrealizable. What would you be worth then? But "grasping Stalin" must attain a certain, maximum degree . . . you are my "benchmark," "axial" friend. . . . If you venture far into the Caucasus, then bring me a nice Circassian girl.

Stalin to Demian August 27: Greetings, friend. You're utterly right that it is impossible to know somebody "inside out" . . . But I am always ready to help you in this respect. [There then follows a ten-page exegesis of Lenin's views of the dictatorship of the proletariat, as distinct from the dictatorship of the party, ending] . . . as for the proletariat, the party cannot be a force for dictatorship. I ask you not to copy this letter of mine, not to make a noise about it.

Demian's reply shows how taken aback he was by Stalin's fanatical outburst: "Instead of a Circassian girl you warmed me up with a treatise."

In response to Stalin's other remarks about his cunning political strategy—attacking leaders of the opposition and then wooing their adher-
ents in order to put an end to fractions and factions—Demian felt
himself on surer ground. Here he and Stalin were cronies again. Demian
wrote: "If the best husband and wife start arguing sharply, even if the
reasons are purely matters of principle, the argument can end with either
the husband fucking somebody else or his wife being fucked by others. I
am sure that you and I will not refuse somebody else's and will not let go
of our own, and if we do let go, then it will be because 'she's a whore,'
even if she's festooned with quotations."

★ ★ ★ The Bedny–Stalin letters convey the contradictions in Stalin's
thinking: coarse in tactics and expression, arcane in professed ideology.

The same duality is apparent in Stalin's relationships with his wives
and children. Some of his behavior is ascribable to Georgian custom: a
wife must never show her husband up in public, must never act disre-
spectfully or frivolously. Children, too, however much loved, must defer
in public. Among Georgian highlanders, a husband makes no display of
affection in public to his wife or children, not even to single out his own
child for rescue from general danger.

Stalin was, even by these standards, an exceptionally unfeeling parent. Not until his second marriage, after the 1917 revolution, did he take
a cursory interest in Iakov, whom he had handed over as a baby to his
sister-in-law and Mikhail Monaselidze, her husband. When, in 1928,
Iakov tried to shoot himself, Stalin greeted him with "Ha, so you
missed!" Iakov fled to his stepmother's parents, the Alliluevs. Stalin
wrote to Nadezhda, his second wife: "Tell Iakov from me that he has
acted like a hooligan and a blackmailer with whom I do not and cannot
have anything in common. Let him live where and with whom he wants."

In 1941, less than a month after the outbreak of war, Iakov was captured by the Germans. Stalin refused Count Bernadotte's offer to negotiate Iakov's release. The refusal was interpreted as putting national
before personal interests, but Stalin went further: he had Iakov's wife imprisoned as a deserter's spouse, and when Iakov's picture was used by the
Germans for propaganda leaflets, Stalin asked the Spanish communist

Dolores Ibarruri "La Pasionaria" to infiltrate undercover agents among Spanish fascists in Germany in order to reach Iakov in his POW camp and presumably kill him. In 1943, however, Iakov was electrocuted and shot dead by the Germans.

To his daughter Svetlana Stalin was at first affectionate, even playful, calling her Khoziaika (housewife) or Satanka, but after she began a succession of ill-judged liaisons, she too fell out of favor and saw little of her father.

Stalin's marital history falls just short of the pathological. The inquisitive mind of a pedant and autodidact, behind a brooding romantic face, attracted women. Old flames flare up in the letters Stalin kept in his archive: "Do you remember the beautiful neighbor Liza, who used to look after you . . . that's me."[32] Stalin's first wife, Kato, made no complaints—she was no mute peasant; she had been educated by private tutors and her brother had studied in Germany—but, a conventional Georgian wife, she kept in the background. Stalin's subsequent liaisons with Onufrieva, Pereprygina, and others, and his second marriage to the seventeen-year-old Nadezhda Allilueva—apart from a preference for adolescent girls and for solitude—do not suggest grossly abnormal sexuality.

Stalin liked female nudity, as his choice of postcards showed. In his marginalia to Anatole France's dialogue on prudery, he underlined the comment, "Few women know how beautiful nudity is," and wrote, "Very original" against the statement that "a plant shows with pride what a human being conceals." When, years later, widowed again, he read the diary that Tolstoi's wife kept for 1910, the last and most unhappy year of a stormy marital life, Stalin found much to comment on, singling out in particular Sofia Tolstaia's entry: "Only the Trubetskoys bathed, husband and wife together in the river, and astounded us by so doing."

After Stalin married Nadezhda in 1917, it was said that he had first raped her; even that he had slept with her mother nine months before Nadezhda was born. The notorious temperament of Olga Allilueva, the fact that both parties had been in the same city in 1900, and the tension toward the end of the marriage support the rumor, though Nadezhda had many other reasons to kill herself in 1932.

Obsessed with pursuing power and crushing opposition, Stalin remained in some areas of his life relatively normal. He was active sexually: Nadezhda had two live births and, her medical records show, ten abortions during their marriage. After her death, to judge by Stalin's well-documented routine, there was little time for sexual relationships. His young housekeeper Valentina Istomina probably met his occasional needs and a few ballerinas and opera singers claimed to have been Stalin's mistresses in the 1930s and 1940s. By all accounts Stalin's sexual behavior was peremptory and rough, but there is no psychosexual theory explanation of Stalin's sadism; it was cold-blooded.

Perhaps in his austerity we can find the key to Stalin's remorseless concentration on the task at hand, his refusal to soften: there were few people close to him whom he was not prepared to destroy and few objects that had any value for him. With the resources of half the world at his disposal he lived in ill-furnished rooms and slept on uncomfortable divans. His wardrobe was sparse, without silk or fur. If not as ascetic (not as chaste and abstemious) as Hitler, Stalin had little interest in physical pleasure. In food he valued simplicity, not delicacy; he checked only that it was not poisoned. His alcohol and tobacco intake was controlled: he made his guests drunk, not himself, and the famous pipe was a rarely lit prop.

One explanation for the Marquis de Sade's need to inflict pain was that he himself was never free of it. Dostoevsky's "Underground Man" proclaims that anyone suffering from toothache badly wants others to feel the same pain. This is plausible in the case of Stalin. The agony he inflicted on others grew out of his own. His medical records imply that he was in constant pain.[33] In addition to his scarred face and webbed toe, his left arm atrophied so much that in his fifties it could barely lift a cup. Stalin's annual checkups in the Kremlin suggest a middle-aged man in chronic pain: in the mid-1920s Stalin had sciatic pain in all his limbs and was plagued by chronic myalgia, arthritis, and eventually muscular atrophy. From 1926 he had irritable bowel syndrome, which caused constant diarrhea and public embarrassment. Prison and Siberia had given him, like other old Bolsheviks, tuberculosis, and although the disease abated, he was left with a weakened right lung stuck to his pleura. His voice was never strong enough to make a speech without a microphone. In the 1920s his teeth rotted and gave him hell: a dentist, Shapiro, extracted eight roots and filed and crowned most of his remaining teeth in Sochi in 1930.[34] In 1921 Stalin was operated on for appendicitis. All the time he held power he had attacks of dizziness, respiratory and bowel infections, and would complain, by the time he took his extended late-summer breaks in the south, of mental symptoms: exhaustion, irritability, inability to concentrate, bad memory.

Stalin's paranoiac suspicions of the doctors who treated him were not entirely unjustified: the misdiagnoses and sudden deaths of Feliks Dzierżyński in 1926 and Andrei Zhdanov in 1948 suggest that the Kremlin professors of medicine were fallible, or worse. Stalin's suspicions caused him to have his medicines fetched from the pharmacy under a false name, and he would have a bodyguard take any medication first. Dr. Shneiderovich was asked by Stalin in 1934: "Doctor, tell me just the truth: do you occasionally feel a desire to poison me?" To Shneiderovich's denial, Stalin responded, "Doctor, you're a timid weak person, you'd never do it, but I have enemies who are capable of doing it." In January 1937 Stalin turned to Dr. Valedinsky at dinner and, apropos of nothing, growled, "There are enemies of the people among the doctors." Fifteen years were to pass before Stalin took a step unprecedented even for tyrants, and had most of his doctors arrested.

While physical and mental pain do not account for the extermination of whole classes and conditions of mankind, they do explain the sudden bursts of fury with which Stalin would turn on loyal servants before he threw them to his wolves.

One simple explanation of Stalin was clear to Trotsky and other victims: they saw him as a bandit, murderer, impostor, traitor—"Genghis Khan who's read Marx," to quote Bukharin. But the boundary between expropriation and robbery, execution and murder, betrayal and tactical maneuver is fuzzy, and most revolutionaries confuse or overstep it. Stalin can be singled out from Lenin, Trotsky, Sverdlov, and the rest only in his willingness to take criminal measures as first, rather than last resorts, and to use them on intimates as well as strangers. The revolution relied on many criminals' lack of inhibitions to seize power and kill their opponents; Stalin can be seen as just a criminal on whose services the revolution was forced to depend.

But Stalin is too easily categorized as a serial killer. Extrapolating twenty years back from the 1930s leads to unfounded allegations such as Roman Brackman's that Stalin hired an ax murderer to kill his father in Telavi in 1906. There were violent deaths among Stalin's companions and enemies that he welcomed, but a causal link is often undemonstrable and even ludicrous.

Stalin is often dismissed as a bandit. In 1907 he sought Lenin's agreement, against the policy of the Social Democrats, Menshevik and Bolshevik, to fund the party by armed robbery; he may also have taken part in wrecking a ship off Batumi. Such expropriations, however, were a vital source of funding, and Stalin's enthusiastic banditry does not set him morally or ideologically apart from most terrorists.

The most odious criminal charge against Stalin (to his fellow revolutionaries) is of cooperating with the Okhranka, acting as a secret police agent, betraying his colleagues and the cause. The evidence is copious but, discounting obvious forgeries which Stalin may have engineered to discredit real evidence, ambiguous. For one thing, collaboration with the Okhranka was often justified. Both socialists and gendarmes wanted a Bolshevik party strong enough to split the left, especially the Social Democrats, and several colonels in the Russian secret service maintained a working relationship with those they were supposed to be jailing, exiling, and hanging. In the 1900s the interpenetration of secret service and revolutionary underground was so tangled that agents of either side could find it hard to remember what aims were paramount in their activities. Stalin's sources of income, his apparent ability to travel from Siberia to Baku without hindrance, even faster than the train timetables allowed, and the ease with which he crossed the Russian, Polish, and Finnish frontiers with dubious papers all make it plausible that he had come to arrangements with the Okhranka.

For the whole of the 1920s and some of the 1930s, Stalin's Okhranka file was considered a bombshell that could destroy him or whoever tried to use it against him while the files of other old Bolsheviks were carefully stored to damn any whom Stalin needed to discard. This however is not enough to categorize Stalin as a traitor. Like Lenin and Sverdlov, only with less hesitation, he used any means for his absolute end. If cooperation with the Okhranka proves that a Bolshevik was an impostor, then the whole of Lenin's Politburo and their revolution becomes a capitalist plot, as absurd and pointless as the legendary last session of the Communist Party of the State of Utah, when it dawned on the seventeen participants that they were all FBI agents.

The striking quality that marks Stalin apart from his comrades is isolation. Before he first saw Lenin in 1905, he worshipped no living human being. There were Georgians at the seminary whom he admired: the murdered thinker and poet Lado Ketskhoveli, for instance. He also admired Seit Devdariani, who led a group of radical students. Devdariani became a philosopher and was in 1937 shot by Beria, unquestionably with Stalin's assent, and the only copy of his manuscript *A History of Georgian Thought* perished, except for a brief fragment, with him. Stalin's serious intellectual rivals in the Tbilisi seminary did not live long.

In Stalin's few friendships he dictated the agenda and he was more loved than loving. Lenin, even after his brain had been shattered by strokes, however, remained a superior being in Stalin's eyes: as ruthless and peremptory as himself, even more charismatic and, above all, with the ability to produce the right words for every theory and the right theory to justify every event, using irony, logic, and abuse to convince. This worship was not fully reciprocated. Lenin saw Koba as "the marvelous Georgian" but had trouble remembering the surname Jughashvili. From the start, Koba stood out from Lenin's comrades as an atavistic executor of the party's, especially of Lenin's, will, balking at nothing, yet calm and collected (when not rude and irritable), a factotum who could even write polemical treatises and expound doctrine, if not an original thinker.

Lenin gave Stalin enough praise to encourage his conceit. From newspaper articles in Georgian, summarizing what he had read in Russian, Stalin in 1913 graduated to treatises in Russian. In Lenin's ruthless cynicism about the means used to achieve the end and in his readiness to take drastic measures, to deceive and manipulate, Stalin found a kindred soul.

Lenin held sacred the famous principle of democratic centralism: decisions reached after a vote in the party's Central Committee were binding on all. (In fact, where necessary, a minority opinion was massaged into a majority opinion.) Stalin was an adept pupil, as he explained to Molotov:

Let's suppose there are 80 people in the Central Committee, of whom 30 take the right position and 50 the wrong one, thus being active enemies of your policy. Why should the majority submit to the minority? . . . A minority has never expelled a majority. This takes place gradually. Seventy expel 10–15, then 60 expel another 15 . . . And gradually, all this being done in the framework of democratic centralism, without any formal infringement of the rules. Actually, this ends with the minority of the majority remaining in the CC.[35]

For all his unprincipled remorselessness, his energy and patience, Stalin needed not just the right moment to take power but the right associates, those willing not just to die, but to kill for him.

TWO

STALIN, DZIERŻYŃSKI, AND THE CHEKA

He will battle to the grave with dark clouds,
Beaten back a thousand times he will rise up
to the end.

— *Feliks Dzierżyński*

Prelude to Power

THE PETROGRAD to which Stalin, Kamenev, Lenin, and Trotsky flocked, in trains from Scandinavia or Siberia, in spring and summer 1917 was unrecognizable to them. Bliss was it at that dawn to be alive, or so it seemed. The removal of Tsar and court left Russia with a parliamentary government of the great, the good, and the reasonable. Aristocratic liberals (constitutional democrats) shared power and platforms with socialists and dormant terrorists. Men like Alexander Kerensky, the lawyer and orator who was leader of the Duma, and effectively prime minister, would have been adequate in a peaceful Scandinavian country. They presided over the total abolition of the death penalty and complete freedom of speech and assembly. They demolished the instruments of oppression: the gendarmerie, the penal system. Crowds filled the streets and made their demands with impunity: housewives wanted bread, workers took over factories, sailors and soldiers rose up against their officers.

In fact a demographic and political disaster had occurred. Millions of peasants had died at the front while the survivors were deserting en masse to seize the land. Hundreds of thousands of officers had perished, some at the hands of their own soldiers. There were too few people left alive to feed the cities or to administer them. Russia was cut off by war from its European allies, except by tortuous rail and ship connections through Sweden and Norway or the interminable route across Siberia, the Pacific Ocean, and the United States. All this was too much for a government of well-meaning men to cope with, especially when faced with the dilemma of whether to withdraw from the war and make peace with Germany, thus provoking the hostility of the British and French and mutiny by the officer class, or to continue the war to "final victory" and doom the country to inevitable collapse and revolution, leaving the Bolsheviks and social revolutionaries to seize power from the ruins.

Kerensky's government dithered, but had it made a firm decision, could not have enforced it. Trapped between the anvil of an officer corps determined to restore order and fight the Germans, and the hammer of workers and soldiers bent on taking power from the Duma to the councils (soviets) that had flourished during the 1905 uprising, Kerensky, enlisting one set of opponents against the other, talked himself into irrelevance.

Lenin and Trotsky, let alone minor players such as Stalin, had no difficulty hiding from halfhearted attempts to arrest them. A demoralized society saw no need to extirpate them. As food became harder to find, as transport and medical services collapsed and life on the streets and at home was endangered by armed marauders, the population became resigned to accepting any force, left or right, that could seize power and take decisions. The spring of euphoria led to a summer of disillusion and an autumn of despair. When in November the Bolsheviks struck, in ten days that shook the world, paralyzing Russia by seizing railway junctions and telephone exchanges, even their most principled opponents put up no coherent resistance, so great was the relief that a group of men had taken on responsibility for the future. However ominous their leaders and ideology, they would put an end to the dithering; they would fill the vacuum.

Feliks Dzierżyński: The First Forty Years

THE PUBLIC OF PETROGRAD and Moscow had heard only of Lenin and Trotsky; other Bolsheviks were shadows emerging from the underground. Stalin was, as backstage manager of the revolution, the least visible of the Bolshevik Central Committee that took power. Leon Trotsky was a genius, creating the Red Army out of disaffected soldiers, workers, and peasants. Vladimir Lenin bullied and cajoled fractious colleagues into a semblance of unity. Nevertheless, the revolution needed a third man against its enemies: it had to be armed against the unseen threat from those on the left and the right who wanted not a Marxist dictatorship but a pluralistic, democratic forum.

Within six weeks of the October revolution, Lenin's men felt surrounded by such hostility that they set up a secret police. Feliks Dzierżyński, a middle-aged Pole, pallid from years in prison, created a punitive, deterrent, and intelligence organization, the Cheka. Dzierżyński became the role model for all future Soviet secret police chiefs, just as Lenin set the example for leaders of the Soviet party and state. It was the symbiosis of Dzierżyński and Stalin which would determine the fate of the USSR after Lenin fell ill and died.

Dzierżyński, who put himself forward for the post despite being as unlikely a leader as Stalin, was the ideal chief for a repressive organization. Like Stalin, he was neither Russian nor an intellectual in the sense that Lenin and Trotsky considered themselves. He had unique experience: nobody had worked as hard in eleven years of prison and exile on unmasking traitors to the revolutionary movement—chairing a committee of prisoners that interrogated suspected provocateurs, as his widow proudly recorded. Nobody was as flamboyantly self-sacrificing for the cause as Dzierżyński: his sense of propriety and duty were hypertrophied. From 1918 on, in his Lubianka office Dzierżyński interrogated prisoners and rummaged through their files and drove out to make arrests—like Stalin taking advantage of the lowest point in his victims' biorhythms; Dzierżyński liked working late at night. The only task he, like Stalin, left to his underlings was executions. Only once did Dzierżyński shoot anybody dead—a drunken sailor who was swearing at him— and this induced a convulsive fit. In power even more ascetic than Stalin, Dzierżyński subsisted as he had in prison, on mint tea and bread, in an unheated office, his greatcoat for a blanket. He rolled cigarettes from rough Russian tobacco. Unlike Stalin, Dzierżyński was a pedantic purist. He threw away pancakes cooked by his sister because she had bought flour from a private trader; he dismissed his niece, and the man who had given her a job, from service on the railways because she had profited from the family name. Dzierżyński fled in indignation on the only occasion he went to an art gallery, never attended a concert and read only Polish romantic poetry or Marxist exegeses. Dzierżyński had his son fostered in a working-class family, where "it is easiest to preserve and enrich one's soul." Dzierżyński's aesthetic sense was sublimated in work. His successor Menzhinsky wrote in his obituary: "Were it not for his artistic nature, his love of art and nature . . . for all his experience underground, he would never have reached the perfection of Chekist art in taking his opponents apart, which made him stand head and shoulders above all his colleagues."

Dzierżyński gave the Cheka and its subsequent acronymic transformations a pseudo-chivalrous image of "sword and flame of the revolution," and the conviction that they should be the central, sometimes supreme, power. The principles—"every communist must be a chekist"—and the extrajudicial powers of the Cheka were established by Dzierżyński, although he always meant it to be subject to the party's leader: to implement and enforce, not create, ideology and policy.

Without Dzierżyński's authority and support, Stalin might never have come to power. In 1922 Dzierżyński would swing the half-million paramilitaries he controlled away from Trotsky's principled "opposition," to Stalin's "loyal support" for Lenin's appeasement of those in the party who wanted civil peace, a partial restoration of capitalism, and the rule of law. From 1917 to 1922, as Lenin's faithful hound, he did more than Stalin for revolutionary unity but sided with Stalin when choices between fractions had to be made.

What brought together these two men of largely incompatible temperament, class, and nationality? Dzierżyński and Stalin were drawn to each other, as other Georgian and Polish intellectuals and rebels always had been. For Georgians, Poland was a congenial part of the Russian empire for university study or exile. Poles and Georgians shared a tradition of eloquence, a cult of honor, and pride in a heroic medieval age of chivalry. Both nations also believed that they had been chosen by God to defend Christian values—the Poles the Catholic faith and Western culture, the Georgians the Orthodox religion and Byzantine civilization—against the barbarians of the East.

Personally, Stalin and Dzierżyński had much in common, apart from dour fathers and doting mothers. From childhood to adolescence they had been destined by their family and temperaments to be priests; the adolescent Stalin could have said what Dzierżyński told his brother Kazimierz: "If I ever concluded that God did not exist, I'd put a bullet through my head." Both at the age of nineteen underwent violent conversion to atheism and revolution. Equally unsmiling and uncommunicative in private life, they spent years of political resistance brooding in prisons and hunting in Siberia. They did not debate in Swiss cafés nor study in French libraries. Unlike the uxorious Lenin and Trotsky, their solitude was broken by only a few months of arid marital life and they both left in their native lands young sons whom they hardly knew. Both had been poets: they declaimed and catechized, they did not expatiate or analyze. Both were shy of public speaking and arcane Marxism. Neither finished his education, and both spoke Russian as a foreign language.[1] Stalin and Dzierżyński prided themselves on their aloofness, and on their nose for treachery. No wonder then that their meeting in Petrograd in summer 1917 after a brief encounter in Stockholm in 1906 led to an alliance.

They were also diametrically different. Feliks Dzierżyński was a Polish noble, even if his family had been reduced to a manor house and some two hundred acres on the borders of Lithuania and Belorussia. Unlike Stalin, Dzierżyński was cosseted by loving siblings—particularly his sisters—and brought up by a well-educated mother. But Dzierżyński had, like Stalin, a harsh father who soon vanished from his life and a religious mother. Above all, he remained affectionately attached to his siblings and his nephews and nieces. Unlike Stalin, Dzierżyński had a dual nature; in April 1919, when the Cheka was slaughtering hostages by the thousand, Dzierżyński could write to his elder sister:

> I can tell you one truth: I have remained the same. I sense that you can't come to terms with the thought that this is me—and, knowing me, you can't understand. Love. Today, as years ago, I hear and feel a hymn to it. This hymn demands war, unbending will, tireless work. And today, apart from the idea, apart from striving for justice, nothing has any weight on the scales of my actions. It's hard for me to write, it's hard to argue. You see only what is, and what you hear about in exaggerated colors. You're a witness and victim of the Moloch of war. The ground you once lived on is subsiding under your feet. I am an eternal wanderer, in motion, in the process of change and creating a new life. You turn your thoughts and soul to the past—I see the future and want, and have, to be in movement. Have you ever reflected what

war really is? You have pushed aside the images of bodies ripped apart by shells, of the wounded on the floor, of the crows pecking out the eyes of the living. . . . And you can't understand me, a soldier of the revolution. . . . My Aldona, you don't understand me—it's hard for me to write any more to you. If you saw how I live, if you looked into my eyes, you'd understand, rather you'd sense that I have remained the same I always was. I kiss you powerfully. Your Fel[2]

Edmund-Rufin Dzierżyński, Feliks's father, earned his living by teaching. He seduced a pupil, Elena Januszewska. They married, but had to leave Lithuania. Edmund-Rufin went to the southern Russian port of Taganrog to teach mathematics, where his pupils included three Chekhov brothers, including Anton. The historian of the Taganrog grammar school, himself a pupil of the hated Pole, reported in 1906 that Dzierżyński senior was "a pathologically irritable man who tormented boys."[3] In 1875 Edmund-Rufin was forced to resign and returned to his family estate.

Feliks was the only one of seven children to rebel; his siblings tried to live middle-class lives. The eldest girl, Aldona, seven years older than Feliks, became a second mother to the family when their father died unexpectedly in 1883. Other tragedies hit the family. When Feliks and his elder brother Stanisław were handling a rifle, one of them killed their fourteen-year-old sister Wanda. This accident may have prompted Feliks's sudden apostasy. He never spoke of Wanda's death but attributed his loss of faith in God and Tsar to witnessing Cossacks attacking Lithuanian peasants in 1893. Like Stalin, Dzierżyński sublimated his fellow countrymen's crusade against their Russian conquerors into hatred for all governing classes. He confessed later, "I dreamed of a cap of invisibility and of the annihilation of all Muscovites."

Feliks's mother, Elena, died in 1896, leaving Aldona to bring up the younger children alone. The Dzierżyński family loved their black sheep: Aldona visited Feliks in prison, sent him parcels and letters, even after his rise to head the Cheka. Aldona married and remained in Poland, personally devoted if politically opposed to Feliks.[4] Feliks's other elder sister, Jadwiga, was to be, together with her daughter (also Jadwiga), his helpmate in Russia. (In 1949 Jadwiga senior died in Stalin's camps.) Stanisław Dzierżyński, who became a biologist, was murdered on the family estate by bandits in 1917.[5] Two of Feliks's brothers, the youngest Władysław, a professor of medicine, and Kazimierz, an engineer, paid dearly for their surname: they were murdered by the Gestapo in 1943 and 1942 respectively. Of Feliks's brothers only Ignacy (1880–1953) died of natural causes.

Feliks, like Stalin, left education just before his final examinations. He plunged into the factories and slums of Vilnius as a Marxist agitator rousing the proletariat to action, for which he learned Yiddish and Lithuanian as well as Russian. Before he was twenty he had made an impact on the Polish social democrats, urging them to abandon Polish nationalism and parliamentarianism in favor of international revolutionary socialism. The adolescent Feliks, like Stalin, combined fanatical rebelliousness with moonstruck romantic musing. Dzierżyński's unpublished poetry echoes the decadence of the "Young Poland" modernists such as his own favorite, Antoni Lange. Typically morbid are Feliks's lines:

> Every night something comes to see me
> Incorporeal and soundless,
> A mysterious vision
> Stands over me in silence.
> It gives me the present of a kiss,
> This gift does not tell me:
> Are you offering me your heart,
> Or are you mocking me, cold Lady?

Dzierżyński, unlike Stalin, remained in thrall to sentimental morbid chivalry, even when acting with cold-blooded ruthlessness. Years of exile and prison blinkered him, and he had little understanding of real life: he was to apply Karl Marx and Lenin to public life with the same naïveté as he adapted Polish romanticism to his private life. On May 27, 1918, he wrote, as if he were a saint in the desert, to his wife (who remained in Zurich until 1919):

There is no time to think of my family or myself . . . the more powerful wheel of enemies that encircles us, the closer it is to my heart. . . . Every day I have to take up more terrible weapons. . . . I have to be myself just as terrible, so as like a faithful hound to tear apart the villain. . . . I live just on my nerves. . . . My thought orders me to be terrible and I have the will to follow my thought to the end. . . .

Like Stalin in Vologda, Dzierżyński in exile attracted women. Stalin played mentor to Polina Onufrieva, while Dzierżyński was the pupil in his relationship with Rita (Margarita Fiodorovna Nikolaeva), a fellow exile three years older than him, in the northern Russian town of Viatka in 1898.[6] Dzierżyński was then twenty-one; this was his first exile and his first love. Declaring himself Rita's fiancé, he volunteered to follow her farther north to Nolinsk. Here, on an allowance of five and a half rubles a month each, they set up house. She was the well-educated daughter of a priest; thanks to her Dzierżyński acquired fluent Russian and even struggled through *Das Kapital.* But classics such as Goethe's *Faust,* Dzierżyński confessed to her, were beyond him.

Dzierżyński had even then discovered his personal power: he wrote to his sister: "When I get carried away and begin to defend my views too ardently, the expression in my eyes becomes so frightening to my opponents that they cannot look me in the face." Twenty years later, in 1919, he told Aldona with relish: "For many people there is nothing so frightening as my name."

The Russian gendarmes found Dzierżyński not frightening but "hot-tempered, irritable, unrestrained." In January 1899 they exiled him farther north, to the settlement of Kaigorodskoe. Dzierżyński spent days with a rifle, shooting game. Fellow exiles gave him a bear cub as a pet; he trained it to dance and it caught him pike perch on command. As the bear grew, it started killing chickens and attacking cows so Dzierżyński chained it. The bear lunged at passersby; he shot his pet dead. The relationship with Rita lingered on through daily letters. She persuaded the authorities to let her settle in Kaigorodskoe with Dzierżyński. He found her, like the bear, troublesome. In August 1899 he made the first of his escapes. This involved little danger: the police circulated just a description of a tall auburn-haired man with a "good figure" whose "exterior gives an impression of arrogance." In a few weeks, Dzierżyński was back in Poland, splitting off from the Polish social democrats the hard-line internationalist and Marxist Social Democratic Party of the Kingdom of Poland and Lithuania. Rita was forsaken.[7]

By 1900 Dzierżyński was behind bars, where another liaison affected him more deeply: he nursed his fellow prisoner Antek Rosół who was dying of tuberculosis. The suffering of Rosół haunted Dzierżyński, and the suffering that he in turn inflicted on his prisoners was undoubtedly justified in his mind to some extent by what the Tsar's government did to Rosół.[8] Two years later Feliks was exiled again, to Arctic Yakutia, after fomenting in a Siberian jail a strike of political prisoners. In Siberia he again spent his days hunting. His wife recalls that he shot a female swan, and when the male returned, fired to put it out of its misery, but missed; the swan then plunged to its death. "Józef [Feliks's underground name] told this with emotion and amazement at the swan's fidelity."[9]

Dzierżyński escaped again in 1903. A few weeks later, now a legendary figure, he was a refugee first in Berlin, then in Kraków, at the time part of Austro-Hungarian Galicia. Dzierżyński's next fiancée, Julia Goldman, was a romantic figure more like the phantoms of his lyrics: she died of TB in 1904. In 1905 Dzierżyński went back to Russian territory, to Warsaw, to stir up violent unrest. Strikes and arrests led to concessions and amnesties from the new Russian parliamentary government. Dzierżyński became a key figure in the Russian social democrat movement: in 1906 he was in Stockholm, where he met Lenin (as well as Stalin, Voroshilov, Rykov, and Plekhanov). Lenin liked Dzierżyński's phenomenal singlemindedness. Like Stalin, in Lenin's eyes Dzierżyński was uncouth but valuable as an unquestioning executive. Years passed before Dzierżyński resented being patronized by Lenin.

In 1908 he was arrested again. This time he spent long enough in prison to become expert in interrogation, denunciation, and retribution. Many instructions he would issue the Cheka ten years later were based on the practices of his own interrogators and wardens or were derived from his observation of prisoner psychology. Dzierżyński was a doctrinaire Bolshevik, arguing with heretics, especially the non-Marxist social revolutionaries, and investigating, calculating, confronting in order to establish which prisoners were stool pigeons, traitors, or double agents—skills which served him well in power.

All this Dzierżyński articulated graphically in his *Diary of a Prisoner* (*Pamiętnik więźnia*), printed in the Polish-language *Red Standard* from May 1908 to August 1909. Ironically for a future hangman, Dzierżyński describes as movingly as Victor Hugo or Dostoevsky the effect of hangings on victims, prisoners, and wardens, emphasizing the utter depravity and horror of the death penalty. One wonders how Dzierżyński could have failed to remember, when ordering the deaths of thousands, lines he had written just ten years previously:

> On the night of the 8th and 9th the Polish revolutionary Montwiłł was executed. While it was still light they took off his leg-irons and moved him to the condemned cell. The trial had been on the 6th. He had no illusions and on the 7th he said goodbye to us through the window as we were taking our exercise. He was executed at 1 A.M. The executioner Egorka got, as usual, 50 rubles for the job. The anarchist K. told me, by knocks on the ceiling, that "they had decided not to sleep all night," and the gendarme told me that just the thought of execution "sends a shiver through you and you can't get to sleep and you keep turning over." And after his horrible crime *nothing here has changed:* bright sunny days, soldiers, gendarmes, changing the guard, exercise. Only in the cells things are quieter, the voices of people singing are not to be heard, many await their turn. . . .

The diary rails at the cruelty of the Tsar's courts, the use of torture to get confessions, and vaunts the discipline of social democrats, so unlike the depravity of anarchists. The reader is struck first by Dzierżyński's fair-mindedness and then by puzzlement that the man who wrote this would soon be a jailer far more ruthless than those whom he denounced. Narrow-minded conceit blinded Dzierżyński to his contradictions. He preened himself, outwitting the gendarmes who interrogated and guarded him; he praised his own psychological subtlety in identifying a female informer, Hanka, who, liberated from a madhouse by radicals, denounced her liberators and blamed another woman for the betrayal.

Eighteen months passed before Dzierżyński was sentenced again to exile in Siberia. The diary stops, but he continued to write in similar vein to his sister Aldona. Again, he escaped within days, and in 1910, after making the revolutionary's equivalent of the hajj—a visit to the radical Russian writer Maxim Gorky on the island of Capri—he was back in Kraków.

That year Dzierżyński married one of his admirers, Zofia Muszkat, the twenty-eight-year-old daughter of a rebellious bookshop worker. Zofia was an acolyte, ready to carry out dangerous archival and secretarial duties for the party; she was resigned to separation and exile. Dzierżyński took her walking in the Tatra mountains. Back in Warsaw, in a room furnished with two iron bedsteads and a table, Dzierżyński fathered a son. He did not see his little Jasiek for years: Zofia was arrested in Warsaw; the baby was born prematurely in prison and suffered from convulsions and malnutrition. Zofia was exiled to Siberia; Jasiek was fostered. Not until 1912 did Zofia escape from Siberia and reclaim her child; by then Dzierżyński had been rearrested.

This time, Dzierżyński was kept in closed city prisons, first Warsaw, then Oriol in central Russia (designated for revolutionary recidivists), finally in Moscow. This experience was far worse than Stalin's exile in Turukhansk. Dzierżyński was kept in leg irons until his muscles tore; clean underwear came once a fortnight; there were over a hundred men in a cell designed for fifteen; tuberculosis was rife. Conditions were nearly as bad as those Dzierżyński would preside over five years later. Dzierżyński had little human contact and few books. By all accounts, he was despondent in Oriol, but he did get a cell to himself and his siblings' gifts of money and newspapers kept him nourished and informed.[10] Like Stalin, Dzierżyński was not released until the revolution of February 1917 suspended all political imprisonment.

Letters to Aldona when world war broke out suggest that Dzierżyński survived on fanatical faith in the future: "When I think of the hell you are all now living in, my own little hell seems so small. . . ." Like Lenin, he approved of this hell, for he wrote to his wife in 1915 from his prison cell: "When I think of what is happening now, about the universal smashing of all hopes, I come to the certainty that life will blossom all the more quickly and strongly, the worse the smashing is today." His siblings' and Zofia's letters sustained Dzierżyński: Zofia used citric acid as invisible ink, and a code based on a poem they both loved by Antoni Lange, "Dusze ludzkie samotnice wieczne" (Human souls eternally alone). Feliks wrote verse for Jasiek:

> Felek has his son on the wall
> in three photographic snaps
> stuck on with prison bread
> If I look at the first, I hear laughter. . . .
> If I look at the second, there, concentrated,
> Jasiek studies the world.
> as though tears had frozen in his eyes.
> And from the child's eyes, at the father
> looks the lonely pain of the mother
> in the anguish of the prisoner's heart. . . .
> Jasiek's father turns and tosses in his dreams
> and stillness embraces his breast,
> and his heart looks for his son's heart
> and tries hard to hear if from afar
> his anguished voice should cry. . . .

Stalin was physically and spiritually toughened by four years of Siberian exile; Dzierżyński was physically weakened and intellectually narrowed by five years of Russian prisons. All that he learned, when moved to the Moscow prison of Butyrki where he was employed in the workshops supplying the army, was to cut and stitch trousers and tunics. Nevertheless, as a leader among prisoners, organizing hunger strikes, protests, and inquisitions, he narrowed the single-minded fanaticism that enabled him to make the Cheka an autonomous body with the desire and ability to control an entire population. But, a guard dog in need of a master, Dzierżyński needed political direction, and it would be Stalin whose guidance he found most intelligible and consistent.

The Extraordinary Commission

THE FIRST CHEKA (Extraordinary Commission) was intended just to guard the revolution's headquarters in Petrograd. But on December 20, 1917, Dzierżyński persuaded Lenin to expand the Cheka to the Extraordinary Committee to Combat Counterrevolution and Sabotage. Not all Lenin's associates applauded Dzierżyński's idea. Leonid Krasin, a factory director who became one of Lenin's most persuasive diplomats and ruthless requisitioners, recorded:

> Lenin has become quite insane and if anyone has influence over him it is only "Comrade Feliks" Dzierżyński, an even greater fanatic and, in essence, a cunning piece of work who scares Lenin with counterrevolution and the idea that this will sweep us all away, him first. And Lenin, I am finally convinced, is very much a coward, trembling for his own skin. And Dzierżyński plays on that.

Lenin's concern for his own skin was not without justification. Sailors who had never forgiven their officers the vicious reprisals for the mutinies of 1905; soldiers who had been sent to die at the front with no boots or rifles while their officers stayed in the rear; factory workers whose wages no longer bought bread and vodka—the urban population would rob, assault, or murder anyone they perceived as an exploiter. Kerensky's provisional government had released thousands of convicted criminals and psychopaths who provided the catalyst in an explosive mixture, and the dissolving Tsarist army not only set loose thousands of men habituated to killing, but more criminals who had been released from penal servitude to serve at the front. Many of these convicts were to become killers on behalf of the new authorities. The Bolsheviks had been swept to power on the wave of violence that swept first Petrograd then Moscow, including the murder of two government ministers in their hospital beds by sailors. The vengeance of the populace was now to be channeled into a judicial and extrajudicial system for hunting down, detaining, and disabling the class enemy. The Cheka was this channel.

The cheapest and surest method of waging this internal war was by shooting. The Bolsheviks had loudly protested when Kerensky's government reintroduced the death penalty for army deserters, but in February 1918, after just two months in power, the Bolsheviks gave the Cheka the formal right to shoot its victims without anyone else's sanction, even without charge or trial. Power of life and death invigorated the Cheka; it spawned offspring with lightning speed. By June 1918 every province and district under a Soviet council of workers and soldiers was setting up its own Cheka. The remit was broad and vague: counterespionage, controlling the bourgeoisie, enforcing Soviet decrees; their character depended on local personalities and feelings. Only gradually, as the White armies withdrew from the center of Russia, were these local groups—frequently barbarous and unpredictable in their behavior but also sometimes controlled by more moderate Marxists and Social Revolutionaries—brought under Dzierżyński's control in Moscow.

Those, like Adolf Joffe, who were attempting to represent the Soviet government abroad as a civilized body, were embarrassed by the Cheka's autonomy and violence. On April 13, 1918, Joffe asked the Petrograd Buro to abolish the Cheka: "Uritsky's and Dzierżyński's commissions do more harm than good and apply completely impermissible, clearly provocational methods. . . ." Even pro-Bolshevik lawyers were horrified. On July 12 V. A. Zhdanov, who had defended the assassin of Grand Duke Sergei in 1903, protested to Professor Vladimir Bonch-Bruevich, who had access to Lenin:

> The absence of control, the right to decide cases, the absence of defense, publicity, or the right to appeal, the use of provocation is inevitably leading the Cheka, and will result in it being a place where a nest of people will be made who under the cover of secrecy and crazy, uncontrolled power will do their personal and party deeds. I maintain that the activity of the Cheka will inevitably be the strongest element discrediting Soviet power.

Shortly before they died, two grand old men of Russian thought and letters, the writer Vladimir Korolenko and the anarchist Prince Piotr

Kropotkin, wrote eloquent protests against the death penalty. In vain: Dzierżyński retained his power of life and death.

As the Cheka became centralized, it divided by fission, evolving into a complex organism that spread over the whole country. It took over counterespionage and control of the armed forces; it oversaw Russia's railways; it intercepted letters and telegrams; it neutralized political opponents including members of other left-wing parties; it fought "sabotage"; it conducted espionage abroad. The handful of party workers, soldiers, and sailors in Petrograd expanded in two years to an organization of 20,000 armed men and women of very varied backgrounds united by the conviction of their rightness, or at least their impunity. When they were not fired by enthusiasm, they were motivated by panic. In Petrograd, under Grigori Zinoviev's hysterical rule, the chiefs of the Cheka were replaced every few weeks, each one more ruthless than the last. *Chekisty* were overworked: each interrogator had a hundred cases to process.

Equipping the Cheka was easy. The First World War had left for both Cheka and Trotsky's Red Army enough small arms, machine guns, and ammunition for three years of civil war and red terror. A consignment of leather coats, sent from western Europe for Russia's air force pilots, was appropriated by Dzierżyński to clothe his men hygienically: the typhus louse that killed so many soldiers preferred woolen greatcoats. Recruiting men who were not disobedient psychopaths was harder. Dzierżyński sought men with "a burning heart, a cool head, and clean hands"; Lenin's remark that for every decent man nine bastards had to be employed was nearer the mark.

At first the Cheka recruited not just Bolsheviks, but left Social Revolutionaries and even a few anarchists. Piotr Aleksandrovich, the leader of the Social Revolutionaries in the Cheka, was a nuisance: he insisted on making the Cheka accountable to local soviets, in which his party still had a say. In summer 1918 the Social Revolutionaries among the Cheka were tricked into mounting a revolt and were crushed. The Cheka then became the unquestioning agent of Lenin's party. Accountability disappeared in March 1919: Dzierżyński was made commissar of internal affairs as well as chairman of the Cheka, thus becoming answerable to himself.

Dzierżyński was not at that time a member of the Politburo, the inner cabinet where seven Bolshevik leaders—Lenin, Kamenev, Zinoviev, Trotsky, Stalin, Rykov, Mikhail Tomsky—and three nonvoting "candidate" members—Bukharin, Molotov, Kalinin—took all major decisions. Lenin dismissed Dzierżyński as a mere organizer.[11] Dzierżyński himself confessed to Trotsky that he "was not a statesman." But voting for the Central Committee of the party shows how respected Dzierżyński was by the party rank and file: in March 1919, Lenin received the maximum number of votes, 262, while Dzierżyński got 241, fewer than Bukharin or Stalin (258) but more than Trotsky (219) or Kalinin (158). Not until 1924 was Dzierżyński made even a nonvoting candidate member.

Dzierżyński therefore needed a close relationship with a Politburo member to influence policy in the Cheka's favor. He edged toward Stalin.

Poles, Latvians, and Jews

THE ETHNIC COMPOSITION of the Cheka aroused as much hostility and terror as its powers. With some justification, émigrés asserted that the Russian revolution was "made by Jewish brains, Latvian bayonets, and Russian stupidity." Up to the mid-1930s Russians were a minority in the Cheka and its successor organizations. A few of Dzierżyński's formidable henchmen were Russians: Ivan Ksenofontov, a former factory worker and army corporal, chaired revolutionary tribunals and organized mass shootings of hostages. Like Dzierżyński a puritan—he tried to ban *chekisty* from drinking alcohol—he too worked himself to exhaustion: by 1922, at the age of thirty-eight, Ksenofontov was known as Grandad. Transferred to the Commissariat for Social Security, he died of stomach cancer in 1926. A more horrifying Russian chekist was the semi-qualified doctor and virtuoso pianist Mikhail Kedrov, who would slaughter schoolchildren and army officers in northern Russia with such ruthlessness that he had to be taken into psychiatric care. Kedrov's consort Revekka Maizel personally shot a hundred White officers and bourgeois and then drowned another 500 on a barge.

The Caucasians in the Cheka were a small, fearsome clique. For a short time, there was a Georgian in the Cheka's governing body, Stalin's close ally Sergo Orjonikidze. A Georgian, Aleksi Sajaia, calling himself Dr. Kalinichenko, tortured prisoners in Odessa. Georgians, Armenians, and Azeris brought to the Cheka a sadism their own country had gotten used to under Mongol and Persian overlords. Georgi Atarbekov, whom Stalin knew well, machine-gunned a trainload of Georgian doctors and nurses who were returning to Georgia from Russian war hospitals; he hacked a hundred hostages in Piatigorsk to death with a saber; he murdered his own secretary in his office; and in Armavir, a town of exiled Armenians, he killed several thousand hostages. Dzierżyński furiously defended Atarbekov's actions.[12]

Dzierżyński surrounded himself with fellow Poles, notably a trusted friend from the Warsaw underground in the 1900s, Józef Unszlicht. Unszlicht was to command the Cheka's 300,000 paramilitaries, an army of "special purpose units" that came into existence despite Trotsky's opposition to splitting up the armed forces and fell upon rebellious civilians, obstreperous peasants, Cossacks, and routed soldiers until 1925. Dzierżyński and Unszlicht anticipated revolution triumphing in eastern Europe and Germany; until Marshal Józef Piłsudski's Poland defeated the Red Army in August 1920, they planned to incorporate Poland into a Union of Soviet Socialist Republics of Europe and Asia. Their dislike of Russia was overridden by a crusade on behalf of the world's proletariat, but the Poland that snatched independence in 1917 was a nationalistic country, led by its landed gentry. The Polish left and Polish Jews who wanted political equality were marginalized by Marshal Piłsudski's state and saw their best chance of power as a Soviet-inspired revolution—hence the prominent role they played in the Cheka.

Latvians were an even more effective ethnic group at both the highest and lowest levels of the Red Army and the Cheka. The Latvian Joachim Vacetis saved Lenin's government in July 1918 when the junior party in the revolution, the Social Revolutionaries, assassinated the German ambassador and kidnapped Dzierżyński. Vacetis's disciplined Latvian troops shelled the building that held the Social Revolutionary division of the Moscow Cheka and destroyed the Social Revolutionaries, who commanded wide support among the peasantry, as a political force.

Repression was no new role for Latvians in Russian tyranny: they had been hired to help Ivan the Terrible and Peter the Great achieve absolute power. The Latvians in the Soviet Cheka were not, however, mere mercenaries. Latvia won its independence in 1919 in the turmoil of world and civil wars, but the new middle-class state had no patience with the left-wing agitators infesting Riga's factories. Militant working-class Latvians became a community of exiles in Russia, numbering perhaps a quarter of a million and living from Petrograd to the Pacific, with their own journals and cultural centers. Some 12,000 Latvian soldiers, from Latgale in eastern Latvia, an area where Russian was understood, fought hard in the First World War, to be abandoned in 1917 by their Russian officers and cut off from their homeland by the Germans. Brutalized by their betrayal, they were natural recruits for the Red Army and the Cheka. In 1919 75 percent of the Cheka's central management was Latvian. When Russian soldiers refused to carry out executions, Latvians (and a Chinese force of some 500 men) were brought in. Latvians won battles in the Urals against the White Army and Vacetis was commander of the Red Army for a year. From their formation in April 1918 to their dissolution in November 1920 the Latvian riflemen had an influence wholly disproportionate to their numbers.

Two formidable Latvians assisted Dzierżyński: Jekabs Peterss and Mārtiņš Lācis. In Riga, Peterss was an agitator among the dock workers; in 1905 he was interrogated by the Tsar's police during which his fingernails were ripped out. He immigrated to London with a group of Latvian and Russian Social Democrats to raise money by armed robbery. Peterss won notoriety in the 1911 Siege of Sidney Street, when three policemen were killed. Peterss was working with so-called anarchists, including two of his cousins, Peter Piaktov (Peter the Painter) and Fritz Svaars. At the Old Bailey Peterss was acquitted, thanks to a barrister hired by the Social Democrat Party and to the laziness of Scotland Yard who, despite eyewitness evidence, let the policemen's deaths be blamed on a dead anarchist. While on the run, Peterss challenged the British authorities: "You had best take care of your Van when riding up to the police station. . . . We mean KILL. . . . I am here in Manchester; We will have that bloddy swine of a Churchill before ere long the days are numbered. . . . Yours, Peters."

Peterss married an Englishwoman, May Freeman, and had a daughter, Maisie, by her. In 1917 he went to Russia to join the Cheka. In Moscow Peterss entrapped the British agent Robert Bruce-Lockhart, who was sounding out possible anti-German collaboration between the Allies and the Bolsheviks. After the assassination of the German ambassador, when Dzierżyński in a hysterical fit resigned his post for two months, Peterss took over as head of the Cheka. He subsequently remained its deputy chief, as head of the Petrograd Cheka. Like other Latvians, Peterss insisted that the Cheka should answer to nobody except the head of the government and that it must be free to carry out "searches, arrests, executions." In Moscow Peterss led raids which killed a hundred anarchists, and in Petrograd he used the prerevolutionary telephone book to round up the middle classes, merchants, civil servants, intelligentsia, and officer corps as hostages for reprisals.

Peterss's brutality earned him a posting to central Asia, where in the early 1920s he took charge of suppressing the nationalist rebellion by the Uzbek and Turkmen Basmachi. Yet, Robert Bruce-Lockhart testifies: "There was nothing in his character to indicate the inhuman monster he is commonly supposed to be. He told me that he suffered physical pain every time he signed a death sentence."[13] Clearly, the pain quickly abated; typical of Peterss was the joint Cheka-party operation with Stalin in Petrograd on June 12–13, 1919, involving 15,000 armed men. Hundreds of suspects, some merely relatives of deserters, were rounded up and shot.

In private Jekabs Peterss was just as ruthless. Releasing Bruce-Lockhart, he gave him a letter to deliver to his wife in London, and in March 1921 May and Maisie arrived in Moscow, to discover that Peterss now had a Russian wife and a son. Peterss refused to let his first family leave the country.[14] The journalist Mikhail Koltsov, writing from the safety of the Ukraine, interviewed Peterss in 1918: "He hunched his shoulders at the spring slush and began pulling his gloves on his big hands. Old, worn-out suede gloves. The fingertips were worn through and sewn up with thick thread, badly, as lonely old men sew. This is how unpleasant sullen bachelors living in sour-smelling nasty low-ceilinged furnished rooms darn."[15]

Lācis was more articulate than Peterss. Before and after the revolution he composed satirical and civic verse and comic plays in Latvian. He wrote a parody of the paternoster, addressed to Tsar Nicolas II: "Our father, Who art in Petersburg, Cursed be Thy name, Destroyed be Thy power . . . " In 1912 he published his poem "The Heart Aches . . . " dedicated to his ancestral mother, Latvia. His investigative work began in the People's Commissariat of Internal Affairs (NKVD), then still the semblance of a normal government ministry. In May 1918 Lācis spectacularly exposed a monarchist conspiracy and was promoted to the Cheka, and in 1919 he distinguished himself in Kiev, where his nephew Paraputs also worked as a chekist and was infamous for appropriating victims' money and jewelry. Lācis and Peterss devised intricate traps, for instance opening in Kiev a "Brazilian consulate" which sold visas for large sums of money and then arrested all visitors in the name of the Cheka; Peterss himself acted as the Brazilian consul. When Kiev was recaptured by the Whites some 5,000 corpses were discovered, and 7,000 other Cheka detainees could not be accounted for.

Lācis became the Cheka's publicist, defending it from the strictures of the People's Commissariat for Justice, and founded a journal called *The Red Sword* to publish execution statistics (grossly underestimated) broken down by gender, social origin, and time of year. He declared:

> The Cheka is not just an investigative organ: it is the battle organ of the party of the future. . . . It annihilates without trial or it isolates from society by imprisoning in concentration camps. Its word is law. The Cheka's work must cover all areas of public life. . . . When interrogating, do not seek material evidence or proof of the accused's words or deeds against Soviet power. The first question you must ask is: what class does he belong to, what education, upbringing, origin, or profession does he have? These questions must determine the accused's fate. This is the sense and essence of red terror. . . . It doesn't judge the enemy, it strikes him. It shows no mercy, but incinerates anyone who takes up arms on the other side of the barricades and who is of no use to us. . . . But it isn't a guillotine cutting off heads at a tribunal's instance. . . . We, like the Israelites, have to build the Kingdom of the Future under constant fear of enemy attack.[16]

Lācis claimed that only 21,000 persons were executed between 1918 and 1920. He exulted in the details, however: the crushing of a Social Revolutionary rebellion in Iaroslavl in July 1918, shooting 57 rebels on the spot and 350 after surrender, after bombing the city from the air and engulfing it in artillery fire from an armored train.

Lācis later became, like Dzierżyński, an overlord of the Soviet economy; he was always pushing the Cheka to extend its remit far beyond security. In his tribute to Dzicrżyński, he declared: "whoever hinders if only by laxness the development of the country's productive forces . . . is liable to eradication and the Cheka must deal with all of this."[17] As his energy flagged Lācis became a member of the Latvian section of the Union of Writers and even saw his plays performed in the Latvian theater in Leningrad. He died, apparently of a ruptured aorta, in 1937, commanding railway paramilitaries in eastern Siberia, just before Ezhov's arrests would have swept him away along with almost every other senior Latvian chekist.

★ ★ ★ The prominent role of Jews in the killings of 1918–21 is a very thorny question, if only because one has to share debating ground with Russian chauvinists and plain anti-Semites.[18] From Trotsky down to the executioners of Odessa, Russia's Jews ruthlessly avenged the victims of a century's pogroms, and the perceived Jewishness of the Cheka, in the minds of not just anti-Semitic fascists but even otherwise fair-minded Russian monarchists and liberals, reflected a widespread view of the Bolshevik party and its Central Committee as a Jewish cabal. We cannot dismiss the upsurge of violence in 1918–21 by Jews against Russians as simply redressing the balance after centuries of Tsarist oppression. One might compare it to the violence in 1947–48 of the Stern gang and Irgun in Israel against Arab inhabitants and British rulers, an explosion of self-assertion after a far worse persecution. The motivation of those Jews who worked for the Cheka was not Zionist or ethnic. The war between the Cheka and the Russian bourgeoisie was not even purely a war of classes or political factions. It can be seen as being between Jewish internationalists and the remnants of a Russian national culture.

In the traditional Russian and Nazi definition of Jewishness, where parentage and surname counts as much as religious and cultural affiliation, such a view is plausible. But what was Jewish except lineage about Bolsheviks like Zinoviev, Trotsky, Kamenev, or Sverdlov? Some were second- or even third-generation renegades; few even spoke Yiddish, let alone knew Hebrew. They were by upbringing Russians accustomed to a European way of life and values, Jewish only in the superficial sense that, say, Karl Marx was. Jews in anti-Semitic Tsarist Russia had few ways out of the ghetto except emigration, education, or revolution, and the latter two courses meant denying their Judaism by joining often anti-Jewish institutions and groups.

The Bolsheviks had strong support among the ordinary Jewish population of the miserable shtetls of western Russia and the Ukraine. Firstly, because for the first years of Soviet power the authorities did not regard Zionism as a heinous crime.[19] Secondly, the Jewish Bund, which many even nonintellectual or pro-Zionist Jews supported, was a socialist party in alliance, like the Bolsheviks, with a wide spectrum of social democrats. And thirdly, the 5 million Jews of Russia, particularly in the thirty years before the removal of restrictions in 1913, had been subject to violent pogroms and fantastical accusations, and were denied access to major cities, civic rights, and the professions. One Russian minister of the 1880s, Konstantin Pobedonostsev, is credited with the remark that Russia's Jews should be dealt with by "one third emigration, one third assimilation, and one third extermination." In the First World War the front line between the Austro-Hungarian and Russian armies had cut through a region of Jewish townships. Over half a million Jews were in 1915 summarily deported east. Between 1918 and 1920, during the civil war, Jews suffered from pogroms at the hands of White Cossacks, Ukrainian nationalists, and Polish invaders; White generals such as Anton Denikin did not always rein in their juniors' anti-Semitism. Among the Red Army, only Semion Budionny's Cossacks consistently committed anti-Jewish atrocities.

In the Cheka and the party, Lenin feared, Jewish brains were as much a drawback as an advantage, and the Jews themselves were only too aware of the backlash they might provoke. Lenin took care to see that Trotsky's name was removed from the commission set up to destroy the Russian Orthodox Church. Zinoviev, visiting the Ukraine, warned that there were "too many Jews." Kaganovich, in the mid-1920s general secretary of the Ukrainian party and a Ukrainian Stalin, cut within three years Jewish representation at Kharkov university from 40 to 11 percent and raised that of Ukrainians from 12 to 38 percent. Any initiative known to emanate from Trotsky or Iagoda could make Russia's smoldering anti-Semitism flare up. Jews loomed large in the repressive organs of government and in the party, while their proportion among the semi-starving, freezing population of Petrograd and Moscow for a while sharply declined. In 1922, they reached their maximum representation in the party (not that they formed a coherent group) when, at 15 percent, they were second only to ethnic Russians with 65 percent.

The Chekist as Intellectual and Organizer

WHEN THE FIRST WORLD WAR ended, the old empires of Britain and France and the largely middle-class governments of the newly independent states of the Baltic and central Europe turned their attention to the threat posed by Bolshevik Russia. The Cheka had to divert resources from internal repression to external enemies, and both espionage and counterintelligence assumed greater importance. The Cheka would need educated linguists as desperately as it had sharpshooters. To deal with spies, to devise propaganda, agents needed skills in disinformation, manipulation, and falsification. For these tasks men with higher education, not just experience in killing, were needed. Jewish recruits best filled this need. Few Baltic or Polish recruits to the Cheka were intellectuals, although Baron Romuald Pillar von Pilchau, a renegade German aristocrat from Latvia, and the fastidious Petrograd lawyer Ronchevsky were outlandish exceptions to the rule.

The Cheka was an essential instrument not just for suppressing counterrevolution or providing intelligence, but for making the shattered economy function. From the start, Lenin and Trotsky secretly planned the totalitarian organization of labor, with mobile labor armies and cooperatives of peasants on state land. In summer 1918 Trotsky organized the first concentration camps in the southeast of the country. Nothing could shake Trotsky's belief that "the unproductive nature of compulsory labour is a liberal myth," but it took a decade for Cheka labor camps to make any perceptible contribution to the economy.

Anticipating Hitler, the Cheka's activities were economically important in more primitive and horrible ways. Desperately needed money accrued to the Soviet state not just from nationalizing banks and businesses; the murdered Tsaritsa's crown jewels, delivered to Moscow in ten suitcases by her killers, fetched about $100 million. When sentenced to be executed, real or imaginary counterrevolutionaries forfeited their property to the Cheka. In late 1919, when the Cheka spawned its provincial and departmental offspring—railways, factories, and military units as well as districts, parishes, and towns got their own Cheka units—executions in the open were abandoned. A shot in the back of the neck in a cellar or garage became standard practice. Victims were first stripped naked and usable clothing stored. Lenin himself received a suit, a pair of boots, a belt, and braces worn by a victim of the Moscow Cheka.[20] Underwear went to Red Army soldiers or Cheka prisoners. Gold teeth were prized from the corpses. (Mikhail Frinovsky, a chekist who was to become notorious in the Great Terror of 1931 and whose teeth were kicked out by a recalcitrant prisoner, had himself a complete set of implants made from the gold teeth of his victims.)

Soviet forces were desperately short of supplies by the end of the civil war; they needed loot to operate. A report to Iagoda from a unit sent to put down a peasant rebellion in Simbirsk runs: "Because of the complete absence mainly of footwear in the Red Army no conspiracies or counterrevolutionary manifestations have been noted."[21] Red Army units would list every trophy they won after successful actions. In 1920, at Kazan, Commander N. Epaneshnikov proudly reported to headquarters that he was sending them "64 ram-rod guns, 17 hunting rifles . . . 86 various rifles, one axe, 16 tanned sheep- and goat-skins, 11 old greatcoats, 1 ripped greatcoat . . . 2 knitted underpants . . . 10 ordinary underpants, 2 sacks of newspaper, 45 raw horse skins . . . a bell . . . and a distilling pipe."[22]

Vladimir Zazubrin, in 1918 a deserter from the White forces and later a lively writer of fiction and memoirs, shot by Stalin in 1938 for his frankness, recalled the hard life of the Cheka executioners:

White, grey carcasses (undressed people) collapsed onto the floor. *Chekisty* with smoking revolvers ran back and cocked the triggers immediately. The legs of those shot jerked in convulsions. . . . Two men in grey greatcoats nimbly put nooses round the necks of the corpses, dragged them off to a dark niche in the cellar. Two others with spades dug at the earth, directing steaming rivulets of blood. Solomin, his revolver in his belt, sorted out the linen of those shot. He carefully made separate piles of underpants, shirts and outer clothing. . . . Three men were shooting like robots, their eyes were empty, with a cadaverous glassy shine. . . .

Like Lācis or Zazubrin, other *chekisty* fancied their talents as writers—just as some writers were later to test their skills as NKVD interrogators. In 1921, in newly conquered Tbilisi, the *chekisty* published an anthology, *The Cheka's Smile*. The contribution by Aleksandr Eiduk, executioner and roving military emissary, ran:

> There is no greater joy, not better music
> Than the crunch of broken lives and bones.
> This is why when our eyes are languid
> And passion begins to seethe stormily in the breast,
> I want to write on your sentence
> One unquavering thing: "Up against a wall! Shoot!"[23]

While in the Moscow Cheka Eiduk admitted "with enjoyment in his voice, like an ecstatic sexual maniac" to a diplomat friend that he found the roar of truck engines, used to drown the noise of prisoners being executed in the inner courtyard of the Lubianka, "Good . . . blood refines you!" Eiduk, shot on Stalin's orders in 1938, was in 1922 assigned by the Soviet government to watch over the American Relief Agency as it fed 10 million starving peasants on the Volga.

More deplorable even than Eiduk's verses were contributions from poets with reputations once worth defending such as Vladimir Mayakovsky, who declared, "Enough of singing of moon and seagull, I shall sing of the Extraordinary Committee . . . " and then advised, "Any youth thinking over his future, / deciding on whom to model his life, I shall tell, without hesitating: 'Base it / On Comrade Dzierżyński.' "

Chekisty and poets were drawn to each other like stoats and rabbits—often with fatal consequences for the latter. They found common ground: the need for fame, an image of themselves as crusaders, creative frustration, membership of a vanguard, scorn for the bourgeoisie, an inability to discuss their work with common mortals. There was an easily bridged gap between the symbolist poet who aimed to *épater le bourgeois* and the chekist who stood the bourgeois up against a wall.

One outstanding intellectual chekist was the twenty-year-old Social Revolutionary Iakov Bliumkin. Joining the Odessa Cheka, he became notorious as "Fearless Naum" and startled the world when he entered the German embassy in Moscow with a mandate bearing Dzierżyński's signature and shot the ambassador, Count Mirbach, dead—allegedly to avenge the humiliating Treaty of Brest-Litovsk and to provoke a breach with Germany and thus world revolution. Bliumkin received only a nominal prison sentence (Had this Social Revolutionary coup in fact been stage-managed by the Bolsheviks?) and reappeared as a Cheka officer in Kiev in 1919.

Bliumkin had genius: he was fluent in many European and Asiatic languages, he wrote verse and, despite the sadistic jokes he played, fascinated admirers with his exploits. Bliumkin personified to the extreme the brilliant intellectual corrupted by the license to kill with impunity. In June 1918, before the killing of the German ambassador, the poet Osip Mandelstam heard Bliumkin boast that he was having a "spineless intellectual" shot and raised a storm of protest. Through Larisa Reisner, Mandelstam, who had a reckless disregard for his own safety, obtained an interview with Dzierżyński. The Cheka boss responded to his indignation: the intellectual may have been saved. Bliumkin also befriended the peasant poet Sergei Esenin and took him to Iran, where in 1920 there was a short-lived Soviet republic thus inspiring Esenin's Persian lyrics. Bliumkin's circle was the first where *chekisty* and poets mingled. Even the principled monarchist poet Nikolai Gumiliov, shortly to be shot by the Cheka, was proud to meet Bliumkin. He wrote in his poem "My Readers": "A man who had shot an emperor's envoy in a crowd of people came up to shake my hand, to thank me for my verses." These asso-

ciations of poet and chekist were mutually destructive. Few of Dzierżyński's men, or Russia's poets, would live out their allotted spans. Esenin
committed suicide and Bliumkin was shot by Menzhinsky for his links
with Trotsky. Mayakovsky was to kill himself, and his Cheka friend
Iakov Agranov was executed.

Whether aghast at power like Mandelstam, who found authority as
"revolting as a barber's hand," or fascinated by it like Mayakovsky and
Esenin, the paths of poets and *chekisty* intersected. In 1919 the greatest
of the Russian symbolist poets, Aleksandr Blok, was interrogated by the
Cheka as a Social Revolutionary and "mystical anarchist" sympathizer.
He periodically interceded, sometimes successfully, for other detainees:
Blok's chekist contact Ozolin, who had himself supervised mass murder
in Saratov, declared himself a fellow poet. Max Voloshin, a poet whose
reputation as a magus overawed both Reds and Whites, who survived
atrocities as the Crimea was conquered and lost by both sides, eloquently
testified in 1921 as to what the demented deposed leader of the Hungarian soviets, Béla Kun, and his consort Rozalia Zemliachka had done:

Terror

> They gathered to work at night.
> They read denunciations, certificates, cases.
> They hurriedly signed sentences.
> They yawned. They drank wine.
> [. . .]
> At night they chased barefooted, naked people
> Over ice-covered stones
> Against a northeast wind
> Into wastelands outside town.
> [. . .]
> They threw them, not all killed yet, into a pit.
> They hurriedly covered them with earth.
> And then with an expansive Russian song
> They returned home to town.

Béla Kun had summoned Voloshin to read through lists of condemned,
ostentatiously deleted the poet's own name, and then invited him to per-

form an act of unbearable complicity: crossing off the name of one man in ten.[24]

It was harder for intellectuals to mix with *chekisty* once the latter began mass killing. "Red Terror" was decreed on September 1, 1918, as a defensive measure which suspended both legality and morality. The pretext was the assassination on August 30 by the young poet Leonid Kannegiser of the head of the Petrograd Cheka, Moisei Uritsky—ironically, Uritsky was one chekist who loathed bloodshed. Lenin was unhappy with Dzierżyński's plans to proceed with mass terror against counterrevolutionaries, but on August 31 he was hit by a bullet allegedly fired by a former anarchist, Fanny Kaplan, and was temporarily put out of action. Kaplan was an unlikely assassin. Not even Lenin's entourage knew until the last moment that he would be speaking at the Moscow factory where he was shot and Kaplan suffered from periodic total loss of sight, caused by an explosion in a terrorist bomb factory a decade before. A revolver was "found" four days later, but could not have fired the bullet extracted from Lenin's neck. Kannegiser, Uritsky's killer, was quickly arrested and confessed, but was interrogated for a whole year in the hope that he would name co-conspirators before being shot. Fanny Kaplan told the Cheka nothing, even when questioned by Peterss, and was handed over to Kremlin interrogators. She was shot a week later in a garage by Pavel Malkov, the Kremlin commandant; the poet Demian Bedny, Stalin's closest friend among the intellectuals, helped Malkov cremate her in a steel oil drum.[25]

Cheka killings escalated. Assassination attempts and advancing White armies, aided by Anglo-French forces invading from the north, the south, and the west, were the pretexts for an orgy of killing that lasted three years. The moral effect on Dzierżyński's organization was horrendous: an explosion of criminal sadism swept the country. In a matter of days, hundreds were shot in Moscow. Uritsky's successor in Petrograd, the redoubtable pervert Gleb Bokii, shot 1,300, although the target set by Dzierżyński was 500.[26] Trotsky and Karl Radek acclaimed the terror; Radek even wanted executions to be public. Lenin in July 1918, before he was fired on, had argued for hangings, rather than shootings, so that the public could better contemplate the corpses.[27]

Killings also arose from the panic and vindictiveness of civil war:

fearful atrocities occurred in cities like Kiev or Astrakhan which changed hands several times between 1918 and 1920. Convicted criminals and certified psychopaths appointed themselves officers of the Cheka and terrorized, raped, and murdered whom they liked. Surrendering White army officers, given safe passes, were summoned to "register" and then shot, burned in furnaces, drowned on barges, or hacked to death. Other executions aimed to improve results on the battlefield by decimating Red Army deserters and retreating units, a party policy that Trotsky, Stalin, and other roving emissaries enforced at the front. Statistics exist only for 1921, a mild year and the last of the civil war, when 4,337 were shot in the army alone.[28] Sometimes a whole ethnic group was declared White and genocide took place. Iona Iakir, a famous Red Army general, had 50 percent of male Don Cossacks exterminated, and used artillery, flamethrowers, and machine guns on women and children.[29] Red Cossacks declared their non-Russian neighbors White and massacred Circassian villagers and Kalmyk cattle-herders. In Moscow, under Dzierżyński's command, indiscriminate mass murder took place. "Counterrevolutionaries" were executed by list; in 1919 all Moscow's Boy Scouts and in 1920 all members of the lawn tennis club were shot.

Not all *chekisty* were men. In the Crimea Stalin's Baku comrade Rozalia Zemliachka and her lover Béla Kun, with Lenin's approval, murdered 50,000 White officers who had trusted Commander Frunze's safe conduct. Zemliachka, a Cheka sadist who would live to enjoy a pension, tied the officers in pairs to planks and burned them alive in furnaces, or drowned them in barges that she sank offshore. She had been educated in a Kiev grammar school and at the Sorbonne.

Two women in the Odessa Cheka were particularly feared: Vera Grebeniukova, known as Dora, who for two and a half months in 1918 mutilated 700 prisoners before shooting them, and the "Pekinese," a Latvian sadist, who was chief executioner. In the Kiev Cheka a Hungarian, Removér, was consigned to a psychiatric ward after she began shooting not just prisoners but witnesses. And in Moscow's central prison in 1919, a woman executioner specialized in fetching the condemned from the hospital ward and whipping them down to the cellars.

Many Cheka killers were convicts, for example Iankel-Iakov Iurovsky, the killer of the Tsar, and the sole black in the Cheka, Johnston of Odessa, who flayed his victims alive. Some of these killers went uncontrollably mad: Saenko of Kharkov, who worked in a special torture chamber, attacked his superiors and was shot; the same fate befell Maga, chief executioner in Moscow. When the killer was of political importance, milder measures were taken. Béla Kun was put in a psychiatric hospital, from where he was released to play a key role in the Comintern. Dr. Mikhail Kedrov, friend and publisher to Lenin and cousin of two Central Committee members, was relieved of his post when, after reenacting the drownings of the French Revolution with captive White officers, he prepared to exterminate the inhabitants of Vologda and other northern towns. Kedrov suffered from hereditary madness; his father, a violinist, had died in a lunatic asylum. The son spent some time in psychiatric care before reemerging to work, just as cruelly, for the Cheka around the Caspian Sea. He retired from the Cheka after the civil war and was head of a neurosurgical institute when Beria arrested him in 1939.[30]

The White armies, too, were guilty of mass murder and terror. The killing of 30,000 Reds by the Finnish Marshal Karl Mannerheim in January 1918 provoked Bolshevik revenge, as did the concentration camps used by the new Estonian and Finnish governments to confine Bolsheviks. In the south of Russia, there were White atrocities, although such lapses were infrequent in the White army, which was staffed with many principled officers and backed up an administration which had not completely discarded its ethics. Insane sadists like Baron Roman Ungern-Sternberg, who killed thousands in Mongolia, were exceptional. Only the Ukrainian "anarchist" Nestor Makhno and some Cossack forces systematically employed terror on a scale comparable to the Red Terror.

Red Terror and civil war thus produced in the USSR a body of men and women for whom summary arrest and execution, often en masse, was a normal, salutary procedure. The holocaust that took place between 1918 and 1922 seems less horrific than Hitler's or Stalin's only because it was directed more at a class than at a race, because most survivors remained cut off from the Western world, because the paper trail has been destroyed, and because, as Stalin liked to say, "Victors are not put on trial." Above all, the terror was never repented, let alone atoned for. In the later 1920s, like a dormant infection, those capable of slaughtering "class enemies" without remorse waited for the moment when they could ravage the body politic again.

The easiest way to comprehend the scale of the holocaust that Lenin, Trotsky, Dzierżyński, and Stalin unleashed is through demographic statistics. We can compare the actual population figures of the USSR in the 1920s with the figures predicted ten years earlier; we can use the reliable 1926 census figures, and extrapolate from figures produced in areas where records were maintained. From 1914 to mid-1917 just under 3 million men of the Russian empire were killed in the war, as were over 300,000 civilians. From 1917 to 1920 the population of European Russia declined by 6 million (5 percent), and proportionately the Ukraine, Belorussia, and the Caucasus suffered equally.[31] Major Russian industrial cities had always had higher death rates than birthrates; they grew by sucking in fresh working forces from the countryside, where on average there were 60 deaths to 100 births before the revolution. But from 1917 to 1920 deaths outnumbered births in the countryside and in the cities mortality more than doubled. Epidemics and famines were bigger killers even than the bullets of the Cheka or Red Army. Lenin in December 1919 declared that, "Either the [typhus] louse will defeat socialism, or socialism will defeat the typhus louse." Tuberculosis, heart disease, and dysentery, arising from malnutrition, cold, and stress, ravaged the country.

Overall, the number of people killed during the revolution and civil war amounted to: nearly 2 million soldiers of the Red Army and Cheka with over 500,000 in the White armies; 300,000 Ukrainian and Belorussian Jews in pogroms by Ukrainian, Polish, and White armies; 5 million dead of starvation in the Volga region in 1921. Moreover, 2 million Russians emigrated to Europe and Asia. This amounts to 10 million fewer inhabitants. How many other human beings should have been alive in the USSR in 1922 but were not is a matter for conjecture. Plausible evidence reveals that the actual numbers executed or sent to death camps vastly exceeded the official figures of 12,000 shot in 1918, and 9,701 shot and 21,724 sent to camps for 1921. The repression that followed the rebellions in Kronstadt or Tambov in 1921 alone resulted in tens of thousands of executions.

The age, class, and gender of the victims aggravated the disaster: soldiers killed were typically men in their twenties, while the émigrés lost to the country were largely members of the professional classes. Those most needed to plow the land, rebuild the factories, and run the economy had gone. Dzierżyński understood this very well. The Bolshevik leadership had lost two generations; their only hope for the future was the children, many of whom were starving, homeless orphans, a waste of human resources and a threat to public order. They would be the raw material of Stalin's Soviet Union. Strategy not sentiment motivated the Cheka, GPU, and NKVD to establish colonies for homeless children. Orphanages, children's communes, and theories of education were a major concern for the secret police; having created the mass of orphaned children, they wanted to use them.[32]

★ ★ ★ The excuse that Dzierżyński, Lenin, and Stalin made for the Cheka's brutal excesses was inexperience. Sailors, schoolteachers, and factory workers could not be expected to maintain professional calm or observe consistent legality in such a furnace of counterespionage and counterterror. In all spheres of government during the first years after the revolution there was a desperate shortage of competent leadership. Men undertook tasks for which they had not the most elementary competence or qualifications. For a soldier, doctor, stoker, or peasant to become a chekist only a short apprenticeship was required to inure him to the violence of the job.

If we take a typical chekist we are as likely to find upward mobility from the dispossessed Jewish shtetl as downward mobility from a Russian middle-class family. Mikhail Frinovsky, for instance, was one of eight children born to comfortably off parents (his father was a schoolteacher and his mother a landowner). Like Dzierżyński the son of a somewhat sadistic man and like Stalin educated in a theological seminary, Frinovsky may seem to have been predestined to rebel. But, like many Russians of his generation, Frinovsky was so patriotic that he falsified his age in order to volunteer to serve in the Tsar's army, and he quickly became an NCO in the cavalry. Disillusioned by the slaughter, he deserted. Once outside the law he gravitated to anarchism and terrorism, and in 1917 took part in torturing a major general to death. He hid from the authorities as a bookkeeper in a military hospital, and when the Bolsheviks took over his crimes were transformed into qualifications for the Cheka. After brief service in the Red Army he became one of the most brutal *chekisty* in Moscow, and then with Stalin was let loose at the front in the 1920 war against Poland.

Then there were *chekisty* like Naftali Frenkel, who, but for the war and the revolution, would have remained a chancer and fixer on the fringes of the building trade and gangster rackets in Odessa. Frenkel had become rich on wartime building contracts and dock work, and when revolution broke out and nobody built or imported anymore, he helped the Cheka take Odessa from the Whites. Most of the gangsters were then shot by their former allies but Frenkel's organizing talents were too good to waste. He was allowed to continue racketeering in the port and also worked for the Cheka until Dzierżyński found the combination too compromising. Frenkel was sent, ostensibly as a prisoner, to the far north, where he became a de facto concentration camp commandant and rose to become the chief contractor on the slave-labor White Sea canal in the 1930s.

There were tens of thousands of Frinovskys and Frenkels in the Cheka. It took in men who ten years earlier had intended to pursue wealth or a career and disseminated those it had corrupted throughout Soviet society. Success in the Cheka meant being delegated to take charge of any failing area, military or economic. Thus executioners and interrogators spread into every sector of government, applying their methods to problems once solved by negotiation and persuasion. From mid-1919 on, Dzierżyński, like Stalin and Trotsky, was sent by Lenin to any part of the front where the army was collapsing, to any province where stores of grain might be requisitioned for the starving cities, to any local party which was becoming fractious—wherever ruthlessness and blind belief in the cause could salvage the situation.

Despite constantly losing men to other commissariats, by mid-1919 Dzierżyński had set up a Union-wide Cheka that could work in his absence. His immediate subordinates, Peterss, Lācis, Ksenofontov, Menzhinsky, and Iagoda—particularly the latter two—were as devoted to the cause as he.[33] The atmosphere was remarkably amicable for such a vipers' nest; the leadership had charisma, and the lower echelons, who knew where their interests lay, showed them loyalty. Together they created a myth that ennobled the sordid bloodshed.

Dzierżyński himself considered that two years in the Cheka was all that could be expected of a recruit, and like Himmler, he saw virtue in the carnage he oversaw. Mārtiņš Lācis declared, "However honorable a man may be, however crystal-clear his heart, Cheka work, carried out with almost unlimited rights and in conditions which have an exceptional effect on the nervous system, leaves its mark." None ever expressed doubts, but their bodies rebelled with fainting fits, colic, and headaches. Like Trotsky, Dzierżyński was prone to hysterical crises which led to breakdowns. Dzierżyński broke down hysterically after the assassination of Count Mirbach in July 1918: detained by Social Revolutionaries, he bared his chest, inviting them to shoot him. When he was released and the Social Revolutionaries had been crushed, he resigned. In autumn, humiliated by his failure to prevent the assassination of Uritsky and the attempt on Lenin's life, Dzierżyński shaved his hair, forged himself Polish papers in the name of Feliks Domański, and turned up in Switzerland at the house where his unsuspecting wife and son lived. Only after an interlude on Lake Lugano did he recover and return to Russia. Dzierżyński's wife and son followed when the Swiss expelled the Soviet diplomatic mission from Bern. From 1919 on, now supported by a wife, a sister, a sister-in-law, and two nieces, but still sleeping in his office and subsisting on bread and tea, Dzierżyński was used by Lenin in a series of special missions. This brought him into Stalin's orbit.

Stalin and Dzierżyński in Tandem

UNTIL THE CIVIL WAR ENDED, Commissar for Nationalities Stalin had little to do except formulate policy. Stalin's real remit was to solve, by any means, supply problems—getting munitions and men to the front, grain to the cities—and to swing the party's weight behind repressive measures taken by the Cheka or Red Army. The first of Stalin's missions was from May to September 1918 with his old friend Klim Voroshilov to Tsaritsyn (later Stalingrad, now Volgograd). Stalin's task was to bring grain from the still-productive south up to Moscow and Petrograd, but instead he and Voroshilov, who commanded an army approaching Tsaritsyn, interfered in the defense of the city against the Whites. Stalin branded the Red commander Andrei Snesarev, who was a protégé of Trotsky, a deserter and a collaborator with the French. Well out of artillery range on the Volga, Stalin and Voroshilov presided over a tribunal which summoned officers from Tsaritsyn. The officers were put on barges on the Volga which were then raked with machine guns. Stalin also commandeered all available troops in the area, including six detachments on their way to Baku to rescue the Bolsheviks there from a takeover by Social Revolutionaries and the British; the deaths of the twenty-six Bolshevik Baku commissars can thus be laid at Stalin's door.

Stalin was accompanied by his new bride, the seventeen-year-old Nadezhda Allilueva, and made his brother-in-law Fiodor take part in the killing of suspected "*spetsy,*" the career Tsarist officers on whose skills the ill-trained Red Army depended. Fiodor Alliluev went mad. Stalin however cemented his alliance with Voroshilov and with the Cossack commander Budionny. Their hostility to professional army officers simmered for almost twenty years before it was to boil over into a campaign of extermination. Stalin, strongly supported by Dzierżyński, clashed with Trotsky over the latter's use of *spetsy.* Trotsky, as commander-in-chief, responded by forcing Dzierżyński to release Tsarist officers from prison for service in the Red Army, their loyalty assured by the threat of imprisoning or shooting their wives and children if they deserted. Dzierżyński was pushed further toward Stalin, who from this point began to replace Trotsky as the ultimate patron of the Cheka.

In the early stages of the revolution Dzierżyński had several times sided with Trotsky. When Lenin caved in to the Germans at Brest-Litovsk in January 1918 Dzierżyński, like Trotsky, refused to endorse what he called "a capitulation of our entire program." Unlike Trotsky, however, Dzierżyński distrusted anyone who had been in Tsarist service: for the Cheka he recruited almost nobody who had served in the Tsar's secret police.

The instant dislike that Stalin and Trotsky had taken to each other in Vienna in 1913 now erupted into a feud that would only end when one killed the other. In 1918 Trotsky countered Stalin's interventions around

Tsaritsyn with a threat: "I order Stalin to form immediately a Revolutionary Council for the Southern Front on the basis of non-interference by commissars in operational business. Failure to carry out this order within twenty-four hours will force me to take severe measures."[34] On the same day Stalin complained at length to Lenin:

> Trotsky, generally, can't refrain from histrionic gestures. . . . Now he's striking a new blow with his gesture about discipline, and all this Trotskyist discipline actually consists of having the most prominent people active at the front watching the behinds of military specialists from the "non-party" camp of counter-revolutionaries and not stopping these people from ruining the front. . . . Trotsky can't sing without falsetto. . . . Therefore I ask now, before it is too late, for Trotsky to be put in his place, given limits, for I fear that Trotsky's crazy commands . . . handing the whole front to so-called bourgeois military specialists who inspire no confidence . . . will create discord between the army and the command. . . .[35]

Shooting commanders *pour encourager les autres* was a strategy common to Stalin and Trotsky. Their overall styles were, however, very different. Trotsky's train carried motor cars, a cinema photographer, and a brass band; stations ahead were telegraphed to lay in butter, quails, and asparagus for the commissar. Shootings of deserters and retreating officers alternated with rousing speeches to the soldiery. Stalin, on the other hand, traveled in ostentatious discomfort; he had no praise for the soldiery, and even less trust: "I must say that those non-working elements who constitute the majority of our army, the peasants, won't fight for socialism, they won't! They refuse to fight voluntarily. . . . Hence our task is to make these elements go into combat. . . ."[36]

The Whites besieging Tsaritsyn ultimately failed to capture the city, but Stalin's brutality had done more damage to his own side than to the enemy. Voroshilov was threatened by Trotsky with a court martial; Lenin concurred, telling the southern army it could appoint anyone as commander except Voroshilov. This humiliation made Voroshilov dependent on Stalin for his military future. Stalin had now collected two men,

Voroshilov and Dzierżyński, whom Lenin and Trotsky had humiliated and spurned.

When demoralized Reds surrendered the Ural city of Perm at the end of 1918 to the Whites, thus allowing British forces to link up with Admiral Aleksandr Kolchak, ruler of Siberia, Stalin and Dzierżyński were dispatched together, in their first collaborative venture, to punish and rally the army. All January 1919, based at Viatka, where Dzierżyński had spent his first exile, he and Stalin were inseparable inquisitors. They were so ruthless that in February 1919 the party's Central Committee had to issue an order releasing the surviving officers "arrested by Stalin's and Dzierżyński's commission to be handed over for the appropriate institutions to deploy."

This, Dzierżyński's first visit to the front, shook his morale but not his resolve, and in April 1919 he wrote to his sister Aldona:

> But you can't understand me—a soldier of the revolution, warring so that there shall be no more injustice in the world, so that war shall not give whole millions of people as booty for rich conquerors. War is a terrible thing. . . . The most wretched nation has been the first to rise up in defense of its rights—and has put up resistance to the whole world. Would you want me to stand aside here?[37]

The following year Dzierżyński moved even closer to Stalin. In 1920, waiting in the Ukraine for the Soviet conquest of Poland, the Dzierżyńskis lived in a dacha near Kharkov with the couple then most intimate with Stalin, the poet Demian Bedny and his wife. That summer, as the Red Army pushed the Poles out of the Ukraine and back to the outskirts of Warsaw, Stalin and Dzierżyński worked together and again showed Lenin and Trotsky their limitations. Stalin had promised Lenin in July 1920 an unimaginable victory: "Now that we have the Comintern, a defeated Poland . . . it would be sinful not to encourage revolution in Italy . . . and in states that are not yet strong like Hungary, Czechoslovakia. . . . In short, we have to loose the anchor and move before imperialism has time to put its broken cart in order. . . ." But for all the brilliance and experience of Commander Tukhachevsky, who had begun his career as a Tsarist officer, by August 1920 the Red cavalry, like that of the Mongols 700 years before, was bogged down in the Polish forests and marshes with neither tents nor coats to keep off the incessant rain. Stalin, however, loudly insisted that the Soviet government should reject David Lloyd George's offer to mediate peace with the Poles on the basis of the Curzon line boundary (today's Polish–Belorussian–Ukrainian border) and grab as much Polish territory as possible before any truce could be negotiated. As a result, the Red Army spent resources besieging Lwów, the capital of the Polish Carpathians. The Poles counterattacked and took 100,000 Russian prisoners, forcing the Soviets to concede a vast belt of territory. The glory went to Poland's ruler Piłsudski, the disgrace to Dzierżyński and Stalin.[38]

Dzierżyński had expected to join the Red Army in Warsaw to help form a Soviet Polish government. He amused his fellow Poles among the Bolsheviks, Karl Radek in particular, by his modest surmise that he might take on the ministry of education in the new Poland, after putting Piłsudski up against a wall. The defeat of the Red Army on the Vistula left him crestfallen. Stalin, Dzierżyński, and Voroshilov had anticipated victory. Now Dzierżyński, like Voroshilov in 1918, was bound to Stalin in disgrace. Voroshilov wrote to Orjonikidze with amazement, "We expected rebellions and revolution from the Polish workers and peasants but got chauvinism and stupid hatred of 'Russians.' "[39]

Trotsky was mercilessly sarcastic about Stalin's lapses—whose treatment twenty years later of the Polish officers who had disabused his dreams would be as barbarous as his reckoning with him. Voroshilov lost for a short time all taste for command: in March 1921 he served as a common soldier, attacking the mutinous sailors of Kronstadt across the ice. In November 1921 he wrote to Stalin, "Working in the war department no longer appeals to me. . . . I suppose I shall be more useful in a civilian career. . . . I'll take any work [in the Don basin] and hope to shake myself out of it, for I've started to get poorly (mentally). I embrace you strongly. . . ."[40]

In February 1921, the Red Army invaded Georgia and completed the reconquest of Transcaucasia. The Georgian communists who gained power were, however, not Leninist puppets and pursued a liberal line—leaving at liberty members of the Menshevik government who had not fled the country. Budu Mdivani and Pilipe Makharadze resisted Stalin's decision to subsume the Georgian republic into a Transcaucasian feder- ation. Likewise, the Soviet detachment of Abkhazia from Tbilisi's rule, making it an autonomous republic amenable to Russian exploitation, upset the Georgians. Stalin often expressed contempt for his native country: "Tbilisi is picturesque, but Baku is more interesting," he would write to Demian Bedny. In 1923 he told Trotsky, "Georgians behave like an imperial power toward Armenians, Abkhaz, Ajarians, Osetians. This deviancy is of course less dangerous than Russian imperialism, but it's still dangerous enough. . . ."[41] Stalin showed such ruthlessness in the Caucasus—in autumn 1920 he supervised the bloody suppression of Circassians and Osetians—that Lenin remarked that there was nobody worse than a "Russified aborigine" at imposing Russification with insen- sitivity.

The task of dealing with the Georgians was handed over to Sergo Orjonikidze, who had demonstrated his ruthlessness by shooting Azeri and Armenian nationalists, whether communists or not. When Georgian communists complained to Lenin, Stalin and Orjonikidze were furious and the latter struck one of them in the face for calling him "Stalin's mule." Lenin was furious with Orjonikidze—"he had no right to the irri- tability that he and Dzierżyński blame everything on"—and put Stalin and Dzierżyński in charge of a commission to investigate and repair the damage. These two, however, exonerated Orjonikidze. Lenin could only attempt to placate the offended Georgians with a short note in March 1923, the last he dictated before arteriosclerosis took away his speech: "Strictly secret. To comrades Mdivani, Makharadze et al. Copy to Trot- sky and Kamenev. Respected comrades! I follow your cause with all my heart. I am indignant at Orjonikidze's coarseness and Stalin's and Dzierżyński's connivance. I am preparing notes and a speech for you."[42]

There were personal reasons why Stalin gathered a coterie around him of men such as Voroshilov, Dzierżyński, and Orjonikidze. Stalin was a loner. During the civil war, he stood out in his isolation. Other Bolshe- viks had intimate allies: wives, sisters, and mistresses. Even Dzierżyński, once Zofia had arrived from Zurich, was eventually cajoled into living in the Kremlin; his wife found work first in the Commissariat for Educa- tion, then as a party propagandist. Wives of leading revolutionaries were placed in inconspicuous but crucial government and party posts. Zinoviev's second wife, Zlata Lilina, was a power in education, while her brother Ionov controlled state publishing in Petrograd. Olga Bronshtein, Kamenev's wife and Trotsky's sister, although she had never been to school, recruited major poets to teach the proletariat to create; later she ran the theaters and then the Lenin museum. Lenin's wife, Krupskaia, was nominally in charge of education: in 1923 she issued circulars banning the publication or teaching of Plato, Immanuel Kant, Arthur Schopenhauer, John Ruskin, Friedrich Nietzsche, and Tolstoi. Trotsky's wife, Natalia Sedova, controlled the State Depository of Confiscated Valuables and the museums.

Divorce and remarriage linked people's commissars to poets, painters, university professors but, despite the Bolsheviks' proclamation of sexual equality, very few free female spirits—Larisa Reisner, Aleksandra Kollontai—roamed the fringes of power. The wives of Bolshevik leaders (but not Zofia Dzierżyńska) had salons where those intellectuals who had not emigrated or were in hiding sought protection from these influential and underemployed consorts. Trotsky, Zinoviev, Kamenev, Radek, and Bukharin—not to mention Lenin—were patrons whose friends, counselors, admirers, and supplicants coalesced, even before the civil war was over, into a new class of hangers-on: the revolutionary intelligentsia. The process worked in reverse, too. The poet Larisa Reisner, who had flirted with Blok and Mandelstam and slept with Gumiliov, became, as soon as revolution broke out, the consort of the commander of a group of Petrograd sailors, Raskolnikov, and later of the wittiest and most cynical of the Bolshevik inner circle, Karl Radek. But she never burned her bridges with the world of poetry and gave such apolitical outsiders as Anna Akhmatova and Mandelstam protection.

Such half-revolutionary, semi-decadent bourgeois circles were alien to Stalin. No intellectual except Demian Bedny would, until Stalin acquired total power, be seduced into a dialogue. Stalin's child bride, Nadezhda, was no use in forging alliances; the only connection she gave Stalin was with the Alliluevs. They were Bolsheviks, but apart from Stanislav Redens, head of the Odessa Cheka and married to Nadezhda's elder sister, they offered Stalin no useful contacts. Even Stalin's underlings Molotov and Voroshilov had wives who opened more doors.

Stalin, however, had one particular resource to win him allies and neutralize enemies: his fellow Caucasians. Apart from Sergo Orjonikidze, he had another boon companion in Nestor Lakoba, the Abkhaz leader famed for his aquiline eyesight and profound deafness. With Stalin's assistance Lakoba, once a junior policeman, detached his small Black Sea homeland from Georgia and made it an island of prosperity in a war-ravaged Caucasus. The Bolsheviks connived at Lakoba's avoidance of reforms and purges; the prerevolution palaces and villas along the coast were neither sacked nor destroyed. Stalin invited Lakoba to stay at his dacha at Zubalovo.[43] When Dzierżyński's mental and physical health faltered and he agreed to take annual breaks, Stalin sent not just him but most of the Cheka leaders to Lakoba.[44] Sergo Orjonikidze wrote to Lakoba on September 25, 1922:

> Dear Comrade Lakoba,
>
> . . . Comrades Dzierżyński, Iagoda and others are coming to stay with you for two months. They must be put in the best villa (clean, with no insects, with heating, lighting, etc.) right on the sea. You must be in all respects a hospitable host worthy of the Abkhaz name, which I do not have the slightest doubt about. The bearer of this note will give you more details. Be well. I shake your hand warmly. Your Sergo.[45]

Caucasian hospitality, after decades of sunless privation, seduced even the ascetic Dzierżyński. Lakoba, whom Stalin cultivated for fifteen years, was his best tool for managing and eliminating rivals. When Lenin's death was imminent, Stalin's close protégé Abram Belenky, then Kremlin commandant, had Trotsky sent off for two months to Abkhazia, ostensibly for his health. Belenky told Lakoba on January 6, 1924:

> I consider the best place for housing him is . . . where you used to put up Comrades Dzierżyński and Zinoviev. The doctors have prescribed Comrade Trotsky complete peace and although our people will provide Trotsky's guards, I nevertheless ask you, dear Comrade Lakoba, with your sharp eye and care, to take Com-

rade Trotsky under your wing, then our minds will be completely at rest . . . we have no need to speak any more on this subject, I am sure you will have understood me completely. Obviously there are to be no meetings or formal parades. . . . Comrades Dzierżyński and Iagoda send you a warm cordial greeting.[46]

By the last year of Lenin's life Dzierżyński shared Stalin's hostility to Trotsky and he actively helped Stalin get him out of the way. A civil war hero, Vladimir Antonov-Ovseenko, who had admired Trotsky's organizational genius, was rebuked by Dzierżyński: "You've gone too far and you are not devoted to the party and revolution . . . keeping the dictatorship of the proletariat . . . demands from the party the greatest unity of ideas and unity of action. . . . And that means Trotsky has to be fought with."

Trotsky's vulnerable point was his hypochondria. Dzierżyński had arranged treatment for him before, and in May 1921 Lenin was worried by Trotsky's symptoms: chronic colitis, arterial spasms, fainting fits. The Politburo decided on April 23, 1921: "Comrade Trotsky is to be told to leave for treatment in the country, taking into account his doctors' prescriptions when choosing the place and time. Supervision of Trotsky's compliance with this decision is the responsibility of Comrade Dzierżyński."[47] Trotsky was sent to the north Caucasus.[48]

On January 5, 1924, as the struggle to dominate the post-Lenin USSR intensified, Stalin saw to it that "leave for Trotsky" was the first item on the agenda for the Politburo. A week later, three days before Lenin died, Dzierżyński made it even clearer to Lakoba that he must keep Stalin's rival away from the levers of power:

Comrade Lakoba! Dear Comrade! Because of the state of Comrade Trotsky's health, the doctors are sending him to Sukhum. This has become widely known even abroad and therefore I am afraid lest there be any attempts on his life by White Guards. My request to you is to bear this in mind. Because of his state of health, Comrade Trotsky will not generally be able to leave his dacha and therefore the main task is not to let any outsiders or unknown persons in. . . .

When Lenin died, Stalin with extraordinary cunning arranged the succession so that his authority would be undisputed. He placated Lenin's leftist heirs, Zinoviev and Kamenev, by joining them in what would be a short-lived triumvirate. The liberal right he reassured by seeing to it that Rykov was chosen as "prime minister," i.e., chairman of the Council of Commissars. Stalin, as the party's general secretary, held the reins of power, and he ensured the Soviet economy came under his control by making Dzierżyński economic overlord. Meanwhile, Dzierżyński's agents sampled public reaction to Lenin's death and reassured Stalin that the Soviet man in the street was most afraid of Trotsky seizing power, bringing back militant communism and ending the New Economic Plan. The NEP allowed private capital to set up small businesses and even operate state concessions; it let peasants farm the land as if they owned it and allowed businessmen and intellectuals to travel abroad. But the authors of the NEP saw it as only a temporary retreat from socialism to allow the economy and population to prepare for the next stage in the creation of a communist society.

While Trotsky languished in the Caucasus, Stalin and Dzierżyński took care of everything from Lenin's embalming to the Politburo's agenda. It dawned too late on Trotsky how disastrous his acquiescence had been. The evening after Lenin died, Stalin composed a telegram: "To Iagoda, to be given immediately to Trotsky. I regret the technical impossibility of your arriving in time for the funeral. There are no reasons to expect any complications. In these conditions we see no necessity to interrupt your treatment. Naturally we leave a final decision to you. . . ."[49] Trotsky saw that he would have no say in the Politburo until May 1924, when Lenin's last will and testament would be read out to the thirteenth congress of the Russian Bolshevik party. This secret "Letter to the Congress," Trotsky hoped, would name him the legitimate heir to power and Stalin unfit to inherit Lenin's mantle. Until then his demands would be modest. "Do you consider my immediate return to Moscow a good idea? My physical state makes it possible to take part in closed sessions, but not in public speeches. Trotsky."[50]

Dzierżyński readily acquiesced in politically disabling Trotsky, who was clearly erratic and divisive, but found Stalin's suppression of other dissident voices within the Bolshevik party harder to swallow. The stroke that silenced Lenin in spring 1923 had deprived the party of the force that could pull everyone together. Lenin, unlike Stalin, allowed others to let off steam before he imposed his own views, and did so without re-criminations. But, at Stalin's insistence, the Cheka moved from suppress-ing other left-wing parties to actions that contradicted the policy of Democratic Centralism preached by Lenin in order to make Stalin's the controlling voice in the Politburo.

Dzierżyński and the Cheka actually had a motivation as strong as Stalin's for repressing dissent: the Cheka needed something to do when peace came or it risked dissolution. In autumn 1919 the White armies had been definitively repulsed from central Russia. Civil war raged for two more years, but the existence of the Soviet state was no longer in doubt. The need for the Cheka came under question. Dzierżyński sought new roles and on May 1, 1920, he had won the Cheka peacetime powers: "The law gives the Cheka the possibility of using administrative measures to isolate those who infringe labor rules, parasites, and persons who arouse suspicion of being counterrevolutionary, persons for whom there is not enough evidence for judicial punishment and where any court, even the most harsh, will always or most often acquit them."[51] In March 1921, Zinoviev, aggrieved by mal-contents in Petrograd's factories, invited Dzierżyński to put Cheka groups in every trade union branch: the unions, which Trotsky had seen as the foundation of workers' power, were emasculated.

Information was the Cheka's commodity in its transactions with Stalin. In 1918 it had been concerned with who people were, not what they thought; now the control of thought and speech offered expansion instead of retrenchment. When Russia's postal services were restored to a shadow of their former glory, the Cheka took on enough perlustrators to intercept and read every item of mail. Information on the public mood—on conversations in queues, on dissident intellectuals, on grum-bling peasants—was gathered from informers into weekly reports for Stalin and the party. But real counterrevolutionaries were now extinct and the surviving populace was too tired, hungry, and dejected. Even though factory workers in 1922 were once again faced with starvation, as inflation ravaged the Soviet economy as badly as Weimar Germany and the authorities looted pay packets for fictitious grain or gold bonds, there was no resistance that would tax even a local Cheka.

Stalin nevertheless needed the Cheka, but one with a changed ethos in order to harass his opponents. For Stalin, Dzierżyński's only defect was fastidiousness: he disliked fabricating evidence. Still less was he willing to repress party members, even when Stalin persuaded him that fractions menaced the party and that all fractious discussion was therefore counterrevolutionary. One reason Dzierżyński's energy was diverted first into the railways and then into restoring the Russian economy was that Stalin needed the services of the cleverer, more inventive, and less principled deputy heads of the GPU (the Cheka's name from 1922), namely Viacheslav Menzhinsky and Genrikh Iagoda, and began to deal with them directly.

From Cheka to
State Political Directorate

DZIERŻYŃSKI SHOT *chekisty* found taking bribes; he deducted alimony from the salaries of unfaithful married men. But the Cheka chiefs did not even mildly reprimand those who shot the innocent or battered prisoners into confessing. The decision to slaughter the Tsar's family in Ekaterinburg and Perm, taken in July 1918 by local party and Cheka officials, was not authorized by the Moscow Cheka but the fait accompli was approved. When the Tsar's family and servants were dead Gorky pleaded, and Lenin apparently agreed, that the killings could stop. But Jekabs Peterss ordered the Cheka to kill the grand dukes imprisoned in Petrograd, including the harmless and respected historian Nikolai Mikhailovich. The grand dukes were beaten, stripped half-naked, and, some on stretchers, shot. Peterss was not even reproved.

Only when cases were fabricated en masse did Dzierżyński sometimes act. In June 1921 at Sebezh on the Latvian border the chekist Pavlovich invented a conspiracy called Tempest (*Vikhr*) and rounded up a hundred victims to be shot. Vasili Ulrikh, who was to preside over Stalin's worst show trials in the 1930s, and Agranov, Dzierżyński's acolyte, believed in Tempest; it took Dzierżyński months to expose the fabrication and have Pavlovich shot. Within a year, however, Dzierżyński stopped such investigations, and a series of fabricated trials in the early 1920s cost hundreds their lives.

In early 1920 the death penalty was abolished. Although, because of the war with Poland, it was reinstated on May 22, the Cheka announced its humanity: a directive of outrageous disingenuousness was signed by Dzierżyński and Iagoda:

> Those arrested in political cases, members of various anti-Soviet parties, are often kept in extremely bad conditions; the attitude taken to them by the administration of places of detention is wrong and often even rough. The Cheka points out that these categories of person must be considered not as persons to be punished, but as persons temporarily isolated from society in the interests of the revolution, and the conditions of their detention must not be of a penal nature.

In 1922 the death penalty was briefly abolished again, except in frontier zones; the Cheka moved its condemned prisoners to frontier zones for shooting. A few surviving grand old radicals still called for the total abolition of capital punishment (the death penalty had been more vehemently opposed in Tsarist Russia than in any other country) and in 1925 the distinguished Tolstoyan Ivan Gorbunov-Posadov pleaded with the Politburo on the hundredth anniversary of the execution of the five Decembrist rebel leaders: "Are we really going to greet the tenth anniversary of the triumph of communists (who began the condemnation of the death penalty) and the coming centenary of Tolstoi with shootings, with laws on bloody reprisals? Are you really going to drag on without end in this way along the inhuman, bloody, senseless path trod by the Tsarist tradition?"[52]

★ ★ ★ The year 1921 had seemed a disaster for the Cheka. In March the Council of People's Commissars cut its funding by a quarter; in November Lenin relegated it "to purely political tasks" and commissioned Kamenev and Dzierżyński to find it less punitive roles. He did this reluctantly, presumably impelled by economic necessity, as he had yielded to pressure to restore private trade in the New Economic Plan. On one note from Kamenev he wrote, presumably about Kamenev's willingness to give way on questions of security: "Poor, weak, timid, intimidated little man."[53]

On February 6, 1922, in a decree encouragingly entitled "On the abolition of the All-Union Extraordinary Commission and on the rules for carrying out searches, confiscations and arrests," the Cheka became the GPU (State Political Directorate) and was made nominally answerable to the Ministry of the Interior. Also encouraging for the Soviet population were the execution statistics: by 1923 executions of political offenders had fallen (officially) to 414 from 1,962 in 1922 and 9,701 in 1920.

Dzierżyński ruled the GPU as he had the Cheka, but he had less scope for his insatiable energy. His time—when he was not ill—was spent restoring the railways, requisitioning grain, and spreading, if not terror, then a spirit of panic in the economy. His tendency to put revolutionary sentiment before economic logic put him at loggerheads with better-educated commissars, on the left and on the right. Kamenev and Rykov in the Union of Labor and Defense set up in 1923 to revive the economy treated him condescendingly. Dzierżyński turned to Stalin for support. He wrote to him on August 3, 1923 (the letter was apparently never sent), "Given my weak voice, which can't reach its goal, another voice must be raised." Doubts left "iron Feliks" hopelessly malleable: "But then there will be cracks in our Soviet building."[54]

Like Stalin, Dzierżyński was impatient and incompetent with economics; he used retribution to tackle economic problems. When workers complained of devalued earnings, Dzierżyński wrote (March 28, 1923) to Iagoda demanding confiscation of all property and the exile from cities of all speculators, bar owners, and money dealers, but the state's own currency operations broke down and the money dealers had to be pardoned.[55] Dzierżyński, however hard he worked, was uneasy with economists. One economist found Dzierżyński's presence at discussions unnerving: "It was hard to keep the thread of one's thoughts in one's head, to keep track of Rykov's objections and to reply to him. I felt that Dzierżyński's cold pupils were boring right through me like X-rays and, after me, were vanishing somewhere in the stone wall." By the mid-

1920s, however, trains ran, factories produced goods, and the public credited these achievements, however shoddy, to Dzierżyński's self-sacrificing energy. To inject life into any sphere of activity, Dzierżyński was made chairman: although he never went to a cinema, he was chairman of a film association and, more appropriately, he was elected chairman of the Society for Interplanetary Relations. Dzierżyński was left desolated and vulnerable by Lenin's death. In a long letter to Stalin and Orjonikidze, he confessed: "I am not a theoretician and I am not a blind follower of persons—in my life I have personally loved only two revolutionaries and leaders. Rosa Luxemburg and Vladimir Lenin—nobody else."[56] The film that Dzierżyński commissioned of Lenin's funeral was the only cinema film he ever watched.

When Lenin died, Dzierżyński's personal power was at its peak: he was at last a member (if nonvoting) of the Politburo; he was people's commissar for transport and soon to become commissar for the whole economy; he was co-chairman with Menzhinsky of OGPU, the United State Political Directorate that consolidated the GPU in September 1923. His attachment to Stalin was not based on affection but panic that the party would fall apart without him. The monosyllabic and unexcitable Stalin seemed to Dzierżyński and many others a calm center in the struggle between the hysterical polemics of the left (Trotsky) and of the right (Bukharin). The left threatened to engulf the USSR in a worldwide revolutionary conflagration; the right seemed ready to abandon the dictatorship of the proletariat for some Scandinavian compromise between socialism and capitalism. Dzierżyński, as a fanatical but fearful Bolshevik, had no choice but to support Stalin.

Like Stalin in the effect of his gaze, Dzierżyński resembled Stalin in refusing to delegate the smallest trifle. Every detail—passengers traveling without tickets, rats in baggage compartments, matchboxes that contained not 100 but 85 matches—bothered him more than the general economic desolation and financial destitution facing the Soviets in 1923. The more Dzierżyński was mocked by Trotsky, the more he relied on Stalin. He asked Stalin for the right to deport "speculators, idlers, leeches" as those responsible for price inflation.[57] Trotsky recalled: "Dzierżyński would catch fire on any question, even a secondary one, his fine nostrils would shiver, his eyes spark, his voice would tense and often break. . . ." Dzierżyński's boast was: "I never ever spare myself. And that is why all of you here love me, because you trust me."

As Lenin lay paralyzed and speechless, the danger of civil war in the Soviet Union between an army that admired Trotsky and a bureaucracy that depended on Stalin had the rank and file of OGPU, itself both an army and a bureaucracy, vacillating. Dzierżyński held a meeting of OGPU functionaries during which he shouted hysterically, "I hate you!" at his co-speaker, the convinced Trotskyist Evgeni Preobrazhensky, editor of *Pravda* and co-author of *The Alphabet of Communism*. By the end of 1923, Stalin's power, still threatened by those closest to Lenin, nevertheless had a wider basis than his rivals.' Stalin thrived, for he held three crucial posts in the party and the government: he was general secretary of the party, the dominant figure in the party's organizational bureau, and he was commissar for national minorities. But Dzierżyński, traveling the length and breadth of the Soviet Union to inspect OGPU, the railways, and the economy, was physically and spiritually flagging. His secretary Vladimir Gerson protested but got no understanding from Stalin's aides. One telegraphed:

> Omsk. Dzierżyński's health is now worse than in Moscow, the work no less. He gets more worked up, he curses more, since things are as bad as they could be. Dzierżyński's presence here is indispensable, otherwise we could have complete collapse. There is no need for medical examination, I don't understand how you, Gerson, can demand he be examined so that he doesn't know, why don't you tell me how?[58]

Dzierżyński was suffering from years of malnutrition, tuberculosis, and a heart condition exacerbated by frenetic work and travel. Once Lenin was dead, only Menzhinsky, Iagoda, and Gerson cared if Dzierżyński wore himself out. Apart from their personal affection for him, he was the only chekist who had any charisma, and they basked in his chivalrous image. In 1925 Stalin instructed Dzierżyński, whom he now no longer needed, to reduce his working week to thirty-five hours; the Kremlin doctors forcibly X-rayed him and tested his blood. Together with Menzhinsky, his neighbor in the country, and Iagoda, Dzierżyński took the waters at Essentuki in the Caucasus. The doctors prescribed warm showers, regular enemas, a semi-vegetarian diet, Caucasian mineral water, and long weekend breaks. Dzierżyński got no better. Typical of his attitude to his health and doctors is a letter to his secretary a year before he died: "I am still coughing, especially at night. I have thick yellow phlegm. Please give me medicine to disinfect my lungs and fix the phlegm. I need not be examined. I can't stand the sight of doctors and will not consent to being examined. I request that the question not even be raised."[59]

On July 20, 1926, in the middle of a rambling, impassioned speech defending the peasantry against the left opposition's program of collectivization, Dzierżyński collapsed; he recovered briefly at home and then died. The autopsy revealed that his coronary arteries were blocked: he died, like Lenin, of arteriosclerosis.

Managing the Soviet economy, Dzierżyński had had to concede that there was no alternative to the market and moved closer to Bukharin's position. He even stopped attacking Trotsky who, as mere chief of science, technology, and trade concessions, was now a spent force. It was dawning on Dzierżyński that Stalin, an apparent advocate of the New Economic Plan, would be the man to undo it. But disillusion with Stalin came too late. Seventeen days before he died, Dzierżyński prophesied in a letter to Stalin's protégé Valerian Kuibyshev:

> Dear Valerian. I am aware that my speeches could strengthen those who will certainly lead the party to perdition, i.e. Trotsky, Zinoviev, Piatakov, Shliapnikov. But what am I to do? I am completely convinced that we will deal with all our enemies if we can find and adopt the right line for managing the country and the economy in practice. . . . If we don't find the line and the tempo, the opposition will grow and the country will then find its dictator the grave digger of the revolution. . . . Almost all dictators now are former Reds—Mussolini, Piłsudski. I am tired of these contradictions.[60]

The phrase "grave digger of the revolution" was Trotsky's sobriquet for Stalin.

THREE

THE EXQUISITE INQUISITOR

In stormy student years he became famous
for his cynical statement at a meeting that
he didn't care about his comrades. . . .
Mixing with people who considered it
shameful to play the piano when people all
round were dying of hunger, Demidov
ardently rushed into music studies. . . .
Indifferent to mockery, indignation or abuse,
Demidov was still not pleased with himself.
He wanted to win total inner freedom.

Viacheslav Menzhinsky,
Demidov's Affair

A False Dawn

IMAGINE IF THE BOLSHEVIK government had been overthrown on Lenin's death in January 1924. Suppose that the surviving Politburo and OGPU chiefs had been brought to trial on charges of mass murder, treason, torture, and robbery. Their lawyers would have advised Trotsky, Stalin, and Dzierżyński to admit guilt, but plead mitigation on five grounds: they were engaged in the overthrow of an unjust and repressive political system; they withdrew from a war that was claiming millions of lives; they were defending themselves against enemies who would have acted as badly or worse; they were fighting foreigners and the ruling classes not the people; they were motivated by the ideal of a just, non-exploitative society in which dictatorship was a temporary phase. And it seems there might have been some grounds for leniency.

After civil war ended in Russia in 1921 there were dramatic drops in executions, enforced labor sentences, political trials, and repressed rebellions. The New Economic Plan (NEP) gave citizens limited rights to engage in trade and manufacture for profit. There was a civil service of a kind. A judiciary and quasi-independent lawyers began to function. The improvements just before and after Lenin's death in 1924 might bear out the claim that the killings and injustices of 1917–21 were an inevitable product of revolution and civil war and not simply instruments by which the Bolsheviks meant to seize and consolidate power. A closer examination of the postwar period, however, shows that there was no real relaxation in the terror. The same men, now at each other's throats, remained in power. The institutions of repression, notably the Cheka-OGPU, had briefly contracted, but they were being more professionally and permanently organized. OGPU was recruiting a new type of officer. They now intended to disable the surviving intelligentsia and bourgeoisie, and their new and better method for doing so was to recruit educated men from these doomed groups.

The approach to the enemy was subtle: not just fear and bullets, but flattery, corruption, and rewards. OGPU evolved from a paramilitary organization which valued heroism and violence into a bureaucratic structure which placed secrecy, hierarchy, and system above revolutionary clichés. This process paralleled OGPU men transferring their allegiance from Trotsky and the commanders of the Red Army to Stalin and his civilian cohorts. Dzierżyński had already shifted OGPU in this direction; his deputy and successor, Viacheslav Menzhinsky, was, however, much better suited by temperament, talents, and origin to the business of turning OGPU into Stalin's chief instrument of power. Menzhinsky ran OGPU for a decade but stayed in the shadows, making no speeches, holding no party posts. No cities were named after him, nor statues raised. A man few have praised and very few have liked, even among Soviet apologists for the Cheka, Menzhinsky has long deserved history's full obloquy.

Viacheslav Menzhinsky's Belated Rise

"WHY MENZHINSKY?" Lenin asked, baffled when Dzierżyński put forward another Pole, Viacheslav Rudolfovich Menzhinsky, in September 1919 to head the Cheka's Special Plenipotentiary Section, which covered intelligence and counterintelligence. "Who else?" Dzierżyński replied. Lenin knew Menzhinsky as a dilettante who had failed to make his mark at law, poetry and prose, in revolutionary politics, music, painting, languages, finance, or diplomacy. The choice was outlandish, but inspired.

Dzierżyński proposed Menzhinsky not as a fellow Pole or friend; before 1917 they had met only once, in 1910, in Paris. True, in the last form he ever filled in, his Moscow electoral card for 1933, Menzhinsky put, under ethnic affiliation, "Polish," but his background, education, and speech were wholly Russian. Menzhinsky's father was a Russified Pole, a professor of history, whose lectures, reproduced on a duplicator, were popular cramming material; his mother was a woman of letters and helped Tolstoyans provide uplifting reading for the Russian peasantry.

Menzhinsky belonged to the ruling classes; his elder brother Aleksandr was an auditor for the Tsar's Ministry of Finances and Viacheslav began his own career as a law student. His dissertation, "Communal Land Ownership in Populist and Marxist Literature," was returned as "unsatisfactory" by one professor who read it and as "unlikely to be assessable by a civilian" by another. The dissertation scornfully surveyed the peasantry whom thirty years later Menzhinsky would help Stalin destroy. "The peasant commune," Menzhinsky asserted in 1898, is "one of the major brakes on Russia's agricultural development . . . the commune is disintegrating, dying a natural death."[1]

In the early 1900s Menzhinsky practiced law, but his literary ambitions drew him into the decadent circle around a notorious homosexual, satanist, and multifarious genius, Mikhail Kuzmin. Menzhinsky left little trace in this circle. He also dabbled in Bolshevism: his mother Maria Nikolaevna was a friend of the great-aunt of Elena Stasova, who was close both to Lenin and to Stalin in his Tbilisi years. On weekends Menzhinsky followed the family hobby of workers' education and preached revolution. The authorities paid him little attention; he was apparently leading a respectable life in a villa in the provincial town of Iaroslavl, employed as a railway administrator. A bourgeois on workdays, a Bolshevik on Sundays, and a decadent at night, Menzhinsky showed remarkable duplicity.

For a decade Menzhinsky was married to Iulia Ivanovna, who had been governess to the Russian branch of the Nobel family and was preoccupied with the theory and practice of bringing up children. The topics of the Menzhinskys' correspondence with their friends the Verkhovskys in the early 1900s are the most bourgeois of any Bolshevik's: office, garden, children. Only Menzhinsky's distress at literary setbacks—his friends insisted on shortening the novel he eventually published—and references to the Nietzschean superman hint at his longing for fame.

In February 1905 the Menzhinskys suffered a trauma: their young daughter died of a cerebral hemorrhage. Menzhinsky left Iaroslavl for St. Petersburg, where he worked with Lenin and Krupskaia, and after the crackdown on Bolsheviks in 1906 underwent two weeks of imprisonment, his only ordeal in the name of the revolution. He went on hunger strike and was released. Menzhinsky's marriage broke up; his wife took the children. She devoted herself to pedagogy and never mentioned Menzhinsky again.[2] Menzhinsky drifted abroad. He roamed France, Italy, and Britain and even the United States for eleven years, working as a bank clerk for Crédit Lyonnais in Paris, as a watercolor painter, as a teacher at the Bolshevik school in Bologna. Like Dzierżyński, Menzhinsky was more deeply attached to his sisters than to any other human being. Neither Vera nor Liudmila ever married. With Vera he hiked over the hills of northern Italy, and the death of Liudmila in 1932 was the worst blow in his life.

What Menzhinsky did in 1909 should have blighted his future prospects with the Bolsheviks forever: in the Russian émigré journal *Our Echo* he attacked Lenin for "appropriating" the proceeds of Bolshevik banditry for his own personal use. Menzhinsky abused Lenin: "another half-mad Tsar Paul I . . . The Bolsheviks' aim is power, influence over the people, their desire is to bridle the proletariat. Lenin is a political Jesuit, twisting Marxism according to his own whim and using it for ephemeral aims. . . . Leninists are not a political group but a noisy gypsy camp. They like waving whips around, they imagine that they have an inalienable right to be the cattle-drovers of the working class." But Menzhinsky shared the views he ascribed to Lenin: a friend recalls him declaring: "the peasantry are cattle to be sacrificed to revolution." Both Lenin and Stalin knew of Menzhinsky's outbursts. Lenin dismissed them with casual contempt as he always dismissed attacks from those beneath him; Stalin, on the other hand, cultivated men who had lapses that made them hostages to fortune. In any case, Stalin likewise saw peasants as "cattle" and Lenin as the "cattle-drover."

Returning to Russia from France in spring 1917 via Britain and Finland, Menzhinsky was a bystander during the October revolution. He played Chopin waltzes on a grand piano in the Smolny Institute when all around him was chaos and panic. The Petrograd Bolsheviks nevertheless found work for Menzhinsky. Thanks to his and his brother's banking experience he was appointed commissar for finance. Lenin first met Menzhinsky fast asleep on a divan in a corridor. To the divan was stuck a label, "People's Commissariat of Finances," and Menzhinsky was so far its sole employee.

Trotsky claimed that Menzhinsky had trouble forcing the banks to disgorge their funds to the revolution so Lenin and Trotsky then tried to utilize Menzhinsky's suave manners and knowledge of languages. In April 1918 he was sent to the Soviet mission in Berlin where, during the mission's seven months of life, Menzhinsky made a positive impression, and not just with his polyglot skills—he spoke most European and several oriental languages—but with his flair for intelligence gathering and analysis. When the Germans expelled the Soviet mission for spreading revolutionary propaganda, Menzhinsky was given riskier work. He spent much of 1919 as commissar for national inspection in the Ukraine, where the Russian Bolsheviks were targets for Ukrainian nationalists. Here Menzhinsky proved his fearlessness, enough for Dzierżyński to make him the third Pole in the Cheka leadership.

A shrewd judge of men and information, a chess player who used real people as pawns and—it turned out—a prodigious fabricator of plots and scenarios, Menzhinsky took over from Dzierżyński even before the latter's death in 1926 and kept his post until his death in May 1934. Apart from People's Commissar for Foreign Affairs Georgi Chicherin (an intimate member of Mikhail Kuzmin's decadent circle), Menzhinsky was the only commissar who looked like a banker, in a three-piece suit, tie, and bowler hat. Like Chicherin, he was also constantly ill. In exile he suffered from kidney infections and a hernia; a car accident in Paris had given him spondylitis, and he was unable to stand or even sit for long. He interrogated prisoners reclining on a divan under a traveling rug which his second-in-command Genrikh Iagoda tucked round his legs. Menzhinsky also had the "Kremlin syndrome": arteriosclerosis, an enlarged heart, and migraines.

Without Menzhinsky's shrewdness, Stalin could not have in the 1920s defeated his enemies abroad and at home; without Menzhinsky's ruthlessness, Stalin could not have pushed through collectivization in 1929, nor staged the show trials of the early 1930s. However far apart in education and origin, Stalin and Menzhinsky had a real affinity. They shared a calm ruthlessness: neither ever raised his voice or spoke at unnecessary length. Menzhinsky cultivated silence to extremes; on the tenth anniversary of the revolution, expected to make a forty-minute speech on the Cheka's glorious role, he mounted the tribune, said, "The main merit of a chekist is to keep silent," and stepped down.

Like Stalin, Menzhinsky had been a poet. Stalin's lyrics reveal a tortured psyche obsessed by the moon, swinging between euphoria and depression, expecting ingratitude and even poison from his audience, and terrified of old age. Menzhinsky's persona is an arrogant and depraved cynic. Perhaps it is significant that Stalin was an adolescent and Menzhinsky in his early thirties when each was first published.

Menzhinsky's published writings give us the best insight into his mentality.[3] His novel *Demidov's Affair* appeared in 1905 in *The Green Anthology* (resembling the English decadent *Yellow Book*) next to thirteen sonnets by Mikhail Kuzmin. Menzhinsky's piece was singled out by one critic as the best in the anthology. The story of Vasili Demidov, "a very elegant youth" who values "only the freedom of the individual," has the blend of depravity and socialism that we find in Oscar Wilde. The novel is narcissistic: its hero is a handsome young lawyer who helps radical women to run workers' Sunday and evening classes but shocks women teachers with blasphemous and erotic lyrics, which he recites at a college gathering. The austere director of the college, Elena, fourteen years older, falls in love with Demidov despite disapproving of him. Their subsequent marriage is strained: the repressed woman and the hedonist prove incompatible. The work mixes decadent amorality with chekist ruthlessness.

Menzhinsky's hero recites a "Poem to the God of Temptation." In this version of the Book of Job, God challenges the poet:

> Can you measure the radiance of my freedom,
> The gravity of the abyss, the joy of being one's self?
> You cower? Stand back. Not everyone can grasp
> The wondrous art of seeing in dreary commandments
> Lighthouses only for bold temptations,
> The goal of happiness in separation, the path to betrayal in friendship.

To which challenge Menzhinsky's Job replies:

> Enough! I have decided. The field is yours.
> I shall build an eternal shrine to you.

When Demidov falls for Anna, a secretary in his office, Menzhin-sky's novel ends in an improbable idyll. Both women are in Demidov's apartment, Elena sorting out rags, Anna dropping clothes on the floor—a realization of the "three-in-a-bed" love lyric which Menzhinsky has his hero recite at a school concert:

> Under passionate searches so passionately
> Your body writhes!
> I, a great artist, laugh,
> No tears, no shame—only yells,
> And sighs and quivering do you know.
> [. . .]
> It has come! I have seen another woman
> With my burning tensed gaze,
> I tickle and kiss her,
> I have bent down, I embrace her, you are next to us.

Demidov's Affair shows how well Menzhinsky understood his future self: when Demidov becomes a legal official, he reflects that he was "the smallest spoke in the chariot of justice and he felt no personal guilt if that chariot crushed anybody."

In 1907, in the anthology *A Thawed Patch* (*Protalina*), in the company of two leading poets—Aleksandr Blok and Mikhail Kuzmin—Menzhinsky published two prose poems, pastiches of the Gospels, "Jesus" and "Barabbas." Menzhinsky's Christ is an epileptic, a suicidal charismatic not a messiah, who takes his disciples to view Golgotha; Barabbas, the killer of tax gatherers, is acclaimed by the mob, released by Pontius Pilate, and discreetly killed by the Romans.

29. There was nobody who would cry out "Release Jesus."
30. But the crowd yelled, "Give us Barabbas, and crucify Jesus."
31. And Barabbas, standing in the crowd, saw Jesus dragged to the place of execution.
32. And Barabbas did not die as a slave on the cross.
33. The Romans killed him in the wilderness and the fifty men who were faithful to him.

34. Barabbas fell with his sword in his hand, and Judaea wept for him, and Galilee tore its hair, groaning:

35. "Barabbas has died, Barabbas the terror of the dishonorable, the destroyer of Romans, the exterminator of tax collectors!"

As in Gorky's play *The Lower Depths,* in Menzhinsky's verses the Christian hero is superseded by the revolutionary bandit.[4] Menzhinsky's verses not only echo Stalin's distrust of an ungrateful mob, they give us an uncanny insight into how Menzhinsky would treat the Jesuses, Pontius Pilates, and Barabbases he would work against, for, and with in Soviet Russia. Messianic obsessions link Menzhinsky to Dzierżyński and to Stalin. What drew them together was repressed Christian piety. All three are unquiet Dostoevskian atheists. Denying God was not enough; they longed to usurp him.

Like Stalin, Menzhinsky, after abandoning creative writing, took a morbid interest in poetry and poets. Both intervened, as patrons, censors, or hangmen, in poets' work and lives but in Menzhinsky's first years in the Cheka, with a blotted ideological copybook, he was precluded from rooting out Social Revolutionaries, Mensheviks, anarchists, or other heretics. He was valued for his ability, rare in an institution largely staffed with illiterates and foreigners, to draft a letter, resolution, or verdict in Russian which combined a lawyer's precision with a poet's elegance. But despite his backroom role, as the Cheka evolved into OGPU, Menzhinsky stood out. Those he interviewed were struck by the hunched body, the spectacles or pince-nez, the couch and the rug. He made much of his long pianist's fingers, rubbing his hands with pleasure, smiling, excruciatingly polite, even—or especially—when he was sending his collocutor to execution.

Repressing Peasants and Intellectuals

IN EARLY 1921 the civil war wound down, the Caucasus was reconquered, and the Poles and the Baltic states signed peace treaties with the USSR. The Cheka, like the Red Army, was opposed mainly by those in whose name it had been fighting as internecine war broke out between Bolsheviks and peasantry. On the Volga grain surpluses and seed corn were confiscated by army and Cheka units to feed soldiers and urban workers, and during the "Antonov" rebellion the peasants were crushed by army units under men like Tukhachevsky, directed by Trotsky, and mopped up by the special purpose units of Dzierżyński's deputy Józef Unszlicht. Tukhachevsky's ruthless slaughter of hostages and rebels worsened the famine brought by war and drought. Few remained alive for the Cheka to torture or kill.

Before the "Antonov bandits" could be shot or sent to camps, the factories and garrisons of Moscow and Petrograd went on strike. Bread rations were at starvation levels; fuel had dried up. The workers, seeing the Whites defeated, could not understand why they were still hungry, cold, out of work, and under martial law. In March 1921, the naval garrison on the fortress island of Kronstadt outside Petrograd demanded free elections, free speech, and land for the peasantry. Their delegation was arrested and Trotsky and Tukhachevsky bullied troops into crushing the uprising. The Petrograd Cheka was in disgrace for not forestalling the rising: Dzierżyński sent a fellow Pole, Stanisław Messing, with another senior chekist, Iakov Agranov, from Moscow to try the rebel sailors, many of whom were shot.

Menzhinsky and his colleague in the Cheka Dr. Mikhail Kedrov drafted a warning to the Central Committee. Lenin, Zinoviev, and Stalin were told that the peasant rebellions were well organized and that if conditions deteriorated the metropolitan workers would strike in solidarity with the peasantry. They also warned that the trade union movement courted by Trotsky—was undermining the party and that the Red Army was no longer a reliable tool. The note recommended that only special purpose detachments—the Cheka's own forces—be used to restore order in army units and factories.

Ensuing disasters proved the Cheka right. Menzhinsky tried to explain this to Trotsky, whom he had previously warned that Stalin was intriguing against him. Trotsky rashly refused to respond—he thought Menzhinsky inconsequential—but he conceded that Menzhinsky was right on one point: the Petrograd Cheka had been secretly sympathetic to the Kronstadt rebels. Menzhinsky's role in liquidating the Kronstadt rebellion had been to dispatch a thousand dissident sailors to Odessa—which nearly led to the subsequent rebellion there. Eight years passed before Menzhinsky took part in more mass repressions.

★ ★ ★ During the early 1920s Menzhinsky oversaw the intelligentsia. In spring 1921 the poets Aleksandr Blok and Fiodor Sologub pleaded for exit visas.[5] Anatoli Lunacharsky, commissar for education and the softest of the Soviet leaders, had himself been a symbolist dramatist. He sympathized: "We have literally driven Blok to the point of no return." Maxim Gorky interceded for Blok and Sologub even though he disliked their verse. For the Cheka, Menzhinsky and Unszlicht took a harsher view: Unszlicht complained of the "completely impermissible attitude of the People's Commissariat for Education on travel by artistic forces abroad. There is no doubt that the overwhelming majority of performers and artists who travel abroad are lost to Soviet Russia. . . . Moreover, many of them conduct open or covert campaigns against us abroad."

Of twenty-four allowed out, only five had returned. Menzhinsky was adamant: "Not just Lunacharsky but Bukharin vouched for Konstantin Balmont [who stayed in France]. Blok is a poetic nature; if anything makes a bad impression on him he will quite naturally write verse against us. I don't think he ought to be let out, Blok should be given good conditions in some sanatorium."[6] Lunacharsky protested to Lenin over Menzhinsky's stance. When the Politburo decided on July 23, 1921, in Blok's favor, the poet was dying. The agony of Russia's best-loved poet embarrassed the Politburo to the extent that it let Blok's close friend Andrei Bely, symbolist poet and novelist, immigrate to Berlin.

Menzhinsky clashed with Lunacharsky again in 1926. He overruled the commissar and banned Mikhail Bulgakov's play *The Day of the Turbins.* Only in his last years did Menzhinsky protect fellow writers: when Mikhail Kuzmin went to see him in 1931, he was promised that his lover Iuri Iurkun would not be harassed by OGPU, a promise that was kept until Kuzmin's death in 1936.

The Cheka accused Petrograd's intellectuals of being the puppet masters of the Kronstadt sailors. Iakov Agranov, Menzhinsky's deputy, constructed out of the sailors' rebellion one of the first imaginary anti-

Bolshevik conspiracies.[7] Agranov first lured back to Russia those sailors who had fled to Finland: Cheka couriers, pretending to be White Guard agents, smuggled sailors across the border to "safe houses" in Petrograd. Then Agranov claimed that the Kronstadt sailors were linked to a "Petrograd Fighting Organization" led by members of the intelligentsia. (The only signs of such an organization were two explosions at monuments to the two Bolsheviks assassinated in Petrograd in 1918, Moisei Uritsky and Moisei Volodarsky-Goldstein.) Agranov employed as provocateur a certain Korvin-Kriukovsky, the scion of a distinguished family, to act as a malcontent chekist and inveigle Professor Vladimir Tagantsev, a soil scientist, into a few symbolic actions including sticking up dissident flyers. The professor was thereupon arrested with his father (an elderly senator), his entire family, and a truckload of others.

Summer 1921 in Petrograd was the Cheka's first successful rehearsal of the techniques for terror perfected in the mid-1930s. In 1921 it took Agranov forty-five days to make Professor Tagantsev accept an ultimatum: to confess and name all fellow conspirators or be executed together with everyone arrested. They signed an agreement on July 28, 1921, ending: "I, Agranov, promise, provided that Tagantsev keeps his side of the bargain, that neither Tagantsev, nor his associates nor any other accused, even the couriers from Finland, will be subject to the death penalty."[8] Tagantsev was given a cell with a shower, meals from the staff kitchen and within a couple of days—one of which he spent being driven round the city to establish the addresses of his contacts—had given Agranov 300 suspects, so many that on the appointed night every motor vehicle at the Cheka's disposal was out rounding them up. After consulting Dzierżyński and Lenin, Agranov broke his bargain with Tagantsev and sentenced over one hundred to death. Tagantsev, the chemist Professor Mikhail Tikhvinsky, and, to widespread public horror when the Cheka published the list of condemned, Nikolai Gumiliov—now Russia's greatest living poet and still growing in stature—were to be shot together with many former civil servants. To accuse Gumiliov of conspiracy, a cavalier monarchist who engaged only in open combat, was absurd.

The sentences produced a flurry of telephone calls, telegrams, and personal visits to Dzierżyński, Lenin, and Krupskaia in Moscow. Krupskaia rescued some victims but Lenin refused to save Professor Tikhvinsky, a man with whom he was on Christian-name terms, saying that "counterrevolution and chemistry are not mutually exclusive." Lenin reacted too late to appeals on behalf of Gumiliov from Gorky and from women admirers. In Petrograd Grigori Zinoviev, atoning for his laxness over Kronstadt, was impatient for blood. The Petrograd Cheka treated the condemned atrociously. Put in a large cell, handcuffed to each other, and left for thirty-six hours without food, water, or lavatory facilities, they were loaded at dawn onto trucks and driven out to a firing range. Tagantsev, Gumiliov, and some eighty others dug their own graves, were undressed, shot by riflemen, and buried, wounded or dead.

A similar trial in Moscow that spring, of the so-called Tactical Center, involved operatives including Menzhinsky who were subtler than Agranov. But these prisoners were braver and more eloquent than Tagantsev: they refused to bargain for their freedom or lives. The accused included Tolstoi's daughter Aleksandra, the philosopher Nikolai Berdiaev, and the historian Sergei Melgunov; the death sentences were commuted. In Moscow Agranov, entrusted only with interrogation, was shamed into silence by the retorts of Tolstoi's daughter.

The prosecution was conducted with a parody of legality by Nikolai Krylenko. Krylenko, who had a law degree, had achieved fame by being appointed the first commander-in-chief of the Russian army after the Tsar's General Nikolai Dukhonin had refused to swear loyalty to the Soviets and been murdered by his troops. In summer 1918, Krylenko went back to the law, which he twisted to fit Soviet requirements. Krylenko had an appreciation of the absurd. In June 1918, after the Soviets had voted to abolish the death penalty, as the prosecutor responsible for sending Admiral Shchastny to the firing squad for not scuttling the Baltic fleet, he declared that the admiral was to be shot, not executed. During the "Tactical Center" trial, Krylenko burst out laughing when the defense exposed the Cheka's absurdity.

Agranov, Menzhinsky, and Dzierżyński—who explained to intercessors that he could not reprieve a major poet without reprieving all the condemned—belatedly grasped that the Petrograd executions of August 1921 had put professionals and intellectuals off working for, as well as against, the regime. The misjudgment was one reason for reforming the Cheka as the GPU in 1922. A revised criminal code, drawn up by Lenin, provided a new punishment for dissidents: deportation from the Soviet Union.[9] In May 1922 this penalty was inflicted on those intellectuals whom a committee—Lenin, Dzierżyński, Menzhinsky, and Unszlicht— classified as undesirables. Stalin, preoccupied that summer with unleashing bloody repression on central Asia and enforcing discipline in Georgia, made no objection to such gentle measures. Even the bloodthirsty Zinoviev supported the venture: "We are now resorting to a humane measure, to deportation; we can resort to a less humane measure, we shall not hesitate to unsheathe the sword."[10]

Hitherto deportation had been voluntary; the first intellectuals granted deportation had been those Jewish writers, headed by Khaim Bialik, who wrote in Hebrew. Jews were encouraged to write in Russian and allowed to write in Yiddish, but Hebrew, the language of Zionism, was banned by Lenin in 1920. In Moscow a hundred Zionist congress participants were arrested and nineteen put in prison. Trotsky's own brother-in-law by his first marriage Ilia Sokolovsky belonged to the Hebrew writers' group. Sokolovsky decided to ask his brother-in-law for "a ticket out of this paradise you are making." Khaim Bialik made a fraught journey through the war-ravished Ukraine to Moscow, saw Gorky and obtained from Lenin the visas that took Hebrew literature out of Russia to Palestine.

Famine as well as Cheka bullets thinned out independent-minded intellectuals: seven academicians including the mathematician Aleksandr Liapunov and the linguist Aleksei Shakhmatov starved to death. Only Russia's Nobel Prize winner, Ivan Pavlov, whose experiments in vivisection were seen as Bolshevism in biology, was given extra rations. Lenin was enraged by "professors and writers . . . counter-revolutionaries, complicit with the Entente, spies, corrupting our youth." Even in 1919 he had written to Gorky about intellectuals "who think themselves the nation's brains . . . actually not brains, but shit." On May 19, 1922, he set Dzierżyński on them but nine days later had his second stroke. Incoherently but intransigently, four days after recovering his handwriting, Lenin scrawled to Stalin on July 17:

Has it been decided to eradicate all the National Socialists? . . . I think all should be deported. They're worse than any Social Revolutionary because they are more cunning . . . . The Mensheviks Rozanov (a doctor, devious). . . . S. L. Frank (author of *Methodology*) . . . A commission under Messing and Mantsev [two senior GPU men] must draw up lists and several hundred such gentlemen should be mercilessly expelled abroad. We'll clean Russia up for a long time. . . . This must be done right away. By the end of the trial of the Social Revolutionaries, no later. Arrest several hundred and without declaring the reasons, "out you go, gentlemen!" All the authors of *The House of Writers,* of *Thought* in Petersburg, turn over Kharkov, we don't know that town, it's abroad for us. . . .[11]

Lenin sent lists of "active anti-Soviet intellectuals" whose names he could still recall for Menzhinsky and Unszlicht to track down, whether they were at liberty or in a GPU prison, and asked Kamenev and Unszlicht for further names. Editors of academic journals who gave contributors too much freedom; doctors who at conferences kept up prerevolutionary traditions of free speech; economists and agronomists with their own ideas on factories and land—all had to go. The expulsion by the dying dictator of the country's greatest doctors anticipated Stalin's "doctors' plot" of thirty years later.

On September 4, 1922, Dzierżyński discussed the list with Lenin and instructed Unszlicht to comb through all contributors to academic and literary journals. Unfortunately, neither Pole knew enough Russian philosophy or literature to judge whom to deport and whom to keep. Dzierżyński wrote:

I think that things won't progress if Comrade Menzhinsky himself does not undertake it. Have a word with him and give him this note. We must work out a plan, constantly correcting and adding to it. We must divide all the intelligentsia into groups. For example: 1) literary writers; 2) journalists and political writers; 3) economists, and here we need subgroups: a) financial, b) energy, c) transport, d) trade, e) cooperatives, etc.; 4) technical (more subgroups): a) engineers, b) agronomists, c) doctors, d) general staff; 5) professors and teachers, etc., etc. Each intellectual must have a file. . . . It must be remembered that our section's task is not just deportation, but active help in straightening out the [party] line on specialists, i.e. causing disintegration in their ranks and bringing forward those who are prepared without reservations to support Soviet power. . . .[12]

In autumn 1922 the cream of Moscow's intelligentsia was gathered at the Lubianka (similar roundups took place in Petrograd, Kazan, Minsk, Kiev). Most were charged with counterrevolutionary activity; a few got their names taken off the list; some were classified essential workers by Soviet institutions. OGPU failed to trace some deportees while others were in their custody awaiting "trial" on other political charges. The detainees did not realize how lucky they were; those who were allowed to stay in the motherland rarely survived more than fifteen years. By the end of September 1922 Genrikh Iagoda had arranged for the remaining 130 or so to be deported to Germany. The German chancellor protested that "Germany is not Siberia" but the consul in Moscow issued visas to those deportees who certified that they were leaving voluntarily. All deportees naturally did so, and, forbidden to take books or manuscripts with them, assembled on the Petrograd docks.

The two shiploads that left for Stettin were Russia's greatest gift to Europe and America. We owe structural linguistics to Trubetskoi and Iakobson, and Christian existentialism to Nikolai Berdiaiev. The historians Sergei Melgunov and Aleksandr Kizevetter were major influences on Western historiography. Prague's Russian Academy and Paris's Sorbonne were enriched by this forced exodus. Conversely, the USSR was deprived of some of its best minds, while those that remained drew the obvious conclusions and withdrew into themselves. The deportations of 1922 were as catastrophic for civic society in the USSR as the executions of 1921.

Negotiating with such eloquent and self-assured victims was an education for the GPU. In one interrogation, Dzierżyński, Menzhinsky, and Lev Kamenev were subjected to an hour-long lecture by the idealist philosopher Nikolai Berdiaiev. Dzierżyński was dumbfounded; he could only mutter, perhaps thinking of himself, "One can be a materialist in theory and an idealist in life or, conversely, an idealist in theory and a materialist in life," after which he ordered Menzhinsky to find a motorcycle and sidecar to take Berdiaev home. In the summer and autumn of 1922, the Moscow and Petrograd *chekisty* were subjected to many more hours of principled refutation of everything they claimed to stand for. When Menzhinsky told the historian Melgunov that he would never see Russia again, the latter retorted, "I'll come back in two years; you won't hold on any longer." Menzhinsky replied, "No, I think we'll last another six."

Appeals and intercessions grated on Lenin. He decided on foreign sanatoria for men like Gorky and Korolenko who opposed his repressions but were too prestigious to execute, imprison, or deport. To Commissar for Health Nikolai Semashko he wrote in March 1922: "Please appoint a special person (best, a <u>well-known</u> doctor) knowing abroad (and <u>known abroad</u>) to send abroad to Germany Tsiurupa, Krestinsky, Osinsky, Kuraev, Gorky, and Korolenko. It needs skillful inquiries, requests, propaganda, writing to Germany, helping <u>the sick</u>, etc. Do it ultra-carefully (taking pains). . . ."

Gorky, however, would neither shut up nor pack up. In August Lenin insisted: "You are having hemorrhages, and not going! Tut, tut, this really is shameful and irrational. In Europe you will have treatment in a proper sanatorium and work three times as much. Really. But we have no treatment, no work—only fussing about. . . . Go away, get cured. Don't be stubborn, I beg you."

★ ★ ★ In October 1921 Gorky left for Berlin and then convalescence in Capri, a paradise from which only Stalin could coax him back.

The executions of Tagantsev and Gumiliov, the deportations of Berdiaev and Gorky, at first seem like monstrous overkill, depriving the state of the very people it needed to entrench and validate it. But these draconian measures had the desired effect. After 1922 few professionals and intellectuals at liberty in the USSR saw any future in living by their traditional codes of free speech and love of humanity. If science or art was to survive in any form, then it had to collaborate with the Bolshevik regime. For the next thirty years, with very few suicidal exceptions, dissent dared not speak its mind, and formerly free spirits sought only terms on which they could capitulate.

But there was no point putting muzzles on the writers without blinders on the readers. Soviet ideology resented the trickle of imported literature and the emergence of private publishers allowed by the New Economic Plan. In summer 1922 Glavlit, the directorate for literature, was set up.[13] It answered to the liberal Commissar of Education Lunacharsky, but Stalin put his own protégé Pavel Lebedev-Poliansky in charge. Lebedev-Poliansky was the same age as Stalin and likewise educated at Church school and theological college. He had to steer an ingenious course between moronic demands from party extremists to ban great classics of literature and philosophy, and the excessive tolerance of liberal socialists.

Glavlit, supervised by the GPU, warned in October 1922: "It is to be deemed indispensable that we move from preliminary censorship to a punitive form of censorship," in other words not just banning undesirable works but punishing those responsible for offering them for publication. Józef Unszlicht of the GPU insisted that publications should also be read by the Politburo, which became a literary committee. Trotsky, the most widely read, was given the greatest load: he read all military and religious literature as well as sharing economics with Lenin. Zinoviev and Kamenev read journalism, philosophy, and fiction. Rykov and Tomsky shared industry and agriculture. Stalin was the least burdened: he shared military works with Trotsky and read works on ethnic minorities. As Glavlit acquired police powers and a monopoly on censorship, the Politburo was able to shift this load. Nevertheless, the highest authority in the Soviet Union—including of course Stalin—never ceased to take a direct interest in literature.

Citizens' private letters were read as thoroughly as publications. Even under the Tsarist regime, although interception of the mail was illegal (as it would be under the Soviet constitution) the government had practiced perlustration, reading 38,000 letters a year by 1882. The GPU created a directorate for political control, run by Ivan Surta, a paramedic.[14] Surta developed the system to such an extent that every correspondent in the USSR could be sure of being read by the GPU: by the end of 1923 5 million letters and 8 million telegrams a year were being read, 250 letters and 2,500 telegrams per perlustrator per day. OGPU's readers, writers, and informants were former soldiers and clerks, men who under the Tsar would have been sucked into the bureaucracy after seven years' schooling, or literate recruits from those who had been adolescents when the revolution broke off their education and their prospects of normal office work.

Control of the Church

The wicked shall go to the sanctuary, with axes and with fire they will break down and burn its doors; and they will take the just men and burn them in the center of the city.

Savonarola, Sermon of 1491

FREEDOM OF RELIGIOUS CONSCIENCE had been a plank in the Bolshevik platform—even the Salvation Army was permitted in Moscow from 1918 to 1920—but the Orthodox Church, the prop of the Tsarist state, met with implacable hostility from Lenin's party. Only Anatoli Lunacharsky hoped to integrate the evangelical wing of the Church into Soviet ideology. In spring 1922, for the final time, Lenin, Stalin, and Trotsky acted in concert—to destroy this last bastion of hostile ideology.[15] Menzhinsky, the GPU's most experienced blasphemer, took charge. This campaign was a logical development of the Bolsheviks' economic and military victory: the Church was singled out not just because of Lenin and Trotsky's anticlericalism or Stalin's, Dzierżyński's, and Menzhinsky's religious complexes, nor just because it was the last element of the old regime with any hold over the populace. The pretext for action was the Church's riches.

War and drought had by the middle of 1921 killed some 5 million peasants, and despite its requests the Russian Church was refused permission to organize famine relief. In August 1921 Lenin authorized the American Relief Agency to distribute wheat in the Volga region with contributions coming from agencies such as Fridtjof Nansen's organization and the Quakers. The ARA's success embarrassed the Soviet authorities: the Volga quickly began feeding the cities again.

At first sight the Church was no danger to the regime; it had failed to give any lead in public affairs, in theology or philosophy, for 200 years. But Orthodox laymen like Aleksei Khomiakov, Konstantin Leontiev, and Fiodor Dostoevsky had revitalized Russian Christianity at the end of the previous century, and it had even competed with social democrats and Marxists for the minds of educated Russians at the time. In 1921 people still remembered the religious-philosophical debates of 1903 and 1904 which had unnerved both the Church hierarchy and the revolutionary movements when they saw with what verve Christians and Marxists could convert each other.

The Church's offer to undertake famine relief now suggested a ploy to the Cheka and the party: the Church would be forced, not encouraged, to hand over its icons, gold, silver, and bronze for sale. In vain Patriarch Tikhon requested that parishes should keep objects used in the liturgy. Lenin believed that billions, not just millions, of gold rubles would be raised by selling Church property—although the Church's land and many of its buildings had already been expropriated—and proposed thus to pay off enough of the Tsarist government's debts to win recognition from European states. Trotsky, convinced of imminent worldwide conflagration, saw the Church's money as a war chest, to be grabbed quickly, before world revolution devalued it.

Both Lenin and Trotsky overestimated the value of the booty: objects were seized so roughly and precious metal scrapped so crudely that barely 4 million gold rubles was realized of which 1 million was spent on famine relief. Dealers in jewelry and works of art did not want to buy the loot; the Bolsheviks, like burglars, could sell only to fences. Protests from liberal Bolsheviks were overridden. Lunacharsky asked Lenin to collaborate with, not antagonize, the hierarchy, "so that we can win over the peasantry in a way that is not dangerous for us." Dzierżyński and Lācis of the Cheka dismissed this argument: "the usual quirks of God-seekers," said Lācis. Dzierżyński announced, "The Church is disintegrating, therefore we must help this process but in no way should we resurrect the Church in a renewed form. Therefore the Cheka must conduct Church policy. . . . Any kind of connection whatever of priests with

other organs will cast a shadow on the party—that is very very dangerous. We've had enough trouble with just the 'specialists.' "[16] Trotsky's
wife Natalia Sedova also remonstrated. She wanted Russian museums to
have items of artistic worth and deplored icons being hacked up for
scrap silver. Lenin was adamant: for the Church he felt a fury as strong
as his contempt for the peasantry and its blind faith in God and the land.
When parishioners rioted, notably in the town of Shuia, the Cheka shot
the ringleaders and Lenin supported extreme measures. On March 19,
1922, he wrote to the Politburo:

> . . . the only moment when we can smash the enemy's head with
> a 99 percent chance of success . . . Now and only now, when
> there is cannibalism in the famine areas and hundreds, if not
> thousands of corpses are lying on the roads, we can (and there-
> fore must) carry out the confiscation of Church valuables with
> the most furious and merciless energy, not stopping at the crush-
> ing of any resistance. . . . A clever writer on political questions
> [Machiavelli] rightly said that if it is necessary for the realization
> of a political goal to go for a series of atrocities, then they must
> be carried out in the most energetic way and in the shortest time,
> for the popular masses will not endure prolonged application of
> atrocities. . . . Therefore I come to the inevitable conclusion that
> it is now that we must give the most decisive and merciless battle
> to the obscurantist clergy and crush its resistance with such cru-
> elty that they won't forget it for several decades.[17]

On only one point was Lenin sensitive: he feared an anti-Semitic
backlash if Jews were seen to be running this "pogrom in reverse"
against Russian Christians, so an ethnic Russian had to be nominally in
charge of crushing the Church. "Any measures whatsoever must be officially announced only by Comrade Kalinin—never under any circumstances may Comrade Trotsky make any public statements in print or
any other way."

In the parishes some 2,700 priests and 5,000 monks and nuns perished. Across Russia there were 1,400 bloody confrontations between
Cheka or Red Army and parishioners, and over 200 trials. On March 20,

1922, the Cheka "indicted" Patriarch Tikhon for counterrevolutionary activity despite the latter's eagerness to compromise; Trotsky wanted to arrest the entire Holy Synod. Tikhon remained free while the evidence was concocted. In Moscow fifty-four senior clerics and parishioners were put on trial, and eleven sentenced to death. In the light of possible international repercussions, Kamenev proposed shooting only two, but was opposed by Lenin, Trotsky, Stalin—"I personally vote against quashing the court's decision"—and Molotov. They compromised: six were shot. Superstition rather than humanity made it hard for the executioners to shoot clergy so the priests were shaved and dressed in civilian clothes stripped from corpses before execution. The Petrograd Cheka, egged on by Zinoviev, put Bishop Veniamin on trial although he had meekly handed over Church treasures, and sentenced him and nine others to death. A Cheka commission reprieved six, but Veniamin and three others, including a professor of theology and a Church lawyer, were shot.

Menzhinsky's GPU men ran puppet breakaway churches including the Living Church, or Church of Renewal, set up before the revolution by the defrocked priest Aleksandr Vvedensky. Most of its priests were GPU agents, and its costs were paid out of the proceeds of looted Church valuables, but their consciences were not entirely extinct. Vvedensky protested to Rykov: "If there are shootings, then we, the Living Church (and I above all personally), will be in the eyes of the mob the murderers of these wretches."[18]

Georgi Chicherin, commissar for foreign affairs, and Vatslav Vorovsky, the plenipotentiary in Switzerland working to win international recognition for the Soviet Union, warned the Politburo that all Europe was incensed by the persecution of the Church, but Stalin and Menzhinsky could not have cared less about foreign opinion, whatever the views of Soviet diplomats. On May 3, 1922, the GPU in Moscow formed a secret commission, headed by Unszlicht, Menzhinsky, and Iagoda, to "summon Patriarch Tikhon to the GPU to receive an ultimatum" requiring him to defrock and excommunicate all émigré Russian clergy. This proposal went to Trotsky and Stalin, who had the Politburo resolve "1) to bring Tikhon to trial; 2) to apply the death penalty to the priests."

For interrogating Tikhon, a quiet but resilient man, the Cheka chose Evgeni Tuchkov. He had won his laurels crushing a rebellion by the Turkic Bashkirs in the Urals.[19] Tuchkov had two missions: to break the Church into warring factions, each controlled by the GPU; to inveigle Tikhon into making treasonable statements.

International protests grew even louder. For the first time in 900 years, the Pope in Rome expressed concern for the Eastern Church; he also offered to buy back all the Orthodox Church's valuables. The Pope was outraged when Polish Catholic priests were publicly tried in Minsk and Bishop Konstantin (Romuald) Budkiewicz was shot. Fridtjof Nansen told Trotsky that if Tikhon was executed famine relief for Russia would stop and an American senator warned that diplomatic relations with the USSR would not be established. Dzierżyński backed down, and proposed calling off Tikhon's trial. Even Stalin wavered.

Menzhinsky tried a new tack: he asked Tikhon to lure the émigré bishops back to Russia where the GPU could arrest them. "Do you think they'd come here?" Tikhon asked. After making all the concessions he could, Tikhon was detained in a monastery 300 miles from Moscow. Tuchkov called a Church synod and GPU agents fixed a vote to depose Tikhon. This failed, since a synod without the patriarch was illegal by canon law. Tikhon died on April 7, 1925, probably unnaturally; Stalin composed the death announcement in *Pravda*. Tikhon's designated successor, Piotr Poliansky, was arrested; Menzhinsky ordered newspaper articles "compromising Piotr" to be printed and Poliansky began a long road to his own Golgotha: a decade of imprisonment culminating in the announcement of his death in 1936 and his execution in 1937. In 1927 Piotr's replacement, Metropolitan Sergi, formally surrendered the Orthodox Church to the Bolshevik party and state. Menzhinsky set up an antireligious commission; a youth movement and a workers' organization called The Militant Godless were formed; Stalin's crony the publicist Emelian Iaroslavsky founded a journal, *The Godless,* to which millions of workers and peasants had to subscribe.

Energetically repressing émigrés, intellectuals, and clerics, Menzhinsky had proved his value; he would now help Stalin crush all opposition, within the party and without.

Stalin's Struggle for Sole Control

Whosoever hath any thing fixed in his person that doth induce contempt, hath also a perpetual spur in himself to rescue and deliver himself from scorn. Therefore all deformed
persons are extreme bold: . . . Also, it stirreth in them industry, and especially of this kind, to watch and observe the
weakness of others, that they may have somewhat to repay.
Again, in their superiors, it quencheth jealousy towards
them, as persons that they may at pleasure despise; and it
layeth their competitors and emulators asleep, as never believing they should be in possibility of advancement. . . .

Francis Bacon, Of Deformity

FROM SPRING 1923 Lenin was a living corpse, unable to call anyone to
order. The New Economic Plan for Lenin had been a necessary but un-
welcome step backward; for the Politburo it represented a weakening of
both the monopoly and the severity of the party's power.

For Stalin, however, this was the time to secure that monopoly for
himself. "Personnel decides everything" ten years later became one of
Stalin's famous slogans. From April 4, 1922, when Stalin secured his own
position as general secretary of the party—a "cook who will make some
hot dishes," Lenin warned—he put this slogan into practice by turning
the secretariat of the Central Committee into a party and state personnel office.

If Stalin had genius, it was as a personnel officer. He recruited apparently mediocre men and used them to great effect. The party's Central Committee became Stalin's instrument: he installed as fellow
secretaries his sidekicks Viacheslav Molotov and Valerian Kuibyshev,
the latter a loyal Stalinist who had shown considerable initiative in the
civil war but was now a malleable alcoholic. Stalin cannily turned the
secretariat from an administrative service into a political powerhouse.
He funneled or withheld information, he compiled agendas, he kept
records, and thus directed the agenda and decided the participants in
party deliberations.

Once general secretary, Stalin appointed another crony, Lazar

Kaganovich, to the party's organizing and distributing section. This section decided which members were posted where, and who would attend party congresses. Stalin already had a second source of authority as a Politburo member where, for the time being, he spoke less and listened more to his eloquent fellow leaders. These two posts gave him a preponderance of power during Lenin's last illness, but Stalin also had his hand on a third lever of power: he was a member of the small Orgburo, the body which decided how and by whom Politburo resolutions were carried out. Stalin dominated the Orgburo: apart from Molotov and Kuibyshev, who always concurred, he had only to win over Dzierżyński and Andrei Andreevich Andreev, a former waiter whom Stalin had made a secretary to the Central Committee, to have his way, with the "liberals" Rykov and Tomsky easily outvoted.

Stalin also controlled the Workers' and Peasants' Inspectorate, which reviewed all government decisions, and ran the Commissariat of National Minorities, which in the early 1920s, against Lenin's intentions, made the Soviet Union a centralized empire rather than a federation of nation-states. As commissar, Stalin oversaw with GPU help the crushing of national rebellions from his native Georgia to Bashkiria. Non-Russian communists were arrested, and some shot, for "nationalist" deviations: they had misunderstood the role of the Russian Federal Republic in the Soviet Union and had taken their own autonomy seriously. They had not heeded Stalin's and Zinoviev's speeches explaining the difference between the Tsar's imperialism and Soviet centralization. Zinoviev in 1919 expressed Stalin's idea with inimitable cynicism: "We cannot do without Azerbaijan's oil or Turkestan's cotton. We take these things which we need, but not in the way that the old exploiters took them, but as elder brothers who are carrying the torch of civilization."

Finally, Stalin dominated the Comintern. Here his cronies the Hungarian sadist Béla Kun and the robotic Finnish journalist Otto Kuusinen ensured blind adherence by most foreign communists to Stalin's line. No wonder, then, that Lenin's famous "testament" of 1922 accused Stalin of concentrating enormous power in his hands.

Lenin's testament reads like a headmaster's report. The six most likely candidates to succeed were all weighed and found wanting. Stalin was singled out for his reckless use of power and capriciousness (his sulks when thwarted) and, in a postscript, for his coarseness and disloyalty. But Lenin advised only that the party should "consider" removing Stalin from his general secretaryship. None of Stalin's faults were, in Bolshevik eyes, grave. Coarseness and impoliteness were virtues in a revolutionary, and Stalin, whenever anyone threw the testament in his face, retorted, "Yes, comrade, I actually am coarse. Ilyich suggested you find somebody else who differs from me by being more polite. All right, try and find him!" Lenin's critiques of Trotsky, Zinoviev, and Kamenev were far more damning: they had all committed heresy by being against armed revolt at some point before October 1917. Bukharin and Piatakov were damned for their poor Marxist credentials: the first was an economist, the second an administrator.

There was no way of holding together the collective leadership that Lenin wanted to succeed him. Trotsky and Stalin, the two leading contenders in the eyes of the party's rank and file, were both set on sole dictatorship; the satraps of Petrograd and Moscow, Zinoviev and Kamenev, saw themselves as a duumvirate but had limited and localized support. Zinoviev was also something of a joke. Few could take seriously a man who resembled Chico Marx and served his guests with a dish of steaming horse meat cooked by himself and within minutes was screaming that he would shoot them all.[20] As for Piatakov and Bukharin, they preferred playing second fiddle, the former to Trotsky, the latter to Stalin, although in the early 1920s Bukharin, the only one of them who might have won a popular election in Soviet Russia, pondered his chances of ruling without Stalin. He even sounded out Stalin's zombie head of state Mikhail Kalinin about the feasibility of dispensing with Stalin's leadership. Kalinin kept silent about this approach but felt guilty and afraid all his life. After he died in 1946, his daughter passed on to Stalin his written confession:

Now I am on the threshold of death I have recalled something from the past which, to be honest, I had not thought significant before. Probably it was in the first year after Lenin died. . . . After a session [of the Politburo] Bukharin invited me to his apartment to look at his hunting trophies. When he was showing me various birds and small animals he asked me, as if by the way, what I would think of a leadership without Stalin. . . . I understood even then that I was being sounded out.[21]

Charisma won few votes in a party congress or on the Central Committee; patronage was decisive. The Bolsheviks were polarized between Trotsky and Stalin. Trotsky's reputation had soared in times of war and danger; Stalin's apparent moderation was attuned to the fatigue that now beset the party after a turbulent decade. In August 1924, to shut out Trotsky, Stalin hived off from the Politburo a group of seven "to agree on the most odious questions," as Kalinin put it. Its membership was approved by a claque of twenty Central Committee members—Stalin and his supporters—who called themselves the governing collective. Stalin was thus able to decide in advance the Politburo's agenda and make it accountable only to his exclusive group of seven.

Stalin's struggle for sole control passed unremarked by the Russian public. They were relieved that 1923 had been a year of relative normality compared to the shocks and upheavals of the past six. The horrors of revolution were best evoked in *The Apocalypse of Our Time* by the philosopher Vasili Rozanov in 1919, who had died that same year of emaciation in the Troitse-Sergeev monastery:

La divina Commedia
With clanking screeching an iron curtain is lowered over Russian
    History.
"The performance is over."
  The audience got up.
"It's time to put on your fur coats and go home."
  They looked round.
  But it turned out that there were no fur coats and no homes.

By the summer of 1923 city trams ran, the theaters were open and there were even casinos; those who had money could buy goods. Books printed in Berlin were sold in Moscow and writers could travel between the two cities. In the countryside the peasantry had enough grain for their own needs, for seed corn and even to sell privately. But compare the

1. "Koba" Stalin, police
photograph, Baku, 1910

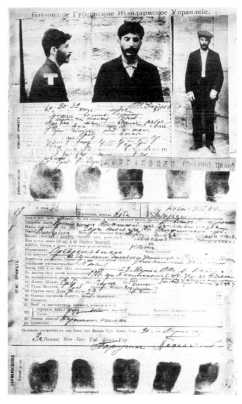

2. Suren Spandaryan and Koba *c.* 1911

3. Stalin (second left, back row) with fellow exiles, Monastyroskoe (Siberia),
July 1915

4. Dzierzyński (center, front), Jakobs Peterss (second left), and senior *chekisty,* 1918

5. Dzierzyński's funeral, 1926. Left to right: Rykov, Yagoda, Kalinin, Trotsky, Kamenev, Stalin, Rakovsky, Bukharin

6. Menzhinsky with his first wife, Iulia, his two daughters, and his son, Rudolf, Iaroslavl, 1904

7. Menzhinsky in the Cheka, *c.* 1919

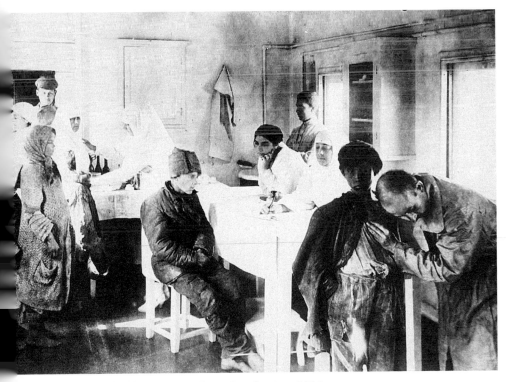

8. American Relief Agency clinic, Volga famine, 1921

9. Left to right: Stalin, Rykov, Zinoviev, and Bukharin at the dacha, 1924

10. Sergei Kirov (left) and Sergo Orjonikidze, north Caucasus, 1920

11. Left to right: Trotsky, Kamenev, and Zinoviev (front), mid-1920s

12. Delivering prisoners to the Lubianka, 1928

13. Boris Savinkov, 1922

14. Menzhinsky, 1925

15. Menzhinsky's funeral, 1934. To the right of the coffin stand Genrikh Iagoda, Menzhinsky's second wife, Alla Semionovna, and Menzhinsky's surviving sister, Vera

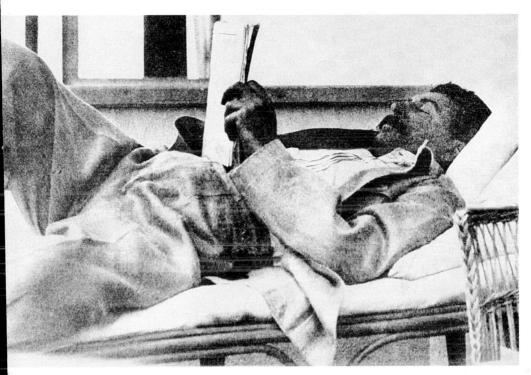

16. Stalin relaxing at the dacha, *c.* 1930

17. Mayakovsky, shortly after his suicide, 1930

18. Pavel Dybenko and Aleksandra Kollontai with Dybenko's sister and parents, 1918

first Soviet Petrograd directory of 1923 with the last Tsarist edition of 1917 and you see a metamorphosis: the addresses and buildings were the same, but only 10 percent of those in the 1917 directory were still there six years later. The city had been drained of its bourgeoisie and filled with soldiers, workers, and peasants. The change in Russia is best summarized in two lines by Nikolai Gumiliov: "Only snakes shed their skins. We change our souls, not our bodies." The populace which the Politburo fought among themselves to control had lost all continuity with Tsarist civic society. By 1923 nobody dreamed of influencing the government; people were reduced to fear, their best hope that they would be left alone.

While Stalin and the Politburo wrangled, the state seemed to retreat and OGPU became more discreet. In 1923, according to official figures, only 414 persons were shot, the lowest number since Tsarist times and until 1947 when Stalin suspended the death penalty.[22] In fact Menzhinsky had retracted one tentacle of OGPU and extended others. The Cheka had shifted its tactics from brutality to more subtle but no less lethal surveillance. Menzhinsky's foreign department concentrated on settling scores with émigrés and was a polyglot elite of imaginatively murderous experts under a chief who enjoyed his métier. In domestic affairs, OGPU took a leaf or two from the book of Dmitri Tolstoi, minister of the interior under Tsar Alexander II, who had designated three classes of men with close contact with the population—schoolteachers, gendarmes, and priests—police informers. OGPU had 40,000 literate employees intercepting mail and telephone calls and thousands of others—20,000 in Moscow alone—informing on citizens' conversations and discussions so that regular summaries of the mood of the public could be compiled. Even with this enormous covert civilian army, OGPU fought for new territory.

Dzierżyński asked Iagoda to write a report on "completely open, obvious profiteering, enrichment and brazenness" to persuade the Central Committee to employ OGPU to expel profiteers and their families from major cities, confiscate their property, and colonize with these people the wildernesses of northern Russia and Siberia. The Politburo took halfhearted action against smugglers and bar owners; the commissar of finances had to protect the urban retail trade from Dzierżyński's narrow-minded obsessions.

A real blow to OGPU came from Bukharin in autumn 1924:

Dear Feliks . . . I consider that we must as soon as possible move to a more "liberal" form of Soviet rule: fewer repressions, more legality, more discussion, more self-rule (under the party's guidance *naturaliter* [Bukharin liked to use Latin]), etc. . . . That is why I sometimes speak out against proposals to widen the rights of the GPU, etc. Understand, dear Feliks (you know how much I love you) that you have no reasons whatsoever to suspect me of any bad feelings to you personally or the GPU as an in-stitution. . . .[23]

Dzierżyński passed the letter to Menzhinsky with his own commentary:

We have to take account of such moods in the Central Commit-tee's ruling circles, and pause for thought. It would be a very great political mistake if in principle the party on the question of the GPU were to surrender to the philistines and give them a holiday—as a party line, as a policy, as a declaration. That would mean giving in to capitalist enterprise, philistinism, tend-ing to the denial of Bolshevism, this would be the triumph of Trotskyism and a surrender of positions. To counteract these moods we must re-examine our practice, our methods and get rid of whatever might feed such moods. This means that we (the GPU) have perhaps to be a bit quieter, more modest, resort to searches and arrests more cautiously, with better evidence. . . . We have to re-examine our policy on letting people go abroad—and visas. . . .[24]

The hangmen had to try a new tack. OGPU was under attack from Commissar for Foreign Affairs Chicherin as its methods undermined his diplomatic efforts abroad. Commissar for Justice Nikolai Krylenko, re-verting to the legality he had been trained in, also put pressure on OGPU: he demanded that crimes, even against the state, be dealt with by the prosecutor's office, the *prokuratura,* under his commissariat. To Zi-noviev, Dzierżyński complained: "A very difficult stage has come for

OGPU. Its workers are mortally tired, some to the point of hysterics. But in the higher echelons of the party a well-known section is beginning to doubt the necessity of OGPU (Bukharin, Sokolnikov, Kalinin)."[25] Dzierżyński complained bitterly that Krylenko was usurping the role of OGPU: suppose, he said, the Commissariat for Justice took over political cases, "that would, at a time when the political circumstances are changing, threaten the very existence of the Soviet Union."[26]

OGPU began to present itself as a band of principled intellectuals, many with legal training, but still executed 2,550 people in 1924. It did, however, clean up its act and find its worst sadists other work. It sent a commission to the special purpose northern camps between Murmansk and Arkhangelsk, extermination camps manned by *chekisty* who had disgraced themselves in metropolitan areas. One camp, Kholmogory, in the hands of a sadistic Lithuanian called Bachulis, was as bad as any of Hitler's would be. The surviving prisoners were sent to the monastery complexes of the Solovetsky islands; the guards went with them. In 1929 Stalin and Iagoda had 600 of them shot, together with many of the prisoners.

This retreat emboldened the liberals in the party: a commission charged OGPU with 826 judicial killings and widespread bribe-taking. To stop depraving soldiers and policemen still further, Lunacharsky, Radek, and Krylenko demanded that only criminals should act as executioners. Mass murderers such as the Siberian bandit Kultiapy were therefore reprieved in 1924 and set to work as prison executioners. A few young sadists, however, were too useful to lose: Mikhail Frinovsky, a man who like Stalin had left theological college to become a murderer, was to rise to ministerial status in the 1930s, while Vsevolod Balitsky, who had tortured and raped in Kiev, became chairman of the Ukraine GPU and then Ukraine's commissar for internal affairs. Stalin would order him to starve the Ukraine's peasants to death.[27]

The top OGPU echelons, if they wanted to keep their fiefdoms, had to serve the intrigues of a new master. In 1925, step by step, Stalin was eradicating his potential rivals: "the superb measurer of doses" as his victims, only belatedly feeling the cumulative effects of his poisons, called him. Manipulating rivals to eliminate enemies, Stalin showed real genius. He used his insight into the base side of human nature, an ability to work while opponents slept or convalesced, a magisterial calmness in the face of righteous indignation, and an understanding of game theory which only the best poker players have. Above all, he assured OGPU of a prominent future role in government.

Trotsky, and others ousted by Stalin, blamed their defeat on *naznachenstvo,* Stalin's fixing of appointments. The posts that Stalin occupied in the party and in government let him determine who went where to serve the state. By 1925 the Soviet bureaucracy was more numerous than that of Tsarist Russia; posts of any importance were reserved for members of the *nomenklatura,* the list of politically reliable party members; and appointments were decided by the party apparatus. As one Central Committee party member put it, "You were hardly likely to vote 'no' if you then got sent to Murmansk or Tashkent." Party gatherings voting on debating points put forward by Trotsky, Stalin, Zinoviev, and Kamenev were packed with those who depended on Stalin's favors.

Stalin prepared meticulously for each encounter. He filled plenary meetings, conferences, and congresses with his claque; he spoke as a prosecutor, forcing his opponents onto the defensive. Stalin's intimates had no doubts of the outcome for all who got in his way. In July 1924 Demian Bedny asked Stalin, long before the latter had Zinoviev removed from the Politburo, "Have you heard the latest joke? The English are willing to let us have Marx's ashes . . . in exchange for Zinoviev's." Stalin's private correspondence with Demian Bedny shows the anti-Semitism behind the campaign against Trotsky. In 1926 Bedny wrote to Stalin:

> If I touch on Trotsky,
> The whole opposition roars.
> What's the problem, ethnic claque?
> Explain it to me carefully:
> If I hit Shliapnikov, I get a brawl!
> If I go for Trotsky it's a <u>pogrom</u>![28]

The differences between Trotsky and Stalin were in style, not substance. They were both Leninists: they believed in the dictatorship of the proletariat, in world revolution, and in turning the peasantry into workers on the land. Where they differed was on emphasis and timing. Trotskyism—a term of abuse devised by Stalin's supporters, who called themselves true Leninists—was nostalgia for the Red Army's glories and the inclination to pour oil on any revolutionary fire, whether in Germany reeling from hyperinflation, in Britain facing a general strike, or in China torn apart by warlords. Stalin had caution and reticence on his side. Trotsky promised to wind up the NEP, to squeeze resources from the peasantry and begin massive industrialization as well as world war. Stalin bided his time, meanwhile letting the right wing, notably Bukharin, relax the state's pressure on the economy so that the peasants built up reserves worth confiscating.

Trotsky and Stalin criticized each other's records of heresy from October 1917 to the end of the civil war, their successes and failures in forcing Red Army commanders on to victory, and the number of occasions each had angered Lenin. In such arguments Trotsky came off worse.

At first Stalin let Zinoviev and Kamenev, who envied Trotsky his military laurels, do the dirty work. On January 4, 1925, Zinoviev drafted a proposal: "To deem it impossible, in the present condition of things that Trotsky has created, for Trotsky to hold such posts as the Chairman of the Military Council and member of the Politburo. . . . " Stalin and Bukharin meanwhile wore masks of neutrality. Trotsky reacted wildly: he declared himself too ill to take part in the plenum and published in *Pravda* a defense against "monstrous accusations," but his sense of party discipline was so entrenched that he obeyed the Central Committee.

Dzierżyński wrote Trotsky off. "The party has had to dethrone Trotsky solely because he, by virtually attacking Zinoviev and Kamenev and other members of the Central Committee of our party, has raised his hand against party unity . . . " he wrote to Stalin and Orjonikidze on October 6, 1925. By now Stalin could dispose of his temporary allies: Zinoviev and Kamenev, used by Stalin to weaken Trotsky's grip, were themselves declared to be a faction. Dzierżyński, as unhappy as a sheepdog whose flock has scattered, hated factional infighting; he accused Zinoviev and Kamenev of self-serving cowardice, of setting the workers against the peasants. He and OGPU were now entirely Stalin's men—there was no other shepherd for the sheepdogs to follow.

The dispute in 1925 and 1926 between Zinoviev and Kamenev on the one hand, and Stalin and Bukharin on the other had real basis. Zinoviev and Kamenev's supporters were Leningrad (as Petrograd had been renamed in 1924) and Moscow factory workers, aggrieved by unemployment and by the low purchasing power of their wages when in work; their real income was half what it had been before the revolution. "What did we struggle for?" was the workers' slogan. The prosperity of the NEP men, who lived by retail trade, gambling, and racketeering, and the peasantry, too poor to purchase manufactured goods but self-sufficient, made the workers resentful. They supported Zinoviev and Kamenev who, within a few months of disarming Trotsky, were arguing for Trotsky's program: winding up the NEP and dispossessing the peasantry for the sake of the urban proletariat who had made the revolution.

In December 1925 at the fourteenth party congress Zinoviev spoke out against Stalin's moderate line on agriculture and industrialization but the brilliance of his oratory was useless. Stalin, not Zinoviev, received an orchestrated "storm of applause." Zinoviev was removed from the Politburo, from his chairmanship of the Comintern, and from his power base in Leningrad. Too late, Zinoviev saw Stalin for what he was: "a bloodthirsty Osetian who doesn't know what conscience is . . . " That remark sealed his fate.

Stalin kicked hardest when his opponent was down; he turned on Zinoviev for neglecting his job in the state planning office. Zinoviev tried to rouse the rabble in his fiefdom in Leningrad.[29] But Stalin's cronies had grudges against Zinoviev and Stalin himself loathed the whole of Leningrad as a nest of opposition vipers.

Opposing Stalin at the party congress, Kamenev chose words more judicious but just as damning as Zinoviev's: "We are against the theory of single rule, we are against creating a 'leader.' . . . I think that our general secretary is not the person who can unite the old Bolshevik headquarters around himself." Kamenev first lost his full membership in the Politburo and then, in January 1926, was made commissar for trade. A few months later he was ambassador to Italy and out of the Politburo.

During their struggle Stalin and the Zinoviev–Kamenev duo had both made conciliatory overtures toward Trotsky.[30] Trotsky was still tempted by power, but his last conversation with Stalin disabused him and he looked for other straws to clutch at. However, Dzierżyński's death in July 1926 removed the last influential Bolshevik who truly believed in reconciliation. In his letter to Stalin and Orjonikidze of October 1925 he had warned them, and Zinoviev and Kamenev:

> Without unity, without this condition, Thermidor is inevitable. . . . The result is inevitable: Leninists, like spiders, will devour each other, as foreseen by the Mensheviks and by Trotsky, who are now coming onto the scene, the first as "equality and democracy," the other as a "communist" Bonaparte. . . . You claim to be the official and sole heirs of the leader [Lenin] of the workers and peasants. Ambition is killing you. . . .[31]

It was too late: the spiders were set to devour each other.

For a few months Trotsky, Zinoviev, and Kamenev forgot the insults they had hurled at each other and formed an opposition. Still unsure that Stalin would win, Menzhinsky was slow to close down their printing presses. In 1926 and 1927 opposition leaflets made it seem, at home and abroad, that debate, even a two-party system, might be burgeoning in the USSR: Stalin and Bukharin would be the conservatives, and Trotsky, Kamenev, and Zinoviev the radicals.

But Stalin had ground his ax. His draft circular to the Politburo shows the care and feeling that he put into his attack: "On a personal question":

1) Comrade Trotsky is wrong to say that Lenin "insisted" on Stalin being removed from the post of general secretary. Actually, Lenin "suggested" the party congress "consider" the question about transferring Stalin, leaving the decision on the question to the party congress. And the congress, after consideration decided unanimously to leave Stalin in the post of secretary, a decision which Stalin was bound to submit to.

2) Comrade Trotsky is wrong to assert than if Stalin had not been secretary "there would not be the struggle we now have." Stalin was not secretary either in 1920 or 1918 when Trotsky waged a frantic campaign against the party and Lenin both in 1918 (Brest treaty) and in 1920 (trade union movement) . . . it

is stupid to attribute discord in the party to a "personal aspect."

3) Comrade Trotsky is wrong to assert that "Stalin is calling him
a revisionist of Leninism." Not Stalin but the thirteenth party
conference . . . Not just Stalin but first and foremost Zinoviev,
Kamenev, and Krupskaia [did so]. . . . [32]

Trotsky's arrogance undid him. He considered Dzierżyński a mindless agent of others' policies, Menzhinsky an effete spook, and Orjonikidze a Caucasian bandit. Dzierżyński and Menzhinsky resented
being patronized by Trotsky and swung the pro-Trotsky element within
OGPU, against all its instinctive revolutionary romanticism, over to
Stalin. At the end of 1927 Trotsky was thrown out of the party with
seventy-five of his prominent supporters including Kamenev and Zinoviev. Zinoviev became rector of Kazan University; Kamenev took on
the scientific and technical directorate of the Commissariat for the
Economy. Trotsky, deluded by his faith in the intuition of the workers
and by his sense of destiny, lost his last post, the fur concession, and was
deported to Kazakhstan.

A New Role for OGPU

IN 1927 OGPU was not yet a centralized, miniature totalitarian state. The
credit (or blame) for the reforms that enabled OGPU to dominate political and economic life in the USSR and made it Stalin's chief instrument
of rule by the late 1920s is Menzhinsky's. Although he never held a revolver or watched an execution Menzhinsky took firm control of the
psychopaths, criminals, or intellectuals who dispatched their victims
with enjoyment in Stalin's cause. Menzhinsky and Genrikh Iagoda
adopted the same motto as Dzierżyński—"a cold head, a warm heart
and clean hands"—in their dirty but vital task, anticipating Himmler, a
man too fastidious to wring a chicken's neck yet who urged the SS on to
slaughter Jews.

The samurai at the head of OGPU had higher politics in mind, while still condoning sadism and class murder in the Russian provinces, in the Ukraine, the Caucasus, and central Asia. Their dual role as political arbiters and repressive policemen caused overwork and illness; they took the waters of the north Caucasus more and more often. Dzierżyński wrote from his sanatorium to Iagoda in summer 1925:

> The most serious attention must be paid to Comrade Menzhinsky's health. I ask for a concilium of doctors, appropriate specialists, to be organized to outline the treatment: where, in what conditions, for how long, etc. . . .
>
> Dear Genrikh Grigorievich! Here I am, the fifth day now. I can feel I am getting better, although I shall only start the Narzan baths on Sunday. Viacheslav Rudolfovich [Menzhinsky] has become considerably better, but to consolidate this improvement and to complete treatment, treatment must nevertheless be prolonged until October 1.[33]

Menzhinsky, with his flair for languages and knowledge of Europe, focused OGPU not on domestic but on foreign enemies although Soviet Russia was now officially at peace with its neighbors. Foreign agents now fell under the remit of the intelligence services, not the Red Army. Dzierżyński's Latvians in the Cheka had coped clumsily with espionage—shooting dead, for instance, the British consul in Petrograd—and had looked on the new nations of Finland, Estonia, Latvia, Lithuania, and Poland, still forming in the crucible of war, as territory for armed forays. Menzhinsky was subtler: for him Tsarist White Guards were not an army to be fought in the field; they were saboteurs to be eliminated in cellars. Activity abroad had to be covert and, if revealed, disavowed.

In the early 1920s there were over 2 million White Russians split into factions spread over Europe and the Far East. Monarchists, liberals, and Social Revolutionaries believed that, with help from neighboring states, they might yet regain power in Russia. As Soviet Russia had only restricted diplomatic representation abroad it was hard to monitor émigré activities and any success by OGPU's counterrevolutionary section came from intercepting the correspondence of small conspiracies inside Russia. Larger exercises were crude and counterproductive. For instance, Lenin had instructed Dzierżyński to send *chekisty* disguised as counterrevolutionaries into Latvia and Estonia: "Cross the border for a kilometer somewhere and hang 100–1,000 of their officials and rich people. . . . Under the guise of 'greens' [nationalist bandits] (we'll put the blame on them) we'll go 10–20 kilometers and hang all the rich peasants, priests, landowners."[34]

Menzhinsky needed lessons in how to do the job better, and he took a step unique in the history of the Cheka. He consulted one of his prisoners, the nobleman Vladimir Dzhunkovsky, the sole senior official of the Tsar's regime to pass on his wisdom to the Cheka. Dzhunkovsky had run the Tsar's gendarmerie and secret services but was highly principled.[35] Unlike Dmitri Tolstoi, he had forbidden the recruitment as informers of teachers, army officers, or anyone with public trust. Dzhunkovsky had even outed his own agent Roman Malinovsky, leader of the Bolshevik faction in the Duma, as a police spy. After the revolution, Dzhunkovsky gave evidence to the tribunal which condemned Malinovsky to death and volunteered his services as a consultant to the Cheka, the one organization, in his view, that could restore stability after the revolution.[36] Dzhunkovsky taught Dzierżyński, Menzhinsky, and Artur Artuzov a technique that had worked spectacularly well under Sergei Zubatov in the Tsar's Ministry of the Interior. This involved creating a puppet legal opposition, supporting factions in illegal opposition and manipulating subversives into working for, not against, the state.

OGPU learned Dzhunkovsky's technique well. Using the skills of the polyglot Artur Artuzov (né Frautschi) and of Latvians such as Pillar and Jekabs Peterss, Menzhinsky set up fictitious resistance movements to lure émigré agents into the arms of OGPU including the Trust, an imaginary counterrevolutionary union of monarchists and Social Revolutionaries. A real counterrevolutionary, a Latvian called Opperput, was offered his life in exchange for mounting a disinformation operation. Under the name Eduard Staunitz, Opperput became the Moscow resident and treasurer of the Trust, which was stuffed with press-ganged ex-officers from the Tsar's army. They were to pose as counterrevolutionaries and were given genuine information to sell to Polish intelligence.

The target in this operation was by far the most fearsome exiled opponent of the Bolsheviks, Boris Savinkov. Menzhinsky and Savinkov knew each other well. They had studied law together in St. Petersburg, and had both made promising literary debuts before descending into the revolutionary underground. But Savinkov had become a Social Revolutionary, believing in terror to destroy the old regime, and in the peasantry to create a new world. He had fled Russia after being sentenced to death for organizing the murders of ministers and generals but returned after the revolution of February 1917 and was a minister in Kerensky's government. After the Bolshevik takeover, Savinkov formed another revolutionary party, the Union of Defense of Homeland and Freedom, which fought the Bolsheviks. Savinkov then left for France and Poland. In France his novels, particularly *The Pale Horse,* won him an international reputation; the romantic view of modern revolutionary politics shared by André Malraux and Albert Camus stems from Savinkov. The novelist Ilya Ehrenburg thought Savinkov "the most inscrutable and terrifying person" he had ever met; Somerset Maugham felt that Savinkov was "what the ancient Romans feared, Fate looking at you." Winston Churchill was struck by "his mortally pale face, quiet voice . . . impenetrable gaze."

After two years' careful disinformation Savinkov fell for Opperput's bait of an anti-Bolshevik underground, a National Union for the Defense of Homeland and Freedom allied to liberal democrats with connections in OGPU waiting for Savinkov to come to Moscow and help them overthrow the Bolsheviks. Together with his mistress and her husband, the Derentals, Savinkov crossed the border. At breakfast in a Minsk apartment he was arrested by his hosts Pillar and Filipp Medved. "Nice work," Savinkov told the *chekisty.* "May I finish my breakfast please?" He then joined his fellow conspirators in a special carriage for Moscow. In the Lubianka, Savinkov and Artuzov treated each other with respect. Savinkov's mistress, Liubov Dikgof-Derental, was allowed to live with him.

In just twelve days Savinkov was tried, pleaded guilty to charges of counterrevolution, and was sentenced to death. However in intensive negotiations with Dzierżyński and Menzhinsky he agreed to write to his associates, insisting that further resistance to the Soviet regime was pointless. He was told that his life would be spared, that he would soon be found work to match his talent. OGPU's bargain was not kept. Savinkov wrote to Dzierżyński on May 5, 1925: "there's no point reforming me: life has reformed me. This was how the question was put in conversation with Menzhinsky, Artuzov, and Pillar: either shoot me or give me an opportunity to work." Dzierżyński had wanted to shoot Savinkov from the start and Menzhinsky's plans to save his rival were thwarted by Stalin after the trial: "I am in favor of a ten-year sentence. This sentence can't be shortened, it's dangerous, the change from death penalty to three years, when applied to somebody like Savinkov, won't be understood."[37]

Menzhinsky had played cat and mouse with Savinkov for eight months before breaking off contact and leaving him to stew. On May 7, 1925, Savinkov fell to his death from the window of a fifth-floor office. The sequence of events suggests suicide, but a casual remark by Stalin in the 1950s implies that Dzierżyński, on Stalin's instructions, ordered the murder.[38] Stalin himself edited the communiqué that Dzierżyński published in *Pravda* announcing Savinkov's death.

The Trust and another OGPU front, Syndicate-2, had other successes before they were wound up by Menzhinsky. In 1925 the British spy and common murderer Sidney Reilly (Shlomo Rozenblium), who had escaped a death sentence in 1918 for counterrevolution in his native Odessa, was lured across the Finnish border. After a number of polite discussions with Jekabs Peterss, Reilly was shot in the back during a walk in the forest on Stalin's orders.[39] In 1926 Menzhinsky's best disinformation exercise was to arrange for the monarchist Vasili Shulgin to visit Soviet Russia in disguise and, escorted by *chekisty* pretending to be counterrevolutionaries, to search for his son, who had in fact just died in a psychiatric hospital. The OGPU agents escorted Shulgin back out of the country, urging him to write a book. This had a double effect: it persuaded readers that there was an underground opposition operating in the USSR and, at the same time, that Soviet Russia was a flourishing state with popular support.

These plots and the successful abduction, assassination, and recruitment of émigrés justified OGPU's existence. Stalin was more paranoiac than Menzhinsky and particularly suspected the British of subverting

Russia, convinced they were taking revenge for Soviet support for the General Strike. When Reilly was caught, and after an explosion in Moscow attributed to British agents, Stalin telegraphed Menzhinsky:

> My personal opinion: 1) London's agents are deeper entrenched here than we think, and their meeting places will persist; 2) mass arrests must be used to destroy English spy links, for recruiting new collaborators among those arrested in Artuzov's department and to develop a system of volunteers among young people to help OGPU and its organs; 3) it would be good to set up one or two show trials in the courts on the lines of English espionage, so as to have official material to be used in England and Europe; . . . 5) the publication of such evidence has enormous significance if you set it up skillfully and find authors of the appropriate articles on espionage in the military, aviation, the navy. When do you plan to publish Reilly's statements? This business has to be set up skillfully. Greetings, Stalin.[40]

Stalin was already fascinated by foreign spies and the prospect of show trials. Menzhinsky and OGPU counterintelligence encouraged this mania and began to frequent Stalin's office. They were often the last to report to Stalin before he went to the Black Sea to rest, and the first to report when he returned, even though, in the mid-1920s, intelligence and foreign relations were not among Stalin's many official remits.

OGPU's widely publicized counterintelligence operations established the Soviet secret services as the most formidable and well funded in the world. Within the Soviet Union there was a conviction that only the Cheka and OGPU worked efficiently, so much so that for every emergency an Extraordinary Commission would be set up. There was even a Cheka for the production of felt boots.

The Tikhon affair of 1922–5 had shown Stalin that Menzhinsky could stage a trial as a theater director stages a play, every actor working from a carefully composed script. When Stalin decided to get rid of foreign and prerevolutionary experts in order to give the party a signal that all dissent was now fatal and the public the message that all failures in the economy were due to sabotage, Menzhinsky was given the task of providing proof. The Shakhty, Prompartiia, and Menshevik trials were not as well rehearsed as the trials of the Great Terror—Menzhinsky and Iagoda would not use physical violence on the accused and could not convince all of them that justice was dead—but Menzhinsky's show trials did require OGPU leaders and underlings to suspend any vestigial notions of justice, morality, or verisimilitude, and to work for months with little sleep.

One important set of documents published in the last five years is the register of visitors to Stalin's Kremlin office from 1924 to his death. We see that representatives of every department of government and party were summoned to his Kremlin office, but that OGPU officers came more often and stayed longer. The records also show that, during his battle for sole control, Stalin felt sufficiently secure to take a month's holiday each year from 1924 to 1926, relying on couriers and encrypted telegrams from Molotov in the government and from Iagoda and Menzhinsky in OGPU to maintain his grip. Once assured that his opponents had been defeated, Stalin was free to devise at leisure grander scenarios for OGPU to stage.

By 1926, Stalin was sure that OGPU depended on him as much as he on them: they had no one else capable of offering patronage. On the other hand, the chiefs of OGPU were not Stalin's men, in that they had not been appointed by him. It would be ten years before Stalin could make OGPU as much his creature as the party Central Committee and Politburo had become. Menzhinsky and Iagoda and their underlings enjoyed the company of sophisticated intellectuals such as Bukharin and Rykov. When Stalin turned against Bukharin and the right he would also need to weed them out of OGPU and replace them with thugs and automatons from his party apparatus.

FOUR

STALIN SOLO

. . . we doubt if any man ever passed
through life, sympathising so slightly with
mankind; and the most wonderful part of his
story is, the intensity of sway which he
exerted over the minds of those in whom he
so seldom permitted himself to contemplate
anything more than the tools of his own
ambition.

John Gibson Lockhart,
Napoleon Buonaparte

Clearing the Terrain

IN MID-JANUARY 1928 Stalin and Trotsky each took trains across the Urals. One traveled by choice, the other by compulsion. Stalin was beginning his first year of tyranny, of ruling without allies; Trotsky was in exile, on the road to oblivion. How had Stalin managed to outmaneuver and silence men more articulate than him, more educated in political theory and economics; men who had thirty years of intrigue and opposition under their belts; men who were better known to, and sometimes better liked by, the public?

Stalin's chief technique had been dissimulation. He was the con man who pretends to be duped. Three forces—Kamenev and Zinoviev's uncompromising Marxist left, Bukharin and Rykov's flexible right, and Trotsky's militancy—aimed to take power after Lenin's death. All three sides had seen Stalin and his cronies as the center ground that had to be captured if they were to overthrow the other two. Kamenev and Zinoviev, certain that they were Lenin's ideological heirs, had embraced Stalin in order to disempower Trotsky. When Trotsky had been sidelined, Bukharin, Rykov, and the other "soft" Social Democrats had supported Stalin against Kamenev and Zinoviev to prevent the New Economic Plan coming to a premature end.

Now in 1928, with Kamenev, Zinoviev, and Trotsky all out of the running, Stalin and his underlings Kaganovich, Molotov, and Menzhinsky turned against Bukharin. In a volte-face, they were going to deal with the peasantry as Zinoviev, Kamenev, and Trotsky had proposed: they would take their grain and their liberty and use their wealth and their labor to create an industrialized and militarized totalitarian society. Only Zinoviev and Kamenev would have no part to play in the industrialization, and Trotsky had been removed from control of the armed forces. The rationale for letting Bukharin share power vanished once liberal economic policies were disavowed and Stalin began a ten-year game that would end with a bullet in Bukharin's neck.

Stalin's skill in ousting all the old guard while implementing many of their ideas shows his profound understanding firstly of the weaknesses of human nature, especially the self-esteem of the intellectual in power, and secondly of the importance of the levers of power, primarily the intelligence apparatus. From January 1928 Stalin gathered the power, as well as the will, to destroy the lives not only of Lenin's Politburo, but of millions of peasants, intellectuals, and workers. There would be no more constraints on his paranoia.

A few months before, in September 1927, apart from on the street and in the semi-legal press, there was just one forum where Trotsky might challenge Stalin, the Comintern. To foreign communists Trotsky repeated Lenin's warnings about Stalin and Bukharin: "Stalin's personal misfortune, which is more and more that of the party, is a grandiose disproportion between Stalin's resources in ideas and the might which the party-state apparatus has concentrated in his hand." Kuusinen and Bukharin parried this attack and Stalin did not need to say a word. The Comintern voted unanimously to expel Trotsky.

Stalin had let Bukharin and Trotsky argue each other to exhaustion; now he used Menzhinsky to deliver the knockout blow. In November 1927, Stalin presented to the Central Committee a sensationally imaginative report by Menzhinsky in which OGPU said it had proof that Trotsky and "the opposition" were planning a coup.[1] The aim was to seize the Kremlin, the post office, and the radio stations, and to blow up railway lines. The conspirators had also supposedly fomented mutiny in army garrisons in Leningrad and the Ukraine. Menzhinsky outbid Stalin: he recommended "liquidating" the opposition leaders "before it is too late."

Stalin postponed any liquidation and kept a moderate face. Three months later, Trotsky was handed his sentence by OGPU: "In accordance with the law punishing any person for counterrevolutionary activity, citizen Lev Davidovich Trotsky is to be deported to Alma-Ata. No time limit for his stay there is indicated. The date for dispatch to exile is January 16, 1928."

Stalin was bombarded with protests from Trotsky's admirers. An anonymous letter of 1927 runs:

Comrade Stalin, . . . You and your colleagues are wrong to curse Trotsky. You're told the workers curse him, not true, not true. Comrade Stalin, I call to you from the depths of the party: <u>Trotsky is more loved than you or Zinoviev, etc. by the workers</u>. . . . Trotsky's been toppled and you're kicking him when he's down. Trotsky is a fighter, he's a force and a decent party member. . . . <u>With the rotten Leninism you've taken up we'll soon collapse</u>. . . .[2]

The last spontaneous demonstration in Moscow for sixty years took place at the railway station where Trotsky's train was waiting, and a dozen OGPU agents were beaten up, although Trotsky was actually still at home. After OGPU came for him two days later, a telegram was sent to Stalin's train in Siberia: "they had to use force and carry him out in their arms, since he refused to come, had locked himself in his room and the door had to be broken down." Trotsky was accompanied by his wife, his elder son, Lev, and thirty followers.

When Trotsky arrived in Kazakhstan, Stalin was in Siberia, implementing his version of Trotsky's policies. The "scissors" problem of the NEP was to be resolved by force. One blade of the scissors was the decreasing price of grain, which deterred peasants from selling surpluses or planting more. The other blade was the sluggishness of Russia's factories, where the incompetently managed workers on their seven hour days and rickety production lines were making too few shoddy goods too expensively: a meter of cotton cloth cost the same as fifteen kilos of wheat. The peasants might survive without goods from the cities, but the workers could not live without grain. By the end of 1927, shortages had led to rationing of basic commodities. Stalin understood sticks not carrots. His solution, to the dismay of Bukharin and other liberals, was not to raise factory productivity or prices for farm produce; it was to terrorize the peasantry into handing over grain and money to the state, to confiscate whatever they hid and arrest those who hid, or traded in, grain.

This policy required the peasantry to be sorted into three categories: the rich peasant or kulak (tight fist) to be eliminated, the poor peasant to inherit the earth, and the middle peasant to be left where he was. A kulak was a peasant who farmed more land than his own family could cope with; a poor peasant was one who had lost his land or was unable to subsist on it, and hired out his labor; the middle peasant, on whom Bukharin wanted to stake the future, produced enough both to subsist and to pay his taxes. At first Stalin's organized pillage of the kulak and middle peasant worked: a million extra tons of grain were collected and famine in the cities was averted in 1928. But over large tracts of Siberia and southern Russia the peasants understood that the years of peace during which, by working hard, they had fed themselves were over.

Stalin's expedition to Siberia in 1928 was a trial run for a crime against humanity. In the next two years, requisition and dispossession under the names of collectivization and "dekulakization" would lay waste virtually all the arable lands of the USSR. Arrests, deportations, and killings escalated, probably beyond what even Stalin and Menzhinsky had anticipated, into a holocaust unmatched in Europe between the Thirty Years' War of the seventeenth century and Hitler. Stalin's attack on the peasantry ravaged Russian agriculture and the Russian peasant to such an extent that for perhaps a century Russia would be incapable of feeding itself. It introduced irrational and unquestioned rule by fear and turned people back into beasts of burden. Stalin was now using OGPU to repress not counterrevolutionaries but a peaceful population.

Most of what Stalin did, however brutal, before 1928 can be ascribed to necessity, to the logic of events. The violence of the civil war can be explained as preemptive self-defense against an enemy who, given the chance, would have hanged Lenin's Politburo from public gallows in Moscow. Stalin's dirty tactics in the battle for the succession to Lenin can be justified by the view, which was not just Stalin's, that only a dictator could rule the country and that his rivals were even worse. But Stalin's collectivization and the eradication of the rich peasant as a class makes little sense on economic grounds. The war on the peasantry that Trotsky, Kamenev, and Zinoviev had proposed and which Stalin implemented was ideological, like Hitler's war on the Jews, but it lacked even the populist basis that underpinned Hitler's extermination of the Jews. Half of Europe could enthusiastically unite behind anti-Semitism, but few Russians blamed the kulak for their misery.

The arbitrary violence of 1928 left the authorities no other option but to go further and enslave the peasantry on collective farms. Russia would never have voluntarily produced surplus grain again, and private trade in grain or withholding it from the state now became criminal offenses.[3] Resistance, even by shouts or a show of fists, was terrorism.

For the first time since the civil war and the last time ever, Stalin traveled the country to enforce a policy rather than take a holiday. He took with him a trainload of OGPU, party, and government workers; his cronies worked in parallel. The Armenian Bolshevik Anastas Mikoyan, to whom Stalin had transferred Bukharin's economic tasks, was terrorizing the grain belt of the north Caucasus; Viacheslav Molotov was taking his train through the black earth of European Russia, the middle and south Volga. At each stop Stalin, Mikoyan, and Molotov mobilized local officials and issued targets for grain. Kulaks, traders, and lax officials were arrested. The poorer peasants and officials in each area did OGPU's dirty work. Sometimes they acted out of fear or in a frenzied mass; sometimes they were covetous or just vindictive. The poor peasant wanted the tools, clothes, houses, and livestock of the rich; the local party or soviet worker hoped to earn himself promotion. In any case, party workers knew that going too far was far less dangerous than not going far enough. They seized even the seed corn for next spring and the sixteen kilos of grain per head per month that the peasant was allotted for personal survival.

OGPU enforced confiscation wherever Stalin, Mikoyan, and Molotov were unable to visit. For example, on January 19, 1928, Menzhinsky telegraphed the GPU chief in Bashkiria: "Communicate by telegraph immediately what you have undertaken to ensure the process of grain requisitioning. What operations have been carried out, how many have been arrested, and who? Has there been any supervision of the movement of factory goods to the country and requisitioned grain to the railways? Are those who buy up coupons for goods in the country being arrested?"

★ ★ ★ Menzhinsky, with Stalin's sanction, was implementing what he had proposed in his university thesis thirty years ago: breaking up the peasant community. All Menzhinsky's senior staff were requisitioned by Stalin for the task in 1928. Iakov Agranov, deputy director of the secret department of OGPU, was taken off his espionage duties and was soon taking his interest down to village level: "Carry out an investigation urgently on the pillaging of the collective farm at Lutsenkovo parish, paying most attention to the leading kulaks. At the same time process the anti-Soviet element in the parish. Inform the secret department of results in detail." Genrikh Iagoda, too, was roped in to see that OGPU, not the courts, dealt with those arrested for speaking out against requisitioning or for "sabotage."[4] OGPU's regular reports also warned Stalin that even from the cowed peasantry there might be a backlash. The Red Army was recruited from the peasantry; the letters soldiers had from home undermined morale and made it unwise to use the army to put down peasant uprisings.

Molotov, touring the Volga, was more cautious than Stalin. He enforced party policy but protested at arbitrary arrests or at local officials using the campaign to settle private scores. Not that there was a grain of humanity in Molotov: he rated bureaucratic efficiency above all else, and blamed party disorganization rather than the kulak for the breakdown in the supply of grain. Stalin used every trick: the peasantry were not allowed to pay in money; every purchase and every tax was in grain. They had to pay taxes in advance and buy government bonds and compulsory insurance until nothing was left. The mills only gave back to the peasants a tiny proportion of their grain as flour.

OGPU was flooded with reports of discontent and open rebellion, as well as abuse from drunken officials "discrediting Soviet power." A few officials were killed by peasants; many were assaulted or had their houses burned down. So many peasants were arrested after Stalin's stay in Novosibirsk that the local GPU could not cope; Iagoda had to hand over kulaks to the militia and the courts.

The peasantry were perplexed by this renewed assault. Was the Soviet Union about to go to war and therefore requisitioning grain? Was the ruble about to collapse and therefore money not being accepted? They concluded, in the words of a letter intercepted by OGPU, "For food we are left with 16 kilos a month per head, but we're against that and we say we'll fight to the death, rather than die of famine." Support for kulaks grew: "Now we shan't vote for the paupers, we voted for them for two years and they ruin everything; we must vote for a well-off peasant who has property as a pledge so that he is answerable," wrote another peasant.[5]

Stalin's entourage was enslaved to doctrine. The kulak was to be eliminated even though he was rarely rich enough to be an exploiter, but often employed the poor peasants, giving them corn to survive the winter and buying them tools. Worse, to meet targets for confiscation, middle peasants were arrested as kulaks. The idiocy of Stalin's policy was that the peasants who could farm the land and worked hard were turned off it, very often to die, and those who could not farm and would not work inherited the earth as members of collective farms. All the achievements of Piotr Stolypin, the prime minister who had in 1908 granted the incentives that revived Russian agriculture and sent wagonloads of butter from Siberia to Britain and grain from Odessa to Germany, were nullified.

Why was there no effective protest from within or outside the party at this campaign of unprovoked violence against the class that all of Russian society had long professed to be the core of the nation? Was it ignorance of what was happening? Did people believe the Stalinist propaganda that the USSR had to become industrially strong, if necessary at the expense of the peasantry? Did dissenters fear deadly reprisals? All three factors deterred intellectuals and party workers from taking a stand. The deafening silence must lead us to conclude that Stalin's apparatus on the one hand and Menzhinsky's OGPU on the other had by 1928 established their reputations for omniscience and ruthless intolerance.

One man did remonstrate with Stalin: Georgi Chicherin, commissar for foreign affairs. Stalin had inherited him from Lenin and for all his allegiance to Marxism-Leninism Chicherin was as fastidious and rational as any traditional minister of foreign affairs. Stalin put up with Chicherin partly because he quite liked him—Chicherin was a genteel decadent in the style of Menzhinsky—partly because there was nobody else as competent as Chicherin or as acceptable to Western governments and partly because Chicherin, mortally ill, would soon vanish from the scene of his own accord. In March 1929, from his sanatorium in Germany, Chicherin expressed lukewarm support for Stalin's "general line in peasant policies" but refrained from judging the details and pointed out that it was Stalin's fault there was no meat to be had in Moscow. He also said, "How good it would be, if you, Comrade Stalin, could change your appearance and travel abroad for some time, with a proper interpreter, not a biased one. Then you'd see reality. You'd learn the value of these outbursts about a final struggle. You'd see the utterly revolting rubbish in *Pravda* in its real nakedness."[6] Chicherin was a voice crying out in the wilderness, but a disinterested one. Bukharin's protests could be dismissed as the whining of a dismissed satrap.

In a typical maneuver, Stalin put right a nominal amount of the damage he had done: by March 1929 a few unjustly arrested and destitute peasants had been amnestied. OGPU also cut down on its executions: officially, in 1928 only 869 were shot in the Soviet Union, a third of the figure for 1927 when Trotskyism was being suppressed. But OGPU noted that "class warfare has now become more acute in the countryside" and they were eager to proceed with mass arrests of the kulaks they had flushed out.

To the July 1928 plenum of the Central Committee, Stalin justified what he had done: Russia had to hit the peasantry hard in order to build railways and hydroelectric power stations. "England squeezed the juice out of all its colonies for hundreds of years. . . . Germany built its industry on 5 billions of reparations after the Franco-Prussian war. . . . America developed its industry by raising loans in Europe . . . our country cannot, must not, go in for robbing colonies or foreign countries. . . ." Extraordinary measures, Stalin insisted, "have saved the country from a general economic crisis." He claimed that in future years there would be reserves of grain and that the requisitions had been a one-off measure. Bukharin bickered about the brutality and Stalin set his cronies on him: "Give us your panacea," shouted Voroshilov. When Bukharin complained that he had to spend two days at OGPU to get the facts, Menzhinsky was asked, "Why did you lock him up in OGPU?" to which Menzhinsky replied, to loud laughter, "For panicking."

Bukharin's group had to grovel in order to hang on to a shred of power. They applauded the first show trials, knowing that the allegations were absurd and the confessions forced; they assented to exporting grain in order to finance industrialization. Only in June 1928, when Stalin decided that the peasantry would have to enter collective farms not just the cooperatives that Bukharin had envisaged, did he protest to Stalin: "Koba, I'm writing to you, not orally, since anyway I am too upset to talk and I fear you won't hear me out, while you will still read a letter to the end. I consider the country's internal and external situation to be very bad . . . people are afraid to talk. . . . I shan't fight and I don't want to. . . . "[7] He was ready, once he had finished presiding over the Comintern, "to go wherever you like, with no fight, no noise, no struggle."

Bukharin knew very well that all his movements and conversations were monitored by OGPU and that Stalin had installed a fifth telephone in his office to monitor calls made by any senior member of the party or government.[8] Stalin had read to Bukharin a transcript of Zinoviev's most intimate telephone conversations. Nevertheless, on July 11, when Kamenev came to Moscow, Bukharin phoned him to arrange a meeting. How did Bukharin imagine that Kamenev and Zinoviev would deal with him after years of relentless hounding in which Bukharin had sided with Stalin? Did Bukharin fear that Stalin, having turned against the peasantry, might bring Kamenev and Zinoviev back into power, in which case Bukharin, Rykov, and Tomsky would be isolated? Bukharin's desperate ploy was to recruit them first.

Kamenev was skeptical and yet gullibly optimistic—he expected a counteroffer from Stalin. He took notes on the conversation in order to brief Zinoviev. Later, Kamenev made sure that Trotsky, too, had a summary. Kamenev had known Stalin for over twenty years; he must have known OGPU and Stalin would find out everything. His behavior was as staggering as Bukharin's, but the prospect, however dim, of retaining power clearly blinded them both to Stalin's inexorable vindictiveness.

In 1930 Kamenev's secretary was arrested by OGPU, who found concealed in a relative's bedstead minutes of the conversation. Bukharin's bridge-building to the left opposition gave Stalin the material in order to destroy, one after the other, the left and right deviations in the party. Only now did Bukharin appreciate Trotsky's point. Calling Stalin a "Genghis Khan who had read Marx" he said, "Stalin knows only one means: vengeance and putting a knife into your back at the same time." Kamenev knew that too; he had been present in 1923 when Stalin told Dzierżyński that his ideal of happiness was to prepare revenge and then go to bed.

During their conversation Bukharin told Kamenev that Stalin had said to Bukharin in 1928, when preparing the Politburo's agenda, "You and I are Himalayas, the rest are nonentities. . . . " When Kamenev asked Bukharin who was backing him, the latter named the rest of his troika, Rykov and Tomsky. Bukharin also said that the deputy head of OGPU, Genrikh Iagoda, and its head of foreign intelligence, Meer Trilisser, were sympathetic, an allegation that was to damn Iagoda and Trilisser in Stalin's eyes. Bukharin posed the dilemma: "1) If the country perishes, we perish; 2) If the country manages to get out of the crisis, Stalin steps back in time and we still perish." Bukharin, Rykov, and Tomsky felt that it "would be far better if, instead of Stalin, we now had Zinoviev and Kamenev."

Kamenev and Zinoviev saw that it was mad to take part in a half-baked plot: there was no hope even of making Stalin revert to the collective leadership of 1923, let alone of his stepping down. When Rykov heard the phrases Bukharin had uttered, and to whom, he yelled at Bukharin (according to Anna Larina, who was to be Bukharin's last wife), "You're an old woman, not a politician!" Gods like Stalin demented their victims before destroying them. It boggles the mind that Kamenev and Bukharin, who had spent decades before 1917 evading detection, could be such bungling conspirators.

Stalin had from Iagoda and Agranov in OGPU a full record of these damning discussions and Kamenev's reflections, too. Just after Stalin gracefully let Kamenev and Zinoviev back into the party, OGPU reported Kamenev speculating, "The only progressive cause that this group (Bukharin, Rykov, Tomsky) can achieve is to remove Stalin from the post of general secretary. . . . I think their chances are less than 25 percent. . . . But actually removing Stalin by this group would mean a right-winger taking Stalin's place. . . . It is extremely likely that when Stalin has beaten the right, he will himself turn doubly right." Kamenev outlined five courses of action of which only one appealed to him: "To seek a union with Stalin on acceptable terms."[9] He decided to avoid Bukharin, to attack him in print, and to contact Stalin—a meeting which Stalin had just refused. Kamenev feared Stalin might outmaneuver him by making a pact with Trotsky and his notes end on a pessimistic note with a very astute prediction of Stalin's future entourage: Molotov, Voroshilov, Mikoyan, Orjonikidze, Kalinin, Kirov.

Martemian Riutin, a Moscow Bolshevik who would mount in 1932 the last attempt to depose Stalin, recalled Bukharin "totally demoralized, in tears" and saying, "I now feel that I have been literally smeared with shit from head to toe." Bukharin recovered sufficiently by the end of 1929 to publish an article, "An economist's notes," denouncing the collectivization of the peasantry as "irresponsible and opportunist." When attacked in the Politburo, Bukharin boldly called Stalin a "petty oriental despot." Bukharin lost his posts. In November 1929 Stalin removed him from the Politburo. Then Bukharin broke. He variously groveled or snorted defiance, as in his letter to Stalin of October 1930:

Koba. After our telephone conversation I immediately left work in a state of despair. Not because you "frightened" me—you can't scare me and won't frighten me off. But because those monstrous accusations you threw at me clearly point to the existence of some satanic, foul and low provocation which you believe, on which you build your policies and which will end badly even if you were to destroy me physically with the same success with which you are destroying me politically. . . .

I consider your accusations monstrous mad slander, crazy and, in the final count, stupid. . . . Or does the fact that I don't lick your behind or write articles in your praise *à la* Piatakov make me "a preacher of terror"? Then say so! God, what hellish madness is happening now! And you, instead of explanations, ooze spite against someone who is full of just one thought: to help in any way, to pull the cart with everybody, but not to turn into a sycophant, there are a lot of them and they are ruining us.[10]

Stalin had paralyzed his opponents. Trotsky still conducted a copious correspondence from Alma-Ata—all the better for OGPU to keep track of the opposition—but he was about to be deported. Zinoviev and Kamenev were grateful for small mercies. Bukharin writhed like a worm on the hook. All would be physically destroyed in a decade; already they were corpses politically. OGPU used provocateurs against them. While Bukharin recuperated in the high Caucasus from the shock of his fall—now he had lost the editorship of *Pravda*—he was doorstepped by a young man called Platonov who claimed to be a Communist Youth member horrified by the treachery of OGPU toward the workers and Bukharin. Platonov elicited enough from Bukharin for Stalin to damn him in the eyes of the Central Committee. In a similar sting, OGPU "unmasked" as a former White Guards officer Trotsky's printer.

The events of 1928 demonstrated the speed and ruthlessness of Stalin as a politician. He had rehearsed his methods for eliminating not only political rivals but also any class from which future opposition might spring. He had one more device still to try out: the fabricated show trial, a spectacle which Menzhinsky and his subordinates including Iakov Agranov had been rehearsing for nearly a decade.

The First Show Trials

With him, pretence was so spontaneous that it seemed he himself became convinced of the truth and sincerity of what he was saying.

Milovan Djilas, Conversations with Stalin

IN 1926 Stalin asked Menzhinsky to stage a show trial that would swing public opinion at home and abroad. Not until 1930 did Menzhinsky do this, although in 1928, under Genrikh Iagoda's less expert supervision, OGPU staged the Shakhty trial of mine engineers from the Don basin in southern Russia. Like the grain requisitions of 1928, the trial was counterproductive. If the country needed grain, why terrorize the producers? If the country needed engineers, why arrest hundreds and put fifty on trial? If foreign specialists were needed to pass on modern technology, why arrest thirty-two German engineers and try three of them? Stalin, accusing others of sabotage, was throwing wrenches in his own works.

Each repression was followed by token relenting: individuals in the judiciary and OGPU were reprimanded for overdoing the persecutions; engineers were praised as a caste whom the state would cherish. Foreigners, however, remained vulnerable: in 1930 British electrical engineers from Metro-Vickers stood trial for sabotage and corruption. The repercussions of such trials forced Stalin to guarantee the safety of foreign specialists and in 1932, when the great Dnepr dams were built, the American engineer Hugh L. Cooper was rewarded not with arrest but with the Red Banner of Labor.

The motives behind the Shakhty trial related to the disparity between promised prosperity and the actual penury of the country. This had to be blamed on someone and foreign saboteurs were an easy target. Moreover Stalin loathed foreign specialists and wanted Soviet citizens to shun them. In addition, the effects of a show trial on the judiciary and public needed to be tested again, and Stalin wanted to see if OGPU could make defendants repeat their confessions in open court before he used show trials on famous old Bolsheviks, not just obscure engineers.

Since Lenin's death the Soviet judiciary and some of Tsarist Russia's surviving defense lawyers had recovered a vestige of self-confidence—at least when OGPU did not express an interest in the outcome. Stalin needed judge and prosecutor able to give his kangaroo court credibility, but wanted to warn off any lawyers who might defend enemies of the state. He was fortunate that Andrei Vyshinsky and Nikolai Krylenko were at his disposal. After sharing a cell with Andrei Vyshinsky, Stalin was sure of his loyalty.

Nikolai Krylenko had conducted with deadly rhetoric prosecutions in the first years of the revolution: he had sent Roman Malinovsky to his death, and arranged trials of Social Revolutionaries and bourgeois intellectuals in the early 1920s. Krylenko, however, was suspect to Stalin: he was a formidable chess player, and organized international tournaments.[11] Krylenko, like Bukharin, also conquered peaks in the Pamir mountains, and he had one named after him. All this implied individualism, cunning, and competitiveness. For all his cruelty and willingness to subvert justice for political expediency, Krylenko, like Bukharin, had a charisma which doomed him in Stalin's eyes and, consequently, in Vyshinsky's.

On any scale of odiousness Andrei Ianuarievich (sometimes called Iaguarovich for his feline predations) Vyshinsky ranks high among Stalin's hangmen. Vyshinsky was of Polish origin. In private life, like

Molotov, he was a loving husband and father, capable of kindness if it did not interfere with politics. Before the revolution he lived a comfortable privileged existence; he had no traumas to avenge and had been trained in one of the world's most idealistic legal systems. He was, however, deeply cynical and sadistic and possessed no gratitude. He had no compunction about sending his former professor of law and many—in fact most—of his colleagues to their deaths. He developed a theory of law in which "confession is the queen of evidence"; he bullied into mute submission defendants whom he knew to be innocent of trumped-up charges. But Vyshinsky had a gift for legalistic phrasing as well as foul-mouthed oratory and proved himself a brilliant organizer in education, law, and eventually foreign affairs.

As a revolutionary in Baku, Vyshinsky had specialized in killing provocateurs and police agents. The chief blot on his copybook, which Stalin valued as a means of blackmailing him, was that, as a youthful prosecutor of the provisional government, he had issued a warrant for Lenin's arrest. After the Bolshevik takeover, Stalin's arrival in Petrograd saved Vyshinsky, who was given a post organizing food supplies. In the party purges, Vyshinsky, as a former Menshevik, was sometimes denied a party card, but by 1925 he was voted in—the sole candidate—as rector of Moscow University.

Vyshinsky's first service to Stalin was in 1927 to arrange the funeral of the neuropathologist Professor Vladimir Bekhterev. The professor's death by poisoning, two days after diagnosing paranoia in Stalin, was suspicious. A few years later Vyshinsky instructed a court to sentence Bekhterev's son to death and his family to the camps. The Shakhty trial was Vyshinsky's first public test, and as he was a prosecutor rather than a judge, the court had to be designated a "special session." Vyshinsky's job was not to decide a verdict or sentence—Stalin had already decided those—his task was to oversee the Shakhty defendants, to rehearse their confessions and court testimony.

Efim Evdokimov, a former convict and OGPU chief in the north Caucasus, had the physical work of wringing confessions from the fifty-three defendants and making them fit for public testimony in May 1928 in the marble Hall of Columns in Moscow, a venue whose theater equipment made it ideal for show trials.

Before the trial Stalin declared all the defendants guilty of sabotaging industry at the behest of French intelligence:

The facts tell us that the Shakhty case is economic counter-revolution, initiated by some of the bourgeois specialists who have already taken control of the coal industry. The facts also tell us that these specialists, organized in a secret group, received money for sabotage from the former owners of the mines who are now émigrés, and from counterrevolutionary organizations in the West.[12]

Nobody in the Central Committee stood up for the accused. Bukharin, now begging Stalin to rehabilitate him, demanded death for all of them.

Not everything went according to plan. Some of the defendants, especially the Germans, naively thought acquittal possible and pleaded not guilty; others pointed out the absurdity of the idea that French intelligence was commissioning sabotage to facilitate an invasion of Russia. The defense lawyers, notably Pavel Maliantovich, who was Vyshinsky's superior and had been minister of justice in the provisional government before the revolution, tried too hard. The six-week trial attracted mockery from the foreign press. Krylenko, to Vyshinsky's amusement, for he resented his rival's flamboyant reputation, allowed his prosecution to flounder in arcane aspects of engineering and of the "class position" in Marxist jurisprudence. Nor was even the Soviet public yet ready to applaud such witnesses as the twelve-year-old boy who demanded that his accused father be shot. Eventually Vyshinsky overrode Stalin's instructions: of the eighteen accused, he let seven walk free, and sentenced only eleven to death. Moreover, international pressure was such that Stalin could only have five actually executed. Three defendants who had refused to testify were shot without trial by Iagoda the following May. Stalin complained to the party that there were still "Shakhty men sitting in all branches of our industry."

After this trial, if the accused became obstreperous in rehearsals, then the trial, if held at all, was behind closed doors, and the public saw only newspaper reports that saboteurs had been sentenced to death.

Thus forty-eight officials in the food industry were shot, and the readers of *Pravda* were left to infer that food shortages were due to subversive state employees. An epidemic of anthrax and distemper among horses was likewise blamed on bacteriologists, who paid with their lives for fighting the epidemic.

Menzhinsky consistently met Stalin's demands for reprisals for imaginary campaigns of sabotage. To every economic problem Stalin had a punitive response. The shortage of consumer goods and the excessive money supply of the second half of the 1920s, said Georgi Piatakov, then chairman of the State Bank, could be solved conventionally by increasing production, importing fewer consumer goods, and exporting agricultural produce. No, retorted Stalin, the money supply could be reduced by confiscating coins from "speculators" who kept small change because the silver content exceeded its nominal value. Stalin had another solution, as paranoiac as it was crass: "Without fail shoot two or three dozen wreckers from the Commissariat of Finance and the State Bank." Five old bankers were sentenced to die. Just one member of the intelligentsia, the poet Osip Mandelstam, last keeper of the public conscience, protested at this judicial murder. To the amazement of all who knew of his protest, the old men were spared. Nobody, however, was inspired by Mandelstam's courage to emulate him. Civic courage in the USSR was dead, and Mandelstam was regarded as mad.

Stalin was undeterred. He fired the chairman of the State Bank and instructed Menzhinsky: "Can you possibly send a memorandum on the results of the struggle (by GPU methods) with speculators in small change (how much silver has been removed, what institutions are most implicated, the role of foreign countries and their agents, how many people have been arrested, who they are, etc.)." Menzhinsky replied humbly: "Your view is correct. There is no doubt about that. But the trouble is that the results of the operation to take out small silver coins are almost deplorable. 280,000 rubles . . . clearly, we had a go at the cashiers and then relaxed, as often happens with us. That's bad."[13]

Under Stalin's watchful eye, Menzhinsky staged at the end of 1930 a show trial in Moscow of eight leading metropolitan engineers and physicists, but first came a summer of arrests, interrogations, and the writing of an elaborate scenario. The first wave of arrests took out Russia's best economists, notably Aleksandr Chaianov and Nikolai Kondratiev, the author of a controversial theory on the relationship of booms and depressions to sunspot cycles.[14] He allegedly led a secret Labor Peasant Party, connected with an émigré Republican Democrat Union and with Mensheviks at home and abroad. Stalin first proposed to Molotov, "Kondratiev, Groman, and a couple or two of other bastards [*sic*] must definitely be shot." He wanted Menzhinsky and Iagoda to link Kondratiev with Bukharin, Rykov, and Tomsky, and when Menzhinsky failed to find a link, Stalin asked OGPU, "Would the gentlemen accused consider confessing their mistakes and cover themselves properly with spit politically speaking by recognizing at the same time the solidity of Soviet power and the correctness of collectivization methods? That wouldn't be bad. . . ."[15]

Kondratiev would not "cover himself in spit," as Stalin saw from the regular statements that Iagoda brought him. Stalin told Menzhinsky, "Delay handing the Kondratiev case to the courts. It is not without its dangers. In the middle of October we'll decide this question together. I have some considerations <u>against</u>." Kondratiev and his fellow accused were dealt with behind closed doors and were finally shot in 1937. Menzhinsky meanwhile went on "checking up and smashing faces," as Stalin phrased it.

"Evidence" from Kondratiev's case fed the Industrial Party (Prompartiia) case at the end of 1930. In this fabrication a deal was struck with the defendants led by Professor Leonid Ramzin. Stalin liked Ramzin; his confessions implicated (and thus silenced) the Soviet head of state, Mikhail Kalinin, and Stalin circulated details to the Central Committee. Leonid Ramzin sang like a canary. In return he was promised his life and full reinstatement.[16] Stalin needed Ramzin's reprieve as an example to more important victims, to get confessions to any accusations, however absurd, in exchange for a reprieve, for the survival of kith and kin—promises that were later rarely kept.

Menzhinsky's success with Ramzin left Stalin hungry for more compromising material for future use. He and Menzhinsky fed each other's paranoia. A letter of October 1930 to Menzhinsky shows Stalin's obsession with micromanaging OGPU's work and an uncritical belief, simulated or not, in universal conspiracies. He writes as if a Franco-Polish-

Romanian army, financed by the Nobel brothers, really proposed invading the USSR. Stalin's cynicism about human behavior is matched by his autosuggestion that the fabrications OGPU had beaten or cajoled from prisoners reflected reality:

Ramzin's statements are very interesting. I think the most interesting thing in his statements is the question of intervention in general, or, in particular, of the date of intervention. It turns out that intervention was planned for 1930, but was put off to 1931 or even 1932. This is very plausible and important. It's all the more important that it comes from a primary source, i.e. from the group of Riabushinsky, Gukasov, Denisov, Nobel [émigré businessmen and alleged co-conspirators, some of whom were in fact dead], a group which is the most powerful social-economic group of all within the USSR, and the emigration, the strongest group in capital and in their links with the French and English governments. It might seem that the Labor Peasant Party or the Industrial Party or Miliukov's party [Miliukov led the Russian Constitutional Democrats, the liberals of the Tsar's Duma] are the main force. But this is not true. The main force is the Riabushinsky-Denisov-Nobel group, i.e. Trade and Industry, [the other parties] are just errand boys for Trade and Industry. . . .

    Hence my suggestions:

a) make the question of intervention one of the most important key points for <u>new future</u> statements by the leaders [of the other parties] and especially by Ramzin: 1) why was the intervention in 1930 put back? 2) is it because Poland was not ready yet? 3) perhaps because Romania isn't ready? 4) perhaps because the Baltic States and Romania haven't yet united with Poland? 5) why has the intervention been put off to 1931? 6) why "might" they put it off to 1932? 7) etc., etc.

[. . .]

d) Make Messrs Kondratiev, Iurovsky, Chaianov et al. run the gantlet, they have been deviously evading the "tendency to intervention," but they are (indisputably!) interventionists and they must be interrogated very severely about dates. (Kondratiev, Iurovsky and Chaianov must know about this just as Miliukov, whom they visited for a "chat," knows.)

If Ramzin's statements are confirmed and fleshed out in statements by the other accused (Groman, Larichev, Kondratiev and Co., etc.) this will be a major success for OGPU, since material we get this way we shall make available to sections of the Comintern and workers of all countries, we shall start a very wide campaign against interventionists and we shall succeed in paralyzing and subverting attempts to intervene for the next year or two, which is very important for us.

Get it? Greetings! I. Stalin.[17]

Ramzin happily clowned at the trial of the Prompartiia: he helped the lame-duck prosecution over many stiles, affirming that he had met the capitalist Riabushinsky two years after the latter's death and that he himself had been briefed by both Poincaré and Lawrence of Arabia. The trial was accounted a success. Five of the eight were sentenced to death but reprieved for performing well in court.[18]

Menzhinsky and Stalin now pressed on with a trial of the harmless remnants of prerevolutionary Russia's law-abiding socialists. The accused had never been, or no longer were, Mensheviks but they had underground experience and OGPU had trouble breaking them. Iagoda threatened to arrest his victims' sick wives and elderly parents—and did so, even after the accused caved in and signed dictated formulaic confessions, sixty volumes of them.

With the benefit of his now considerable experience Menzhinsky could see that only fourteen of the 122 accused would perform reliably in open court so the rest were dealt with behind closed doors. Even so, Nikolai Krylenko, prosecuting, was wrong-footed in court. One Menshevik who had escaped abroad, Rafail Abramovich, was said to have visited Russia to brief the conspirators but was able to prove that he was in western Europe all that time and successfully sued two German newspapers that printed reports of the trial. Even loyal Bolsheviks had trouble suspending their disbelief at the ludicrous testimony. One noted in his diary:

A hall flooded with lights, microphones, sound recorders, judges, stenographers. One impression only: a trial that had been over-rehearsed. Ramzin was examined when I was there. He was led across the hall. . . . A heap of correspondents filling the front rows fired their cameras at him for several minutes, sitting on top of each other. Ramzin was wearing a white collar, a jacket buttoned up to the neck, standing by the microphone and not waiting for questions from the prosecution, spent at least a whole hour giving his evidence. He said really shattering things. . . .[19]

Bringing the Writers to Heel

IF THE SOVIET PEOPLE had any hope of intercession at the end of the 1920s, before everyone's conscience and common sense was obliterated by terror, that hope lay with the creative intellectuals, especially the writers. For over a hundred years, from Pushkin to Tolstoi, Russian poets, novelists, and philosophers had stood up for the people against oppression, enduring prison, exile abroad or in Siberia, poverty, and obloquy. But if the novelist Leo Tolstoi and the philosopher Vladimir Soloviov had courted repression to save the lives of those whom the Tsarist state proposed to kill, their successors Vladimir Mayakovsky and Mikhail Bulgakov stood back from the brink. Five years of the New Economic Plan had given them back a semblance of the security, prestige, and prosperity poets and novelist had once enjoyed but they had not recovered the moral security destroyed by the civil war. They might intervene for close friends, and would still protest when OGPU purloined their diaries or when Glavlit banned their works, but they did little more.

Not a single writer with the exception of Osip Mandelstam now had the courage to confront Menzhinsky and Stalin on any matter; to stand up for liberty of conscience, let alone free speech or the right to life, liberty, and the pursuit of happiness. True, poets and philosophers all had friends, wives, mistresses, and children who would go down with them; " 'I have a wife and children' is the best cog in the machinery of tyranny," said the Slovak novelist Jan Johanides. Undoubtedly, Stalin was more terrible than Nicholas I or Alexander III. So much worse then, the crime of conniving at his atrocities than assenting to the Tsarist oppression of the nineteenth century. The cowardice of Soviet intellectuals led to a punishment as terrible as that which moral courage would have incurred.

Stalin was now preparing to deal with the intelligentsia, but because he regarded himself as a creative mind, because he depended on writers, cinematographers, and composers for his entertainment, he moved stealthily. New cadres of engineers could be trained, peasants replaced by tractors, and the Politburo was easily replenished from the eager ranks of the Central Committee. It was far harder, Stalin knew, to find new writers, composers, actors, and painters; the young proletarian writers to whom the old guard had been ordered by Lunacharsky and Gorky to pass on their skills, produced, as Stalin knew, little but trash.

Stalin took great interest in the arts from 1928. The theaters, cinemas, concert halls, and publishing houses of Moscow and Leningrad were thriving but the quarrelsome intelligentsia were like headless chickens; their patrons—Trotsky, Bukharin, Zinoviev, Kamenev—had fallen from power. As NEP foundered under taxation and persecution, independent publishing vanished and authors were cut off from Russian culture abroad, writers were left to the mercy of editorial boards and state publishers, controlled by Glavlit's censors.

In 1927 Lebedev-Poliansky of Glavlit, reporting to the Central Committee, called for Stalin's intervention. Lebedev-Poliansky had shown vulpine deviousness in letting through, for certain audiences at certain times and places, a few books or plays of artistic merit such as Isaak Babel's civil war stories *Red Cavalry,* and Mikhail Bulgakov's drama *The Days of the Turbins.* In this he had set himself against Lenin's widow Krupskaia and his sister Maria, two bigots who exercised fundamentalist censorship in the Commissariat for Education. But censorship grew oppressive. It was now retrospective: secondhand-book shops had their stocks weeded, and libraries were purged of ideological impurity, although state libraries were allowed special closed holdings of banned books. Lebedev-Poliansky complained of "walking on a razor's edge" between political and artistic criteria. He knew that Glavlit was hated and quoted a prose writer: "There is a general groan over the whole front of contemporary literature. We cannot be ourselves, our artistic conscience is constantly being violated. . . . If Dostoevsky were to appear among us today . . . he too would have to put all his manuscripts back in the drawer with a 'prohibited' stamp from Glavlit." The great poets—Voloshin, Akhmatova, Mandelstam—abandoned verse. Pasternak had stopped writing lyrics. Sergei Esenin had hanged himself, leaving a farewell poem written in his own blood. Bulgakov's satirical prose on the Soviet mission to transform nature had fallen foul of the censor: "Fatal Eggs" portrayed imported Marxism as irradiated reptile eggs brought in by mistake as hens' eggs, whose hatchlings devastated the country instead of feeding it; "The Heart of a Dog" depicted *Homo sovieticus* as a vicious hybrid between a dog and a human being. Stalin himself took umbrage at much of what he read. Pilniak's story "Tale of the Moon Extinguished" recounted the death of the civil war commander Mikhail Frunze, implying that his fatal abdominal operation had been ordered by Stalin.[20] Author, editor, and journal were severely punished.

Nevertheless, a few literary decisions in 1928 were benevolent. Two of Bulgakov's plays were authorized for performance, on the grounds that one gave experience to young actors and the other was the sole source of income for a small theater. Stalin's most liberal authorization was for an edition of all Tolstoi's work (eventually ninety volumes). Tolstoyans imprisoned and exiled by OGPU were partially amnestied, despite the opposition to Bolshevism that Tolstoi's religious and philosophical work enjoins. Tolstoi's disciple Vladimir Chertkov, deported by the Tsar to Great Britain in 1896, had an audience with Dzierżyński in 1920 and with Stalin in 1925. He persuaded Dzierżyński that Tolstoyans, like other nonviolent sectarians, were harmless to the state. Chertkov's argument to Stalin was ingenious: he warned that Tolstoi's works would be published abroad if the Soviet authorities did not preempt this. Tolstoyans suffered in the collectivization; their communal working of the land could not coexist with Stalin's measures but Chertkov, and after his death in 1936 his son, secured for Tolstoi's work and his followers indulgences that Stalin granted to no other unorthodox believers.[21]

One group of writers, the Russian Association of Proletarian Writers and the Proletarian Theater, had already appointed themselves the secret police of poetry; they were nonplussed by Stalin's apparent liberalism. They protested about performances of Bulgakov's *The Days of the Turbins* and *Flight,* both showing the plight of the Whites in the civil war with some sympathy. A commission of the Central Committee, including Krupskaia and Rozalia Zemliachka, demanded instead mass printing of works by specified communist authors.

Stalin made himself the arbiter of literary disputes. Wearing his mask of tolerance, he told proletarian playwrights that concepts of right and left did not apply to "such a nonparty and incomparably broader sphere as is artistic literature, the theater, etc." Stalin "would have nothing against the staging of Bulgakov's *Flight* if he added to his eight 'dreams' one or two more showing the inner social springs of the civil war." *The Days of the Turbins* was a good play, because it leaves the impression that "if even people like the Turbins are forced to lay down their arms and submit to the will of the people . . . then the Bolsheviks are invincible," and if Bulgakov's plays were staged frequently that was because proletarians couldn't write good plays. "Literature should progress not by bans, but by competition."[22]

Talking to Ukrainian writers in February 1929, Stalin applauded literature in local languages and prophesied that when the proletariat conquered the globe French not Russian would be the universal language. Stalin even conceded: "You can't insist that literature be communist."

Stalin not only loved theater, he and Menzhinsky learned from it. OGPU developed Stanislavskian theories of acting and the theater in a direction more barbarous than Konstantin Stanislavsky could ever have dreamed of for their show trials, aiming to make their victims act as if they believed in their own guilt. The Bolshoi Theater for opera and ballet, and for drama Stanislavsky's Moscow Arts Theater, were Stalin's, and thus the Politburo's, regular haunts. Few performers from either ended up in the Lubianka, except as informers. Stanislavsky, once the owner of cotton mills, was forgiven his past but was not allowed to forget it. His brother and nephews had been shot in the Crimea, and in the next few years he would lose a dozen nephews and other relatives to the GULAG and the executioner's bullet. Chekhov's widow, Olga Knipper, was forgiven her tours abroad during the civil war, and her letters of 1918 cursing the Bolsheviks as power-crazed killers. Her nephew the actor Mikhail Chekhov was allowed by Iagoda to leave for Germany and the United States, and his ex-wife Olga Tschechowa became one of Hitler's and Goebbels's favorite actresses. Stalin forbade reprisals against the family and Olga Knipper and at least one of her nephews became NKVD informers. Other theater directors, however left wing, were damned for their failure to bend their experimentalism to Stalin's conformist tastes. The theater director Vsevolod Meierkhold, however outspokenly pro-Soviet, annoyed Stalin intensely with his modernism, which Stalin called in 1929 "affectation, mannerisms." He was doomed.

The Russian theater had always lived on state patronage; now the Soviet authorities controlled the repertoire, the funding, and the fate of actors, authors, and directors. Literature was a more private and independent activity. Control required deep penetration by OGPU; writers had to be recruited to detect undercurrents that a simple chekist might miss. Poets acquired OGPU friends: Esenin had Iakov Bliumkin to report on his activities, while Mayakovsky was handled by Iakov Agranov—who gave him the revolver that he was to shoot himself with—and by his mistress's husband, Osip Brik, on whose door someone once scrawled:

> The man who lives here, Osip Brik, is
> Not just a linguist and a critic.
> He's a grass, a police dog who
> Interrogates his friends for OGPU.[23]

Skilled *chekisty* wrote poor poetry; talented poets were bad secret policemen. One Bohemian "proletarian" poet, Ivan Pribludny, Esenin's friend, was hauled in for his incompetence and in 1931 repented:

I formally took upon myself the obligation to be an OGPU collaborator some years ago, but I have done virtually no work and haven't wanted to, because the demands I had to meet as a collaborator interfered with my private life and my literary creativity. When I was summoned to OGPU on May 15, I asked the comrade who summoned me permission to go to the lavatory. When I got permission, I went there and wrote the following on the door: "Lads, ring Natasha [his wife] on South Moscow

17644 and tell her I'm not there." . . . I confess that I thus broke the conspiratorial status obligatory for me as a secret collaborator of OGPU. . . ."[24]

Certain genres of literature had priority for the Soviet state: writers of history were subjected to special ideological rigor. Mikhail Pokrovsky, an old Bolshevik who had edited Lenin's work, helped set up a Communist Academy and an Institute of Red Professors; he worked until his death in 1932 to suppress conventional historical research. He recognized only his own doctrines, which saw even the Middle Ages as an era of proletarian struggle, and rejected all national history. Russia's major historians lost first their right to publish, then their teaching jobs, and finally their liberty.

One institution of Tsarist Russia was not yet destroyed: the Academy of Sciences. Its membership had shrunk through emigration, execution, deportation, and starvation but enough men of international prestige survived for Stalin and OGPU to be circumspect with this last bastion of independent thought. Unlike the state and government, the academy remained in Leningrad until 1934, and not until 1925 did it even change its name from "Russian" to "All-Union." Until 1934 it elected members from capitalist states including Lord Rutherford from Britain and Albert Einstein from Germany. Stalin's Politburo tried to pack the academy with its own candidates and bribed academicians with trips abroad but in 1928 ungrateful academicians blackballed three communists. They had to hold a new ballot.

Even Bukharin, an economist of some standing, was blackballed— by the physiologist Ivan Pavlov—on the grounds that "Bukharin's hands are covered in blood." Only when Bukharin burst in, uninvited, on Pavlov's family having dinner, inspected his butterfly collection and proved that he was a knowledgeable lepidopterist, did Pavlov relent: the Politburo had one representative in the academy. Ivan Pavlov, famous for making dogs salivate at the sound of a bell, enjoyed unique immunity: Lenin ordered Zinoviev in 1920 to ensure that Pavlov had whatever he needed to keep his staff and animals alive. By 1928, Pavlov, born in 1849, was so unafraid of death that he could proclaim Jesus of Nazareth, not Lenin, to be the greatest human being, and tell Molotov with impunity that the Soviet government was "shit." In 1929, on the hundredth anniversary of the birth of the biologist Ivan Sechenov, Pavlov began a speech: "O stern and noble comrade! How you would have suffered if you had remained among us! We live under the domination of a cruel principle: state power is everything, the individual personality is nothing. . . . On this foundation, gentlemen, no cultured state can be built, and no state whatsoever can hold out for long."

★ ★ ★ Hundreds remembered that speech. Pavlov asked his audience to stand and, quivering with fear, they did so. In the 1930s Ivan Pavlov was the only prominent citizen in the Soviet Union apart from Stalin who spoke his mind with no regard for the consequences.[25] Academicians quaked whenever Pavlov spoke as they knew that Stalin's vengeance would be wreaked on them.

OGPU left Pavlov alone, but harassed as "spies" academicians who had "foreign collaborators." In the academy 15 percent of the tenured academics and 60 percent of the untenured lost their jobs. Then Menzhinsky prepared a show trial of 150 leading scholars and scientists. The academy was alleged to be hiding state secrets in its archives. Arrests began in October 1929: OGPU first took four leading historians, among them Sergei Platonov. Platonov was, like Pavlov, very old. He admitted that he was a monarchist by conviction; in his youth he had taught the Tsar and his brothers.[26]

The academy case was conducted by hardened *chekisty* like Agranov and Jekabs Peterss. After auditioning the 150 detainees, they chose sixteen victims, mostly historians, for public trial. Menzhinsky took a pedantic interest, even correcting the German grammar in statements from the historian Evgeni Tarle, who confessed that academicians kept guns and ammunition in the Pushkin House in Leningrad, and titillated the Bolshevik historian Pokrovsky with statements squeezed out of the detained academics (Menzhinsky and Pokrovsky had been friendly as exiles in Paris). OGPU did all it could to help the "Professor with the Pike," as Pokrovsky was called, to bring the academy under the heel of his Institute of Red Professors.

Academicians who would not incriminate Platonov were put in cells infested with typhus-bearing lice. They were promised leniency for testimony and crippling beatings for silence. Platonov was frail and his death under interrogation would have been politically embarrassing. As it was, international protests at his detention provoked Maxim Gorky to write in *Pravda* that foreign critics were silent about arrests and trials of communists in their own countries but raised a hue and cry about the fate of monarchists like Platonov, who was then given a room with clean sheets in the remand prison where he was even allowed to have his cat with him. After a year he confessed to running an underground military organization and to receiving large sums from the Polish government.[27] Platonov, like Tarle, was spared public trial and given a mild sentence of exile. When Pokrovsky died and Stalin reverted to the old monarchist view of Russian history, these two were still in good health and were rehabilitated.

It took another decade to drag the academy to Moscow, where it would be under the nose of the party, and to interest Stalin more keenly and balefully in the academy's research into mathematics, genetics, and linguistics. Then the NKVD would terrorize the academy into surrendering its greatest members to the Lubianka and accepting scoundrels like Vyshinsky as members. But for the first half of the 1930s the Academy of Sciences was the last beacon of free thought in the USSR.

Operations Abroad

OGPU, UNDER MENZHINSKY AND STALIN, spread its wings abroad as an organization parallel to the Soviet diplomatic corps. After entrapping Boris Savinkov, OGPU set up more fictitious centers of resistance but, once bitten twice shy, émigrés no longer fell for them. Agent Opperput was sent, or perhaps fled, to Finland and persuaded the Russian General Warriors' Union that he had changed sides again. They backed Opperput's botched attempt to blow up a GPU hostel in Moscow but Opperput's group was finally gunned down near Smolensk. The only retaliations the union mounted were the assassinations of a Soviet diplomat in Warsaw and a chekist in Belarus, and the bombings of a Leningrad Communist Party club and the Lubianka reception room.

The more the émigrés proved that they were too weak and disunited to be any threat to the Soviet regime, the more OGPU nurtured Stalin's obsessions. His suspicions fed by the first defectors from his inner circle, Stalin decided that no citizen who fled the Soviet Union should be left unpunished; no activists among the White army in exile should be left alive. On New Year's Day 1928 Stalin's personal secretary Boris Bazhanov slipped across the Iranian border, evading his GPU pursuers. He wrote a sensational memoir of his time in Stalin's office, but lived. Shortly afterward Georgi Agabekov, OGPU resident in Turkey, also defected and wrote a book about the Cheka; it took nine years for Stalin's killers to reach him.

Stalin was hindered by his diplomats, especially by Chicherin, who reminded him how badly he needed capitalist financial credits and technology, from taking violent action against all defectors and ill-wishers abroad. Although in 1927 Britain broke off relations because of Soviet support for the General Strike, Weimar Germany and the Soviet Union enjoyed throughout the 1920s a close but covert military relationship. There was also an understanding between the Abwehr and OGPU. In the early 1920s, Atatürk's Turkey and the Soviet Union had together fought off dismemberment by the British and French, though this friendship turned sour when Atatürk suppressed Turkish communists. For seven years, the Soviet secret services and military had intervened in China, in the strife between the Kuomintang, communists, and warlords. OGPU had also kidnapped the Cossack leader Boris Annenkov and a White general.[28] OGPU's success in China collapsed when the Soviet resident Mikhail Borodin, with Stalin's approval, backed a communist coup, against diplomatic and military advice. Chiang Kai-shek slaughtered the Shanghai communists and—to cries of "I told you so" from Trotsky—Soviet influence in China evaporated. Only in Poland did OGPU mount successful attacks. In 1923 Józef Unszlicht took pleasure in blowing up the Warsaw citadel where he had been a prisoner; the explosion killed over a hundred and nearly obliterated Warsaw's Jewish quarter.

Russian émigrés and defectors were concentrated in France, which also had a large communist movement and became OGPU's main base. In February 1927 the French Sûreté arrested over one hundred Soviet agents, but the French government stopped short of a full purge lest it harm trade with the USSR. In 1928 and 1929 two cautious émigré leaders in France, General Piotr Vrangel and Grand Duke Nikolai Nikolaievich, died; the Russian General Warriors' Union was now led by General Aleksandr Kutiopov, whose slogan was, "We cannot wait for the death of Bolshevism, we must annihilate it." In January 1930 Kutiopov was kidnapped by OGPU agents and delivered in a wooden box to a Soviet cargo boat waiting offshore. He died from the chloroform that the kidnappers used.

OGPU corrupted many in the Russian diaspora: General Nikolai Skoblin, fallen on hard times, was induced by his wife, the singer Nadezhda Plevitskaia, a woman of no political convictions or scruples, to help OGPU kidnap other Tsarist generals; the businessman Sergei Tretiakov was offered concessions in Russia if he handed over to OGPU refugees and defectors who sought his help. Other émigrés were exploited: the Tsar's ambassador to London Nikolai Sablin sent to another former Tsarist ambassador, Mikhail Giers, better information on British foreign policy than any Soviet agent could obtain; copies went to Moscow. OGPU usually managed to smooth over the diplomatic rows provoked by trails of corpses across France and Switzerland. Their expertise in political murders had no peer among international secret services.

Menzhinsky was busy with fodder for show trials; his deputy Iagoda was repressing the kulaks and turning overflowing concentration camps into a pool of slave labor. Meer Trilisser ran foreign operations in 1930. Trilisser had organized terror in the civil war in Siberia and despised Iagoda as an "office rat." Their quarreling, and Stalin's dislike of the bespectacled, giggling Jewish chekist, led to Trilisser leaving OGPU.

While Trotsky was in Alma-Ata, OGPU summarized for Stalin hundreds of letters and telegrams that linked him to a network of unrepentant supporters. Menzhinsky then stopped Trotsky's correspondence, arrested his courier, and forbade Trotsky even to shoot pheasants around the city. Trotsky was cut off from his younger daughter, Nina, who, harassed by the police and refused medical help, died of tuberculosis in June 1928. Stalin wanted Trotsky out of the country but Politburo members balked at setting such a precedent for the treatment of a former leader. Stalin spoke mildly: "I propose to send him abroad. If he comes to his senses, the way back won't be barred."

Only Turkey agreed to accept such a notorious deportee. On December 16, 1928, OGPU called on Trotsky and told him that they were raising "the question of a change of address for you." A month later Trotsky was transported across Russia, avoiding railway stations where demonstrations might be held. Trotsky protested by calling his towel Iagoda and his socks Menzhinsky. He, his wife, and elder son were delivered to Istanbul where, after an unhappy stay in the Soviet consulate, he was allotted a magnificent brick villa in which Sultan Abdul Hamid's chief of security had once lived, on the island of Büyükada in the Sea of Marmara.

Menzhinsky's and Iagoda's mistake was to let Trotsky take most of his archive. That archive, despite raids by Stalin's agents, gave ammunition to Trotsky for a ten-year propaganda barrage. During his four years on Büyükada, Trotsky was a magnet not just for OGPU's agents but for dissident socialists, Soviet and European. Iakov Bliumkin, forgiven for murdering the German ambassador in 1918 and now OGPU's most flamboyant agent, was operating, as Sultan-Zadeh, in Istanbul, trading in Hebrew incunabula (he spoke fluent Hebrew, Turkish, and Persian). In 1923 Bliumkin had worked in Trotsky's secretariat, editing articles on the civil war to reflect the glory of Trotsky's command of the Red Army. Bliumkin remained, despite the danger, so drawn to Trotsky that he not only visited him, but took back to Moscow a letter from Trotsky instructing his supporters how to act.

Bliumkin thus became a hare to his own hounds. His mistress was set up to ensnare him, and a former Trotskyist whom he told about the letter denounced him to Stalin. Bliumkin shaved off his beard, hijacked a car, but was caught and interrogated—"with prejudice," as Stalin instructed. The sentence was dictated by Stalin to Menzhinsky. Iagoda coopted his hated rival Trilisser, Bliumkin's protector, onto the OGPU troika that condemned Bliumkin. Menzhinsky and Iagoda outvoted him and imposed the first death sentence carried out for Trotskyism. In autumn 1929 Bliumkin had thus made history again as the first senior OGPU man to be killed by Stalin. The rest of OGPU drew its conclusions.

Otherwise, deporting Trotsky was a success. His supporters were demoralized and Trotskyists in the USSR could now only carp at the "empirical" (i.e., brutally inefficient) way in which Stalin's henchmen were carrying out the policies they had advocated. Some Trotskyists were tired of provincial exile and, like Kamenev and Zinoviev a year earlier, wanted to worm their way back into power and the metropolis. If Stalin stopped using Article 58 of the criminal code (anti-Soviet crimes from agitation to treason) against them, they would reunite with the party. Four of Trotsky's supporters announced a "rupture, in ideas and organization, from Trotskyism": Ivan Smirnov, who had opposed Stalin since 1923; Ivar Smilga, a libertarian Latvian; Evgeni Preobrazhensky, who with Trotsky had opposed the Brest-Litovsk treaty and who had overseen the killing of the Tsar and his family; the party's wit and cynic Karl Radek.[29]

Stalin did not deign to speak personally to penitent Trotskyists. Emelian Iaroslavsky, secretary to the party's Central Control Commission, Stalin's panegyrist and nicknamed for his militant atheism "the Soviet priest," had them sign a public recantation. Not all Trotskyists gave in. The Bulgarian communist Khristian Rakovsky, who had been Soviet ambassador to Britain and France and felt that, despite being exiled to Saratov, he was shielded by his prestige in the Comintern, demanded democratic discussion within the party. Some 500 "oppositionists" in ninety-five labor colonies and prisons supported Rakovsky's demand, but by shooting Iakov Bliumkin, the messenger, Stalin and Iagoda had made contact with Trotsky a capital offense.

In 1929 Stalin's fiftieth birthday was celebrated with sycophantic posters and eulogies. Stalin stopped mediating between left and right and veering from one to the other. He named 1929 the year of the "great turnabout" (*perelom*— the word also means fracture). In April the first five-year plan of industrialization began, incorporating the projects that Stalin had denounced, when Trotsky put them forward, as absurd: "As if a peasant who'd saved a few kopecks for a new plow were to go and buy himself a gramophone." Economists knew what was demanded of them: they proposed doubling in five years the output of coal, steel, electricity, and gold. Stalin took the wildly optimistic figures and doubled them again, campaigning to achieve the five-year plan in four.

New ways were needed to approach these targets. Foreign invest-
ment, given Stalin's hostility to foreigners as saboteurs, played a minor
part, although Henry Ford greedily offered assembly lines for tractors
and trucks. Capital reserves were too small. In the world depression,
Russia's oil and timber fetched less than ever. Grain had to be taken
from the peasants even more ruthlessly. Russia had vast reserves of coal,
gold, and rare minerals in its frozen far north, but even the one and a
half million unemployed in the cities could not be lured there. Despite
the losses of the First World War and the civil war, Russia had labor in
plenty—but it had to be forced.

Enslaving the Peasantry

> And behold, seven other kine came up after them out of the
> river, ill-favored and leanfleshed; and stood by the . . .
> brink of the river. And the ill-favored and leanfleshed kine
> did eat up the seven well-favored and fat kine. So Pharaoh
> awoke.
>
> *Genesis 41: 3–4*

STALIN'S CAMPAIGN of 1929 against the peasantry might be seen by a
cold-blooded cynic as a long-overdue cure for an overpopulated countryside. In the nineteenth century Europe had sent surplus peasantry to
its colonies. In the twentieth century Stalin had Siberia and Kazakhstan
to absorb the peasants of Russia and the Ukraine who, despite the terrible mortality of the civil war, were still too numerous for the land to support. The suffering that ensued has few parallels in human history; it can
only be compared in its scale and monstrosity with the African slave
trade. But whereas the British, French, Spanish, and Portuguese took
200 years to transport some 10 million souls into slavery, and kill about
2 million of them, Stalin matched this figure in a matter of four years.

This was an act of unprecedented monstrosity, and the almost total
silence and indifference of Europe and America to the fate of the Russian peasantry suggests that the rest of the world, like Lenin, Stalin, and

Menzhinsky, considered the Russian peasant hardly human. The Nazi persecution of the Jews began as Stalin completed his genocide of the Russian peasant. We are still shocked today by Europe's connivance at Nazi racism but, compared with Europe's indifference to the introduction of slave labor in Russia and to the eradication of the Russian peasant, its murmurs about Nazi atrocities seem like an outcry. The Soviet authorities tried to confine journalists and diplomats to Moscow but could not stop them looking at the countryside from train windows; nor could it prevent foreign technicians working on projects in the provinces from talking. A few European journalists—Nikolaus Basseches in Germany, Gareth Jones and Malcolm Muggeridge in England—reported accurately and extensively, but their voices were drowned by the disgracefully bland reassurances of such experts as the British professor Sir Bernard Pares or the American journalist Walter Duranty that nothing untoward was happening. Some journalists, notably Duranty, had been suborned by Iagoda and retailed Stalin's propaganda not just to secure privileged access to commissars but also to avoid unpleasant revelations about their own activities.

Stalin, the party, and OGPU were not worried. Apparently, putting a dozen foreign technologists on trial hurt Soviet prestige, but enslaving and exterminating millions of Russian and Ukrainian peasants did not. In January 1929 the Politburo instructed Menzhinsky, Nikolai Ianson (then commissar for justice), and Krylenko to combine forces, "to ensure maximum speed in carrying out repressions of kulak terrorists."[30] In May a Politburo resolution entitled "On the use of the labor of criminal convicts," strictly secret and signed by Stalin, was addressed to Iagoda in OGPU and to Krylenko in the prosecutor's office. It runs: "To move to a system of mass exploitation for pay of labor by criminal convicts with a sentence of less than three years in the regions of Ukhta, Indigo, etc."[31] In July "concentration camps" became "corrective labor camps"; the GULAG came of age.

In April 1930 Stanisław Messing, Menzhinsky's deputy and a Polish veteran of the suppression of the Kronstadt uprising, set up a vast economic empire. Its nominal head was Lazar Kogan, who had run OGPU's border guards; Kogan's deputies were Matvei Berman, the most ruthless exploiter of unskilled labor in history, who would at the age of thirty-four take over the GULAG, and Iakov Rapoport, one of just two GULAG pioneers who would survive Stalin.

Most of the inmates who flowed into these camps were not convicts, but "socially dangerous elements" by OGPU's criteria: kulaks of the first category, in other words prosperous farmers who might resist dispossession. Arrests and deportations at first nearly overwhelmed the system. Menzhinsky and Iagoda atoned for their mishandling of the first show trials and of Trotsky's departure by taking energetic measures to provide a pool of labor, albeit unskilled, for the mines of the far north. Iagoda's strategy, which Stalin backed, was to change the raison d'être of OGPU's empire from a political to an economic one. Political prisoners had formerly been idle playthings for sadistic, disgraced Cheka officers. As Menzhinsky sickened, Iagoda took the initiative and replaced feral camp administrations with more subservient ones; he directed prisoners' physical strength into whatever earned, or saved, foreign currency: logging, mining, and finally massive construction projects like the White Sea canal.

Arrests and executions carried out by OGPU soared: 162,726 persons were arrested in 1929, mostly for "counterrevolutionary activity," 2,109 were shot, some 25,000 were sent to camps and as many again into exile. In 1930 arrests doubled to a third of a million and executions increased tenfold to 20,000.[32] The camps received over 100,000. By 1934 there would be half a million slave laborers. The camp economies, with their terrible mortality and relentless thirst for expendable laborers, would come to dictate the number of arrests.

Stalin's five-year plan involved urbanization, and depopulating the countryside was the obvious method. The grain requisitioning of 1928 and the taxation that had beggared every farmer gave the peasantry no incentive to stay on the land and the state continued to pillage and terrorize the countryside. The "great turnabout" announced by Stalin in November 1929, a program of total collectivization in grain-producing regions, was the next step. Collectivization had been officially under way since 1921, but less than 5 percent of peasants had joined, even on paper, collective farms.

Skirmishes escalated into civil war in the winter of 1929–30, with hundreds of thousands of peasants armed with pitchforks and shotguns against OGPU paramilitaries with machine guns. In many areas, despite Menzhinsky's fears about their loyalties, Red Army units used artillery and aerial bombardment. In the Ukraine, the civil war commanders Iona Iakir and Vitali Primakov led punitive raids. All resistance, even demonstrations in which communist activists were merely beaten up, was met with overwhelming force. A few army men defected to the peasantry and on one occasion pilots were shot for refusing to bomb rebellious villages. Even OGPU men revolted: in March 1930, in the Altai mountains of Siberia, Fiodor Dobytin, the district GPU plenipotentiary, arrested eighty-nine party members, shot nine of them, and liberated 400 imprisoned kulaks, whom he armed with rifles.[33]

The last opposition in the Politburo, Bukharin and his liberal economists, was gagged, while the capitalist world, indifferent to the holocaust, seemed happy to sell machinery and technology for Soviet industrialization. Stalin did as he wished. Targets for collectivization were stepped up as the process became irreversible. Over 27,000 party activists were mobilized. Molotov urged Stalin to even more severe measures and in mid-January 1930 took overall charge, on a commission with Krylenko, Iagoda, and one of OGPU's most bestial men, Efim Evdokimov.

These men were interested only in class war, in eradicating kulaks, although less than 2.5 percent of Russia's peasantry were prosperous enough to be classified as such. But Iagoda, Evdokimov, and Krylenko marked out over 5 percent of peasants for destitution, deportation, and, in many cases, extermination. Kulaks were divided into three categories: "hostile"—to be shot or put in camps, "dangerous"—to be exiled to nonarable land in the far north or to Kazakhstan, and "not posing a threat"—to be dispossessed and released in their own region. By the end of January 1930, Molotov's commission had put 210,000 households, 1.5 million human beings, in the first two categories. Kulaks were evicted into the freezing winter, their neighbors forbidden under pain of sharing their fate to give them food or shelter. Their money—even their savings books—was confiscated together with any property not in their hands or on their backs. Those that survived the trains to Siberia were at the mercy of one of OGPU's most vicious chiefs, Leonid Zakovsky, who had not built even shacks to house them.

On paper the campaign was a success: by mid-February 1930 Molotov was able to report that some 13.5 million households—over half of the peasantry—had handed over land, livestock, and tools to collective farms. Given that the kulaks had left everything behind, the poor and middle peasantry should have prospered since they now had more arable land and equipment per head. Some poor peasants were given warm clothes and shoes stripped from kulaks—gifts that Iagoda hoped might win their loyalty. In fact, many collective farms existed only on paper, in regions where all that had happened was decimation of the population and disruption of the economy. The peasantry slaughtered that winter half the draft and meat animals in the country. "For the first time they are eating all the meat they want," commented a Red Army officer. But the promised tractors had not been built, and when they were many did not work—and now there were often no horses to pull the plows.

The fate of those left on the land was grim; that of the kulaks was as horrific as the fate of Poland's Jews under Hitler—"Auschwitz without ovens" as one survivor later put it—the only saving grace being Iagoda's improvised tactics which left enterprising or lucky kulaks with the hope of escaping death. Iagoda's letter to his subordinates Stanisław Messing and Gleb Bokii had a Stalinist logic: "The kulak understands splendidly that collectivization of the countryside means that he must perish, he will resist all the more desperately and viciously, which we see in the villages. From planned uprisings to counterrevolutionary kulak organizations and terrorist acts."[34] The kulak, Iagoda argued, must have "his back broken" by spring. Gleb Bokii was to organize more camps and locate wildernesses, some well above the Arctic Circle, where deported kulaks could be left unguarded to die, out of earshot or sight, of starvation, cold, and disease.

There were difficulties in moving over a million peasants. Trains of cattle trucks—each train carrying up to 2,000 deportees and watched over by guards who killed at the slightest provocation—crawled over Russia's railways, already overloaded in a country virtually without motor roads. The inhabitants of provincial cities were horrified by the spectacle at their railway stations of crowds of starving and louse-ridden kulaks, middle peasants who had been rounded up to meet the targets, and poor peasants classified as "subkulaks" for expressing pity for the kulaks. Urban workers steeled themselves to walk over corpses on the pavements. OGPU was worried only when areas hitherto unscathed were panicked by tales of what was about to happen.

At all times Stalin knew in detail what was happening. Iagoda gathered almost daily for Stalin and Molotov statistics from all over the country on arrests, deportations, executions. Naive young communists wrote letters describing the sickening atrocities on the trains to Siberia and in the Arctic tundra. To counter resistance, more OGPU cadets and frontier guards were rushed in. Food, tools, even barbed wire failed to arrive; there was no funding. Junior OGPU officials, motivated by fear of responsibility rather than pity for their victims, complained about the Commissariat of Trade, which failed to provide food. Even the theoretical rations per adult kulak could not stave off death in unheated barracks in a Russian winter: 300 grams of bread, 195 grams of potatoes, 100 grams of cabbage, 75 grams of salt herring—1,300 calories.

In the south the liquidation of the kulaks turned into ethnic warfare as Don Cossacks who had survived the 1920 genocide were murdered as kulaks by their impoverished neighbors, Ukrainian peasants. All over the north Caucasus "spontaneous" atrocities, spurred on by OGPU, flared up: Cossacks were burned alive in cinemas, Chechen shepherds and beekeepers were gunned down as "bandits." Frinovsky, head of OGPU's border guards, arrived to quell national uprisings, allegedly provoked by kulaks. He reported, after putting the uprisings down, that corpses choked the rivers flowing into the Caspian Sea. A few communities were hard to crack: the million German farmers who had lived for two centuries on the left bank of the Volga rallied behind their church pastors. Not until 1941 were Stalin's men able to dispossess the Volga Germans. Inspired by their mullahs, the Tatars also withstood attempts to separate out the kulaks, but they could not hold off OGPU, and dreadful retribution was exacted.

The Ukraine suffered worst, for anti-Muscovite feeling fueled resistance so widespread that it took Stalin two years to devise adequate reprisals. There was more violent resistance in the Ukraine than in the rest of the Soviet Union; of all kulaks deported, a quarter were Ukrainian.

There were now virgin lands in Kazakhstan on which to begin an arable experiment; they were won, like the American west, by exterminating the nomads who had lived on them for centuries. Unlike the American west, however, Kazakhstan received new settlers with no money, clothes, seed corn, or tools, and many would freeze or starve to death. Other Kazakhs fled with their animals into China. Perhaps 2 million emigrated, even though their fellow Kazakhs in China had no pasture to spare, and half of the refugees died.

The information dam erected around the country by OGPU still leaked. Until 1935, when rural post offices stopped accepting letters for abroad, Cossacks wrote to their relatives scattered from Uruguay to China. But Westerners in general were too gullible or indifferent to protest about the holocaust among the Russian peasantry and Cossacks. As one Kuban Cossack wrote to his relatives abroad: "Various delegations come from abroad, all communists of course. They are fed well and told stories. If they see people queueing and ask why, 'our' lot explain that these are poor people come for a free meal. And the foreigners go home and probably talk about miracles in the land of the Soviets."

In 1930 a Terek Cossack woman described to an émigré cousin her life over the last ten years:

> You reproach us for not writing to you, but we'd be glad to have a correspondence, except it's impossible. You probably heard we were deported in 1922. . . . We were scattered over the wide world, each going where he could, to the Ingush, the Chechens, Osetians, Georgians—so that we relatives don't see each other. . . . Your family was chased out in 1923 and on the night of December 10 outside Grozny all six were shot, but S. was killed right on the street. The next morning all your farm was looted—the house was blown up, the sheds, barns and gates went to the Chechens. . . . When we were expelled we wrote to you that many had died, they were all shot.
>
> Our Cossack station has been divided into three categories. "Whites"—the males have been shot and the women and children scattered wherever they could save themselves. The second category is "reds"—they were deported, but not harmed. And the third, "communists." Nobody in the first category was given anything, reds were allotted one cart per family to take every-

thing they wanted, while communists had the right to take over all their movable property. . . . Don't send any money, because the collective farm gets it and we just sign for it. Our deported men are in the infantry and very few come home—everyone says they've died.[35]

Ordinary peasants could write only to party bosses or the newspapers, and Soviet newspapers referred letters they did not print to OGPU. Kulaks had nothing to lose—they wrote to Stalin. For instance:

Dekulakization happens like this: 15 people come at night and take everything. They stole pickled berries, salted gherkins and even the meat from the saucepan. They ripped my only fur coat off me, I resisted and was arrested on the spot. . . . Many people perished when the kulaks were deported, at –40° they took families by horse-drawn cart to Tiumen and Tobolsk. In Tobolsk alone about 3,000 are buried, these are completely innocent victims, it is like the order that King Herod once gave to slaughter babies under six months. . . . Comrades Bukharin, Rykov, Frumkin and Tomsky are right, they know peasant life and peasant thinking better than you.[36]

Molotov was well pleased with the campaign of 1929–30. All targets were exceeded, many by well over 100 percent: 140,000 had been arrested, twice the figure suggested by the Central Committee at the end of January; the far north had received 70,000 deportees for slave labor in mines and forests, twice the number budgeted for. Twice as much grain as targeted had been requisitioned, leaving even the remaining poor and middle peasants with too little to eat, let alone to sow in spring. The monetary supply was under control, by annulling kulaks' savings and confiscating their silver.

Iagoda's final report on liquidating the kulak, circulated to the Politburo on March 15, 1931, is a proud compilation of disgraceful figures.[37] The party and police had nearly lost control: in 1929 and 1930 thousands of anti-Soviet leaflets and posters had circulated, some 14,000 mass demonstrations and 20,000 acts of "terrorist violence" had occurred, and there had been 3,000 incidents of grain being burned rather than handed over. Resistance reached its peak in March 1930. The figures reported by Iagoda omit atrocities in the north Caucasus, the Urals, and Siberia, and OGPU's 20,000 executions omit the slaughter of women and children in villages which offered armed resistance. In 1929 the Buriat Mongols, despite their Buddhist faith, rose up. Their own historians agree on a figure of 35,000 Buriats shot in the course of "pacification." Figures for Bashkirs, Chechens, and Cossacks are still guesswork. To judge by OGPU's informants, the peasantry were bewildered about what political course to take. Some shouted their support for Bukharin, Rykov, and Tomsky, acclaim which helped to doom the right in Stalin's eyes; some called for the Industrial Party (an invention of Stalin and Menzhinsky) to assume power. In remote areas, kulaks resorted to partisan warfare against OGPU and the collective farms.

No wonder that Stalin later told Churchill in 1945 that collectivization had caused him more anxiety than the Second World War. To stem the chaos, Stalin blamed his subordinates for misleading him. Russian tsars had defused popular resentment by accusing their ministers of pulling the wool over their eyes. A desperate peasantry, unable to conceive of a mind so evil that it would deliberately inflict so much suffering, believed a god who blamed his fallen angels. There was no longer a left or right "deviation" to blame, although they would be resurrected as bogeymen and scapegoats, so Stalin blamed his overenthusiastic subordinates. His article "Giddiness from Success" in *Pravda* on March 2, 1930, signaled that the worst was over. "Collective farms cannot be imposed by force. . . . Who needs these distortions, this bureaucratic decreeing of a collective movement, these unworthy threats against the peasants? Nobody but our enemies." Then came an equally hypocritical decree from the Politburo, "On the struggle against distortions of the party line in the collectivization movement." The peasantry were so encouraged by these texts that they deserted the collective farms. By summer 1930 the country was only 20 percent collectivized. Peasants left the collectives, even though they lost the animals and tools they had brought with them and were then allotted the worst land to farm.

The activists who had followed instructions from Stalin, Molotov, and Iagoda did not understand the shift in tactics and were nonplussed by this ungrateful disavowal. They were reluctant to apologize to the peasantry but Stalin judged that party discipline required testing the obedience of his subordinates.

There could be no real going back. Land had been redistributed (and often left fallow), houses burned, horses slaughtered, families split up, and heads of households killed. At least half a million people were facing malnutrition in camps or "special settlements," and a million dispossessed kulaks begged for food, bribed officials for new papers, or sought work in the towns. OGPU's own reports stressed the hopelessness in barracks in Astrakhan and Vologda, where 20,000 former kulaks were dying of typhus and hunger. Tens of thousands of victims, particularly middle peasants caught up in the waves of arrests, appealed to the judiciary. A few thousand were freed from the camps and sought work in the enormous building sites springing up in the Urals and on European Russia's rivers.

OGPU recorded executions that followed a written sentence but left uncounted deaths with no paper trail. For want of censuses in the early 1930s, the mortality of the first collectivization campaign has to be guessed. The figures point to a catastrophe even before the terrible famine of 1932–3: a drop in the birthrate from 45 to 32 per thousand between 1928 and 1932, and a climb in the death rate with 620,000 more deaths in 1931 than in 1928. The groundwork for the famine, the greatest demographic catastrophe to hit the peasantry in Europe since the Middle Ages, was laid by Stalin in 1929, for the survivors were so weakened, physically, morally, economically, that they were doomed to die. For want of horses, women pulled plows; there was precious little grain and, with half the livestock slaughtered, no meat.

But Stalin had stepped back simply in order to advance much further. In September 1930 he told Mikoyan to force the tempo of grain exports to "establish our position on the international market" and instructed his faithful acolyte Poskriobyshev, the secretary of the secret section of the Central Committee, to receive warmly the American engineer Hugh L. Cooper, who would accept increased grain exports from the USSR in exchange for help with producing tractors. By 1931, from a starving countryside, over 5 million tons of grain was being exported to pay for turbines, assembly lines, mining machinery, and the funding of communist parties all over Europe, Asia, and America.

The silence of the West, which emerged from its economic depression at least partly as a result of orders from the Soviet Union paid for by the blood of millions of peasants, is a blot on our civilization. Diplomats and journalists may well have shared Stalin's view that the Russian peasant was a subhuman brute; Western businessmen were eager for the contracts that Soviet industrialization was bringing their way. As the late British historian Christopher Hill said seventy years later of the Ukraine in 1933: "I saw no famine."

The silence of the Russian intelligentsia, bludgeoned and cajoled by OGPU and the party, is more excusable. When writing about the civil war, Soviet novelists and poets could talk of atrocities on both sides and mourn the waste, but on this second civil war there was no leeway. Nevertheless, a handful of Russian poets could not blind themselves to what everyone knew was happening. The young poet Nikolai Zabolotsky lost his freedom and his health for speaking of the horrors in his ironically entitled "Triumph of Agriculture": he let the Russian peasant protest through the mouth of a horse:

> People! You are wrong to believe that I cannot cogitate, if you thrash me with a stick, after putting a breast band on my neck. A peasant, his legs gripping me, gallops, lashing horribly with the *knut,* and I gallop, though ugly, my hungry mouth gasping for air. All around nature is dying, the world is rocking, impoverished, flowers are dying, weeping, swept away by a blow of the legs.

The Peasantry: The Final Solution

IN FEBRUARY 1933 Stalin told a congress of handpicked peasants that the collective farms had snatched at least 20 million of them from the clutches of the kulak and pauperdom. Each household, Stalin promised, would have one cow, once the kulaks were finished off. Stalin's final words ring true, read with or without irony: "This is an achievement such as the world has never known before and which no other state in the world has tried to achieve."

Stalin told Churchill that collectivization cost 10 million lives. OGPU counted the deaths by starvation and disease only for a few months; they kept records only of peasants shot, arrested, or deported as kulaks, their mortality rates, their escapes, their recapture. A few registry offices in the worst-affected areas along the Volga kept track of who died from what. In some villages and Cossack stations, abashed officials and a few courageous peasants tried to keep a toll. Today's statisticians can estimate the losses from the age and sex structure of the generation that lived through this catastrophe. Another basis for calculation is the difference between the population predicted in 1926 for 1937 and the real figures (some 20 million less) obtained in 1937 by the census takers—they were shot for their honesty. Allowing for famine, violence, hypothermia, and epidemics caused by the disruption, the number of excess deaths between 1930 and 1933 attributable to collectivization lies between a conservative 7.2 and a plausible 10.8 million.

The surviving peasants were enslaved for two generations. On December 27, 1932, the Soviet state issued internal passports to its citizens but not to the peasants, who were left unable to leave their collective farms. For them the civil war had come back, but with no Whites or Greens to defend them. Provincial towns suffered, too: refugees brought epidemics of typhus—there were nearly a million cases in 1932. Food shortages in many cities made ration cards meaningless. Rickets, scurvy, and dysentery killed children; in many areas more than half the infants under one year old died.

The kulaks began dying the moment they were dispossessed: in trains that took them north and east, over 3 percent died of disease and privation. Despite the annual influx of deportees, the population of the "labor settlements" actually fell from 1932 to 1935. Of 1,518,524 kulaks in exile in 1932, nearly 90,000 died.[38] The following year was worse: 150,000—13 percent of deportees—died and a quarter of the escapees were recaptured. Only in 1934 did mortality drop below 10 percent. The death rate in Iagoda's labor camps gave prisoners a one-in-three chance of surviving a ten-year sentence. Not counting the victims of the Great

Terror, in the 1930s, over 2 million persons were deported to labor settlements in hitherto uninhabited areas of the north and Siberia. Kulaks were followed by the inhabitants of frontier zones and other undesirables. Of the 2 million, well over 400,000 died, including 50,000 "repressed" by OGPU and the NKVD, and over 600,000 fled into anonymity or to the building sites of the Urals and Siberia (a third of these were recaptured). To the casualties of the subsequent famine, we have to add half a million kulaks who died outside the grain-producing regions.

Stalin had full reports from commissariats, party, and OGPU. All June, July, and August of 1930, 1931, and 1932 he spent recuperating on the Black Sea coast, supervising Kaganovich and Molotov by courier and telegram. In August 1933 he went south again for a two-month break, traveling slowly by train, riverboat, and car, taking a week to pass through the worst-affected regions. Stalin saw abandoned villages, victims of famine and of typhus epidemics. "Koba," Voroshilov wrote to Abel Enukidze, "like a sponge, kept soaking it all up and there and then, after a little reflection, sketched out a series of measures."[39]

Politburo members were flooded with protests: on June 18, 1932, a twenty-year-old Ukrainian Communist Youth activist wrote to Stanislav Kosior, the Ukrainian party secretary:

> Imagine what is now being done around Belaia Tserkov, Uman, Kiev, etc. Enormous areas of fallow land . . . In the collective farms where there were 100–150 horses there are now only 40–50 and those are falling down. The population is starving terribly. . . . Tens and hundreds of cases when collective farmers go to the fields and vanish and a few days later the corpse is found and without pity, as if it were quite normal, is buried in a pit, and the next day they find the corpse of the man who buried the first one. . . .[40]

Kosior was so shaken that he held back the grain that Moscow demanded from his starving region. This damned him in Stalin's eyes and for the time being he was demoted to deputy commissar for heavy industry.

Stalin did not relent. He gave detailed instructions to intensify the campaign: "deport from Kuban region in twenty days 2,000 rich kulak families who are maliciously preventing sowing," he instructed Kaganovich on November 22, 1932.[41] In December Stalin and Molotov told Iagoda, Evdokimov, the army commander Ian Gamarnik, and the secretary of the lower Volga region, Boris Sheboldaev, to expel from a north Caucasus Cossack station, "the most counterrevolutionary, all inhabitants except for those genuinely devoted to Soviet power . . . and to settle this area with conscientious Red Army collective farmers who have too little land or bad lands in other regions, handing them the land, the winter wheat, buildings, deadstock and livestock of the deportees."[42] Sheboldaev had to commandeer railway depots to cope with this resettlement. He complained to Kaganovich that the peasants who were starving to death were concealing grain hoards, that out of sheer malice they were letting their horses and cows die of starvation.

Stalin conceded a few adjustments to give peasants incentives to produce a surplus for the market, but the hungry were kept away from food. On September 16, 1932, Stalin's draconian law "of five ears of corn" came into force. To stop uprooted kulaks from "shattering our new structures," it punished by death or prison any peasant taking just a handful of grain or a cabbage from the land for themselves. Capitalism, Stalin argued, overcame feudalism by making private property sacrosanct; socialism must overcome capitalism by making public property "inviolable." Under this law within a year 6,000 had been shot and tens of thousands imprisoned—prison at least held out the prospect of daily rations for the thieves.[43]

At Stalin's behest, Menzhinsky concentrated on procuring grain from the starving regions and seeing that OGPU got it to the ports or, if there was no cover and no transport, that the peasantry were prevented from looting the piles of grain rotting in the rain. Menzhinsky's part in the famine of 1931–3 makes him responsible for more deaths than can be laid at the door of Dzierżyński, Iagoda, Ezhov, or Beria. Iagoda, unlike Menzhinsky, was shaken by the enormity of what OGPU had enabled Stalin to do. On October 26, 1931, he wrote to Rudzutak, then commissar for the Workers' and Peasants' Inspectorate:

The sickness rate and mortality of the deportees is too great. . . .
The monthly mortality equals 1.3 percent in Northern Kazakhstan and 0.8 percent in the Narym [Siberia] region. Among
those that have died there are a particularly high number of
younger children. Thus of those below 3 years old 8–12 percent
of the group has died every month, while in Magnitogorsk it has
been even more, up to 15 percent a month. It must be noted that
on the whole the high mortality is not due to epidemic illnesses
but to the lack of arrangements for housing and equipping these
people, and child mortality climbs because of the absence of the
necessary food.[44]

Menzhinsky and Iagoda had from the north Caucasus figures for
deaths from starvation and disease and for cannibals or corpse eaters. In
March 1933 they were informed:

Citizen Gerasimenko ate the corpse of her dead sister. Under interrogation Gerasimenko declared that for a month she had
lived on various rubbish, not even having vegetables. . . . Citizen
Doroshenko, after the death of his father and mother was left
with infant sisters and brothers, ate the flesh of his brothers and
sisters when they died of hunger. . . . In the cemetery up to 30
corpses have been found, thrown out at night, some gnawed at
by dogs. . . . several coffins have been found from which the
corpses have disappeared. . . . In Sergienko's apartment was
found the corpse of a little girl with the legs cut off, and boiled
meat. . . .[45]

For once, Menzhinsky and Iagoda's men—Georgi Molchanov, who had
organized terror in the north Caucasus and now headed OGPU's secret
political sector, and Genrikh Liushkov, Molchanov's deputy and later a
defector to Japan—decided not to punish the cannibals, and requested
food, medicine, and doctors to be sent. In other areas, Molchanov and
Liushkov found that even working collective farmers were dying: "On
March 16 farmer Trigub, an activist, 175 days' work credited, died of
hunger. He applied several times to the farm administration for an issue

of food, but received no help. For the same reason groom Shcherbina (185 days' work) and carpenter Volvach died."[46]

Not only the authorities were brutalized. Surviving peasants turned on each other and the starving. In summer 1933 a GPU man from the north Caucasus reported:

> On Malorossiiskaia farmstead a boy was caught in a vegetable garden: he was killed there and then by the collective farmers. . . . At Ivanovskaia farmstead a cultivator and five collective farmers detained a workman on the rice farm whom they tortured, cutting off his left ear; they put his fingers in a door and broke them, then threw him alive down a well. After some time they dragged him out barely alive and threw him into another well which they filled with earth. At Petrovskaia homestead a keeper at the Stalin commune detained an unknown woman on the collective farm area for stealing ears of wheat, took her into a straw barn, tied her to a pillar and burned her and the barn. He buried the corpse where the fire was.[47]

Soviet intellectuals had to be blind and deaf not to know of these horrors. Very few even hinted at them.[48] Osip Mandelstam, safe from censorship now that he was unpublishable, noted in a short lyric of 1933 that "Nature doesn't recognize its own face, / and the terrible shades of the Ukraine and the Kuban [. . .] / On the felt earth hungry peasants / Guard the gate, not touching the handle." Nikolai Kliuev, in his vision of starving Russia *The Country of Burnt-Out Villages,* had prophesied:

> The day chirped with sparrows, when as if to go looking for mushrooms, the infant was called to the yard. For a piece of beef and liver a neighbor gutted the boy and salted him with gray salt along his birdlike ribs and sinews. From a joist under the beam an old woman washed away the blood with her mop. Then, like a vixen in a snare, she burst out barking in the storeroom. And the old woman's bark was terrible, like a lullaby, or like magpies' chattering. At midnight the grandmother's suffering rose over the poor hut in the shape of Vasia's head. Peasants, men and

women, crowded round: "Yes, the same curls and pockmarked nose!" And suddenly the mob howled at the moon for mortal guilt. Parfion howled, so did thin Egorka, and the massive wolf echoed them on the eaten-out backyards. . . .

The Ukraine suffered worst from cannibalism, a crime for which Soviet law had made no provision. Cannibals were summarily executed by OGPU.

Stalin's concern was to make sure the foreign press got no wind of these horrors. "Molotov, Kaganovich!" he wrote furiously in February 1933, "Do you know who let the American correspondents in Moscow go to the Kuban? They have cooked up some filth about the situation in the Kuban. . . . This must be put a stop to and these gentlemen must be banned from traveling all over the USSR. There are enough spies as it is. . . . "[49] Very few foreign correspondents saw the famine firsthand and their reports met with disbelief. Who in peacetime would destroy his country's peasantry?

One person was able to get Stalin's ear, and that was the young Cossack writer Mikhail Sholokhov. Stalin responded, however perfunctorily, to Sholokhov's boldness when other interventions exasperated him. Sholokhov wrote of the horrors he witnessed at his own Cossack station, Veshenskaia: he described collective farmers left destitute after grain, clothes, and houses were taken, deportees forced to sleep in the freezing cold, children shrieking, a woman with a baby at her breast begging in vain for shelter before both died of the cold. He described mass floggings, torture in frozen pits or on red-hot iron benches, mock executions, women stripped naked on the steppe. "Do you remember, Iosif Vissarionovich, Korolenko's sketch, 'In a pacified village'? Well, this 'disappearance' was done not to three peasants suspected of stealing from a kulak, but to tens of thousands of collective farmers."[50] Sholokhov hinted that if he had no response, he would use the material in his second novel, *Virgin Soil Upturned*. Stalin thanked Sholokhov and sent out Matvei Shkiriatov from the Workers' and Peasants' Inspectorate. One or two torturers from OGPU were given nominal prison sentences. Stalin told Sholokhov, "your letters create a somewhat one-sided impression . . . you have to see the other side . . . your respected Cossack farmers were being saboteurs and didn't mind leaving the workers, the Red Army without grain."

The region that suffered most from Soviet collectivization was the Mongolian People's Republic, which was in the hands of a Russian puppet, the future Marshal Khorlogiin Choibalsan, a drunken psychopath who connived at the murder of his entire Politburo. Mongolia was not just a cordon sanitaire between the Soviet Union and Japanese Manchuria; it was a laboratory in which Stalin's antireligious and anti-kulak campaigns were tested. The Buddhist lamas, a third of the adult male population of Mongolia, were slaughtered, the cattle herders dispossessed. In spring 1932, its population reduced by a third, Mongolia revolted and Stalin had to retreat. The government was partially replaced, the rebel leaders declared Japanese agents and their followers promised an amnesty; trainloads of consumer goods were sent and a squadron of aircraft repainted in Mongolian insignia was sent to bomb the insurgents.

In Russia too there were rebellions, though remarkably few. Within a day's journey of Moscow, on April 10, 1932, thousands in the town of Vichuga rose, burned down the police station, and occupied the party and GPU headquarters, seriously injuring fifteen police. Kaganovich came down to organize the reprisals. In the grain belt the new motor tractor stations became police headquarters not machinery centers. Together with OGPU, MTS "chekas" arrested kulaks, "disorganizers," and "wreckers." But even when the tractor stations had tractors available to replace dead horses and plowmen, the collective farms had no money to lease them. "I consider it impermissible," Stalin wrote to Kaganovich, "that the state spends hundreds of millions on organizing MTS to serve the collective farms and still doesn't know how much the peasantry is going to pay for their services."[51]

Down in the Ukraine what disturbed Stalin was not the deaths of millions of his subjects, but vacillating local leaders who grumbled that plans for grain procurement were "unreal." "What is this? This isn't a party, it's a parliament, a caricature of a parliament," he wrote to Kaganovich. His own brother-in-law Redens, he grumbled, was "not up to conducting the battle with counterrevolution in such a big and peculiar republic as the Ukraine."[52] Stalin claimed to fear another Polish invasion: "Piłsudski's agents in the Ukraine are not slumbering, they are much stronger than Redens or Kosior thinks. Bear in mind too that the Ukrainian Communist Party (500,000 members, ha-ha) contains quite a few (yes, quite a lot?) of rotten elements, conscious and unconscious agents of Petliura, even direct agents of Piłsudski." Stalin asked Menzhinsky to remove Stanislav Redens and put in the field the most brutal GPU man available, Balitsky. The Ukraine was to be "within the shortest time a real fortress."

By 1934 the main slaughter was over, and a relatively good harvest provided enough grain for the surviving peasants and the townspeople. Effectively, the war of Stalin, the secret police, the party, the army, and the city workers against the peasants was won. Even those who had witnessed the horror tried to put it all behind them. Sholokhov gave *Virgin Soil Upturned* a happy ending. Gorky, novelists, and filmmakers of the Soviet Union celebrated a countryside feeding industrial workers the calories they needed to build paradise. The only exception was Nikolai Zabolotsky, who imbued "The Triumph of Agriculture" with a Swiftian irony that misled the censor for a few years. Into a horse's mouth Zabolotsky put the peasant's *De profundis:*

All around nature is dying, the world is rocking, impoverished . . . now, bowlegged with pain, I hear: the heavens howl. Now a beast trembles, predestined to turn the wheel's system. I beg, reveal, reveal it, friends: are all people really lords over us?

Collectivization had brutalized victims and perpetrators to such a degree that civilized society no longer existed in the USSR. The cruelty and passivity it induced in Soviet citizens made it possible for Stalin and his hangmen to proceed to an even more violent campaign in the party and among the urban population.

FIVE

IAGODA'S RISE

. . . if you magnified an ordinary flea several thousand times you'd get the most fearful animal on earth which nobody would be strong enough to control . . . But history's monstrous grimaces produce such magnifications in the real world, too. Stalin is a flea which Bolshevik propaganda and the hypnosis of fear have magnified to unbelievable proportions.

Gorky's diary,
according to witness[1]

Toward Sole Dictatorship

The Czar can send any of his officials to Siberia, but he cannot rule without them, or against their will.

John Stuart Mill

FORCED COLLECTIVIZATION confirmed Stalin's tyranny. Not just public opinion, but the party, the Central Committee, and now the Politburo could be set aside. From 1930 onward, all power in the USSR flowed from Stalin's Kremlin office, ten minutes' walk from his chief executive agency, Menzhinsky and Iagoda's OGPU. Stalin's office, together with those of his closest circle in the Kremlin, was the nerve center from noon to about two in the morning, and spent annually nearly a million rubles on secretaries and OGPU couriers, encrypted telegrams communicating Stalin's decisions, and generous rations of food, tea, and cigarettes.[2]

Stalin entrenched himself in an office that worked better after dark. A spider at the center of a web, he was alert to any disturbance and could neutralize any threat. In the Council of People's Commissars (Sovnarkom) and in the Workers' and Peasants' Inspectorate, Stalin had only his cronies appointed. Kalinin, head of state, the last remaining leader appointed in Lenin's time, blackmailed for his promiscuity in private, his liberalism in politics, and a dossier that proved he had been an informant for the Tsar's gendarmerie, was enslaved to Stalin. Once Stalin ousted the last of the right, Rykov—"He was getting under our feet," Stalin wrote to Gorky—he made Molotov chairman of Sovnarkom, effectively prime minister. Key commissariats were in Stalinist hands: Orjonikidze controlled the super-ministry for the economy, while Voroshilov held, to the army's contempt, the Commissariat for War.[3]

All power in the Soviet Communist Party's four organs—Politburo, Secretariat, Orgburo, Central Control Commission—was in Stalin's hands. After Bukharin's removal, only vestiges of the right remained in the Politburo, which was controlled by men who never disagreed with Stalin—Molotov, Voroshilov, Kalinin—backed up by equally loyal candidate members like Andreev, Kaganovich, and Mikoyan. As general secretary, Stalin controlled the party's agendas and membership, and Stalin, Molotov, and Kaganovich—the Secretariat—formed a triumvirate that brooked no contradiction. The party's Orgburo was dominated by the same triumvirate. Stalin sat everywhere but on the Central Control Commission, which purged party membership, but since Orjonikidze was the chairman and Stalin's sycophant Iaroslavsky was a secretary, this too was Stalin's instrument.

Stalin's cronies were chosen on the same principles that a lion tamer chooses his lions: "the lion that is the most amenable . . . is the omega animal," as Yann Martel's hero remarks in *The Life of Pi*. Generally, Stalin reciprocated the loyalty of his omega animals; they remained in post even if they lost wives, brothers, and friends to the GULAG and the executioner. Ever since 1912 Stalin had sensed what others missed in Molotov, the uncommunicative pen pusher. Others knew Molotov as "stone arse" for his desk-bound outlook.[4] Molotov lacked human warmth outside his immediate family and his passion came to the fore only when he signed death warrants. Even his own underlings he protected only if he thought them irreplaceable and defensible. His initials VM also stood for *vysshaia mera* (highest measure), the death sentence; on lists of the condemned Molotov would append not just "VM" but "Bastards" or "They deserve it." Molotov remained an unapologetic believer until his death in 1986, forgiving Stalin even the arrest of his beloved wife, Polina.[5]

Lazar Kaganovich likewise surrendered his family to Stalin: his brother shot himself on learning of his impending arrest. He took over from Stalin the organizational and distributive section of the party, so that acolytes took key posts and the untrusted were sent to the ends of the earth. As Stalin's double—general secretary—in the Ukraine Kaganovich was so crass that he had to be recalled to Moscow. He was insensitive to others' suffering (his father's trade had been driving cattle to slaughter) and was vicious when it was safe to be so—he beat his crippled secretary, Misha Guberman. Kaganovich was a single-minded factotum who could govern while Stalin rested, and whose bullying forced the pace of any enterprise, such as building Moscow's underground. Kaganovich genuinely adored Stalin. Unlike Molotov, Kaganovich was embarrassed by his inability to spell or to punctuate, and unlike Molotov, who used a dry workmanlike tone, Kaganovich became more servile every year. Responding to instructions in 1932, he wrote, "Comrade Stalin, you have put the question from the party point of view so broadly and clearly that there can be no serious vacillations. And anyway you have not only the official political, but also the comradely moral right to dispose of someone whom you have formed as a politician, i.e. me, your pupil."

Of these Stalinists, only Sergo Orjonikidze had eventually to go. A fellow Georgian, Orjonikidze argued with Stalin and physically wrestled with him. His energy and self-confidence and his feudal loyalty to his protégés would lead to a head-on collision with Stalin, but for seven years, with brutality and ingenuity, he forced workers to turn some of the fantasies of the five-year plans into reality.

Two centers of power alone still evaded Stalin's control: the Red Army and OGPU. Voroshilov coped as best he could with generals more distinguished than he: the Red Army was too vital for protecting the state against imaginary foreign enemies or real peasant rebels, and the alliances with German and Chinese generals that Tukhachevsky, Iakir, and Vasili Bliukher used to modernize and train the army were beyond the competence of Stalin's acolytes to supervise. Only in 1937 was Stalin ready to crush the military. OGPU, like the Red Army, was run by men whom Stalin had not appointed, even if they worked closely with him. Menzhinsky, however ill, went to Stalin's office many times between 1928 and 1931, especially when show trials were being prepared. These meetings were not minuted but the correspondence they generated suggests they resembled a Hollywood scriptwriters' session, in which director and scriptwriter would agree on storylines and interpretations. These performers were more gladiators than actors. Pasternak, in a poem of 1932, saw Moscow like Nero's Rome: "which, / Instead of rubbish and twaddle, / Demands from the actor not a reading / But full perdition in earnest. / When a line is dictated by feeling, / It sends a slave onto the stage, / And art ends there / And soil and fate breathe."

Stalin usually saw Menzhinsky and Iagoda separately in his office as their functions were distinct. Menzhinsky dealt with words and fictions: counterintelligence, show trials, maneuvers against the left and the right in the party. Iagoda dealt with numbers and physical violence: organization, repressions, gathering incriminating evidence, exploiting convicts, mayhem, and murder. Some days when Iagoda visited, Stalin saw nobody else. On other occasions, Iagoda brought to Stalin his grimmest associates. Stanisław Messing, Gleb Bokii, and Efim Evdokimov, who had personally tortured, executed, and raped, sat with Stalin to discuss operations. The only OGPU officials who disgusted Stalin were those who handled foreign intelligence. Meer Trilisser was rarely admitted, and Artuzov was not invited until 1933, when Hitler's advent to power forced Stalin to talk personally to OGPU's foreign department.

Despite hours closeted together, Stalin kept Iagoda at a distance. Iagoda was related by blood, marriage, and friendship to circles hostile to Stalin, both left and right. By 1930 Stalin had for Iagoda's post his own candidates. So far they merely monitored OGPU; very soon they would oversee and then veto and eventually direct it. At no point, however, did Stalin foresee a diminishing role for OGPU; when one enemy was crushed, he sought a new one.

Stalin looked on hostile elements as a homeopath views a drug: the more diluted the dose, the more powerful the effect. Stalin constantly asserted that the nearer to victory and homogeneity a socialist society was, the more desperate the battle with the remnants of capitalism and the bourgeoisie. For this reason he closely watched OGPU. In August 1931, when OGPU declared that it "remained the unsheathed sword of the working class and has accurately and skillfully smashed the enemy," Stalin put the last phrase in the present tense: "is striking at the enemy."

Stalin gathered information—the chief source of his power—not just from Menzhinsky and Iagoda but through his own channels. Through his secretariat he double-checked information from the party, the commissariats, and OGPU. His secretaries Ivan Tovstukha and Aleksandr Poskriobyshev were the only recourse for citizens to whom nobody else listened. Tovstukha, a discreet, cunning sifter of rumors, had been Stalin's trusted aide since the leader had been just commissar for ethnic minorities. Poskriobyshev channeled the information that could have inundated Stalin into a manageable flow. Unlike Tovstukha,

Poskriobyshev without demur organized and covered up murders. Stalin could not have ruled as he did without the particular unscrupulousness of Molotov and Poskriobyshev.

Bodyguards, assigned to Stalin by the operative department of OGPU, were another source of information. Karl Pauker, a hairdresser and makeup artist in the Lwów operetta when the city was in Austria-Hungary, deserted to the Russians in the First World War and headed Stalin's guard for thirteen years. An uproarious clown at Stalin's parties, Pauker told Stalin the OGPU gossip that Menzhinsky or Iagoda thought unfit to pass on.

Stalin's final information channel was the press. In 1930 Stalin replaced Bukharin as editor of *Pravda* with an Odessa Jew, Lev Mekhlis. Mekhlis had been Stalin's chief assistant in the party secretariat and, despite his Zionist background, was as valuable as Poskriobyshev, operating over a range of posts staggering for a former office boy and schoolteacher. Mekhlis made *Pravda* Stalin's mouthpiece, turgid but compulsory reading. Like Stalin's secretariat, *Pravda* was a magnet for citizens' complaints and, like OGPU, was snowed under by denunciations. Mekhlis's summaries of letters received but not printed were even more use to Stalin than those that Iagoda supplied.

By 1931 OGPU's independence was weaker. Menzhinsky's diseased back, heart, and kidneys forced him to delegate his work. In his last two years, mental distress after the death of his beloved sister Liudmila disabled him. Menzhinsky had no scruples; he had even before the revolution called the peasantry "cattle," and his Nietzschean adoration of the strong kept him loyal to Stalin, but he liked neatness in the tragedies he engineered. A Jacobean fifth act, strewn with corpses, was not his style. The ground that Menzhinsky had prepared for Stalin—staging show trials, creating the strongest foreign spying organization in history, using forced labor, getting OGPU troops to do what the Red Army might not, and, furthest from the original remit of the Cheka, repressing dissent within the party—all this would be cultivated by Iagoda, who lacked Menzhinsky's authority and was easier to command.

The scale and duration of Menzhinsky's work belies Trotsky's casual dismissal of him as an intellectual dilettante caught up with professional thugs. More intelligent than Dzierżyński, more educated than any other head of the Cheka, polite and sensitive, he was Stalin's enabler for the crucial period between the death of Lenin and the murder of Kirov, when Stalin was still working toward total control.

Bringing Up a Guard Dog

AS MENZHINSKY'S HEALTH deteriorated at the end of the 1920s, Stalin had to deal more frequently with his deputy Genrikh Iagoda. Stalin's tone to Iagoda was far cooler, while Iagoda's responses and reports were guarded, fearful, and dull. Stalin had reasons for disliking Iagoda. He had been a protégé of the first Soviet head of state, Iakov Sverdlov, with whom Stalin had quarreled as early as 1913; Iagoda had maintained friendly relations with such enemies as Bukharin and, worse, had been named by Bukharin as one man in OGPU on whom the opposition could rely, should Stalin be overthrown. However, Iagoda not only knew where all the corpses were buried; he was a hardworking, unscrupulous, and compliant henchman. It would take Stalin five years to be sure that he had a replacement; someone who would be loyal not to OGPU but to him, who would be ruthless and energetic, and who would willingly face down the hostility of professional *chekisty* to an outsider. This man would be Nikolai Ezhov.

In the meantime, Iagoda had neither Dzierżyński's fanaticism nor Menzhinsky's erudition. He was evasive and self-serving—a "guard dog on a chain," he called himself. He had no creative talent, even if in later life he liked to recite poetry with pathos. Iagoda's private letters are strained and inexpressive. He was an awkward provincial in the metropolis, both envious and enamored of those more suave than he. But he understood Stalin well enough to fear the future. His last years gave his sulky personality a tragic aura; one's revulsion is tinged by pity.

Genrikh Iagoda came from a Polish Jewish family.[6] He was born in 1891 in northern Russia, in Rybinsk where his family had just moved, nobody knows from where. In 1892, the Iagodas settled in Nizhni Novgorod, a city officially closed to Jews. Gershon, Genrikh's father, was a cousin of Movsha, the father of Iakov Sverdlov. Gershon Iagoda was a printer, and ran, with Movsha Sverdlov, a shop making seals and stamps to authenticate fake documents for revolutionaries. Genrikh had two brothers and six sisters. The family was impoverished, but Genrikh completed six years of secondary school, probably paid for by his future father-in-law the merchant Leonid Averbakh, two hundred miles east in the city of Simbirsk. Iagoda's spelling and general knowledge suggest he was a poor pupil.[7]

Leading Bolsheviks such as Dr. Nikolai Semashko, Lenin's future commissar for health, frequented the Sverdlov–Iagoda printshop. Nizhni was the hometown of the then-notorious radical writer Maxim Gorky. In 1904 the printshop was raided and a visitor with manifestos and thirty kilos of type seized, but the Sverdlovs and Iagodas were left in peace, a fact which fed rumors that Genrikh may have been, at thirteen, a police spy.

Iagoda, like Lenin, was traumatized by the death of his elder brother: in 1905 Mikhail Iagoda, a bystander, was hacked to death by Cossacks at Nizhni's barricades. (In 1916 Iagoda's other brother, Lev, an army recruit, was shot for insubordination.) Like Dzierżyński and Menzhinsky, Iagoda as a youth depended emotionally on his sisters; one gleans the impression that Genrikh was an unloved son, even more so after the deaths of his brothers, and that the only affection he received, or at least reciprocated, came from his five sisters. Certainly, his subsequent eager allegiance with leading Bolsheviks and *chekisty* shows the ingratiating clinging sycophancy of a boy chronically starved of parental love. Iagoda's elder sister, Esfir, worked in a shop in St. Petersburg. Another older sister, Roza, was at nineteen an assistant pharmacist in Moscow and an anarchist. Under Roza's wing Genrikh worked as an apprentice pharmacist for six months—hence his reputed expertise in poisons—and joined anarchist circles. Nizhni's anarchists were led by a police informer, Chembarisov. The young Iagoda would never cause serious trouble and was benignly watched by the gendarmerie and Okhranka both in Nizhni and in Moscow.

Iagoda in his callow adolescence was recalled as "thin, middling height, hunched shoulders, with long black hair . . . Unsociable, introverted, sullen." To another he seemed "a wolf cub at bay." (His adult demeanor, with an unsmiling Velásquez face and a toothbrush mustache, was that of a cornered rat.) Police spies code-named him "Little Owl" or "Lonely." The police description of 1910, when Genrikh visited his sister in Moscow, conjures up a very un-Bolshevik Iagoda: "Wearing white shirt with long white tie, greyish jacket, black trousers, large grey tie pin . . . long hair." Iagoda, as a pharmacist, was supposed to procure explosives for bombs to rob a bank in Nizhni, but he was so inert that the police did not bother to arrest him until May 16, 1912. They found nothing incriminating beyond false papers and did not even link Iagoda with the notorious Iakov Sverdlov. Iagoda was sent to Simbirsk for two years under police supervision.

In 1913 the Romanovs celebrated their tercentenary and Genrikh was amnestied. He moved to Petersburg, where Nikolai Podvoisky, a newspaper editor who became the first Bolshevik minister for the armed forces, impressed by his connections to the Sverdlovs and by his eagerness to please, found him work in the health insurance office of the Putilov steelworks. Podvoisky was a fruitful contact: he was the brother-in-law of two future Cheka chiefs, Kedrov and Artuzov. Iagoda secured even better connections by marrying in 1914 Ida Averbakh, Iakov Sverdlov's niece and the daughter of his possible childhood benefactor. Ida was intelligent, but too unprepossessing to reject such a lowly suitor as Iagoda. For Genrikh, however, she was a catch; her ambitious brother Leopold Averbakh would dominate Soviet literary politics.

In 1915 Iagoda was conscripted. He rose to lance corporal, was wounded, and discharged. When revolution broke out, Iagoda joined the Bolsheviks, backdating his membership to 1907. Just before his death in 1919, Iakov Sverdlov wrote to Dzierżyński recommending Iagoda for the Cheka rank and file. Dzierżyński valued reliability above education or intellect and quickly promoted Iagoda. Sverdlov had also found Iagoda work in the Supreme Military Inspectorate. In disputes between Trotsky and Stalin over military policy, Sverdlov's military inspectorate took Stalin's side. Iagoda was soon editing with Stalin a soldier's edition of *Pravda*. He was now indissolubly linked to Stalin and to the Cheka.

Like Stalin, Iagoda traveled all over Russia, inspecting the military from the safety of the rear. Iagoda also had a post in the Commissariat for Foreign Trade, where he befriended a con man, Aleksandr Lurié. Lurié and Iagoda both had sticky fingers and Lurié interested Iagoda in everything foreign, from fine wines and dildos to literature and spies. Iagoda rescued Lurié from prisons in Russia and Germany, and Lurié helped Iagoda profit from lucrative concessions, notably the diamond trade. The Cheka and Foreign Trade Commissariat were linked since one confiscated the valuables which the other sold abroad for hard currency. What marked out Iagoda from Dzierżyński and Menzhinsky was that he was corrupt and acquisitive. This did not disqualify him in Stalin's eyes. Quite the contrary: a Iagoda vulnerable to blackmail was more malleable. Without intellectual distinction or convictions, Iagoda fitted the mold of Stalin's acolytes. He intuited the wishes of his masters, he questioned nothing, and he worked tirelessly day and night.

Iagoda also came to Lenin's attention as he knew a lot about medicine and was expert at finding sanatoria where Bolshevik leaders could get their overtaxed hearts and minds treated. Iagoda's links with doctors, some of whom he intimidated into committing murder, would make him indispensable to Stalin.

As the civil war ended, Iagoda rose to the top of the Cheka. On June 6, 1921, Dzierżyński wrote to Unszlicht: "I suggest that Comrade Iagoda should be appointed deputy to Comrade Menzhinsky, who because of his health needs to have a limit on his working hours in the Cheka." Soon Iagoda was on warm terms with both Dzierżyński and Menzhinsky, whom he treated with perhaps genuine affection: "Dear Viacheslav Rudolfovich, I am sending a cab driver with a fur coat [confiscated from a detainee]. I think you may need it. On the whole, it's quiet in the republic. . . . I'm not writing to you, and I shan't do so, about cases and new appointments, I'm told it has a bad effect on the health. . . . G. Iagoda."[8]

When Stalin became general secretary, Iagoda grasped that the Georgian would succeed Lenin. He began reporting to Stalin directly, bypassing the GPU's channels and playing deftly on Stalin's suspicions.[9] Iagoda also curried favor with Stalin's cronies such as Voroshilov.

When the Cheka faced peacetime contraction, its salaries paid late, its uniforms and rations withheld, Iagoda lobbied for money. He had an accountant certify that the GPU's financial position was "catastrophic" and scared the government with the prospect of "mass desertion" from its ranks, "incidents of demoralization, bribe-taking and other sins."

Such energy made Iagoda liked by both Dzierżyński and the lower ranks. He was good at fund-raising; he arrested persons who had wealthy relatives in neighboring states such as Latvia, where Russian exiles had little legal protection, and extorted ransoms.[10] Stalin was also impressed by Iagoda's manipulation of displaced persons: White Cossack refugees in Bulgaria and Turkey fell for Iagoda's reassurances of amnesty if they went back to their ravaged farms. Helped by the Bulgarian secret police, Iagoda filtered out anticommunists and suspected spies from the returning Cossacks before resettling them and persuaded the League of Nations to bear the costs. OGPU obtained experience that would be used more ruthlessly when many more Cossacks were repatriated after the Second World War.

Iagoda did, however, blunder. He let the head of the Tsarist police, Alexei Lopukhin, leave for France; Lopukhin understandably failed to return. In the 1920s and 1930s a number of defections infuriated Stalin, even if the defectors were of no importance. Worse, Iagoda took visible steps to insure himself lest Stalin lose power. Iagoda naturally gravitated to the right opposition of the party, mainly because Bukharin, Rykov, and others on the right were better company. Unlike the puritanical left, they patronized writers, musicians, and artists; they spoke about Europe (which Iagoda knew only from their stories), they drank good wine and mixed with attractive women. Iagoda loved courtship from the literati, who asked him how to behave if they fell into his clutches. He told Babel, "Deny everything, whatever charges we may bring. Say 'No,' only 'No,' deny everything, and we are powerless." But Iagoda feared retribution for his proclivities. Ivan Gronsky, editor of *Izvestiia,* noticed, "Iagoda was terribly afraid of the Central Committee."[11]

By 1929, with Menzhinsky's connivance, Iagoda had all sectors of OGPU staffed with his own protégés: Frinovsky in the special department, which hunted down deviant party and government members; Iakov Agranov in the secret department, created in 1923 to control intellectuals; and Karl Pauker in the operative department, which guarded Stalin. As Menzhinsky lay dying, OGPU feared that either Kaganovich or Mikoyan, both Stalin's creatures, would be put in charge of them. Iagoda, Frinovsky, Agranov, and Pauker did their utmost to block outsiders from chairing OGPU.

Disaster struck Iagoda when Bukharin sought out Kamenev to propose an anti-Stalin coalition. Bukharin's total words were: "Iagoda and Trilisser are with us." OGPU knew Stalin had his own informants so they had to get in first with an explanation. On February 6, 1929, Menzhinsky, Iagoda, and Trilisser reported to Stalin Kamenev's "nonsensical slander either of Comrade Bukharin or of us, and whether or not Comrade Bukharin said anything of the sort, we deem it essential to refute this slander categorically in front of the party." Henceforth, Iagoda avoided Bukharin, but Stalin's trust, once lost, was irretrievable.

From 1929, Iagoda felt more and more vulnerable. In response, he aimed to be indispensable. He and Agranov infiltrated the intelligentsia so thoroughly that by 1932 the party was able to take complete control of all the creative arts. Iagoda and Frinovsky devised ambitious enterprises for the GULAG that made it vital to Stalin's industrialization. From this frantic activity, Iagoda sought Baudelairean relief in *luxe, calme et volupté,* falling helplessly in love with Gorky's daughter-in-law.

The inventory of Iagoda's possessions, compiled by two lieutenants, two captains, and a brigadier of the NKVD who arrested him, says much about Iagoda and Ida's lifestyle:

1. Soviet money 22,997 rubles 59 kopecks, include savings book for 6,180.59
2. Various wines, 1,229 bottles, most foreign and of 1897, 1900 and 1902 vintages
3. A collection of pornographic photographs—3,904 items
4. Pornographic films—11
5. Cigarettes, various foreign, Egyptian and Turkish—11,075
6. Foreign tobacco—9 boxes
7. Men's coats, most foreign—21
8. Fur coats and squirrel fur jackets—9
9. Ladies' coats, various foreign—9
   [. . .]
57. Foreign shirts, Jäger—23
58. Foreign underpants, Jäger—26
59. Gramophones, foreign—2
60. Radiogram, foreign—3

61. Gramophone records, foreign—399
    [. . .]
76. Silk ladies' shifts, mostly foreign—68
77. Knitted cardigans, mostly foreign—31
78. Ladies' panties, silk, foreign—70
79. Cosmetic boxes in leather suitcases—6
80. Foreign children's toys—101 sets
    [. . .]
87. Fishing equipment, foreign—73 items
88. Field binoculars—7
    [. . .]
92. Various revolvers—19
93. Sporting guns and small-arm rifles—12
94. Infantry rifles—2
    [. . .]
99. Automobile—1
    [. . .]
102. Pipes and cigarette holders (ivory, amber, etc.), most porno-
     graphic—165
    [. . .]
105. A rubber artificial phallus
    [. . .]
116. Antique crockery—1,008 items
    [. . .]
123. Various foreign objects (ovens, refrigerators, vacuum cleaners,
     lamps)—71
    [. . .]
126. Foreign sanitary and hygienic objects (medicines, contracep-
     tive sheaths)—115
127. Pianos—3
    [. . .]
129. Counterrevolutionary Trotskyist, fascist literature—542
130. Foreign suitcases and trunks—24[12]

Dzierżyński and Menzhinsky had fatal flaws and arrogance, but
their probity was never doubted, and they received solemn state funerals.

Compared to them Iagoda was a petty figure; his arrogance and his cruelty reflected an inner insecurity, which was to be his undoing. His ashes would be thrown in a nameless pit, not placed in a mausoleum.

The Trophy Writer

One night a werewolf slipped away
From wife and child and went to see
A village teacher in his grave
And asked him, "Please, will you decline me?"
The pedagogue climbed up and out
Onto his coffin of brass and lead
And spoke to the werewolf, who, devout,
Crossed his paws in front of the dead. . . .

Christian Morgenstern

IN 1929 STALIN put the littérateur Menzhinsky in charge of crushing the peasantry, and chose the provincial ignoramus Genrikh Iagoda to bring the literati to heel. The choices follow Stalinist logic: the hangman should have nothing in common with, and no sympathy for, the condemned, although, for all his ignorance, Iagoda had two links to the literary world. His brother-in-law Leopold Averbakh was a critic, and Iagoda himself was virtually a kinsman of Russia's most prestigious left-wing writer, Maxim Gorky. In 1928 Iagoda's career was boosted when Stalin used him to bring Maxim Gorky back to the USSR. For six years, ostensibly for his health, Gorky had lived on the island of Capri.[13]

Gorky had his reasons to return. While he was widely read in the Soviet Union, his reputation in the West was waning. The sagas he now composed about decaying Russian merchant families were dreary; Stalin himself found *The Artamonov Business* hard going.[14] Homesickness and penury bothered Gorky while OGPU and Stalin felt that Gorky on Capri was a magnet for undesirable heretics. Stalin had always found Gorky unreliable; he had crossed swords with him in 1917, calling his protests "geese cackling in intellectual marshes," but he longed for a sage to validate his actions, a bard to laud his genius. Stalin had silenced the USSR's wittiest political panegyrists, Kamenev and Bukharin, and needed better flattery than Demian Bedny's doggerel or the proletarian hacks' stilted dramas. Gorky had written encomia to Tolstoi and Lenin; he could do the same for Stalin, who now put off other potential hagiographers.[15] Stalin calculated that in Gorky's wake intellectuals from Britain, America, France, and Germany would flock to the USSR.

The conversation of Voroshilov, Kaganovich, and Molotov (Gorky privately called them "camp-following trash") must have stultified Stalin, who now had no literate penfriend. Demian Bedny, slow to follow changes in Stalin's taste, had disgraced himself by writing the anti-Russian satire, *Get off the Stove!* and Stalin had broken off their friendship. Stalin began to discuss in letters to Gorky the plays he had read. Their correspondence reads like exchanges between a publisher's reader and a copy editor, or the reports of a minister to a president. Stalin wrote, "We're moving the cart: of course, it squeaks, but we are moving ahead. . . . Transport is in a poor state (too overloaded), but we'll get it right very soon."[16]

Both Iagoda and Stalin baited Gorky with secret material on "wreckers" for a play: "I've gathered some new material," wrote Stalin, sending transcripts from OGPU's questioning of the economist Kondratiev and of the Mensheviks. Gorky enthused about the punishment meted out but never wrote the promised play. In return Gorky fed Stalin flattering snippets: Moura Budberg, Gorky's mistress, had told him that London's bestselling book was a treatise on the Soviet five-year plan and that Bertrand Russell had declared that only in the USSR could scientists experiment on human beings. Gorky advised Stalin to publish a book on how laws are made in the Soviet Union.

In December 1931 Gorky showed Stalin how much he cared:

There is particular verbal raging from monarchists and their terrorist organizations. All in all, they are stalking you intensively, one can't help thinking that now efforts will increase. And you, dear comrade, I hear and I have seen, behave rather carelessly, you drive at night to No. 6 Nikitskaia [Gorky's apartment]. I am completely sure that you have no right to behave like that. Who would replace you if the bastards knock you off? Don't be angry, I have a right to worry and give advice.

The Politburo subsequently passed a resolution, after a communication from OGPU, that Stalin should cease going about Moscow on foot. With Gorky's help, Iagoda had secured a major victory: Stalin could no more play Harun-al-Rashid, walking the streets, dropping in unannounced to see writers and commissars. His contacts outside the Kremlin were overseen by OGPU, and he was as much a prisoner of OGPU as its overlord.[17]

Gorky's chief asset as a writer was curiosity, his weakness vanity. He was lured back to the USSR with promises that he would be told everything. His jubilee would be celebrated, all the literary initiatives begun under Lenin would be resumed. He would revitalize Russian literature. For the first five years after his return he spent May to September in Russia and the winter in Capri for his lungs. From 1933, when Hitler's rise made it even less conscionable for a Soviet writer to live in fascist Italy and Stalin feared that Gorky could be infected by Trotskyism, Gorky was kept in golden cages in Moscow and the Crimea. His hometown Nizhni and Chekhov's Moscow Arts Theater would both take his name but the tribute he most appreciated was Stalin's establishment of the Gorky Literary Institute, which was to nurture gifted writers.

Without Iagoda, Stalin could not have coaxed Gorky back. Iagoda had recruited Piotr Kriuchkov, Gorky's secretary, into OGPU. Through Kriuchkov, Iagoda not only learned everything about Gorky's life; he could also feed Gorky with ideas and books that inclined Gorky to see Soviet Russia as the only bulwark against fascism.

Iagoda made Moura Budberg, previously the mistress of Robert Bruce-Lockhart and of H. G. Wells, indispensable to Gorky. No woman who entered Gorky's orbit ever left it. His legal wife, Ekaterina Peshkova, who had the thankless task of running the Soviet Red Cross for Political Prisoners, still adored him. So did the actress Maria Andreeva, a long-standing Bolshevik from the Moscow Arts Theater; Iagoda retrieved Maria Andreeva from exile in Berlin to join the harem in Capri. Moura Budberg had been beholden to the Cheka ever since she had been blackmailed by Jekabs Peterss over her marriage to an aristocrat and her affair with the British agent Bruce-Lockhart in 1918. She engineered the return of Gorky, and his archive, to the Soviet Union.

Gorky looked on Iagoda not just as a fellow countryman from Nizhni, he was kith and kin. In the 1890s Gorky had adopted Zinovi, Yakov Sverdlov's rebellious brother, who was both third cousin and uncle by marriage to Iagoda. Zinovi took Gorky's surname, Peshkov.[18]

OGPU kept Gorky's household on Capri under surveillance, as did Mussolini's secret police. Both Moura Budberg and Gorky's son Max Peshkov worked for Iagoda (Max confided to the poet Khodasevich that he was once given a confiscated stamp collection by Dzierżyński as payment for helping the Cheka make arrests). Gorky felt that returning to Moscow would give him peace but on his first homecoming in 1928 his Moscow apartment, which belonged to his wife, was effectively controlled by Iagoda. It seethed even more than Capri with competing women: Ekaterina Peshkova, Maria Andreeva, the nurse Lipa Chertkova (once wardrobe mistress in the Moscow Arts Theater), and Timosha, Max's wife, who many suspected preferred her father-in-law to her feckless husband. Gorky remarked, "I never had luck with women. There've always been a lot, but did any sense come out of it?"

Stalin broke Gorky in gently; the writer was not at first told of the Shakhty death sentences. Iagoda moved him to a dacha that had belonged to the merchant Savva Morozov, who had financed the Moscow Arts Theater and the Bolsheviks before the revolution. Back in Europe Gorky found himself ostracized by Russian émigrés for shaking Stalin's hand. He tried to make the best of his ambiguous position: from Sorrento he wrote to Iagoda, asking for reprieves for an ornithologist in the Urals, an elderly Ukrainian littérateur, and a Siberian Esperantist. Iagoda proved more responsive than Dzierżyński to Gorky's appeals. When in May 1929 Gorky returned to Moscow Iagoda had more intimate reasons to stay close: he was infatuated with Gorky's daughter-in-law Timosha. Despite this, Genrikh and Ida's only child Garik was born that year.

Iagoda sent Gorky, supervised by an OGPU major from Nizhni, to the special purpose camps in the former monasteries on the Solovetsky islands. Gorky willingly put on his blinkers. He met famous academics dying in the frozen north, but all he and Timosha expressed to Iagoda on their return was their delight at the clean sheets, good food, daily newspapers, and rehabilitation which OGPU officers gave their prisoners. Emboldened by Gorky's appreciation, Iagoda responded: "Some frontier guards have asked me to send you a collection of their poems for your opinion. This is their own work, there is some pretty good verse. . . . I personally add my voice to theirs. That's all I ask. But I would so much like to see you. . . . You seem to have forgotten your 'intimate friend.' Perhaps you'll write, eh? Timosha also is upsetting me—she's quite, quite forgotten me!"[19]

Gorky was, he willingly admitted, two-faced and sly; he had always played up to his patrons, whether rich merchants or OGPU chiefs. He was, he confessed to Chekhov, "absurd . . . a locomotive with no rails," but he drew the line at writing a preface to poetry by frontier guards. They were, he told Iagoda, "graphomaniacs" who would be mocked by the critics. But Gorky would write admiringly about frontier guards. He could not write fully about the Solovetsky camps for the Cheka had purloined his notebooks, but by 1932 he was writing "about the unprecedented, fantastically successful experiment of re-educating socially dangerous people in conditions of free socially useful work."

Stalin appreciated the gloss that Gorky put on the camps and he wanted Gorky as commissar for literature. The present commissar, Anatoli Lunacharsky, once a decadent poet and a relatively liberal even principled man, was dying. The literary atmosphere had darkened. Iagoda's brother-in-law Leopold Averbakh was terrorizing literature, attacking in print and in letters to Stalin any non-proletarian, unengaged writing. Averbakh believed himself untouchable: he was Sverdlov's nephew and Iagoda's brother-in-law, while his wife, Elena Bonch-Bruevich, was the daughter of an old friend of Lenin's. Averbakh believed he had the party and OGPU behind him. But his Association of Proletarian Writers stifled creativity and the proletarians wrote no plays Stalin could watch with pleasure or novels which depicted heroes convincingly. Stalin's chief of cavalry, Budionny, wanted Isaak Babel shot for his portrayal of marauding Cossacks in *Red Cavalry,* Pilniak infuriated Stalin by implying he was a murderer, and Zoshchenko put caricatures of Stalin in his stories but they entertained Stalin, and he even read Zoshchenko out loud to his daughter. Gorky's homecoming raised hopes that Averbakh's grip on literature would loosen.

Through Gorky, Iagoda now had access to artists who could speak to OGPU chiefs. Iagoda loved directing writers' lives. He never achieved the understanding dialogue that, for instance, Iakov Agranov had with Mayakovsky, but he had the satisfaction of dispatching Mandelstam to the Urals and Nikolai Kliuev to Siberia. Writers who had not yet fallen foul of OGPU were intimidated by Iagoda's "magpie's eyes." The novelist Leonid Leonov was aghast: "Once Gorky and I were at the same table. Iagoda stretches across the table toward me, drunk, flushed with cognac, his eyes popping and literally croaks: 'Listen, Leonov, answer me, why do you need hegemony in literature? Answer, why do you need it?' I then saw in his eyes such spite that I knew I would fare ill if he could get me."

Suborning Gorky was Stalin's triumph over the imagination. The party now corrupted lesser writers using reassurance, even affection. Small services—material to be used, approaches to be taken—were requested and paid for, and soon the victims accepted with joy whatever was forced on them.

Much blame for the loss of their honor and conscience attaches to Soviet writers, who had even before the revolution aped revolutionary parties by forming mutually warring groups, ostracizing those who would not accept their ideology. Theater directors taught Menzhinsky, Iagoda, and Stalin how to run their show trials. Meierkhold and his Georgian acolyte Sandro Akhmeteli treated actors as the party treated its members. In 1924 Tbilisi's Rustaveli theater actors signed pledges: "I shall have no brothers, sisters, parents, friends, or kith and kin outside the membership; I submit absolutely, and always will, to the corporation's decisions, I sacrifice my life and future to the corporation's will." It was easy for such bullies and cowards to adjust to Bolshevik dictates.

Soviet writers irretrievably abased themselves in 1932 when they took a cruise on a government mission along the White Sea canal, 140 miles from Lake Onega to the White Sea. The canal had been built on Iagoda's initiative by OGPU's political prisoners, kulaks, and convicts. Even the engineers were prisoners. Iagoda prided himself on the speed and cheapness with which he built this canal—under two years, for a fifth of the budget—which showed Stalin what OGPU might do for the economy. The death toll was well above 100,000. Some 300,000 prison-

ers—underfed, freezing in winter, tormented by midges in summer—
had cut through bogs and granite. There was little reinforcing iron for
the concrete; human bones and tree branches were used. All for nothing. The canal was too shallow for ships that could withstand the Arctic Ocean; it was ice-free only for half the year and in any case the canal
duplicated an all-weather railway to Murmansk and Arkhangelsk. Before it was finished it was crumbling and has since been reconstructed
twice.[20]

Iagoda saw the White Sea canal as a personal triumph. His brother-
in-law Leopold Averbakh, with Semion Firin, deputy chief of the
GULAG, and Gorky, led boats laden with Soviet intelligentsia. Averbakh, Firin, and Gorky contributed to a book glorifying OGPU's humanity and expertise, and the re-education of criminals and subversives
by labor. Among the writers who volunteered for, or were cajoled into,
this act of prostitution were the "Soviet Count" Aleksei Tolstoi and the
satirist Mikhail Zoshchenko. Prince Dmitri Sviatopolk-Mirsky, recently
repatriated from England, and the innovative Victor Shklovsky were two
literary critics on the flotilla of ships, and the graphic Hemingway style
of the 600-page panegyric to slave labor betrays the latter's hand. Imprisoned writers like the futurist Igor Terentiev were presented to the
tourists as seekers of redemption by labor. Nobody on board could have
been fooled. The statistics in *The Stalin White Sea–Baltic Canal* are lies:
a figure of 100,000 laborers is given—the number at any one time and a
third of those actually used. Fewer than 13,000 of the survivors were
freed when the canal was finished.

Only one contribution to this volume can be read without revulsion:
Mikhail Zoshchenko wrote "History of a Re-forging," the biography of
a con man, Abram Rottenberg, a Jew from Tbilisi. Rottenberg's cosmopolitan adventures end on the White Sea canal, but unlike other prisoners portrayed Rottenberg is reluctant to redeem himself, and
Zoshchenko concedes that he could take up fraud again. Apart from
Zoshchenko, who refrained from murderous slogans, every contributor
also valiantly called, like Gorky and Stalin, for "the enemy to be finished
off."[21]

The one foreign correspondent who wrote objectively about forced
labor, the German journalist Nikolaus Basseches, got short shrift from

Stalin. Kaganovich and Molotov, who had "like idiots put up with this capitalist shopkeepers' puppy," were told "to pour filth on the pages of *Pravda* and *Izvestiia* over this capitalist scum, and after a short time chase him out of the USSR."[22] Just one major Russian poet, Nikolai Kliuev, beggared and ostracized, living on the charity of friends and foreigners, wrote the truth about the White Sea canal. The lines only survive because he later quoted them under interrogation by the NKVD in Siberia:

> That was the White Sea canal of death
> Akimushka dug it,
> So did Prov from Vetliuga and Auntie Fiokla.
> Great Russia got soaked
> To the bones with the red shower
> And hid its tears from people,
> From others' eyes in alien bogs
> [. . .]
> Russia! Better to be in smoke and soot
> Than the blood of canal locks and the lice of brushwood causeways
> From Ararat to the Northern seas.

Before 1931, when Stalin still roamed the streets late in the evening, he, Molotov, and Voroshilov would stroll over from the Kremlin, sometimes several times a week, to see Gorky. They stayed, eating, drinking, and talking, until late at night. A motley group of writers came to these gatherings and many were awed by Stalin's modest bonhomie. Conspiratorially cautious as ever, Stalin always sat facing the door. He fed the gathering tidbits of inner party gossip: "Lenin knew he was dying. Once, when we were alone, he asked me to bring him potassium cyanide. 'You're the cruelest man in the party, you can do it,' he said." Stalin invited writers to speak their minds.[23] "There will be unity only in the cemetery," he told them, but few appreciated how close they were to that cemetery. Like Mao Tse-tung and his slogan "Let a thousand flowers bloom," Stalin wanted to mark out the weeds in his literary garden.

A few writers were emboldened by the relaxed atmosphere. One declared that Politburo members should not be portrayed as demigods, that Stalin should be shown with his pockmarks. Another interrupted a toast, declaring that Stalin must be fed up with all this acclaim. Neither survived very long. Korneli Zelinsky noted: "When Stalin talks, he plays with a mother-of-pearl penknife. . . . When he laughs, his eyebrows and mustache move apart and something cunning appears. . . . He has caught everything on the radio station of his brain, which operates on all wavelengths. . . . But be on your guard if he is being charming. He has an enormous range of anesthetics at his disposal."

While Stalin, Molotov, and Voroshilov enjoyed the company of writers, and did not mind meeting Menzhinsky, Iagoda, and other OGPU agents at Gorky's, they loathed crossing paths with Bukharin and Kamenev, of whom Gorky was fond. Gorky tried to reconcile them, even forcing Bukharin and Stalin to kiss. Offering his lips for the kiss, Stalin said: "You won't bite?" "If I bit you," said Bukharin, "I'd break my teeth; you have iron lips."[24]

Gorky persuaded Stalin to give the two opposition leaders a respite before "finishing them off" (*dobit,* Stalin's favorite verb). Bukharin became editor of the government newspaper *Izvestiia,* while Kamenev ran the publishing house Akademiia. Kamenev published memoirs and world classics of a quality and with an objectivity not seen in the Soviet Union before or since. Bukharin made *Izvestiia* as readable a newspaper as censorship and Stalin would permit. From Stalin's point of view only on Zinoviev was Gorky sound: Gorky never forgave Zinoviev his lust for intellectuals' blood. In 1935 Zinoviev was in prison awaiting his first trial, accused of "moral responsibility" for Sergei Kirov's murder. He was allowed to appeal to Gorky:

> . . . to be honest, I have often thought that personally you have never liked me. But a lot of people write to you. So let me too, one of the most unhappy persons in the whole world, turn to you. You are a great artist. You know the human soul. You are a life teacher. . . . I beg you, think hard for a minute what it means for me to be now in a Soviet prison. . . . Of course I realize that the party cannot fail to punish me very severely. But still I fear more than anything ending my days in an asylum for the insane. . . . I end this letter January 28, 1935, in remand prison,

and today I'm told I am being taken away. . . . I don't know where yet. Help, help![25]

Gorky did not intercede for Zinoviev, but he did for Kamenev and Bukharin, which disgruntled Stalin. Iagoda was told to isolate Gorky further. Dubious figures were visiting Gorky including Prince Sviatopolk-Mirsky, the literary historian and son of a Tsarist minister who had converted to communism while a lecturer in London. He was denounced to Iagoda as a British agent and only Gorky's favor delayed his arrest.[26] Similarly, the Franco-Russian journalist Victor Serge, arrested for protests against repressions, was released when Gorky and Romain Rolland combined forces.

Gorky's glorification of Stalin's terror—"If the enemy doesn't surrender he is to be annihilated"—was a betrayal but he was able to rescue some. He had Chinese herbs brought by diplomatic courier to treat an illness that was apparently threatening Sholokhov's life and commended him to Stalin's protection; Evgeni Zamiatin, unable to publish in the USSR, was allowed to leave for France; the Moscow Arts Theater was ordered to employ Mikhail Bulgakov, and OGPU had to return to Bulgakov the notebooks it had impounded.[27] Even Vladimir Zazubrin, the celebrator of Cheka executioners but now in disgrace, was, thanks to Gorky, brought back from Siberia and given a job in publishing (he was shot in 1938). Gorky begged Stalin not to punish the editors who attacked Gorky's "softness." He lobbied for publishing nineteenth-century Russian classics even when they repudiated communist ideology.[28]

Stalin now devised an obligatory ideology for all the representative arts, "socialist realism," and in 1932 set up the Union of Writers. Gorky agreed to preside over its first congress in 1934 although, despite his brilliant table talk, he floundered on public platforms. To his credit, Gorky loathed those writers, such as Aleksandr Fadeev and Vladimir Stavsky, whose chief talent was political wrangling and who dominated the new union. Gorky's price for conducting the first congress was that Stalin should let Bukharin take a leading role in the proceedings.

Gorky sent a draft of a frank opening speech for Stalin's comments. On August 14, Kaganovich, an unlikely critic, reported his misgivings to Stalin, who was relaxing in the Caucasus:

As it is, the lecture won't do. Above all, its construction: three quarters, if not more, is taken up by general historical philosophical reflections, and those are wrong. His ideal is primitive society. . . . Clearly this position is un-Marxist. . . . Soviet literature is almost unmentioned. . . . In view of the seriousness of our alterations and the danger of the lecture going wrong, we (I, Molotov, and Voroshilov) went to see him and after a fairly long chat he agreed to introduce corrections and changes. His mood seems to be bad. . . . It's not just that he started talking about difficulties . . . but the taste his objections left.[29]

Gorky was clearly not completely reliable and the congress had to be carefully orchestrated. In August 1934, Kaganovich and Stalin's Central Committee satrap for the arts, Andrei Zhdanov, decided which writers should run the union. Of the thirty-three men and one woman nominated for the union presidium, only a handful—Gorky, Aleksei Tolstoi, Mikhail Sholokhov, and the Georgian novelist Mikheil Javakhishvili—had any distinction, the rest were party apparatchiks. Fifty-nine writers of various ethnic affiliations were chosen for the plenum. For Buriat Mongolia, Yakutia, and Karelia, Kaganovich and Zhdanov could not suggest anybody. Overall, there were a few real writers—Boris Pasternak, Ilya Ehrenburg, Samuil Marshak (the children's writer and translator of Burns), and Paolo Iashvili, the Georgian poet—but the majority were either hacks or thugs. Some, like Demian Bedny or Zazubrin, were both.

The union's self-government was a sham. Iagoda controlled those writers who were OGPU agents and Andrei Zhdanov oversaw the congress. Zhdanov and others nervously listened to Bukharin's speech but restrained the Stalinist left from howling it down. Foreign delegates including André Malraux were stopped from circulating freely. As the congress began, OGPU found nine copies of an anonymous leaflet addressed to foreign delegates, apparently composed by a group of Soviet writers:

. . . We Russian writers remind one of prostitutes in a brothel, with just one difference, that they trade their bodies and we trade our souls; just as they have no way out of the brothel, except death by starvation, neither have we. . . . At home you set up various committees to save victims of fascism, you assemble antiwar congresses, you make libraries of books burned by Hitler, all very well. But why do we not see you acting to save victims of our Soviet fascism, run by Stalin? . . . Personally we fear that in a year or two the failed seminary student Iosif Jughashvili (Stalin) will not be satisfied by the title of world-class philosopher and will demand, like Nebuchadnezzar, to be called at the very least the "sacred bull." Do you understand the game you're playing? Or are you, just like us, prostituting your feelings, conscience, duty? But then we shall never forgive you for that, never ever. . . .[30]

The authors of this manifesto were never identified, nor did any foreign delegate speak of it. OGPU informers summarized participants' private comments for Stalin's perusal:

Isaak Babel: The congress proceeds as dead as an imperial parade, and nobody abroad believes in it. Our press can inflate its stupid fictions about the delegates' colossal enthusiasm. But there are foreign correspondents who will shed the right light on this literary requiem. Look at Gorky and Demian Bedny. They hate each other, but they sit at the congress together like turtledoves.

Iagoda and Agranov had unsettling feedback: Malraux had reacted to honors bestowed as "a coarse attempt to bribe me"; writers were signing an appeal for the return of Nikolai Kliuev; a parody of Aleksandr Pushkin's tribute to Gavriil Derzhavin was circulating: "Our congress was joyful and bright, / And this day was terrible nice— / Old Bukharin noticed us / And, seeing us off to the coffin, blessed us."

The Politburo dictated the congress's final resolutions: the writers' mission was to glorify the crushing of class enemies and the leadership of Stalin, and the union's "leading organs" were to improve and increase production of "works of art of high artistic standard, imbued with the spirit of socialism."

Nobody at the congress spoke of the two suicides that had shaken the Russian literary world. Esenin had hanged himself from a heating pipe in December 1926, and Mayakovsky, who had reproached Esenin for "taking the easy way out," had in spring 1930 shot himself, an act that Pasternak daringly called "Mount Etna surrounded by cowardly hillocks." Just as Tsar Nicholas I had been blamed for the fatal duels of Pushkin and Mikhail Lermontov, so OGPU was implicated in both suicides. Esenin had been led astray by Iakov Bliumkin, and Mayakovsky by Iakov Agranov, who gave him the fatal revolver. Esenin and Mayakovsky had felt themselves rejected. By 1926 peasant poets like Esenin were being condemned as the voice of the kulak. Mayakovsky, in his late play *The Bedbug,* depicted a future puritanical communist society in which poets are as undesirable as bedbugs.

For letting Bukharin speak freely at the congress, as well as earlier blunders, Stalin sent Iagoda a signal in June 1931 by temporarily demoting him from first to second deputy head of OGPU. Now Iagoda needed Gorky's advocacy if he was to succeed Menzhinsky as head of OGPU.

Iagoda made strenuous efforts. He manipulated Gorky into praising show trials. It is said that Gorky accused Iagoda of murdering innocents when he heard that forty-eight officials accused of sabotaging food supplies were shot, but archive documents show Gorky approving such reprisals. Gorky did not read exposés in the Western press that proved OGPU's falsifications. Gorky's letters to Iagoda, "Dear Friend and Fellow countryman," ooze sadism, sycophancy, and, worse, sincerity: "I'd very much like to come to the trial and look at the ugly mugs of these 'people come down in the world' . . . at these crushed villains . . . . I have been reading the statements of these sons of bitches about organizing terror and was extremely astounded. If they hadn't been such vile cowards they might have shot at Stalin. And you [Iagoda], I hear, walk quite carefree down the streets. You walk and drive about. An odd attitude to your life. . . ."

Iagoda, knowing that Stalin would read copies of these letters, wrote pathetically to Gorky:

Like a dog on a chain, I lie by the gates of the republic and chew through the throat of anyone who raises a hand against the peace of the Union. . . . Do you know, Aleksei, what pride stirs one when one knows and believes the party's strength and how enormous the party's strength is when it falls like lava on any fortress; add to this the leadership of a million-strong party by such an exceptional leader as Stalin. True, I have something to live for, to struggle for. I am very tired, but my nerves are so tensed that you don't feel the tiredness. Now, I think, the kulak has been finished off, and the peasant has realized, and thoroughly so, that if he doesn't sow, if he doesn't work, he'll die, and there is nothing more to be hoped for from counter-revolution. . . . I'm almost alone now, Viacheslav [Menzhinsky] is ill. . . .[31]

The events in Russia during Gorky's winters on Capri—the roundups of Trotskyists, the deportation of kulaks, the suicide of Nadezhda Allilueva—were conveyed to him by Iagoda as acceptable if unfortunate events in a heroic war. Gorky kept Iagoda's letters with pride. He, his son, and his daughter-in-law, Timosha, were caught in Iagoda's web. Gorky became devoted to his captor: "I have got very 'used' to you, you have become 'one of the family,' and I have learned to value you. I very much love people like you. There aren't many of them, by the way. Please give a cordial greeting to Menzhinsky. . . ."

Timosha became Iagoda's mistress. (Max was complaisant.) Stalin was assured that Gorky would settle permanently in the USSR, organize writers into "engineers of the soul," and create an international chorus to praise the leader. But when Gorky asked Stalin to spare Shostakovich the vicious tirades in *Pravda* which he had commissioned, he had gone too far. Moreover, he was disparaging the cult of Stalin in his diary, which his secretary Kriuchkov was certainly leaking to Iagoda. Gorky would now pay for his golden cage. On May 11, 1934, his son Max died of pneumonia after lying outside all night on the grass. He had been drinking *iorsh*—beer and vodka—with Piotr Kriuchkov, Gorky's secretary. Iagoda was later accused of murdering Max. It is true that Iagoda, in love with Timosha, had an interest in Max's death, and neither he nor Dr. Leonid Levin, appointed by OGPU to look after Gorky's family, discouraged his drinking. Iagoda and Stalin tried to comfort the inconsolable father; the latest giant passenger aircraft was named *Maxim Gorky*. It crashed.

A luxury river cruiser, also named *Maxim Gorky,* staffed with an OGPU crew, took Gorky down the Volga and away from human contact. He saw nothing of the famine that had depopulated the Volga the previous year. The journey must have been unbearable for Iagoda, who had secured adjacent cabins on the boat with Timosha and had an intercommunicating door knocked through between them. Timosha however was still in shock from her husband's mysterious death and very likely overcome by revulsion for her lover. Iagoda, grim and silent, left the cruise at the first stop. He remained as infatuated with Timosha as he was hypnotized by Stalin, but from that summer of 1934 he became even more of a cornered rat than before. He sensed that he would be compelled to frame and murder the people to whom he was drawn: the intellectuals of the party and the professionals. They could not be called his friends—Iagoda had no friends—but they provided respite from his dark, hangman's life and offered him the comforts of wine, beautiful women, poetry, witty conversation. Always a stranger at the feast of life, at least he could be a spectator. As Stalin's policies grew grimmer and Iagoda was directed to repress those closest to him, and as those closest to him—Gorky's family—began to sense the degree to which he was their jailer not their protector, Iagoda became more withdrawn, sluggish and melancholy, less and less capable of taking any measures that would avert Stalin's wrath.

★ ★ ★ Gorky died on June 18, 1936. In 1938 Iagoda, together with three doctors—Leonid Levin (who had attended Dzierżyński), Dmitri Pletniov (Russia's leading cardiologist), and Ignati Kazakov (an unorthodox therapist patronized by Menzhinsky)—would be accused of killing him. Like Chekhov, Gorky had worn out his heart, pumping blood through lungs ravaged by tuberculosis. On June 8 he was semiconscious; given a massive dose of camphor he then had an impassioned discussion with Stalin on his future plans.[32] For nine days Gorky read and wrote. A witness (the testimony is thirdhand) claims that on June 17 Iagoda's car brought Moura Budberg to the dacha, and that Gorky then died.

The circumstances of Gorky's death repay study.[33] First, Dr. Levin was an NKVD doctor whose diagnoses were often suspiciously at odds with autopsy reports; Stalin had foisted him on Gorky, even sending him at Christmas 1930 to Capri for six weeks. Second, Stalin's office diary for June 17, 1936, mentions no visitors to his office except for a stenographer. Third, Stalin was now about to try Kamenev and Zinoviev for their lives and Gorky would have protested. Fourth, there were four sudden deaths of writers who had displeased Stalin—Panait Istrati, Henri Barbusse, Gorky, and Eugène Dabit.[34] Fifth, Moura Budberg vanished to London after Gorky's funeral. Budberg, Timosha, and Ekaterina Peshkova refused all their lives to discuss his last days.

At Gorky's funeral Iagoda stood in the guard of honor, Stalin bent over the coffin and his brother-in-law Stanislav Redens controlled the crowds outside.

Fellow Travelers Abroad and Dissent at Home

General good is the plea of the scoundrel, hypocrite and flatterer.

William Blake

WHY DID SOVIET WRITERS let themselves be penned in like sheep by the party shepherds and OGPU dogs? Some, a decade earlier, had proved their indomitable courage. Isaak Babel, a bespectacled Jew, had ridden with, and then written about, Cossack cavalry attacking Ukrainian gentry, Polish invaders, White Guards, and the Jews of western Russia. But even he adopted the "genre of silence."

In 1934 a mass protest against Stalin's apparatchiks might still have made an impact; when the survivors saw what came of their acquiescence in 1937 they must have regretted their falling in line behind Gorky and the party minions. They had betrayed the Russian peasantry, for whom the major classic Russian writers, from Pushkin to Chekhov, had made a stand. With just a few exceptions—Zabolotsky, Mandelstam—they had disowned the truth and applauded lies about the society whose conscience they were supposed to guard. Excuses can be made: the tour of the White Sea canal had confronted the conformists with writers whose integrity had made them doomed slaves digging frozen bogs. After 1929 exile was not an option. A German writer protesting against Hitler might do so from the safety of asylum in the United States; a Soviet writer against Stalin could not.

But there can be no excuse for the Western observers who attended Soviet Union of Writers' banquets in 1934. A few quibbled, like Malraux, but none disseminated the truth about collectivization, famine, arrests, and executions. If Louis Aragon, Romain Rolland, Lion Feuchtwanger, Bertolt Brecht, George Bernard Shaw, and H. G. Wells had chosen to be honest, what risk would they have run? They chose to fawn on Stalin and lie with impunity. Iagoda had no trouble assembling a chorus of Stalinist flatterers from the left wing of Western writers.

For French writers, as for Gorky, Iagoda found beautiful, polyglot women. In France Romain Rolland's fame was waning after *Jean Christophe,* his *roman-fleuve,* so Iagoda commissioned a twenty-volume Russian edition of his works and recruited the enchanting Maria Kudasheva to translate them. Rolland married Kudasheva but found Iagoda hard to like. "An enigmatic personality. A man who looks as if he is refined and cultured. . . . But his police functions inspire horror. He speaks softly to you as he calls black white and white black, and his honest eyes look at you with amazement if you begin to doubt his word," he wrote in his diary. But he was bewitched by Stalin. Rolland's conversations with Stalin in 1935 are on record, and the respective gullibility and cynicism are breathtaking.

Rolland: Why are twelve-year-old children now subject to adult criminal penalties?

Stalin: We discovered in our schools groups of ten to fifteen boys and girls who aimed to kill or to debauch the best pupils, the prize scholars. They drowned them in wells, inflicted stab wounds on them, terrorized them in every way. . . . We have in the Kremlin women librarians who visit the apartments of our executive comrades in the

Kremlin to keep their libraries in order. It turns out that some of
these librarians had been recruited by our enemies for carrying out
terror. We found that these women were carrying poison, intending
to poison some of our executive comrades. Of course we have
arrested them, we don't intend to shoot them, we are isolating
them. . . .[35]

Henri Barbusse, a nobler figure than Rolland, had won fame with
novels on the First World War and in old age took part in the Congress of Friends of the USSR in Cologne in 1928. Barbusse interviewed
Stalin three times in his Kremlin office and wrote an adulatory short
biography. But Barbusse's admiration for Trotsky worried Iagoda and
for this reason on his 1932 visit to Moscow he was not even met at
the station. But when celebrations of the fortieth anniversary of Gorky's
literary debut began, Stalin rose from his seat on the stage, had
Barbusse brought up from the stalls and surrendered his seat to the
Frenchman.

The communist poet Louis Aragon married Elza Triolet, the sister
of Lili Brik, a known OGPU agent and the inamorata of Mayakovsky.
Other Frenchmen were more elusive: Malraux and Gide ultimately
double-crossed Stalin.

Rolland, Barbusse, and Aragon were the decoys for Europe's intellectuals. Warier luminaries like George Bernard Shaw and H. G. Wells
asked more awkward questions. Stalin declared that handling Shaw had
proved "rather more complicated" but gained his fatuous approval,
which carried more weight than Rolland's or Barbusse's. Wells entered
Stalin's study a wise man—"This lonely, overbearing man, I thought,
may be damned disagreeable, but anyhow he must have an intelligence
far beyond dogmatism"—and came out three hours later none the
wiser.[36] Stalin discovered that inviting established writers for mutual flattery was even more effective than direct propaganda.

Just a few dogs did not bark in the Soviet night. Two of Russia's
greatest poets, Mandelstam and Akhmatova, did not join the union.
When Mayakovsky, who had supported the revolution so vociferously,
preferred death to life in the USSR, the shock was profound. Pasternak
and Mandelstam felt liberated from lies: they both wrote lyric verse

again, Pasternak's *Second Birth,* Mandelstam's *Armenian Cycle.* To para-phrase John Cleese's character in *Clockwise,* "The despair they could take; it's the hope they couldn't stand."

Mandelstam sensed that in the stillness of a Moscow midnight a typewriter was always writing out denunciations. OGPU had been build-ing up dossiers in which painters and poets with any avant-garde inter-ests—once the darlings of the revolution—were linked to former White officers, émigrés, former gendarmes. Hitler's views on "degenerate art" coincided with Stalin's. The Ukrainian GPU had a dossier of 3,000 vol-umes named "Spring"; one of their first victims was Igor Terentiev, sent to dig the White Sea canal.[37] As the son of a gendarme and the brother of an émigré, he could have easily been shot. Terentiev later became a free worker on the Moscow–Volga canal; not until 1937 were capital charges pressed against him.

Probably the last year in which lyricism was even conceivable in the USSR was 1932. In Pasternak's *Second Birth,* his finest book, Stalinism met a covert rebuke:

> But only now is it time to say
> Contrasting the comparison with the greatness of the day:
> The beginning of the glorious days of Peter the Great
> Were darkened by rebellions and executions.

It was also the last year in which Mandelstam saw his verse in print: the ending of his poem "Lamarck" proclaimed too loudly the end of human freedom:

> Nature has stepped back from us,
> As if she didn't need us,
> And she has put the dolichocephalic brain
> Like a sword back in its sheath.
>
> And she has forgotten, left it too late
> To lower the drawbridge for those
> Who have a green grave,
> Red breath, supple laughter . . .

Poetry after 1932 had to be written "for the desk drawer," or, since drawers were searched, committed to memory. Pasternak veered away from political reality. Mandelstam confronted the reality but shunned the perpetrators: he called on Bukharin but never went to meet the Politburo at Gorky's. For Mandelstam Stalin was a malevolent god, even an alter ego, another Joseph. But the sight of the humanoids on Stalin's Politburo was, for Mandelstam, unbearable. On the eve of the writers' congress, he lost his liberty for the lines:

> And round him is a rabble of scraggy-necked leaders,
> He plays with the services of half-human creatures
> Some whistle, some meow, some snivel,
> Only he alone pokes and prods.

Iagoda liked Mandelstam's lampoon well enough to learn it by heart and recite it to Bukharin. Proletarian poets, however, dismayed him by betraying their class. The drunken Pavel Vasiliev was lucky to escape with a warning for writing in 1932 of Stalin:

> Cutting thousands of thousands of nooses, you got your way to power
>   by violence.
> Well what have you done, where have you pushed to, tell me, stupid
>   seminary student!
> These sacred texts should be put up in lavatories . . .
> We swear, o our Leader, we shall strew your path with flowers
> And stick a wreath of laurels up your arse.[38]

Otherwise, irreverence was to be heard only in the folk quatrains of slaves on the collective farms and in the camps.

For the Soviet literati the bitter pill was sugared. Writers who conformed got apartments, dachas, guaranteed print runs, translation into the major languages of the Soviet Union and tours to the Caucasus or Pamirs. Compliant Russians, Georgians, Ukrainians, Armenians, and Kazakhs lived on mutual translation, "taking in each other's washing." Translation, like children's literature, for a few years became a haven: readers benefited as poets and prose writers took cover behind another writer or language. "An alien tongue will be an embryonic membrane for me," Mandelstam put it. Stalin encouraged translation. Italian authors—the USSR saw itself, in opposition to Mussolini, as the guardian of Italian culture—were recommended. Dante, a poet under sentence of death entangled in feuds between Guelfs and Ghibellines, edified Soviet poets. Stalin had Machiavelli retranslated. Mikhail Lozinsky, Gorky's protégé and Mandelstam's friend, spent the 1930s translating *Inferno*, and completed *Paradiso* after a spell in the camps.

Behind the scenes OGPU was tightening its grip. Glavlit came under OGPU's direct control and censorship became secretive.[39] Only six copies including one for Stalin of lists of "major withdrawals, retentions, and confiscations" of publications from bookshops and libraries were printed. Any information could count as divulging state secrets: mentioning unemployment, food shortages, grain exports, suicides, insanity, epidemics, even weather forecasts were hostile propaganda. It was forbidden to mention OGPU, the NKVD, or even the telephone number of the Registry for Births, Deaths, and Marriages. Almanacs with addresses and telephone numbers of householders in Moscow and Leningrad, published since 1923, were stopped in the early 1930s. Directory inquiries were made at a street kiosk, which took fifteen kopecks (and their names) from inquirers. The censors forbade naming cows and pigs "Commissar," "Pravda," "Proletarian," "Deputy," "Cannibal," or "Yid." So that animals would still come when called, Glavlit suggested phonetically similar substitutes: "Anesthetic" for "Commissar," "Rogue" for "Pravda."[40] The censor mutilated the classics, too: lewdness in Pushkin was "pornography." Folktales, where heroes chose between the left road and the right road, were rewritten so that heroes now chose between a side road and a straight road.

Even accidental dissidence was to be repressed. Under Stalin, misprints were declared "sorties by the class enemy." All over Europe misprints had been disingenuously used by typesetters to annoy authority. Queen Victoria was reported to have "pissed" over Waterloo Bridge; Nicholas II at his coronation had a "crow" put on his head, later altered to "cow." Correction slips in Soviet books listed all mistakes and who made them. Writers or typesetters could die for one misplaced letter, as Andrei Tarkovsky's film *Mirror* suggests unforgettably. Substituting one

consonant made Stalin "pisser" or "shitter" (*ssalin, sralin*), Stalingrad
could be set to read "Stalin is a reptile" (*Stalin gad*). Printing "Lenin had
kittens" (*okotilsia*) instead of "Lenin went hunting" (*okhotilsia*) was
punishable. Captions in newspapers were a favorite target for the censors: "Stalin by the beating-up [instead of electoral] urn"; "We must
guard the life of comrade Stalin and the lives of our leaders" placed opposite "Annihilate the reptiles so that not a trace remains on Soviet
land." Translation into other languages of the Soviet Union was unreliable. "Who does not work, does not eat," in Turkmeni became, "Who
does not work, won't bite."

In the early 1930s the semiliterate troika of censor, propagandist,
and OGPU man went through every public library, removing some 50
percent of the books, including major classics. Poetry, apart from
Pushkin, Nikolai Nekrasov, and Demian Bedny, was devastated.

In 1932 publishing, book distribution, even the secondhand book
trade were all placed under the control of the party's Central Committee.
Antiquarian and foreign books sold by diplomats or returning Russians
were confiscated by inspectors. As enemies of the people were identified
and removed, their books were destroyed and their names excised or
inked out from every copy of encyclopedias; more persons were employed in censoring literature than in creating it. The political line
changed frequently, so that antifascist literature, for instance, or literature on anti-Jewish pogroms, would suddenly have to be destroyed.
Stalin's *Short Course* (a history of the party) went through successive
editions as the heroes of the revolution became unpersons. Foreign publications, on which technological institutes relied, were frequently confiscated; polyglots were arrested as spies. So few censors were left who
could read English, French, or German that foreign newspapers and
books were destroyed wholesale in the post office.

Prose writers suffocated under mindless censorship and complained.
When in March 1930 Bulgakov complained to Stalin, his letter fell first
into Iagoda's hands. Iagoda underlined certain lines—with sympathy or
disapproval, we do not know. "Fighting censorship, of whatever kind
and under whatever regime, is my duty as a writer, just as calling for freedom of the press is. I am an ardent supporter of this freedom and I believe that if any writer were to try to prove that he doesn't need it, he

would be like a fish publicly declaring it doesn't need water." Zamiatin in desperation published his anti-utopia *We* abroad and protested to Stalin the following year: "The author of this letter, sentenced to the highest measure of punishment [death], turns to you with a request for this measure to be substituted by another [exile]."

From Unity to Uniformity

IN THE EARLY 1930s the party was too preoccupied with purges within its ranks to even think of debating the human cost of collectivization. Better to be accused of genocide than be suspected of loyalty to Bukharin, Kamenev, or Trotsky. From spring 1930 to autumn 1932 the party could see where Stalin's policies, which they had endorsed, were leading. Many feared the consequences of collectivization and the impossibly ambitious industrial projects, and believed that strikes and uprisings could encourage the USSR's neighbors to invade. Yet what alternative was there to Stalin? Bukharin, Zinoviev, and Kamenev had by recanting their deviations lost all credibility and had nothing in common but their demand for "democracy" within the party. New men were known only to one region of the country or within one field of industry, the bureaucracy or the party.

Undoubtedly, there was discontent, dismay, and even moral turmoil among party members, especially the middle and older generations who owed little to Stalin. But they failed to act. They had no leaders with any leverage on power; they had no clear idea of how to industrialize the economy without violence against the peasantry. Above all, they had no political principles, no civic beliefs and, consequently, little civic courage. Most were just sick of the bloodshed and feared for their own lives at the hands of the Politburo and OGPU.

Doubters knew that Stalin had to be voted out if policies were to change. They also knew that such a vote, if it failed, would be suicidal, and no more than a quarter of the members of the Central Committee, which Stalin had packed with his cronies, would vote against him. The only other recourse—which had been suggested to, and rejected by, Trotsky a decade earlier—was armed force. Some Red Army commanders like Bliukher deplored Stalin's policies but others such as Marshal Tukhachevsky had no inhibitions about slaughtering peasants, and without Trotsky there was no political figure the army respected enough to follow in revolt. In any case, senior officers were so closely shadowed by party commissars and OGPU agents that any conspiracy would almost certainly be nipped in the bud. OGPU, citing denunciations from teachers at the military academy, warned Stalin that the army had "rightist" sympathizers at its highest levels—including Tukhachevsky— who might try to arrest Stalin and seize power. On September 10, 1930, Menzhinsky, who thrived on exciting his leader's suspicions, advised Stalin, then resting in the Caucasus, to get his blow in first:

> It is risky to arrest the members of this grouping one by one. There can be two ways out: either immediately arrest the most active participants of the group, or wait for you to arrive, and meantime just use surveillance, so as not to be caught unprepared. I consider it necessary to note that at the moment all rebel groups get ready very quickly and the second solution carries a certain risk.[41]

Stalin, for once, was skeptical; he consulted nobody except Molotov, and wrote only to Orjonikidze after musing over Menzhinsky's warning for a fortnight: "Tukhachevsky, it appears, has been in thrall to anti-Soviet elements among the right. . . . Is that possible? Apparently the right are ready to have even a military dictatorship in order to get rid of the Central Committee. . . . This business can't be dealt with the usual way (immediate arrest, etc.). We have to think it over very carefully. . . ."[42] In the chaos of collectivization Stalin needed the military to back up OGPU and dared not let his suspicions carry him away. Stalin and the military did nothing except grumble and speculate about each other.

★ ★ ★ Between 1930 and 1932 there were two serious explorations of how to overthrow Stalin. Both were quickly detected and crushed, and

Stalin by all accounts was not much shaken. The first centered around Sergei Syrtsov and Beso Lominadze, neither rightists or leftists. The serious dissident was Syrtsov, an economist and candidate Politburo member, party secretary in Siberia and possessor of impeccable Stalinist credentials: in the civil war he had slaughtered Cossacks, and in 1928 facilitated Stalin's grain requisitioning expedition to Siberia. Lominadze was a handsome young Georgian and a friend of Sergo Orjonikidze. In 1924 Lominadze had been removed from the Georgian government for nationalism, in other words leniency toward anticommunists. Stalin, lenient in turn, found him work in the International Youth Movement, and in 1930 let him go back to the Caucasus.

Syrtsov had disliked Stalin's "great turnabout." From autumn 1930 he protested at OGPU's proposals to use short-term prisoners as slave construction workers. He criticized the bad quality of industrial output, the waste of resources, the falsification of statistics, the bureaucracy— the latter a keyword for Trotskyist critics of Stalinism. Syrtsov was backed by other economists, particularly in Siberia. Beso Lominadze in the Caucasus, where agriculture was largely small-scale sheepherding and fruit-growing, went further. His "Address from the Transcaucasian Party Committee" called collectivization "pillage" and blamed Stalin personally.

In autumn 1930, while Stalin was away on the Black Sea coast, Lominadze was summoned to Moscow to explain himself. There he and Syrtsov joined forces as "Marxist-Leninists" or, as Stalin was to call them, the "Left-Right Fraction." They decided to try to remove Stalin at the December plenum of the Central Committee and Central Control Commission.

The Politburo banned Syrtsov from publishing his criticisms of the economy and dismissed his demand that Stalin be recalled from the Caucasus to deal with the economic crisis. Lev Mekhlis, editor of *Pravda,* heard about Syrtsov and Lominadze's plan to "remove" (*ubrat*) Stalin. This word meant to Stalin and many of his circle one thing only: kill. Mekhlis denounced Syrtsov as a dissident. On October 21, 1930, the day after Stalin received the denunciation, Syrtsov was hauled before an interrogating commission chaired by Orjonikidze, which included the butcher of the Crimea, Rozalia Zemliachka. The commission bullied

Syrtsov and Lominadze into admitting "antiparty" activity, and by December they had been expelled. Stalin now had a pretext to get rid of any rightists still in office. He replaced Rykov, chairman of the Council of Commissars, with his automaton Molotov. Disarmed so rapidly, Syrtsov and Lominadze realized that their fellow conspirators must have been planted on them by OGPU.

Syrtsov and Lominadze were at first dealt with mildly, perhaps because of Orjonikidze's affection for the latter. Orjonikidze found Syrtsov work in the Urals. Here he lived until the Great Terror, despite being denounced in 1935 for commenting, "Stalin is paving his road to power on Kirov's bones."[43]

In the Great Terror, Stalin turned against his old ally Orjonikidze principally because he had shielded Lominadze:

> Comrade Orjonikidze had a very bad, unpleasant and un-party-like letter from Lominadze. He came to see me and said, "I want to read you Lominadze's letter." "What's it about?" "Something nasty." "Give it to me, I'll bring it to the Politburo's attention, the Central Committee must know what sort of people it has working for it." "I can't." "Why not?" "I gave him my word."[44]

Orjonikidze packed Lominadze off to the Urals too, employing him in industrial Magnitogorsk. But Lominadze was a fellow Georgian, and his disloyalty had insulted Stalin who, it is said, envied Lominadze's guardsman height. On the evening of May 29, 1934, Stalin summoned Lominadze, with Orjonikidze, for a two-hour dressing-down.[45]

> He made me wait for two hours in the reception room. When I went in . . . he didn't look up, didn't raise his head. I lost my temper. How could he treat someone so, degrade someone? I stood on the threshold and thought of turning round straightaway and leaving forever. Too late. He raised his head, made a vague gesture as if to say, "Come on in, why are you standing?" I went up to him and said hello. He didn't even nod in reply to my greeting. He gave a harsh laugh and said haughtily, "What have you got to say for yourself, know-it-all?" . . . He flung his

black pipe at me and swore at me in Georgian. . . . Since then I have been waiting for the ax to fall.

Lominadze, like other Georgians threatened by Stalin, did not wait for the ax to fall. His chauffeur reports: "We were driving onto the Upper Urals high road . . . both in sheepskin jackets, warm and comfortable. Suddenly I heard a sharp bang like a shot. I stopped, turned to Lominadze and said with annoyance, 'A tire's burst.' He said, 'No, it's not a burst tire, I've put a bullet in my chest. . . .' "[46] Lominadze was buried in Magnitogorsk; the monument was soon torn down, the grave leveled, and all of his staff arrested.

The second challenge to Stalin came in 1932. Martemian Riutin, who had once worked in a candy store and was now secretary of the Krasnaia Presnia district of Moscow, mounted, from this lowly post, a challenge to Stalin's dictatorship. Like Syrtsov, Riutin had been a career Stalinist, telling Zinoviev and Kamenev in 1927 that "the party will walk over the opposition's head and the opposition will be thrown onto history's rubbish heap." Like Syrtsov, Riutin was sickened by Stalin's destruction of the Siberian peasants.

In June 1932 two documents circulated around Moscow, written by Riutin as a member of the "Union of Marxist-Leninists" within the Bolshevik party. The papers became known as the Riutin Platform. One document of 167 pages was called "Stalin and the Crisis of Proletarian Dictatorship." Riutin was not the sole author; others—identifiable outcasts from both right and left—had left stylistic and ideological traces in his text. A lecture by Riutin called "Crisis in the Party and Proletarian Dictatorship" was worked into a short "Address to the Party." This manifesto demanded "liquidation of the dictatorship of Stalin and his clique," new elections to party organs, an immediate party congress and elections to the soviets, a new judiciary, a "decisive" purge of OGPU, and slower industrialization. Stalin had turned party leaders, according to Riutin, into "a band of unprincipled, mendacious, cowardly intriguers. . . . Not even the boldest and most brilliant provocateur could have devised a better way to destroy proletarian dictatorship and to discredit Leninism than Stalin and his clique's leadership."

Copies of the Riutin Platform reached academics and party members and were read in the Ukraine, Belorussia, even Poland. Stalin's wife, Nadezhda, read the manifesto, which circulated in the industrial academy where she was studying. Stalin's suspicion that she had read the document and said nothing was one of the straws that broke the back of their marriage.

Menzhinsky and Iagoda mishandled the Riutin Platform, which OGPU did not show to Stalin until September 1932. A wave of arrests and a purge of half a million party members ensued. Balitsky and Molchanov of OGPU interrogated Riutin, who quickly recanted. His daughter, who brought him fresh underwear, was convinced from the state of his linen that he was being physically tortured. At Riutin's premises OGPU "discovered" documentation that incriminated Zinoviev, Kamenev, and Bukharin.[47]

On October 11, 1932, Menzhinsky, Iagoda, and Balitsky, with an OGPU prosecutor, sentenced Riutin to death. In 1932 death sentences on party members still had to be confirmed by the Politburo. It is believed that only Stalin voted for shooting Riutin; his subordinates Kirov, Kuibyshev, and Orjonikidze voted for ten years' solitary confinement, while Molotov and Voroshilov abstained. Riutin went to prison.[48]

The fates of Syrtsov, Lominadze, and Riutin discouraged other overt opposition. Stalin could by the end of 1932 be sure that, whatever the horrors in the countryside, no internal force could shake his rule. He was now cocooned in the Kremlin and his dachas, moving between them in bulletproof cars escorted by heavily armed convoys. He no longer visited intellectuals or incited them to speak their innermost thoughts. He no longer needed to charm or persuade anybody. Intimidation had proved quicker and more reliable.

On November 9, 1932, Stalin's last remaining tie with normality was severed. His wife, Nadezhda, was found dead—they slept in separate rooms in the Kremlin—in a pool of blood, a small pistol which her brother had given her by her side. The previous evening at a party Stalin became, or acted, drunk and had thrown bread, cigarette ends, and orange peel at her, shouting, "Hey you, drink!" "Don't 'hey' me," she said, and left.[49] Bukharin, Molotov, Marshal Budionny, and Nikita Khrushchiov all had explanations for her suicide: Stalin had another woman; he uttered violent threats to her; she was a typically neurotic Alliluev; she was horrified by what she heard about ordinary citizens' lives and wanted to punish her husband for his crimes against the people.

The letters that Stalin and Nadezhda exchanged in 1930 and 1931, when Stalin was in the Caucasus without her, show mutual affection, mingled with fearful resentment on her part and wrathful impatience on his. She showed jealousy: "I've heard about you from a young attractive woman who said that you looked splendid, she saw you at dinner at Kalinin's, you were in remarkably good spirits and teased everyone mercilessly who was embarrassed at being there with you." She interceded for those she felt were unjustly treated. She hinted at hardships: "The public's mood in the trams and other public places is bearable; they grumble, but good-naturedly. . . . I must say that the mood about food supplies, among students and teachers, is only average, everyone is worn out by the queues. . . . Prices in the shops are very high, that's why there are a lot of goods. Don't be angry at such details, but I'd so much want these disparities to vanish from people's lives. . . ."[50]

These were tame objections. Nadezhda applauded Stalin's extreme actions, such as the demolition of the cathedral of Christ the Savior. His replies were curt and sometimes sarcastic—"For some reason recently you have started praising me. What does this mean?"—but his letters to Nadezhda also often ended in baby language—"kiss you wots and wots." Whatever tipped the balance and made death better than life with Stalin happened in summer 1932 but the letters for that year have disappeared. Had Nadezhda grasped how much he was responsible for the miseries of the countryside? Did she agree with the Riutin Platform?[51]

Stalin forbade an autopsy, allegedly because, "All the same, it will be said that I killed her." The death certificate signed by Dr. Vladimir Rozanov, one of Lenin's doctors, who had treated Stalin for the previous ten years, states, "Committed suicide by a shot to the heart"; Dr. Boris Zbarsky, who had mummified Lenin and prepared Nadezhda's body for her lying-in-state, told a friend a year before he died that he had masked a wound in her temple.[52] Reports of Stalin's behavior after her death are contradictory. He attended or he stayed away from the funeral; he kissed her body during the lying-in-state or he pushed the coffin angrily away. Over Stalin's immediate circle her death cast a pall; the notion that he might have murdered his wife or driven her to suicide, as he had provoked his son Iakov to shoot himself, made his allies nearly as fearful as his opponents.

Stalin, a consummate actor, could not hide his bitterness. For him all suicides were betrayals. To the army commander Budionny he complained, "What normal mother would leave her children orphans? I didn't have time to give them attention, and she has left me bereft. Of course, I was a bad husband; I didn't have time to take her to the cinema."[53] Not grief but murderous vindictiveness overcame Stalin. Those who had found Nadezhda's body were soon in camps or condemned cells, as were most of her relatives and friends and, apart from Nikita Khrushchiov, her fellow students.

Kaganovich recalled that he had known Stalin as five or six different persons, and that a new personality began in 1932 and lasted until 1940.[54] Stalin now felt vulnerable to assassination. Riutin had proposed "removing" him, then a year later at Sochi his motorboat came under fire from the shore—either because the frontier guards had not been notified that the boat would leave Soviet waters or because his host, the Georgian chekist Lavrenti Beria, was trying, as OGPU had the previous year, to impress on Stalin that he needed protection from assassins. After Nadezhda's death, Stalin charged those he singled out for death with plotting his assassination.

★ ★ ★ The year 1934 seemed to Soviet citizens and foreign observers to mark a change, perhaps for the better. To the Soviet public, the British and French were no longer portrayed as devils, although a worse devil, Hitler, was consolidating his hold on Germany. News, even visitors, from abroad seeped through. The harvest was good: the collective farms, supplied with working machinery and with several million fewer mouths to feed, delivered more food to the cities; OGPU executed a mere 2,000 for counterrevolution, down from 20,000 in 1930 and 10,000 in 1931. A record number, 139,000, of counterrevolutionaries had gone to the GULAG in 1933 and deaths in the camps shot up five times to more than 62,000, but these casualties were invisible to those in the cities. When the writers wound up their congress in September 1934 they assumed that Stalin had dealt with his opponents and had carried off, albeit by the skin of his teeth, his risky economic enterprise. They believed that they could breathe freely.

As for Iagoda, long before Gorky's death his days were numbered. On October 29, 1932, Menzhinsky visited Stalin's office for the last time; thereafter, he worked desultorily at his dacha. Stalin's notes to Menzhinsky show that he, not Iagoda, had Stalin's confidence:

> Comrade Menzhinsky! I ask you to keep secret the content of our conversation about affairs in OGPU (for the time being!). I mean by this the OGPU collegium (including Iagoda), whose members must not know for the time being the content of our conversation. As for the secretaries of the Central Committee, you can talk to them completely freely. Greetings! I. Stalin.[55]

But Menzhinsky's days were numbered too. In summer 1933, at a sanatorium in Kislovodsk, he was watching only himself. His notebooks end: "No work. Just lie there for 24 hours a day, with an ice pack or a hot-water bottle on your chest, bath or massage. This is death. You lie all day in a hammock . . . what a pleasure it is to watch life passing! I've been forced to live, to take up psychology. . . ." He died on May 10, 1934, at the age of fifty-nine of heart and kidney disease, and his family was looked after.[56] Iagoda was later accused of poisoning Menzhinsky (and others) with mercury vapor, and Menzhinsky's nephew Mikhail Rozanov declares that to this day he can remember the smell of the lethal wallpaper Iagoda had installed in their apartments.

Iagoda helped organize Menzhinsky's funeral. Not until July did Stalin, after sounding out other candidates, decide that he had, as yet, no alternative. In August OGPU underwent metamorphosis: Iagoda became the head of the giant NKVD (People's Commissariat of Internal Affairs) ministry of police and security.

Iagoda might have felt promoted had he not sensed the watchful eye of Stalin's devoted favorite, the boyish chief of the Central Committee's personnel department, Nikolai Ezhov.

SIX

MURDERING THE OLD GUARD

The more innocent they are, the more they
deserve to die.

Bertolt Brecht

The Killing of Sergei Kirov

Gherkins are green, tomatoes are red,
Stalin in a corridor shot Kirov dead.

Folk couplet of 1934

AT 4:30 P.M. on December 1, 1934, a shot was fired in Leningrad. In the next four years its ricochets would kill not only Genrikh Iagoda, but most of the party elite, commissars, judges, prosecutors, senior army officers, captains of industry, and over a million others. Leonid Nikolaev, a former employee of the Leningrad party, shot Sergei Kirov point-blank in the head. Kirov was Stalin's protégé, the Leningrad party secretary, a member of the Politburo and secretary of the Central Committee. This was the first and last assassination of a Politburo member in Soviet history. After fifteen minutes the doctors gave up resuscitation and telephoned Stalin. Nikolaev had turned his gun on himself but missed; after two hours in hysterics, he shouted out, "I have avenged myself."

When the news reached Stalin, he was closeted with Molotov, Kaganovich, and Andrei Zhdanov—whom he immediately appointed to succeed Kirov. He summoned his chief bodyguard, Karl Pauker, Iagoda, and a dozen members of the Politburo and secretariat; even Bukharin, now editor of *Izvestiia*, was called in. Stalin ordered a special train to take him to Leningrad and immediately drafted a decree to deal with "terrorists." Kalinin as head of state and Abel Enukidze as secretary of Kalinin's presidium then signed Stalin's draft into law:

> The case of those accused of preparing or committing terrorist acts is to be dealt with in an accelerated way; judicial organs may not hold up the carrying out of death sentences because of appeals for mercy from criminals of this category. The organs of

the NKVD are to carry out death sentences passed on criminals of the above categories as soon as the court has pronounced sentence.

When Stalin got back from Leningrad, the law was made more specific:

1. The investigation of such cases must be completed in no more than ten days;
2. The charges will be handed to the accused twenty-four hours before the court examines the case;
3. The case will be heard with no participation by other parties;
4. No appeals for quashing the verdict or for mercy will be allowed;
5. The death sentence is to be carried out as soon as it has been pronounced.[1]

Stalin made this ruthless decree the basis for dispatching hundreds of thousands until more legalistic measures were introduced in 1939.

Many believe that Stalin drafted this law and ordered his special train to Leningrad before Kirov's murder, in other words that he had planned it. Stalin's office register shows, however, that the law was signed by Kalinin and Enukidze between 6 and 8 p.m., and the railway archives that the train was booked after the murder.[2] Party commissions between 1956 and 1990, witnesses' testimonies, and archival searches have not proved Stalin's complicity, and the simplest explanation seems the best: that Leonid Nikolaev was a demented, aggrieved killer acting on his own, aided only by luck in encountering Kirov when he was unguarded.

Stalin had several times in the 1920s shown that he could order the death of a man whom he had only days before embraced, but he began to terrify his inner circle only after 1934. Why should he turn on Kirov, whom he had sent to replace Zinoviev in Leningrad and whose record since the revolution had been to consistently follow and applaud his policies? Some of the very few delegates to the seventeenth party congress of spring 1934 who survived Stalin alleged that there were meetings of malcontents—one in the quarters of Sergo Orjonikidze, then Stalin's closest friend—plotting to vote for Kirov rather than Stalin as general secretary. In the event there were, it seems, only three votes against Stalin. Some say that Stalin had several hundred ballot papers burned. Others allege that Kirov told Stalin of the plot and then despaired, convinced that his "head was on the scaffold," that "Stalin would never forgive" his being nominated. But these accounts emanate from persons, such as Kirov's sister-in-law Sofia, who were not close to him, and they contradict known facts. It is true that three surviving delegates who counted ballots agree that there were two or three votes against Stalin and that there were about 300 fewer ballot papers than delegates, but had papers crossing out Stalin's name been destroyed or had some delegates failed to vote?

Nobody saw a burned ballot paper and its seems unlikely that Kirov would have let his name go forward. Kirov shunned high-level politics; although a good orator, he preferred contact with the party and factory workers in Leningrad, as he had in the north Caucasus. He had no vision of his own. He had last seen Stalin on November 28 when they had been to the theater together and Stalin saw him off at the railway station. The Kirovs had been family friends of the Stalins for years. After Nadezhda's suicide, Kirov and Orjonikidze kept Stalin company through the night. During summer breaks in the Caucasus Kirov and Stalin took the Matsesta mud baths together. Kirov was one of only two men in front of whom Stalin would undress. (Nikolai Vlasik, Stalin's bodyguard, enjoyed the same intimacy.) They played skittles together, Stalin partnering a kitchen worker, Kirov partnering Vlasik. The only blot on Kirov's copybook was that he had been a versatile and open-minded journalist on a politically middle-of-the-road Vladikavkaz newspaper before the revolution, but Stalin liked his subordinates to have a questionable past.

Nikolaev's disturbed behavior before the murder aroused comment. He had been detained in the party building in October, carrying a gun and acting suspiciously, but released as the Smolny Institute was not a restricted building and Nikolaev had had a license for a sporting weapon since 1924. His diary shows a man driven by bitter conceit. After running over a pedestrian on his bicycle he was demoted from his post as a party instructor, then dismissed for refusing manual work. He hated depending on his wife's earnings and felt he was an unnoticed genius. His diary is full of inept epigrams and ominous ambitions: "There are a lot of people, but there's little difference between them. . . . I want to die with the same joy as I was born with." The diary has detailed notes of times, addresses, distances, and shot angles for an assassination of Kirov: "After first shot, run to his car: a) smash window and fire; b) open door. In Smolny: at first encounter take a grip on my spirit and decisively. . . . My path of thorns . . . letter to the Central Committee . . . Lack of prospects. 8 months' unemployment . . . Moment and penitence; historic acts. We and they . . ."

Would Stalin and Iagoda have used such a loose cannon as Leonid Nikolaev when they had professional killers at their disposal?[3] Moreover, as the historian Adam Ulam asks, why should Stalin get rid of Kirov by having him assassinated, and thus allow people to believe that a party leader, even himself, was assailable? If Stalin wanted to eliminate a rival, the latter was first branded a traitor, then arrested, tried, and shot; or else he was reported ill, poisoned, or found dead in a crash.

★ ★ ★ Stalin's train raced through the night along 700 kilometers of track guarded by thousands of NKVD men. In the morning, accompanied by the heads of every branch of the power structure—Voroshilov, Molotov, Zhdanov, Iagoda, Ezhov, Khrushchiov, Karl Pauker, Vyshinsky, and Aleksandr Kosarev—Stalin left the train.[4] He was greeted by Filipp Medved, head of the Leningrad NKVD and a friend of Kirov. Stalin struck him in the face and called him an asshole.

Iagoda and Vyshinsky set up an investigation. Stalin decided to interrogate personally Nikolaev and Kirov's bodyguard, Mikhail Borisov, the chief witness. Kirov insisted on walking the streets and loathed being followed by bodyguards and Borisov had lagged behind when Kirov unexpectedly went back to party headquarters. Stalin told the NKVD to bring Borisov but nearly all their vehicles were busy and only a truck with a broken front spring was left. Borisov sat on the edge of the open back, and when the truck veered his head was smashed against a lamppost.[5]

What Stalin and Nikolaev said to each other is not minuted. Molotov, who in reams of dictated reminiscences said little that was even half true, recalls Nikolaev as "a miserable specimen to look at . . . He said he'd meant to kill, for ideological reasons. . . . I think he seemed to be embittered by something, expelled from the party, a chip on his shoulder. And he was used by the Zinovievites. . . ." Nikolaev's behavior at the trial has also been cited as proof that Stalin ordered the murder. Nikolaev, according to a Cheka guard, when the sentence was delivered, exclaimed, "Cruel!" and, "I've been deceived." However, the reason Nikolaev cried out was most likely that Stalin's promise to him had been broken. Stalin and the NKVD frequently bargained with the accused and promised them their lives—or the lives of their loved ones—if they testified as they were told to. With each successive trial, as the accused incriminated themselves and yet still suffered the death penalty, together with their relatives, these promises lost their effect. In December 1934, the bargain still seemed sincere. Presumably, for a promise that he would not be shot, Nikolaev incriminated Zinoviev and Kamenev, and gave Stalin the material he needed for a final judicial solution.

Arrests and trials followed. Iagoda declared that Nikolaev was acting for émigré agents; over one hundred alleged White Guards already in NKVD hands were shot, their deaths reported in the second week of December. Iagoda clearly did not believe in a conspiracy. He pursued the case languidly. Ezhov instructed him that Stalin wanted Zinoviev and Kamenev targeted. When Iagoda failed to get the right testimony, Stalin—as Ezhov would boast when Iagoda fell from power—telephoned him: "Look out, or we'll smash your face in." After three weeks' interrogation, Nikolaev was made to confess to links with Trotsky through the German consulate and, as his wife, Milda Draule, was Latvian, with Latvian espionage. The others arrested were Zinovievites loyal to the old Leningrad party apparatus. Through guilt by association, Iagoda established—but not to Stalin's satisfaction—that Nikolaev was acting for, if not at the behest of, Zinoviev.

A few months before, another loner, Artiom Nakhaev, had attempted violence against the Bolshevik leadership, and after three months' interrogation by Agranov had confessed that he was the tool of émigrés and foreigners. On August 5, 1934, just outside Moscow, Nakhaev, an artillery commander, had called on a squad of cadets he was training to seize firearms from an arsenal and attack the Kremlin. "The state is enslaving workers and peasants. There is no freedom of speech, Semites are running the country. Comrade workers, where are the factories you were promised, comrade peasants, where are the lands you were promised? Down with the old leaders, long live the new revolution!" The cadets froze in horror. Nakhaev swallowed poison, but was resuscitated and arrested. Stalin ordered Nakhaev to be "annihilated," and instructed Iagoda to fabricate a conspiracy. A few days before Nikolaev, the demented Nakhaev was shot after being indicted as an emissary of a Tsarist general in the pay of the Estonian consulate in Moscow.[6] Stalin raged to Kaganovich:

Nakhaev's case is dastardly . . . Of course (of course!) he's not a loner. He must be pressed to the wall, made to talk, to give the whole truth and then be punished with all severity. He has to be a Polish-German (or Japanese) agent. *Chekisty* are becoming ridiculous when they discuss his "political views" with him (call that interrogation!). A mercenary scoundrel has no political views—else he wouldn't be an agent of outside forces.

On December 4 Stalin returned to Moscow with Kirov's body. He seemed distressed at the lying-in-state and was heard to say, "Sleep in peace, my dear friend, we'll avenge you." Stalin's revenge was the trigger for a mass psychosis that would rage through the Soviet Union for four years.

Today's Stalinists and even a number of non-Stalinists argue that everything Stalin had done, however murderous and cruel, until Kirov's murder was ultimately necessary and for the best. They maintain that the USSR had to become industrially strong, to deter its external enemies, and that in the wake of the Great Depression its exports were insufficient to buy the technology necessary for industrialization. They also argue that the USSR's only realizable asset was grain, and the peasantry would not produce enough for export unless they were collectivized. The proof of Stalin's success is that in 1943–5 the USSR defeated Hitler and deterred Japan. Humanity, the Stalinist argument runs, should therefore be grateful for Stalin's strength of purpose, for had Adolf Hitler and Admiral Isoroku Yamamoto shaken hands somewhere in the Urals in 1942, the whole world would have been enslaved by fascism for generations to come, and would have endured a genocidal holocaust far worse than Stalin's purges.

But until 1937 nobody was planning armed action against the USSR, except in Stalin's paranoiac fantasies. Moreover, when the earning potential of the USSR's natural resources, even in the depressed 1930s, and the success of such programs as Roosevelt's New Deal in converting inefficient agricultural workers into builders of dams and factories, are considered, the revenue justifications for collectivization collapse. An evil action can have good consequences, and vice versa, but it needs exceptional generosity of spirit, not to say naïveté, to ascribe to Stalin's pursuit of total power and the murder of millions humanitarian motives.

Events in the USSR after 1934 defy logic as well as morality. With the exception of Viacheslav Molotov, who maintained to his death that Stalin and he had exterminated a fifth column that would have betrayed the USSR to the Nazis, nobody has been able to rationalize Stalin's vengeance for Kirov's death. His murder was the trigger to exterminate every Bolshevik who had opposed Stalin, or who might conceivably take his place. If Kirov had not been killed, we can reasonably suppose that some other event would have provided a pretext.

There had been no loud protests against the events of 1929–34, because there was virtually no civil society left in the USSR. The Church had been reduced to a few frightened priests hiding in ruins. The legal profession had nothing left of its former power but its rhetoric. The prestigious medical profession was suborned to the Kremlin hospital. The creative intellectuals had been exiled, imprisoned, terrorized, driven to ramshackle ivory towers, or bought off. But the *total* absence of protest after December 1934 is still amazing, if for no other reason than that the hangmen must have guessed from Stalin's actions that they were now themselves in danger. To many in OGPU, the party, and above all the armed forces, the escalation of terror, as Stalin breached one taboo after another, was palpable. He was insisting on death for political dissenters, real or imaginary. What was there to lose by stepping up dissent into rebellion? What held back Iagoda in OGPU, Tukhachevsky in the Red Army, or Sergo Orjonikidze in the Politburo from attempting to neutralize Stalin? Why did they not get their blow in first?

Back in the Kremlin in December 1934, Stalin took a pencil and sketched out a scheme. Opponents were assigned to a "Leningrad center" and a "Moscow center" and alleged to have conspired to assassinate Kirov. This time some thirty-three persons were gathered in Stalin's office, among them Ivan Akulov, the chief prosecutor, his deputy Krylenko, and the inventive legislator Professor Andrei Vyshinsky. The fabrication of the two "centers" and the indictment of their supposed members took another month.

Removing Zinoviev and Kamenev

The works [of Machiavelli] have thus played a prominent role in the great work of revealing the true nature of power in a class society, a work which has been taken to its end only today, in the works of Marx and Engels, Lenin and Stalin.

> *Lev Kamenev, Introduction to Volume I of the* Works of Machiavelli

ZINOVIEV AND KAMENEV were in 1934 contrite hacks, hoping to rise again when Stalin's anger and suspicion had been allayed. Zinoviev began writing on Marx and Engels. Stalin kept a vengeful eye open and on August 5, 1934, condemned Zinoviev's commentary on Engels in *The Bolshevik:* "We can't leave *The Bolshevik* in the hands of morons which Comrade Zinoviev can always make dunces of. Those guilty must be found and removed from the editorial office. Best of all to remove Comrade Zinoviev."[7]

Stalin treated Kamenev more subtly. Their early acquaintance was founded on Kamenev's gift to Stalin of Machiavelli's *The Prince;* the last inch in the rope that Stalin allowed Kamenev was a foreword to the first volume of a new edition of Machiavelli. Kamenev's essay shows belated insight into what he and Stalin had inherited from Cesare Borgia, Lorenzo de' Medici, and Niccolò Machiavelli:

Machiavelli made of his treatise a strikingly expressive and wide-ranging catalogue of rules, which a ruler of his time must be guided by in order to win power, keep it and victoriously resist all attempts against him. This is far from being the *sociology* of power, but this set of recipes gives us splendidly the *zoological* features of the struggle for power. . . . The immorality, the criminality, the cruelty of Machiavelli's book about *The Prince* is entirely contained by the fact that he decided . . . to speak out about things as they are.[8]

When Kamenev and Zinoviev were charged with Kirov's murder, the new edition of Machiavelli was stopped, and the volume with Kamenev's foreword was pulped.

Weeks passed before Zinoviev and Kamenev were charged. First, Stalin and Iagoda replaced the disgraced Leningrad NKVD men with their Moscow chiefs. Iakov Agranov, who had fabricated conspiracies ever since 1921, conducted the main interrogations assisted by an articulate prosecutor, Lev Sheinin, who made a good living writing up his investigations in the style of Sherlock Holmes stories. Agranov and Sheinin, a sledgehammer and a crowbar, broke everyone who had unluckily befriended, or merely met, Leonid Nikolaev. Soon a worse ogre than Agranov appeared. Nikolai Ezhov, although officially a Central Committee not an NKVD man, came to interrogate some of the accused.

Stalin personally wrote out the indictment of Nikolaev and his alleged associates. Stalin's text delighted Vyshinsky, who had only to add the finishing touches. The indictment stated that the accused were wreaking vengeance on Kirov for crushing the Zinovievites. The decree of December 1 was made retroactive. The trial started at 2:40 p.m. on December 28 and sentence was pronounced at 6:40 the next morning. On December 25 Vasili Ulrikh, by now a notorious hanging judge, had visited Stalin to find out what sentence to pass. Nevertheless, Ulrikh telephoned Stalin twice during the trial, so perturbed was even he by Nikolaev's insistence that he had acted alone. Ulrikh's fellow judges and his common-law wife both recall that he wanted to refer the case for further investigation, but that Stalin was adamant: "No further investigation, finish the trial . . . they must all have the same sentence—shooting." This snuffed out the last spark of legality in Ulrikh. He never demurred again.

All fourteen were shot that same morning. Agranov and Vyshinsky stood by the cells as the victims went to the death cellar. Nikolaev's executioner reminisced: "I picked Nikolaev up by his trousers. I was crying. I was so sorry for Kirov." The last to be shot was the second arrested, Ivan Kotolynov. Agranov and Vyshinsky asked him, "You'll be shot now, so tell the truth, who organized Kirov's murder, and how?" A guard testified twenty-two years later that Kotolynov replied, "The whole of this trial is nonsense. People have been shot. I'm going to be shot now. But none of us, except Nikolaev, is guilty of anything."

These executions were only the beginning. In March, Nikolaev's wife, sister-in-law, and brother-in-law were shot. Leningrad party officials were told to list former Zinoviev supporters. They replied that it would be easier to list those who had not supported Zinoviev.[9] Throughout December 1934 and January 1935, the Leningrad party was cleared of those who had worked under Zinoviev: 663 were exiled to Siberia, 325 to other cities in European Russia. Almost every Bolshevik who had belonged to a fraction, even before Lenin's death, was expelled and hundreds of "democratic centralists" and trade unionists were sent to the backwoods, effectively holding pens for the condemned. After Leningrad's NKVD and party came the former aristocrats, civil servants, merchants, and bourgeois who were still at large: several trainloads left Leningrad in early 1935.

Stalin closed in slowly on his quarry; Kamenev was even included in the guard of honor at Kirov's funeral. He and Zinoviev avoided each other. On their reinstatement in the party in 1933, when each was received by Stalin in his office for the first time in four years and the last time ever, they had decided never to say or do anything that OGPU could use against them. Kamenev had, thanks to Gorky, found refuge in literary work. Zinoviev, however, scorned journalism: only political power interested him.

At the seventeenth party congress in February 1934 both right and left oppositions had prostrated themselves. Bukharin proclaimed Stalin "a mighty herald not just of economic but of technical and scientific progress on the planet . . . a glorious field marshal of proletarian forces" and qualified his earlier statements as "Parthian arrows bordering on the criminal." Kamenev made an act of contrition: "We aimed our most powerful sting, all the weapons we then had, at the man who hit us harder, who more penetratingly than anyone pointed out the criminal road we had taken, at Comrade Stalin." Zinoviev excelled them both: "Stalin's report was . . . a chef-d'oeuvre which joined the treasury of world communism the moment it was pronounced."

As Zinoviev's apartment was being searched by OGPU on December 16, 1934, he penned a letter to Stalin: "In no way, in no way, in no way am I guilty before the party, before the Central Committee or before you personally. . . . I beseech you to believe my honest word. I am shaken to the depth of my soul."[10] A week later, the NKVD was still ferreting for evidence against Zinoviev and Kamenev. The two were rearrested in mid-January 1935, when a former supporter broke down under questioning. The subsequent first trial of the "left opposition" was a travesty, even by Soviet standards of the 1930s. Kamenev was told as the trial opened that if he repeated his confessions his life would be spared. Ulrikh gave Zinoviev ten years in prison, and Kamenev five. Later Iagoda applied tougher interrogation techniques, and Zinoviev and Kamenev faced capital charges. Meanwhile, seventy-seven alleged members of "the Zinoviev Leningrad opposition group" went to prison or into exile, and another 12,000 members of the "exploiting classes" were deported from Leningrad.

Before finishing off the left opposition, Stalin took a broom to his own stables. Iagoda's men combed the Kremlin, arresting cleaners, librarians, secretaries, and guards for plotting to murder Stalin, their pretext that relatives of Kamenev worked in the Kremlin. There was one surprising victim of this operation: one of Stalin's most trusted friends, a Georgian he had known in Baku, Abel Enukidze.[11] Expelled from the party for "depravity," he found himself a niche running the spas around Kislovodsk. Stalin then demoted Enukidze to running road transport in Kharkov, where he was arrested two years later. Enukidze was the only rightist victim of 1935, and was presumably victimized for personal reasons. Stalin first eliminated the remnants of the left, after adopting their policies of forced collectivization and industrialization, because those on the left were close to Trotsky, and despite Trotsky's impotence in exile, Stalin feared them more.

Stalin had other reasons to strike again at enemies he had knocked down eight years before. In February 1935, during the Kremlin purge, Iagoda arrested Mikhail Prezent, the secretary of the journal *Soviet Construction*. Prezent was small fry except that he was Abel Enukidze's friend. Prezent was not shot; deprived of insulin, he died in prison in three months. His diary was a bombshell. Iagoda passed it on to Stalin.[12] Prezent knew Gorky, Demian Bedny, and many Trotskyists, whose gossip he recorded from their fall in 1928 to their partial rehabilitation in the early 1930s. Stalin annotated the diary and, where it exasperated him, tore pages out before returning it to Iagoda. Trotsky was described as the last intelligent man in Soviet politics, someone to whom "today's barking pack of dogs used to hand his galoshes and brush the dust off his suit." Prezent recorded sarcasms at Stalin's expense, some from favorites like Demian Bedny and the journalist Mikhail Koltsov making fun of Stalin's uncouth habits such as opening uncut pages in books with his greasy thumb. Prezent's diary showed that the semi-rehabilitated left felt that they still mattered. Their jokes did not amuse Stalin. One he underlined: "Trotsky decided to commit suicide, so sent Stalin a letter challenging him to socialist competition."

If Kirov's death was tragedy, Prezent's diary was the farce preceding the massacre, but Iagoda seemed increasingly unlikely to be the one to conduct it. His lapses of vigilance were disqualifying him.[13] Soft sentences on the Leningrad NKVD and on Zinoviev and Kamenev looked like inertia. Iagoda stuck out like a sore thumb. Younger men brought in to replace the ousted old Bolsheviks were not inhibited by the unwritten rules that had settled party disagreements bloodlessly. They had been children in the civil war; often they had lost or left their parents. Stalin was their father and Stalinism the only ideology they knew. They saw nothing sacred about Bukharin or Kamenev and nothing absurd in the idea that Lenin's cohorts might be spies and saboteurs.

Stalin had a new framework for repression. As well as the law of 1932 which had put stealing a handful of food on the level of treason and accelerated the procedure for trying terrorists, a wider concept of treason, "betraying the motherland," now applied to citizens who left the country or failed to return: their relatives, cohabitants, and dependents were punished by five years' exile. "Special sessions" (*oso*) had first been introduced by Tsar Alexander III to exile revolutionaries; under Stalin an *oso* could execute its victim. Each *oso* consisted of an NKVD man, a prosecutor, and a party official. Hundreds of thousands of prisoners a year could be processed as quickly as cattle through a slaughterhouse.

The lawyers mutely assented. Krylenko agreed with Stalin that there was an emergency, that the fewer class enemies there were left, the harder they would resist. Only the chief prosecutor, Ivan Akulov, whom Stalin had in 1931 thought tough enough to replace Iagoda, demurred. Akulov ran the first trial of Kamenev and Zinoviev but would not condemn them for Kirov's murder. In mid-1935 he was transferred to less blood-thirsty work.[14]

Ulrikh and the other hanging judges never questioned the sentences prescribed. Only to embarrass Iagoda did the Politburo periodically display token leniency. In September 1934 a committee was set up to "free innocent persons who have suffered . . . to purge OGPU of those who use 'specific techniques' [torture] and to punish them, whoever they are." A few defense lawyers had previously taken on cases where the NKVD was prosecuting; one was Nikolai Borisovich Polynov, editor of *The Lawyer* (*Iurist*) before the revolution. Before 1933 he occasionally secured an acquittal, even when the verdict had been dictated by OGPU, but now defense lawyers were appointed by the prosecution.

Only one traditional legal skill was upheld by Andrei Vyshinsky. Koni and Plevako, two eminent Russian lawyers of the nineteenth century, had loved the sound of their own rhetoric and published their speeches. But Koni and Plevako had been defense lawyers whereas Vyshinsky's genius for invective was placed exclusively at the prosecution's service. Vyshinsky and Krylenko fought to dominate the legal system and in 1935 attacked each other in print. Vyshinsky triumphed, passing to Stalin Krylenko's fatal remark that legal decisions need not heed Stalin's speeches. Krylenko was no saint but he did publish in *Soviet Justice* a feature called "Black Tables," exposing miscarriages of justice or failures to observe the policies of the Commissariat for Justice. Another column called "Red Tables" lauded judicially or politically correct actions. Just one of Vyshinsky and Krylenko's colleagues—Faina

Niurina—took justice seriously. She lobbied for the independence of the investigator from the prosecution—a tradition of the Tsarist legal system. Her naive energy and "token woman" status took her some way until, in 1937, she fell foul of Vyshinsky and was shot a year later. Of six judges in the Court of Appeal, five were killed and one sent to the camps. Soviet justice was virtually extinct.

Hitler's Lessons

HISTORIANS ARE TEMPTED to take Hitler and Stalin in tandem, as parallel studies of the psychopathic dictator. In fact, they differ from each other as much as either differs from a normal human being. They are alike as totem figures of evil, striving to dominate the world, brooking no contradiction, unconstrained by remorse or affection. They are unlike in all other ways: Hitler left, as much as he could for his purposes, Germany's social, legal, and economic structure unchanged; he chose an ideology, anti-Semitism, that appealed to all classes in Germany, to the Christian churches, to the European nations he would conquer; he used rhetoric and armed force as his main instruments. Stalin finished Lenin's mission of demolishing the social, legal, and economic structure of Russia's society; he made revolutionary socialism a hollow container for his own fascism—he was no more a communist than a Borgia pope was a Catholic; he expressed himself in silences, gestures, and clichés, and, except for two years at the height of the Second World War, no dictator did more to keep his armed forces under his heel. Hitlerism was like a cancer on the body politic, letting the body apparently function normally until the cancer destroys it; Stalinism was more like the larva of a parasitic wasp—devouring and converting to itself the body politic that it has invaded. But despite their differences and their enmity, Hitler and Stalin had common interests for a decade, from 1932 to 1941.

For most of the 1920s Germany and the Soviet Union, the two nations left hungry at the feast of the Treaty of Versailles, had an understanding that went beyond common diplomatic and commercial interests. When Hitler took power on a program hostile to the USSR,

Stalin naturally had to sound out new alliances and Hitler became a valuable bogeyman. From 1932 until 1939 the USSR and the Comintern, managed by Stalin's puppets Kuusinen and Béla Kun, depicted Hitler's Germany as a menace so great that all antifascists had to overlook Soviet blemishes. Was not the USSR now the sole defender of peace, the Jews, and the workers? Correspondingly, Hitler made the Bolsheviks into a bogeyman for all anticommunists: were not the Bolsheviks and international Jewry the source of all the world's evils?

But antagonism concealed respect, although Hitler seemed at first to Stalin, as he did to Western leaders, a malleable buffoon. Because he thought he would be able to manipulate Hitler, Stalin's Comintern forbade German communists to join the social democrats in resisting the rise of the Nazis. Stalin thus helped Hitler to gain power, just as his vendetta against other parties of the left helped General Franco defeat the republic of Spain.

Hitler's first political actions imitated Stalin: setting up concentration camps, attacking homosexuality and "degenerate art." Stalin had outlawed male homosexuality after Iagoda reported on December 19, 1933:

> While liquidating recently a union of pederasts in Moscow and Leningrad, OGPU has ascertained the existence of salons and dens where orgies have been arranged. . . . Pederasts have been recruiting and debauching completely healthy young people, Red Army men, navy men and students. We have no criminal law to enable us to prosecute pederasts. . . . I would consider it essential to issue an appropriate law to make pederasty answerable as a crime. In many ways this will clean up society, will rid it of nonconformists.[15]

Hitler impressed Stalin when he burned down the Reichstag in summer 1933, then framed communists for the arson. Hitler had not sufficiently suborned German judges to carry off the fabrication, but he was imitating Menzhinsky's show trials. Stalin sent two Soviet journalists to cover the Reichstag trial.[16] Commissar for Foreign Affairs Litvinov was traveling via Berlin, and was happy, "if Hitler desires, to talk with him too . . . if they propose signing a protocol that all conflicts are settled, then we can agree to that, if they express in an apologetic form regret for a number of incorrect actions. . . ."[17]

In summer 1934 Hitler's Night of the Long Knives also excited Stalin's admiration. Hitler killed the leader of the brownshirts, Erich Röhm, with scores of his followers, thus getting rid of his own left deviation. Stalin exclaimed, it is reported, "Clever man, that's how to deal with opposition, cut them out in one go!" Stalin told his army intelligence, "The events in Germany . . . must lead to the consolidation of the regime and to the strengthening of Hitler's own power."[18] He drew analogous conclusions for himself.

At the Nuremberg rallies of summer 1935 Goebbels and Rosenberg berated the Soviet Union. Stalin held back Kaganovich and Molotov: "My advice is not to make a hysterical noise in our press and not to give in to the hysterics of our newspapermen. Nuremberg is a response to the Communist International, if you recall that the Comintern congress poured filth over them and besmirched them. Let *Pravda* criticize them in a principled, political way, but without street language." In Hitler's virulent anti-Soviet Reichstag speech Stalin saw "no basis for protest."[19]

The differences in principle between Hitler's national and Stalin's Leninist socialism can be reduced to Hitler's declaration: "My socialism is not the class struggle, but order." However, Stalin's socialism converged with Hitler's in that it too became national. From 1933 Stalin encouraged Russian chauvinism, implying that Russians were politically and culturally superior—elder brothers to the other peoples of the USSR and the Slavs, just as the Germans were a superior race among the Aryans. True, Stalin's anti-Semitism was inconsistent, but only in temperament were Hitler and Stalin diametrically opposite.

Once Hitler secured power, Stalin nevertheless sought friendlier relations with Britain and France; he was hedging his bets. To sever economic relations with Germany was not, however, in the Soviet Union's interests. Some in Hitler's entourage, particularly Goering, felt that it was not in Germany's either. The countries had shared political goals: the crushing of Poland, for both Hitler and Stalin an upstart and a usurper of national territory. Germany and the USSR also remained territorial victims of the Treaties of Versailles and Genoa. They still felt the grievances against Britain and France that had allied them in 1922 when they signed the Treaty of Rapallo. A militarily revived Germany in Stalin's eyes could provoke a war which would destroy Western capitalism and thus initiate a world proletarian revolution. Even in 1935, Marshal Tukhachevsky speculated that Hitler's anti-Soviet rhetoric was "just a convenient umbrella to cover up revanchist plans against the west and the south."[20]

Hitler was always anti-Bolshevik. Some of his ministers, however, believed that Stalin was extirpating the worst, in other words the Jews, in Bolshevism. Karl Radek, the Bolshevik most appreciated in Germany, where he spent many years either in exile or in secret negotiations with government ministers and with revolutionaries, famously joked, "What's the difference between Moses and Stalin? Moses got the Jews out of Egypt, Stalin is getting them out of the Politburo." In the 1930s Jews were to disappear—at Stalin's behest—from the NKVD and the Commissariat for Foreign Affairs until only two remained in Stalin's entourage, Kaganovich and Lev Mekhlis. Mekhlis lurked in the shadows, and Kaganovich, as Joachim von Ribbentrop remarked with relief, "had nothing Jewish about him at all." Goebbels and Ribbentrop overlooked the fact that Stalin was repressing ethnic Germans with even more alacrity.

In the late 1920s military collaboration was the backbone of the German–Russian alliance. Forbidden by the Treaty of Versailles to modernize its forces, Germany obtained, as well as naval facilities, three bases in Soviet Russia: Lipetsk, 300 miles southeast of Moscow, to train its air force; Kazan in Tataria, 400 miles east of Moscow to test tanks; and Tomka for experimenting with chemical weapons.

Collaboration had its teething troubles. The first Soviet agents with one hand negotiated the purchase of naval vessels and with the other incited the workers of Hamburg to rise up in the "Red October" of 1923 against their government. But by 1926 dealings were more professional: Józef Unszlicht, Dzierżyński's colleague, went to Germany and established relations with Admiral Wilhelm Canaris, who would head Hitler's Abwehr. The security services of the two countries, when the time came, found cooperation easy.

In return for providing Germany with testing grounds and bases,

Russia received technology for high-quality steelmaking, and was helped to build tanks, artillery, and airplanes. German facilities in Kazan and Lipetsk trained Soviet troops and airmen, and their technology promised better aviation. Stalin had difficulty with aircraft: throughout the 1930s Soviet aircraft were so unsafe—there was at least one crash on most days—that party officials who were not pilots were forbidden to fly; Stalin himself did not board an aircraft until 1943. Stalin feigned concern for human life on June 24, 1932, when he wrote to Voroshilov: "The most alarming thing is the accidents and the deaths of our pilots. The loss of airplanes is not as terrible (to hell with them) as the death of living people, pilots. Living people are the most valuable and most important thing in all our cause, especially in aviation." The only pilots whose lives Stalin willingly ended were those who complained of having to test "flying coffins." High-ranking officers commuted between the two countries; the Red Army under Tukhachevsky developed jointly with the Germans blitzkrieg tank tactics.[21]

France could not offer Stalin comparable help. Although after Hitler came to power imports from Germany dropped to less than a tenth of their 1931 level, when Stalin exchanged grain for steel, in 1934 Stalin bought for some 64 million marks military hardware and technology.[22] Stalin's trade representative in Berlin, even in autumn 1934, was permitted by the Nazis to visit all plants and factories supplying goods to the USSR.[23] Hitler did close the German army's operations at Lipetsk, Kazan, and Tomka, but on the nonideological pretext that he had to cut spending. By 1936 Soviet imports of technology from Germany were doubling again.[24]

From 1934 to 1937 Stalin had a secret go-between with Hitler: a Georgian, David Kandelaki, whom Stalin knew through his first in-laws, the Svanidzes. Kandelaki had been educated in Germany. Officially, he headed the Soviet trade mission to Germany and Scandinavia, but he answered to neither the Commissariat of Foreign Affairs nor the NKVD. His remit went beyond trade.[25]

Two Nazis looked eastward. Hermann Goering's cousin Herbert wanted to work with the Soviet Union against France and Britain. Dr. Hjalmar Schacht, the finance minister, despite planning to invade the Soviet Ukraine and share it with Poland, offered Stalin 500 million marks' credit in exchange for oil for Germany's military. "Tell Kande-laki," Stalin told Kaganovich in September 1935, when Germany and the Soviet Union were disowning each other publicly, "to insist on get-ting from the Germans everything we need for military purposes and for dyes."

Whether or not Stalin thought peaceful coexistence possible with Hitler, he eagerly stirred up rivalry between France and Germany for the Soviet Union's support. "The old entente has gone," Stalin wrote to Kaganovich and Molotov on September 2, 1935. "Instead two ententes are forming: that of Italy and France on one hand, and of England and Germany on the other hand. The worse the fight between them, the bet-ter for us. It is not at all to our advantage for one of them to smash the other. Our advantage lies in their fight being as prolonged as possi-ble, without a quick victory for one over the other."

Social democracy or Trotskyism stuck in Stalin's throat far more than fascism. In September 1933 Mussolini and Stalin added neutrality and friendship to their nonaggression pact; in 1936, Mussolini's press ac-claimed the shooting of Zinoviev and Kamenev as proof of Stalin's con-version to views compatible with Italian fascism.

By 1937, Stalin had become so confident of Hitler's strength and France's and Britain's weakness that he had Kandelaki draft a pact with Hitler. The author was rewarded with the Order of Lenin, but was shot a year before the pact was signed.

Women and Children

THE FATE OF ZINOVIEV and Kamenev and the mystery around Kirov's murder were enough to convince anyone in the Central Committee of the party, let alone the Politburo, of the lethal consequences of dissi-dence. However, one group, barely represented in the top echelons, could still risk speaking out: women. Under the Tsars women had been promi-nent in opposing tyranny—with guns and bombs as well as words—and the state, with some remnant of chivalry, had hesitated to come down on them with the same force that it applied to male revolutionaries. In the

USSR the voice of female protest was far weaker, but it could still be heard until the mid-1930s.

Stalin removed women from power as assiduously as he dismissed Jews. Women Trotskyists shared exile with male Trotskyists, and the wives of Stalin's real or imaginary political opponents were subjected to measures only a degree or two milder than were their husbands, unless they had renounced and divorced them. Nevertheless, 95 percent of those sentenced to the camps or to death for counterrevolutionary activity were men.

Three dowagers exerted vestigial influence. The most important was Nadezhda Krupskaia, Lenin's widow. In the mid-1930s she remained a deputy commissar for education and sat on party commissions. Stalin had loathed her ever since December 1922, when he had abused her for taking dictation from Lenin against doctors' orders. She had begged Kamenev and Zinoviev to "protect me from coarse interference in my private life, from unworthy cursing and threats. . . ." Since then Krupskaia had been overridden by Stalin on every question including the mummification of Lenin and the cult of his name. "If you want to respect Lenin's name, then build nurseries, kindergartens, houses, schools, and so on," she had said.

Krupskaia had first gravitated to Zinoviev and Kamenev, the most Leninist in education and outlook of the leadership. When Zinoviev and Kamenev were ousted, Krupskaia, like Lenin's sister Maria, moved right, to Bukharin. When collectivization began in 1929 Krupskaia took Bukharin's side, claiming that Lenin had intended cooperatives, not collective farms, to supersede the peasant smallholder. Krupskaia, the daughter of an army lieutenant and a governess, was a narrow-minded bigot compared to whom, on questions of culture and education, Stalin was a liberal, but she could not tolerate the repression of Lenin's colleagues. She protested at Stalin's falsification of party history; he lambasted her for idolizing Trotsky. Stalin saw to it that foreign visitors were kept away from her and even threatened to declare the compliant old Bolshevik Elena Stasova Lenin's real widow if Krupskaia did not cave in. "In what way actually is Comrade Krupskaia different from any other responsible comrade?" Stalin asked, calling Krupskaia's speech at the fourteenth party congress "pure rubbish."[26]

Krupskaia's protests became fainter as Stalin's recriminations became harsher. On March 19, 1935, for the first and last time, she was summoned to Stalin's office where she remained for two hours. Agranov, Iagoda's deputy, and Nikolai Ezhov, shadowing the NKVD for Stalin, had arrived two hours earlier. To judge from the gaggle of NKVD and commissars present that afternoon, the subject was the forthcoming prison sentences to punish Zinoviev and Kamenev for "moral" responsibility for Kirov's murder. Krupskaia was mute when Kamenev and Zinoviev were tried for the third time and shot. After that she connived at Stalin's murders and was too compromised to speak out. In 1937, on a commission with Politburo members to decide Bukharin's fate, Krupskaia even voted for the harshest proposal: expulsion, arrest, and shooting.[27]

Krupskaia received hundred of letters from victims—often children—of Stalin's repression who hoped that she could make Stalin set injustices right, but her only protests were against Russian chauvinism: she deplored the damage to minority languages from having Russian compulsorily taught in all schools.

Lenin's youngest sister, Maria Ulianova, was the second dowager. She was even more peremptorily disempowered (though she had always disclaimed privilege). Ulianova was a close friend, as well as political ally, of Bukharin and, on his breach with Stalin in 1929, she lost her post of secretary to *Pravda*. She died, ostracized in semi-exile, in 1937. Stalin rendered harmless a third widow without having to imprison or kill her.[28] Until 1939 Gorky's legitimate widow, Ekaterina Peshkova, ran the Political Red Cross, which in the 1920s had been able to monitor and even alleviate the conditions in which some political prisoners were held by OGPU. While Iagoda was in office—if only because he was in love with her daughter-in-law—Peshkova secured a few reprieves, or at least relief, for the repressed and their families, but when he fell, Peshkova offered only guarded sympathy.

One woman, and the least likely, was singled out by Stalin for a real political role. Aleksandra Kollontai, daughter of one Tsarist general and, by her first marriage, the wife of another, left her husband and child in 1898 to become a feminist, a libertine, and a Bolshevik. Exceptionally beautiful and a talented writer, although six years older than Stalin she enchanted him, as she did many men and women. She suspended his Georgian predilection for discreet, silent, and chaste women.

Trotsky loathed Kollontai, and perhaps Stalin loved her for this alone. When revolution broke out, she began a torrid affair with a man seventeen years her junior, Pavel Dybenko, a muscular Ukrainian sailor who became commissar for the navy. Sailors ignored orders from Trotsky unless Dybenko confirmed them and Trotsky had Dybenko court-martialed. Kollontai, now commissar for social security, begged prosecutor Nikolai Krylenko to release Dybenko. Krylenko made her abjure her principles and become Dybenko's wife. Kollontai's love letters were copied by the Cheka to the Politburo and the couple inspired scabrous verse in Petrograd:

> Russia has turned into a brothel,
> The Bolsheviks' orchestra roars out,
> And various scum is dancing
> A Soviet can-can with no knickers.
> The crook Lenin greets the guests.
> The glasses are brimming over,
> And seeing the blood in them, hysterically
> Bawls that whore Kollontai.

Kollontai had to be sent away until the scandals died down. Stalin appointed her a semiofficial envoy to Sweden and Norway; the latter was persuaded to recognize Soviet Russia partly because it had herrings to sell. Kollontai—an exemplary socialist—charmed the Scandinavian bourgeoisie and proved herself the Soviet Union's most effective diplomat, even though the Swedes expelled her for political and sexual profligacy (she had long since cast off Dybenko). Thanks to Kollontai, the USSR secured half a million tons of Norwegian herring, and a grateful fishing industry stopped the Oslo press calling her a whore.

In 1925, however, *Pravda* began attacking Kollontai's depravity. She had helped write the first Bolshevik family code, which recognized a woman's right to abortion and divorce on demand, but the party's mood had changed. Again, Kollontai turned to Stalin for protection, professing loyalty to the "general," in other words Stalinist, line. *Pravda* fell silent. Kollontai's carefully edited diary shows that she was a genuine Stalinist, loyal to his every political twist, although she did admit to lingering unhappiness about the lack of democracy within the party.[29] The memoirs of her lovers and the diary pages that she failed to edit suggest that her fondness for Stalin was like her infatuation with Dybenko: a love of coarse, self-assured authority. Her mind, however, was as clear as her conscience was murky. Stalin, she told one lover, lacked Trotsky's culture and oratory but had two merits: "hellish patience" and insight. She found Molotov, eventually commissar for foreign affairs and thus her boss, "the incarnation of greyness, dullness and servility," but she still preferred Stalin's entourage to the intellectuals of Zinoviev's or Bukharin's circles. She broke with anyone like Karl Radek who incurred Stalin's disapproval. In 1923, with prescience, Kollontai asked Stalin never to link her name with Dybenko's again.

Stalin enjoyed blackmailing Kollontai: he showed her a letter for his eyes only from Dzierżyński. The letter contained a semiliterate peasant's complaints about the orgies at a Siberian peasant commune named after her. Kollontai rode out the storm: she went to Mexico City for a year before returning to Scandinavia. From Oslo Kollontai sent a photograph of herself to Stalin and consoled him for the deaths of Sergei Kirov and, two months later, Kuibyshev:

> Dear, much respected Iosif Vissarionovich. On a day when two persons close to you have been ripped out of life, I couldn't help having warm personal thoughts about you and what you are going through. Many years ago you helped me so responsively and simply at a very, very bad moment in my life. I shall never forget it.[30]

By 1935 Kollontai had many responsibilities including monitoring "deviations" in the Norwegian Communist Party. When Trotsky was seeking asylum, Kollontai persuaded Stalin that assassinating Trotsky in Norway would be "too noisy" and suggested a solution: to stop purchases of herring until he had been expelled to a country where Stalin's NKVD could operate freely against him.[31]

Kollontai writhed in private: "Executions . . . They are always, invariably, my grief and agony," she wrote in the original version of her diary.[32] She even wondered if Stalin was paranoiac. Soviet instructions often made her a laughingstock in Oslo, for instance when she asked the Norwegian government to ban performances by the émigré ballerina Anna Pavlova. Norwegians began to shun her; Stalin transferred her to the Stockholm embassy, where the military attaché and first secretary had just defected. Here too Kollontai looked foolish; the Swedes refused to hand over the two defectors. She confessed her failure to Stalin in terms that he would accept: "I consider the main reason for defection to be the presence of opposition in the party and the intensification of provocative work by foreign forces hostile to us." Kollontai remained an asset to Stalin: she soothed the Scandinavians even when Stalin invaded Finland.

No Soviet ambassador had so much leeway from Stalin as Kollontai. When she complained that OGPU's arrest of a Swedish engineer, Rossel, undermined her position, Stalin telephoned Menzhinsky: "Make sure that Rossel is not on Soviet territory within twenty-four hours." In Moscow Stalin, with schadenfreude, invited Kollontai to dine with him and with her former husband Dybenko. Stalin poured wine and made Dybenko (whom he soon had shot) sing Ukrainian songs. When dinner was over, Stalin asked, "Why did you break up with Kollontai? You did a very stupid thing, Dybenko."

★ ★ ★ Stalin disempowered women but empowered children. Stalin's corruption of tens of millions of young people is perhaps an even greater evil than the premature deaths of so many millions of innocent adults.

When all ideological resistance had been crushed there still remained instinctive, family values. These had always been a hindrance to Russian tyrants. In medieval times the notion of "mutual responsibility" (*krugovaia poruka*) held spouses, parents, children, even neighbors of miscreants responsible for their actions. Lenin and Dzierżyński reintroduced *krugovaia poruka* to keep Tsarist officers loyal to the Red Army; Stalin extended it to defectors and any "traitor to the motherland." A spouse had to divorce a counterrevolutionary immediately if they hoped to escape their fate. Such evil idiocies reached their nadir when in 1936 Georgi Piatakov, deputy commissar for heavy industry and under investigation, begged Nikolai Ezhov to let him shoot his convicted wife.

Children were induced to transfer their affections from their families to Stalin; children who denounced their parents were lionized. Lenin had abolished the prerevolutionary Boy Scouts and shot their leaders; Stalin had by 1931 formed the Pioneers to replace them.

In rural areas the Pioneers were unpopular and it needed an act of terror to promote them. In 1932, in the Urals village of Gerasimovka—though the Pioneers had not yet reached the area—OGPU fabricated a Pioneer martyr, Pavlik Morozov, who had fought and died for his Soviet principles against grain-hoarding kulaks. The Pioneers became a mass movement. Pioneers all over the Soviet Union called for "Murdering kulaks to be shot!"

Maxim Gorky acclaimed the martyr: "Pavlik Morozov's heroic action . . . could have had very broad social and educational significance in the eyes of Pioneers. Many of them would probably realize that if a 'blood' relative is an enemy of the people, he is no longer a relative, but just an enemy and there are no further reasons to spare him." Every Soviet child for the next fifty years would be indoctrinated with the Morozov legend.

The real story was unearthed in a thorough and very brave investigation by Iuri Druzhnikov from the 1950s to the 1980s, when witnesses in the Morozov affair were still alive.[33] Pavlik Morozov's father, Trofim, was for a time the chairman of the village council, trying to balance the authorities' demands for grain against the villagers' desire to survive. Gerasimovka was surrounded by camps for displaced kulaks from southern Russia who were desperate to flee and offered bribes for false papers. Meanwhile, the prosperous peasants of Gerasimovka were themselves being deported to the Siberian tundra. In November 1931, Pavlik denounced Trofim to OGPU for protecting kulaks; Trofim went to a camp for ten years.

Pavlik did not benefit by his actions—his own family's property was confiscated as part of Trofim's punishment—but he began to denounce any villager hoarding grain, selling potatoes, or expressing discontent. He was ostracized by the villagers until his reign of terror ended on September 4, 1932, when his body and that of his brother Fedia were found under cranberry bushes deep in the forest.

The authorities acted with alacrity: the boys were buried with no autopsy. After three months' imprisonment, their grandparents (in their eighties), a nineteen-year-old cousin, and an uncle were put on trial in the village hall—to which journalists and an audience from the nearest town were bused. The defense counsel abandoned his clients; the prisoners, admitting nothing, nevertheless pleaded guilty. The prosecution berated kulaks generally. After the verdict, the four were led to a pit, undressed, and shot. Trofim Morozov was apparently shot in the camps after hacking out his grave in the permafrost.

Pavlik and Fedia Morozov were, most likely, dispatched by the bayonet and rifle butt of an OGPU killer, Spiridon Kartashov.[34] The order to stage such a murder must have come from Iagoda, and probably from Stalin; such a fabrication was too important to be left to local initiative. The subject remained very sensitive for the Soviet censors; when Sergei Eisenstein made a film about the child martyr, using the title of Turgenev's story *Bezhin Meadow,* Stalin was furious at the iconographic portrayal of Pavlik Morozov and his uncle as Isaac and Abraham and the film was largely destroyed. Stalin henceforth forbade making any film without every word in the script being vetted.

There were more Pavlik Morozovs. Druzhnikov found fifty-seven cases in the 1930s. Denunciations overwhelmed the NKVD: some denouncers asked for a month's stay in a sanatorium as a reward for their tireless efforts. Adults even denounced children. Childish absurdities were taken seriously. For instance, on July 5, 1935, little Niura Dmitrieva from Volsk on the lower Volga sent Stalin a ten-page letter listing in detail "all the children who have been teasing, hitting, and making fun of me." Niura also denounced her teacher for assigning too much homework. Stalin had a commission sent to Volsk to punish the guilty and bring the girl to an elite boarding school in Moscow.[35]

Pigs in the Parlor, Peacocks on Parade

A GENERATION OF CHILDREN had grown up in the USSR with no memories of life before the revolution. Their education, apart from exposing them to a few Russian classics, gave them no hint that there was any morality, let alone conscience, outside Stalin's Communist Party by which they should be governed. They grew up believing, many of them fanatically, that foreigners were spies, that the children of the bourgeoisie, the rich peasantry, and the clergy were renegades, that all political prisoners were guilty, that the NKVD and the courts were infallible.

The new generation was strongly represented in the NKVD. The *chekisty* of the civil war period had moved into the bureaucracy and into industry, carrying with them their belief in ruthless repression as the best means of administration. Some, who persuaded themselves that they had not lost all semblance of humanity, retired into academia or literature. Their places were taken by the orphans of the civil war, by party workers who had been drafted into, or felt drawn to, an organization where their authority would be unquestioned. The new intake was ethnically more Russian and less Jewish, Latvian, or Polish; it was less well educated, often semiliterate. It had no interest in, let alone sympathy for, the ideas of Trotsky or Bukharin, or any ideas at all. It saw itself as a punitive weapon in Stalin's and Iagoda's hands. Under Nikolai Ezhov it would prove itself a mindless tool of a paranoiac murderer. Even in 1935 the NKVD no longer questioned the most absurd indictments and directives from above.

By mid-1935, except for a few Chechen outlaws, the entire population of the USSR was under the NKVD's total control. Iagoda had knuckled under to Stalin's new favorite Nikolai Ezhov and was concocting material for the show trials of those opposition leaders who were still alive, some even at liberty. Ezhov began writing for Stalin a pamphlet entitled "From Fractionalism to Open Counterrevolution." He was instructed to argue that Trotsky had made terrorists of ideological opponents like Kamenev and Zinoviev and to blame Iagoda for lack of vigilance.[36]

Lazar Kaganovich had now covered Moscow with asphalt and furnished it with an underground railway. The city began to impress foreign visitors. Iagoda cleared Moscow of its 12,000 professional beggars: instead of going back to their villages, where begging was a respected profession, they were sent to Kazakhstan. Thanks to the GULAG's output of timber, coal, and nonferrous and precious metals, the Soviet economy was growing. The camps had over 500,000 inmates in 1934, and 750,000 in 1935. The GULAG was also more efficient: inmates' annual mortality dropped from 15 percent in 1933 to 4 percent in 1935. Deported kulaks added their labor as industrial workers or farmers in Siberia and Kazakhstan. Their death rate also dropped to a fraction of the appalling 13 percent of 1933.

Iagoda was rewarded; the NKVD got new ranks and uniforms. On November 26 Iagoda became general secretary (a rank that hitherto only Stalin had enjoyed) of state security, equivalent to an army marshal. He ordered himself a tunic covered with gold stars and raspberry-striped dark blue trousers; his underlings were only slightly less garish. They exemplified William Cobbett's "pigs in the parlour, peacocks on parade." Secret police the NKVD were not.

Iagoda should have known that these marks of favor augured doom. Stalin had never forgotten that Iagoda had been named by Bukharin as a potential supporter of a right coup. He also failed to provide the forced labor he had promised for the Moscow–Volga canal and the Moscow underground; these projects were completed with paid and voluntary labor. The economic uses of the GULAG were limited.

In October 1935 the curious case of the old army commander Gai Gai-Bzhishkian exhausted Stalin's patience with Iagoda. Gai had told a drinking companion, "Stalin has to be gotten rid of." He was denounced and sentenced to five years in prison. On the train taking him away, his guards let him go to the lavatory, where he smashed the window and leapt onto the track. Gai, Iagoda had to admit to Stalin, had escaped. Two days later, he was found by a peasant.

Stalin was furious. He raged:

> To catch one sniveling wretch the NKVD mobilized 900 men
> from frontier guard school, all their own workers, party members, Communist Youth, farmers and made a ring that must

have consisted of several thousand people over 100 kilometers. One wonders who needs a Cheka and why it exists anyway if every time, in every trivial case, it has to ask for help from Communist Youth, farmers, and the whole population? Moreover, does the NKVD understand how disagreeable for the government is the uproar created by such mobilizations? . . . I think that the Cheka part of the NKVD is suffering from a serious disease. It's time we started treating it.[37]

Iagoda received from Gai in prison a tearful letter of penitence: "I miss nothing, not my family, my little daughter, nor my invalid elderly father, I miss to the point of burning pain my old name, Gai, combat commander of the Red Army. Comrade Iagoda, it's very painful for me to talk about this to you. . . . Give me the chance to atone for my guilt with blood. It's dark in the cell and tears make it hard to write."[38] Iagoda had Gai examined by the Kremlin doctors, who diagnosed pneumonia. On November 7, 1935, a note, signed by Agranov not Iagoda, reported to Stalin that Gai had died. In fact he was very much alive. Stalin must have found out Iagoda's deceit, for Gai was shot two years later.

Typically, Stalin pretended to forgive Iagoda's lapse and made him general commissar of state security. Important tasks were, however, taken out of his hands. While Iagoda's men summoned Kamenev and Zinoviev from prison for further interrogation, Stalin, with Kaganovich and Ezhov, rewrote their confessions and dictated the course of further questioning. Iagoda and the NKVD now came under the party secretariat's control. The forthcoming show trial was outlined by Stalin more minutely than the wreckers' trials which Menzhinsky had prepared under his supervision.

Nothing shifted Stalin from his determination to physically "finish off" those he had destroyed politically. Kamenev, whose sentence had been increased from five to ten years, kept a stoic silence, bargaining with his persecutors only for his family's survival. Zinoviev showered the Politburo with appeals from his prison cell. On one occasion he begged Stalin to let him publish the memoirs he was writing in prison and to help his "academically talented" Marxist son. To his oppressor he wrote:

One desire burns in my soul: to prove to you that I am no longer
an enemy. There is no demand which I would not meet in order
to prove that. . . . I am reaching the point where I stare for long
periods at portraits in the newspapers of you and other members of the Politburo with the thought: look into my soul, can't
you see that I am no longer your enemy, that I am yours body
and soul, that I have understood everything, that I am ready to
do everything to earn forgiveness, mercy?[39]

Stalin had however decided to show that Zinoviev and Kamenev
were Trotsky's agents, aiming to overthrow the Soviet state by violence.
He would prove to socialists abroad that Trotsky was a terrorist and a
Gestapo collaborator. Formally, in July 1936, Iagoda and the chief prosecutor, Andrei Vyshinsky, asked Stalin for the go-ahead to retry Kamenev
and Zinoviev on the grounds that they had secured light prison sentences
in 1935 by concealing their guilt. Iagoda arrested Zinoviev's former secretary Pikel and an old associate of Trotsky, Dreitser, and broke them by
sleep deprivation into signing the necessary statements. Zinoviev and
Kamenev were not, strictly speaking, tortured although Zinoviev was
kept in overheated cells, where he suffered from asthma and liver pains.
He was a broken man; perhaps he believed assurances that Stalin "would
not shed the blood of old Bolsheviks."[40] Kamenev was resigned.

So well did Kaganovich and Ezhov supervise Iagoda that Stalin
could spend all August and September on holiday in the Caucasus, while
the fantastic Trotsky-Zinoviev "Moscow center" was set up and then
demolished. Kaganovich, like Ezhov and, one suspects, Stalin, was able
to hypnotize himself into believing his inept conspiracy fantasies. On
July 6, 1936, Kaganovich announced to Stalin:

I've read the statements by those bastards Dreitser and Pikel.
Though it was clear before, they are revealing with all details the
true bandit face of the murderers and provocateurs Trotsky, Zinoviev, Kamenev, and Smirnov. Now it is absolutely clear that
the main inspiration of this gang is that mercenary shit Trotsky.
It's time I think to declare him "outside the law" and to shoot
the rest of the swine whom we have in our prisons.[41]

Iakov Agranov worked viciously on those of Zinoviev and Kamenev's codefendants who had not yet broken. Ivan Smirnov, a Siberian civil war veteran and former supporter of both Zinoviev and Trotsky, had in 1927 publicly called for Stalin's removal. He went on hunger strike. So did the Armenian Vagarshal Ter-Vaganian, who slit his wrists and wrote to Stalin in his own blood: "People are slandering, slandering vilely, shamelessly, their slander is shriekingly obvious. . . . Nevertheless I am powerless against these brazen lies." Agranov force-fed both men. Other defendants were designated to show that Trotsky worked for the Gestapo. Four German-Jewish communists stood trial for their lives—Moise Lourié, W. Olberg, G. B. Berman-Jurin, and I. I. Fritz-David. They had taken refuge in the USSR., not dreaming that Stalin would kill far more German communists than Hitler.

In August 1936 Kaganovich told Stalin that he, the prosecutor Vyshinsky, and Judge Ulrikh had fully rehearsed the trial for performance from the 19th to the 22nd, and Kamenev and Zinoviev would appear as the seventh and eighth of sixteen abject penitents. "The role of the Gestapo is to be brought out in full. If the accused name Piatakov and others [on the right] they will not be stopped." On the first day Zinoviev confessed to knowing all about Kirov's murder as it happened, and Smirnov admitted receiving instructions from Trotsky. The second day, Kaganovich and Ezhov reported, went even better. All defendants were singing the same tune and Zinoviev's demeanor was "more depressed than any of the others." Only Kamenev—Kaganovich underlined this point—was "keeping up a pose that was defiant compared with Zinoviev's. He's trying to put on airs, acting the leader." Best of all, the victims' statements would damn every other of Stalin's opponents: Rykov, Tomsky, Bukharin on the right; Radek, Grigori Sokolnikov, Piatakov, and Leonid Serebriakov on the left were all mentioned.

So vile were the smears that on the last day of the trial Mikhail Tomsky shot himself—as Stalin's former secretary Boris Bazhanov had predicted he would—at his dacha. The suicide note ran:

> . . . here is my last request—don't believe Zinoviev's brazen slander . . . Now I end this letter after reading the court's resolution that I should be investigated. . . . I feel that I shan't be able to en-

dure that, I am too tired for such shocks as being put in the same dock as fascists. . . . I ask forgiveness from the party for my old mistakes, I ask that Zinoviev and Kamenev be not believed. . . . P.S. Remember our nighttime conversation in 1928. [At a barbecue in Sochi a drunken Tomsky had warned Stalin, who was grilling the kebabs, "Our workers will soon begin firing at you."] Don't take what I blurted out seriously—I have been repenting that deeply ever since. But I couldn't change your mind, for you'd never have believed me. If you want to know the names of the people who pushed me down the road of right-wing opposition in May 1928, ask my wife personally, then she'll say who they were.[42]

Maria Tomskaia, the widow, would not talk to the NKVD's secret department so Stalin and Kaganovich sent Nikolai Ezhov with the suicide note to her. She hinted that Iagoda had "been playing a very active role in the trio who led the right [opposition] . . ." A niche was ready for Tomsky's ashes in the Kremlin wall and his death mask was taken. But Stalin, who unlike Hitler hated disgraced comrades to commit suicide, ordered him to be buried in his garden; the body was later dug up and disposed of. Two years later the rest of the right opposition could only envy Tomsky.

Tomsky's suicide note, Ezhov told Stalin, implicated Iagoda:

. . . who has played a very active part in the guiding troika of the right and has regularly provided them with material about the state of play in the Central Committee . . .

A lot of failings have been shown up in the NKVD and in my view they can in no way be tolerated anymore. . . . Among the ruling clique of *chekisty* moods of self-satisfaction, complacency, and bragging are more and more blatant. Instead of drawing conclusions from the Trotskyist case and criticizing their own faults and correcting them, these people are dreaming now only of medals for the case they have cleared up. . . .

We'll have to shoot quite an impressive quantity. Personally I think that we have to face up to this and once and for all finish with this scum [Zinoviev and other defendants].[43]

All the defendants received death sentences. Most declared that they expected nothing less. Even Kamenev ended abjectly: "The practical management of organizing this terrorist act [killing Kirov] was carried out not by me, but Zinoviev." Vyshinsky excelled himself in the absurdity of his rhetoric: "In their dark cellar Trotsky, Zinoviev, and Kamenev throw out a vile call: get rid of him, kill him! An underground machine begins to work, knives are sharpened, revolvers loaded, bombs assembled." Vyshinsky attacked Zinoviev as a "villain, a murderer weeping for his victim." Not a scrap of evidence was produced, and, thanks to Iagoda's carelessness, the confessions could easily be proven false. One minor defendant, E. S. Goltsman, alleged he had met Trotsky's elder son in 1932 in the Copenhagen Hotel Bristol; Lev Trotsky junior was taking his examinations at the time in Berlin, and the hotel had been demolished in 1917.

Ulrikh took twenty-four hours to deliver the verdicts. Stalin in Sochi insisted on editing them and told Kaganovich:

> It needs stylistic polishing . . . you must mention in a separate paragraph of the verdict that Trotsky and Sedov [Lev Trotsky junior] are liable to trial or being tried, or something like that. This has great significance for Europe, bourgeois and workers. . . . You must cross out the final words: "The sentence is final and cannot be appealed." These words are superfluous and make a bad impression. We mustn't allow an appeal, but it is stupid to put that in the sentence. . . .

The next morning fifteen of the sixteen petitioned Stalin for a reprieve, which was immediately refused. All were shot a few hours later. Nikolai Ezhov was present. He extracted the bullets from the corpses and wrapped these souvenirs in paper slips with the condemned men's names. Kamenev and Smirnov walked to the execution cellar stoically, but Zinoviev clung to the boots of his guards and was taken down by stretcher. This scene was reenacted several times at supper at Stalin's dacha, the bodyguard Karl Pauker playing the part of Zinoviev—begging for Stalin to be fetched and then crying out "Hear, o Israel"—until even Stalin found the charade distasteful.[44]

Writers within the USSR put up little or no opposition to the trial and the executions. Ehrenburg, Sholokhov, and Aleksei Tolstoi had clamored for the execution of their former patrons whom they knew to be innocent, at least of the crimes of which they were convicted. A very few, like Pasternak, withstood the pressure to sign petitions demanding that the accused be shot. Ehrenburg's and Sholokhov's compliance is more pardonable than the complicity of Western intellectuals and observers. Some had watched Hitler's Reichstag trial, admired the spirited defense put up by the Bulgarian communist Dimitrov, and applauded his acquittal. They claimed that Vyshinsky and Ulrikh's pastiche of European legal proceedings could not have been wholly falsified, that the Soviet judiciary had not sold its soul to Stalin.

Kaganovich reported to Stalin on the second day of the trial that all the foreign correspondents' telegrams made a special point of the evidence incriminating the right wing. The best-informed outside observer, Trotsky, was gagged; the Norwegian government feared a Soviet boycott of its herrings, and Kaganovich drafted a letter from Stalin to Norwegian minister of justice Trygve Lie, naming Trotsky as the main organizer of terrorism in the USSR and demanding his removal. Trotsky, the first foreigner to be interned and held incommunicado in Norway, was not allowed to sue those European newspapers that repeated Vyshinsky's slanders from the trial.

Western radical opinion in 1936 had no desire to annoy Stalin. Hitler had invaded the Rhineland; General Franco had risen against the Spanish republic; Japan was invading China; the USSR was sending a delegation to a European peace congress. Democrats believed that in the cause of fighting fascism critics of Stalin's judicial murders had to be muzzled. Historians, jurists, and diplomats assured the European public that the trial had been legally impeccable. Writers like Theodore Dreiser and Bernard Shaw vouched for Stalin's character. Bertolt Brecht, on the other hand and with impenetrable cynicism, told a friend perplexed by the confessions of Kamenev and Zinoviev: "The more innocent they are, the more they deserve to die."[45] Kamenev and Zinoviev knew what Stalin had done and what he might yet do: if they were innocent of plotting his death, they had sinned by not committing tyrannicide, an act which even St. Thomas Aquinas condoned: "God looks with favor upon the physical elimination of the Beast if a people is freed thereby." Bertolt Brecht probably meant something else, but if ever tyrannicide was a moral imperative, then in 1936 failing to assassinate Stalin was a crime that deserved the death penalty.

Iagoda's Fall

... this leader had usually a favourite as like himself as he could get, whose employment was to lick his master's feet and posteriors ... This favourite is hated by the whole herd, and therefore to protect himself, keeps always near the person of his leader. He usually continues in office until a worse can be found; but the very moment he is discarded, his successor, at the head of all the Yahoos in that district, young and old, male and female, come in a body, and discharge their excrements upon him from head to foot.

Jonathan Swift, Gulliver's Travels

THE FALLOUT from the trial had not been enough for Stalin. All September he had complained to Kaganovich, Molotov, and Ezhov that *Pravda* was explaining the case badly:

It reduces everything to the level of personalities: that there are nasty people who desire to seize power, and nice people in power. ... The articles should have said that struggling against Stalin, Voroshilov, Zhdanov, Kosior, and others is struggling against the soviets, against collectivization, against industrialization, therefore a struggle to restore capitalism in the towns and villages of the USSR. For Stalin [he spoke of himself in the third person] and the other leaders are not isolated persons, but the personification of all the victories of socialism in the USSR ... i.e., the personification of the efforts of workers, peasants, and hard-working intellectuals to smash capitalism and let socialism triumph.

Stalin ended this self-deification on a religious note: "Finally it should have said that the fall of these bastards to the state of White Guards and fascists was the logical consequence of their Fall from Grace [*grekhopadenie*] as oppositionists in the past. . . . This is the spirit and the direction in which agitation ought to have been conducted. . . ."[46]

Promises to spare family members were broken. Within days Kamenev's wife, who was also Trotsky's sister, was in the Lubianka. The worst fears of the right wing were confirmed. Piatakov, Orjonikidze's right-hand man in the Commissariat for Heavy Industry, was, at Stalin's insistence, moved to the Urals, a prelude to arrest. Bukharin and Rykov were told that "the investigation had not found a legal basis for holding them criminally responsible," a hint to both of them that this basis would soon be found. Within days of the executions, Kaganovich told Stalin, "I have the impression that perhaps Bukharin and Rykov did not maintain a direct organizational link with the Trotsky–Zinoviev bloc, but in 1932–3 and perhaps afterward they were informed of Trotskyist business. The right clearly had its own organization." Kaganovich claimed that in purging Trotskyists from the railways, his remit as commissar for transport, he had uncovered right-wing saboteurs, too.

On September 25, 1936, Stalin finally pounced on Genrikh Iagoda. Together with Andrei Zhdanov, in whose hand the directive was written, and using a channel closed to the NKVD, Stalin telegraphed Kaganovich, Molotov, and the rest of the Politburo:

> One. We deem it absolutely essential and urgent to appoint Comrade Ezhov to the post of commissar of internal affairs. Iagoda [not Comrade Iagoda] has blatantly shown himself not to be on top of his job in exposing the Trotsky-Zinoviev bloc. OGPU is four years late in this business. All the party workers and most of the provincial representatives of the NKVD are saying this. Agranov can stay as Ezhov's deputy in the NKVD. Two. We deem it essential and urgent to remove Rykov from the Commissariat of Communications and to appoint Iagoda to the post. We think this needs no explaining since it is clear as it is. [. . .]
> Four. As for the Party Control Commission, Ezhov can be left

concurrently as its chairman, providing he gives nine tenths of his time to the NKVD. . . .

Five. Ezhov agrees to our proposals.

The Politburo was overjoyed: Kaganovich wrote immediately from his spa to Orjonikidze: "Our latest main news is Ezhov's appointment. This the remarkably wise decision of our Parent [as Kaganovich now called Stalin] has come to fruition and has had an excellent reception in the party and country."[47] The coup was carefully prepared: Ezhov had talked to Agranov, whose loyalty to his chief Iagoda was frayed. Agranov later reported, "Ezhov summoned me to his dacha. I must say that this meeting was conspiratorial. Ezhov passed on Stalin's remarks about faults which the investigation had allowed to happen with the Trotskyist center case and instructed me to take measures. . . ."[48]

Stalin sent Iagoda a separate telegram. Iagoda was too clever a rat not to smell the poison in the sweet:

To Comrade Iagoda. The Commissariat of Communications is a very important business. This commissariat has defense significance. I don't doubt you will be able to put it on its feet. I ask you particularly to agree to work in the Commissariat of Communications. Without a good commissariat we feel helpless. It can't be left in its present state. It has to be put on its feet urgently. I. Stalin.

For a little while Iagoda kept his rank of general commissar of state security and Kaganovich was worried that the NKVD might remain loyal to him. Kaganovich told Stalin on October 14, on the eve of the latter's return to Moscow:

Ezhov's affairs are going well. He has gotten down to the rooting out of counterrevolutionary bandits firmly and energetically, he conducts interrogations remarkably well and with political competence. But it seems that some of the apparatus, even though it has now quieted down, will not be loyal to him. Take for example a question which has a lot of meaning for them, that of rank. There is talk that Iagoda still remains General Commissar, while Ezhov, they say, will not be given that rank and so on. . . . Don't you think, Comrade Stalin, that it is essential to pose this question?

Iagoda fell to his doom with excruciating slowness. In 1934 he saw Stalin almost weekly when the latter was in the Kremlin; these meetings often lasted two hours. In 1935 and the first half of 1936 Stalin saw him on average once a fortnight, usually for no more than one hour. In 1934 his rival Ezhov would see Stalin as frequently, but for shorter visits. In the course of 1935 and 1936, Ezhov met Stalin more and more often and they were frequently together for three hours at a time. On July 11, 1936, Iagoda had his last meeting in Stalin's office.

Iagoda did not take his new commissariat seriously: he spent October and November 1936 on sick leave. When he did turn up, he came late and sat idly at his desk, rolling crumbs of bread into balls or making paper airplanes. In the NKVD, Ezhov was arresting Iagoda's subordinates, both those he had trusted and those he had quarreled with. Of Iagoda's close associates only Iakov Agranov was still in post in the new year.

In January 1937 Iagoda lost his general secretary's rank and on the evening of March 2 was summoned to a plenary meeting of the Central Committee of the party to admit responsibility for the failings of the NKVD: he should have unearthed the conspiracies in 1931 and thus saved Kirov's life; he had ignored Stalin's directions; his departments had lacked agents. Iagoda was bawled out by Ezhov and mocked by a menacing newcomer, Lavrenti Beria, who had the hall in uproar when he called Iagoda's NKVD a "company for producing worsted wool." In desperation, Iagoda blamed his subordinates—Molchanov, for example, was a traitor—and the White Sea canal, which had distracted him from police work. More of Stalin's jackals made frenzied attacks. Stalin joined in, as did his brother-in-law, Stanislav Redens.

Iagoda had to endure worse harassment the following morning, when he could only get in a few phrases of disavowal. He and Agranov blamed each other. Zakovsky, a Latvian Jew who had taken over the Leningrad NKVD after Kirov's murder and who was almost the only one of Menzhinsky's appointees brutal enough to be acceptable to

Ezhov, fell upon Iagoda, who was reproached for quarreling with Efim Evdokimov, the GPU chief of the north Caucasus. Finally Evdokimov assessed Iagoda's performance:

> A rotten, non-party speech . . . Iagoda, we know you're no lamb. . . . Thank God, I know Iagoda well. It's he who cultivated a very odd choice of people; I ask, now you Iagoda were once my boss, what help did I get from you? . . . Stop blustering, you never gave me help in my work. . . . Iagoda, you were in bed with Rykov and his influence on you shows. . . . Iagoda must be made to answer. And we must think hard about whether he should remain in the Central Committee.[49]

The only words in Iagoda's defense came from Litvinov, commissar for foreign affairs, who praised, albeit faintly, NKVD counterintelligence, and from Vyshinsky, who acknowledged Iagoda's "objective material" for trying foreign wreckers. Ezhov finished off, claiming that if he and Stalin hadn't threatened to "smash Iagoda's face in," Kirov's murderers would not have been caught. The session ended by condemning NKVD slackness. It was the worst day in Iagoda's life but even worse was to come.

On March 28, 1937, Frinovsky, whom Ezhov had made his deputy, searched Iagoda's dacha. Iagoda was picked up the next day at his Moscow apartment. He was taken to the Lubianka and the apartment was ransacked for a week by five officers. Little public action had to be taken. There were no paintings or statues of Iagoda and very few photographs to destroy; he was responsible for only one publication, *The White Sea–Baltic Canal,* which was pulped; three sites named after him—a railway bridge in the Far East, a training school for frontier guards, and a commune—were renamed. When Trotsky was expelled and Zinoviev arrested, dozens of towns changed names, millions of books were withdrawn, photographs airbrushed, paintings retouched. Iagoda went down with barely a ripple.

Under interrogation, Iagoda admitted his sympathies for Bukharin and Rykov and his distress at Stalin's policies; he confessed to furnishing friends' dachas using over a million rubles of NKVD funds. But a month passed and he still would not admit espionage and counterrevolution,

nor did the interrogators find jewelry thought to have passed through his
hands. When Ezhov complained of Iagoda's recalcitrance, Stalin sug
gested that Efim Evdokimov, who had not been an NKVD employee for
three years, should take over the interrogation. Evdokimov sat opposite
Iagoda—now a pathetic figure, his hands handcuffed behind his back,
his trousers falling down—downed a vodka, rolled up his sleeves to show
his apelike biceps, asked, "Well, international spy, you're not confessing?" and boxed his former chief's ears.

From this point truth blends with fiction in Iagoda's statements.[50]
He seems to have seen the pointlessness of holding back and confessed
to attempting to overthrow the state with the help of the Kremlin guard
and the military, revelations which gave Stalin and Ezhov plenty of material for future use. He said he had poisoned, with the help of Dr. Levin,
the NKVD doctor, virtually everyone he knew who had died in the last
four years: Menzhinsky, Gorky, Gorky's son, Kuibyshev. He even confessed to impregnating Ezhov's office with mercury vapor. The only accusations he balked at—even though the promise of his life was dangled
in front of him—were spying and murdering Kirov. As he cleverly declared at his trial, "If I were a spy, dozens of countries could have closed
down their intelligence services."

Some of Iagoda's statements ring true. He called himself a skeptic,
"wearing a mask, but with no program," who had followed Stalin rather
than Trotsky out of calculation not conviction. As Iagoda's interrogation proceeded, a second show trial of Zinovievites took place, the Red
Army's marshals, generals, and colonels were purged, and the arrests of
Bukharin and his supporters provided more material, some true, most
false, to force Iagoda into total self-incrimination. To Iagoda's credit, he
incriminated first himself, then others who were already arrested and
doomed, and avoided saying evil of those who might yet be at liberty.

The most hurtful evidence against Iagoda came on May 17 in a letter from his own brother-in-law, Leopold Averbakh, to Ezhov:

> Iagoda directly propelled us into maximum involvement in
> the struggle against Gorky. . . . Iagoda several times talked of
> Voroshilov's invariably bad view of him, and he did so in a
> tone of outright hatred. . . . In private conversation with Gorky
> you could feel that the topic of conversation was beyond

Iagoda. . . . Iagoda needed Gorky as a possible weapon in political games. . . . I am writing this statement to you since I am
obliged to reveal to the utmost and in every way the utterly
loathsome personality of Iagoda and everything I know of his
inimical activity . . . so that the party can cauterize this gangrene fully and wholly and cleanse Soviet air of this scum and
stench.

This mendacious letter bought Averbakh perhaps a year's extra life.

For some months Iagoda was left to stew in his cell. In December,
the NKVD went for him again, this time to make him admit that he had
conspired to poison Max Peshkov, his mistress's husband, and then
Gorky himself. Iagoda's confession was ambiguous: he had encouraged
Kriuchkov to make Max drink and to take him for drives in an open car,
to let him sleep out on dew-covered benches, and then let Dr. Levin treat
the resulting pneumonia with lethal medicine. Iagoda's doctors had likewise hastened Menzhinsky's end, and he had hurried both Gorky and
Kuibyshev to their deaths—the former dying from the effects of his return to Moscow from the warm Crimea, the latter by making a trip to
central Asia. When the doctors were confronted by the interrogator with
Iagoda, they admitted guilt but could not say how they had finished off
their patients. They said that Iagoda would have killed them had they
disobeyed him.[51]

Interrogation was over. Early in 1938 one of Averbakh's associates,
the playwright Vladimir Kirshon, was put in Iagoda's cell as a stool pi-
geon. Kirshon reported Iagoda's conversations to Major Aleksandr
Zhurbenko, one of Ezhov's short-lived star interrogators. Not for a
decade had Iagoda spoken so sincerely. Iagoda wanted only to know
what had happened to his wife, Ida, to his mistress, Timosha, and to his
eight-year-old son, Genrikh. He expected death any day. He denied poisoning Gorky and his son, not just because he was innocent but because
of the hurt it would cause Timosha. As he was to die anyway he was inclined to deny everything, were it not that "this would play into the
hands of counterrevolution." He could endure the trial if he were allowed to speak to Ida; he dreamed of dying before the trial; he felt mentally ill. He wept constantly, he fought for his breath.[52] Iagoda even
fumbled for his Judaic roots. An NKVD guard reports him exclaiming,

"There is a God. From Stalin I deserved nothing but gratitude, but I
have broken God's commandments ten thousand times and this is my
punishment."

On March 9, 1938, Iagoda took the stand at the last of Stalin's three
great show trials. As Trotsky commented, if Goebbels had admitted that
he was the agent of the pope, he would have astonished the world less
than Iagoda's indictment as the agent of Trotsky. Only Bukharin and
Iagoda dared to hint to the public that the trial was a sham. Iagoda refused to elaborate on his role in the death of Gorky's son. As for Kirov's
death, he asserted that he was as a matter of principle against such terrorism. Any version that Vyshinsky proffered, he parried, saying, "It
wasn't like that, but it doesn't matter." He claimed to have seen Dr.
Kazakov, allegedly his agent in killing Menzhinsky, for the first time in
court. Iagoda called Dr. Levin's and Kriuchkov's incriminating evidence
"all lies." Vyshinsky did not press Iagoda, a man who knew how little
Stalin's promises meant and who had nothing to lose. "You can put pressure on me, but don't go too far. I shall say everything I want to. But
don't go too far."

At this point there was an interval, after which Iagoda looked as if
he had been beaten. "He read his next statement from a piece of paper,
as if he was reading it for the first time," an eyewitness remarked. Iagoda
admitted everything except killing Max Peshkov and spying for half a
dozen foreign states. His last word was a plea to be allowed to work as a
laborer on one of his canals. On March 13, 1938, he was sentenced to
death and shot two days later. In July Iagoda's wife was sentenced to
eight years in the camps, and condemned to death a year later. His sister
Lili was first exiled to Astrakhan and jailed, then shot. The sister closest
to Iagoda, Rozalia, got eight years, then another two, and died in the
camps in 1948. One sister, Taisa, survived; in 1966 she asked in vain for
Iagoda's sentence to be quashed.

Iagoda's father had written to Stalin:

Many happy years of our life during the revolution have now
had a pall cast over them by the very serious crime committed
against the party and the country by the only son we still have
living—G. G. Iagoda. . . . Instead of justifying the trust placed
in him, he became an enemy of the people, for which he must

bear the punishment he merits. . . . I am now 78. I am half blind and incapable of working. I have tried to bring up my children in the spirit of devotion to the party and revolution. What words can convey all the weight of the blow that has struck me and my 73-year-old wife, thanks to the crime our last son has committed? . . . We consider it essential to tell you that in his personal life for the last ten years he has been very far from his parents and we cannot have any sympathy for him, nor can we be held responsible, all the less since we have had nothing to do with his deeds. We old people ask you to see that we can be assured of a chance to live out our life, now so short, in our happy Soviet country, for we find ourselves in difficult moral and material circumstances, with no means of existence (we receive no pension). We ask you to protect us, sick old people, from various oppressions by the house administration and the district council, who have begun to take over our apartment and are clearly preparing other measures against us. And this evening, June 26, when we have just got down to writing this letter, we have been ordered to leave Moscow within five days together with several of our daughters. This repressive measure against us seems unmerited and we call upon your sense of justice, knowing your profound wisdom and humanity. . . .[53]

Deported 800 miles south to Astrakhan, Iagoda's parents were then arrested. His father died within a week of arriving in the camps, his mother shortly afterward. Timosha Peshkova was left untouched, and lived until 1988. Of Iagoda's kin, only little Genrikh survived. Two women in the orphanage where he was placed took pity on him and gave him a new surname, under which the Iagoda family line still lives on.

Monolithic Power

BETWEEN THE MURDER of Kirov and the dismissal of Iagoda, Stalin operated with maniacal energy and cold, calculated purpose. Everything he did gave the Soviet state what later observers believed was its magical source of strength: its monolithic power. Stalin eliminated, politically and then physically, all politicians who had shown a capacity to act or even think independently. He set in stone a pyramidal power structure: himself, his Politburo, the NKVD, the party's bureaucracy. He asserted total control over every government commissariat, from foreign policy to culture and light engineering. He structured the population so that there was no social basis for any revolt or dissent: the peasants were crushed, the intelligentsia suborned or terrified, the workers tied to their workplaces. Only the army remained self-governing, and not for long. Stalin pushed women away from power; a few token women did his bidding on the Central Committee but the valkyries of the revolution were all disarmed. He made divorce difficult, abortion nearly impossible, and homosexuality illegal. There was no prospect of a new generation shattering the monolith; children and adolescents were organized into the Communist Youth Movement, which kept a tight grip on their activities and ideology from puberty to adulthood. The class system was allegedly abolished although actually a caste system was emerging. The party became self-perpetuating. There were no more spectacular mésalliances like the marriage of Kollontai and Dybenko; party, NKVD, and intelligentsia interbred: Gorky's granddaughter married Beria's son and Stalin's grandson Fadeev's daughter.

A few genuine scientists, as well as a horde of charlatans, still contributed to Soviet thinking, but Stalin had congealed thought too. Genetics and modern physics were declared heretical. Music not in C major, poetry not paraphrasable, painting and cinema not monumental or strictly representational, were all banned. The whole country even began to look alike: from standard-issue clothing to standard housing and transport, Stalin created a seemingly unchangeable world where Everyman's monotony was broken only by the garish pageants and uniforms of the party and police elite. Stalin's precautions against his assassination reached absurd levels. Nothing but an invasion by outside forces—and here Stalin was convinced that his own cunning was defense enough—could shake the foundations of the world he seemed to have created single-handedly in 1935–6.

SEVEN

THE EZHOV BLOODBATH

A camel claimed political asylum on the Polish border: "They're exterminating all the rabbits in the USSR." "But you're a camel," said the border guard. "You try proving you're not a rabbit!" replied the camel.

19. Genrikh Iagoda and Maksim Gorky, 1934

20. Famine, Kharkov province, 1932

21. Stalin and Voroshilov fishing, Abkhazia, 1933. Left to right: Voroshilov, Stalin, unknown bare-chested figure, Beria

22. Stalin and his second wife, Nadezhda Allilueva-Stalina, *c.* 1928

23. Right to left: Stalin; his daughter, Svetlana, and second son, Vasili, 1936

24. Stalin's NKVD guards, Sukhum, 1933

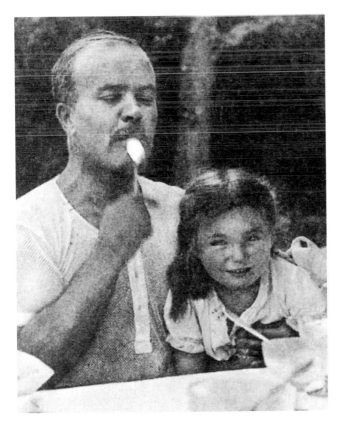

25. Molotov and his daughter, Svetlana, c. 1930

26. Leonid Nikolaev, killer of Sergei Kirov, *c.* 1933

27. OGPU boss Filipp Medved, White Sea Canal, 1931

28. Kirov in his coffin, December 1934

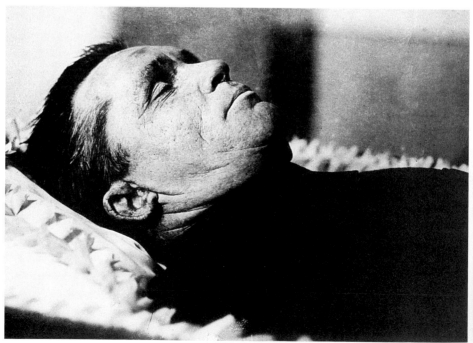

29. Prisoners at work, White Sea Canal, 1933

30. Svirlag corrective labor camp, Leningrad province, 1936

31. Judges at Menshevik trial, 1931

32. Andrei Vyshindky, chief prosecutor in the 1930s show trials

33. Faina Niurina, acting chief prosecutor of the Russian Federation in the 1930s

34. Rykov (front left) and Bukharin (center) on their way to trial, 1938

35. Nikolai Ezhov (right) with his brother, Ivan

36. Ezhov (left) conferring with Stalin, 1937

37. Ezhov and Orjonikidze at the dacha, 1936. Left to right: Ezhove's foster daughter Natalia, Ezhov, Ezhov's second wife, Evgeniia, Sergo Orjonikidze, Orjonikidze's wife, Zinaida, and assistan, Semushkin

38. Red Army leaders in the late 1920s. Left to right: defense commissar Klim Voroshilov, Marshal Tukhachevsky, Nokolai Muralov, chief of staff Aleksandr Egorov

39. Lazar Kaganovich, early 1930s

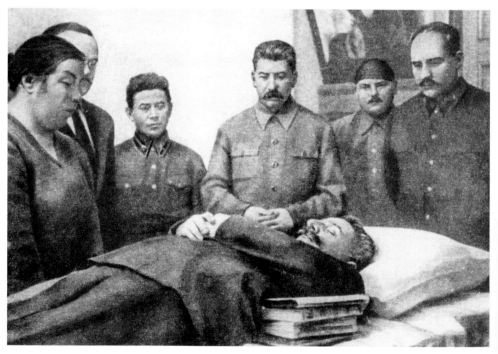

40. Sergo Orjonikidze very shortly after his suicide or murder, February 1937. Left to right: his widow, Zinaida Orjonikidze, Molotov, Ezhov, Stalin, Zhdanov, Kaganovich, Mikoyan, and Voroghilov

The Birth of the Great Terror

May my prayer be received
As incense before Thee,
Raised up by my hand,
A Vespers sacrifice.
Hear me o Lord

Orthodox hymn occasionally
sung by Stalin, Voroshilov,
and Molotov in the 1930s

AS STALIN was condemning the last of the old Bolshevik guard to death, he was also preparing his own remedy for dissidence and free thought in the general population. The ensuing "Great Terror" raged across the Soviet Union from spring 1937 to autumn 1938 and resulted in around 750,000 executions and twice as many sentences to lingering death in the camps. What minds could conceive then organize such a massacre? More puzzling still: how could a literate urban population submit to a reign of terror and actively, even enthusiastically, collaborate in offering victims up to it?

Stalin in the 1930s exemplified the degenerative psychotic who, with every enemy exterminated, saw yet more enmity to be extirpated and whose serial killing progressed not arithmetically but geometrically. Then there was Nikolai Ezhov, who was promoted to conduct the terror and then removed when the ravages were complete. We shall try to unravel something of the psyche of Nikolai Ezhov. As for Kaganovich and Molotov, their murderousness, like that of other Politburo members who survived Stalin including Malenkov, Mikoyan, and Khrushchiov, stemmed not from any inner compulsion to kill, but from a total, doglike submission to their psychopathic master. The difference between the terror of 1937–8 and the killings that had gone before was its cannibalism. The two main instruments of terror, the 4-million-strong Communist Party and the NKVD, were also its victims.

As for the Soviet population of the mid-1930s, it is necessary to understand how every bond linking one human being to another had been shattered by twenty years of Soviet rule and a decade of Stalinism. Hitler had to negotiate with the Protestant and Catholic churches and even make minor concessions to them over, say, euthanasia for the congenitally ill; he had to soothe, admittedly with no difficulty, the relict ethical scruples of the military, of the business community, the legal and academic professions. Only in the furor of wartime, and by allowing the civil population to pretend that they were not complicit in mass murder, could Hitler proceed to his campaigns of mass extermination.

Stalin had to make no such compromises. The Orthodox Church had been crushed. The Red Army had no coherent code of behavior; it had slaughtered civilians in the civil war and peasants in 1929–32. The intelligentsia was abroad, in prison, or compromised and bribed. There was no communal ethic left alive outside the party. The population had simply to endure each crisis and hope peace and stability would ensue. In 1917–18 they had acquiesced to the Bolshevik coup, in 1926 to the replacement of the collective leadership by a dictator, in 1929 to the enslavement of the peasantry. In 1937–8 effectively every tenth adult male in each city or town would vanish; surely Stalin and the party would then have finished and the survivors, like the Saved in an Anabaptist world, could live in paradise.

The population had incentives to collaborate with its oppressors. If you did not run with the hounds you were a hare to be torn apart by them, and those who disappeared left behind vacant jobs, rooms to live in, clothes, food and drink to be consumed. The terror also hit hardest those between thirty and forty-five in managerial and professional jobs. Like the war against the peasant, the urban terror pitched the young, the dispossessed and unskilled against the middle-aged who had riches and skills. Whether an anonymous slanderer or an arresting NKVD officer, the oppressor often had a personal vendetta or something to gain.

Stalin understood the worst in human nature and motivated his executives and the population accordingly. By installing Nikolai Ezhov, he had acquired the ideal instrument. Undoubtedly, had Ezhov refused to carry out the terror, Stalin would have used Kaganovich or Molotov or his newer acolytes Andreev or Zhdanov instead. But the terror was amplified by Ezhov's uniquely maniacal compliance and the stimulation that he and Stalin applied to each other. We know a little more today about Ezhov than we did, and he merits a biographical excursion.

How the Hedgehog Got Its Prickles

... the lion that is the most amenable to the circus trainer's tricks is the one with the lowest social standing in the pride, the omega animal.

Yann Martel, Life of Pi

IN HIS PARTY DOCUMENTS it is repeatedly stated that Nikolai Ivanovich Ezhov was born in St. Petersburg on May 1, 1895, that he started work as an apprentice metalworker at the Putilov works in Petersburg in 1906, and was called up by the army in 1913.[1] Ezhov once wrote that he had had only two years' elementary schooling and had taught himself to read and write. In the 1920s he read so much that he acquired the sobriquet of "Nick the Bookman" (Kol'ka-knizhnik). He was thus literate by the modest standards of Stalin's Politburo.

Under arrest in 1939, Ezhov said his father, Ivan, was an army bandsman in Lithuania and later ran a Petersburg teahouse of ill repute.[2] When Ezhov filled in his party card, he claimed to know some Polish and Lithuanian. Evdokia Babulina-Ezhova, in her sole contribution to our knowledge of her infamous brother, recalled spending holidays in the Suwałki-Mariampol region on the Polish–Lithuanian border. Ezhov's mother, Anna, was a bandleader's maid. Ethnically Russian, she had lived in Lithuania.

Possibly, Ezhov was born in 1892 in Suwałki; the only Ivan Ezhov listed in the St. Petersburg directory for 1895 ran a public house. Certainly, Ezhov was wise to invent a wholly Russian and wholly proletarian origin for his career under Stalin. When he took over the NKVD from Iagoda, citizens hoped that a genuine Russian worker would mitigate the fanaticism of the Russophobe Poles and Jews who had run the Cheka and OGPU.

The Nikolai Ezhov of the 1920s is recalled as a considerate, friendly lad. Bukharin's and Orjonikidze's widows insisted that their husbands' executioner was a good man fallen into bad company, a helpless marionette in the hands of a master puppeteer: "You don't blame the rope for hanging you," another survivor said. But Ezhov in his forties was Hyde to his younger Jekyll—an alcoholic prone to violent outbursts against his drinking companions, a voracious sexual predator, an active and a passive bisexual, seducing any woman or underage girl he came across—with not a drop of sentiment, loyalty, or remorse.

We know even less of Ezhov's first twenty years than we do of Iagoda's or Menzhinsky's. Whereas their initiation into mass killing came in the bloodiness of the civil war and revolutionary terror, Ezhov cannot be blamed for many deaths until Stalin in 1936 put him in charge of a machine that slaughtered hundreds of thousands. No doubt Ezhov's service in the Tsar's army scarred him deeply, and at the height of his brief reign of terror he still liked to sing, with deep feeling and beautiful intonation, the traditional song of the fatally wounded soldier:

> Black raven, black raven,
> [. . .]
> Why do you spread your talons out
> Over my head?
> Fly home to my land,
> Give this bloodstained cloth
> To my young wife.
> Tell her she is free . . .

Ezhov, like Iagoda, owed his promotion to talents as a bureaucrat; his revolutionary honors, like Iagoda's, were minor. He was, it seems, an agitator at the steelworks and later the artillery repair shop where he worked. When revolution came to Vitebsk in Belorussia, with its Russian, Jewish, and Polish populations, Ezhov joined the Red Guard and the Communist Party and helped disarm by bluff a large Polish corps on its way to fight the Bolsheviks in Petrograd.[3]

From 1919, when Ezhov joined the Red Army, the facts are verifiable. Barely five feet tall and unfit for the front, Ezhov was sent to a radio-telegraphic school in Saratov on the Volga. He became secretary of the garrison Communist Party in Saratov, brushed up his thick auburn hair and wore built-up heels to add to his height. From Saratov, as the Whites approached, Ezhov's school retreated up the Volga to the Tatar city of Kazan. Despite a reprimand for recruiting deserters into the school, he was promoted, and then in 1921 put in charge of party propaganda in central Kazan. Here Ezhov had to reconcile, under Lenin's cosmetic multinationalism, the national aspirations of the Tatars with the Muscovite orientation of the Russians.

The latter half of 1921 is a blank in Ezhov's record. He may have taken part with Malenkov in the Red Army's suppression of an uprising in Bukhara in October 1921, which would account for his closeness to Malenkov in the mid-1930s. Certainly Ezhov was ill; all his life he had a hacking cough and feverish bouts followed by spells of treatment for tuberculosis. In Kazan Ezhov married Antonina Titova. Like Ezhov's mother and adopted daughter, she miraculously survived him. She is not known ever to have spoken of her husband. The daughter of a village tailor, she was studying science at Kazan University when the revolution disrupted classes; she found secretarial work in the party. Small but muscular after working in a foundry, Nikolai Ezhov was an appealing suitor. For eight years they seemed a normal couple.

The Kazan party recommended Ezhov to Moscow from where he was sent to Ioshkar-Ola (then Krasnokokshaisk) in the Mari republic on the north Volga, where half the population was Mari, a Finnic people. Ezhov was to allay ethnic tensions. He arrived in March 1922, when the Mari held key appointments in the party and better-educated Russian communists seethed with resentment. The local party boss Ivan Petrov contemptuously called Ezhov in Mari Izi Miklai (Little Nick). Ezhov responded with techniques that later made him formidable: he created a secretariat, staffed with his own men, to usurp Petrov's power; he reported to Moscow on the "ideological mess" of Petrov's party organization, uncovered fraud and called in from Moscow a commission to deal with the Mari. Ezhov then raised the stakes: he appointed his wife, Antonina, to manage the party organization and attacked Petrov and Mari "nationalists": "Petrov has to be reigned in. I enclose documents." The conflict ended with both Petrov and Ezhov given indefinite leave, but his appeals to Moscow had introduced Ezhov to men of power around Stalin, and Kaganovich had Petrov deported.[4] Kaganovich and Ezhov had worked together before the Petrov affair. Kaganovich met Ezhov in 1917 in Vitebsk, where the former was rabble-rousing at the railway workshops. The boyish Ezhov, to Kaganovich's amazement, was the Vitebsk station commissar.

Ezhov was moved in 1923—by Kalinin, Rykov, and three of Stalin's satraps, Kaganovich, Kuibyshev, and Andreev—to another ethnic hornet's nest: Semipalatinsk, then a city in the vast Kazakh-Kirgiz republic. Ezhov, at most thirty years old, became the party chief of a province ravaged by starving Turkic nomads, bandits, and deserters. He coped, and was moved to Orenburg, then capital of Kazakh-Kirgizia; by 1926 he was a senior party official and a delegate to the fourteenth congress of the All-Union party. The Kazakhstan archaeologist and writer Iuri Dombrovsky, who survived several spells in the camps, liked Ezhov. "Many of my contemporaries, especially party members, came across him personally or through their work. There wasn't a single one who had anything bad to say about him. He was a responsive, humane, soft, tactful person. He would always try to sort out any unpleasant personal problem privately, to put the brakes on things." Another Kazakhstan party secretary, back from the GULAG, recalled that Ezhov "sang folk songs with feeling."

At the end of 1925, at the party congress in Moscow, Ezhov stayed in a hotel with Ivan Mikhailovich Moskvin. As he was at daggers drawn with Zinoviev, Moskvin was the sole member of Leningrad's administration whom Stalin promoted—to running the party's organization and distribution section, headhunting administrators. Moskvin took to Ezhov as a fellow Leningrader. Ezhov wanted a Moscow posting, for Antonina had resumed her studies there in 1926, and in February 1927 Ezhov joined Moskvin's section, where he amazed even the ascetic Moskvin by meeting every deadline and by his appetite for paperwork. After seven months, Ezhov became Moskvin's deputy and almost an adopted son in the Moskvin family: Moskvin's wife, Sofia, called him "sparrow." Cuckoo would have been more appropriate, for ten years later Ivan and Sofia Moskvin would be shot, Ivan as a freemason, Sofia for no specific reason, on Ezhov's orders. Moskvin's son-in-law the writer Lev Razgon recalls Ezhov in 1927: "not at all like a vampire, he was a thin little man, always dressed in a cheap crumpled suit and a blue satin tunic. He would sit at the table, quiet, taciturn, a little shy, he drank little, did not interrupt, just listened, his head slightly inclined." What Moskvin told Lev Razgon about Ezhov was clairvoyant: "I don't know a more ideal worker, or rather executive. If you entrust him with any-thing you need not check up, you can be sure: he will do it all. Ezhov has only one fault, admittedly a fundamental one: he doesn't know when to stop. . . . And sometimes one has to keep an eye on him in order to stop him in time."

Ezhov was a real talent. The Tatar party secretary, a Russian Jew, asked for Ezhov as "a tough lad . . . to sort out the Tatars." Kaganovich picked Ezhov to help in the collectivization campaign of autumn 1929 when 25,000 party members were mobilized to intimidate the peasantry; as deputy commissar for agriculture, Ezhov was among the most intimi-dating. Antonina, absorbed in her research into sugar beets, saw less and less of her husband. Ezhov, his temper frayed by overwork, looked else-where for consolation. The Ezhovs were nevertheless observed together in 1930 in Sukhum by Osip and Nadezhda Mandelstam; they were all staying, courtesy of Nestor Lakoba, at a villa near the Black Sea. Ezhov was to sanction Mandelstam's last and fatal arrest; his widow would find it hard to believe that this "modest and rather pleasant man" who had given them lifts to town in his car and who danced with a limp, had be-come the organizer of Stalin's holocaust. In Sukhum the Mandelstams heard of Mayakovsky's suicide, an event that reawakened Mandelstam's lyric inspiration. Russian party officials went on dancing; Georgian guests remarked that *they* would never dance on the day their national poet had died. Nadezhda Mandelstam relayed this to Ezhov, who promptly stopped the party.[5] Ezhov played billiards with Lakoba, he danced, he sang—with perfect pitch and great feeling—he let his wife take Abkhaz peasant children for rides in his car, he obligingly took back with him to Moscow zoo a bear cub that Lakoba had been given. The amiable Antonina lounged in a deck chair, and Ezhov cut roses for more responsive women.

The previous year, at a sanatorium in Sochi, Ezhov had met a woman any man working for Stalin should have avoided like the plague. Evgenia Feigenberg was not just Jewish and twice married; her present husband, Aleksei Gladun, a Moscow editor, had lived in America until 1920, and the couple had worked in the London embassy in 1927. Evgenia was only a typist but she had literary connections that fascinated Nick the Bookman: she had been and would be again Isaak Babel's mistress. Gladun later testified: "He was hopelessly infatuated with her and wouldn't leave her room. . . . My wife explained to me that Ezhov was a rising star and that it was to her advantage to be with him, not me. . . ." The Ezhovs divorced and Nikolai married Evgenia in 1931. The divorce saved Antonina's life—she died at the age of ninety-one—but not Gladun's. Evgenia became editor of *The USSR on the Building Site,* and in Moscow the new couple moved to Strastnoi (Passion) Boulevard.

In November 1930 Ezhov got Moskvin's job and was for the first time closeted with Stalin. In autumn 1932 he had six such meetings; by 1933 they were occurring at roughly fortnightly intervals. Stalin directed Ezhov "to take a special interest in strengthening and increasing the personnel of OGPU's regional apparatus as part of the drive to consolidate collective farms and drive out the kulaks."[6] By then Ezhov ran the commission for purging the party, organizing checks on documents and past records, which threw out nearly half a million members or one eighth of the party. He combined many functions in the party's Orgburo, supervising OGPU and heavy industry, and placing party cadres. The more Stalin railed at old Bolsheviks for their "arrogance as grandees who have grown too big for their boots," the more he promoted younger acolytes whose indebtedness to him compensated for their lack of Bolshevik credentials.

By the early 1930s Stalin was expressing avuncular concern for the young protégé. He called Ezhov Ezhevichka (little blackberry). Lavrenti Beria, taking Stalin's cue, called Ezhov Iozhik (little hedgehog). In August 1934 Ezhov's health worsened. Stalin sent him first to Berlin, then to an Austrian spa for treatment. The Austrian doctors diagnosed a stomach disease and Stalin had Kaganovich send them a telegram asking them "to refrain from operating on Ezhov unless there is an urgent need to."[7] Stalin telegraphed the Soviet embassy in Berlin: "I ask you very much to pay attention to Ezhov: he is seriously ill, he underestimates the seriousness of his situation. Give him help and surround him with care. Bear in mind that he is a good man and a most valuable worker. I shall be grateful if you regularly inform the Central Committee of the progress of his treatment. Stalin." Ezhov's symptoms persisted, and in 1935 Stalin wrote to him, "You must take leave as soon as possible—to one of the spas in the USSR or abroad, as you wish, or as the doctors say. Go on leave as soon as possible, if you don't want me to raise a scandal about it." As a result the Politburo allowed Ezhov and Evgenia two months' leave and 3,000 gold rubles for treatment abroad.[8] Ezhov was treated, as were several of the Soviet elite, by Dr. Carl von Noorden, who had only recently fled from Germany to Vienna. Nobody else in Stalin's circle, not even Molotov, caused Stalin so much concern as Ezhov.

After May 10, 1934, with Menzhinsky dead and Iagoda in sole charge of OGPU, Stalin considered it imperative to subordinate OGPU and then the NKVD to his own men. Kaganovich and Ezhov found fault with Iagoda's every action and, worse, his every failure to act. Ezhov went behind Iagoda's back to his underlings Iakov Agranov and Efim Evdokimov, and reported in withering terms to the Politburo on the state of the NKVD. Ezhov's devastating reports doomed Iagoda. They ensured that within months Ezhov would move from overseeing the NKVD to full control, with a remit to purge it as no Soviet institution had yet been purged.

Purging of the Guard

The white bread is spread thick with caviar,
The tears are hotter than boiling water.
Hangmen also get sad.
People, have pity for hangmen!
Hangmen have a very bad time at night,
If hangmen dream of hangmen, and as in real life, but even harder
Hangmen hit hangmen across their mugs.

Aleksandr Galich, "Dance Song"

EZHOV MAY NOT HAVE BEEN first choice to replace Iagoda; Stalin had considered someone very different, his Abkhaz friend Nestor Lakoba, who had very little blood on his hands and genuine popularity among his people. In the summers of the early 1930s Stalin, Beria, Lakoba, their wives and children played together in villas and on beaches at Sukhum or in shepherds' huts on the shores of Lake Ritsa. Stalin trusted Lakoba enough to go hunting wild boar with him. Lakoba was a crack shot, whose party trick was shooting a raw egg off his cook's head. It was on one such occasion that Stalin made his famous quip "Me Koba, you Lakoba." Lakoba sent Stalin hundreds of lemons and planted mandarin trees around his villa. Nadezhda Allilueva gave Sarie, Lakoba's wife, the gift traditional for the highest ranks of OGPU, a gold-plated pistol.

Stalin talked at greater length to Lakoba than to anybody else.[9] In 1930, Stalin had exempted Abkhazia from collectivization, criticizing officials who did not "take account of the specific peculiarities of Abkhaz social structure and made the mistake of mechanically transferring Russian models of social engineering to Abkhaz soil." Nevertheless, Stalin did gently note Lakoba's errors: "despite his old Bolshevik experience, he mistakenly lets his policies rely on all layers of the Abkhaz population (that is not a Bolshevik policy) and finds it possible not to submit to the provincial committee's decisions. . . . I think that Comrade Lakoba can and must free himself from this mistake."[10] Although not the idyll of Fazil Iskander's novel *Uncle Sandro from Chegem,* Abkhazia under Lakoba was cunningly steered between Stalinism and its ancient pagan traditions.

Surviving relatives say that when Stalin asked Lakoba to take on the NKVD in Moscow Lakoba refused. Why did Stalin ask? Lakoba, like Sergo Orjonikidze, was as personal a friend as Stalin could have and, as a fellow Caucasian, Stalin could judge his intonations and responses with certainty. But it was inconceivable that Lakoba would turn the NKVD into the slaughterhouse that Stalin wanted. Certainly, Stalin's behavior in autumn 1936, when Lakoba last saw him, just before Ezhov's appointment was announced, was grim; hell had no fury like Stalin spurned.

The blots in Lakoba's copybook would have damned others long before. In 1924 he had guarded Trotsky, another fine marksman, and come to like him. Even in 1926 the Lakobas had sent affectionate letters to Lev Davidovich. A Caucasian vendetta, hidden behind smiles, raged between Lakoba and Lavrenti Beria, who wanted Abkhazia back under Georgian rule. Beria showed his duplicitous character in letters to Lakoba.[11] Beria's servility wore thin in 1935 when Lakoba's half-brother Mikhail put a Brauning revolver to his temple after Beria had uttered an obscenity in the presence of women.[12]

On November 20, 1936, Lakoba went to Moscow with Orjonikidze to see Stalin. They resurrected the long-standing suspicion that Beria had in 1920 been a genuine, not a double, Azeri nationalist agent.

But by this time Stalin's trust in Lakoba had evaporated. Lakoba found it hard to grasp that his position had changed and that he was no more exempt from Beria's control than any local Caucasian leader. On December 26 Beria summoned Lakoba to Tbilisi where his wife pressed Lakoba to come to their apartment for dinner. Lakoba was reluctant; a few months earlier a girl had been found dead in Lakoba's villa, shot with his handgun, and Beria's inquest implied that she had been Lakoba's mistress. Beria's wife and mother cooked Lakoba a trout. Two hours later at the opera, Lakoba doubled up and died in convulsions.[13] The body, minus its vital organs, was returned to Sukhum, where Beria and his wife were chief mourners, and Lakoba was ceremoniously buried in the botanical gardens.

The doctors who autopsied the victim were arrested. A month later Lakoba's tomb was flattened and the body exhumed. Lakoba was declared an enemy of the people; Sarie, his widow, was charged with plotting to kill Stalin with the pistol Allilueva had given her and tortured for two years until she died. Lakoba's mother was bludgeoned to death by Beria's hangman Razhden Gangia. Beria slaughtered almost the entire Lakoba clan, keeping the children in prison until they were old enough to execute. Lakoba's young son Rauf was tortured in Moscow by the notorious Khvat, sentenced to death by Ulrikh and shot in 1941. One brother-in-law and two nieces survived. Most of the Abkhaz intelligentsia perished; Georgians and Mingrelians colonized southern Abkhazia. Beria's revenge was directly sanctioned by Stalin without Ezhov's signature. After Lakoba's murder Stalin stayed away from the Caucasus for nine years.

⋆ ⋆ ⋆ In autumn 1936 Ezhov first had to complete Iagoda's tasks: to prepare two show trials, which would dispose of those, first on the left, then on the right, implicated at the trial of Kamenev and Zinoviev. To make the NKVD do as Ezhov wished it was to be purged; the hangmen themselves were first in line for the gallows. Each previous new leader had made a smooth transition. Even when Iagoda took over from Menzhinsky, quarreling with many who disliked his "sergeant-major" rudeness, OGPU-NKVD had remained cohesive. On that occasion Stalin had removed only a handful—Stanisław Messing, Meer Trilisser—whom he either disliked or needed for other work.[14] Just a few—Efim Evdokimov, Iakov Agranov—genuinely objected to Iagoda's style. They disliked the fabrications in the early 1930s not because they found them distasteful; they wanted more sophisticated methods of falsification.

Ezhov laid waste the NKVD, as he would the party, the army, the intelligentsia, and the urban population. He first removed the most prominent—sometimes letting them stew for a few months in provincial demotion. The moment Ezhov took over, a chief of the secret political directorate, I. V. Shtein, killed himself. After Iagoda's arrest, Gleb Bokii, the terror of Petrograd and Turkestan, was seized. Georgi Molchanov, Iagoda's head of the secret political directorate, was arrested a month before Iagoda and shot "by special arrangements," in other words without formal interrogation or sentence, after violent questioning from his colleagues Nikolai Nikolaev-Zhurid, the Latvian Ans Zalpeter, and Sergei Zhupakhin, the axman of Vologda, who would themselves soon follow their victim. Molchanov, a handsome man, was beaten into a shadow of his former self and must have found execution a relief. One of Stalin's candidates for Iagoda's post, Vsevolod Balitsky, was shot by Ezhov as a Polish spy.

Neither his acumen, nor having Stalin as his neighbor at Zubalovo, nor helping to topple Iagoda, saved Iakov Agranov. He helped Ezhov settle in, prepared Radek and Piatakov for trial, and after three transfers in seven months was arrested in July 1937. Agranov was tormented for over a year before being shot. Efim Evdokimov, whom Stalin had proposed to Ezhov as the interrogator of Iagoda, was also ill rewarded: in May 1938 he was transferred to the Commissariat of Water Transport, which had now become death row for *chekisty*. Soon Lavrenti Beria would exterminate Efim Evdokimov and all the north Caucasus men who owed their careers to him. Iagoda's head of the Gorky (Nizhni Novgorod) NKVD, Matvei Pogrebinsky, shot himself when Iagoda was arrested; a few days later I. I. Chertok, Iagoda's deputy head of counterespionage, jumped to his death. Even one of Ezhov's favorites, Commissar of State Security third rank Vladimir Kursky, who took over from Georgi Molchanov, killed himself on July 8, 1937; the last straw for him was the order to interrogate and dispatch Zinaida Glikina, Ezhov's unwanted mistress. The last aristocrat in the NKVD, Pillar von Pilchau, was arrested as a Polish spy. Of Iagoda's 110 most senior men, ninety were arrested by Ezhov. Most perished. Ezhov arrested 2,273 *chekisty* at all levels and, by his own count, dismissed another 11,000.

The NKVD purge first hit non-Russians. Jews and those who had affiliations with Germany and with the so-called *limitroph* countries, Poland, Romania, the Baltic states—countries where communists could expect no protection—were marked men. The NKVD paid heavily for its cosmopolitanism. In recent years only two senior NKVD officers, Bliumkin and his friend Rabinovich, had been shot; many non-Russian *chekisty* had voluntarily or involuntarily changed careers. In vain: every famous Latvian—such as Peterss—and Pole—such as Messing and Unszlicht—in the economy or in cultural life followed their former colleagues into oblivion.

Rank and file NKVD men were dismissed or transferred; arrest and shooting were largely reserved for senior staff. Fear spread through the service. The new NKVD—Beria would finish what Ezhov began—would look very different. On October 1, 1936, of the 110 senior operatives, only 42 were Russians, Ukrainians, or Belorussians; 43 declared themselves Jews, there were nine Latvians, five Poles, and two Germans. By September 1938, just before Ezhov fell, senior staff had increased to 150, but Russians predominated with 98; there were no Latvians and only one Pole, while Jews had diminished to 32. A year later, under Beria, there were 122 Russians and only six Jews. The only significant non-Slavs were Beria's 12 Georgians.[15]

Ezhov's Russification of the NKVD reflected Stalin's conversion to Tsarist chauvinism. Operations abroad, already crippled when Stalin in

1936 closed down the NKVD network in Germany to avoid annoying Hitler, became a shambles for they depended on polyglots of Baltic, German, or Jewish origin. Ezhov got rid of Abram Slutsky, the head of the foreign directorate of the NKVD, with a lethal injection as an arrest might have frightened Slutsky's subordinates into defecting. Ezhov then had Artur Artuzov, his best counterintelligence officer, arrested; he was half-Swiss, half-Estonian, and had lived next door to Iagoda.

Ezhov also homogenized the NKVD's class structure. Iagoda had employed more white-collar executives; under Ezhov, the workers and peasants took over, a trend that Beria accelerated. Iagoda had used former gentry and petit bourgeois, even a former priest and a Baltic baron; under Ezhov they were almost all purged. Likewise, the educational level of the NKVD's senior men changed. Those with just elementary schooling still formed 35–40 percent of the personnel (Beria was to reduce this by half by introducing two-year courses in literacy and arithmetic), but Ezhov reduced the proportion of staff with higher education from 15 to 10 percent. Beria then recruited intellectuals, so that over a third of the NKVD's management had degrees by 1939. These purges meant promoting younger officers and drafting in new staff from Communist Youth and orphanages. Between 1937 and 1939 the average age of senior NKVD men dropped from forty-two to thirty-five. The promotion of youth over age, of Slav over non-Slav, of peasant over white collar reflected Stalin's bias toward persons with no outside ties and no past.

Those few who held on to their posts in the NKVD cadres after Iagoda's and Ezhov's falls were low-fliers: rarely seen at headquarters, they skulked in remote regions. Typical of these lucky few was Dmitri Orlov, in charge of exiled kulaks on the steppes of northern Kazakhstan. NKVD men realized that a summons to Moscow for a posting or an award was in fact a death sentence. Surprisingly few tried to evade their fate. Some committed suicide after a telephone call from Ezhov: for instance, Vasili Karutsky, who had just been promoted to run the Moscow province NKVD, or, at the end of Ezhov's reign, Daniil Litvin, who had conducted the slaughter of nearly 50,000 in Leningrad during 1938. Some defected, like Genrikh Liushkov, who crossed the Manchurian border in thick fog ostensibly to meet an agent, and then worked for the Japanese until they dispensed with him in 1945. The commissar of the Ukrainian NKVD, Aleksandr Uspensky, faked suicide, adopted a new identity, and raced the length and breadth of European Russia, sheltering with mistresses or old friends for five months, before he was caught outside the left-luggage office at a remote station in the Urals.

Most NKVD men, like Ezhov, drowned fear for their own fates in alcohol and sadism: they hated the innocents who were slow to confess, for the interrogator who failed to secure a statement might follow his prisoner to the executioner. Nobody now called Ezhov "blackberry" or "hedgehog"; the lasting pun on his name was *ezhovye rukavitsy,* literally "hedgehog-skin gauntlets" or "rod of iron."

In 1937 Stalin authorized the use of active physical torture and the horrors at the Lubianka were replicated in dozens of provincial centers.[16] The NKVD archives of Novosibirsk in central Siberia tell a grim story.[17] Novosibirsk was praised by Ezhov as the second most efficient city outside the capital for the numbers of spies, wreckers, and hostile social elements it filtered out of the population—probably some 10 percent of the male adults and adolescents of the area. Many kulaks and Trotskyists had been exiled to Novosibirsk so targets for arrest were easily met. In April 1937 Ezhov sent out one of Iagoda's men, Lev Mironov, to arrest as many as he could in the army garrisons and railway depots of the region. Two months later, exhausted, Mironov was arrested. Karl Karlson, a Latvian chekist, formerly deputy commissar of the Ukrainian NKVD and ranking second to Ezhov, went to central Siberia in August 1937. By January 1938, he too had been arrested. The experienced Grigori Gorbach replaced Karlson; he lasted less than a year. Gorbach terrified his colleagues: Ezhov had instructed him to find enemies not just in central Siberia but within the Novosibirsk NKVD.[18] After Gorbach came Major Ivan Maltsev, the most demented of all; he was to die in the camps.

Novosibirsk bonded its men in blood; all officers took part in mass executions called "marriages." One officer, Konstantin Pastanogov, denounced his own uncle but demurred when ordered to shoot him. He survived only because Lev Mironov took pity on him. The special and secret political directorates of the Novosibirsk NKVD were at half strength from purges within their ranks. The deficit was made up with men who found writing up statements more laborious than beating victims into signing them. Ezhov sent out fifty students from Moscow's NKVD school to help.

Targets for Extermination

What have the little piglets done
That they should be slaughtered year after year, just
To keep these foxes in luxury? The very sacred Dragon
In the ninefold depth of his pool, does He know
That the foxes are robbing him and gobbling up His little piglets,
Or does He not?

Bertolt Brecht, after Po Chiu-i

IN SPRING 1937 terror spread from the party leadership to the urban population. Ezhov assigned targets (*limity*) to each region for arrests, executions ("Category 1"—73,000 in all), and imprisonment ("Category 2" —just under 200,000) of enemies of the people. Eighteen months later these targets had been exceeded ninefold. The Smolensk NKVD chief was told by Ezhov, "better to overdo it than not do enough." Novosibirsk soon exceeded its target of 5,000: by October 4 the local NKVD had arrested 25,000 and sentenced 13,000 of these to death. As Novosibirsk had, until 1938, Japanese and German consulates, thousands were designated spies. The NKVD was backed up by the militia, which was diverted from detaining thieves and hooligans to hunting enemies of the people. They arrested anyone who came to a police station, even on an innocent errand; they visited farms and removed a percentage of peasants as saboteurs. In 1937 the Novosibirsk militia arrested 7,000 people in this way.

There was some official resistance: one prosecutor, M. M. Ishov, arrested the most eager hangmen including Maltsev and freed their victims. Ishov was soon arrested himself, with his brother and colleagues, and badly beaten by Maltsev although, extraordinarily, he lived to be reinstated. Even at the end of 1938, when Ezhov's writ no longer ran, and memoranda from Moscow rebuked the NKVD for illegal procedures,

Maltsev could not stop. When Beria finally removed the incorrigible heads of the Novosibirsk NKVD, the region was left to the mercy of their juniors, psychotic drunkards who beat their wives, fell down mine shafts, stole public and private property, and were sent away to prisons or sanatoria. In southern Russia and the Caucasus, even before Stalin authorized torture, the sadism was such that the living envied the dead; few of those tortured were fit for the GULAG.

For one measure Ezhov won popularity: he reversed the Soviet policy of treating common criminals as redeemable brothers of the working class. In April 1937 Ezhov proposed, to Stalin's approval, rearresting recidivists and career criminals, who would now be deported and executed. By July 40,000 common criminals, mingled with kulak refugees, had been arrested. Of these 8,000 were shot. The streets of Moscow and Leningrad were still dangerous at night, but now that banditry was punished almost as severely as telling anti-Soviet jokes, some of the public regained confidence.

Ezhov sent those he spared the bullet into the GULAG, which he expanded into a hitherto unimaginable inferno. When Iagoda fell, over 800,000 slaves were working in the GULAG, while NKVD prisons held another quarter of a million and many hundreds of thousands of exiles worked in conditions indistinguishable from slavery. By 1936 annual mortality in the GULAG had dropped to about 20,000 and in Iagoda's last year of power the NKVD recorded only 1,118 executions.[19] This was, in the poetess Anna Akhmatova's phrase, a "vegetarian" era, compared with the carnivorous Ezhov period.

Under Ezhov the growth of the camps was limited only by the harsh terrain of the Soviet Arctic and the logistics of transporting, housing, guarding, and exploiting prisoners. Purges within the NKVD killed off the GULAG's best managers. In December 1938 the GULAG population passed the million mark, and there were nearly as many in the prisons and other labor colonies. In 1938 mortality in the GULAG— overcrowded, chaotic, run by inexperienced and frightened administrators—soared to 90,000 or 10 percent of the inmates. Even so, the camps could not keep up with the mass arrests; those detained in grotesquely overcrowded prisons often died of typhus, dysentery, heat, malnutrition, or torture before they could be executed.

Stalin and Ezhov therefore decided that the percentage of "enemies" sentenced to death rather than forced labor must rise from 0.5 to 47 percent. In 1937 and 1938 the NKVD's own records show that 1,444,923 persons were "convicted" of counterrevolutionary crimes, and of these 681,692 were shot. The flow to the camps was halved, but processing so many prisoners—who had to be beaten into incriminating others and thus provide further fodder for the NKVD—was still unmanageable. The NKVD ran out of paper to record sentences and executions.

Prisoners could be shot expeditiously—200 in a night was the average in Leningrad, and experienced butchers could manage this number single-handed—but disposing of the corpses, given the shortage of bulldozers and open spaces in cities, was harder. Sometimes victims were taken to areas where NKVD officers had dachas; they dug their own graves, on which pine trees would be planted and wooden chalets built. From December 1937 the NKVD stopped sending its corpses to hospital morgues to be processed with those who had died naturally. Three times as many bodies now had to be disposed of daily in Leningrad. The NKVD took over twenty-seven acres of forestry land at Pargolovo near the closely guarded Finnish border, where 46,771 corpses were buried.

Thanks to the efforts of a few dedicated men and women, we now have full knowledge of what happened in Leningrad and in parts of Moscow. The *Leningrad Martyrology* gives details of the 47,000 men and women of the city and the province who perished at the hands of the NKVD over eighteen months.[20] None of the arrests resulted from an investigation. The target set by Ezhov for Leningrad had been 4,000 shot and 10,000 sent to the camps over four months from July 1937. Ezhov instructed all NKVD headquarters that all former kulaks, common criminals, Germans, Poles, and those repatriated from Manchuria after the Japanese seizure were to be rounded up and results reported to him every few days, with the warning: "If in the coming days the present position is not put right, the appropriate conclusions will be applied to you."

Certain categories of the population were more vulnerable to arrest than others: 95 percent of those shot were men. Xenophobia was key: non-Russians, only 18 percent of the population, provided 37 percent of the victims. Poles, Finns, Estonians, and Latvians were singled out to the extent that the USSR in 1937 had half as many ethnic Poles and Balts as it had in 1926. Virtually all ethnic Poles—some 144,000—were arrested and three quarters of these were shot.

Ironically, Zakovsky, head of the Leningrad NKVD from the murder of Kirov until March 1938, was a Latvian—his real name being Štubis. Aleksandr Radzivilovsky, who began his Cheka career in the 1921 bloodbath of the Crimea, revealed his instructions when interrogated by Beria's men in 1939:

> I asked Ezhov how to carry out in practice his directive on exposing the anti-Soviet Latvian underground, and his reply was that there was no need to feel embarrassed by the absence of concrete material, but I should mark out several Latvians who were party members and beat the necessary statements out of them. "Don't beat about the bush with this lot, their cases will be decided in batches. You need to show that Latvians, Poles, etc. in the party are spies and saboteurs." Frinovsky recommended that I should, in cases where I failed to get confessions from detainees, sentence them to shooting just on the basis of indirect witness evidence or simply unchecked informants' materials.[21]

Manual workers and peasants made up 24–28 percent of the victims; 12 percent were professional workers, a much smaller group within the population. The Leningrad purges (and they were typical) thus hit hardest skilled professionals doctors, veterinary surgeons, agronomists, engineers—and priests, as well those previously accused of counterrevolution. Blue-collar railway workers, thanks to Kaganovich's vigilance, also suffered badly. Some minority peoples effectively faced genocide, but only the Chechen and Ingush in the high Caucasus took up arms against Ezhov's NKVD.

Anyone who lived in the same building as arrestees or was related to them was natural prey. NKVD men scanned lists in concierges' offices and arrested those with unusual surnames as spies. Just possessing a desirable apartment or furniture was a motive for arrest. Most victims were sentenced by a troika or a joint commission of the Public Prosecutor and the NKVD; some received quasi-judicial sentences from the Military Collegium of the Supreme Court. Nearly all were sentenced under Arti-

cle 58, covering counterrevolution, of the Soviet criminal code. Most of
Ezhov's victims were charged with those crimes (Article 58, Paragraphs
10 and 11) that needed least evidence—"propaganda and group activity"—offenses which could be committed by a chance remark or playing
cards with friends.

Because it had so many officials, professionals, and persons from
other regions and countries, Moscow province and city, with twice the
population of Leningrad, had three times as many casualties. Here too
the executioners were overstretched. In 1937, some time before Hitler,
Stalin's NKVD hit on gassing as a means of mass execution. Trucks ad-
vertising bread drove around the Urals, pumping exhaust gases into the
rear compartment where naked prisoners lay roped together in stacks,
until their loads were ready for the burial pits.

The society called Memorial has traced 21,000 buried just in the Butovo military area south of Moscow. The victims include hundreds of
local peasants, most of the monks and priests of the Troitse-Sergeev
monastery in Zagorsk who had survived earlier purges, inmates from the
Dmitlag—the camps which supplied the labor force for the Moscow–
Volga canal—and thousands from central Moscow prisons. Many professionals vital to the economy, such as Leopold Eikhenvald, a professor
of radio-electronics, had naturally studied and researched abroad; their
"spylike way of life and anti-Soviet agitation" doomed them. There was
no gratitude: the Tsar's head of gendarmerie, the elderly General
Dzhunkovsky who had taught the Cheka all he knew about countersub-
version, was shot. Any contact with Europe was lethal. The Commissariat of Foreign Affairs lost ten diplomatic couriers to the pits at
Butovo. Forty-seven Austrian refugees from Hitler were shot as Nazi
spies, as were 600 Germans and over 1,000 Latvians. Butovo specialized
in artists: over a hundred painters, iconographers, sculptors, and design-
ers, the 1920s Moscow avant-garde, perished in December 1937 and January 1938.

As men and women were shot, their names were struck off endless
typed lists which bore the signatures of an NKVD troika or, if the condemned were of any importance, of Politburo members. Attached to the
lists were photographs of harrowed and beaten faces, taken shortly after
arrest—the NKVD owned perhaps the world's largest photographic

archive, of some 10 million faces. The execution orders bore just one instruction: "When carrying out the sentence it is obligatory to check the person against the photograph."

Butovo was a killing ground from August 8, 1937, to September 19, 1938. The flow of corpses peaked in September 1937 (3,165) and March 1938 (2,335), and varied from a handful to 474 victims in one night. Most of the 21,000 were executed by a small team of NKVD hangmen: M. I. Semionov, I. D. Berg, and P. I. Ovchinnikov. Most killers in the NKVD never rose high and few were ever held to account; their usual punishment was alcoholism.

When Ezhov vanished—unmourned, unmentioned in the press—and the terror paused before taking new directions, it was assumed that Stalin had reasserted control over the purges which he had temporarily lost. But now it is indisputable that he was aware of all Ezhov's actions in detail and in advance. Ezhov not only enthusiastically sought authority to purge more and more spheres of industry or classes of person; Stalin himself spurred Ezhov on, pointing out, for instance, the Baku oil fields as an area likely to be harboring great numbers of saboteurs and spies. Whenever senior party members or key professionals were sentenced, lists went to the Politburo—to Stalin, Kaganovich, Molotov, and Voroshilov—for their emendations. The names of some 7 percent of the victims of the Great Terror—40,000—were perused by one or more of these four. Occasionally Stalin crossed out a name or substituted imprisonment for death; Molotov, for reasons he would not later recall, did the opposite. All four added comments: "deserves it," "prostitute," "scum." On one day they confirmed over 3,000 death sentences. Georgi Malenkov had, as the Central Committee's personnel officer, a hard job finding replacements and Stalin told each new commissar to appoint two deputies to take over if he was arrested. From time to time Stalin would gently apply the brakes, requiring a party secretary or prosecutor to sanction certain arrests.

Ezhov exercised all his ingenuity to keep up the pace. His original target, agreed with Stalin, of 200,000 arrests and 73,000 executions, was exceeded ninefold, with Stalin's full cooperation. Moreover, Stalin's younger acolytes Malenkov, Khrushchiov, and Andreev never deviated from his line by a millimeter, and starred in the troikas that sent thousands to their death. Stalin brought Ezhov into the Politburo in October 1937 and saw him almost every day. In 1937 and 1938 they spent over 840 hours working together. Only Molotov saw more of Stalin at that time.

Either Ezhov needed a tight rein or Stalin found mass murder so enthralling that he could not delegate, but in 1937 and 1938 Stalin forwent the annual break of two months or so that he had taken in the Caucasus or on the Black Sea ever since ousting Trotsky from the Politburo. After terror came war, and Stalin would not take a holiday again until October 1945.

The Last Show Trials

Freedom of the person lies largely in protection from questions. The strongest tyranny is the one that allows itself the strongest question.

Elias Canetti, Mass and Might

SHOCK WAVES from the show trials by which Stalin got rid of the last remnants of the old Bolsheviks swept away up to three successive administrations in all districts of the Soviet Union; tens of thousands of loyal Stalinists were devoured by the leviathan that they had engineered and lauded. The last show trials of 1937 and 1938 were the epicenter, but the greatest suffering was at the periphery, among workers with no political interests.

Ezhov had a secondary role in the two show trials that would get rid of the last traces of opposition. He could beat prisoners into submission, but had no gift for devising scenarios for foreign journalists to observe. Stalin therefore settled with Andrei Vyshinsky what the prosecution and the accused would say in court. Stalin left Ezhov, together with Kaganovich, to bark at Central Committee plenary meetings; Ezhov's underdogs would bully the defendants into learning the scripts that Vyshinsky would devise.

Despite sleep deprivation and other torments, it took a month to break the defendants of the "Parallel anti-Soviet Trotskyist Center" to be tried from January 23 to 30, 1937. Karl Radek, the only victim for whom Stalin had any residual respect, agreed to plead guilty only if he could write his own part; Radek's desire to have memorable lines was stronger than his will to live. According to Stalin, he said, "You can shoot me or not, as you like, but I'd like my honor not to be besmirched." Others in this trial had already been broken by a previous trial of Trotskyists in Siberia. Piatakov was prepared not just to damn his own wife as a traitor, but to shoot with his own hand those convicted in the first show trial. Stalin politely declined, explaining that in the USSR executioners had to remain anonymous.

Despite 400 pages of documentation, this second show trial was even more shoddily fabricated than that of Kamenev and Zinoviev in 1936. Piatakov was alleged to have flown to Oslo but the Norwegian authorities stated that no foreign aircraft had landed there at the time. The crimes were more implausible than Zinoviev's and Kamenev's "assassinations," Vyshinsky pathetically citing a signalwoman crippled in a train crash arranged by Trotsky's agents. All but four of the accused were shot although the lucky four lived only a few years. Radek, who had teased Vyshinsky in court with the implausibility of the evidence and whom Stalin reprieved, was murdered in prison in 1939. Before the trial Radek read Vyshinsky his proposed last words. "Is that all?" Vyshinsky asked. "No good. Redo it, all of it. Try and admit this and that. . . . You are a journalist after all!"[22] Radek sent his wife a letter which the NKVD interpreted in one way and she, no doubt, in another: "I have admitted I was the member of a center, took part in its terrorist activity. . . . I don't need to tell you that such admissions could not have been extracted from me by violent means nor by promises."[23]

Vyshinsky was rewarded with the dacha of Leonid Serebriakov, former commissar for roads and one of those he had condemned to death.

Western reaction to this second trial was muted: the Spanish Civil War made it unseemly for the left to criticize Stalin, the Spanish republic's last supporter. British MPs and journalists assured the public that the accused had confessed because the evidence was overwhelming. Japanese and German correspondents declared the trial an outrageous fabrication, but because they were fascists, they were not believed in Britain or America. Any improbabilities which Western observers had noticed in the confessions, explained the exiled German writer Lion Feuchtwanger, were due to faults in translation. In court Karl Radek denied that he had been coerced: "If the question is raised whether we were tortured during interrogation, then I have to say that it wasn't me who was tortured, but the interrogators who were tortured by me, since I caused them unnecessary work."

Why did the accused not retract their confessions in court? The guards would not have beaten them in public and they certainly could not have trusted Stalin's promises to spare them or their families; they knew of the extermination of Kamenev, Zinoviev, and almost all their kin. Were they unsophisticated enough to believe that it was their duty to admit guilt as a sacrifice for the party? They didn't appear to have been drugged. The full dossier covering their interrogation is not yet in the public domain, and in any case it may have been largely falsified. Either their torturers made threats which we can only guess at, or they had motives for complicity which surpass our understanding. Fear alone does not explain the defendants' behavior, unless they had been threatened with tortures even more unspeakable than what they had endured.

The third great show trial of this series, in 1938, of Bukharin, Rykov, Iagoda, and their fellow defendants, took a whole year to organize. Was the delay due to Ezhov's inability to devise scenarios, Iagoda's recalcitrance, or Stalin's sadism? Was Stalin loath to end an amusing game of cat and mouse with Bukharin, who remained editor of *Izvestiia* even while the newspaper called for his demise? His letters to Stalin in 1936 and 1937 have a psalmodic quality, perhaps a key to the martyr complex of the defendants. "If you could only really know my 'soul' as it is now!" he wrote in February 1936. "I still want to do <u>something good</u>. And now I must tell you straight: my <u>only hope is you</u>."[24]

In spring 1936 Stalin had even let Bukharin go abroad to retrieve the archives of the now banned German Social Democratic Party. Bukharin spoke fatalistically to the émigré historian Boris Nikolaevsky, Rykov's brother-in-law, and wrote saccharine letters to Stalin: "You keep swelling, so that anyone can see how needed you are now—perhaps

more than ever, my dear!" In August Stalin let Bukharin go moun-
taineering for the last time in the Pamirs. In autumn 1936 the net closed
and Radek was arrested. Bukharin stood up for Radek as someone
"ready to give his last drop of blood for our country." The more
Bukharin's name figured in indictments of others, the more he pleaded
to Stalin:

> I ardently beg you to allow me to come and see you. . . . There is
> no greater tragedy than when one is surrounded by hostile dis-
> trust and one is guilty of nothing, not a jot. . . . Only you can
> cure me. . . . I ask not for pity, not for any forgiveness, for I am
> not guilty of anything. But the atmosphere is such that only a
> super-authority (only you) can take on yourself to the end the
> boldness of saving an innocent man who because of the tactics
> of the enemy has got into an exceptional situation. . . . Interro-
> gate me, turn my skin inside out. . . .

When Stalin told him to stay on at *Izvestiia* Bukharin sent him "A
Poem About Stalin in Seven Cantos" that he had composed "in one of
my sleepless nights." In blank verse, it begins with the death of a genius—Lenin—and continues with Stalin's Great Oath, his Path of Fire
and Struggle, and Victory. Canto Five is The Leader:

> Here he stands, in gray greatcoat, the leader
> Of innumerable creative millions . . . And powerfully
> Gives a mighty strength
> To the momentum of a new triumphant life.

The poem ends with Friendship of Nations and Trumpet Signals, at
which Stalin leads armies to fight fascism: "And wisely he looks afar,
staring with testing gaze / At the hosts of enemies, Great Stalin."

Once *Pravda* was unleashed against him, Bukharin asserted his innocence "in word, deed, and thought." When Kamenev and Zinoviev
were executed, Bukharin groveled. He told Vyshinsky, "I am terribly
glad the dogs have been shot." Three *chekisty* came to evict him from his
apartment in the Kremlin, but a phone call to Stalin got rid of the in-

truders. The year 1937, however, was all despair. The death of Sergo Orjonikidze in February 1937 deprived Bukharin of his last friend in
power. He admitted to Stalin:

> . . . I was <u>embittered</u> against you (that's true): I didn't under-
> stand your objective political rightness. . . . But I am not the
> person I was. I cannot even weep over the body of an old com-
> rade. On the contrary, his death will serve as a pretext for certain
> people to dishonor me. . . . I know that you're suspicious and
> often happen to be very wise in your suspiciousness . . . but I am
> a living person walled up alive and spat on from all sides. . . . I
> repeat to you my request that I shouldn't be harassed and should
> be allowed to "live out the rest of my days" here.

The February–March 1937 plenum of the Central Committee was
surely one of the most grotesque meetings in the history of humanity.[25]
Two thirds of the 1,200 delegates would be dead within the next two
years, yet, in a frenzy, they called for terror against more enemies.
Bukharin and Rykov, fresh from confrontations with former associates
beaten by the NKVD into incriminating them, were thrown into the
ring. To this mindless throng, presided over by a taunting Politburo—
Stalin, Molotov, Kaganovich, and Voroshilov—Bukharin pleaded for
compassion: "Comrades, I beg you not to interrupt me, because I find it
very hard, it's simply physically hard to speak. . . . I haven't eaten for
four days . . . because it is impossible for me to live with such accusations. . . . Understand it's hard for me to live." To which Stalin inter-
jected, "It's easy for us, is it?" Bukharin dared not parry Stalin's assertion
that all previous defendants had freely confessed and provoked only
laughter when he declared that everything in the trials of the Trotskyists
was plausible except that which incriminated him. Stalin intervened
more than anybody else—a hundred times—during this witch hunt. At
times Stalin softened: "You must not, you have no right to slander yourself . . ." he said. "You must see it our way. Trotsky and his disciples Zinoviev and Kamenev used to work with Lenin and have now come to
terms with Hitler." Bukharin claimed he was mentally ill. "Excuse and
forgive . . . So that's it," retorted Stalin. Rykov attempted a more spirited

self-defense, but when he tried to defend Bukharin, Stalin interrupted: "Bukharin hasn't told the truth even here."

Ezhov had the last word: he accused Bukharin of keeping a file of anti-Soviet utterances hidden from the GPU, and promised to arrest him: "The plenum will allow Bukharin and Rykov to convince themselves in reality of the objectivity of the investigation and to see how investigations are conducted." A commission of thirty-five would decide their fate: they agreed to expel and arrest the two. Ezhov proposed shooting them; a minority voted for ten years' imprisonment. Stalin, wearing his arbiter's mask, had the commission "direct the Bukharin–Rykov case to the NKVD" which meant that he had instructed Ezhov to annihilate them. When the plenum voted on the commission's remit only Bukharin and Rykov abstained.

Stalin and Ezhov allowed Bukharin a cell where he could smoke and write before standing trial with twenty others in March 1938.[26] This trial strained even Vyshinsky's imagination. He had to tie together Genrikh Iagoda, Bukharin's right-wing opposition, three Kremlin doctors, three former Trotskyists, and Gorky's and Kuibyshev's secretaries on charges dating back to 1917 of serial murder, sabotage, induced famine, treason, and terrorism on behalf of the intelligence services of every major European and Asiatic state. When tried before the carefully screened audience, Bukharin adopted the same tactics as Iagoda: he pleaded guilty in general but cast doubt on every detail. Like Iagoda, he rebutted Vyshinsky's efforts to blacken him as a foreign spy. Nevertheless, Bukharin ended his ordeal with utter self-abasement: the only reason for not shooting him, he said, was that "the former Bukharin has now died, he no longer exists on earth." An observer of the show trials would have had to conclude that all Lenin's party except for a tiny circle around Stalin had for some reason carried out a simulated Bolshevik revolution at the behest of world capitalism.

Bukharin had at least come to understand why he had to die:

Stalin has some big and bold political idea of a general purge
a) in connection with the prewar period and b) with a transition
to democracy. This purge takes in a) the guilty, b) the suspect,
c) potential suspects. In this case I couldn't be excluded. Some

are made harmless one way, others another, others a third
way . . . great plans, great ideas, and great interests outweigh
everything and it would be petty to raise the question of my own
person in the face of universal-historical tasks that weigh first of
all on your [Stalin's] shoulders.[27]

Nevertheless, Bukharin still hoped for mercy: "if I am given a death
sentence . . . instead of shooting, let me have poison in my cell (give me
morphine to go to sleep and not wake up) . . . Have pity! I beseech you
for this." In other letters he offered to go to the Arctic camps for twenty-
five years and found universities and museums there, or to America for
an indefinite time where he "would smash Trotsky's face in."

Bukharin's final note to Stalin began, "Koba, why do you need my
life?" This note Stalin did not put in his archive; all his life he kept it
under a newspaper in a desk drawer at his dacha. On March 15, 1938,
Bukharin's decade of torment ended. Together with Iagoda and all but
three of the other defendants at the third great show trial, he was shot.
The three were shot in Oriol prison in 1941. Five days too late, Romain
Rolland wrote to Stalin, "a mind like Bukharin's is a precious resource
for his country, he could and ought to be preserved for Soviet science
and thought." He invoked Gorky's name and warned Stalin of the remorse which the French, even Jacobins, had felt after guillotining the
chemist Lavoisier. Stalin did not reply.[28] Instead, he screened a film, *The
Court's Sentence Is the People's Sentence,* which starred Vyshinsky at his
most rabid. Of Bukharin's family, only his first wife was shot. His second
and his third teenage wives went to the GULAG, his son went to an
NKVD orphanage and grew up not even knowing who his father had
been.

Other damned men including Abel Enukidze and Jan Rudzutak, despite torture, would not or could not give public testimony; they were
tried in secret and shot separately.[29] Elsewhere, the trials of others whom
Stalin distrusted had already taken place. Beria had already exterminated Budu Mdivani, Orakhelashvili, and most of the older Georgian
communists.

Fewer Western observers—with the spectacular exception of the
American ambassador, Joseph Davies, who informed his government of

"proof beyond reasonable doubt to justify the verdict of guilty"—were deceived this time. Romain Rolland was shaken. Stalin was wrecking the unity of the antifascist left with the internecine murders his NKVD carried out in Spain and with this trial. He could now resort only to accommodation with Hitler for his security. Mussolini's organ *Popolo d'Italia* mused: "Has Stalin become a secret fascist?" *Il duce* was rubbing his hands because "nobody exterminated so many communists as Stalin."

Disarming the Army

. . . there were two guiding rules. One: the more harm a leader does, the more good he does for the fatherland. If he abolishes learning, good; if he burns down a city, good; if he terrifies the population, even better. . . . Two: to have as many bastards as possible to do your bidding. . . .

Then [the leader] gathered the "bastards" and said to them: "Bastards, write denunciations!" . . . They write denunciations, draw up harmful plans. . . . And all this semi-literate stinking matter gets to the zealous leader's office. . . .

[The leader] gathered the "bastards" and said: "Tell me, bastards, what do you think real harm consists of?"

And the bastards replied unanimously: ". . . That the harm we bastards do should count as good; and good, if done by anyone else, count as harm. That nobody should dare to say a word about us bastards, while we bastards can yap what we like about whomever we want to. . . ."

Mikhail Saltykov-Shchedrin,
The Tale of the Zealous Leader
(*Stalin's own underlining, c. 1951*)[30]

STALIN WAS NOT only carrying out a cull of everything suspect in the general population; he made the February–March plenum of 1937 endorse a yet more demented campaign that would threaten to cripple the economy. The logic was that every commissariat must be badly infested by enemies. Kaminsky at health and Orjonikidze at heavy industry de-

murred; their commissariats, they were sure, were clean. These denials
cost them their lives. Kaminsky was arrested, and on February 18, 1937,
Orjonikidze, the last man to talk to Stalin as an equal, either shot himself or was shot by Stalin's emissary.[31]

At first Voroshilov, war commissar, also resisted Stalin and Ezhov's
thesis. Voroshilov argued that the army took only the best sons of the
people, but then changed his mind and announced to the assembled
Central Committee news that "will make even your steel-hard hearts
shake." Several commanders were under arrest. At the plenum forty-two
army officers spoke up in support of Voroshilov and against their comrades—thirty-four of them were to perish. Voroshilov was to preside
over the murder of the army's commanders, but he hung on to their gifts,
cushions embroidered by their wives.[32]

Beheading the Red Army was certainly a successful preemptive
strike. An army of NCOs could never mount a coup d'état, nor would
the killing of army officers stir up the same horror among the intelligentsia as the slaughter of the peasantry or the urban professional
classes; like Kamenev and Zinoviev, Tukhachevsky and his fellow civil
war commanders were up to their necks in blood. And Stalin's blow at
his own power base had its paranoiac logic. The army was the last force
outside Ezhov's NKVD that could conceivably overthrow Stalin and it
still contained officers from the Tsarist army. In addition, most Red
Army commanders had been appointed by Trotsky and many despised
the performances of Stalin and Voroshilov in the civil war—two had
published accounts of the 1920 campaign against the Poles that showed
Stalin at his worst. Moreover, for fifteen years the officers had collaborated with the German army in tactics and technology and, who knows,
in ideology. Stalin especially distrusted the supreme commander, Marshal Mikhail Tukhachevsky. The marshal had charisma, and was so admired abroad that the German and the émigré Russian press had called
him the USSR's future Bonaparte.

Tukhachevsky had been arrested in 1923 and, with other commanders, came under Menzhinsky's suspicion in 1930. Suspect officers
were sent abroad as attachés, which in 1937 made them foreign spies. Did
they really plot against Stalin? In his dotage Molotov insisted that
Tukhachevsky had planned a coup; the NKVD defector Aleksandr

Orlov alleged that Tukhachevsky had gotten hold of a document proving that Stalin had been an Okhranka agent. Tukhachevsky must have considered a coup d'état at some point. But, given the all-pervading NKVD—every two senior officers were monitored by a political commissar—and its overwhelming strength around the Kremlin, a coup could not be discussed, let alone mounted.

Stalin's ingratitude toward the Red Army, without whose brilliance and energy he could have died on the gallows in 1919 or 1920, is attributed by some to a German sting. Soviet agents in the 1930s reported Nazi leaders mooting an officers' plot against Stalin; in early 1937 *Pravda* received reports, which Stalin saw, that Alfred Rosenberg was cultivating anti-Semitic Red Army officers. The Gestapo and Abwehr allegedly concocted documents proving that Tukhachevsky's staff was in German pay, and fed them to the NKVD through Beneš, the Czechoslovak foreign minister.[33]

Eight outstanding commanders—Tukhachevsky, Iona Iakir, Ieronim Uborevich, Avgust Kork, Robert Eideman, Boris Feldman, Vitali Primakov, and Vitovt Putna—were "tried" on June 11, 1937. Ezhov's penciled notes of Stalin's wishes has their names with "a" for "arrest" and a tick for "arrested." A ninth victim, Gamarnik, bedridden, shot himself before the NKVD came. Stalin sadistically appointed, under Ulrikh's chairmanship, the victims' comrades as judges: Jekabs Alksnis, Vasili Bliukher, Ivan Belov, Semion Budionny, Pavel Dybenko, Nikolai Kashirin, and Boris Shaposhnikov. Before the trial began, the accused were beaten into making incriminating statements against their judges. Just two of the judges—the superannuated cavalryman Budionny, famous for the slaughter of Poles and Jews by his Cossacks in 1920, and the untalented Shaposhnikov—survived; the rest were executed within eighteen months.[34] All the accused except Boris Feldman were badly tortured by Ezhov's men. Feldman said whatever his interrogator wanted to hear,[35] and had a comfortable cell, cigarettes, apples, even biscuits with his tea.

For months Tukhachevsky had had forebodings: his trip to London for the coronation of George VI had been canceled "in case of an assassination attempt by German and Polish agents." On May 13, 1937, Stalin received him in the Kremlin for forty-five minutes in the company of

Ezhov, Molotov, Voroshilov, and Kaganovich; possibly Stalin at this meeting offered him his life in exchange for a confession. Nine days later he was arrested and, after a week, battered by the truncheons of Ushakov and Izrail Leplevsky, he told Ezhov in person that he had conspired with Trotsky. He then had to concoct his plan to let Germany defeat the Red Army; this, with everyone else's statements, was sent to Stalin to edit. Tukhachevsky's statements are stained with his blood. Ushakov later boasted how he worked without sleep right until the day of the trial, forcing Feldman, Tukhachevsky, and Iakir to incriminate each other. By June 7 all eight had ceased to deny the charges, and Stalin, Kaganovich, and Voroshilov summoned Ezhov and Vyshinsky to plan the trial. On June 9 Stalin received pleas for mercy. On the most heartfelt of them, Iakir's, the Politburo scribbled their observations: "Swine and prostitute, I. Stalin," "A perfectly precise definition, K. Voroshilov," "For a bastard, scum, and whore there is only one punishment—the death penalty, L. Kaganovich." That evening Stalin was visited by Vyshinsky, Ezhov, and Lev Mekhlis, editor of *Pravda.*

At the trial the accused apparently—the transcript is "edited"—kept to their scripts. When the discomfited judges sought further details, the accused said they were unable to add any. Feldman alone spoke at length, in support of the prosecution. Budionny made regular reports to Stalin; another judge, Ivan Belov, told Voroshilov that the accused "had not told all the truth, they have taken a lot to the grave." Feldman was the only prisoner to nurse any hopes: "Where is the concern for the living human being if we're not reprieved?" he asked. At 11:35 p.m. on June 11 Ulrikh sentenced all eight to death. Ezhov and Vyshinsky asked each condemned man if he had anything to say as they were led off one by one to be shot by Vasili Blokhin, the Lubianka's senior executioner.

NKVD investigators received medals. A campaign was launched by Stalin and Voroshilov to advertise a new army "cleansed of rotten gangrene down to healthy flesh," an army from which 34,000 officers, not counting NCOs and rank and file, were dismissed in the following eighteen months.[36] The death toll was comparable to that of a major war, except that the highest ranks had a casualty rate typical of the rank and file. The lower the rank the smaller the chance of dismissal, and the greater the likelihood of avoiding subsequent arrest and execution. Of ninety dismissed *komkory* (generals) only six survived; of 180 divisional commanders dismissed just thirty-six escaped. Of captains 7,403 were dismissed and 5,613 escaped arrest, although a few received GULAG sentences and in 1941 were retrieved, variously crippled, to fight Hitler.

Even after Ezhov's fall, when investigations were aborted and some interrogators arrested for falsification, Lavrenti Beria went on executing army officers. Some, like Bliukher, were beaten with a brutality exceeding even Ezhov's. Bliukher died on November 9, 1938, under interrogation, blind in one eye, of a blood clot in the lung, after his abdominal organs had been reduced to pulp. Beria then telephoned Stalin, who ordered Bliukher to be cremated.

Slaughtering generals and sparing lieutenants could, a cynic might think, reanimate rather than demoralize an army. One can argue that the Red Army's fiascos—the attack on Finland in 1940 and the retreat from Hitler in 1941—were compensated for by the prowess of its youthful command in 1943. But not even Voroshilov could have believed that the surgery he, Stalin, and Ezhov inflicted on the Red Army would make it fitter to defend the USSR. Paranoia and resentment, not military logic, dictated Stalin's purge.

For potential opponents in Japan, Germany, Poland, and the Baltic states, the Red Army purge was a godsend; the Soviet public, however, applauded the murders of civil war heroes only feebly. They had gotten used to seeing Trotsky, Kamenev, Zinoviev, and Bukharin as opposition, but the Red Army leaders had remained official heroes right until their arrests. It was hard to regard Tukhachevsky, who in 1935 had written on the menace of Hitler's new army, as a German spy. The intelligentsia, whose salons had sought out the suave Tukhachevsky at a time when it was suicidal to seek patronage from the old Bolshevik guard, composed no hosannas for this slaughter.

Stalin then gave his neighbors in eastern Europe a second present: he purged the Comintern, throwing foreign communists and their Soviet controllers to Ezhov's wolves, in particular to Aleksandr Ivanovich Langfang. Langfang worked with excessive enthusiasm: he beat Jaan Anvelt, the Estonian communist leader, to death on December 11, 1937, and was reprimanded for "hindering by clumsy actions the exposure of a dangerous state criminal." The Yugoslav Josip Broz (Tito), the Bulgarian Dimitrov, the Czech Klement Gottwald, the Italian Ercoli (Palmiro Togliatti), the German Wilhelm Pieck, the Finn Otto Kuusinen survived only by denouncing rivals. Survival came by Stalin's whim: Langfang extracted incriminating evidence on everyone in the Comintern—Mao Tse-tung, Chou En-lai—and even some of the Politburo—Andreev, Zhdanov, and Kaganovich. Comintern members tried to show Stalin that they were his, body and soul: Kuusinen's son was arrested, and when Stalin asked why he had not protested, Kuusinen replied, "No doubt there were serious reasons for his arrest." (Kuusinen junior was released.) Some, like Harry Pollitt of Britain or Jacques Duclos of France, survived because their countries' embassies did not wash their hands even of communists.

Stalin claimed that the Comintern was infected with Trotskyism and cosmopolitanism. Osip Piatnitsky, former secretary of the Comintern, and his friend Commissar for Health Kaminsky at the 1937 plenary meeting called Ezhov "a cruel man with no soul."[37] Stalin gave Piatnitsky two weeks to recant.[38] In a vote condemning Piatnitsky, only Krupskaia and Litvinov abstained. At a banquet in November 1937 for the depleted Comintern under Dimitrov's secretaryship, Stalin proclaimed, "We shall destroy every enemy, even an old Bolshevik, we shall annihilate his kith and kin."

Martyrdom for Poets

IN 1937, EVERY ORGANIZATION, from writers' unions to collective farms, held, under the supervision of local party and NKVD officers, a miniature version of the February–March Central Committee plenum. Writers, composers and artists, engineers, doctors, and academics sentenced each other to expulsion and arrest. Panicked ranks offered up, in propitiation, their most talented members for sacrifice.

Writers were already at loggerheads with the Politburo. Ezhov's acolyte V. Ostroumov collated reports on the conversations, regardless of prestige or talent, of authors from Babel to Demian Bedny. Babel, a

lover of Ezhov's wife, attracted special attention.[39] He had, said an informer, spread rumours that Gorky had been murdered on orders from
above. On Trotsky Babel had remarked, "it's impossible to imagine the
charm and the strength of his influence on anyone who encounters
him"; on Kamenev, "the most brilliant connoisseur of language and
literature." Pasternak had been praised by Bukharin, had relatives
in Britain, had complimented André Gide, and was repeatedly denounced.[40]

Ostroumov informed Stalin that the poet Mikhail Svetlov had said,
"everyone's being rounded up, literally everyone. Commissars and their
deputies have moved to the Lubianka. But what is ridiculous and tragic
is that we walk among these events without understanding a thing about
them. . . . What are they so afraid of? . . . we are just pathetic remnants
of an era that has died . . . This isn't trial, but organized murder."

Demian Bedny again missed an ideological about-face: he produced
an operatic satire, *Mythical Heroes,* which set a burlesque medieval Russia to music by Borodin. But Stalin now thought medieval Russia an ed-
ifying prelude to his own rule and approved of the conversion to
Christianity in the tenth century. Demian's opera was banned, and he
was excluded from the party for "moral degeneracy." His reaction, according to the NKVD source, was suicidal:

> The oppression and terror in the USSR are such that neither lit-
> erature nor science is possible. . . . It seems I've been in a party,
> 99.9 percent of whom were spies and provocateurs. Stalin is a
> horrible person and is often motivated by personal scores. All
> great leaders always created around themselves brilliant pleiades
> of comrades in arms. But whom has Stalin created? He's exter-
> minated everybody, there's nobody, everyone's been annihilated.
> Only Ivan the Terrible did anything like that. . . . The army is
> completely destroyed. . . . The peasants are afraid of nothing
> because they think that prison is no worse than the collective
> farm.[41]

Stalin mercifully let his old friend die in his bed of diabetes. He penned a
note to be read aloud to Demian, saying that "we Soviet people have

enough literary junk anyway, so it is unlikely to be worth your while increasing the layers of such literature with yet another fable . . ." and apologizing to "Demian-Dante for my involuntary frankness."

Three of Russia's greatest poets, Osip Mandelstam, Nikolai Kliuev, and the young Nikolai Zabolotsky, were marked out for destruction. The writers' union secretary, Vladimir Stavsky, wrote to Ezhov on March 16, 1938:

> In a section of the writers' milieu the Osip Mandelstam question has been discussed with a great deal of apprehension. As you know, for obscene libelous verses and anti-Soviet agitation, Mandelstam was exiled to Voronezh three or four years ago. The term of his exile has ended. He now lives with his wife near Moscow (outside the 100-kilometer zone). But in fact he often visits his friends, mainly literary people, in Moscow. They support him, collect money for him, make him into a "martyr," a poet of genius whom nobody recognizes. . . . The question is about the attitude of a group of prominent Soviet writers to Mandelstam. And I am turning to you, Nikolai Ivanovich, with a request for help.
>
> Mandelstam has just written a series of poems [the Voronezh notebooks that became famous thirty years later]. But they have no particular value—even in the general opinion of the comrades whom I have asked to take a look at them (especially Comrade Pavlenko, whose report I enclose).[42]

Piotr Pavlenko, both police spy and critic for years, confirmed that Mandelstam was dispensable—"not a poet, but a versifier . . . his language is complex, obscure, and smells of Pasternak." In May, at a sanatorium to which he was lured, Mandelstam was arrested and given ten years in the camps, a sentence which not even a healthy man could expect to survive. He died in his first Vladivostok winter.

Stalin rarely bothered to inquire about the fate of those the NKVD sent to the GULAG, even when he himself sanctioned the arrest. They were "camp dust," as good as dead to him. Stalin took only an initial predatory interest in Mandelstam. But nobody understood Stalin better than this other Joseph. In 1937 Mandelstam imagined Stalin as a dehumanized prisoner of the Kremlin:

> Inert, inside a mountain lies an idol
> In thrifty, boundless, happy rooms,
> And from his neck drips the fat of necklaces,
> Guarding the ebb and flow of dreams . . .
>
> The scattered bones are tied into a bundle,
> The knees, the hands, the shoulders humanized.
> He smiles with his most serene mouth,
> He thinks in bone and feels with his brow
> And tries to recollect his human guise.

Many Leningrad writers were also engulfed; the NKVD invented a conspiracy linking children's writers, translators, and poets to the civil war poet Nikolai Tikhonov. The NKVD and the editor Nikolai Lesiuchevsky, who advised them, as Pavlenko did in Moscow, were however disconcerted when Stalin and Tikhonov took a shine to each other at the Pushkin jubilee celebrations. The NKVD nevertheless drove mad the surreal poet Daniil Kharms, who had recently written his best-known lines for children:

> He kept going straight and ahead, and kept looking ahead.
> He didn't sleep, he didn't drink, he didn't drink,
> He didn't sleep, he didn't sleep, drink or eat.
> And then one day at sunset he entered a dark forest,
> And since then, since then, since then he has vanished.

They also arrested the maverick poet Nikolai Oleinikov. His interrogator, Major Iakov Perelmuter, himself shot in 1940, told him, "I know you're innocent, but the lot has fallen on you and you must sign this fake statement, or else you will be beaten until you sign it or die." Oleinikov was shot as a Japanese spy on November 24, 1937.

Nikolai Zabolotsky was luckier: on March 19 he was arrested and tortured, but his vivid imagination caused him to go mad. His tormentors were bored by psychiatric cases and Zabolotsky was sent to the GULAG. His charm and talent as a draftsman saved him from hard labor; he was the only important poet to survive the camps and convey what he experienced:

> So here it was, the land of melancholy,
> The Hyperborean barracks,
> In which Pliny the Ancient had seen
> An orifice stretching into hell!

Any poet who had, like Mandelstam, been exiled by Iagoda was certain of death from Ezhov. Nikolai Kliuev, denounced to Iagoda by Gronsky, editor of *Izvestiia,* was in the wilds of Siberia. His appeals to the Political Red Cross and to Kalinin went unanswered even though he recanted: "I respect and exalt the Great Leader of the world's proletariat, Comrade Stalin!" Kliuev was moved 300 miles nearer Moscow, to Tomsk where, half-paralyzed, he was embroiled by the Tomsk NKVD in the fictitious "Union for the Salvation of Russia." After months of agony Kliuev was shot in a batch of hundreds on waste ground outside Tomsk around October 24, 1937. When the victims were exhumed in 1956, in the presence of Kliuev's arresting officer, now rector of Tomsk University, Kliuev's suitcase with his last manuscripts was found by his bones.

The theatrical world was handled more gingerly as the party bosses valued theater for relaxation. The Bolshoi and Moscow Arts theaters, which provided ballerinas for the Politburo's beds and informers for the NKVD, received awards and pay increases. Other theaters trembled— Stalin exploited directors' egos, inducing Vsevolod Meierkhold and Aleksandr Tairov to denounce each other—but of all Leningrad's and Moscow's directors and theaters only Meierkhold and his theater were doomed, partly because the actress Zinaida Raikh, Meierkhold's wife, wrote to Stalin on April 29, 1937:

> I keep arguing with you in my head, trying all the time to prove how wrong you sometimes are about art. . . . You are being so infinitely, infinitely deceived, they hide from you and lie to you

that you have now rightly addressed the masses. For you I am now the voice of the masses and you have to listen to the bad and the good from me. . . . I have planned a meeting with you for the 5th of May, if you can. . . . I shall now write to Nikolai Ezhov about organizing this meeting. . . .[43]

Two prose writers—Pilniak and Babel—had a year or two to wait before martyrdom, although terror had already silenced both. Andrei Platonov was ostracized, and his adolescent son arrested. Only Bulgakov, dying of kidney disease, still worked, dictating to his wife the last part of *The Master and Margarita* with its Manichaean vision of Stalin as Satan, the Professor Woland whose cosmic evil is the artist's refuge against the mundane evil of his enemies.

One writer alone—Mikhail Sholokhov—dared denounce, at length, Ezhov's horrors to Stalin.[44] Sholokhov's dogged courage, or blind despair, may have steered Stalin toward thinking that the Great Terror had done enough, and that Ezhov could now go. Living with servants, a motor car, and his own livestock like a feudal lord among the Cossacks who furnished the material for *Quiet Flows the Don,* Sholokhov would not stay quiet. With his friends he sat on the district party committee and ran his Vioshenskaia Cossack station as best he could. Unable to finish *Quiet Flows the Don,* he feuded with the NKVD and party authorities that ruled the Cossacks from Rostov on the Don. The enemy was Ezhov's ally Efim Evdokimov. Sholokhov's associates and a cousin were charged with counterrevolution and tortured. Sholokhov got his closest friend released, and took the war onto Ezhov's territory.

The previous autumn Sholokhov had been received by Stalin twice, on both occasions with Molotov and Ezhov; they talked for over two hours. On February 16, 1938, Sholokhov sent Stalin a twenty-page letter. He accused the local NKVD of aiming to "destroy all the Bolshevik leadership" in the district and told Stalin, "it is time to unravel this tangle." He denounced Evdokimov, the torture and the falsifications. Absurdly, Sholokhov's cousin, a schoolmaster, had been accused of uprooting 10,000 fruit trees from school grounds of less than an acre. Stalin admired the power of Sholokhov's portrayal of Cossacks divided by revolution and collectivization, even though Sholokhov's querulousness exasperated him. Stalin had Sholokhov's friends released, but made only perfunctory gestures to relieve the fear gripping Vioshenskaia and its Cossacks.

Stalin scrawled over Sholokhov's letter, "Check this!" He sent Matvei Shkiriatov from the party Control Commission to investigate. Shkiriatov freed only three of the hundreds arrested around Vioshenskaia and found no reason to punish any NKVD officers. Sholokhov came to Moscow and saw Stalin twice more, getting his word in before Ezhov entered the office. The second time, on October 31, 1938, with him were two delegations, one of persecuted officials from Vioshenskaia, the other from the Rostov NKVD. In the presence of Beria, Ezhov was grilled by Stalin. In Moscow Sholokhov took even more extraordinary risks: he visited Ezhov and then, like Babel, slept with Ezhov's wife. Their lovemaking in the Hotel National was recorded and a transcript given to Ezhov.[45] But by October 1938 Ezhov was enfeebled: he could not take retaliatory action without Beria's countersignature, although only Stalin's intervention saved Sholokhov from the fate of others who had slept with either of the Ezhovs.

Sholokhov's was a lone voice. Others blocked out their terror by celebrating the mirage of happiness over the Soviet horizon. Using Bukharin's drafts, Stalin had in 1936 promulgated a constitution that promised secret ballots, freedom of speech, inviolability of the person, and privacy of correspondence. The census figures of 1937 were pulped; the demographic catastrophe that had happened was denied. Some memoirs of the mid-1930s evoke a golden age. The new Soviet elite with its special shops, sanatoria, villas, and servants could pretend, if it drank enough, to be secure. Just as elderly Germans maintain that they were unaware of the fate of their Jewish neighbors and recall in the mid-1930s only full employment, national pride, and public order, so some elderly Russians, often the pampered children of the new bureaucracy, deny being afraid for themselves or sorry for others at that time. Today's cynical neo-Stalinists argue that the terror affected barely 1.5 percent of the population and that this price was worth paying to guarantee victory in the Second World War.

But what Soviet family or community was not scarred by Stalin's tyranny? Was the price of victory not so high because the country's morale, population structure, and armed forces had been crippled? Diaries of the 1930s, even when lyrical and hedonistic, have false, hysterical tones that betray fear and guilt.[46]

The Soviet glitterati and their attitude to the NKVD remind one of the Eloi in H. G. Wells's *The Time Machine*—frolicking on lawns by day, sleeping in frightened huddles at night when out of subterranean shafts come apelike, pasty-faced Morlocks, the "human spiders" who snatch and eat them. Vladimir Stavsky, as he was snaring Osip Mandelstam for the NKVD, was enthusing to his diary about rescuing his cat, about rabbits and mice in the snow, the star-studded sky, Moscow's new skyscrapers, and Lazar Kaganovich's athletic physique. But Stavsky was bothered by his inability to write a single sentence of artistic worth, and in the summer of 1938 the beaches of Sochi, once crowded with the families of officials, were deserted. The prisons, camps, and mass graves overflowed. Institutions were breaking down for want of skilled workers.

Even though Stalin intervened directly in the management of terror, it still destroyed the very people that he needed to preserve. The USSR lost its astrophysicists when the Pulkovo Observatory in Leningrad was raided; Moscow's low-temperature physics laboratory could have exploded when its physicists were taken by the NKVD. One also wonders what went through Stalin's mind when he learned from a despairing relative's letter in April 1938 that of the many thousands of women whom the NKVD had plucked from the streets in Moscow and lost in the camps one was his own daughter, Pasha Mikhailovskaia, the first of his illegitimate children.[47]

In autumn 1938 the terror seemed to stop, as suddenly as it had started eighteen months before. Stalin had for some time been giving Ezhov conflicting signals. He was awarded the Order of Lenin in July 1937—he shaved his head for the occasion—and was brought into the Politburo in October. But he knew that promotion from Stalin often foretold a favorite's doom. On December 20, 1937, when Ezhov was the star of the evening at the Cheka's twentieth-anniversary celebrations, Stalin stood Ezhov up; Anastas Mikoyan delivered the encomium to the "Iron Commissar." Ezhov had been put on a pedestal as high as Dzierżyński's—panegyrics were commissioned from folk poets in Dagestan, towns named after him—but Stalin had snubbed him.

Ezhov's worsening drinking bouts forced the Politburo to grant him leave in December 1937. In February 1938 Ezhov took his protégé Uspensky to Kiev to install him as commissar of the Ukrainian NKVD. With Nikita Khrushchiov's help, Ezhov and Uspensky, often too drunk to stand, decimated the Ukrainian *chekisty.* Ezhov was now arresting his own appointees. Some perished for complicity with Iagoda; some, like Iakov Deich of Rostov on the Don and Piotr Bulakh of Vladikavkaz, were arrested on the previously inconceivable pretext of "excesses." "Excesses" were condoned again in September 1938, when local NKVD chiefs were told by Stalin to pass death sentences without referring them to the center, in other words to Ezhov. This last frenzy—105,000 shot by regional troikas—was, however, limited to two months. Its end was also Ezhov's.

Disposing of Ezhov

> George's son had done his work so thoroughly that he was considered too good a workman to live—and was, in fact, taken and tragically shot at twelve o'clock that same day— another instance of the untoward fate which so often attends dogs and other philosophers who follow out a train of reasoning to its logical conclusion. . . .
>
>   *Thomas Hardy,* Far from the Madding Crowd

EZHOV KNEW his game was up in April 1938, when he was also made commissar of water transport, rather as Iagoda had been transferred to communications; the previous water transport commissar had been shot within a month of appointment. For two months Ezhov nevertheless plunged into water transport, as only he knew how, arresting much of the commissariat and bringing in his NKVD men to replace them.

NKVD overseas operations had suffered in the purges. Ezhov had failed to kill Trotsky, although he had infiltrated Trotsky's inner circle in Paris and stolen parts of his archives. Ezhov's last competent agent was Sergei Shpigelglas, who specialized in liquidating defectors and émigrés.

Shpigelglas's final action was to murder Trotsky's son, Lev Sedov, as the latter convalesced from an appendectomy.[48] This last murder was counterproductive: it alerted Trotsky and made him warier. Shpigelglas also left such a blatant trail of blood that he damaged Franco–Soviet and Swiss–Soviet relations.

Worse for Ezhov's reputation were the defections of some NKVD men he had recalled to Moscow in order to arrest. Giorgi Liushkov on June 12, 1938, went over to the Japanese, Aleksandr Orlov on July 14, to the Americans. Liushkov published in Japanese frank accounts of Stalin's crimes. Orlov offered Ezhov and Stalin a deal: he would keep quiet about Stalin's crimes in exchange for the lives of his relatives; if he or they disappeared, his lawyers would reveal what the NKVD had done in Spain and in the USSR.

Voroshilov, who had caught the change in Stalin's mood, began talking of the NKVD as forcing everyone, regardless of guilt, to confess. Within the NKVD Ezhov had shot by August any subordinates who might testify against him, even his staunchest henchmen Zakovsky of Leningrad and Lev Mironov of Siberia, while Stalin was disposing of others—launching Frinovsky, too, into water as commissar for the navy. Like Iagoda before him, Ezhov seemed to take no steps to avert his fate. He had even fewer options than Iagoda: there was nobody left alive with whom he could have plotted a coup, there were no old Bolsheviks to whom he could gravitate. His own Cheka feared and hated him; Ezhov had murdered his own appointees, not to mention the old guard. He was alone except for a few old companions with whom he could seek solace in vodka and sodomy. The only person he still loved was his eight-year-old foster daughter, and she could hardly have comforted or advised him.

On August 22 Stalin appointed Lavrenti Beria, who was already boss of Georgia and de facto NKVD satrap for all Transcaucasia, head of the NKVD directorate of state security. Now that Lominadze and Orjonikidze were dead, Stalin had in Moscow no close ally to whom he could speak privately in Georgian. He had watched and promoted Lavrenti Beria for nearly fifteen years and had groomed him to succeed Ezhov, just as Ezhov had been chosen to replace Iagoda.

Beria finished his purges in Georgia in September 1938 and handed over the remnants of the Georgian party and intelligentsia to the easier-going Kandid Charkviani and its NKVD to Akvsenti Rapava, a Mingrelian cobbler's son who had crushed Abkhazia after Lakoba's murder. He then came to Moscow and saw Ezhov straightaway; their affable relationship in Lakoba's villa six years before now became a standoff. Beria had brought his NKVD men from Georgia, figures as vile as Ezhov's. Without Beria's countersignature, Ezhov could issue no orders. Holed up in his dacha with wife, daughter and nanny, Ezhov was now drinking too heavily to counterattack. From September 1938 Ezhov's remaining associates fell victim to Beria. On Red Square on November 7 Beria stood in Ezhov's place. The faked suicide and flight of Aleksandr Uspensky that same month was another nail in the Ezhov coffin.

Winding up the terror was presented to the public as redressing the balance between Andrei Vyshinsky's law-abiding judiciary and the lawless NKVD. Ezhov had unsettling meetings at the Kremlin and in his own office with both the scheming Vyshinsky and the crusading Sholokhov. These discussions led on November 17 to a resolution, "On Arrests, Procuracy Supervision, and Conduct of Investigation," as a result of which the NKVD was no longer prosecutor, judge, and executioner. In theory if not practice the NKVD would arrest, they would torture, and they would execute; Vyshinsky's organs now took over the intermediate processes of indictment and trial. Local troikas lost their right to shoot prisoners. The Politburo disavowed their own "unfounded arrests" as the work of "foreign spies and enemies of the people."

Both Ezhovs were desperate. Evgenia had been mentally ill since May and had rarely left the dacha. Ezhov challenged her about her affairs with Sholokhov and Babel. Ignoring his own sexual intercourse with her friends and their daughters, with his subordinates and their wives, he decided to divorce her. She appealed to Stalin on September 19, 1938, to reconcile her husband to her. Ezhov abandoned divorce proceedings but shot both of his wife's previous husbands, her closest confidante's husband, and her former boss.

On October 29 Evgenia was sent to a sanatorium. She left a note at home: "Darling Kolia. I beg you, I insist you have all my life checked out. I can't reconcile myself to the thought that I am suspected of two-faced behavior and crimes I have not committed." She again appealed to Stalin: "Dear, beloved Comrade Stalin, I may be calumnied, slandered, but you are dear and close to me. . . . Let my freedom, my life be taken, I won't object, but I shan't give up my right to love you. . . . I feel I am a living corpse. . . ." On November 21, she died of an overdose of sleeping tablets which she had asked Ezhov to bring her. Ezhov's oldest friend and long-standing lover, Vladimir Konstantinov, later testified that Ezhov had said, "I had to sacrifice her to save myself."

After Evgenia's funeral—which he did not attend—Ezhov brought a letter of resignation with him to a four-hour meeting with Stalin, Molotov, and Voroshilov. Accused of doing too much, Ezhov blindly flagellated himself for having done too little, for "lack of Bolshevik vigilance" in leaving so many spies and conspirators untouched, in letting Liushkov and Uspensky escape arrest, in failing to consult the party. By December Ezhov had only three posts left: secretary of the Central Committee, chairman of the Party Control Commission, and commissar for water transport. He never entered Stalin's office again. He appeared at some public occasions, but Stalin did not shake his hand. Ezhov went on another binge with Vladimir Konstantinov and others.

He should have spent the new year handing over the Lubianka to its new master but was too drunk to turn up and left behind the dossiers he had compiled on Politburo figures. Beria gathered the evidence to destroy him. In Ezhov's office were found hidden behind books six vodka bottles, three full, two empty, and one half empty, and the four used revolver bullets wrapped in paper inscribed "Kamenev," "Zinoviev," and "Smirnov" (shot twice). Ezhov owned more handguns than Iagoda, but his library contained only 115 books. Even water transport was now beyond Ezhov; he was formally reprimanded for incompetence by Molotov. On January 21, 1939, Ezhov's picture appeared for the final time in *Pravda* and he attended his last Politburo meeting eight days later. He was not elected to, and not allowed to speak at, the eighteenth party congress in March; a penciled plea to Stalin for a talk was ignored. His arrest on April 10 went unreported. Those following the announcement of appointments merely saw new commissars of sea and river transport. Ezhov and his commissariat vanished. The citizens of Ezhovsk-Cherkessk woke up on April 11, 1939, to find their town renamed Cherkessk.

Ezhov was taken to the secret prison of Sukhanovka outside Moscow, which he himself had had converted from a monastery and in which the church had been converted to an execution chamber with an oil-fired crematorium where the altar had been. Ezhov had hysterics; he was beaten. He was interrogated by Beria's deputy Bogdan Kobulov, then by Kobulov's assistant, the sullen and vicious Boris Rodos.[49] Rodos had crippled other detainees and was warned not to kill this frail, tubercular alcoholic. Ezhov was charged with spying, conspiring to overthrow the government, murder, and, worse in Stalin's eyes, sodomy. Ezhov penciled an appeal to Beria: "Lavrenti! Despite all the harshness of the conclusions that I have deserved and which party duty compels me to accept, I assure you in all conscience that I remain devoted to the party, to Comrade Stalin, to the end. Yours, Ezhov."

Mentally and physically painful interrogations went on throughout June; Ezhov admitted virtually everything. In July questioning shifted from treason to degeneracy. None of this—unlike Iagoda's sins—was made public, although because of Beria's prurience and desire to disillusion Stalin with his "little blackberry," Ezhov was forced to write his sexual autobiography. After that, the accusations of sabotage seemed banal.

In autumn 1939 Ezhov was handed over to a quieter interrogator, Esaulov, a man who neither hit prisoners nor drank before interrogating them. Ezhov now retracted his confessions to spying. In January 1940 he nearly died of pneumonia and kidney disease and had to be rushed to the hospital. Back at Sukhanovka, Ezhov was handed over to Military Procurator N. P. Afanasiev, who would oversee both trial and execution. On February 1, 1940, Ezhov was charged with five capital crimes. He threatened to retract his confession in court unless he could talk to a member of the Politburo. Ezhov was taken to Beria's office in the prison. Beria gave Ezhov the first glass of vodka he had tasted in nine months and promised that his relatives would live—Ezhov's brother Ivan and at least one nephew had in fact been shot two weeks previously. As for Beria's reassurance, "Don't think you will inevitably be shot. If you confess and tell everything honestly, your life will be preserved," Ezhov knew its value; he had often given such promises.

The next day, February 3, Ezhov was tried by Ulrikh, who had a year ago brought him brandy and flowers. Ezhov admitted everything except terrorism and espionage—sodomy had been dropped from the charges. He was allowed an unusually long last word of twenty minutes. He complained of Rodos's beatings; he admitted only neglect, in purging too few—14,000—in the NKVD. If he had been a terrorist, he could have easily killed members of the government with his own "technology." His moral degeneracy, he argued, was irrelevant; he had worked like an ox. He ended:

> Shoot me peacefully, without agonies. Neither the court nor the Central Committee will believe I am innocent. If my old mother is still alive, I ask for her old age to be provided for and for my daughter to be brought up. Please do not repress my relatives, my nephews, since they are guilty of absolutely nothing. . . . Please tell Stalin that everything that has happened to me is just a coincidence of circumstances and it is quite possible that enemies whom I missed have had a hand in it. Tell Stalin that I shall be dying with his name on my lips.[50]

The judges pretended to deliberate for half an hour. Ezhov fainted at the verdict, then scrawled a petition for mercy; it was read out over the telephone to the Kremlin and rejected. Ezhov was taken in the dead of night to a slaughterhouse he himself had built near the Lubianka. Dragged screaming to a special room with a sloping cement floor and a log-lined wall, he was shot by the NKVD's chief executioner, Vasili Blokhin. Beria gave Stalin a list of 346 of Ezhov's associates to be shot. Sixty of them were NKVD officers, another fifty were relatives and sexual partners.

Ezhov's mother, Anna Antonovna, and sister, Evdokia Babulina-Ezhova, survived. The Ezhovs' adopted daughter, Natalia, was, like Iagoda's son, taken to a provincial orphanage and given a new surname. In 1958 she voluntarily went to live in the GULAG world of the Kolyma, where she taught music. All her life Natalia Khaiutina has demanded Ezhov's rehabilitation, arguing that he was no more guilty of murder than other Politburo members who did Stalin's bidding.

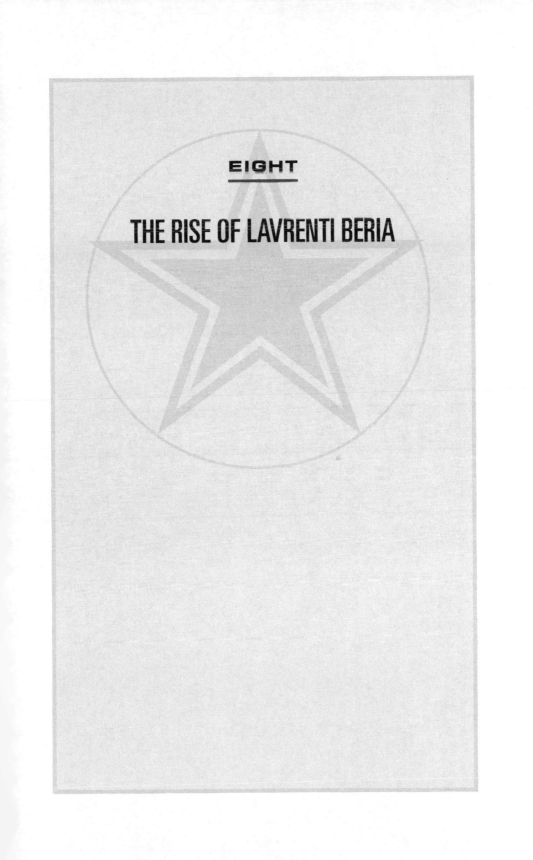

EIGHT

THE RISE OF LAVRENTI BERIA

Why Beria?

IN MID-1938, surveying a country where most were paralyzed by terror and many fired by suspicion and fanaticism, where the only initiative shown was in writing denunciations, a state bereft of its best professionals—army officers, physicists, translators, engineers, agronomists— Stalin may have paused for reflection. His own world had also been devastated: his wife had made the ultimate gesture of rejection; his two sons, terrified and repelled, avoided him; he had put to death two of his most trusted Georgian friends, Abel Enukidze and Sergei Orjonikidze. The yea-saying conversation of his loyal robots Kaganovich, Molotov, Voroshilov, Andreev, and Zhdanov provided little consolation; the note of comradely affection disappears from Stalin's missives.

Clearly, the center of power had shifted. The NKVD was no longer the chief agency of Stalin, the Politburo, and the party, but a power that could bring down the highest echelons.

Stalin's choice of Lavrenti Beria first to oversee then replace Ezhov was a logical decision. It worked on a personal plane: Stalin knew all about Beria, from the stains on his character to his fifteen-year-long record of intelligent, flexible, and ruthless efficiency. Unlike Ezhov, Beria knew when to hold back, when to step back. Beria was not just a vindictive sadist, he was an intelligent pragmatist, capable of mastering a complex brief, and one of the best personnel managers in the history of the USSR. With very slight adaptations, he could have made himself a leading politician in any country of the world.

Beria had proved himself as the Stalin of the Caucasus, murdering and terrorizing like Ezhov and Stalin combined but managing the economy more skillfully than Kaganovich, and the intelligentsia more masterfully than Andrei Zhdanov. Beria combined Ezhov's energy and unscrupulousness with Menzhinsky's intelligence and finesse. He could sustain the atmosphere of terror and yet repair the damage caused to the

USSR's economic and military strength. Only the disgust Beria aroused in almost every Bolshevik had stopped Stalin bringing Beria to Moscow before. But now that those who knew the worst about him—Sergo Orjonikidze, Sergei Kirov, Abel Enukidze—were dead, nobody in Stalin's circle was so fastidious as to object to working with such a murderous, devious, ambitious, and utterly unscrupulous lecher. Fifteen years would pass before Kaganovich, Molotov, and Voroshilov would be as frightened of Beria as they had been of Ezhov.

Beria in the Caucasus

LAVRENTI BERIA WAS BORN on March 29, 1899, to Pavle and Marta Beria in Merkheuli, a village near Sukhum, the capital of Abkhazia. The Berias were peasants and Mingrelians, a people related to the Georgians, and lived in a three-walled hovel with a hole in the roof for a chimney. Lavrenti, like Stalin, was the third and only healthy child of the marriage.[1] Marta was by birth a Jaqeli, a family related to the Dadiani, feudal princes of Mingrelia. She was a fine seamstress, a talent which kept her family from starvation, while for a time the young Beria helped by working as a postman. Like Stalin's mother, Marta Beria was pious and determined to educate her son; he studied at Sukhum City College. Beria became a hydraulic engineer, a trade he practiced when conscripted in the summer of 1917, and which then took him to the oil fields of Baku, where he enrolled in technical college in 1918.

Beria's revolutionary credentials in Baku are murky. In 1919 and for part of 1920 he was an intelligence agent for the Azeri nationalist party, the Musavat, which collaborated with the British forces then occupying Baku and repressed Bolsheviks. Later Beria insisted, probably truthfully, that he was working in the Musavat as a double agent on behalf of the Bolsheviks. No conclusive proof is yet available, but suspicions never abated.[2] In 1920 Sergei Kirov proposed shooting Beria; in 1926 Dzierżyński investigated him; in 1931 Georgian communists, and in December 1936 Lakoba's widow, brought Orjonikidze in Moscow a dossier. Each time Beria thwarted his accusers with worse allegations against them.[3]

By mid-1920 Beria was in independent Georgia, where he was arrested in Kutaisi as a Soviet spy. Sergei Kirov, then ambassador to Georgia and preparing for the Soviet 11th Army's invasion, bullied the Georgian government into releasing Beria, who returned to Baku. There he was detained by the new Azeri Cheka and then released by its head, the future satrap of Azerbaijan, Jafar Bagirov. Cheka headquarters in Moscow disliked the local organization. Mikhail Kedrov, fresh from ravaging Arkhangelsk, went to Baku to eradicate local nationalism and attacked both Beria and Bagirov for corruption. They were drinking with the local clergy, Christian and Muslim, oppressing Armenians and Russians, favoring Azeris and Georgians. Beria was saved from arrest on Anastas Mikoyan's intervention.

By October 1922, eighteen months after the Soviets had invaded Georgia, Beria was head of secret operations in the Georgian Cheka. He married a girl of sixteen, Nina Gegechkori, whom the Cheka had arrested after an anti-Soviet demonstration. In Tbilisi, as in Moscow, the Cheka was staffed largely by outsiders: Latvians and Russians. Beria, speaking Georgian, Russian, Mingrelian, and a little Azeri, was invaluable in this polyglot city.[4] His references from his seniors deplored his cowardice but praised his persistence, and Józef Unszlicht, deputy chairman of the GPU, was impressed enough to award Beria an inscribed Brauning revolver in 1923. Beria made his mark in 1924, stage-managing the bloody suppression of a Georgian national uprising, although he apparently had tried to warn the rebels.

That warning suggests the survival of vestiges of humanity in Beria, and in 1924 he applied to leave the Cheka. He wanted to resume his career as a hydraulic engineer and, hoping to be sent to Belgium for training, asked to move to the oil fields in Baku. But the Cheka could not do without him. Remaining in the organization, Beria advanced rapidly, disgracing and transferring his rivals. The dislike that Beria aroused made many Georgian *chekisty* seek work elsewhere in the USSR.

Beria's rise was speeded by sudden deaths among his colleagues, and he acquired a reputation for murder and falsification. In 1925, in an accident that baffled three commissions of inquiry, a Junkers aircraft crashed near Tbilisi, killing Beria's superiors, the chairman of the Transcaucasian GPU, Solomon Mogilevsky, and Stalin's favorite killer of the

Caucasus, Georgi Atarbekov. Beria composed an obituary for Mogilevsky: "I cannot believe, I don't want to believe that I shall never hear again Solomon Grigorievich's soft voice. . . . I remember his especially attentive concern for me and the Azeri Cheka's work: 'We here rely on you,' he said in his friendly chats with me."[5]

Beria, loyal to his underlings and ruthless to his rivals, later found more subtle methods to oust his bosses. In 1926 Stalin's brother-in-law, the Pole Stanislav Redens, who had during the civil war proved ruthless if erratic in Odessa and the Crimea, became head of the Transcaucasian GPU. Redens knew no Georgian and Beria, as head of the Georgian GPU, took advantage. Redens committed one blunder in March 1929: ignoring Beria's advice, he made the Georgian Muslims of Ajaria close their religious schools and uncover their womenfolk's faces. Armed rebellion ensued, and ended only when Beria undertook to settle the Ajarians' grievances. Beria's political rating rose; Redens's fell. Beria finally disgraced Redens in 1931, when, after a scandal, Redens was sent by Stalin to the Ukraine.

By 1931 Beria had his own gang of henchmen, Georgians and especially fellow Mingrelians from western Georgia. His efficiency and his personal modesty—he drank only wine and dressed appallingly—in a country notorious for its leaders' nepotism, self-indulgence, and laxity, impressed Stalin. The rebellions that swept Azerbaijan in the wake of collectivization were calmed by Beria with maximum cunning and minimal firepower.

Whatever Moscow did, Beria's Tbilisi imitated. After Menzhinsky's dispossession of the Russian Church, Beria attacked the Georgian Church, sending Catholicos Ambrosi to prison for nine years. In 1927 Beria "elected" the compliant Kristopore as Georgian patriarch and then stopped his "leftist" colleagues oppressing the remaining clergy. Caucasian technical specialists suffered in the 1930s at Beria's hands, just as Russian scientists suffered from Menzhinsky and Stalin: Baku's oil fields were allegedly run by counterrevolutionaries working for the British consulate and their prerevolution owners the Nobel brothers. In Georgia too, both left and right oppositions were exposed and smashed. For Stalin, the Caucasus was a microcosm of the USSR, and in Beria he had a viceroy to rule it with rigor. Beria did lessen the burden of collectivization on Georgia, but the only rebuke he had from Stalin was for failing to eradicate vine pests.[6]

Beria fawned on Stalin. His intermediary was Nestor Lakoba, with whom Stalin spent some weeks every summer. Beria swallowed his antipathy to the Abkhaz and tried to overcome the aversion Lakoba felt for GPU Georgians who came from Tbilisi to visit Sukhum. One such was Nadaraia, soon to be a virtuoso executioner at Tbilisi's main prison and later employed as Beria's pimp. Beria's first notes to Lakoba of 1928 are already phrased in intimate terms; they are requests for various comrades from the GPU to have their crimes and failings overlooked and forgiven:

> Dear Comrade Nestor! I send you greetings and our best wishes. Thanks for the letter. I would very much like to see Comrade Koba before he departs. If you get a chance it would be good if you could give him a hint about this. I have ordered Comrade Nadaraia to be recalled. Instead, a good chekist will be coming. Greetings, Your Lavrenti.

In January 1929, Beria thanked Lakoba in the only way he knew: "Dear Nestor, I am sending you my own revolver and 250 cartridges. Don't let its appearance bother you—the revolver is a competition one. With a greeting, Your Lavrenti." Later Beria took great trouble to find a fine edition of Jules Verne for the twelve-year-old Rauf Lakoba.

In 1931 Stalin lost patience with Georgian leaders, especially the husband and wife Mamia and Mariam Orakhelashvili, who had run both the party and the Russian-language press since 1929. They were lenient to Georgian Mensheviks and Trotskyists, and offhand about Stalin's heroic role in the Caucasus.[7] Beria seemed the only real Stalinist in the Caucasus.

In March 1931 Menzhinsky gave Beria an encomium:

> . . . the ten years that the GPU has existed in Georgia have left a glorious page in the history of the Cheka-OGPU . . . full of self-sacrificing, heroic struggle with enemies of the proletariat . . . this enormous, intensive work has basically been done by local

cadres, brought up, educated, and tempered in the fire of battle under the unceasing leadership of Comrade Beria . . . exceptional intuition . . . always finding his bearings precisely even in the most complex circumstances.[8]

Beria was on his way up. In 1931 Lakoba sent Beria notes of discussions with Stalin (Koba) and Sergo Orjonikidze:

Koba: Will Beria do for Transcaucasia?
Me: The only person who works properly is Beria. Perhaps we are biased toward him.
Sergo: Beria's a fine chap, he works. . . .
Sergo: Well, are you pushing Mamia out?
Me: Mamia doesn't organize anybody or anything, he doesn't call anybody to order, he doesn't get a hold on anything. . . .
Koba turns to me, asks: He (indicating Sergo) says Polonsky ought to be put in charge of the Transcaucasian Committee. What do you think?
Me: That would be a very bad mistake.[9]

Beria thus became first secretary of the Georgian party and yet kept de facto control of the GPU in Transcaucasia. To become both the Stalin and Iagoda of the Caucasus, he now had only to take over the secretaryship of the Transcaucasian party. In summer 1932, from Gagra on the Black Sea, Lakoba reported to Beria Stalin's thoughts:

Koba: . . . Does Beria want to get a voice on the Politburo? . . . when is Beria coming? (He put that question at the beginning of the conversation. . . .)
Me: If needed, Beria will come right away.
Koba: We have freedom of movement, there's no law against coming by any particular time.[10]

In October 1932 Beria was duly appointed first secretary of the Transcaucasian party. Now, by direct appeal to Stalin, he might overrule anyone in the Politburo or the Caucasus. His wife's cousin Aleksandra Nakashidze now kept house for Stalin in Moscow and fed Beria information for the next ten years. Summer 1933 Beria spent with Lakoba and Stalin and their families. He sat the motherless Svetlana Allilueva on his knee; he flaunted his loyalty, waving an ax at the shrubs in Lakoba's garden as if they were the heads of Stalin's enemies. Despite an unfortunate episode during a cruise when border guards fired on their launch, the three following summers the Berias, Lakobas, and Stalin vacationed together, hunting and playing skittles; only Beria's flirtations with his womenfolk alarmed the patriarchal Abkhaz.

Beria as Satrap

IN TBILISI BERIA commissioned a history of the Bolshevik movement in the Caucasus. Unwilling himself to read a book from cover to cover let alone write one, he selected the university rector and chairman of the Union of Georgian Writers, Malakia Toroshelidze, and the commissar for education, Eduard Bedia, to gather and falsify material on Stalin as the Lenin of the Caucasus. After Stalin's editorial amendments, Beria assumed the authorship, and the book became required reading in colleges throughout the Caucasus. Beria had not committed the fatal lapse of Abel Enukidze, who had dared to produce a *History of Underground Printing in the Caucasus* in which Stalin's name did not loom large.

Conducting the Great Terror on his home ground, Beria outshone both Stalin and Ezhov, with his knowledge of Georgia's technological and creative elite. Many of the old party guard had been driven out or arrested by Iagoda or Ezhov; the rest were arrested by Beria in 1936 and 1937, their appeals to Stalin, whom many had known as a friend, unanswered. In 1935, when Stalin came to see his mother in Tbilisi, Malakia Toroshelidze had linked arms with Stalin and Beria while they sang folk songs.[11] On December 16, 1936, his daughter Susanna begged Stalin: "My father, mother, and elder brother have been arrested. . . . I am seventeen . . . my other brother has been expelled. You can understand, Uncle Soso, my brother Levan has always been highly strung. . . . Uncle Soso, we worship our father."[12] Toroshelidze and his co-author Bedia were shot.

While Beria ruled Transcaucasia—this "super-republic" was on paper dismantled in 1936—he was as ruthless with Armenia as with Georgia and its minorities, Mingrelian, Ajarian, Osetian, or Abkhaz. Jafar Bagirov, by himself, made Azerbaijan a living hell. In July 1936 Beria personally shot dead Khanjian, secretary of the Armenian party, and five months later he poisoned Nestor Lakoba and thus crushed the Abkhaz.[13] Stalin and Ezhov packed the Moscow Politburo and NKVD with Russians; Beria put Georgians in charge of Georgia, purging the minorities mercilessly.

Older Georgian Bolsheviks had close links to the intelligentsia. After dealing with them, Beria turned on Georgian writers, artists, musicians, and actors directly and with deadly effect. Between 1936 and 1938 a quarter of the members of the Georgian Union of Writers were destroyed; the survivors lost their capacity to speak or write. The writers were so easily conquered because they were so divided. Before Beria, the poets Paolo Iashvili and Titsian Tabidze had sat in judgment on the works of others. The files of the union are a list of altercations: a drunken remark, quarrels over the union's Ford car, spawned feuds to which Beria's purges gave fatal outcomes. Few saw the threat that Beria represented.

Beria's relations with Georgian intellectuals were forged at parties and during altercations. He liked to walk into theater rehearsals; he liked to summon writers to meetings. In summer 1937 a dozen prominent writers were arrested. "Some of you," said Beria, "still have undeclared links with enemies of the people. I omit the surnames." Then Beria called the poet Titsian Tabidze over: "Among the omitted surnames, Mr. Tabidze, was yours."

Old Bolsheviks like Beso Lominadze had been to school with poets like Paolo Iashvili and Titsian Tabidze, the founding members of the "Blue Horns" school, so called because it aimed to reconcile the blue of French symbolism with the drinking horns of Georgian hedonism and then make them amenable to Bolshevik ideology. Beria's rise had at first encouraged poets. In 1934 Beria put Paolo Iashvili on the Transcaucasian Central Committee; the poet Galaktion Tabidze joined the Georgian Central Committee; even the feckless Titsian Tabidze sat on the Tbilisi soviet. When they realized the price of participation it was too late to step back.

The previous Georgian regime between 1929 and 1931 had inclined leftward. The Georgian classics had been banned: Shota Rustaveli as a feudalist, Ilia Chavchavadze as a bourgeois. Beria announced celebrations of the centenaries of both Rustaveli and Chavchavadze, sweeping aside Trotskyist fundamentalism and Russian chauvinism at the same time.

Beria showed theatrical talent: his first purge outside the party involved the director of the Rustaveli Theater, Sandro Akhmeteli. Akhmeteli fled to Moscow, only to find that Beria had powers of extradition. The director was imprisoned as a British spy who had plotted to kill Beria and Stalin. He was tortured until mute and paralyzed, then shot, on June 28, 1937, Beria's final touch being an auction of all his goods in the theater.

Beria's next target were Blue Horns poets. Their leader, Grigol Robakidze, his wife, and adopted daughter had been allowed by Orjonikidze to travel abroad. Robakidze defected to Germany, where he wrote novels set in Georgia. One, *The Murdered Soul,* has Stalin's "horoscope," a devastating psychopathological study: "Consumed with activity, Stalin sat in the Kremlin, a power-holder, not a ruler: the power line of revolutionary forces, a being, not a human being. A power cable with the warning 'Danger of Death' . . . He towered, full of cruel current, undefeatable, the cold, blind fate of the Soviet land and perhaps of the whole world. . . ."[14] Robakidze's defection was to provide Beria with all the excuse he needed to kill his friends.

In 1936 Georgian writers competed to offer hospitality to André Gide when he visited Tbilisi, Tsqaltubo, and Sukhum with a party of French communists. Those authors who gave Gide dinner and fulsome praises were, after *Retour de l'URSS* was published, indicted as fascists. The novelist Mikheil Javakhishvili had remarked, "André Gide has some good ideas." Paolo Iashvili admitted that hospitality to visiting dignitaries was his sycophantic recidivist disease, and wrote a poem, "To the Traitor André Gide": "Treacherous, black-faced Trotsky's cur, following your master." But to no avail. Nothing that Georgian poets did could exempt them from mass damnation in May 1937.

The journal *Literary Georgia* was Beria's mouthpiece. It devoted a whole issue to Beria's review of the progress Georgian writers had made in reforming their verse and behavior to meet his demands and those of Stalin. Giorgi Leonidze was the first of several Georgian writers to compose a work on the childhood of Stalin. The idea was typical of Beria's bidding system, in which almost every writer participated and in which only bids that were neither too innovative nor too trite succeeded. In 1934 every Georgian capable of versification contributed to a luxuriously produced anthology on Stalin; in 1935 offers were invited for "artistic biography." By 1939 those that survived had all produced a novel or a poem.

Beria reminded Georgian writers that while the Germans were burning Heine he was reprinting Rustaveli. He insisted on the supremacy of his patronage above all other reasons for writing. By 1937 what was not attributed to Beria was dedicated to him. A young sycophant, Grigol Abashidze, wrote:

To Lavrenti Beria

You are everywhere, wherever coal is cut
Or open meadows heartily plowed,
You lead in front and in our land
Stalin's idea has become fact.

The great blow came on May 15, 1937, in Beria's report to the party. Under a photograph of Beria in NKVD uniform came a list of works published or aborted, like trees planted or uprooted, coalfields exploited or abandoned. Achievements and failures in poetry, prose, drama, and criticism were enumerated group by group. Beria's venom was reserved for critics who had misled fellow writers. The first arrest was of Benito Buachidze, a critic trying to live down the connotations of the name he had chosen when Benito Mussolini was admired by Russian poets. Buachidze had terrorized non-proletarian Georgian writers with his hard-left criteria; ironically, his strictures were plagiarized by Beria.

To Davit Demetradze, an ineffectual critic, Beria entrusted the conduct of writers' union sessions from May to October 1937, at which writers had to incriminate themselves and others. Only two stayed away: Georgia's most popular poets, Galaktion Tabidze and Ioseb Grishashvili. Beria exempted them as Stalin had exempted Pasternak, and controlled them as Stalin controlled his protégés.[15] Everyone else underwent sessions that went on from 7:00 p.m. until 3:30 in the morning.[16]

After ritual adulation of Beria's speeches, writers had to confess their links to those previously arrested. The wretched victim was then led off by NKVD agents waiting in the foyer.

Blue Horns poets incriminated themselves, or exculpated themselves and incriminated others. Nikolo Mitsishvili, who had recruited Osip Mandelstam as a translator and thus brought his own poetry and Tabidze's to the attention of Russian readers, was arrested during the proceedings. Mitsishvili's apogee had been in 1934: his panegyric had been printed on the first page of Beria's anthology of poetry to Stalin and then translated by Pasternak. His nemesis followed a drunken party where he said what he thought of Soviet leaders; he was the first Blue Horn to be shot.

The Georgian poet whose doom most horrified Russian poets was Paolo Iashvili—friend of Pasternak, translator of Pushkin. Seated on a white horse, Iashvili had in 1921 greeted the communist invaders at the city boundaries. Iashvili's downfall was precipitated by his intimacy with Red literati from Moscow and Paris, leading scientists such as Gogi Eliava and Volodia Jikia, and discredited party leaders. Iashvili had shouted loudest for Kamenev and Zinoviev to be shot, but sensed his vulnerability, replying to his fellow writers' interrogation: "What is a Soviet writer supposed to do when he is drinking wine in some dubious cellar and some drunk, a stranger, stands up and makes an insincere speech to you, praising your literary achievements to the sky and you are forced to stand up and publicly respond with a speech of thanks to a man who is very often extremely suspect?"

On July 22, 1937, during a session debating his expulsion, Paolo Iashvili pulled out a concealed gun and shot himself dead. The writers' union plenum then passed a resolution expressing the wish that Iashvili would be remembered with "unbounded loathing" and condemning his "treacherous work." Titsian Tabidze walked out of the proceedings and was denounced for decadence and for loyalty to the defector Robakidze. Titsian resigned himself to his fate, and his lyric genius returned:

> Many more races will pass,
> Perhaps the Pontus Euxine may dry up,
> All the same the poet's throat, slit from ear to ear,
> Will live in the atom of verse.

Tabidze was slowly tortured to death.

At these meetings Georgia's finest prose writer, Konstantine Gamsakhurdia (father of Georgia's future president), defended Titsian Tabidze from abuse and refused to speak unless NKVD agents were silenced. He reported an assurance received from Orjonikidze that dissident intellectuals would not be sent to concentration camps, "because this would be imitating Hitler." Gamsakhurdia was a Mingrelian, like Beria, and had been the independent Georgian government's envoy in Germany. He had been sent to the Solovetsky islands as a bourgeois nationalist. On his return he had translated Dante's *Inferno* and then written an outrageous novel about collectivization, *Stealing the Moon,* in which a Beria-like party activist rapes his mother and murders his father. Beria nevertheless gave Gamsakhurdia an inscribed revolver, and when he was arrested for an affair with Lida Gasviani, the "Trotskyist" director of the state publishing house, he was released. Gamsakhurdia's relations with Beria were based on mutual respect and detestation. Gamsakhurdia was the only living Georgian novelist whose work Stalin, despite scribbling abuse in the margin, admired.

Georgia's other major novelist, Mikheil Javakhishvili, was a marked man. On July 26, 1937, the union voted: "Mikheil Javakhisvili, as an enemy of the people, a spy and diversant, is to be expelled from the Union of Writers and physically annihilated." One brave friend, Geronti Kikodze, walked out of the hall.[17] Javakhishvili was beaten in Beria's presence until he signed a confession; he was shot on September 30. His property was looted, his archives destroyed, his brother shot, his widow turned into a recluse for the next forty-five years.

Beria wiped out most of the major writers of Armenia, Abkhazia, and Osetia but he could not touch any Russian writers except for those already arrested. On December 10, 1937, Beria addressed the survivors. He linked all his victims—engineers, theater directors, poets—with a plot to spread typhoid, to sell Ajaria to the Turks, and to kill Lavrenti Beria.

★ ★ ★ Like Ezhov, Beria seduced or raped women by first arresting their husbands, lovers, or fathers. Unlike Ezhov, he made his sexual predilections public. Sandwiched on the backseat of an open-top Buick between two guards—appropriately named Sikharulidze (son of joy) and Talakhadze (son of mud)—Beria curb-crawled Tbilisi, abducting schoolgirls. On moving to Moscow, Beria at first refrained from these expeditions, but soon after the war his black car and two guards, now Sarkisian and Nadaraia, the latter the executioner of Metekhi prison, resumed cruising for young girls. Beria inspired loathing among his party colleagues, many as murderous as he, largely because of his predilection for their wives, mistresses, and daughters.

Mopping Up After Ezhov

TWO MONTHS AFTER ARRIVING in Moscow, Beria refined the terror. After November 15, 1938, victims were no longer chosen at random, but, as before 1936, for their links to others. Purges that Ezhov had begun in the armed forces, the NKVD, the Communist Youth Movement, the Ministry of Foreign Affairs, and the intelligentsia were either wound up or stepped up. The NKVD was, after Ezhov's appointees had been shot, also a happier place. They now had a leader supposedly trusted by Stalin and, instead of Ezhov's unpredictable and scorpionlike ingratitude to his own juniors, a Caucasian set of relationships between boss and underlings: treachery was cruelly punished, but Beria stood by his men and loyalty was rewarded.

Beria learned faster than Ezhov, but had at first to seek Stalin's advice—he lacked his predecessors' familiarity with the Moscow elites: writers, journalists, army officers, diplomats. From September 1938 to Stalin's death there were few periods when Beria and Stalin did not meet at least twice a week—and often daily. At first the meetings lasted less than an hour but by spring 1939 the two were talking for two hours at a time. In 1940, Beria was sometimes closeted with Stalin from 6:00 p.m. until 5:00 the next morning. Even after 1949, when Stalin was seventy and saw fewer people for less time, Beria usually visited weekly for two hours.

Beria's first task was to purge the NKVD of Ezhov's appointments and the remnants of Iagoda's men. From September 1938 to February 1939 ninety-seven NKVD bosses were arrested, as many as in the whole two years of Ezhov's rule. Most were shot in 1939, well before Ezhov died, but some were milked for two years to provide material for future arrests. Among the victims was Beria's former boss Stanislav Redens. Beria personally signed the warrant. Vacancies were filled by Beria's own men.

In the lower ranks, in one year Beria dramatically raised the educational level of the NKVD: graduates rose from 10 to over 35 percent, while those with no secondary education fell from 42 to 18 percent. Ezhov's Slav chauvinism was mitigated by the transfer of half a dozen men, not all of them Georgians but mostly from Tbilisi's NKVD, notably Sergo Goglidze, a commissar of state security under Ezhov, and Goglidze's deputy Mikeil Gvishiani. Beria sent Goglidze to Leningrad and Gvishiani to Vladivostok as his satraps. The Belorussians came under the control of Lavrenti Tsanava.[18] The Uzbeks too were policed by a Georgian, Aleksi Sajaia. Twenty years before, under his pseudonym Dr. Kalinichenko, Sajaia had been notorious as the most sadistic chekist in Odessa. In 1939 the whole of the USSR could be said to be controlled by Georgians and Mingrelians.

Notable among Beria's parvenus were the Tbilisi Armenian brothers Bogdan and Amayak Kobulov, Vladimir Dekanozov, a Georgian from Baku, and Solomon Milshtein, a Vilnius Jew who had joined the Transcaucasian Cheka with Beria and whose promotion of physical education in Tbilisi made him into the fittest of Beria's torturers. Amayak Kobulov soon became councilor at the Soviet embassy in Berlin, and Dekanozov also went to Germany, as Stalin's ambassador to Hitler. Bogdan Kobulov, a man who rationalized his brutality by seeing himself as part of an elite with a right to rule, graduated to be Beria's deputy.[19] Solomon Milshtein was to oversee the USSR's railways.

The intellectual in Beria's team was a Caucasian Russian, Vsevolod Merkulov, who had studied physics for three years at St. Petersburg University and had proved his mettle in quelling the Ajarian rebellion of

1929. Beria's most violent henchman, a Jew from Tbilisi, Leonid Raikhman, held a key post in the NKVD's training school. Someone whom Beria genuinely liked and brought to Moscow was Prince Shalva Tsereteli, a brave dimwit who had been in prison with Beria in Kutaisi in 1920, escaped to become a bandit and joined the Georgian Cheka as a professional killer. As under Iagoda, the secret police again included a token aristocrat. Beria also brought from Tbilisi the Latvian A. P. Eglitis. Two men who would have a future in the KGB were picked by Beria from the Red Army: Sergei Kruglov, a tank mechanic, took charge of NKVD personnel, and Ivan Serov, the butcher of Budapest in 1956, learned his trade as commissar of the Ukrainian NKVD.

Beria kept on very few key figures from Ezhov's regime: Pavel Meshik, a Ukrainian specializing in state security, was too talented to shoot and still young enough to retrain as an economist for the NKVD; Iakov Rapoport, the only long-lived Latvian Jew in the NKVD elite, continued to build canals with GULAG labor; Leonid Fokeevich Bashtakov, chief disciplinary officer in the OGPU and NKVD training schools, was chosen by Beria to deal with extrajudicial killings, euphemistically called special operations. Lev Vlodzimirsky, a Russian despite his Polish surname, had ruled the north Caucasus under Iagoda, been brought to Moscow by Ezhov, and was now promoted by Beria to take charge of the directorate for investigations.

Beria kept on especially talented interrogators such as Esaulov, who questioned Ezhov. Lev Aronovich Shvartsman, a semiliterate promoted by Ezhov for his talent in beating prisoners and editing their statements, was promoted. So was his close colleague Boris Veniaminovich Rodos, who battered Ezhov into submission. Rodos enjoyed Beria's confidence, and his purview included all who had ever brought up Beria's role as a double agent in Baku. On Beria's behalf Rodos tortured and dispatched many Caucasians including Betal Kalmykov, first secretary of the Kabarda-Circassian party, and Sergo Orjonikidze's younger brothers and secretaries. The miracle is that Beria let Rodos, who knew so much, outlive him.

Beria let Rodos loose on the central Asian party leadership in spring and summer 1939. Working in the specially equipped Moscow prison of Lefortovo and scorning the usual truncheons, drugs, or electrodes, he trampled victims with his boots or urinated into their mouths. Another of Ezhov's men Beria singled out, Aleksandr Langfang, made a brilliant career. A former concrete pourer, he was known for his brutality as a "chopper" (*kolun*), reducing many former diplomats and Comintern representatives into unrecognizable pulp. Even more fearsome was Shvartsman, who specialized in torturing women and then editing their incoherent confessions, despite his lack of education, with an elegance and grammatical correctness unrivaled in the Lubianka.[20]

NKVD men who had fled to other areas of government were hounded down, as they had been by Ezhov; almost none previously arrested were spared by Beria. Béla Kun underwent another year's interrogation before being shot in November 1939. His consort Rozalia Zemliachka kept her post in Party Control. Stalin shielded her for sentimental reasons—in 1903 she had been almost the first of Lenin's emissaries to contact the young Jughashvili.

A very few NKVD men arrested by Ezhov were retrieved by Beria. Andrei Sverdlov, the son of the first head of the Soviet state, had as a boy stolen Iagoda's cigarettes and later been found work as the GPU's youngest interrogator. Ezhov, no doubt at Stalin's behest, had Sverdlov arrested. He was interrogated unusually gently and delivered to the Lubianka. Beria apologized to him on behalf of the Central Committee and appointed him assistant to the man who had just interrogated him. Sverdlov, at twenty-eight, became Beria's specialist in academicians, poets, and the wives of arrested old Bolsheviks; he was noted for mixing physical violence with sophisticated conversation.

Beria was resisted by only one veteran chekist, Mikhail Kedrov, now head of an institute of neuropsychology. Kedrov's son Igor, a serving NKVD officer, was horrified at Beria's promotion and urged his father to tell Stalin what he had last said in 1923—that Beria had been an Azeri police agent. Beria arrested Mikhail Kedrov in February 1939 and Igor two months later. Kedrov senior was, to Beria's fury, acquitted by the USSR's supreme court. Not until October 1941, when Beria evacuated a trainload of prisoners to Saratov on the Volga, could he shoot Kedrov out of hand.

Beria extinguished the last spark of humanity in Ezhov's satrapy. Lefortovo prison, which broke prisoners who held out in the Lubianka, had a hospital where torture victims were restored so that interrogation could resume. Anna Anatolievna Rozenblium, the "good fairy of Lefortovo," reverted to the Tsarist tradition of compassionate prison doctors, like Dr. Haas who had nursed the young Dostoevsky back to sanity in Omsk. Anna Rozenblium in two years' service at Lefortovo certified forty-nine cases in which prisoners died under torture and nursed many more back to health. The few who survived Lefortovo and the GULAG remember her as the last human being in the NKVD. On January 31, 1939, Beria arrested Anna Rozenblium, and Boris Rodos trampled her. Convicted as a Polish spy, she emerged fifteen years later from the GULAG to testify against her torturers.

The NKVD was superficially reformed: officers still took the furniture and apartments of those they arrested, but Beria now stipulated "that the furniture is to be stock-checked and temporarily given to employees quartered in these apartments," although no NKVD or KGB man ever gave back to rehabilitated survivors the possessions they stole. Prisoners were no longer driven about the streets in marked vehicles, but were discreetly transported in vans signed "Vegetables" or "Meat," thus serving two propaganda purposes at once.

Beria decided to give the NKVD the same cultural gloss as the Red Army, establishing the world's only secret-police song and dance ensemble. It was to perform for Stalin's official sixtieth-birthday celebrations in December 1939.[21] This ensemble would give in 1941 an unlikely refuge to the satirical dramatist Nikolai Erdman, who had infuriated Stalin in the 1920s with his play *The Suicide.* In 1933 Erdman had incurred arrest and three years' exile in Siberia by inducing the actor Vasili Kuchalov to recite in front of Stalin his fable:

> The GPU arrested Aesop
> And smashed his glasses and his teeth up.
> The moral of our fable's this:
> Don't ever dare to take the piss.[22]

The belief that Beria would restore justice and moderation to NKVD activities was fostered by the release of prisoners when an NKVD investigator was arrested or dismissed. Those released were able to protest their innocence and denounce illegal torture; little did they know that in 1939 Stalin repeated in writing the telegraphed authorization he had in 1937 given the NKVD to use "physical methods of influence."

The chief prosecutor, Andrei Vyshinsky, easily adapted to Beria's regime. He staged public demonstrations of legality: a group of veterinarians accused of spreading anthrax among horses found a lawyer, Boris Menshagin, to defend them and were released.[23] Vyshinsky himself moved into government, as deputy chairman of the Council of People's Commissars. As always, Vyshinsky survived by throwing his colleagues to the wolves. In the previous two years he had denounced any prosecutor with a sense of legality or conscience to Ezhov. Faina Niurina, vulnerable as a woman and a Jew, had signed her own death warrant in 1937 when she quoted the guillotined French revolutionary Olympe de Gouge: "If a woman has the right to mount the scaffold, she has the right to join the tribunal."[24] Now the ruthless Grigori Roginsky, whom Vyshinsky had used to dispatch rival prosecutors such as Krylenko, was sanctimoniously handed over to Beria as a counterrevolutionary. Beria put Roginsky in the hands of his hardest men, Bogdan Kobulov and Lev Vlodzimirsky.[25] By 1940 the *prokuratura* was run by Viktor Bochkov, an army officer who knew no law but had advised Ezhov on which army officers to arrest. Beria could rely on Bochkov to fit the law to the NKVD's needs.

Arrests in the Red Army dwindled under Beria in 1939. That year only 847 officers were dismissed and forty-one arrested; under Ezhov some 38,000 had been dismissed of whom nearly 10,000 were repressed. The naval officer Piotr Smirnov-Svetlovsky, arrested in March 1939, was perhaps the last accused conspirator in the armed forces. In 1939 Beria even had some 5,570 dismissed officers reinstated.[26] Two years later the NKVD recorded at least 18,000 Red Army men alive in its prisons and camps, and some were retrieved for service in the Second World War.

The GULAG population nevertheless grew relentlessly—by January 1, 1939, to 1,344,408, with another 315,584 in corrective labor camps and the same number in prison. The courts began to acquit some of those accused of counterrevolution; convictions for political crimes fell to a tenth of the 1938 figures. Shootings also tailed off. Beria and Stalin cut counterrevolutionary executions from 328,618 in 1938 to 2,552 in

1939 and a mere 1,649—if the murder of 21,000 captured Poles and the thousands of shootings in the GULAG camps are ignored—in 1940. The mortality of prisoners in the GULAG fell to 50,000, half the 1938 figures. Beria is credited with an amnesty, but in reality fewer (223,622) were freed from the GULAG in 1939 than had been in 1938 (279,966). In 1940 over 300,000 were let out. These figures however pale beside the influx of new prisoners: 749,647 in 1939 and 1,158,402 in 1940. Terror under Beria was just as massive, only less immediately deadly.

Stalin wanted a more pliable, not a more humane, NKVD, and on occasion gave Beria orders to kill without arrest, let alone trial. Under Iagoda and Ezhov such killings had been largely done abroad; now they happened in the USSR. The first victim, in July 1939, was the Soviet ambassador to China, Ivan Bovkun-Luganets. He was not to be arrested lest his colleagues still in China panic and defect. Beria and Bogdan Kobulov reserved a Pullman railway carriage to take Bovkun-Luganets and his wife, Nina, to Georgia, to the mountain resort of Tsqaltubo. Three senior NKVD men shared the carriage, two of Beria's acolytes, Lev Vlodzimirsky and Shalva Tsereteli, and the bodyguard Veniamin Gulst, an Estonian Jew. Tsereteli killed the ambassador with a hammer, Vlodzimirsky battered the ambassador's wife, and Gulst strangled her. At Kutaisi station the bodies were unloaded in sacks. The head of the Georgian NKVD, Akvsenti Rapava, had the bodies driven into the mountains. An accident was staged. The driver of the car was shot and all three bodies were buried in Tbilisi. The ambassador and his wife— but not the chauffeur—were then exhumed and reburied with full honors on Stalin's orders.

The same summer Stalin decided that Marshal Grigori Kulik must be punished for protesting at the army killings in 1938. But because of the Finnish war of winter 1939–40 the marshal himself, an artillery specialist, seemed temporarily indispensable. It was decided in 1940 just to kill his wife, and for two weeks the killers of the Bovkun-Luganetses, Vlodzimirsky, Tsereteli, and Gulst, staked out the marshal's apartment until she came out alone. She was interrogated by Beria and, believing she had been recruited as an agent, sent by Kobulov to be shot by Blokhin at Sukhanovka prison. Marshal Kulik reported her as a missing person.[27] Vlodzimirsky and Tsereteli were given medals; Gulst was made deputy commissar for internal affairs in newly conquered Estonia. Stalin had Beria put on hold plans to kill Commissar for Foreign Affairs Maksim Litvinov and the nuclear physicist Piotr Kapitsa. For the first lover of Stalin's daughter, the film director Aleksei Kapler, Beria's men merely arranged a beating.

The Last of the Intellectuals

THE FIRST BIG PROJECT assigned to Beria by Stalin was the show trial of a vast network of alleged spies. Dozens of intellectuals and party officials made hundreds of confessions, incriminating virtually every writer who had not yet been arrested and every ambassador and official of the Ministry of Foreign Affairs. Between the first arrests and the final executions two years would pass but Stalin finally decided against the show trial itself. At the end of 1939 his pact with Hitler and the partition of eastern Europe would occupy the limelight. In any case, some of those incriminated might yet be of service to the Soviet state.

The scapegoat was the journalist Mikhail Koltsov. If *Pravda* featured a readable piece in the 1930s, Koltsov was probably the author. His versatility and courage—he was a pioneer pilot and had been a a frontline war correspondent from Kronstadt to Barcelona—belied his frail appearance and made him genuinely popular. Koltsov could toe the Stalinist line and would even help the NKVD murder "enemies of the people" with whom he was acquainted, but in his writing he could be bitingly satirical.[28] He was also famous in Europe for his *Spanish Diary,* which had recorded as graphically, if not honestly, as George Orwell the corrupted idealism of the Spanish Civil War. The USSR had been officially neutral in this war and Koltsov had invented an alter ego, Don Miguel, for his fighting role.

Stalin, Ezhov, and Beria distrusted Soviet participants in the Spanish war. Military advisers like Vladimir Antonov-Ovseenko, the Soviet general consul in Barcelona, and journalists like Koltsov were open to infection by the heresies, especially Trotsky's, prevalent among the republic's supporters. NKVD agents sent to Spain were therefore keener on abducting and murdering anti-Stalinists among republican leaders and International Brigade commanders than on fighting Franco. The defeat of the republic, in Stalin's eyes, was caused not by the NKVD's diversionary efforts, but by the treachery of the heretics.

Stalin had twenty years' worth of grudges against Koltsov. He had spent 1918 in his native city Kiev, where under Kaiser Wilhelm's benign occupation the Ukrainian press had printed his liberal and anti-Bolshevik articles. In 1923, against Stalin's wishes, Koltsov had printed in *Ogoniok*—the magazine he founded and which outlasted the Soviet Union—a photomontage "A Day in the Life of Trotsky." When Koltsov organized the world 1935 congress of writers in support of culture against fascism, he had failed to make the participants praise Stalin as loudly as they condemned Hitler. Moreover Koltsov had made Stalin give in to blackmail: unless the USSR sent real writers such as Babel and Pasternak not just Soviet party hacks—all dressed in identical coats and suits ordered for the occasion—the French delegates would walk out.[29] Koltsov was friendly with French leftists like André Malraux, who were distancing themselves from Stalin, and had invited André Gide to Russia, let him meet Soviet intellectuals unmonitored by the NKVD, and had failed not only to stop Gide publishing his *Retour de l'URSS*, but also to refute Gide's "slanders."

Stalin greeted Koltsov jovially on his return from Spain and on May 14, 1938, summoned him for an hour's meeting with himself, Voroshilov, and Ezhov to discuss why republican Spain was losing the war to the fascists. Koltsov was alarmed by his parting exchange with Stalin: "Do you own a revolver?" "Yes." "You're not thinking of using it to shoot yourself, are you?" Koltsov told his brother that he read in Stalin's eyes the judgment "too smart." Arrested on December 13, 1938, Koltsov found his interrogator, who could not write two words without three spelling mistakes, convinced of the existence of a conspiracy by all Russia's major prose writers and poets still at liberty. Koltsov's arrest was sensational; nobody believed that a man admired all over Europe could be disgraced.

Whenever a writer was arrested, Stalin would summon the novelist Aleksandr Fadeev, secretary of the presidium of the Union of Writers, to accept complicity in the repression.[30] Fadeev saw Stalin reading two files of the statements that Koltsov had been tortured into making and perused them himself. "Now do you believe in his guilt?" Stalin asked. Koltsov was accused of being recruited by both French and German intelligence, together with his French friends and German communists in Russia including Koltsov's refugee German girlfriend, Maria Osten. Babel, Pasternak, Ilya Ehrenburg, and Aleksei Tolstoi were implicated in Koltsov's statements.

Questioned by clever interrogators, Beria's notorious Shvartsman and Raikhman, Koltsov admitted links with those already shot or about to be shot: he had been a friend of Karl Radek; he had known Iagoda's deputy Georgi Prokofiev and had employed his wife as a journalist; he was the employer and lover of Ezhov's wife; he had known the NKVD defectors in Spain, Valter Krivitsky and Aleksandr Orlov. Shvartsman and Raikhman gave Koltsov a list of those living and at liberty whom they needed to incriminate. His conscience suffered little when he named the secretary of the Union of Writers, Vladimir Stavsky, and he did no harm by naming André Malraux as a spy. But by May 1939 Koltsov had been tortured into implicating people he respected: Vsevolod Meierkhold, the charismatic director of experimental theater, five Soviet ambassadors—Vladimir Potiomkin and Iakov Surits in Paris, Ivan Maisky in London, Boris Shtein in Rome, Konstantin Umansky in Washington—and Commissar for Foreign Affairs Litvinov. These "cosmopolitan intellectuals" had supposedly been corrupted by Western intelligence services.

To back up Koltsov's admissions, Beria arrested Evgeni Gnedin, the press officer at the Commissariat of Foreign Affairs. Gnedin miraculously lived to publish his memoirs: "Beria and Kobulov put me on a chair and sat on either side and punched me on the head, playing 'swings.' They beat me horribly, with the full force of their arms, demanding I give evidence against Litvinov." By August the NKVD could confront Gnedin and Koltsov and make them leaders of an anti-Soviet conspiracy of intelligentsia and diplomats.

Late at night on February 1, 1940, Mikhail Koltsov was tried before Vasili Ulrikh. He retracted all his confessions but was, of course, found guilty and shot that night. The same night Vsevolod Meierkhold was dragged out—both his legs had been smashed—to be shot. Meierkhold also retracted his confessions at his trial and wrote a protest to Andrei Vyshinsky:

> I was placed facedown on the floor, beaten on the heels and back with a truncheon; when I sat on a chair I was hit by the same rubber truncheon on the legs (from above, with a lot of force) the pain was such that I thought they had poured boiling water on the injured sensitive parts of my legs (I shouted and wept with pain).[11]

A week later Ulrikh sentenced Isaak Babel to death. All three were shot by Vasili Blokhin, and their ashes thrown into Burial Pit No. 1 at the Donskoe cemetery. Ulrikh smilingly assured Koltsov's brother that the official sentence of "ten years without right of correspondence" meant that Koltsov was alive in a camp in the Urals.

Many in the Koltsov affair survived untouched. Ehrenburg was allowed to return to live in France. None of the diplomats named were shot: Maisky remained ambassador to London. Litvinov lived, but was replaced by Molotov in May 1939; the Nazi Ribbentrop would not have signed a pact with so prominent a Jew as Litvinov.

In a separate case, Stalin had the novelist Boris Pilniak shot, revenge for Pilniak's *Tale of the Extinguished Moon*. Russia's last prose writers were dead or cowed. Mikhail Bulgakov was blind and dying, Andrei Platonov deeply depressed. After Meierkhold's arrest and the gory murder of his wife, Zinaida Raikh, Russia's theater directors came to heel. Stalin decided personally to oversee cinema directors like Sergei Eisenstein.[12]

★ ★ ★ For all his engineering training, Beria was—at least until world war broke out—as vicious to technologists or scientists as to writers. In Georgia he had killed a world-class bacteriologist, Gogi Eliava, whose mistress he fancied, and a great engineer, Volodia Jikia. In Moscow the first arrests that Beria ordered included those of Andrei Tupolev, Russia's most productive aircraft designer, and Sergei Koroliov, the pioneer of rocket engineering. Beria realized quickly enough the importance of such men and reprieved them. They did their engineering in special technical prisons, the carrot being: "The plane flies, you get a Stalin prize and freedom," the stick: "It crashes and you're shot."

In 1939 and 1940 some mice, thinking that the NKVD cat was away, played. Censorship became so lax at times that one might have thought it abolished. The state printed the bawdy and irreverent letters written to Anton Chekhov by his oldest brother, Aleksandr, and even set in type Anna Akhmatova's poetry of the last thirty years. All over the USSR journals printed material which a year ago would have doomed both editor and author. In Georgia the young Ivane Ioseliani published "Teimuraz III," a pathetic tale of the last pretender to the Georgian throne; the *Soviet Geographical Journal* published the homosexual love letters of the great explorer Nikolai Przhevalsky to his favorite Cossack.

Beria's false dawn soon ended. With advice from Andrei Zhdanov, Stalin's new favorite, who both literally and figuratively played the piano while Stalin sang, Beria clamped down. The editor of Aleksandr Chekhov's letters, Ivan Luppol, died in the camps; Akhmatova's collected verse was pulped. "It is simply a disgrace, if I may say so, when collections of verse appear. How could this Akhmatova 'fornication to the glory of God' appear? Who promoted it?" Zhdanov scribbled in rage on a report which cited a hundred of Akhmatova's best lines as damning evidence.[33]

A few scientists and scholars were freed from prison in 1939 by Beria, including the soil specialist Academician Boris Polynov and the professors who specialized in the western and southern Slavonic languages—Czech, Polish, Church Slavonic, Serbo-Croat, and Bulgarian. This group had been repressed in the late 1920s and early 1930s because their subject linked them to the bourgeois governments of eastern Europe and the Balkans, and because of the medieval texts their students studied. Andrei Vyshinsky, as rector of Moscow University, would not concede that a student of Church Slavonic had to read the Gospels. By 1939 Stalin's view of Russian history and of Russia as the elder brother in the Slavonic family overrode Marxist ideology, and the Slavonic linguists now dominated academia.

Whatever Marx and Engels had not foreseen in modern science

upset Stalin's minions. Einstein's relativity and Max Planck's quantum mechanics clashed with materialism, denied the infinity of time and space, and distorted the Newtonian symmetry of Marxism. Stalin and Andrei Zhdanov, to whom Stalin referred questions of philosophy, were tactfully told that Einstein and Max Planck were indispensable to modern electronics and in the exploitation of atomic energy. With ritual denunciations of bourgeois idealism, physicists continued to work on bourgeois theories. Nevertheless, the German physicist Hans Helman, a refugee from the Nazis who had published *Quantum Chemistry* in Russia in 1937, was shot, and his colleagues Iuri Rumer and Nikolai Fuchs were arrested, one by Ezhov, the other by Beria. Lev Termen, the pioneer of television and inventor of one of the world's most unearthly musical instruments, the theremin, was sent to the GULAG in July 1938. Three brilliant theoretical physicists, Matvei Bronshtein, S. P. Shubin, and Aleksandr Vitt, were shot or died in the camps in 1938. Professor Ivan Bashilov, the only scientist refining radium from uranium in the USSR, was arrested in July 1938 and sent to dig ditches around the radium refinery he had set up. When the plant, under NKVD management, could not work without him Bashilov was returned, as a prisoner, to his own laboratory.

Beria can take no credit, at this stage, for rescuing the Soviet atom program; first he wrecked it. Just one major nuclear or low-temperature physicist, Piotr Kapitsa, avoided arrest. Kapitsa argued with both Stalin and Molotov that they would never find a physicist to replace him. In 1934 Kapitsa was forbidden to return to Lord Rutherford's Cavendish laboratory at Cambridge or to see his family. By sheer force of personality he made the Soviet government buy a replica of his Cambridge equipment and intervened with Ezhov, Beria, and Vsevolod Merkulov, Beria's educated underling, to save his colleague Lev Landau and one of Russia's finest mathematicians, Nikolai Luzin.

Medicine and biology in the USSR fared worse than physics. The Soviet medical profession was disgraced, not so much when Professor Dmitri Pletniov was sentenced to twenty-five years on the charge of having killed Gorky and his son, but when Pletniov's pupils Drs. Vladimir Vinogradov and Meer Vovsi perjured themselves by testifying that Pletniov was indeed a murderer. Biology died with collectivization. Desperate to restore grain production after the murder of the kulaks, Stalin believed, or feigned belief, in miracles. There were ill-fated experiments to breed rabbits—the breeding stock was eaten by the peasants—and even kangaroos; at Askania-Nova in the Ukraine, zoologists tried to domesticate African eland; in the north they harnessed moose to plow. The maddest solution of all captured Stalin's imagination: Trofim Lysenko, a Ukrainian peasant with a horticultural diploma, claimed to have discovered the secret of training cereals to adapt to poorer soils and climates. Lysenko, unwittingly, had resurrected the evolutionary theory of Jean-Baptiste Lamarck, who had held that evolution occurs by changes in behavior passed on to progeny. If cosmologists had announced that the earth was a disc resting on the back of a giant tortoise, they could hardly have been more obscurantist than this. Lysenko incarnated Jonathan Swift's Academician of Lagado who promised:

> All the fruits of the earth shall come to maturity at whatever season we think fit to choose, and increase an hundred fold more than they do at present, with innumerable other happy proposals. The only inconvenience is, that none of these projects are yet brought to perfection, and in the mean time, the whole country lies miserably waste, the houses in ruins, and the people without food or clothes.

Modern genetics was discarded and declared counterrevolutionary. Lysenko was awarded a doctorate and made an academician, although to judge by his mocking comments scribbled on Lysenko's articles, Stalin knew he was a charlatan. His influence outlasted Stalin and completed the ruin of Soviet agriculture.

The few biologists who dared denounce Lysenko as a charlatan were arrested as saboteurs. The internationally acclaimed geneticist Nikolai Vavilov prepared microscope slides of the chromosomes whose existence Lysenko denied; Lysenko would not even look. Genetics was by 1939 a Jewish-bourgeois heresy called "Weissman-Morganism." In June 1939, Lysenko's henchman Isai Prezent wrote to Molotov—Lysenko had poor spelling and grammar; he appended his signature to Prezent's letter. Ostensibly the letter was about the seventh international genetics congress, held in Edinburgh in 1939, with the honorary president's chair, for Vavilov, left empty. Lysenko wanted Vavilov arrested.

> Recently our own Morganists have begun adding their voice to the choir of capitalist yapping dogs. In a series of public speeches Vavilov has been declaring that "we shall go to the stake," representing the situation as if Galileo's times had been resurrected in our country. . . . The behavior of Vavilov and his group has recently taken on an intolerable nature. Vavilov and the Vavilovites have really taken their gloves off, and the conclusion is inescapable that they are trying to use the international genetics congress to strengthen their positions. . . . Vavilov has recently been doing everything he can to portray our country as one where science is being persecuted. . . . The congress could become a means for struggling against the turn our Soviet science is taking toward pragmatism, to the needs of socialist production. . . .[34]

Using this letter, on July 16 Beria asked Molotov for permission to arrest Vavilov as "the leader of the bourgeois school of 'formal genetics.'"

Vavilov was picked up in August 1940, and after 1,700 hours of interrogation by the notorious Lieutenant Aleksandr Khvat, confessed to being a saboteur working for Iakov Iakovlev, the executed commissar of agriculture. Vavilov's elderly teacher, Academician Dmitri Prianishnikov, appealed to Beria. Prianishnikov had a little leverage as he was supervising the dissertation that Beria's wife, Nina, was writing. Vavilov was sentenced to death; after two appeals the sentence was commuted to twenty-five years. In Saratov Prison Vavilov was offered a milder regime and work in a laboratory but, wrecked by torture and famine, he died of malnutrition in January 1943.[35] Two experimental biologists, Vavilov's associates Nikolai Koltsov and Nikolai Ivanov, died suddenly and mysteriously on December 2 and 3, 1940. Prianishnikov begged Beria at least to release Vavilov's followers and save what was left of biology and genetics in the USSR. Beria did not respond.

Nikolai Vavilov's younger brother Sergei was a physicist. In June 1945 Stalin made him president of the Academy of Sciences. Stalin liked to have in the highest posts people whose brothers, sons, or wives were in prison or had been executed. Sadism apart, Stalin felt safer when he held his appointees as moral hostages. Vavilov wanted to know his brother's fate so Stalin telephoned Beria and let him listen in: "Lavrenti, what's happened to our Nikolai Vavilov? He died! Oh, how could we have lost such a man!"

Lysenko was not the only charlatan Stalin cultivated. In linguistics Stalin was much taken with Nikolai Marr, the son of a Scottish adventurer and a Georgian peasant girl. Marr achieved a professor's chair for discovering and editing a Georgian translation of a lost Greek commentary to the Song of Solomon. After 1917, Marr invented Marxist linguistics, the Japhetic theory, which grew from an idea about the unity of Caucasian languages into sheer lunacy: all language, he stated, had developed with the evolution of social classes from the four magic syllables "sal," "ber," "yon," and "rosh." Marr died in 1934. His ravings did include intuitions about language that were far ahead of his time, but his protégés, mediocre sorcerer's apprentices, made Marrism their road to promotion. Linguists who kept to the mainstream were for fifteen years denounced as the dupes of émigrés and foreign intelligence.[36]

Ethnic Cleansing

IN 1939 STALIN, as Kaganovich would reminisce, changed personality. The mass cull of his own citizens stopped and he started to leave not just the day-to-day administration but many major political decisions to his henchmen, especially Molotov and Beria. Stalin viewed the storm gathering over Europe as good weather for the USSR: Germany, Britain, and France would fight each other to exhaustion while Russia would peacefully benefit, economically and territorially. To judge by his scribbles in the margins of books, Stalin devoted much of his time to reading: he devoured and annotated film scripts, historical novels and monographs, Georgian and Russian literature, linguistics. His cultural tastes became markedly conservative, his politics more nationalistic than socialist.

In spring 1939 Stalin broke off overtures to Britain and France and made an accommodation with Hitler. The gigantic administrative and policing tasks that ensued from the division of Poland and the annexation of the Baltic states, which Stalin and Hitler secretly agreed to in May 1939, left Lavrenti Beria no time to pursue his purge of the intelligentsia and the diplomatic corps. If Russians now slept better at night, non-Russians became insomniacs. What Ezhov had unleashed on Soviet citizens, Beria turned on Poles, Ruthenians (Western Ukrainians), Moldavians, Lithuanians, Latvians, and Estonians, not to mention German and Jewish refugees from Hitler.

Beria's was not the first ethnic cleansing in the USSR. Genrikh Iagoda and Nikolai Ezhov, at Stalin's behest, had already singled out those ethnic groups that straddled the USSR's borders and those within the country which might have allegiance to another state.[37] Between Leningrad and the Finnish border had lived 200,000 Inkeri Finns. After Kirov's murder, their Finnish-language schools, newspapers, collective farms, and village councils were shut down, and in spring 1935 Iagoda had 30,000 deported to northern Russia and Tajikistan. Leningrad lost the dairy products that the Inkeri Finns had supplied. Then 45,000 Poles and Germans were deported to Kazakhstan from the frontier areas of the Ukraine. In 1937 Ezhov had singled out Poles and Latvians living, usually as Soviet citizens, in Russia's cities for extermination. The next stage was to dispense with any pseudo-legal framework of arrest, trial, and sentence, and to move whole peoples away from border areas to the steppes of Kazakhstan and other areas of Siberia and central Asia, where pastoral nomads had been virtually eradicated in the early 1930s.

The first to suffer were Koreans living between Vladivostok and the Korean border, and elsewhere in the Far Eastern region. They had been highly regarded immigrants: some were Orthodox converts who had moved to Russian territory at the turn of the century after being threatened with beheading by the Korean emperor. Later waves were fleeing the Japanese, who colonized Korea in 1910. The Koreans had supported the Bolsheviks in 1917; they supplied most of the USSR's rice and soybeans and underwent collectivization with less suffering than other ethnic groups. They had lost in the purges some of their intelligentsia and party leadership, but they hoped for political autonomy and, despite ominous accusations in *Pravda* that Chinese and Koreans were tools of the Japanese secret services, never expected to be told in August 1937 that all 180,000 of them were to be deported to Kazakhstan and Uzbekistan.[38]

Soviet Koreans were better equipped, morally and physically, and luckier than later deportees. Each was allowed to take sixty-five pounds of luggage, and most chose rice and soybean seeds so as to start farming again in central Asia. Few spoke Russian, let alone Kazakh or Uzbek, but they were welcomed by the central Asian party leaders, who had not yet been purged, and they adapted to growing cotton and watermelons as well as rice. Nevertheless, some died on the slow train journey across Siberia, and many froze to death in their first central Asian winter. In 1938 they suffered further. Korean-language schools were closed, as were all their newspapers except one. A process of forced assimilation had begun that after two generations would kill the Korean language in central Asia. The land from which the Koreans had been driven was seized by NKVD frontier guards and a few thousand Russian peasant deportees.

In winter 1937 and 1938 it was the turn of the Kurds, especially those living in the enclave of Nakhichevan on the Turkish–Iranian border. A people without a state for 600 years, hounded by Turkey, Iran, the British rulers of Iraq, and the French in Syria, the 48,000 Kurds from Nakhichevan and as many more from the rest of Azerbaijan and Armenia were given twenty-four hours to get into the trains the NKVD had marshaled. They had none of the Koreans' luck, going in summer clothing to open steppes in temperatures of −40°. They were split up, two or three families to a Kazakh village, and the senior male of each household was taken by the NKVD, never to be seen again. Only in prison and the GULAG were groups of Kurds able to support each other; the resistance of 140 Kurds who used their boots as weapons against the thieves and bandits who ran a camp barracks is celebrated in a Kurdish folk ballad.[39] Statistics, if kept, have not been found, but forbidden to speak their language, to meet each other, let alone to return home, survivors believe that about 40 percent of the Kurds perished.

In February 1938 all Iranians in the USSR, refugees from the Shah or not, were marked out for arrest. Once again, numbers are unknown. That spring, as party leaders were building dachas around Sochi and in the mountains of the western Caucasus, Ezhov deported several thousand local Greeks. A few escaped to Greece; most shared the fate of the Kurds.

The open and secret protocols of the Molotov–Ribbentrop pact gave the USSR almost everything that the Tsar and Lenin had lost: the Baltic states and Poland's eastern territories. Beria's task was to filter out from 20 million new citizens all who would in the USSR have been purged. From September 1939, when Poland was invaded by Hitler and Stalin, to June 1941, when Hitler attacked the USSR, these new Soviet citizens were sorted by two criteria: ethnic and sociopolitical. Poland's eastern territories were predominantly populated by Jewish townspeople, Ukrainian and Belorussian peasants, and ruled by Polish landlords, administrators, and urban intelligentsia. At first the Ukrainians and Belorussians were treated gently, collectivization being the worst they underwent. Some even welcomed liberation from their Polish overlords. The nationalist Western Ukrainians or Ruthenians, however, hated both Soviets and Poles, and were reclassified by Beria as hostile.

In the Baltic states, the Soviets removed all government employees, those who owned land or factories, or who belonged to noncommunist parties, and those whose intellectual prestige fostered national pride. Too little time was left between the Soviet invasion of June 1940 and the Nazi counterinvasion for Beria to do more than begin this task.

For Stalin, humiliated so badly in 1920, Poles were the prime target. In dealing with them Stalin had Hitler's full cooperation. Both sides thought the Polish state "an abortion of the Versailles treaty"; both planned to reduce the Polish population to a subservient minority. Hitler, unlike Stalin, had singled out the Polish Jews for extermination, but his "Aktion A-B" to reduce the Polish intelligentsia and military to insignificance was halfhearted compared with Stalin and Beria's policy. Some 400,000 inhabitants of pre-1939 Poland—Poles, Jews, Ukrainians, and some Belorussians—were deported east to camps and hard labor in three major operations during spring 1940.[40] One in six died in their first year of exile.[41] The deportees, however, were luckier than those Poles detained in camps in western Russia.

The Katyn Massacres

THE KATYN MASSACRES, in which 22,000 Polish officers, policemen, and civil servants were murdered by the NKVD, are probably the most notorious and senseless of Stalin's crimes. Ezhov probably shot more ethnic Poles in 1937 and 1938, but they were Soviet citizens. The Katyn murders show lack of foresight: the USSR would be held internationally accountable. Even if Poland was wiped off the map, did Stalin really believe, like Hitler, that he could do such a thing and suffer no consequences at all?

The documentation suggests that the decision to kill the Poles was taken at leisure—four months after the surrender—and repented in haste—when the Soviet authorities found they could not cover up their waste of a valuable resource for the coming war against Hitler.[42] The surrender of Polish army units which had neither been captured by the Germans nor broken through to neutral Romania had not been planned for, and the prisoners of war were handed over by Voroshilov to Beria's NKVD, which knew how to set up prison camps. The military had no food for the prisoners and wanted to let go at least those who were ethnically Belorussian or Ukrainian, but Lev Mekhlis, now Stalin's political commissar in the army, had objected. The only prisoners repatriated by the Soviets were German soldiers captured by the Poles.

Beria set up eight camps in western Russia and put one of his secretaries, Piotr Karpovich Soprunenko, in charge. Soprunenko had been for ten years an army machine gunner, ideal for what the NKVD had in mind for the Poles. Camps were set up at Kozelsk in the monastery of Optina wilderness, at Starobelsk in a former nunnery, at Ostashkov in the St. Nil wilderness monastery on Lake Seliger, at Putivl in the Safronii monastery, in an old TB asylum and an orphanage. Here prisoners starved and froze in pigstys and derelict sheds. So many died that Mekhlis decided to release those who were ethnically or politically unobjectionable, and 43,000 who came from German-occupied Poland were handed over to the Nazis. Another 25,000 NCOs and soldiers were marched off as forced labor to build highways in the Carpathian mountains near the new border with the German Reich and 11,000 went to the

Ukrainian mines. Only the Jews could count themselves lucky; they had from the Soviets what Hitler would deny them, a chance to live.

Senior Polish officers, although robbed of their watches by Red Army officers, were at first treated gingerly; Beria ordered those above the rank of lieutenant colonel to be given separate bunks and adequate nutrition and to be addressed politely. Privileges were accorded to those to be sent back to German-occupied Poland lest they speak badly of the Soviet regime. All were assured that their detention was temporary. The Polish officer contingent was very heterogeneous as it included recently mobilized journalists, academics, artists, doctors, judges, and priests—Poland's professionals and intellectuals—as well as its military caste. There were also a few women, notably Janina Lewandowska, the Polish aviator.

In Lithuania 3,000 more Polish officers had been interned; the NKVD went there to collect them. By December 1939 the camps had been infiltrated by NKVD informers planted among or recruited from the prisoners, but their reports of Polish intransigence angered Beria. The NKVD was unused to prisoners who knew their rights and international conventions. Polish officers wrote letters pointing out that either Poland was at war with the USSR, in which case they were POWs, or it was not, in which case they were illegally detained. Their wives and mothers, either still living in eastern Poland or exiled to Kazakhstan and Siberia, flooded the NKVD and Stalin's secretariat with inquiries about their missing menfolk. There were 135,000 Polish deportees, mostly women and children, who were tolerably treated: each family was allowed to take half a ton of possessions into Siberian exile.

The NKVD began making arrests: a beekeeper who gave his fellow officers lectures was removed for "counterrevolution." The camp authorities broadcast recordings of Molotov's speeches, put on films and lectures, arresting Poles who asked "casuist" questions of the lecturer. Playing cards and money were confiscated; chess sets were issued. Hospitals were set up, and in some months in some camps mortality dropped to zero. A few provisions of the Soviet decree on treatment of POWs, a pastiche of the Geneva convention, were observed.

The Polish officers expressed no gratitude for small mercies. In Starobelsk camp a group of colonels demanded protection from a foreign embassy with a Polish interests office and from the Red Cross; they wanted their relatives informed and, if arrested, they wanted formal charges. They asked to be spared watching films that "offend our national feelings." They were indignant at the infrequency of mail. (Those in German captivity received all the letters they wanted and could write once a month.) The more reasonable the requests, the more brutal the response. By January 1940, in the Ostashkov camp, on Beria's orders the NKVD had photographed and fingerprinted all the prisoners in order to charge them with "struggling against the international communist movement." Intransigent individuals were sent to Kiev or Moscow for trial. Other camps followed suit in February. The NKVD contemplated deporting the officers together with other Polish prisoners, a total of 140,000, across Arctic Siberia to the permafrost of the Kolyma. Nevertheless, some lists of names were given to the Red Cross in February 1940.

Overwhelmed by his charges and expecting more prisoners from the war against Finland, Soprunenko was the first to suggest "unloading" (*razgruzka*) the camps. He recommended releasing the old, the sick, convinced (or convincing) communists, and murdering frontier police, staff, and intelligence officers. Beria passed this on to Merkulov, who relieved Soprunenko of some of his burdens by recommending moving 22,000 civil servants and landowners to city prisons. But the camps were still crowded.

Beria finally made an unambiguous recommendation to Stalin on March 5, 1940: "They are all thoroughgoing enemies of Soviet power, saturated with hatred for the Soviet system . . . the only reason they wait for liberation is to be able to take up the fight against Soviet power. . . ." The inmates of three camps, 14,700 POWs, and 11,000 Poles held in prisons "should be dealt with by special measures and the highest measure of punishment, shooting, should be applied to them." The victims were not to be informed of the charges or the sentence. The Politburo voted the same day in favor of murder. Stalin signed first, then Voroshilov, Molotov, and Mikoyan; Kaganovich and Kalinin agreed by telephone.

What made Stalin's inner circle so eager to murder these officers who the whole world knew were in NKVD hands? Clearly, neither Stalin nor Voroshilov had ever gotten over the defeat which the Red Army, under their direction, had suffered at the hands of these same men in

1920. Now, with the Finns also wreaking havoc on the Red Army, they were doubly frustrated by their incompetence.[43] The age-old mutual hatred of Poles and Russians, nations that straddle the fault line between Roman Catholicism and Orthodoxy, only inflamed the viciousness. Russians had never appreciated being portrayed as the barbarians against whom only Polish chivalry shielded western Europe.

Beria may have initiated this solution. Stalin, when he could tear himself away from his books, was depressed to the point of inertia by the defeats that the Red Army—an army without generals—was suffering at the hands of the well-trained, well-armed, and highly motivated Finns. The only meetings Beria had in Stalin's office in February and March were with army marshals and it is unlikely that Polish POWs figured much on the agenda. Stalin did however make a curious amendment to Beria's proposals: from the troika—Beria, Merkulov, and the head of special operations Bashtakov—that would sign the death sentences, Stalin crossed out Beria's name and substituted that of his subordinate Bogdan Kobulov. Did he foresee the operation going wrong and want to spare Beria becoming a scapegoat, or was mass murder too routine an operation for the commissar of the NKVD and Stalin's best adviser when a world war was in the offing?

Bogdan Kobulov held a conference in Moscow of a dozen NKVD officials, where it took a week to plan the killings. All victims' families had to be deported at dawn on one day, April 15, to Kazakhstan for ten years. Inquiries had to be made of Hitler's authorities to ensure that Poles from central Poland were returned to the Germans. Kobulov, Merkulov, and Bashtakov drew up identity slips with the death sentences for each of 22,000 victims. About 600 men were reprieved, some at the request of Pavel Sudoplatov of the NKVD's foreign directorate, because their military experience would be crucial in a future war with Germany or because they were candidate puppets to rule a future communist Poland; their families were also exempted from deportation. Three future generals, Władysław Anders, Zygmunt Berling, and Jerzy Wołkowicki, thus lived to form new Polish armies a year later.

Fifty Poles of international renown, including the impressionist painter Józef Czapski, were rescued by Mussolini and other influential Westerners. Hitler's government begged the life of Wacław Komarnicki, who would ironically become minister of justice in the exiled London government. Polish fascists, even if virulently anti-Bolshevik, were handed over unharmed to the Germans. A few were saved so late that they witnessed NKVD atrocities: Professor Stanisław Swianiewicz, on a death train, was identified as an expert on the German economy and removed.

To transport all the prisoners to the execution sites in the forest around Katyn, Beria's railways boss Solomon Milshtein timetabled trains and laid on trucks. The executioners of the Lubianka and Sukhanovka under Vasili Blokhin had in March 1940 finished the elimination of Ezhov's men and the intellectuals implicated by Mikhail Koltsov, so a contingent was assembled and equipped with German weapons and ammunition.[44] Soprunenko went off to exchange prisoners with the Finns and the work of compiling lists fell on Arkadi Gertsovsky, one of the main managers of the massacres.

Eleven generals, an admiral, 77 colonels, 197 lieutenant colonels, 541 majors, 1,441 captains, 6,061 lieutenants and other ranks, 18 chaplains, and the Polish army's chief rabbi were all to be shot in April, together with the remnants of the Polish civil service and bourgeoisie. The condemned were joined by other Poles who had attracted adverse attention, such as Ludwig Helbardt, dying of stomach cancer in a Ukrainian hospital, who had written to Molotov asking to be reunited with his destitute family. Few suspected what was awaiting them. Many were distressed, some to the point of suicide, by being deprived of all mail from March, but when the trains were marshaled in mid-April some wrote in their diaries that they were going home, although they feared being returned to German-controlled Poland.

Some executions were carried out more humanely than usual by Blokhin and his men. In Kalinin (Tver), where the Ostashkov prisoners were killed one by one, each Pole was taken into the prison club room and his identity carefully checked, before being handcuffed and led into a neighboring soundproofed chamber and shot in the back of the neck. The bodies were then dragged through a back door, thrown into covered trucks and taken to the countryside at Mednoe, to the grounds used for the NKVD men's dachas, a site chosen by Blokhin. A total of fifty executioners was used, Blokhin in his leather apron, helmet, and gauntlets taking a leading part. Each evening a body count was telegraphed to Merkulov in Moscow.

The same procedure was used in Kharkov, the bodies disposed of in the grounds of an NKVD sanatorium next to the secret-police dachas, where a large number of Soviet victims had already been buried.

The victims buried in Katyn forest—4,143 bodies were exhumed by the Germans in 1943—left graphic memorials: one victim had carved in a piece of wood a diary of his last days; another diary ends, "they have taken away my rubles, my belt, my penknife." These men suffered: they were stood in groups by open pits, many of them had their hands bound with barbed wire and some had nooses around their necks. Others, notably some Catholic priests, buried at Katyn had been shot in Smolensk prison in an underground execution chamber and their bodies stacked in the pits.

As the shootings ended, in mid-April, the unsuspecting families were deported east. Many died of starvation and cold. Surviving Polish men were assigned to a group of 135,000 prisoners sent to the Arctic to build a railway to the coal mines of Vorkuta. One NKVD man, Daniil Chekholsky, showed a spark of kindness. Sacked for letting Poles post letters as they went off to execution, he admitted sending telegrams to relatives: "Your husbands have left. We don't know the address. . . ." Other NKVD men took to drink. In October Beria rewarded the executioners with an extra month's salary, while the organizers all received medals and awards.

The camps now had space for prisoners from Lithuania, Latvia, and Estonia as Stalin had delayed his takeover of the Baltic republics until mid-June 1940, when the Finnish war was over. The NKVD had few Estonian, Latvian, and Lithuanian speakers left, and the Baltic republics had few resident communists to collaborate with the new authorities. The Soviet occupiers needed many months to identify the nationalists, the intellectuals, the property owners who could be deported. Apart from the deportees, some 60,000 Estonians, Latvians, and Lithuanians were killed; only the outbreak of war halted the slaughter. Until then, western Russia's railways were crowded with trains. One week before Hitler attacked, over 17,000 Lithuanians and the same number of Latvians left for Siberia, Kazakhstan, and the Komi republic; seven trainloads of Latvian and Lithuanian prostitutes went to Uzbekistan. On the previous night, from the territories grabbed from Romania—Bessarabia and the Bukovina—another 30,000 were deported. Until June 20, 1941, Poles and nationalist Ukrainians were still being railroaded east.

No sooner were the killings in Katyn over than the consequences began to emerge. Thousands of letters from wives and children reached Moscow, and some leaked abroad. When Hitler defeated France and Soviet intelligence began to admit to itself, if not to Stalin, the probability of war with Germany, they realized it had been madness to slaughter the cream of the Polish army. In August 1940, first the Hungarian, then the International Red Cross began to ask about missing persons. They got no answers.

The survivors, gathered at Griaznovtsy camp, numbered a few hundred officers. In October 1940 they were suddenly well treated and Lieutenant Colonel Berling was sent first class to Moscow to talk to Beria and Merkulov about forming a Polish army on Soviet soil. Berling said, "Fine, we have magnificent staff for an army in the camps." Merkulov replied, "No, not those. We made a big mistake with them." Berling was put in a luxurious dacha near Moscow with other senior Poles. By November Beria dared tell Stalin that he had a nucleus of twenty-four anti-German Polish officers, who would cooperate if Władysław Sikorski's government in London authorized them. Stalin feared antagonizing Hitler but Beria went on regardless. More Poles, interned in Latvia, were retrieved in August 1940, and although many went to the GULAG, Beria formed two Polish brigades of officers.

After war between Germany and the USSR broke out in June 1941, about two thirds of the Polish soldiers sent to the GULAG were retrieved to fight against the Nazis. Most opted to serve alongside the British in North Africa and Sikorski continued to press for news of the missing officers. Stalin pretended to telephone Beria about them and then claimed that they had walked to Manchuria or had not been reported by lazy camp commandants. Vyshinsky claimed they had been freed in Poland. Stalin told General Anders that the Germans must have captured them. In 1942 100,000 Poles with their families left the USSR through Iran; tens of thousands remained in Russia, increasingly harassed.

On April 13, 1943, the Germans began exhuming Katyn, and Stalin added falsification to prevarication. The Germans called in the Swiss Red Cross, but to their disgrace the British and Americans denounced the Swiss report and concurred with the Russian version, that the Germans had buried old newspapers with the corpses to calumniate the innocent Soviets. In January 1944, the Soviets set up their own special commission, from which the party and the NKVD were conspicuously absent. Two academicians, a metropolitan bishop, the chairman of the Soviet Red Cross, and the writer Aleksei Tolstoi connived to produce "witnesses" to prove German "provocation." A film was also made. Aleksei Tolstoi, as perceptive as he was unprincipled, warned Nikolai Shvernik, Stalin's head of anti-German propaganda, that the film "is not only unfit for showing but can even have a negative effect . . . the witnesses seem to be repeating a lesson they have learned by heart . . ."

When in March 1946 at the Nuremberg trials Goering's defense tried to bring up Katyn, the Soviet commission led by Vyshinsky protested forcibly. Katyn was not discussed. In Minsk, German officers were hanged for allegedly massacring Polish officers at Katyn. The lying went on until 1988.

The treatment of two Polish Jews taken prisoner in October 1939 was just as calamitous as Katyn for Soviet credibility and the war effort. Henryk Erlich and Wiktor Alter were leaders of the Jewish socialist Bund, effectively the heart and mind of a Jewish anti-Hitler committee. They were taken to Moscow and charged as Polish spies and hostile critics of the Molotov–Ribbentrop pact. Beria's men worked slowly; the war with Germany had been raging for a month by the time Alter was sentenced to death. Instead of death, however, Erlich and Alter were first given ten years' imprisonment and then offered their freedom if they would head a Jewish antifascist committee. By mid-September they had offices in the Hotel Metropol and were looked after by Beria's Polish liaison officer. Beria proposed Erlich as president and Alter as secretary, while the world-famous Yiddish actor Solomon Mikhoels would be vice president. But things did not go according to Beria's plan. Erlich and Alter used their initiative: they worked with the British, Polish, and American ambassadors, and proposed a Jewish legion to fight alongside the Red Army. They also began to search for missing Polish officers.

Beria sent Leonid Raikhman to arrest them on December 4, 1941, this time as Nazi agents spreading pacifism. Erlich hanged himself in prison the following May while Alter wrote letters to Stalin threatening suicide. Only in early 1943, when the discovery of Katyn ruined relations with the Poles and Stalin felt he had little to lose, did Molotov reply to the inquiries of Albert Einstein and other distinguished Americans and instruct Litvinov to announce that both Erlich and Alter had been shot for treason on December 23, 1941. Beria in fact had Alter shot three days after this announcement. Sergei Ogoltsov, head of the NKVD in evacuation at Kuibyshev, personally supervised the execution and the burning of his possessions. Roosevelt and Churchill both silenced protests in their own countries, but Jewish trust in Stalin as their savior collapsed.

★ ★ ★ In 1940 and 1941 Stalin's instincts and cunning had completely failed him. Initiating a winter war with Finland when the Red Army had been lobotomized by the NKVD ruined his prestige. Sanctioning the murders of Poland's officer corps and two internationally respected Jewish activists were acts as stupid as they were atrocious. Appearing to dismiss as Anglo-American disinformation all the reports that his intelligence received about Hitler's intentions was his most catastrophic failure. About the first two lapses Stalin was uncharacteristically unvindictive. He quarreled with Voroshilov over the latter's inept conduct of the Finnish campaign, but when Voroshilov in fury retorted, "You killed all the senior officers!" smashed a plate and stormed out, Stalin did nothing. Voroshilov was replaced as commissar and given less crucial defense posts—where he performed with equal incompetence—but never fell from favor. Nor did Beria, Merkulov, and Bogdan Kobulov suffer for killing those Polish officers who would have been so useful a year later.

What was going through Stalin's mind in 1940? All his enemies dead, with Beria running internal affairs and Molotov external affairs, as hopeful as Neville Chamberlain that he had brought "peace in our time," Stalin withdrew into what he took to be philosophy. He had taken Hitler seriously enough to have had *Mein Kampf* translated and studied. Stalin read the same books as Hitler—Clausewitz's *On War* and Otto von Bismarck's memoirs—but drew different conclusions. Reading Clausewitz,

Stalin could well have concluded that no German leader would repeat Napoleon I's mistake of invading Russia; reading Bismarck, that no German leader would dare fight another war on two fronts. Stalin and Hitler were both gamblers: Stalin was a calculating player; Hitler, staking everything on one card, blitzkrieg, played a different game.

While his minions ruled, Stalin recast both history and himself. Since the Marxist historian Pokrovsky had died, the moving force of history had, for Stalin, reverted from class struggle to kings and queens. Soviet textbooks in the 1930s reflected this change by showing Russian nationalism and empire building in a positive light. In 1938 Stalin had the "newly literate" languages of the USSR switch from the Roman to the Cyrillic alphabet. Tsarism was now "progressive": it had built a multiethnic centralized nation. Anniversaries of Russian classic authors were celebrated with pomp and ceremony throughout the USSR; generous Stalin prizes were awarded to any composer, painter, film director, or writer who glorified Russia's past as the prelude to an even greater future. Andrei Zhdanov commissioned patriotic operas, films, and novels.

The cinema became for Stalin the supreme art. Sinners among film directors were forgiven. He even let Kapler, who had been beaten for kissing Svetlana Allilueva, work, although in 1943 he was sent to the camps for ten years. Sergei Eisenstein, who had come close to arrest for his years in America and for his religious portrayal of the peasantry in *Bezhin Meadow,* was recruited. Together with Lev Sheinin, Vyshinsky's favorite interrogator, Eisenstein proposed a film about the trial and acquittal of the Jew Mendel Beilis, accused in Kiev of drinking a Christian infant's blood for Passover. But a Jewish project was anathema to Stalin; anti-Semitism was part of his Russian chauvinism. Eisenstein was directed to make a film not about honest Russian jurymen, but about Ivan the Terrible. Stalin saw himself too as a harsh, divinely appointed ruler who would save his country in a war on two fronts: the Germans and the Japanese of 1941 were reincarnations of the Livonians and Tatars of 1540. Aleksei Tolstoi, with clairvoyant perception of what Stalin wanted, drafted a three-part drama on Ivan. Stalin edited the first published version until Ivan came across as sufficiently stable and unrepentant for his taste.

Not Ivan the Terrible, but Russia's great generals obsessed Stalin in

1940. A film was proposed glorifying Catherine the Great's General Aleksandr Suvorov, who had fought Swedes and Turks with equal success. Stalin read the script and told the director to make Suvorov less kindly. Stalin's Suvorov was in his own image as generalissimo:

> The script doesn't reveal Suvorov's characteristic policies and tactics: 1) correctly taking into account the enemy's faults, and knowing how to exploit them fully; 2) a properly thought-out and bold attack combined with a diversion to strike the enemy in the rear; 3) the ability to choose experienced and bold commanders and to direct them to the object of attack; 4) the ability to promote boldly to senior posts those who excel, without regard to rank, taking little notice of the official seniority or origins of those promoted; 5) the ability to sustain in the army harsh, truly iron discipline.[45]

Trotsky's End

KATYN HAD BEEN BERIA'S WORST MISTAKE, but in August 1940 he had a resounding success: he had Trotsky killed. For seven years, since Trotsky had left Turkey for France, the NKVD's pursuit of the only enemy Stalin took seriously had been a gruesome farce. The French authorities were fed up with the trail of bullet-ridden corpses and the émigrés and diplomats who helped the killers; the NKVD, apart from killing Trotsky's children, his parents, his sister, his sister-in-law, and some of his political followers, had murdered eight secretaries. When in January 1937 Trotsky moved to Mexico, the NKVD could plan anew as the Stalinist Mexican Communist Party had influential supporters, and Mexico's refugees from Spain included NKVD collaborators. Stalin's determination was not lessened by Trotsky's newly conciliatory position toward him. To the dismay of his followers, Trotsky had approved Stalin's division of Poland with Hitler, on the grounds that the USSR was a workers' state and that the Baltic states and Poland would now benefit by joining a proletarian empire.

Beria had inherited from Ezhov a few Spanish Civil War adventurers. One was Naum Eitingon, who had operated as a guerrilla with the republican forces under the name of General Kotov, and who took over from the defector Aleksandr Orlov as the NKVD's main agent in Spain.[46] Eitingon was assisted by Iosif Grigulevich and by a new recruit to the NKVD's main directorate, Pavel Sudoplatov—the only one of Beria's men to publish a full, if mendacious, account of his activities. They were allotted $300,000 to mount their operation, which produced two plans, both using new agents unknown to Trotsky. One, organized by Grigulevich, was an amateurish machine-gun attack on May 24, 1940, by Mexican Stalinists led by the painter David Siqueiros and assisted by the treachery of Trotsky's last secretary, Robert Sheldon Harte. Siqueiros's men riddled Trotsky's room but failed to search it. The Trotskys hid under the bed.[47]

Eitingon's plan was more subtle. His agent Ramón Mercader was a fanatical Stalinist, physically strong but morally weak, and had fought in Spain. His mother, Caridad, had for three years been an NKVD agent. Mercader had many aliases: the Belgian Jacques Mornard, the Canadian Frank Jackson. Sudoplatov and Eitingon instructed him to court Trotsky's assistant Sylvia Ageloff, to express no interest in Trotsky or Trotskyism, and to insinuate himself into the house as her apolitical husband. Despite Mercader's lack of credentials, political knowledge, or personal charm, Trotsky was too polite or too resigned to assassination to investigate him or to avoid being alone with him. On August 20, 1940, Mercader smashed an ice pick into Trotsky's skull. Mercader was caught; Eitingon and Caridad Mercader were already on their way to California. If there was any doubt that Trotsky's death was Stalin's doing, it was unwittingly dispersed by *Pravda*'s triumphant announcement before even the Mexican police knew that Trotsky had been killed "by a member of his inner circle."

Stalin was so pleased by this success that he personally assured Naum Eitingon, "not a hair will ever fall from your head."[48] Three weeks later Stalin's magnanimity went further: he told a Central Committee meeting that enemies should be portrayed in films

not as monsters, but as people hostile to our society, but not devoid of some human characteristics. The vilest villain has

human traits, he loves somebody, he respects somebody, he
wants to make sacrifices for somebody. . . . Why not represent
Bukharin, however much he was a monster, but he did have
some human features? Trotsky is an enemy, but he is [corrected
to "was" in the stenogram] a capable man, without argument,
represent him as an enemy who had negative features, but he
also had good qualities, because without argument he did.[49]

Having disposed of Trotsky, on January 30, 1941, Beria became general commissar of state security. It did not worry him that he might last
no longer than Iagoda or Ezhov after Stalin had awarded them that
rank.

NINE

HANGMEN AT WAR

41. Lavrenti Beria, mid-1920s

42. Beria's guards, chauffeurs, and pimps Nadaraia and Sarkisov

43. Caucasian Party caucus, 1935. Left to right: Pilipe Makharadze, Mir-Jafar Bagirov, Beria

44. Sailing on the Black
Sea, 1933. Left to right:
Lakoba's wife, Sarie; Nina
Beria; Lavrenti Beria;
Lakoba's son, Rauf. On
right, with her arm on the
captain's shoulder, Stalin's
daughter, Svetlana

45. Party conference, 1935: head of Abhkaz Party, Nestor Lakoba; Beria, head of
Armenian Party, Agasi Khanjian

46. Lakoba's funeral, January 1937. The message on the wreath reads "To our close friend Comrade Nestor from Nina and Lavrenti Beria." Bottom: Nina and Lavrenti Beria

47. Vasili Blokhin, chief executioner
at the Lubianka, 1940s

48. Meeting, 1936. Front row, left to right: Khrushchiov, Zhdanov, Kaganovich,
Voroshilov, Stalin; second row, first from left: Georgi Malenkov

49. Head of SMERSH Viktor Abakumov, *c.* 1946

50. Abakumov after his arrest, 1951

51. Latvians being deported to Siberia, 1946

52. Show trial of 1938

53. Vsevolod Meierkhold

54. Meierkhold and a portrait of his wife, Zinaida Raikh

55. Charlatan biologist Trofim Lysenko, late 1930s

56. Geneticist Nikolai Vavilov, Lysenko's victim, late 1930s

57. Marina Tsvetaeva and her daughter, Ariadna, 1925

58. Nuclear physicist Piotr Kapitsa (left) with Jewish actor Solomon Mikhoels, 1946

59. Nine NKVD men:

a. Leonid Zakovsky (Štubis), head of Leningrad NKVD, 1937

b. Genrikh Liushkov, head of secret political section, defected to Japan, 1938

c. Baron Pillar von Pilchau, last aristocrat in NKVD

d. Anatoli Esaulov, who interrogated Ezhov

e. Vsevolod Merkulov, physics graduate and Beria's deputy

f. Akvsenti Rapava, head of Georgian NKVD, after his second arrest, 1953

g. Bogdan Kobulov, Beria's associate and NKVD representative in East Germany

h. General Vlasik, chief of Stalin's household and tutor to his children, after his arrest, 1952

i. Iakov Agranov, NKVD's specialist for intellectuals and associate of Mayakovsky

"Brothers, Sisters!"

Hitler's attack on the USSR on June 22, 1941, did not alter Stalin's view of his people. When he had recovered from the shock of Hitler's "treachery" and the humiliating rout of the Red Army, Stalin broadcast to the nation in terms he had never used before and would never use again, speaking like a Christian, calling on his "brothers and sisters." However, nothing significant had changed in Stalin or his hangmen. Beria and Merkulov's secret police went on shooting prisoners, including those arrested for anti-German statements. Absurdly draconian measures were announced to deter troops from surrendering or retreating, however inevitable or logical such a tactic might be.

What altered on June 22, 1941, was the attitude of the Soviet people. German cannon and SS extermination squads, scorched earth, and starvation neutralized fear of the party and NKVD. Some gave vent to despair. Anna Akhmatova was heard declaring, "I hate, I hate Hitler, I hate Stalin, I hate those who are bombing Leningrad, I hate those who are bombing Berlin, I hate everyone who is conducting this absurd, horrible war." Some felt uplifted by the suffering of a just war. Pasternak's poem "A Terrible Fairy Story" announces that "The fear that has furrowed faces / Will never be forgotten," but anticipates, as did very many Soviet citizens, that for this suffering there would be a compensation: "A new better age will dawn." What made the horrors of the 1940s more tolerable than those of the 1930s was that everyone's fate was bound together. If the Soviet people gave in to the Nazis, Stalin and all his henchmen would go down with them. For once, the leaders of the country depended on the people, and had to show it. Pasternak called the war "a purifying storm, a stream of fresh air, a wafting of redemption." The Leningrad poet Olga Berggolts exulted: "In mud, dark, hunger, grief, / Where death followed our heels like a shadow, / We felt such happiness, / We breathed such stormy freedom, / That our grandchildren would envy us." For free speech, people still paid with their lives—in punishment battalions or by firing squad—but the fear had abated.

War forced Stalin to dismantle his monolith. Within months he had learned that he could not micromanage a successful response to blitzkrieg, that generals and colonels had to make their own decisions. He had to allow the Church to rally the people. He could not win without the support of the hated West, and he had to make concessions. At times Stalin even had to tell the truth to his people. In his decree of July 28, 1942, he admitted: "The population is beginning to be disillusioned by the Red Army, and many curse it for handing our people to the yoke of the German oppressors, while retreating to the east . . . we no longer prevail over the Germans in human resources or supplies of grain." British and then American officers had to be allowed to walk the streets of Moscow and the northern ports, even fraternizing with Soviet officers and befriending Soviet women. Winston Churchill set aside all his knowledge and hatred of the Bolsheviks and welcomed Russia as an overnight ally, the first ray of hope for a beleaguered Britain. German planes would for a time have no more fuel from the Soviet oil fields, and the troops poised to invade Britain were now pouring east. Roosevelt, when six months later the United States joined the war, had no hesitation in embracing Stalin as an ally—or at least a deterrent—to tie down a significant number of Japanese divisions. Just as pragmatically, Stalin had to mask his contempt for Western statesmen and make some concessions in order to receive from his new allies leather, meat, vehicles, munitions, and information that might stem the German tide. Stalin pretended to forget about Anglo-American intervention against the Bolsheviks in 1919; the British and Americans enforced silence in their own countries about Stalin's crimes against humanity.

Stalin's hangmen abandoned prophylactic killing; they had to see to their own survival and the nation's. For a short while they encouraged Stalin to avenge the army's defeats by shooting one hapless general after another, but within a year, like Stalin, they understood that professional officers, engineers, and administrators were too precious to waste. The blood of the rank and file, civilians or soldiers, was still shed prodigiously, but the hangmen observed a truce in their war of attrition against the professional classes.

Beria Shares Power

IN 1941, AS WAR LOOMED, Stalin began to manipulate his henchmen in a new way. The dangers of arrest and execution receded, but so did the security of power. Stalin began to duplicate powers, to split commissariats, to switch his favors from one to another, to make his underlings jealous and suspicious of each other. The change in Stalin can be ascribed to his realization that his mental and physical powers were waning—he was now sixty-two years old—and that, for the first time since he had achieved power, his plans were going awry. The Red Army almost defeated by the Finns, Hitler sweeping through the Balkans, first isolating, then threatening the USSR, all proved his fallibility. He could no longer crush every obstacle in his path. He trusted nobody—not even himself, as he told Khrushchiov—and saw a potential assassin in every guard and every associate. Even more than before, he duplicated the channels that fed him information and avoided written instructions, often even verbal ones. A clenched fist to his teeth, a raised eyebrow was an order which could more easily be disavowed. Stalin began to be unpredictable and his hangmen reacted accordingly. They too hesitated to take any course of action that could not be stopped or reversed. They cooperated less and watched each other more. Even the old circle of Kaganovich, Voroshilov, and Molotov lost its coherence.

Beria was better equipped, by personality and intelligence, than anyone else to cope with an aging Stalin, but even he must have been dismayed on February 3, 1941. Days after making him general commissar of state security, Stalin sliced his empire in two. Beria remained commissar for internal affairs, but his remit was now mundane: traffic police, firemen, and the GULAG empire. A separate Commissariat for State Security was hived off and Stalin appointed Beria's loyal deputy, Vsevolod Merkulov, to the new commissariat. Beria had been warned not to monopolize power, but he was not in as precarious a position as Iagoda and Ezhov had been when they had lost sole command of state security. Beria and Merkulov were after all old allies; their working and personal relationships remained close.

Vsevolod Merkulov's appointment was typical of the new tactics. Stalin was throwing several scorpions into the box to see if one would kill the others. Another of Beria's subordinates, Viktor Abakumov, replaced Merkulov as Beria's deputy and was subsequently put in charge of military counterintelligence. After the war, a couple of lesser scorpions from the security services, Rukhadze and Riumin, were thrown in to counteract these three.

Experience with Iagoda had taught Stalin that the security services could be controlled only by appointing someone from outside their remit. Stalin therefore promoted his former secretary and the editor of *Pravda,* Lev Mekhlis, into an intelligence and security overlord. Stalin was also tinkering again with the machinery of state. The party Politburo became a dead letter; decision-making passed to the government, the Council of Commissars, and, when the Germans invaded, to the State Defense Committee, which comprised Stalin and his closest cronies. Apart from Molotov, Stalin now tended to prefer younger men—Beria, Zhdanov, Malenkov, Khrushchiov. Their servility was balanced by ruthless infighting that ensured they would never conspire together. Kaganovich was shifted away from the center of power to terrorize the coal and oil industries and occasionally rally the armed forces' morale with firing squads. Voroshilov was given tasks where he could do the war effort least damage.

Beria was too energetic and efficient to be dispensable. Stalin jokingly called him "our Himmler," but he was also the Soviet Union's Albert Speer. Like Kaganovich and Mekhlis, Beria used executions to terrify the hesitant, cowardly, or incompetent; unlike them, he grasped military and technical arguments and was a canny judge of character and ability. Beria remained cool in the face of opposition and danger.

Merkulov, the most articulate and least repulsive member of Beria's inner circle, throughout the war supplied foreign intelligence. He was an officer's son and had been a second lieutenant in the Tsar's army. In Tbilisi Merkulov had taught for three years in a school for the blind and in September 1921 he joined the Georgian Cheka. He faithfully stuck to Beria until the last day of their lives. At the height of the terror Merkulov cannily left the NKVD for trade and transport. When in September 1938 Beria took Merkulov to Moscow and back into the NKVD, he at first balked at the physical torture of detainees. He was teased by Beria—"Theoretician!"

After dutifully organizing the killing of Poles at Katyn, Ostashkov, and Smolensk, Merkulov's next mission was in summer 1940, when he went incognito to Riga to purge Latvia's middle classes. On his appointment as commissar for state security Merkulov found the Soviet intelligence service laid waste by Ezhov's purges with the remnants too frightened of Stalin to tell him unpalatable truths. The NKVD's best spies, including Richard Sorge, were not trusted.[1] Two of Beria's acolytes, Amayak Kobulov, Bogdan's younger brother, and Dekanozov, were stationed in Berlin, Kobulov from September 1939 as first secretary and intelligence officer, Dekanozov from November 1940 as ambassador after spending the summer terrorizing Lithuania. Neither spoke German. The German Foreign Ministry did not know whether to be insulted or amused that the Soviet Union had sent such a physical and mental dwarf as Dekanozov, a toad with stubble, to match their urbane ambassador to Moscow, Count Schulenburg. Amayak Kobulov, on the other hand, was charming but dim, which made him an ideal conduit for Nazi disinformation. Vsevolod Merkulov thus transmitted to Stalin on May 25, 1941, what Stalin wanted to hear: "War between the Soviet Union and Germany is unlikely. . . . German military forces gathered on the frontier are meant to show the Soviet Union the determination to act if they are forced to. Hitler calculates that Stalin will become more pliable and will stop any intrigues against Germany, but above all will supply more goods, especially oil."

Stalin had sent Molotov to Berlin in November 1940 to negotiate terms on which the USSR might become an ally of Germany, Japan, and Italy but the talks foundered on Molotov's insistence that the USSR should take over Iran and western India. If Hitler contemplated letting the USSR take over parts of the British Empire, then, Stalin reasoned, the USSR was safe. Even Hitler's attack on Yugoslavia in spring 1941 left Stalin unperturbed.

Beria himself had completed Ezhov's work destroying Red Army intelligence: everyone of the rank of colonel or above had been shot. A few terrorized majors remained, their credentials having ethnically Russian surnames and knowing no foreign languages. To guess Hitler's next move, they relied on gossip gleaned from central European military attachés or drunken SS officers. They drew no conclusions even when the German embassy in Moscow packed its furniture and families off home. They miscalculated the number of German troops on the Soviet frontier as 40 percent instead of 62 percent of all Hitler's forces. As late as March 1941, Lieutenant General Filipp Golikov, the squat, bald, scarlet-faced blimp who now headed Red Army intelligence, perversely concluded: "Rumors and documents that speak of the inevitability of war against the USSR this spring must be assessed as disinformation emanating from English and even perhaps from German intelligence."[2]

When war broke out, Vsevolod Merkulov had the wit to steal others' intelligence. Naum Eitingon was entrusted with nurturing five traitors in the British intelligence services—Burgess, Maclean, Philby, Blunt, and Cairncross. Through them, once the British had cracked the German Enigma encoding machine, Merkulov obtained for Stalin and his generals information on German armaments and plans. There were Soviet spies in Nazi Germany, but their warnings were dismissed and they were so carelessly handled that the Gestapo soon caught them. Moreover, Stalin insisted on raw intelligence; in his conceit, he would not let professionals analyze the information they gathered.[3]

Even as commissar for state security, Merkulov devoted time to creative work. He had already written a pamphlet about Beria, "Loyal son of the Lenin-Stalin party." Using the grandiose pseudonym Vsevolod Rokk (all-powerful fate), Merkulov staged his play *Engineer Sergeev* to applause all over Russia from 1942 to 1944. In the first disastrous months of the war, Sergeev has to blow up the electricity station he built. German agents, a former kulak, a White Guard, and a Baltic German officer try to stop him. Helped by an NKVD lieutenant Sergeev destroys his beloved power station, killing himself and the German agents.

After Hiroshima, when Stalin conceded that the USSR had to have its atom bomb, Merkulov came into his own. With his education in physics, he understood what questions to ask his spies in Britain and America. Until then, Merkulov performed best his traditional NKVD work: reporting to Stalin on everything writers and filmmakers said when they thought they were not overheard. Stalin and Zhdanov's attack on the intelligentsia in 1946 was fueled by intellectuals' utterances during the war, when they felt courted, even treasured, and began to think aloud.

Beria's other rival was Viktor Semionovich Abakumov. Supposedly born in 1908 to a hospital boilerman and a laundress, and without formal education, Abakumov matched Merkulov's patrician style but was violent, uncultured, and devious.[4] Outside secret police work, Abakumov, tall and handsome, was interested only in women and luxury. In his early days Abakumov was called "Foxtrotter" but in 1934 his career faltered when he began taking dancing partners to OGPU safe houses, not only for sex but to make them denounce whomever he next proposed to arrest. He was demoted to GULAG guard. In 1937 he found a new niche in the secret political and operational directorates of the NKVD for whom he installed listening equipment, and made searches and arrests. His physical strength and love of the job attracted the attention of Bogdan Kobulov, who induced Beria to let Abakumov run the turbulent southern city of Rostov on the Don. In February 1941, when Beria's empire was cut in two, Stalin arranged for Abakumov to replace Merkulov as Beria's deputy in the NKVD.

At first Abakumov ran border guards, uniformed police, and fire brigades, but when war began, Stalin put Abakumov in charge of military counterintelligence. Here Abakumov made an impact. He answered directly to Stalin and could ignore Beria. In spring 1943, as the fortunes of war turned in Russia's favor, counterintelligence became a powerful force. Abakumov became deputy to Stalin, who made himself both commissar of defense and supreme commander. Abakumov's organization, even more dreaded than Beria's, was SMERSH (Death to Spies). It had seven branches: it conducted surveillance over the army staff and all forces, it pursued and killed deserters and self-mutilators, it formed "blocking squads" to shoot retreating soldiers, it supervised quartermasters and field hospitals, it filtered suspected collaborators in reoccupied territory, it watched over contact with allies and the enemy. SMERSH terrorized the army and all who lived in combat zones, and squeezed everything it could from German prisoners. SMERSH made death in battle preferable to retreat for Russians and to surrender for Germans, but as an intelligence organization it was a liability. Most of its men were as aggressive and ignorant as Abakumov; they shot or hanged many loyal and able officers and men.

Abakumov controlled his empire from a building opposite the Lubianka, from which he would emerge to stride the streets of Moscow, flinging 100-rouble notes to beggar women. Like Beria, Abakumov was considered just, even compassionate, only by his subordinates. In 1945 Stalin put Abakumov on the Soviet commission to prepare for the Nuremberg trials of German war criminals. In 1946 Abakumov took Merkulov's place as minister of state security, and held it until 1951. Beria, absorbed by the campaign to build atomic weapons, was no longer a rival, but although Abakumov oversaw two purges and numerous murders for Stalin, even he ultimately proved insufficiently vicious.

The Red Army had not just the enemy and SMERSH to fear; the military collegium of the Soviet supreme court also traveled the front, holding courts-martial and issuing death sentences on the most trivial pretexts.[5] It was headed by Ulrikh's deputy I. O. Matulevich; he and his men, hardened by the terror of 1937–8, typed thousands of death sentences on slips of cigarette paper. A soldier had only to admire the quality of German aircraft design or to roll a cigarette in a German leaflet he had picked up, a nurse had only to treat a wounded German, to be shot. In such a terrible war some soldiers greeted the firing squad with indifference, even relief, and so on April 19, 1943, Stalin took a leaf from the Germans' book and brought in execution by public hanging: "Shooting is abolished because of the leniency of this punishment." This measure resulted in spectacles that revolted even Matulevich: destitute civilians would strip the bodies of the hanged for their clothes. But public hanging was a punishment Stalin kept in his arsenal until the end of his life.

Stalin's least-known but most vicious scorpion—whom the army loathed even more than they did Beria, Abakumov, and Matulevich—was Lev Mekhlis. Stalin had met him on the southwestern front in the civil war, where Mekhlis was a political commissar who detested former Tsarist officers as deeply as Stalin did. Mekhlis helped Rozalia Zemliachka murder captured White officers in the Crimea.[6] From the Crimea Mekhlis moved to join Stalin in the Workers' and Peasants' Inspectorate, and then, with Bazhanov and Tovstukha, became Stalin's secretary. In 1926, Mekhlis was sent with Nikolai Ezhov to be educated at the Communist Academy, where he contrived to adopt and, at the right time discard, the Bukharinite views of the academy's teachers. By 1931 Mekhlis was literate enough to become editor of *Pravda,* which he turned into Stalin's mouthpiece, receiving material from Stalin on former party leaders to be denounced in the paper and then arrested by Ezhov. For seven years Mekhlis took not a single day off and dragged into the paper, against their better judgment, fine writers such as Mikhail Koltsov, to make *Pravda* more readable.

Mekhlis was the sole new member of the party's Central Committee of summer 1937 who survived the terror. In December of that year, with the purge of the Red Army under way, Stalin made Mekhlis head of its political directorate. Mekhlis traveled across Siberia to pick out officers and political commissars for arrest.[7]

There was a wave of suicides in Mekhlis's wake: in 1940, over a thousand Red Army men killed themselves "for fear of being held responsible." Mekhlis spoke to Stalin over the head of Voroshilov. Officers hated Mekhlis for his bullying and denunciations, even if they grudgingly conceded his courage. Like Voroshilov, Mekhlis was unafraid of bullets; he made political commissars hold their propaganda meetings at the front, not in the safety of the rear. By summer 1940, however, Stalin judged that the army had suffered enough. He created for Mekhlis a new Commissariat of State Control, primarily to frighten the Soviet bureaucracy—an institution three times the size of the Red Army into a semblance of honesty, efficiency, and frugality. Here Mekhlis worked with Malenkov to build up a small army of 4,500 inspectors. By the time war broke out—to his disbelief, as much as Stalin's—Mekhlis could investigate or veto any expenditure or plans by any of forty-six other commissariats.

To replace the military intelligence apparatus he had destroyed, Mekhlis recruited thousands of men in his own image, many from his old school, the Institute of Red Professors. They acted as political commissars and brought back dual command, political and military, to the Red Army. This system of command contributed to the defeats of 1941 and 1942, and Stalin and Mekhlis reluctantly rescinded it.

Mekhlis had army officers trained on the basis of Stalin's textbook, *The History of the Communist Party of the Soviet Union—A*

Short Course, a book which singled out Mekhlis for praise, while the rank and file learned slogans glorifying Stalin. Mekhlis worked almost without sleep as Stalin's troubleshooter and Stalin backed him on most points, balking only at issuing arms to untrained "communist squads." Over two years, Mekhlis raced thousands of miles across the fronts, killing as many Red Army generals as the Germans. His cruelty was legendary: if the Germans used human shields of Russian POWs or women and children, the Red Army was to mow them down. The NKVD was to slaughter all prisoners in cities that lay in the enemy's path. A solider who answered back to a sergeant was to be shot in front of the ranks.

Mekhlis was as ridiculous as he was atrocious: when he found captured Germans with playing cards depicting naked women, he printed 11 million leaflets to shower on the enemy: "How Hitler is depraving his army." Officers were arrested not for fighting badly, but because they had been arrested before, had received secondary education under the Tsar, or were sons of priests. General V. Kachalov, who had already been killed in his tank, was sentenced to death because he was seen putting into his pocket a German leaflet as he drove off to the front; the general's wife and mother-in-law went to the GULAG.

A real test came in the Crimea, which in 1942 the Red Army was trying to hold against the Germans. Never had Mekhlis been so frenetic in giving battle orders, recruiting political workers, and dismissing officers; this was ground he had conquered twenty-two years ago. Now everything went wrong. Mekhlis was responsible for the disaster of May 1942, when the Russians were swept off the peninsula by a German army half their size. Mekhlis escaped without a scratch but with a besmirched military reputation. A key territory, 400 tanks, 400 aircraft, and nearly half a million men had been lost. Stalin sent a menacing telegram:

> You hold a strange position, as if you were a bystander or observer not responsible for the deeds on the Crimean front. This position is very convenient, but it is rotten through and through. . . . If you had used attack aviation against tanks and enemy forces, and not on sideshows, the enemy would not have broken through the front. . . .[8]

Oddly, back in Moscow Mekhlis was not court-martialed; Stalin set up a party military and political propaganda unit, in which he could do less harm. He nevertheless continued to range over the fronts, encouraging blocking squads to shoot retreating soldiers and moving on when he had enraged local commanders. When political commissars were abolished, the panic had abated, and victory over Hitler seemed certain, Mekhlis became just a bogeyman, and commanders could even appeal against his slanders. Now they might be demoted, but not shot.

★ ★ ★ War had changed Soviet society. Initiative had been encouraged, even rewarded when it succeeded. Victory over a real enemy, not some Trotskyist chimera invented by Stalin, had restored the individual's faith in himself. The Red Army—into which nearly a quarter of the entire population had been recruited—had become more powerful, more supportive, and more worth fighting for than the party. Above all, German bullets had steeled men and women to overcome their fears. It would need a very heavy hand indeed after victory in 1945 to return the population to the servile and gullible state of the 1930s. Stalin, Abakumov, Beria, and Mekhlis would have to use all the punitive force at their command to get the population back into its cage.

Like Stalin, Mekhlis was more perturbed than jubilant when the Red Army moved into central Europe: "Not just in the history of the Soviet Union, but in the history of our Fatherland, <u>for the first time</u> millions of people have visited abroad. They will bring back all sorts of things. Much of what they will see makes no sense to our people. . . . And what would they say if they'd been to America (skyscrapers, industry)?"[9] Stalin and Mekhlis were right. The sight of prosperity beyond a Russian soldier's dreams, even in war-ravaged Germany, Hungary, and Czechoslovakia, did have an effect on his mind. Mekhlis would have to combat the corrupting effect of capitalism on the army of occupation. This prompted Stalin in March 1946 to make him once again minister of state control, where he could cut out the rot in the bureaucracy and the officer caste.

Evacuation, Deportation, and Genocide

Send, o Lord, the Soviets Thy help,
And from the master race protect our land,
Because Thy sacred Ten Commandments
Are broken more by Hitler than by us.

Nikolai Glazkov

BERIA, LESS EASILY FOOLED by Hitler than was Stalin, took in what he heard from Sorge in Tokyo and Dekanozov, who in 1940 shuttled between Moscow and Berlin. In Moscow the German ambassador, Schulenburg, a Russophile, told Dekanozov Hitler's plans. Stalin ordered that bearers of bad tidings should be told to "fuck their mothers." Beria sycophantically concurred; even on June 21, 1941, the night before German tanks crossed the Bug River, he promised that "accomplices of international provocateurs will be ground into GULAG dust." He had the gall to ask Stalin to recall his own protégé Dekanozov from Berlin for "bombarding" him with reports of imminent attack. To judge by the change in Beria and Bogdan Kobulov's treatment of Polish officers from summer 1940, they well knew that war was looming; when in spring 1941 General Wołkowicki asked for permission to fight the Germans in Yugoslavia, Beria was sympathetic. But Beria never confronted Stalin, who had made up his mind that Hitler would not attack the USSR until he had finished off Britain.

In the panic and despondency of July 1941, Stalin kept Beria close by, using him as his number two on the State Defense Committee. Beria took specific responsibility for the defense industry as so many of its factories and workers were part of the GULAG empire. Another of his tasks was to liquidate potential collaborators and to scorch the earth wherever the Red Army was in retreat, so that Hitler, like Napoleon 130 years before, would find neither food, fuel, nor sympathizers.

The NKVD was one of the first commissariats to set up, together with the diplomatic corps shepherded by Andrei Vyshinsky, in evacuation at Samara on the Volga. Of 3,000 prisoners sent to the Volga from Butyrki prison the 138 most important were shot in October. They included Abram Belenky, Lenin's chief bodyguard and one of Stalin's oldest cronies, Béla Kun, Mikhail Kedrov, the chekist and neuropsychologist, several air force generals whose planes had been destroyed on the ground in the first hours of the war, and the last head of Red Army intelligence, Iosif Proskurov, who shared the fate of his six predecessors. Generals who survived the first attacks on the western front were arrested by Vsevolod Merkulov and also shot in Samara.

From Oriol prison, reserved for prominent political prisoners—Dzierżyński had spent four years there—154 were taken into the forests and shot. They included an unusual number of women, among them Trotsky's sister Olga Kameneva and the legendary Social Revolutionary Mariia Spiridonova, as well as victims of the show trials who had been promised their lives such as Gorky's doctor, Pletniov. These murders Beria assigned to the organizers of the Katyn killings, Bogdan Kobulov and Leonid Bashtakov. Worse were the massacres perpetrated on Beria's orders in the newly acquired Western Ukraine: perhaps 100,000 civilian prisoners were shot in Lwów as the Red Army retreated.[10] When the Germans captured a city very rapidly, as at Poltava, the local NKVD, to make flight easier or to avoid leaving behind anyone who might welcome the invaders, would kill prisoners and "untrustworthy" citizens on its own initiative. Other deaths were ordered from Moscow: in November 1941, in eight days, 4,905 persons were shot on Beria's orders.

The losses of men in 1941—2,841,900 of the Red Army killed or captured in summer and autumn alone—forced Beria to limit executions and to retrieve military manpower from wherever he could. Two generals in the GULAG, Kirill Meretskov and Boris Vannikov, were patched up in a sanatorium and sent to their commands. Meretskov was one of the few who had fought well in the Finnish war. He was so crippled by torture that he became the only general allowed to report to Stalin sitting down. Vannikov had been commissar for the defense industry until his arrest two weeks before war broke out; he recovered from his ordeals better than Meretskov and eventually provided the military coercion for Beria's atom bomb project.

Only in November 1941 did Stalin dare trust Sorge's assurances from Tokyo that Japan would not attack and move Siberian troops to the European front, but prisons and GULAG resources—more than 80 per-

cent of the 2 million prisoners were men of military age—were still un-
tapped. However, just 3,000 kulak exiles were considered safe material
for the Red Army and in 1941 over 200,000 more peasants and "socially
dangerous elements" had been exiled east for forced labor. From 1941 to
1944 over a million men out of a total of 29 million conscripted into the
Soviet forces during the war were taken from the GULAG to the front.
The NKVD's executioners were still busy. Officially, only 1,649 counterrevolutionaries not including Polish officers were shot in 1940; in 1942
the toll was 23,278, excluding untold thousands shot out of hand by
NKVD or military tribunals. Long after the rout of 1941, Stalin still had
senior officers shot. The choice of victim was arbitrary: some, like General Kozlov, who had lost the Crimea and nearly lost the Caucasus to the
Germans, lived on.

Beria had one major deportation to undertake: 1,500,000 ethnic
Germans, most skilled farmers in an autonomous republic on the left
bank of the Volga, were moved. On August 3, 1941, Stalin, hearing that
these Germans had fired on retreating Soviet troops, sent a note to
Beria: "They must be deported with a bang." It is said that Beria and
Molotov had already tested the loyalty of the Volga Germans by sending in parachutists in German uniform and rounding up every household that gave them shelter.[11] The deportation—by the standards of
Beria's later operations, even the standards of the British and American
internment of enemy aliens—was humane: each family could take up to
a ton of possessions and was given vouchers for the livestock they left
behind, although these were rarely honored. Some 900,000 ethnic Germans were deported, largely to Kazakhstan; the rest were recruited into
labor armies. Like the Koreans before them, the Germans had a strong
social and religious structure and were respected by the Kazakhs. Their
mortality in Kazakhstan was low, and the land around Alma-Ata flourished under their care.

Stalin twice sent Beria, in August 1942 and March 1943, to stiffen the
Russian defense of the Caucasus. Stalin complained to Roosevelt and
Churchill that he often had to visit the front, but in fact went only twice
in the war as the noise of gunfire loosened his bowels. Beria showed no
such cowardice, but the regular army had no faith in him.[12] In the winter
of 1942–3 the Germans failed to take the passes over the Caucasus de-

spite, or because of, Beria's measures. Beria was no general: he replaced Caucasians—Armenians, Azeris, Dagestanis—in the ranks with Russians, and maintained a strong presence of NKVD troops, even if this meant denying arms and transport to the regular army battling on the passes with Hitler's Edelweiss mountain units. Beria's actions could always be disavowed. This is why Stalin let Beria's men contact the Bulgarian ambassador and the short-lived pro-German Yugoslav government to sound out Hitler's terms for peace. Beria also supervised experiments in bacteriological warfare and excelled himself moving the defense industry to the Urals, with the help of the GULAG and a labor army composed of those ethnic groups not trusted to fight. The production of steel and electricity soon exceeded that of the areas lost to the Germans.

In summer 1943, with the factories in the Urals working and the German tide ebbing, Stalin again hived off state security as a separate commissariat under Merkulov. This was not a diminution of Beria's power; Stalin was allocating him some new tasks.

Several peoples of the USSR were branded as collaborators. First came the Turkic shepherds of the northwest Caucasus, the Karachai. In the winter of 1942–3 they had allegedly shown German patrols the mountain passes into Georgia and joined Nazi militias. Like many Caucasian peoples, some Karachai had hoped that Hitler would free them after twenty years of terror. Even after the Germans left, a Karachai national committee, fewer than a hundred desperadoes, fought a guerrilla war. But most Karachai did not collaborate: many families in the mountains even hid evacuated Russian Jewish children. During the brief German occupation, Colonel Unukh Kochkarov, the leader of the Karachai Red partisans, had been captured. When he escaped and rejoined the Red Army he was shot by the NKVD. Beria and his deputy Ivan Serov were interested only in the fiction of a "traitor-nation." Serov and Mikhail Suslov, the NKVD controller of partisans, personally led the repression. In mid-October 1943 the Karachai autonomous district was abolished and 53,000 NKVD troops moved in to deport 69,267 Karachai, mostly women and children, to Kazakhstan. They were joined by their menfolk when the latter were demobilized. The deportation was cruel: no possessions, even warm clothing, were allowed. A million sheep were left untended. On the long freezing rail journey to Kazakhstan and on the central Asian steppes, 40 percent of the deportees, including 22,000 children, perished.

Then it was the turn of the Kalmyks. These Buddhist Mongols whose land lies between Volgograd and the Caspian Sea had been for centuries a football kicked between the Russian and Chinese empires. On December 27, 1943, they were accused of handing over their cattle to the Germans and their autonomous republic was also abolished. The Kalmyks were to be scattered from the Arctic to eastern Siberia, steppe cattle herders used as forced laborers in forestry and dam building. With one hour's notice, without clothing or food and in terrible cold, over 90,000 Kalmyks were deported, to be followed by 20,000 of their menfolk still fighting in the Red Army. The trucks taking the Kalmyks to the railheads were American war aid.

On April 2, 1944, Beria reported to Stalin that the deportation had been carried out "without events or excesses."[13] The Kalmyks were so dispersed that any figure for the number of dead must be guesswork but the 1953 census located only 53,019. In 1939 there had been 134,000. In some areas only one in fifteen families survived, eating grass and twigs. On discharge, Kalmyk soldiers were treated worse than GULAG prisoners—forced to labor all day for 700 grams of bread. In November 1944 Beria was compelled by complaints from the Siberian authorities to ask Anastas Mikoyan to provide 36 tons of soap, 18 tons of tea, 90 tons of salt, some wool and cotton so that survivors might last through the next winter. Molotov, in the name of the Council of Commissars, insisted that the destitute Kalmyks pay.

Solomon Milshtein boasted to Bogdan Kobulov that, by banning baggage and cutting space, as half the deportees were children, he had cut the number of trains to 194, each of 64 carriages, to deport 150,000 Karachai and Kalmyks; the typhus that broke out was not, in his view, his fault.

Two successful genocidal operations led Beria to undertake a more difficult deportation: that of the Ingush and Chechens. These two related peoples (the Vainakh) had for 200 years fought a guerrilla war against the Russian invaders. In Soviet times the resistance, particularly of the eastern Vainakh, the Chechens, had been fierce. Chechen rebellions in the 1920s and 1930s, when they captured whole towns and drove out the GPU and Red Army, had not been forgiven by Stalin; nor had the Chechens and Ingush forgotten the NKVD's violence against them. Some educated Chechens looked to Germany. Hitler's ideologists had declared Chechens, Circassians, and other indigenous Caucasians proto-Aryans, and the Germans promised recognition as human beings, even political autonomy.

As Georgians, Stalin, Beria, and Kobulov detested the Ingush and Chechens with that antipathy of lowland townsmen to highland warriors that goes back to the dawn of history and is still felt in Georgia. The NKVD chiefs who conducted the Chechen and Ingush operation were also predominantly Georgian. On February 17, 1944, Beria announced that he would deport 459,486 people in eight days; as well as Chechen and Ingush, some of their Osetian, Dagestani, and even Russian neighbors would be rounded up. Beria requested leave for this "serious operation"; he wanted to take personal part.

Copying Hitler's techniques with the Jews, Beria forced the Chechen leaders and mullahs to dissuade their people from resisting. All accessible villages were surrounded by NKVD troops and the villagers called to an assembly from which a few were allowed back to the houses to fetch possessions. This time, the deportees were allowed to take half a ton of possessions per family. As a result, 14,200 carriages and 1,000 open wagons crowded the railways to the Urals and to Siberia at a time when military supplies and troops needed the tracks. Nineteen thousand troops, horses, and American trucks—brought in through Iran—were mustered; bridges and roads were repaired; Siberian and Kazakh authorities were warned of the influx. Beria sent Stalin telegrams assuring him that the operation was going smoothly. It was not. Heavy snow meant some villages could not be evacuated, so Beria's men, determined to finish the operation in eight days, burned the villagers alive in barns, stables, and mosques. Mikeil Gvishiani flew from Vladivostok to help Beria. At Khaibakh, near Nashkh—the heart of Chechen culture and the center of resistance—Gvishiani locked several hundred villagers, from newborn babies to men of 110, in stables and set fire to them, machine-gunning those who broke out.[14]

The Chechen and Ingush deportees, toughened by highland life and allowed to take some possessions, stood up to deportation better than the Karachai and Kalmyks. As Dostoevsky had noticed in prison in

Omsk and as Solzhenitsyn was to remark, Chechens and Ingush had the mettle necessary to endure. Even so, by October 1945, of the half-million deported, a fifth had perished. Chechnya and Ingushetia were wiped from the map: parts of the territories, like that of the Karachai, were added to Georgia, some given to the Lak people of Dagestan. For their efforts the Supreme Soviet awarded Beria, Bogdan Kobulov, Kruglov, and Serov the Order of Suvorov (first degree); Gvishiani, Merkulov, and Abakumov received less prestigious decorations.

As he received his award, Beria was deporting yet another Caucasian people, the Balkars, Turkic shepherds like the Karachai. The Balkars had suffered badly from the 37th Red Army on November 28–9, 1942: suspected of collaborating with German patrols, over 500 Balkar villagers—mostly women and children—in the Chereke valley had been shot in their houses. On March 7, 1944, the Balkars were given thirty minutes to get into the NKVD's Studebaker trucks. In the Kabarda-Balkar capital of Nalchik, Beria informed the local Circassians that the Balkar lands would be given to Georgia. Three weeks later the Balkars were unloaded from trains in the frozen Kirgiz steppes, where they were ostracized as traitors. Of the 37,000 who had left the Caucasus, about 2,000 died on the journey or soon after. Some Kabarda Circassians had been accidentally deported and were sent back, some of them to be deported again with other Kabarda later that year.

The Crimean Tatars were next. In April 1944, Kobulov and Serov drew up for Beria an ethnic map of the Crimea and accused Tatar soldiers of deserting to the Germans.[15] Beria informed Stalin of "the undesirability of Crimean Tatars residing any longer in a frontier zone" and arranged with the Uzbek authorities for them to be moved 2,000 miles across central Asia. Stalin's State Defense Committee issued a resolution—which no Crimean Tatar saw for forty-five years—confiscating their cattle and requiring them to pay for their transportation. The NKVD and NKGB allocated 32,000 men to round them up and the government ordered 75,000 planks for the cattle wagons in which the 165,000 Tatars were to travel. The Uzbeks were allocated 400 tons of fuel to truck the Tatars to the remote villages where they would be confined under threat of twenty years' hard labor in the camps if they moved more than three kilometers. By May 18, two weeks ahead of the deadline, Kobulov and Serov, under Beria's direction, had deported all the Tatars, mostly children and their mothers. Some went to northern Russia as forced labor for cellulose factories; 6,000 were arrested as anti-Soviet elements, and 700 shot or hanged as "spies."

When Churchill, Roosevelt, and Stalin met in Yalta in February 1945, not one of these indigenous inhabitants of the Crimea was left. Their fishermen's houses and their vineyards had been torn down to build villas and sanatoria for Russian party officials. The ethnic cleansing of the Crimea was completed by deporting 15,000 Greeks, 12,000 Bulgarians, and 10,000 Armenians. By the end of 1945, nearly half the deported Tatars had died of cold, hunger, disease, and despair. Many died on the journey and were buried in sand and ballast by the railway tracks. Their barracks in Kazakhstan had no glass in the windows; the bread ration was cut to 150 grams a day. There were no schools for the children; dysentery and scabies, as the NKVD admitted, raged. Those Tatar men who survived the war, however many medals they had, were dispatched on demobilization into exile. The only Tatars released were women married to Russians.

Beria still had some mopping up to do. Muslims in the Caucasus were again the victims. In 1944 47,000 Meskhi, Turkish-speaking Georgians living near the Turkish border, were dispatched to central Asia, as were 1,400 Hemshins (Muslim Armenians), the 9,000 remaining Kurds in Armenia, and some 30,000 people of unspecified nationality. Again, over half of the deportees were children. Between 12 and 33 percent of these deportees died. A few hundred Laz, a Muslim people living around Batumi and related to the Georgians, were mistaken for Meskhi and also deported but the Laz intellectual Mukhamed Vanlishi succeeded in persuading Beria to repatriate, and even compensate, the survivors a year later. In this final phase 413 NKVD men received medals for "bravery" and "fighting merit."

Prisoners of War

THE DEATH AND MISERY inflicted on the USSR between June 1941 and May 1945 are of course primarily Hitler's responsibility. In all,

11,285,100 Soviet citizens in the armed forces were killed, reported missing, or taken prisoner. Of these, 939,700 missing reappeared and about half came back of the 3 million prisoners of war—the POW figure is a round one since the Germans and Soviets used different definitions. Thus, over 8 million men and women—predominantly young men—in uniform were killed. Civilians under German occupation fared even worse: the figure of 9,987,000 deaths produced at the Nuremberg trials is roughly correct. Perhaps 4 million—mainly Jews—were shot; the remainder died of cold, disease, famine, and massacre as a result of the German occupation exacerbated by the Soviet scorched-earth retreat. Thus approximately 18 million deaths in the USSR from 1941 to 1945 can be attributed directly to the Nazis.[16]

But how much blame must Stalin and his hangmen take? Did Stalin criminally shed the blood of his armies in futile attacks or last stands? Was the scorched-earth policy a legitimate means of denying the enemy sustenance? Beria, Abakumov, Merkulov, and Mekhlis shot and hanged soldiers, civilians, and prisoners indiscriminately to a level far exceeding the official figure of 40,000 executions for the four years of war. The conditions in Soviet camps became atrocious, as bad as Dachau or Buchenwald. In 1942 alone, 352,560 prisoners, a quarter of the GULAG, died. Some 900,000 GULAG prisoners died of maltreatment during the war, though their camps were thousands of miles from the front. Civilian mortality in both cities and countryside in the unoccupied part of the USSR soared. At the worst periods, the spring of 1942 and the winter of 1943, in some areas half the infants died before their first birthdays. During the blockade of Leningrad, 750,000 perished.[17] The actual 37 million civilian deaths in the occupied and unoccupied areas of the USSR from 1941 to 1945 exceed by some 23 million the expected number, had mortality stayed at peacetime levels. The structure of the surviving population was distorted to the extent that in some country areas there were three women for every man left alive. Moreover, the draconian retribution exacted on the Soviet population in reconquered areas cannot be blamed on Hitler, while the deaths of half a million deportees and of one and a half million German POWs are entirely due to decisions made by Stalin and carried out by Beria and other commissars.

About half the Soviet prisoners in German hands and just over half the German prisoners in Russian hands survived. Both sides felt untrammeled by the Geneva convention. The atrocities committed by the German army from the very start of the war made the Russian military disinclined to take prisoners; particularly when retreating, they shot surrendered Germans. Red Army men knew the Germans shot all Soviet prisoners who were Jewish or who held party posts. Most Soviet prisoners were captured in the first years of the war and had to endure four years of starvation and abuse before liberation; the vast majority of German prisoners were captured only in the last eighteen months of the war. The annual mortality of German POWs in Soviet hands was twice as high as that of Soviet POWs in Germany.[18] Until mid-1943, when the Soviets were sure of victory, their treatment of POWs was horrific. A typical document dated May 4, 1943, sent to Major General Ivan Petrov, who ran the NKVD's Main Directorate for POWs and Internees (GUPVI), reads: "I inform you of the movement of POWs to Pokrovskoe camp 127. From March 4 to 13, 1943, we had three trainloads of POWs totaling 8,007. Of these by May 1, 1943, 6,189 died, including 1,526 en route. . . . Causes of death: dystrophy 4,326, typhus 54, frostbite 162, wounds 23, others 98. . . ." Of the 91,000 Germans who surrendered at Stalingrad, 27,000 died within weeks, although von Paulus's army was starved and frostbitten when captured, and only 5 percent, mainly officers, survived.[19]

In 1943, after Stalingrad, tens of thousands of Germans flowed into the GULAG, and the authorities began to see some point in keeping them alive. Soprunenko, who had managed what were in essence death camps, was replaced by Ivan Petrov, who had worked with Beria in the NKVD blocking forces in the Caucasian passes. Petrov picked out from the POWs those capable of useful work. German prisoners of late 1943 and 1944 were fresher, and as civilians had often been artisans; 80 percent of them could be used. As the war progressed, Russian guards became more forgiving. German artisans had a work ethic, and in mines, forestry, and construction outshone even free Soviet workers. In the camps German prisoners staged operas, carved ornaments, and grew tomatoes: their 50 percent survival rate over several years was higher than that of civilian prisoners thanks to their contributions to the GULAG economy and to the comforts of the camp commandants.

The work ethic of the German prisoners was also their undoing. When the war ended Stalin was reluctant to lose this workforce so 35,000 of the best POWs were charged with crimes—plotting to invade the USSR, aiding world bourgeoisie—and given twenty-five-year sentences. In the last months of the war, the number of prisoners virtually doubled and 1,500,000 foreign slave workers doubled the output of the GULAG, just as Hitler's program of *Ostarbeiter* slavery had boosted the German war effort. Most POWs in the USSR built roads and railways, many worked for the Ministry of Defense. In the postwar period, it is calculated that 8 percent of Soviet GNP came from POW labor. By 1950 they had contributed a billion working days to the Soviet economy, and had rebuilt several main highways and a dozen ruined cities.

German war guilt was thus partially expiated, but Nazis who had committed atrocities were prosecuted haphazardly. Trials began with three SS officers and their Russian driver in Kharkov in December 1943; they were hanged for massacring hospital patients and wounded POWs. Some 37,600 Nazi POWs were sentenced for war crimes: of these only 400 were executed, the others receiving twenty-five-year sentences so that their knowledge or skills could be exploited. Many known perpetrators of atrocities were treated benignly. Those publicly hanged in Kiev and a dozen other cities were not necessarily the most guilty while the Germans hanged in Minsk could not have committed the Katyn atrocities for which they died.

Only after 1946 could POWs receive mail or Red Cross parcels, and the repatriation process dragged out until the end of 1955. By then, however, there was a new source for the camps, millions of former Soviet citizens and other east Europeans garnered by the Red Army, SMERSH, and the NKVD.

Liberating Europe

IN 1944–5, AS THE WAR ENDED, Beria's NKVD met resistance even on Soviet territory. The Chechens and Crimean Tatars had submitted without a fight, but in the western Ukraine and the Baltic states, particularly Lithuania, there was desperate partisan resistance. It would take the NKVD nine years to liquidate the Ukrainian nationalists and the Lithuanian "green brotherhood," who had been joined by deserters from the Red Army and were supported by men of the Polish Home Army (Armija Krajowa), whom the Soviets had first betrayed and then turned on. In six months' mopping up after the German retreat, 40,000 Ukrainians were killed and nearly as many taken prisoner. Beria let Bogdan Kobulov and Lavrenti Tsanava, his commissar in Belorussia, run this antiguerrilla war. Some 200,000 Ukrainians, Belorussians, and Poles were killed in 1944 5; the NKVD lost fewer than 3,000 men.

In the recaptured Baltic states, Beria resumed the arrests and deportations interrupted in June 1941. About 100,000 kulaks were deported from the Baltic to Siberia. All ethnic groups other than Lithuanians and their Russian colonizers were deported from Lithuania. In Latvia 2,000 "forest cats" and other guerrilla groups fought the NKVD. There were massive reprisals. Estonia offered less armed resistance, but still lost most of its remaining intellectuals and middle class to the Siberian camps.

In summer 1944, with the Red Army back in Poland and Stalin determined to consolidate his conquests of 1939–40, Beria was fully stretched. As the German troops retreated, followed by millions of civilians fleeing East Prussia, the Armija Krajowa, loyal to the Polish government in London, tried to take control. This partisan army, supplied with light weapons, radios, and uniforms by British and American airplanes, numbered over a quarter of a million. For them the Red Army were occupiers, not liberators, though the Poles recognized the Soviets' right to pursue the Germans across Poland. The USSR had broken off relations with the London government and the Armija Krajowa in 1943, when the latter had accused the NKVD of the Katyn murders.

When the Red Army entered Vilnius, helped by two Polish partisan regiments, the eighty-year-old Polish bishop greeted them with a cross in his outstretched hands. He was arrested by the NKVD. The Poles were told that Vilnius was now the Lithuanian capital, even though the Lithuanians had collaborated with the Germans in exterminating the Jews and oppressing the Poles, who had together been the ethnic majorities in the city. The Red Army was accompanied by its own puppet Polish Ministry of Security and army under Zygmunt Berling.

There were so few communist Poles, particularly officers, that this army had been stiffened with Russian officers with Polish surnames. The intelligence service of the communist Polish army was entirely Russian. As the NKVD took over each city they disarmed, arrested, and sometimes shot members of the Armija Krajowa. Ivan Serov, Beria's deputy in Poland, branded the Armija Krajowa criminals and British agents. Serov could not cope with all Poland. In Lublin and Łódź, for example, Viktor Abakumov of SMERSH and Lavrenti Tsanava of the NKVD worked in parallel. Their main concern was ethnic homogenization: tens of thousands of Belorussians, Ukrainians, and Lithuanians, as well as millions of Germans, were deported from Poland, while similar numbers of Poles were driven out of the Ukraine, Belorussia, and Lithuania. This cleansing accorded with the Armija Krajowa's nationalism, but did not reconcile them to communist rule.

In summer 1944 the Armija Krajowa led an uprising in Warsaw against the Germans, banking on help from the Red Army dug in on the opposite bank of the Vistula. However, the Soviets chose to watch idly as the Germans brought in heavy artillery and over two months destroyed Polish resistance and, block by block, Warsaw itself. After the surrender of General Bór-Komorowski, the new commander of the Armija Krajowa, General Leopold Okulicki, disbanded his men into autonomous partisan groups.

By the time the Soviets reached Berlin, Beria's men had arrested 27,000 Poles, mostly resistance fighters against the Germans. The unreliability of the puppet Lublin Polish forces, who deserted to their families or to the partisans at the first opportunity, forced Beria and Serov to use cunning. In March 1945 Beria had Serov invite General Okulicki and seven key figures in the Polish resistance to talks with the NKVD at which, guaranteed immunity from arrest, they would meet a General Ivanov and fly with him to London to reach a compromise between the London and Lublin governments with the terms agreed by Russian, American, and British representatives. On March 28 the eight Poles were taken to an airport. There was no General Ivanov; the plane flew them to Moscow, where they went straight to the Lubianka to be interrogated by Beria's deputy, Vsevolod Merkulov. They were followed by 113 other Poles. Okulicki had been in the hands of the NKVD before, from 1939 to 1941 in Lwów. He confessed that he had been waiting for the war to end in order to join with the British in a battle against the USSR. On June 18 sixteen Poles were tried by Ulrikh, who was for this delicate occasion restrained, on Stalin's orders, by Molotov, Beria, and Vyshinsky. The Poles were allowed defense lawyers; the sentences were mild. Leopold Okulicki came off worst with ten years' imprisonment. However, Okulicki and two others soon died in prison. Poland had had the first taste of the techniques Beria and Abakumov would use all over eastern Europe to secure Stalin's control.

Bolesław Bierut's government was nervous about reaction to Okulicki's fate and interceded for Armija Krajowa members and for judges, professors, schoolboys, and others among the thousands arrested. Stalin granted most an amnesty. Bierut's government included a number of Jews; endemic Polish anti-Semitism flared up. In Kraków Polish policemen joined in a pogrom. On July 4, 1946, in Kielce, a runaway Polish child, Henryk Blaszczyk, was induced by state security officers to say that he was fleeing from Jews who meant to eat him. A crowd of some 15,000, again led by policemen, slaughtered forty-two Jews. These pogroms, which in total killed perhaps 2,000 Jewish survivors of the Holocaust, were led by Poles who saw Jews and communists as one and the same. A 1947 leaflet in Bydgoszcz declared, "a handful of degenerate Jews have taken over the state." But the Soviet-backed Polish Ministry of Security joined the frenzy: one of its bulletins read, "Once again a nine-year-old girl has disappeared. It may be that Jews from Rzeszów have eaten her. . . ." Poles complained that Russian films had been dubbed into Polish by Jews so the Soviet authorities employed Dzierżyński's widow and son to check the dubbing actors for Jewish accents.

Other countries that the Red Army invaded caused the NKVD fewer headaches. In Bulgaria elections were rigged to give Dimitrov's communists and their Soviet advisers control by the end of 1945. In Czechoslovakia, where even noncommunists revered Stalin as the leader of the Slavs and the USSR as the sole country that had not betrayed them at Munich, the survivors of the prewar communist party, strengthened by the Moscow nominees Gottwald and Clementis, needed less assistance than Polish communists and infiltrated Eduard Beneš's social democrat government. The communists took over policing, public and secret, and banished or murdered politicians who stood in their way. The Red Army and the NKVD helped the Czechs in their most popular enterprise: to drive out 3 million Germans from the Sudetenland. The government handed over the land to Czech peasants and the factories to Red Army engineers for dismantling and removal to the USSR.

By the end of 1944, the Soviet authorities had installed in Romania their nominee Gheorghe Gheorghiu-Dej. As in Czechoslovakia, they needed three years to disable other political parties. (One minister, Gheorghe Tatarescu, said, "We shall put some in prison, liquidate others, and the rest we shall deport.") Romania, unlike Poland or Czechoslovakia, was not to be ethnically homogenized: the Hungarian-speaking west of the country was kept intact, and many Romanian Jews had survived. Stalin insisted on Gheorghiu-Dej giving ministerial posts to a Jew, Ana Pauker, and an ethnic Hungarian, Vasile Luca—although both were soon purged.

Hungary, as a German ally, was treated with special caution. The British and American contingents on the Allied Control Commission and a shortage of skilled NKVD operators slowed Stalin's takeover. Elections in 1945 were free and resulted in a majority for a peasant-based smallholders' party. For two years Hungary seemed destined for the happy neutral status of Finland, where the prospect of serious armed conflict and of bad relations with Sweden kept Stalin from using force. In Hungary, however, which the Allies had tacitly assigned to the Soviet sphere of influence, there was no reason not to apply the salami tactics used on Czechoslovakia.

Viktor Abakumov's SMERSH, far worse informed than Beria's NKVD, followed the Red Army into Hungary. There Abakumov made a blunder whose repercussions for Soviet foreign policy were as baleful as the murders committed by Beria and Merkulov at Katyn. In Budapest Abakumov detained Raoul Wallenberg, the Swedish consul who had saved thousands of Hungarian Jews from the camps. He was sent to the Lubianka. In Soviet eyes he had been an intermediary between the Germans and Americans exploring the possibility of a separate peace. Wallenberg had also helped the Soviets barter valuable metals and had played a part in Finnish–Russian negotiations. Nikolai Bulganin, then reporting to Stalin as deputy minister of defense, signed the order for Wallenberg's arrest. When SMERSH was wound up and Abakumov became minister of state security on May 4, 1946, Wallenberg remained his prisoner. Wallenberg, according to Pavel Sudoplatov, was interrogated forcefully at Lefortovo prison then housed in the Lubianka and invited to become a Soviet agent. He refused. On Molotov and Vyshinsky's instructions, Wallenberg was killed, probably by a lethal injection from the toxicologist Professor Grigori Mairanovsky in the laboratory adjoining the Lubianka on July 17, 1947, and cremated. The Soviet cover-up was inept: claims that Wallenberg had suffered a fatal heart attack were undermined by Dekanozov blurting out to the Swedes immediately after Wallenberg's arrest that he was in the Lubianka. Like the Katyn murders, Wallenberg's murder was obfuscated by the Soviets for another forty years and the records of his interrogation have almost certainly been destroyed.[20]

Beria's main task in 1945–6 was to install a Soviet regime in each of the conquered territories. Viktor Abakumov's was easier, if equally large in its scale: SMERSH had to repatriate about 4 million Soviet citizens— and some wretched ethnic Russian noncitizens—from western and central Europe. The largest contingent were the 1,836,000 surviving POWs. Despite their fragile state they went to filtration camps, and from there mostly to the GULAG as "traitors to the motherland." The next largest contingent were Ukrainians and Russians, largely women, sent to Germany as forced labor. Only those who had at least two children by marriage to a foreigner escaped repatriation; the rest suffered the same fate as POWs, no matter how involuntary their stay in Germany. To aid the war effort Beria had reduced the number held in the GULAG from nearly 2 million in January 1941 to just over 1 million by January 1946. Abakumov's SMERSH repatriated so many Soviet citizens that by the end of 1949 the GULAG's population had climbed to an official 2,561,351. As in 1938 and 1942, so in 1947 the GULAG could not cope: the annual mortality rate doubled to nearly 4 percent. In 1947 alone 66,830 prisoners died.

Abakumov was especially harsh to Soviet citizens and ethnic Russians who had fought on the German side. Unlike those Poles and Hungarians who had served with the Germans, they were not treated as POWs. The Russian Liberation Army formed by General Vlasov was handed over to the Soviets in its entirety, even though the British and Americans knew that Vlasovites were being executed on the dockside in Odessa and in the filtration camps in Austria. Vlasov's men in some cases had turned against the Germans: the Vlasov army had liberated Prague before Marshal Konev's men entered the city and on the island of Texel in Holland Georgian Vlasovites had allied themselves with the Dutch resistance. The Allies' return of the Vlasovites was legally dubious and morally wicked.

Worse, in July 1945, the Allies handed over at Judenburg and Sankt Valentin 50,000 Cossacks and White Russians, together with their women and children, who had never been citizens of the USSR. Individual Cossacks had been guilty of atrocities, particularly against Serbs, but in an operation worthy of Stalin, a whole community was sent for extermination. The menfolk were killed before they reached the GULAG; the women and children were in eastern Siberia by October 1945. All traces vanish after 1949. Cossack commanders, who had operated under General von Panwitz, were personally interrogated by Abakumov and their statements read by Molotov and Stalin before they were tried. They were hanged in January 1947.

The Scent of Freedom

IT IS A TRUISM that after losing a war any Russian government makes concessions to its population, and after winning a war the ungrateful regime turns on its own people. Stalin in 1945, only a thousand times more brutally, did what Alexander I had done in 1813 and crushed his nation's hopes that its loyalty and suffering would be rewarded.

In Russia's western provinces and the Ukraine, the Soviet authorities faced a problem unique in Europe: they sometimes had to deal with people nostalgic for the German occupation. All German administrators of occupied territory had been murderous to Jews and communists; many had treated the rest of the population as subhuman slaves. Some, however, especially in the regions adjoining the Baltic, had given small towns and villages their first experience of good administration. Peasants had had their land restored and the tithes they had to supply the German occupiers with were not unduly onerous. These memories had to be eradicated. The peace that came with Germany's unconditional surrender in May 1945 was illusory east of the Elbe. Stalin turned his war machine on his own minorities, on eastern Europeans who sought to revive their prewar independence, and, as in the 1930s, on his own too buoyant intelligentsia and party. The bourgeois contagion that the Anglo-American alliance had brought had to be scrubbed out.

The Red Army, however, was stimulated to unsocialist behavior by Stalin's own policies. What remained of German industry and infrastructure was dismantled and sent back to the USSR as the beginning of war reparations. Not only industrial plants, but art galleries and museums were looted, sometimes recovering what the Germans had looted from the east. When Soviet soldiers raped German women and took German watches, bicycles, crockery, and clothes, they were only imitating the state. Officers packed whole trains with loot: cars, dinner services, books, even herds of cattle for their dachas. Stalin said that he saw nothing wrong with rape, and he tolerated the massive looting, noting that if he had to arrest a senior Red Army officer he could now easily find a pretext. The criminalization of the Red Army began in 1945. The USSR was flooded with foreign currency and consumer goods: American aid, from Jeeps to secondhand shoes; German loot, from prize cattle to cameras. The black market, which had virtually vanished in the mid-1930s, reappeared. Nothing that Stalin or his successors threatened could kill it off. Likewise, the underworld, so badly damaged by Ezhov, thrived on postwar inequalities. The cities were infested with deserters, demobilized soldiers, and thugs freed from the GULAG; in 1947 there were 10,000 murders and hundreds of thousands of violent robberies in the USSR.

Alliance with the Western democracies shook communist ideology and brought about the rehabilitation of the Russian Orthodox Church. When Easter bells rang out, on Stalin's orders, in Moscow in 1942, the effect was astounding. On September 5 Metropolitan Sergi, accompanied by two senior bishops, all wearing ordinary suits, and by Molotov and Vsevolod Merkulov, talked to Stalin while Beria, Malenkov, and Mikoyan waited outside. The result was the restoration of Church property, generous funding, and permission to print the Bible. Andrei Vyshinsky was entrusted with finding a censor who could purge the Bible of anti-Soviet sentiments. The choice fell on the dramatist Nikolai Virta, who was paid 500,000 rubles by the Church and declared both the Old and New Testaments to be completely in accord with party ideology.

The Church was now, like that of Ivan the Terrible or Henry VIII of England, an arm of the state. In Stalin's first broadcast to the Soviet people after the outbreak of war, he had flabbergasted his listeners by addressing them not as "comrades" but, like a Christian pastor, as "brothers and sisters." Promoting Orthodoxy had been more effective in galvanizing the nation to fight than reiterating the slogans of Stalinism. Stalin may also have listened to an American envoy, who had pointed out that Congress would not hesitate to send the USSR military aid if religious suppression stopped. Right until Stalin's death Russian metropolitan bishops were delivered in large black limousines to appear on international platforms, such as peace congresses, in the company of such stalwart atheists as Fadeev and Ehrenburg.

Russian intellectuals recalled reacting with relief to the outbreak of war. Some had hoped for defeat, hoping that Hitler would establish a puppet Russian state as tolerable as Vichy France; most longed for victory, forgetting that after every major victory the Russian state had tightened the screws. For rallying round, Soviet intellectuals expected gratitude, even though Stalin's remark "Gratitude is a dog's virtue" was widely quoted. Even the peasantry assumed that Stalin would have to pay for Anglo-American support: rumors swept the country that Churchill and Roosevelt had demanded the abolition of collective farms as the price of help.

Writers, composers, and painters had been treated with a care they were no longer used to. Very few were stranded in blockaded Leningrad; most were evacuated not to the Volga and Urals, where the government and heavy industry were relocated, but to the warmth and relative plenty of central Asian cities such as Tashkent. Scarce resources were allocated to print poets such as Akhmatova and Pasternak. Symphonies were commissioned; public readings turned writers into stars. Those who reported from the front, such as Konstantin Simonov or Ilya Ehrenburg, were treated like party leaders. No major writer was imprisoned or shot, although the very few still alive in the GULAG were not released. Only Nikolai Zabolotsky, after Ilya Ehrenburg, Samuil Marshak, and Nikolai Tikhonov wrote a letter to Beria in March 1945, was taken off heavy labor and given work as a draftsman which would enable him to survive.

One major poet died a tragic death. Marina Tsvetaeva, lured back to Russia in 1939 despite Pasternak's warnings of 1935, found herself a pariah. Her husband, one of Beria's contract killers, was shot, her sister and daughter arrested as French spies, and she was barred from publishing. Evacuated with other writers to Elabuga near Kazan and starving in a garret, washing dishes in the canteen where favored writers ate, she hanged herself. Almost her last poem is a reproach to her fellow poets, none of whom—not even the repentant Pasternak—had dared to be a Good Samaritan:

> And there is no coffin!
> There is no separation!
> The table's spell is broken, the house is woken.
> Like death to a marriage feast,
> I am life that has come to a supper.
> You are nobody to me: not brother, son, husband, or friend—
> and still I reproach you:
> you, who laid the table for six *souls,*
> without giving me a seat at the far end.

Pasternak, who had once thought himself in love with Tsvetaeva, wrote a poem in her memory, which he dared in 1943 to read to audiences. Its grief is understated almost to the point of callousness:

> In the silence of your departure there is an unexpressed reproach.
> Losses are always enigmatic.
> In the fruitless searches which are my reply
> I agonize without result: death has no outlines.

Oh, Marina, it's long been time, and not such a terrible trouble,
to transfer your neglected ashes from Elabuga in a requiem.

Returning to Moscow in spring 1943 by riverboat, Pasternak dared
to write in the captain's journal, "I want to have a bath and I also thirst
for freedom of the press." The free speech of the writers was carefully
recorded by those of their friends who reported to the NKVD. In 1943
and 1944 Vsevolod Merkulov collated the remarks for Stalin's perusal.[21]
The most loyal communists had views that strangely anticipate those of
many modern Russians: ". . . it's an irony of fate that we are shedding
blood and devastating our country in order to strengthen Anglo-
American capitalism . . . So Hitlerism has played its historic role, for it
has saved capitalism from death," remarked a literary critic, Boris Valbe.
Others were more sanguine: the grandson of the great Maecenas Savva
Morozov, a journalist who had by a miracle not paid for his ancestry
with his life, declared, "it's clear that after the war life in this country
must change radically, under the Allies' influence the government will be
forced to make decisive changes internally. It's very likely that opposition
parties will emerge in the country." In summer 1943 many writers believed that the generals who were winning the war—Zhukov and
Rokossovsky—would gain such political clout that they could become
dictators, that the returning soldier would demand the dissolution of
collective farms and Soviet power.

Only the hardbitten like the critic Viktor Shklovsky—his brother, a
priest, had been shot—had an inkling of what Stalin would do: "Victory
will give us nothing good. . . . Our regime has always been the most cynical of any that have ever existed; the anti-Semitism of the communist
party is just delightful. . . . I have no hope of the allies exerting any ben-
eficial influence. They will be declared imperialists the moment peace
talks begin." Even a conformist like Aleksei Tolstoi feared that "when
war comes to its completion we shall still have to fight our allies for the
partition and remaking of Europe." The novelist Sergei Golubov was
equally grim:

Any kind of changes for the better, any freedom of thought, of
artistic creation is out of the question for us, for we have the in-

ertia of power, of an order which has been established for all time. The authorities are incapable, even if they wanted to, of the slightest concessions in public life or the collective farms, the economy, for that might make a crack into which all the dissatisfaction that has piled up would gush.

Like many writers, Golubov was overwhelmed by poverty: "Where else, except in the USSR, can a writer be asked such a crazy question as: 'Are you suffering from malnutrition?' A writer can be gratified with a sack of potatoes or a pair of trousers."

By summer 1944, optimism was fading. Books were not passing the censor; writers were being reprimanded by cretinous party officials. Kornei Chukovsky, the translator and much-loved children's poet from Leningrad, complained of

> the most terrible centralization of literature, its subordination to the tasks of the Soviet empire. . . . I am living in an anti-democratic country, in the country of despotism. . . . The dependence of our press today has led to the silence of talents and the squawk of the sycophants. . . . With the fall of the Nazi despotism, the world of democracy will find itself facing our Soviet despotism.

Stalin and Merkulov cracked down on the self-assertion of intellectuals as mercilessly as they had on the national identity of the Chechens or Crimean Tatars. Merkulov announced that all writers who had expressed rebellious opinions were being "worked on." The monthly journals, their main outlet and source of income, were brought to heel. Stricter editors were installed. Writers and film directors were told to produce epics showing Stalin's wise and heroic conduct of the war.

Stalin's younger acolytes Georgi Malenkov and Andrei Zhdanov, relatively well-educated members of the Politburo, were told they had to restore order in the arts. The Leningrad journal *Zvezda* (*Star*) annoyed them most. Leningrad, despite its authoritarian rule by Andrei Zhdanov, nurtured the illusion that its extraordinary suffering during the war entitled it to speak more freely. The poetry in *Zvezda* spoke too much of the realities of war: "bridges made of frozen corpses," "a rotten scum of bile and anguish," tuberculosis, and prostitution. Contributors failed to see that the alliance with America was over and continued being conciliatory to religion and the bourgeoisie. Nikolai Aseev, otherwise a Stalinist poet, had written to the Americans: "You have an Abraham, we have a Joseph . . . let's make a new Bible."

The self-esteem of the intelligentsia and of the Red Army's generals had to be crushed; Stalin was preoccupied with preventing his satraps getting above themselves. Beria, Abakumov, Molotov, and Malenkov all found their freedom of action and their certainty of power curtailed. Stalin had gotten all he wanted from the Allies in Potsdam in summer 1945 and had quickly joined the war against Japan in August, but in that same month everything changed with the American detonation of two atom bombs over Hiroshima and Nagasaki. Arguably, these bombs saved many more lives than they took. Not only were the Americans spared the loss of life that an invasion of Japan would have cost, but, having lost the atomic race, the Soviets could no longer contemplate overwhelming the smaller forces of the British and Americans in Europe and realizing Lenin and Trotsky's dream of a Soviet Union from the Atlantic to the Pacific.

Stalin had not had a break nor seen the Caucasus since the autumn of 1936. On October 9, 1945, he left Moscow for Sochi and stayed so low and so long that rumors began to spread that he was ill, that Molotov would take over the reins of power. Now nearly sixty-seven and suffering from arteriosclerosis, Stalin was exhausted. He had summaries of British and American newspaper reports of his health sent to him in Sochi; he was both irritated and amused by the speculation but held out until mid-December before returning to Moscow.

TEN

THE GRATIFICATION OF CRUELTY

Our Ninika has aged,
His hero's shoulders have failed him.
How did this desolate grey hair
Break an iron strength?

Sozeli (I. Jughashvili)

Senescence

THE LAST SEVEN YEARS of Stalin's life and rule are distinguished by a process of petrifaction, a hardening of the arteries at all levels. For all that he tinkered with the organization of party and government, the changes were more in nomenclature than in reality. While new henchmen were promoted, the old, for the most part, were retained. Stalin's main concern was to establish his power structure in a perpetual state of balance and counterbalance, and his technique was to stimulate mutual jealousy and suspicion, and an overriding fear of himself, among his underlings. As 1947 approached, the suspicion and fear grew; every year ending in a 7 marked ten years since the revolution. In 1927 Stalin had jettisoned Trotsky, Zinoviev, and Kamenev and made the party overwhelmingly Stalinist; in 1937 he had launched the Great Terror; in 1947 his hangmen expected a new purge.

Yet Stalin was now a less energetic man, less able to see his measures through to the end. His memory began to let him down and the postwar world demanded far more attention than even the most paranoiac workaholic could devote. In the 1930s foreign policy had been a matter of balancing Germany against western Europe and keeping an eye on Japan. Now America and NATO were a hostile bloc; the Chinese revolution and the Korean War demanded massive Soviet involvement; the disintegration of the French and British colonial empires was creating instability around the world while eastern Europe had to be incorporated into a new Soviet empire; and the USSR, its morale, its economic, agricultural, and industrial might severely damaged by war, had to be reconstructed.

Stalin thus had to delegate, but he simultaneously immersed himself in areas that were esoteric for him including linguistics and biology, interfering simultaneously in favor of a dogmatic Marxist approach that defied all modern science but also in favor of pragmatic common sense.

Similarly, in politics, Stalin pursued both a consistent doctrinaire line of vindictive repression and a logical pragmatic one of flexible incentives. His decisions and policies were not motivated by the desire to achieve the best or the most efficient outcome. He wanted to paralyze opposing views by limited support and limited condemnation of both sides, so that neither the fanatical Marxist nor the pragmatic realist would dominate in any field. That paralysis of Soviet thought and initiative which would eventually bring about the downfall of the USSR was Stalin's way of disabling the succession. His henchmen understood this; they hedged their bets and quietly tried to build their own power bases.

Exploding the Bomb

STALIN RETURNED from his long holiday on the Black Sea to Moscow in December 1945. On December 1, still in Sochi, he had received a letter from his daughter Svetlana, to whom he had uncharacteristically sent a box of mandarins. "I'm very, very glad you're well and resting well, because Muscovites, unused to your absence, have begun to circulate rumors that you are very gravely ill."[1] Svetlana continued: "the last six weeks bandits and hooligans have started robbing and killing Muscovites horribly." Stalin was sure that without him chaos threatened. He was yet more contemptuous of his underlings. Stalin reassembled the mechanics of power. Kalinin, the head of state, was dying; his replacement, Shvernik, who had headed the trade unions, was even more of a cipher. Since 1941, Stalin had headed all three branches of power: the legislature, on the Supreme Soviet, as Shvernik's puppet master, the party as general secretary and Politburo dictator, and the executive as chairman of the Council of People's Commissars. He began to look for more malleable acolytes. War had required technocrats like Beria and Malenkov; after the war, Stalin sought ideologists to restore a totalitarian state.

Prewar henchmen were demoted: Kaganovich was moved down from transport to building materials, Marshal Voroshilov became the Soviet overlord of Hungary. While Stalin had been on holiday he had delegated power to Beria, Malenkov, Mikoyan, and Molotov. In December 1945 Molotov's star fell. Stalin telegraphed his four commissars from Sochi:

December 5: I warned Molotov on the telephone that the Foreign Commissariat's press department was wrong to pass *The Daily Herald*'s reports from Moscow setting out all sorts of fantasies and slanderous thoughts about our government, about the relations between members of the government and about Stalin. Molotov answered me that he thought foreign correspondents ought to be treated more liberally. . . . Yet today I read a report . . . in *The New York Times* . . . in a still coarser form. . . .

December 6: I consider your telegram completely unsatisfactory. It is the result of the naïveté of three of you and the sleight of hand of the fourth, i.e., Molotov. . . . None of us had the right to decide on his own matters involving a change in our policy. But Molotov did usurp that right. Why, on what basis? Is it not because libelous slanders are part of his work plan? . . . I have become convinced that Molotov does not value very much the interests of our state and the prestige of our government as long as he can get popularity in certain foreign circles. I can no longer consider such a comrade to be my first deputy[2]

Beria, Malenkov, and Mikoyan read the telegram aloud to Molotov They reported: "We summoned Molotov . . . after some thought he said that he had made a whole pile of mistakes but thinks this mistrust unfair, there were tears in his eyes."

Molotov had angered Stalin by failing to secure a Soviet veto in the allied consultative commission on the future of Japan; in London he had let France and China have a say in peace treaties with Germany's allies. Molotov was banished to New York, as envoy "Mr. Nyet" to the United Nations. Mikoyan also incurred Stalin's wrath for failing to report on the new harbors and rich fishing grounds of the newly acquired Kurile Islands.

In March 1946 the Supreme Soviet renamed commissariats ministries. Stalin told the Council of Ministers, "A people's commissar . . . reflects a period of unstabilized system, the period of civil war, of revolutionary breakup etc., etc. . . . The war has proved our social system is very strong . . . it is appropriate to change from people's commissar to minister. The people will understand this easily because there is a plague of commissars."[3]

Whether commissar or minister, any pretext—rain falling after fine weather was forecast—sufficed for Stalin to abuse his underlings. These bouts of anger did not always have the fatal outcomes of 1937 or 1938 but they shook men once confident of their hold on power.

Malenkov was unseated. The pretext was a letter sent to Stalin by his surviving legitimate son, Vasili, a drunken hooligan promoted to air force commander. Other pilots had paid with their lives for telling Stalin that Soviet aircraft were "flying coffins"; Vasili, although his father detested him, spoke freely about the Yak-9 fighter and its crashes. Stalin knew that half the 80,000 Soviet aircraft lost in the war had crashed due to mechanical failure. Abakumov also fed Stalin statistics comparing the deadly exploits of the Luftwaffe with the Soviet air force's failures. Stalin dismissed Aleksei Shakhurin, minister for the aviation industry, within days of his return to Moscow and in spring had Abakumov arrest him together with Marshal of Aviation Aleksandr Novikov. They spent seven years in jail.

A Politburo resolution on May 4, 1946, pointed at the real culprit:

1. To confirm that comrade Malenkov, as the boss of the aviation industry responsible for certifying aircraft and for the air force, is morally answerable for the appalling failings which have been uncovered in the work of these departments (producing and certifying substandard aircraft), that he, knowing of these appalling failings, failed to make the Central Committee aware of them.

2. To deem it essential that Malenkov be removed from the Secretariat of the Central Committee.[4]

In March Malenkov, hitherto at only forty-five the rival of Andrei Zhdanov as Stalin's heir apparent, was packed off to Kazakhstan.[5]

Beria alone seemed safe. In 1946 he left his ministry in order to manage the atomic weapons project, but from the Politburo he still oversaw internal affairs. The minister, Sergei Kruglov, was an unimaginative, spasmodically brutal bureaucrat. His main tasks for Stalin were to develop the GULAG and build more canals with slave labor. On Stalin's insistence he put 200,000 political prisoners into special camps to be worked to death in harsher conditions, their only consolation being that they were moved away from the common criminals who had raped, robbed, and murdered them.

Beria lost his subservient, urbane minister for state security, Vsevolod Merkulov; Stalin wanted a more forceful minister. Viktor Abakumov came from SMERSH and reported direct to Stalin. Beria and Abakumov had no time for each other. Abakumov brought with him to the Ministry of State Security (MGB) two SMERSH generals, although Beria's position in the Politburo left him with a little leverage over Abakumov, who retained several of Beria's henchmen. One was Sergei Ogoltsov, who had cannily declined to be minister on the grounds of "lack of knowledge and experience"—disingenuous considering that he had joined the Cheka at the age of eighteen, had terrorized the Ukraine and Kazakhstan, and in winter 1941–2, under siege in Leningrad, had shot thirty-two prominent academics as "counterrevolutionaries." Abakumov, like Beria, stood by his staff however much he abused them verbally; he even kept on the NKVD's token Latvian, Eglitis, as well as two Georgian satraps of Beria's, Goglidze in the Far East and Tsanava in Belorussia. In Georgia, however, he got rid of Beria's nominee Rapava.

Beria took the atomic bomb project over from Molotov, who had failed to organize even a supply of uranium. Until Hiroshima, Stalin had paid little attention to his physicists' warnings of the Allies' and Germans' progress. Now Stalin gave Beria first call on all resources as long as he got a bomb. If Beria failed, he would undoubtedly be shot.

In the event, Beria's four years' managing atomic weaponry were impressive. He seemed to get as much enjoyment from engineering projects as from arresting and killing enemies of the state. The atmosphere in which Soviet physicists and engineers worked was electric, and rather more luxurious than Los Alamos. This was Stalin's one project where almost nobody was arrested and where all deadlines were met.[6] There were many unnamed victims: thousands died mining uranium. More prisoners built laboratories, villas, garages, railway lines, even whole cities. Tens of thousands—three generations—of Kazakhs were condemned to death and radiation sickness when the bomb was tested in 1949. For once, however, the scientific community in the USSR felt valued.

The Soviet atomic bomb was built from information provided by Western scientists—some because they were communists, some believing that world peace would be secured by both sides in the cold war possessing nuclear deterrents, a few for mercenary reasons. Beria and NKVD men like Sudoplatov took the credit; Soviet foreign intelligence had revived in the ten years since Ezhov had annihilated it. The NKVD learned nuclear physics from Klaus Fuchs, metallurgy from Melita Norwood. Germany was scoured for scientists, students of Werner Heisenberg, who could enrich uranium and produce heavy water, and for the engineers who had built the V-2 rockets that would develop into intercontinental ballistic missiles. Physicists were retrieved from the GULAG and POW camps to be well fed and housed on the Black Sea.

First Beria located his uranium. In June 1946 Ivan Serov and another close associate, General Mikhail Maltsev, founded a company called Bismuth staffed by MGB troops. It took over twenty-seven sites in Upper Saxony and by October they were mining uranium from the old silver and lead mines. More uranium came from the Urals and the Russian Arctic.

Next Beria assembled his personnel. General Boris Vannikov, who had been tortured and then released in the first months of the war, maintained discipline; he clumsily bullied the physicists with a loaded revolver on his desk. Pavel Meshik, an old hand of Beria's, came fresh from SMERSH and the subjugation of Poland. He ensured hermetic secrecy around a project employing 100,000 persons. Beria kept constant watch, traveling the length and breadth of the USSR in a specially adapted train to dozens of sites in Siberia, the Urals, the Caucasus, and Kazakhstan. Physicists were rewarded with a freedom to publish rivaled only by the Orthodox Church.[7]

The physicist who adapted Western information to Soviet resources was Igor Kurchatov. Piotr Kapitsa, used to working for the tactful Lord Rutherford, would not be bossed by Beria. In November 1945 he complained to Stalin: "Comrade Beria's weakness is that a conductor has not only to wave his baton around, he has to understand the score. That's where he's no good . . . marking proposed resolutions with a pencil in his chairman's armchair does not amount to managing a problem."

Kapitsa urged Stalin to let the physicists run the project themselves: "scientists are the leading force, not the subordinates in this business." After Beria visited him in person Kapitsa withdrew from the project, and when Beria demanded his arrest, Stalin replied, "You're not to touch him." Kapitsa spent seven years working in his own laboratory at his dacha.

In summer 1949 Igor Kurchatov took a nickel hemisphere with a critical mass of plutonium to the Kremlin. Stalin stroked it and felt the heat. The Soviet bomb was tested in Kazakhstan at 7:00 a.m. on August 29, 1949, eleven years earlier than American experts had predicted. Beria's euphoria was spoiled only by Stalin, who, woken at 4:00 a.m. in Moscow, responded "I already know" to the news. Kurchatov and Beria distributed dachas, cars, and fat bonuses to all those involved. According to Kurchatov, Beria had a notebook which listed each person's punishment—from shooting to the camps—if the bomb failed: the rewards were calculated accordingly.

Crushing the Last of the Literati

THE LITERATI were unluckier than the physicists. Andrei Zhdanov was told to bring them to book. Zhdanov began with Leningrad, working closely under Stalin's supervision. The propaganda apparatus of the Central Committee undertook literary criticism. They found war stories objectionable if the soldier heroes were downcast, poems deplorable if they lamented ruined cities. Humor was utterly beyond Zhdanov. Targeting the Leningrad journal *Zvezda,* he picked on one of the satirist Mikhail Zoshchenko's funniest stories, *The Adventures of an Ape,* and raged at the idea of an ape escaped from the zoo becoming an example for human beings.

On August 9, 1946, Stalin himself, with Zhdanov and a rehabilitated, chastened Malenkov, railed at *Zvezda*'s unfortunate editor, Vissarion Saianov, for printing a parody of the nineteenth-century civic poet Nekrasov.[8] A parody, said Stalin, was "a trick, the author is hiding behind someone." Stories like Zoshchenko's, said Stalin—even though he had read him to his daughter Svetlana—proved that the editors were "tiptoeing after foreign writers . . . encouraging servile feelings." Others, notably the playwright Vsevolod Vishnevsky, joined the attack: Zoshchenko's autobiographical tale *Before Sunrise,* Vishnevsky told Stalin, was "undressing down to his dirty underwear," Zoshchenko's heroes were "drunks, cripples, invalids." Stalin damned Zoshchenko as "the preacher of non-ideology," his stories as "malevolent rant." Anna Akhmatova was called by Stalin "nothing but an old name." One editor stood up for Akhmatova, saying that if rejected by *Zvezda* she would be printed in *Znamia,* to which Stalin retorted, "We'll get round to *Znamia* too, we'll get round to the lot of them." Finally, Stalin conceded that there were "diamonds mixed with the dung" but the Akhmatova and Zoshchenko cult was blamed on Leningrad's unsound ideology. The journals were put under new editorship; Akhmatova, one of Russia's two greatest living poets, and Zoshchenko, its best short-story writer, were outlawed. The next day the MGB denounced Zoshchenko's "anti-Soviet" views, his doubts about victory, his remark that "Soviet literature is now a pathetic spectacle," and his bad influence. Zoshchenko was not however arrested; possibly he was saved by writing an emotional but dignified defense to Stalin.

Also on August 9 Stalin made a speech to the party's Orgburo on the films he had seen. Scenes that showed homeless coal miners after the war should be thrown out of films. He compared Russian scriptwriters unfavorably to Charlie Chaplin.[9] Soviet poets were lazy compared to Goethe who had worked for thirty years at *Faust* (*Faust* was always a literary benchmark for Stalin). He disliked the second part of Eisenstein's *Ivan the Terrible* with its remorseful Tsar and its carousing secret police whom Eisenstein had depicted as "the lowest mangy rabble, as degenerates, something like the American Ku Klux Klan."

Stalin's rant signaled a crackdown: the ninety-volume edition of Tolstoi which had been coming out since 1928 was shortened, Tolstoi's Christianity neutralized by Leninist prefaces. The novelist Fadeev, complicit in the execution of so many writers in 1937–8, was made general secretary of the Union of Writers. Access to foreign literature was strictly limited to those who Stalin felt had a need to see corrupting matter.

Literature was crushed but Stalin was gentler with the cinema, the Politburo's main source of relaxation. On February 23, 1947, late at night, Eisenstein and Nikolai Cherkasov, who had played Ivan the Terrible, were brought to see Stalin, Molotov, and Zhdanov in the Kremlin.[10] Everything that Stalin said was self-revelation. He lectured Eisenstein on history, and then criticized his Ivan: "you made him too indecisive, like Hamlet." Ivan, said Stalin, had been the first ruler to nationalize all foreign trade. It was right to show Ivan as cruel, Stalin told Eisenstein and Cherkasov, but wrong not to show why he had to be cruel. His only mistakes were "not cutting the throats of the last five feudal families" and "letting God get in the way and spending a long time repenting and praying." "Of course," said Stalin, "we're not very good Christians, but we can't deny the progressive role of Christianity." Stalin showed a grasp of cinematography; Zhdanov and Molotov could only add puerile remarks. By midnight the atmosphere was amicable. Cinema and music were the only two art forms where Stalin forgave an artist's mistakes.

★ ★ ★ By autumn 1946, like naughty schoolboys, Malenkov, Mikoyan, Molotov, Kaganovich, and Voroshilov had been punished and reinstated. Under Beria's supervision, they could be left to run the country while Stalin took another break of over three months in Sochi. The Politburo was not popular; the population had to endure frozen wages, raised prices, lower food rations, higher collective farm quotas, and rampant crime. Some things, however, were going well. The Nuremberg trials had run smoothly; the German defendants had not alluded to Stalin's war crimes. No British or American politician or lawyer had remarked in public that half of the Soviet commission for trying Hitler's war criminals belonged in the dock with them. Stalin had not let victory go to his generals' heads. Marshal Zhukov, the conqueror of Berlin, ran Germany as his fiefdom only until March. Stalin had Abakumov and Beria collect evidence against Zhukov who, like most senior officers in the Red Army and the NKVD, had furnished his dacha and house with German loot, and even considered casting him as a British spy. Like Tukhachevsky eight years earlier, Zhukov was given an intimation of his mortality by demotion to a provincial command; unlike Tukhachevsky, Zhukov was not pushed over the precipice.

Despite fearful anticipation, 1947 did not bring a return to terror; it was the most stable year of Stalin's regime. There were no sudden falls from grace or tergiversations of policy. Andrei Zhdanov was on his way out, drinking himself to death, and the promotion of other juniors whom Stalin consulted more and more, such as Nikolai Voznesensky from the State Planning Ministry and the charismatic Leningrad party boss Aleksei Kuznetsov, did not yet alarm the established satraps.[11] Stalin reinstated prewar foreign policy by forbidding American capital in the form of the Marshall Plan to "enslave," as Vyshinsky was told to put it, the economies of eastern Europe.

In 1947, those who cooperated with Russia's wartime allies suffered. Two cancer specialists in Leningrad, Professors Nina Kliueva and Grigori Roskin, had been offered equipment by the American ambassador in exchange for sharing their research into crucin, an antitumor drug. Zhdanov called this a betrayal of state secrets and revived in a nastier form the prerevolution "court of honor" to deal with professional misconduct, after which the wretched professors were handed to Abakumov's MGB. The Ministry of Internal Affairs and MGB were also busy hunting down Ukrainian partisans; they killed some 3,000 and sent 13,000 to the GULAG. Hundreds of Abakumov's most experienced officers were now "advisers" to the new security services of Poland, Czechoslovakia, Hungary, Romania, Bulgaria, and Albania, where they sometimes had to hold back, not egg on, the local recruits. Yugoslavia needed no advice; Tito had a secret police as ruthless as Stalin's.

The year was unusual in that more refugees entered the USSR than left it. After the defeat of the communists in the Greek civil war, five Soviet ships went to Durrës in Albania and evacuated thousands of guerrillas, their families and orphans. The Greeks were bitterly disillusioned when, like Soviet Greek deportees, they were settled in Kazakhstan. From Iran, a Kurdish army led by Mustafa Barzani fled to Soviet territory; Stalin understood the potential of a Soviet-trained Kurdish force to topple the pro-British Iraqi regime, but the Kurds too were dispatched far away, to the outskirts of Tashkent.

Stalin nevertheless surprised the world. On May 26, 1947, he abolished the death penalty, except for collaborators with the Germans. In no country has capital punishment been so often and so briefly abolished as in Russia: twice in the eighteenth century by the Empresses Elizabeth and Catherine, once, unofficially, by Tsar Alexander I, once by the provisional government in February 1917, and once in the 1920s. This time the state abstained from executions for nearly three years. The substitute sentence, twenty-five years' hard labor, was imposed very frequently—nearly 37,000 sentences in 1948 as opposed to 12,000 in 1946—so that the mortality of those convicted of capital crimes actually rose, since around 3 percent of such prisoners died each year.

Jews and Cosmopolitans

BUT 1947 was to be the calm before the storm. Although Stalin had in 1931 pronounced anti-Semitism to be "like cannibalism" and he would continue to condemn it even up to his death, he nevertheless turned on the USSR's Jews.

Stalin's anti-Semitism was not like Hitler's or that of the Tsar's governors. It had no racial, let alone religious, basis and it took root slowly. The Leninists he had exterminated were Leninists first and Jews second, but Stalin's rise to power was interpreted by the Russians who took control of party and secret police as the repression of a Jewish cabal. When Trotsky, Zinoviev, and Radek were ousted and then killed, the party was Aryanized; when Iagoda was replaced by Ezhov and Beria, the NKVD too was purged of Jews. For Stalin Jews became associated with polyglot intellectuals who resisted political direction. After Hitler, Stalin began to suspect them as internationally recognized martyrs, a people who might seek protection from the whole world, not just from the USSR. Once the State of Israel emerged and the Jews of the USSR acquired an alternative homeland, Zionism became a crime and all Jews suspects.

Stalin's anti-Semitism showed itself in his personal life. His elder son, Iakov, and his daughter, Svetlana, both had liaisons with Jews. Iulia Meltser, Iakov's wife, and Aleksei Kapler, Svetlana's admirer, were made to suffer. The seventeen-year-old Svetlana was yelled at: "Couldn't you find yourself a Russian?!" Svetlana's first husband, Grigori Morozov, who introduced her to his friends, prominent Jews, was seized by the police in May 1947. The couple's passports were replaced with new ones that canceled their marriage. Svetlana then married Zhdanov's son in 1949, and Stalin told her, "Zionists used your first husband to trap you. . . . The whole older generation is infected with Zionism, and they're teaching the younger generation."

Some of Stalin's in-laws, married to the Svanidzes and Alliluevs, whom he had shot, were Jewish. Other Alliluevs, Nadezhda's sisters-in-law, were friendly with the critic Lidia Shatunovskaia, who was in Solomon Mikhoels's circle. Stalin's dislike of Jews was fed by fear that details of his private life would be leaked abroad, but above all by his hatred of any element that had bonds with foreigners. For Stalin, the Jews experienced no proper class struggle; even when they abjured their religion, their ethos and solidarity survived. Stalin had been ambiguous about exploiting the Holocaust even for purposes of propaganda. He had imprisoned and murdered Erlich and Alter, the Polish Jews who had wanted to rally Jews in Britain and America to the Soviet cause. He had been reluctant to let the only internationally known Soviet Jew, Solomon Mikhoels, accompany the Yiddish poet Yitzak Fefer to extract from American Jews $45 million toward the USSR's war effort.

Even during the war, atrocities against Jews were rarely mentioned; the Nazis were portrayed as bent on exterminating all Soviet citizens. References to Jews were eliminated from the published text of a diary found on a German corpse in September 1941:

Actual text

24 June: Passing through a *shtetl* I took part in clearing a Jewish shop.

5 July: At ten we were in Krusko. At first I didn't feel like setting off looking for quarry, but after I'd read all the cheap novels, I got up too and began searching the houses the Jews had abandoned. The doors were broken down with crowbars, axes and other tools. Broody hens and pigs ran around. Our food was poor, so after dinner it began again. Again we set off for the Jewish quarter.

Text in *Pravda*

24 June: Passing through Slonim Walter and I took part in clearing shops and apartments.

5 July: At ten we were in the township of Kletsk. We set off straightaway in search of quarry. We broke doors down with axes and crowbars. Anyone we found locked inside we finished off. Some used pistols, some rifles, a few bayonets and butts. I preferred to use a pistol.[12]

Stalin's conversation with the Polish president, Sikorski, the ambassador to Moscow, Stanisław Kot, and General Anders on December 3, 1941, the day before Erlich and Alter were rearrested by Beria's Colonel Leonid Raikhman, is also revealing:

Anders: I think I shall have about 150,000 men at my disposal, but a lot of Jews don't want to serve in the army.

Stalin: Jews are bad soldiers.

Sikorski: The Jews joining the army include a lot of black-marketeers and smugglers. They'll never make good soldiers. I don't need that sort of people in the Polish army. . . .

Stalin: Yes, Jews are bad soldiers.[13]

During the war Solomon Mikhoels and his partner in the Jewish Antifascist Committee, the writer Shakhno Epshtein, boldly deplored anti-Semitism within as well as outside the USSR. The Soviet press omitted such outbursts. Soviet Germanophobia broadened into xenophobia; patriotism narrowed into Russian chauvinism. A stream of reports reached the party protesting that ethnic Russians were underrepresented in the arts, education, and medicine. What Ezhov had done in the NKVD was now done in every official sphere: Jews were restricted. For example, few documents state this, but most memories agree that from 1944 a ceiling, usually 10 percent, was set for admitting Jews to higher education.

Statistics of ethnic affiliation were kept at every level of Soviet society and leave no room for doubt that in the postwar period Stalin discriminated against Jews. In 1945 Jews held about 12 percent of the senior posts in the bureaucracy, the economy, the mass media, and education; by the end of 1951 they had less than 4 percent. By 1950 only 8 of over 1,100 delegates to the Supreme Soviet were Jewish. By the end of 1951 there was just one Jew among over 1,000 party secretaries.[14] Wherever Soviet officials had contact with foreigners, as in the news agency TASS, Jews were dismissed. Ivan Maisky, former ambassador to London, awaited arrest. In Nazi Germany only a Goering could declare, "I decide who of my subordinates is a Jew." In the USSR Jews were self-certified. Kaganovich declared he was a member of the leadership not the Jewish community; Litvinov declared himself an ethnic Russian.

Russian literary circles radiated schadenfreude at the discrediting of the Jews: Fadeev abolished the Jewish section of the Union of Writers as joyfully as he had created it. The censors pulped anthologies of Jewish poetry and books about Jews in the revolution. As in the 1930s, literary critics bore the brunt. A report prepared for Malenkov and Stalin in 1949 accused "an anti-patriotic bourgeois-aesthete group . . . only 15 percent Russians" of monopolizing criticism in literature and the theater.

In the 1890s, Russian writers had periodically grumbled that they were the victims of Jewish literary and theatrical critics. Even Anton Chekhov had confided to his notebook in 1897, "Writers like Leskov . . . cannot please our critics, because our critics are almost all Jews who don't know the core of Russian life and are alien to its spirit, forms, humor." In 1949 Sergei Vasiliev composed "Without Whom Can One Live Well in Russia," a viciously chauvinist parody of a famous nineteenth-century poem by Nikolai Nekrasov, "Who Lives Well in Russia." Vasiliev wrote of "twelve vicious eggheads of our Soviet criticism" and endowed them with typically Jewish names: Gurevich, Berstein, Finkelstein, Munblit, Holzmann. Vasiliev accused them of corrupting Russian literature with decadent and imperialist influences from such figures as James Joyce and Rudyard Kipling, and of supporting dubious Russian poets like Akhmatova and Pasternak. The parody ends with the Jews being taken by the ear and thrown out of literature "in the Russian way of Lenin and Stalin." Vasiliev's poem was not printed but was set in type and read out, after approval from state security officials, to a meeting of the Union of Writers.[15]

For some time Jews remained in the MGB, including Raikhman, Eitingon, and Grigulevich, but eventually they too would go.[16] Had Jewish composers and filmmakers been purged, Russian music and cinema would have become a wasteland. The nationally important work of the Soviet Academy of Sciences and the conscience of some academicians also inhibited the anti-Semitic purge. In physics, the proportion of Jewish graduates had increased during the war from around 50 to 98 percent, and the atomic bomb project then exempted them from dismissal. Kaganovich and Mekhlis hung on to power, but their spheres of action were narrowed, and the Jewish wives of satraps such as Molotov, Andrei

Andreev, and Stalin's secretary Poskriobyshev were demoted, exiled, or shot, a fate that their husbands apparently accepted without protest.

In propaganda the USSR was still portrayed as the home of European Jews, or at least non-Zionist Jews. Odessa was in 1950 the last city in Europe where Yiddish could be heard on the streets. Stalin dithered. On the one hand, since his first treatise on the subject in 1913, Stalin had maintained that the Jews were not a nationality, since they had no homeland, and must therefore assimilate. On the other, he created on the Manchurian border an alternative Zion, an autonomous Jewish territory, Birobidjan, where he settled a few thousand token Jews.

Stalin had no use for the Jewish Antifascist Committee after the war; it was too closely connected with Zionism. Stalin held back in 1947, for in November the United Nations voted to establish a Jewish homeland in Palestine. Stalin supported the founding of Israel, as although it depended on American capital and was a powerful magnet for Soviet Jews, many of Israel's founding fathers had been born in the Russian empire and been members of socialist or communist movements and Stalin hoped to influence them. On May 18, 1948, within hours of the United States, the USSR recognized Israel. Soviet Jews were forbidden to migrate but Romania and Czechoslovakia happily met their own anti-Semites' and Stalin's demands by letting 10,000 Jews leave every month. This was one move by Stalin that enjoyed international approval.

In September 1948 the new Israeli ambassador, Golda Meir, arrived in Moscow. Meir knew no Russian, but her counselor Namir and her attaché Ratner did. Meir received an ovation at the Jewish theater in Moscow. Her visit to the synagogue drew a crowd that blocked nearby lanes and, worse, Molotov's wife, Polina Zhemchuzhina, whose robotic Stalinism had not extinguished all spontaneous emotion, suddenly addressed Golda Meir in Yiddish: *"Ich bin a yiddische Tochter!"* Other Soviet Jews were warier than Zhemchuzhina: Ilya Ehrenburg told Golda Meir he hated Russian Jews who only spoke English.

A year later Polina Zhemchuzhina was arrested—she and Molotov had divorced at Stalin's suggestion a few days before. Stalin loathed Zhemchuzhina; as the closest living friend of Nadezhda Allilueva, she knew what had prompted her suicide. Molotov abstained from voting for her expulsion from the Central Committee but her career was over, and

Molotov, despite apologizing for his abstention, lost the Foreign Ministry to Vyshinsky. By imprisoning Zhemchuzhina, Stalin pinioned Molotov as he had Kalinin. Kalinin's Estonian wife had been tortured in 1938 and, despite his appeals in 1944, the wife of the head of state was still delousing shirts in the camp bathhouse as he lay dying.

The Soviet–Israeli idyll did not last long: communists won only four seats in the Israeli Knesset; the MAPAM party lobbied for the right of Soviet Jews to emigrate. Israel became a client state of the United States.

Palestine was not the only country mooted for the survivors of the Holocaust. Stalin had allowed Mikhoels and Fefer, during their wartime visit to America, to suggest the Crimea. In the 1920s and 1930s some $30 million had been contributed by Americans to aid Jewish settlers in the north Crimean steppes. Molotov was dubious: he thought Jews an urban people who "couldn't be put on a tractor." But Mikhoels pushed the idea, tactlessly telling Stalin that Soviet Jews needed a refuge from Russian anti-Semitism.

Like Erlich and Alter in 1941, the leaders of the Jewish Antifascist Committee had presumed too much. Stalin preferred a murderous solution to the aspirations of Soviet Jewry. To arrest Solomon Mikhoels, the committee's president, would have made him a martyr, so Stalin would have Mikhoels killed, and Zionists would confess to murdering him for his loyalty to the USSR. Viktor Abakumov provided a pretext: under torture, I. I. Goldshtein, a friend of Svetlana's first husband, confessed that Solomon Mikhoels was giving the Americans information on Stalin's family. Abakumov was ordered to liquidate Mikhoels. Despondent at the arrest of friends and at a flood of abusive letters, Mikhoels told a leading actor that he sensed he would soon die. He went to Minsk with a friend, the critic Vladimir Golubov-Potapov, who also worked for the MGB. Three senior hangmen arranged the killing for January 13, 1948: Abakumov's deputy Sergei Ogoltsov, Shubniakov of counterintelligence, and Beria's crony Lavrenti Tsanava, head of the Belorussian MGB. Golubov-Potapov was instructed to get Mikhoels out of his hotel. The two were snatched and taken by car to Tsanava's dacha. They were laid on a road, and a truck driven over them. The corpses were then dumped in the snow in a suburb of Minsk.

Civil police came from Moscow to certify accidental death. Rumors spread that right-wing Poles or fanatical Zionists had killed Mikhoels. Killers and victims were at first both honored: Tsanava, Shubniakov, and the MGB drivers got medals; Mikhoels an obituary in *Pravda*. Albert Einstein and Marc Chagall sent condolences. Polina Zhemchuzhina came to the funeral, Ehrenburg spoke, and Peretz Markish recited a poem ending, "Out of the ditches and stinking pits / Six million innocent tortured victims will arise to give you reverence." Kaganovich's niece came and warned Mikhoels's relatives, "Never ask anyone anything."

In spring 1948 Abakumov drew up for Stalin a list of Jewish activists, concentrating on those linked with the Jewish Antifascist Committee, and those designated British and American spies. The committee was officially dissolved in November, when Israel took a "hostile" stance toward the USSR. Abakumov searched the Jewish theater and "proved" that Mikhoels had been an American Zionist agent. Dozens were arrested and tortured with red-hot metal rods; some held out for months. One interrogator, Colonel M. T. Likhachiov, explained to his victims, "I'm going to wring your necks, otherwise I'll get my head cut off." Abakumov's secretary V. I. Komarov later wrote to Stalin (when he and Abakumov were behind bars): "I especially hated Jewish nationalists and was merciless to them, for I saw them as the most dangerous and spiteful enemies."

Polina Zhemchuzhina was abandoned to Abakumov's mercies. He broke her by making two male officials confess in her presence that they had had group sex with her.[17] Stalin had these statements read out at the Politburo in Molotov's presence. Zhemchuzhina was then sent to Kazakhstan.

The Jewish antifascists were shown no mercy. Many were accused of crimes that became capital when in 1950 Stalin brought back the death penalty. The biologist Lina Shtern, who through her American brother had imported streptomycin to treat TB patients, was declared a spy, as was the famous biochemist Iakov Parnas, who died in his first week in prison. One academician, Nikolai Gamaleia, who was ninety and ready to die, courageously wrote to Stalin: "something very wrong in respect of Jews is happening in our country . . . Anti-Semitism now comes from persons occupying top positions in governing party organs. . . ."

The interrogations and torture dragged on, then abruptly stopped in

1949. Abakumov's men had a more urgent purge of Leningrad's party leaders to conduct. Half of the Jews were sentenced to the camps, but fifteen of the remainder were saved for a major trial, and their "leader," Yitzhak Fefer, was in 1950 transferred to a new special prison, supervised by Malenkov and Shkiriatov, for dangerous political prisoners. The fifteen, when they finally came to trial, had the consolation that those who had arrested them were now held in the same prisons.

Vengeance on Leningrad

I not only detested pure words
And the strictures of higher judges,
I basked in flatterers' hypocritical duplicity,
I encouraged slanderous intentions
And pronounced false condemnations.
I had no pity for widows' tears
Nor for orphans' inarticulate sobbing,
I did not clothe the loins of paupers . . .

King David of Georgia (the Builder),
"Hymn of Penitence VII"

IN THE LATE 1940s Stalin's entourage noted with alarm his weakened concentration each time he returned to Moscow from his three months' autumn holiday. He now abandoned one project before starting another and new favorites were as liable as old colleagues to incur wrath and distrust. Stalin became more secretive, and set members of the Politburo against each other. Tired, he looked only at selected papers and suspected that facts were being hidden from him. He wrote very few notes; instructions, often ambiguous and contradictory, were conveyed by a few words or gestures during dinner and drinking bouts at Stalin's dacha.

Stalin sensed ideological betrayal all around. One traitor was Professor Petre Sharia, secretary for propaganda in the Georgian party, who was editing and translating into Russian all Stalin's Georgian prose. In 1943 Sharia's twelve-year-old son, Dazmir, was killed by a car and the boy's English teacher gave Sharia Tennyson to read for consolation. Under Tennyson's influence Sharia wrote, in Russian, a poem which, the Politburo reported, "recognizes the immortality of the soul and the reality of life beyond the grave." Worse, in 1948 Sharia let his deeply moved friends secretly print seventy-five copies on state printing presses. Sharia went to prison despite his defense that grief had driven even Karl Marx to throw himself into his first son's grave.

When in August 1948 Andrei Zhdanov died of heart disease despite or because of the attention of several leading Kremlin doctors, Stalin reacted with strange equanimity. Zhdanov had looked after ideology and had kept Leningrad free of heresy, enduring the blockade, albeit in his well-supplied bunker. In the first weeks of the siege, however, Zhdanov had organized the defense of the city and an evacuation of civilians. Stalin had countermanded his plans, complaining in his telegrams of Leningrad behaving as if it were "an island in the Pacific," not a part of the USSR. Moreover, after Zhdanov's son became Stalin's son-in-law, both father and son were suspected of intriguing against Stalin. In any case, with or without Zhdanov, Leningrad still seemed to Stalin, as in the 1930s, a nest of vipers.

Abakumov set to work in 1949 to prove that the Leningrad party had planned to make the city the capital of a Russia autonomous within the USSR. Some Leningraders, notably the ideologist Mikhail Suslov and Aleksei Kosygin, had the foresight to abandon the Leningrad party as soon as Zhdanov died and align themselves in Moscow with Malenkov and Beria. Thousands of Leningrad officials lost their jobs and 200 were arrested. Aleksei Kuznetsov had been congratulated by Stalin for his leadership in Leningrad, moved to the Kremlin, told that "the motherland will never forget you," and put in charge of party personnel. He had no inkling of his fate until he got into a lift with Malenkov, who cut him dead. Andrei Voznesensky, the former head of state planning, was arrested as he came home from a cordial supper with Stalin. He, Kuznetsov, and several dozen others were kept without sleep in the new Moscow special prison, Matrosskaia tishina (Sailor's Silence), watched over by the head of party control, Matvei Shkiriatov. For torture they were driven at night to Lefortovo prison, where the airplane engines in an adjacent factory drowned out their screams.

However unscrupulous, Abakumov had no aptitude for falsification and preferred factual charges: Voznesensky's indictment was for losing ministry papers. Abakumov ignored Kuznetsov's links by marriage to other leaders which could have brought down Mikoyan, Aleksei Kosygin, and General Gvishiani. Stalin was impatient with this pettifogging investigation. He had Voznesensky's brother and sister shot.

On January 12, 1950, "in view of requests from the national republics, trade unions, peasant organizations, and figures in the arts," the death penalty was reintroduced "as an exception" for "traitors to the motherland, spies, subversive wreckers." Kuznetsov and his fellow prisoners, convicted of slander, of defying the Central Committee, of squandering funds, just qualified for death. In the early hours of October 1 the Leningrad victims were sentenced, taken by electric train outside the city, shot, and buried. The Leningrad purge of 1949 was cruel, but smaller by several orders of magnitude than Ezhov's purge of eleven years before. Dozens, not tens of thousands, were shot; hundreds, not hundreds of thousands, imprisoned. Older victims could have reflected that they were atoning for their own parts in much more murderous frame-ups.

The Leningrad sentences were not made public and the arrests petered out. Moreover the arrests of Jews and other "cosmopolitans" had not produced fabrications strong enough to withstand a public show trial, despite the efforts of several dozen interrogators. Lev Sheinin, the short-story writer and *prokuratura* interrogator, who in the 1930s had whipped up public enthusiasm for the NKVD's purges, failed—he himself was Jewish—to compose a scenario that would persuade even an anti-Semitic public. Sheinin was dismissed and imprisoned with Abakumov's men.

In June 1951 Stalin found a more ruthless hangman, Lieutenant Colonel Mikhail Riumin, and a more compliant minister, Semion Denisovich Ignatiev.[18] Viktor Abakumov, to his own and his henchmen's amazement, had to go.[19] Riumin wrote to Stalin accusing Abakumov of corruption and suppressing evidence. Sitting in Ignatiev's office, he had copied out what his masters had drafted—the real author being Malenkov's aide Dmitri Sukhanov.[20] Riumin had been easily blackmailed: he had left secret files on a bus, he had concealed his dubious background—his father had been a cattle dealer, his siblings convicts, his father-in-law a White officer.

Riumin's allegations were partly true. Abakumov had spent a fortune, the proceeds of plundering Germany, on an enormous apartment where he lived with his second, trophy wife. Abakumov had also in November 1950 arrested, at Stalin's instigation, a Jewish doctor, Professor Iakov Ètinger. The professor read the English *Jewish Chronicle,* and his aspersions on Stalin to his stepson had been recorded. Being Beria's physician did not save Ètinger; he died in Lefortovo prison after being put in a specially refrigerated cell, a torture Abakumov had copied from the Gestapo. Riumin accused Abakumov of suppressing Ètinger's confession that he had conspired with other doctors to murder party leaders using inappropriate treatment.

Riumin had found the piece missing from Stalin's jigsaw puzzle. The show trial of 1938 had put in the dock a chief hangman, Iagoda, with a mainly Jewish cast of Bolshevik intellectuals and three murderous doctors to do their bidding. The forthcoming trial would have the same mix.

The key piece of evidence was a letter from Lidia Timashuk, a cardiologist in the Kremlin hospital. In 1948 she had administered the dying Andrei Zhdanov's cardiograms and ordered him to stay in bed. She was overruled by Stalin's doctor, Professor Vladimir Nikitich Vinogradov, who told Zhdanov to go for walks, even to the movies. The cardiograms prove Timashuk right.[21] On August 30 a heart attack killed Zhdanov. Timashuk had long been an MGB informer but the letter she wrote, with her minority diagnosis, was meant to cover her back, not damn the Kremlin professors. The professors' postmortem report confirmed their diagnosis, and they did what they could to silence Timashuk.[22] Timashuk's letter was set aside not by Abakumov, but by Stalin, who read it and sent it to his own archive.

Abakumov, like Ezhov before him, found himself friendless. Beria, Malenkov, Ignatiev, and Shkiriatov all signed a warrant for his arrest on July 12, 1951. Ignatiev took over the MGB, with Riumin, now a colonel, as his deputy. Abakumov became "No. 15" in the special prison; his wife, a baby at her breast, was in another Moscow prison. Like Ezhov's first wife, Abakumov's previous wife was lucky to have been deserted: she was evicted from her apartment but not arrested. The purge in the MGB struck at a handful of Abakumov's colleagues: Lev Aronovich Shvarts-man, as a Jew, was doomed; Naum Eitingon, despite Stalin's promise and thanks for killing Trotsky, was also arrested.

Abakumov's torments were to last for three and a half years. When given pen and paper, he wrote to Stalin, neither groveling nor remon-strating, but Stalin then ordered full sets of interrogation records for himself, Beria, and Malenkov every ten days. Egged on by Riumin, three interrogators worked with rawhide whips to generate enough material to keep Stalin happy. *Chekisty* like Abakumov, as Stalin reminded his henchmen, needed extra beating to break them. Abakumov and his un-derlings were first made to confess to beating their own prisoners. Abakumov was put into leg-irons and handcuffed; he had no cell mates; he was hungry and cold. On April 18, 1952, Abakumov appealed to Beria and Malenkov: "Dear L. P. and G. M. . . . I've never ever seen such bestiality and I didn't even know there were such refrigerated cells in Lefortovo, I was misled. . . . This stone sack can kill, cripple, or cause terrible illness. . . . I kept asking who authorized such nasty tricks to be played on me. . . . I realized that it was Riumin."

Lev Shvartsman, who had previously composed statements for inco-herent victims of torture to sign, now went mad—or simulated madness. Sent for more interrogation, Shvartsman then took another tack: he confessed that he was the leader of the Jewish nationalists, that he had sodomized Abakumov, the British ambassador, and his own son, as well as slept with his daughter. This time he was certified insane.

Riumin worked slowly, too slowly for Ignatiev's composure or Stalin's pleasure. However dim, Riumin knew that once the case was over, he would be disposable; he was in no hurry to conclude interroga-tions. He took a year to extract statements that Abakumov had framed the aviation minister in order to embarrass Malenkov, that he was in league with the Leningrad renegades whom he had sent to their deaths, that he was planning a coup d'état. All Riumin lacked was proof that Abakumov was a Jew. By April 1952, Abakumov, still refusing to con-fess, was a cripple and Riumin risked killing him if torture continued. Riumin nevertheless indicted him on November 3, 1952, as the leader of the MGB's Jewish nationalists. Eleven days later, Stalin, after angrily penciling comments on Abakumov's halfhearted confessions, dismissed

Riumin and sent him to join the other failed state security ministers among the accountants at the Ministry of State Control.

It was now Ignatiev's chance to shine, but he preferred his desk to visiting the Lubianka. Stalin roared at him, "You want to keep your hands clean, do you? You can't. Have you forgotten Lenin ordered Fanny Kaplan to be shot? And Dzierżyński said Savinkov had to be annihilated. If you're going to be squeamish, I'll smash your face in. If you don't do what I tell you you'll be in a cell next to Abakumov's."[23] Ignatiev had a heart attack. When he recovered, he moved Abakumov to Butyrki prison, to a cell surrounded by five empty cells. A guard and a doctor watched Abakumov, who was beaten a little less violently than the Jewish doctors and the recalcitrant MGB officers.

Yet more astonishing arrests were made: General Vlasik, Stalin's confidant, chief bodyguard, and tutor to his children, had been dismissed in spring 1952 for squirreling away dinner plates and caviar, and carousing with loose women. He was arrested in the autumn. Not even a dog could have been more devoted than Vlasik. Was Stalin demented? And, if so, could Beria and Malenkov now seize power?

Stalin's End

> . . . he worried as he felt all power ebbing from him—then Stalin was just Soso Jughashvili, a simple Georgian. He recalled far-away Georgia, of which he retained just the taste of turkey in walnuts, the taste of Kakhetian wine, the song "Live ten thousand years" and the Georgian curse: *magati deda ki vatire,* "I should make their mothers weep."
>
> *Grigol Robakidze,* The Murdered Soul

DEMENTIA EXPLAINS Stalin's decision to add his own doctor, Vladimir Vinogradov, an ethnic Russian despite gossip his real name was Weintraub, to the Jewish doctors' conspiracy. On January 19, 1952, Vinogradov examined Stalin for the last time and advised him, in view of his arteriosclerosis, to stop working. Stalin sent a note to Beria: "Sort out

Vinogradov," and along with fourteen other Kremlin doctors, not all of whom were Jewish, he was arrested. Lidia Timashuk was interrogated and awarded a medal. Vlasik was accused jointly with Abakumov of suppressing Lidia Timashuk's warning of the incompetence of the Kremlin doctors, something which Stalin himself had in effect done.

Abakumov was in a bad way. Goglidze, working for Ignatiev as happily as he had for Ezhov, Beria, Abakumov, and Riumin, accepted a doctor's report: "Prisoner No. 15 seems to have heart disease and can be interrogated no more than 3–4 hours and only in daytime . . . if necessary, urgent medicine can be given to restore his health so that he can be actively interrogated when acute methods have to be used." Abakumov's interrogator now wanted to know why he had not warned Stalin that Tito was splitting Yugoslavia from the communist bloc. The question was ridiculous: Stalin himself had given Tito a series of ultimatums in 1947 and 1948, demanding that he subordinate Yugoslavia's foreign and domestic policies to the USSR. Stalin had underestimated Tito's enormous ego and the strength of his army and secret police; when Yugoslavia broke away from the Soviet bloc in summer 1948, it was not for want of intelligence from Abakumov.

Leaving Abakumov to stew, Stalin had the Kremlin doctors handcuffed and tortured. Riumin carried this out in the Lubianka, in a specially equipped room. The interrogators explained, "We don't use red-hot iron rods. But we do thrash people." The doctors understood pain only too well. Some quickly confessed to killing not only Zhdanov but the Bulgarian communist Dimitrov, the French Maurice Thorez, and even to harming Stalin's children. One doctor claimed that he had learned euthanasia from Dr. Pletniov's killing of Gorky. They were told that they would be hanged unless they said which plotters they were working for.[24] Dr. Meer Vovsi, a cousin of Mikhoels, confessed to being simultaneously a Nazi and a British agent, even though the Nazis had killed his family. Vinogradov and Vovsi, the indictment concluded, meant first to poison Stalin, Beria, and Malenkov, and then fire on their limousines.

Stalin was so absorbed in the Jewish doctors' plot that he took no break at all in 1952. His paranoia accelerated as his physical health declined, and in February 1953 he dismissed his secretary and last real devotee, Poskriobyshev, who had not even complained when Stalin had his Polish-Jewish wife shot. On December 1, 1952, Stalin made his last speech to the Presidium of the Central Committee. As usual, he said that the more successful the party, the more enemies would sabotage it. He called Jews agents of American intelligence, warned that many were doctors, and then turned on the MGB: "They've admitted themselves that they are sitting in dung." In eastern Europe the inevitable finale to the Kremlin doctors' plot was being rehearsed: eleven alleged Zionists in the Czechoslovak party were hanged on December 3, 1952, for using doctors to shorten their leader's life. On January 9, 1953, *Pravda* featured a sensational headline: "Murderers in White Gowns." Jews would now be tried on a wave of public panic and hatred. Twenty-eight more doctors were arrested, and nine spouses.

Rumors of a massive pogrom raged among Moscow's anti-Semites, Jews, and diplomats. In the MGB Goglidze collected these rumors: after the doctors had been hanged in Red Square, 400,000 Jews would be deported to Siberia to "save" them from the people's wrath; cattle wagons were ready in Moscow's railway marshaling yards. There was no basis for any of this: the railway archives show no deportation preparations, and even a senile Stalin would have forbidden anything as spontaneous as a pogrom. However, a letter to *Pravda* was prepared, and sixty prominent Jews were told to sign it—they included the physicist Lev Landau, the poet Samuil Marshak, the novelist Vasili Grossman, and the film director Mikhail Romm. The signatories demanded the eradication of "Jewish bourgeois nationalists" and "spies and enemies of the Russian people." Kaganovich chose to sign a separate version of the letter. Ilya Ehrenburg signed only after writing to Stalin to warn him that the letter might "confuse people who are not yet aware that there is no Jewish nation."[25]

Seven weeks before his fatal stroke Stalin lost interest in the whole fabrication, and it fell apart before he was declared dead on March 5. Most of the doctors were lucky: two died under torture, but the others, physically and psychologically traumatized, were released a few weeks later by Beria. None of Stalin's heirs was in such good health that they could afford to alienate the country's leading medical consultants.

The Jewish antifascists were less fortunate: their interrogators such as P. I. Grishaev, a polyglot lawyer, were fresh from the Nuremberg trials. Some were beaten to death by the "choppers" while Grishaev wrote up his doctoral dissertation; others were executed by Abakumov in November 1950.[26] The rest were saved for trial, and Yitzhak Fefer was even produced in the Hotel Metropol when the American singer Paul Robeson came to Moscow and asked to see him. Fourteen, including Fefer, Peretz Markish, and Academician Lina Shtern, survived long enough to be tried in secret, with neither defense nor prosecutor but with "expert" witnesses and at surprising length—from July 11 to 18, 1952. The trial was held in the secret-police Dzierżyński club room inside the Lubianka. The judge, Cheptsov, later claimed to have had doubts about his verdicts, which he attributed to Abakumov's, Riumin's, and Grishaev's incompetence rather than the defendants' innocence. Fefer acted as bellwether; others spoke defiantly, but all were shot except Lina Shtern, the sole survivor to tell the tale.

Even Beria's power seemed to be waning. After 1949, when the atom bomb had been tested and Soviet physicists were at work on the world's first hydrogen bomb, Beria had time to spend in Stalin's company at the Kuntsevo dacha and in Sochi. However, as Stalin aged, his nocturnal meetings became shorter and he now rarely saw Beria without Malenkov, Mikoyan, or Molotov. Stalin told Beria to replace the Georgian household staff at his dacha with Russians. In autumn 1951, while on the Black Sea coast of the Caucasus, Stalin brought a party commission to Georgia to arrest Beria's Mingrelians in the party for bribery and nationalism. Worse for Beria was the next wave of arrests: Gegechkoris—relatives of Beria's wife—and at least one of his mistresses were caught in the net. Teimuraz Shavdia, a son of the family which had brought up Nina Beria-Gegechkori, was sentenced to twenty-five years in the GULAG. Shavdia had deserted from the Red Army and fought with the Nazi SS before joining the French Maquis; inexplicably, he had been living openly in Tbilisi.

Beria's subordinates sensed his power ebbing and helped Ignatiev and Stalin undermine him. After Beria's appointee Rapava fell, an eastern Georgian, General Nikolai Rukhadze, took over the Georgian MGB. He dined with Stalin at Sochi and was told to report direct. Rukhadze, like Riumin, disappointed Stalin: he boasted to his cronies of privileges but was uninventive. He alleged that Beria was Jewish but could not follow up Beria's connections with Georgian émigrés in Paris. Nevertheless, a Politburo resolution of November 9, 1951, named a Gegechkori as the target of American intelligence. On March 27, 1952, another Politburo resolution did more damage: Kandid Charkviani, to whom Beria had entrusted the Georgian party, was replaced by another eastern Georgian, Akaki Mgeladze.[27] Apart from Beria only one other Mingrelian still retained power outside Georgia: Lavrenti Tsanava in Belorussia, the murderer of Mikhoels. He too was dismissed in June 1952. Lastly, Stalin threw out Beria's sole ally in the Red Army, its chief of staff, General Sergei Shtemenko, who had with Beria held the Caucasian passes against the Germans. By June 1952 Beria was cowed. Thousands of Mingrelians were arrested and their language was banned from official use. Before 1952 Georgians had represented less than 1 percent of the population of the GULAG although they were 2 percent of the population of the USSR; the Mingrelian affair rectified this anomaly.[28]

Rukhadze very quickly overreached himself: Stalin transferred Georgian state security to another candidate and brought Rukhadze to Moscow where "his fate will be decided."[29]

Beria's fawning now grated on Stalin, but he was irreplaceable. Few others, certainly neither Riumin nor Rukhadze, met Stalin's essential criteria: "clever, active, and strong." Only Andrei Vyshinsky approached Beria in Stalin's esteem. Since 1949 Vyshinsky had been no less intransigent and rather more eloquent a minister of foreign affairs than Molotov. Vyshinsky's part in the judicial murders of the 1930s was notorious, but the disgust he inspired at international conferences was in Stalin's eyes an asset. MGB men looked down on Vyshinsky as "the Menshevik," but Vyshinsky was important enough for his Kremlin office, like Stalin's, to have a telephone which let him monitor all calls in the complex.[30]

Even Vyshinsky must have blanched when Stalin gave a rambling ninety-minute speech to the Central Committee on October 16, 1952. One by one, Stalin berated his closest associates in tones that had always presaged a fall. The unsinkable Mikoyan—"from one Ilyich [Lenin] to the other [Brezhnev] without heart attack or paralysis"—for once turned pale. Stalin damned Molotov: "What about Molotov's offer to hand the Crimea to the Jews? . . . Comrade Molotov respects his spouse so much that hardly have we in the Politburo taken a decision on an important political question than it quickly becomes known to Comrade Zhemchuzhina. . . . Clearly such behavior by a member of the Politburo is impermissible."

Even as Stalin railed in Moscow his puppets in Budapest, Prague, Bucharest, and Sofia were carrying out his instructions. Stalin had insisted on purges in eastern Europe partly because he was furious at the failure of the MGB to destroy Tito. Stalin had said, "I have only to move my little finger, and Tito is finished," only to find Tito and his security minister Ranković more than a match for him. East European leaders who thought Stalin and Molotov too intransigent toward Tito—all but the Hungarians and Albanians were slow to follow Stalin's line—were branded Titoist, Trotskyist, and Zionist. In Tirana, Enver Hoxha, supervised by an MGB officer, was the first to mete out a death sentence: in June 1949 Koci Xoxe, the Albanian Beria, was shot.

Władysław Gomułka, the Polish general secretary who had spent the war underground, was too soft. Stalin had Bierut remove Gomułka, who eventually accepted an invitation to see Stalin at Kuntsevo in December 1948 and managed to charm him. Gomułka kept his life and liberty, even though Stalin and Ogoltsov had forty state security men preparing a dossier.

Among Bulgarian communists, as among the Poles, those who came to power with the Red Army and the MGB were at loggerheads with wartime resistance communists. At the end of December 1948 Georgi Dimitrov, hero of the Reichstag fire trial and villain of Stalin's Comintern, had Stalin's sanction to dispose of two men who had spent the war in the Bulgarian resistance, one of them the deputy prime minister, Traicho Kostov. Dimitrov had gone back to Russia to die and Stalin trusted only a Moscow Bulgarian to take over. Lev Shvartsman led a team of MGB men to Sofia, where they tormented Kostov and a dozen others. Interrogation records in Bulgarian and Russian were sent for Stalin to peruse. Some victims were economists trained in the West, and Stalin's hatred of "specialists" imbues his comments: "The Kostov affair will help purging these agents and all hostile elements."[31] Abakumov proposed framing Kostov as an agent of Tito, and Sergei Ogoltsov flew down with three regiments of MVD troops in civilian dress to draw up an indictment, which they did not even bother to translate into Bulgarian. Kostov was hanged in December 1949 and a thousand Bulgarians went to prison.

In Hungary Rákosi longed to be rid of his rival, Minister of Internal Affairs László Rajk, who had graduated from a Nazi concentration camp, not from the Comintern. It took years for Rákosi to persuade his Soviet masters, who doubted his sanity, to help but in May 1949 they arrested Živko Boarov, an attaché at the Yugoslav embassy in Budapest, and an American journalist, Noel Field, who traveled between Budapest and Prague collecting material for his articles and had in 1943 refused to collaborate with the NKVD. Field's and Boarov's interrogators in Budapest forced them to implicate Rajk as an American and Yugoslav agent but used such terrible tortures that the confessions they extracted were too wild even for a Soviet-style trial. Rákosi, like Stalin, wanted Rajk charged with trying to assassinate him and asked Andrei Vyshinsky and Stalin for a Yugoslav prisoner as an additional witness.[32] Soviet advisers reined back the Hungarian torturers and Rajk admitted to being a fascist for twenty years and a Yugoslav agent for ten. Abakumov wrote the indictment for Rákosi; Rákosi and Stalin then hammered out a draft for TASS. On September 22, 1949, Stalin wrote to Rákosi: "I consider that L. Rajk must be executed since any other sentence won't make sense to the people." Rajk and two others were hanged; over a hundred others imprisoned.

Rákosi's fertile imagination concocted for Stalin a list of over 500 communists of all nationalities from Austrian to Australian but mostly Czechs and Slovaks to be repressed. Rákosi asked the Poles to try Gomułka. He asked the Czech leader, Gottwald, to arrest all Czech communists who had lived in the West. Polish and Czechoslovak secret policemen collected Rákosi's dossiers from Budapest. The Poles merely dismissed Gomułka; the Czechoslovaks asked Moscow to send them the advisers who had worked so well in Bulgaria.

Klement Gottwald was no more anxious than Bierut to arrest his ministers but was more cowardly; the Soviet MGB men had to find a Czech equivalent to Rajk. Preliminary arrests under Abakumov's instructions soon brought the necessary "evidence." Gottwald was happily imprisoning and murdering social democrats, but extending the purge to "cosmopolitan" communists created in Prague from 1949 to 1952 an atmosphere grimmer than anywhere else in eastern Europe. By February 1951, sixty Czech and Slovak communists were in prison. Gottwald knew that if he showed mercy or courage he too would fall victim to Rákosi and Stalin so laid down the lives of his friends to save his own. Rákosi and Enver Hoxha then began new purges; Rákosi's own deputy János Kádár was jailed.

In Yugoslavia Tito neither hanged nor shot his Stalinists, but tens of thousands of pro-Soviet Yugoslav communists went to concentration camps to be broken physically and morally. The USSR did not intercede for these Yugoslavs; Stalin, Abakumov, Rukhadze, Riumin, and Ignatiev were preoccupied with their own purges in Leningrad and Mingrelia. By the end of 1951, when they looked west again, Zionism was the main foe, and in any case Viktor Abakumov was in prison and Moscow had nobody with Abakumov's competence. It was left to Rákosi to make the running. He was equal to the task and produced a list of Jews to be removed which included those who had helped him torture the "Titoists." The Czechoslovaks too were told by Moscow to eliminate their Jews. Rudolf Slánský was the ideal scapegoat, a Jew who had appointed other Jews and who could be blamed for economic failures in Czechoslovakia. Klement Gottwald was awarding Slánský the Order of the Republic on his fiftieth birthday when Stalin sent the order to arrest him. A year later, Gottwald met Stalin at the nineteenth plenum of the Soviet Central Committee in October 1952 and within a month Slánský and ten others had been hanged in Prague.

Only the Romanians dawdled. Gheorghiu-Dej told the Soviet ambassador that he knew of no Romanians linked to Slánský. When pressed, the Romanian leader threw three members of his Politburo—two Jews and one Hungarian—to the wolves. They were luckier than the Czechoslovaks: Stalin's death let Gheorghiu-Dej off the hook. One victim died in prison; the other two were set free.

★ ★ ★ It is no wonder that Malenkov, Molotov, and Beria let thirteen hours pass before they called for doctors, when on March 2, 1953, they were summoned to Stalin's semiconscious body, which had been lying on the floor in vest and pajama bottoms for over twenty-four hours. They waited to be sure that the stroke was fatal and then Beria called to his driver, "Khrustaliov, the car!" and raced off to the Kremlin.

Beria's Hundred Days

> "All power," said a moron in his cups,
> "Tends inevitably to corrupt,
> And absolute power corrupts absolutely."
> Clever men should think astutely,
> And not repeat a thought so feeble,
> Power in fact is corrupted by people.
>
> *Iuri Andropov*
> *(KGB chairman 1967–82)*[33]

THERE WERE BROADLY THREE reactions to the news of Stalin's death. Many workers, peasants, children, and students were hysterical with grief; they felt bereft of certainties and abandoned to the mercy of enemies and intriguers, domestic and foreign. GULAG prisoners smiled, laughed, tossed their caps into the air; this was their first ray of hope, the first time they had seen their guards discomfited. The party apparatchiks and hangmen calculated how power would be inherited and began a waiting game, while the leadership maintained, for the time being, the semblance of unity essential for their immediate survival.

Stalin's achievement may be measured by the ease with which the state survived his demise. Four days after his death Beria, Malenkov, Bulganin, and Khrushchiov amicably reallocated power. The leaders from eastern Europe who came for Stalin's funeral were reassured. Malenkov was "prime minister" on the Council of Ministers; Molotov took over foreign affairs, Beria internal affairs, and Bulganin was defense minister, with the former minister Marshal Vasilevsky staying on as his deputy. Khrushchiov ran the Central Committee of the party, which now became the servant not the master of the government. Mikoyan and Kaganovich had posts that preserved their self-esteem; Voroshilov basked in the empty title of head of state.

But Beria was taking the helm with formidable speed and fearlessness. Like the east European communists, he understood the Ministries of the Interior and of State Security to be the focus of power. He made the Ministry of State Security what it had been before 1941, a department of the Interior Ministry. Sergei Ignatiev quietly stepped aside. Beria first needed to win from his colleagues, the party, and the Red Army what they most begrudged him: trust and popularity. Immediately after Stalin's funeral, he had Polina Zhemchuzhina flown back to Moscow to be remarried to Molotov. He rehabilitated Kaganovich's brother Mikhail, and awarded his widow a pension. However, neither Molotov nor Kaganovich showed any gratitude.[34]

Less than a week after Stalin's funeral, Beria set up four commissions to report to Kruglov, Kobulov, and Goglidze within two weeks. One commission acquitted the surviving Kremlin doctors, the second rehabilitated state security officers whom Riumin had brought down, the third liberated artillery officers purged by Stalin, the fourth freed the Mingrelians imprisoned or exiled by Rukhadze. Beria himself then rehabilitated Solomon Mikhoels. He was extraordinarily unvindictive: of Mikhoels's murderers, only Ogoltsov and Tsanava suffered; Riumin was traced to his shack outside the Sevastopol post office, arrested, interviewed by Beria for fifty-five minutes and promised his life if he confessed everything, then handed over to Vlodzimirsky and Khvat. On March 24 he wrote to Beria, "When I have to die, regardless of why or in what circumstances, my last words will be: I am devoted to the party and its Central Committee! At the moment I believe in the wisdom of L. P. Beria . . . and hope my case will have a just outcome." In a second interview with Beria Riumin was told, "You and I shan't see each other again. We are liquidating you." Riumin fell ill with despair, but then Beria forgot about him.

Others who had actually worked against Beria or whom he had undermined—General Vlasik, Rukhadze, who had engineered the Mingrelian arrests, Abakumov, and a handful of Abakumov's most brutal interrogators—remained in prison, but they were left in peace. Beria interviewed Rukhadze in his office in March 1953, and Rukhadze groveled to Beria from the Lubianka:

I weep, I am in agony, I repent everything that has happened. I feel very, very sad. Please believe me, Lavrenti, that I had no hostile intent. The circumstances I was in, and my loneliness, had a big part in my sins. . . . I turn to you with a plea, as to my own father and tutor, and on my knees with tears in my eyes ask you to spare, forgive, and reprieve me. For my children's sake let me have the chance of dying in freedom, after seeing them for the last time. You and only you, Lavrenti, can save me.[35]

At first Beria had support from his closest ally, Malenkov, who in April drafted a speech deploring, without naming Stalin, the "personality cult" of Stalin's last years. The party meeting was postponed and the speech never made.[36] The biggest shock came on March 26, when Beria sent a note to Malenkov proposing the world's biggest amnesty: it would empty the GULAG of a million prisoners. Half, Beria pointed out, were there because of Stalin's 1947 law prescribing long prison sentences for all kinds of theft. Everyone with sentences of under five years was to be freed and their slate wiped clean. Sentences over five years would be halved. All women who had children under ten or who were pregnant were to be freed, as were males over fifty or under eighteen. The Ministry of Justice had one month to come up with alternatives to prison for most crimes.

The motive was purely practical. As Beria pointed out, the judicial system was flooding the GULAG with 650,000 new prisoners every year. Political prisoners—some half a million, except for a very few with short sentences—would still serve their time.[37] Two months later Beria abolished the special sessions, the troikas of MVD, prosecutor, and party secretary that since 1934 had sentenced millions to deportation, imprisonment, or death. Beria washed his hands of the whole penal system and handed it to the Ministry of Justice except for the special prisons and camps that still held 220,000 of the political prisoners and war criminals.[38] Beria had, in theory, established the rule of law in the USSR but the irony is that he let the measures be called the Voroshilov Amnesty. Over 1,200,000 prisoners were in fact freed and nearly half a million prosecutions were aborted. By summer 1953 Russian cities were being plagued by amnestied thieves, muggers, and rapists, while political prisoners and their families went on suffering.

On April 3, 1953, thirty-seven doctors were publicly rehabilitated; Ignatiev was disgraced and Lidia Timashuk lost her medal. Beria sent a secret memorandum to the Presidium with statements from Abakumov, Ogoltsov, and Tsanava admitting the murders of Mikhoels and his friend Golubov on Stalin's orders. Lest the typist be shocked by the lèse-majesté, Beria inserted Stalin's name by hand. Again, the killers had their medals taken away. On April 4, 1953, Beria prohibited torture. The chambers in Lefortovo prison were dismantled and all instruments destroyed; the poisons laboratory, however, remained. Four days later the Presidium received a long document from Beria expressing concern for his native Georgia. In consequence, the Mingrelians purged by Rukhadze and Stalin were rehabilitated, as were 11,000 unfortunate Georgian citizens who had been deprived of all their possessions and deported. This document too had Stalin's name inserted by hand wherever the chain of responsibility led to the top. There were no revenge arrests; Akaki Mgeladze, whom Stalin had put in charge of the Georgian party, went to manage a tree nursery in northeastern Georgia. Beria made a rehabilitated Mingrelian, Aleksi Mirtskhulava, the Georgian party leader.

Beria brought back conventional economics: he told army generals the military was costing too much; he stopped work on gargantuan civil engineering projects—canals in the central Asian deserts, railways over Arctic permafrost—dear to Stalin's heart, which drained the budget and took thousands of prisoners' lives. The savings would be used to pay the peasants more, and charge consumers less for food.

In May, Beria surpassed even the amnesty when the May Day parade in Red Square took place without the usual giant portraits of the leaders. Was the age of idolatry over? Beria remarked that Canadians had no internal passports and proposed abolishing most restrictions on movement. All closed cities would now be open, except for three naval bases, and anyone gainfully employed would have the right to live in Moscow and Leningrad. Thanks to Beria, the inhabitants of 300 cities and the frontier zones rejoined the outside world.

Beria was driving the ship of state so fast its crew feared it would break up, and as if he knew that he had but little time, he gave orders that inevitably provoked mutiny. At the end of May he proposed handing power in the western Ukraine and Lithuania to officials native to the area. As a result, Ukrainians took charge of the local party, a move that won Beria popularity among Ukrainian writers and filmmakers, but not among the Russified party elite. In Lithuania all official proceedings, Beria insisted, had to be in Lithuanian, and Russian party secretaries who did not speak the local language had to go.[39] Belorussia and Latvia benefited in the same way.

Malenkov and Khrushchiov saw this as the wrecking of the USSR and Beria's next straws broke the camel's back. On June 2 he tabled measures "for creating a healthy political climate in the German Democratic Republic." The GDR was in crisis. Riots took place as the East Germans saw West Germany overtake them and achieve prosperity, and in two years half a million people—including 3,000 party members and 8,000 police—had fled west. Beria proposed negotiating the reunification of a "democratic, peace-loving independent Germany" by letting German communists talk to West German social democrats. Private capital was to be allowed, cooperatives disbanded, harsh punitive measures abolished, and prisoners freed. The aim, Beria admitted, was to further "the peaceful settlement of international problems," and he demonstrated this in Hungary by forcing Mátyás Rákosi to take on as his prime minister a Soviet agent, the gentler Imre Nagy. Beria also canceled Stalin's plans to assassinate Tito and tried to mend relations with him. In the east, Beria urged the Chinese and North Koreans into peace talks to end the Korean War. He recalled all the MVD's intelligence agents to Moscow, allowing back out only those who passed an examination in the language of the country where they were posted.

Beria was jeopardizing party rule, Russian dominance, and the integrity of the USSR and its eastern European empire. He had to go. The reasons for removing him, Khrushchiov would argue later, were moral: Beria was utterly ruthless and depraved. This was undoubtedly true, although more went to their deaths on Molotov's or Khrushchiov's signature than on Beria's. The vital difference was that they killed with a stroke of the pen or a touch of oratory whereas Beria got blood on his shirt. As for Beria's legendary sexual proclivities, he was certainly guilty of many rapes—usually by blackmail rather than force—and of violating young girls. On the other hand, some of his mistresses were fond, or at least respectful, of him. By the standards of some Soviet leaders, who used the Bolshoi Ballet as a brothel, or even compared to J. F. Kennedy or David Lloyd George, Beria was not beyond the pale, even if at intervals during meetings he ordered women to be delivered to his house, as modern politicians order pizzas.

The Hangmen's End

The wild plums blossom in Tbilisi—
A joy for Molotov to see,
For Voroshilov all the merrier.
But not for L. P. Beria.

Lavrenti Pavlych Beria
Has failed the main criteria.
A heap of ash, *Deo volente,*
Is all that's left of our Lavrenti.

Anonymous, 1953

BERIA KNEW EVERYTHING about everyone, but from March to June 1953 he gave no hint of intending to use his knowledge to slaughter his colleagues. Never had there been fewer arrests in the USSR, and there were virtually no executions. Beria had lost his taste for blood. Dismissed party secretaries became ambassadors or managers. The MVD halted its assassinations abroad. Beria's threat was not to Khrushchiov and Malenkov, but to the system that kept them in power.[40] The mystery is why Beria did nothing to protect himself. For thirty-three years he had been one of the most skillful political operators on earth, and now he let a group of mediocrities forget their differences and topple him.

Personal popularity in the USSR, even among the secret police, counted for little; in any case, even if Beria had brought relief to the surviving 2 million Jews and dozens of professors of medicine, yet another Georgian governing a fundamentally Russian state would have been intolerable for the rank and file of the party. Beria started building a holiday village of dachas for government and party officials near Sukhum, but to many this bribe looked like a trap.

East Germany gave Khrushchiov an opportunity. Beria's proposals to defuse the tension had come too late and rioting workers in Berlin and other cities had been crushed, on Beria's own orders, by Soviet tanks. To Molotov, minister for foreign affairs, this proved Beria's incompetence. Fear overrode caution, Molotov joined the conspiracy and his seniority ensured its success.

Khrushchiov had first to detach Malenkov, often photographed arm in arm with Beria but now worried by the demotion of many of his protégés. Khrushchiov then battled with Voroshilov's timorousness and Kaganovich's vacillation. The plot was hatched in parks and on the streets, lest Beria's men were tapping their telephones or bugging their apartments. By the end of June, the Presidium was won over, although Mikoyan and Voroshilov, likewise sated with bloodshed, wanted Beria not killed but sent back to Baku where the party had found him, as minister for oil production.

Two armed forces had to be won over: at least part of the secret police and the army. In the MVD Sergei Kruglov and Ivan Serov willingly betrayed their master; they hated Beria's Caucasians—the Kobulovs, Goglidze—being promoted over Russian heads. Khrushchiov sounded out the army through Bulganin. Beria had a few friends in the Red Army, but men like General Shtemenko, whom he had made chief of the general staff, were shunned, and many senior officers had never forgiven or forgotten Beria's torture and murder of Bliukher in 1938. Khrushchiov won over Marshal Moskalenko and carefully seduced Marshal Zhukov, who had been demoted by Stalin and saved from death by Beria, with promises of glory.

It was hard to gather armed men without alerting Beria's agents. In May, Bulganin sent army officers who might not have cooperated to the provinces on exercises while Malenkov and Molotov encouraged Beria to pay a flying visit to Berlin with army generals. Beria was suspicious and discovered a Presidium meeting was to be held. He flew back; the conspirators were in disarray and the meeting confined itself to tedious agricultural questions. Some witnesses report Beria alerting groups of parachutists outside Moscow and arming party workers in the Caucasus.

The coup was staged on June 26 during another Presidium meeting. Only Malenkov, Bulganin, and Khrushchiov knew what would happen.

Each Kremlin guard was shadowed by an army officer, ostensibly for training purposes. Bulganin brought his trusted generals in his limousine, all except Zhukov carrying handguns, against the rules, into the Kremlin. Marshal Zhukov, the generals, and a dozen party men lurked in the waiting room outside Stalin's study. Khrushchiov told them to enter when a bell rang twice.

Beria arrived late, wearing a crumpled gray suit and no tie. He asked about the agenda, and was told "Lavrenti Beria." Malenkov's notes for the start of the meeting are the only surviving document:

> Enemies have tried to place the MVD above party and government . . . Ukraine, Lithuania, Latvia. Are these measures necessary? . . . Beria . . . controls the party and government. This is redolent of great dangers, if delayed, too late to put right. . . . <u>We need a monolithic collective</u> and we have one. . . . Comrades are not sure who's eavesdropping on whom . . . make him minister of oil production. Next! . . . Who wants to discuss it?[41]

A farcical meeting began. Beria was replying to the abuse when Malenkov rang the bell and Marshal Zhukov entered with four officers. They stood behind Beria, two men putting revolvers to his head. Beria sat and wrote the word "alarm" nineteen times. He was taken to the anteroom and searched. His pince-nez, which he never saw again, was removed.

Beria was driven first to an army barracks. The next day he was visited by his former deputy Kruglov, who now took his job. Because of the rumored parachutists, Beria was moved to an underground concrete bunker. Army officers occupied the Lubianka. Tanks entered Moscow and Bulganin told the soldiers that Beria, Abakumov, and the rest of the old MGB were planning mass terror. The tanks left town to disarm two divisions of MVD troops before returning to surround the city center.

Beria's portraits were removed from all offices. Three MVD men swept the contents of Beria's safe into a sack; most papers were burned for fear of what they might contain. In Berlin Ulbricht breathed a sigh of relief as Beria's agents were recalled and the danger of the GDR merging with West Germany receded.

In his first week in the bunker Beria obtained from his warder, General Batitsky, scraps of paper and a pencil. He appealed to Malenkov at once: "Egor do you really not know I've been picked up by some strange people I want to set out the circumstances when you summon me." Two days later, he sent another slip of paper: "Egor, why don't you answer?" Beria asked for his selfless work to be remembered, for forgiveness "if there was anything to forgive during these fifteen years of hard, intense work together," and for his mother, wife, and son to be looked after. Beria's son, pregnant daughter-in-law, and two grandchildren had been arrested the same day; Nina Beria followed them. Beria's deaf-mute sister and elderly mother were for a time left alone.

On July 1 Beria wrote to Malenkov and his other accusers a rambling penitential letter: "My behavior toward you, where I am 100 percent in the wrong, is especially bad and unforgivable." He reminded Malenkov that they had agreed on some of the reforms, and that his mistake had been to circulate Interior Ministry documents that might embarrass Khrushchiov and Bulganin. He regretted his proposals to free East Germany and his actions against Rákosi. Beria could not rouse Malenkov's conscience but he could appeal to his sense of self-preservation. The letter hinted that they might go down together.

To convince Molotov that he had always spoken well of him, Beria begged him to contact his family. He also reminded Molotov how they had gone to see Stalin when war broke out to rouse him to action. He appealed to Voroshilov, Mikoyan, Kaganovich, Khrushchiov, and Bulganin: "I've never done anything bad to you." Beria wanted badly to live and offered to work on a farm, a building site.

The next day self-pity turned to panic: "Dear comrades," Beria wrote, "they are going to get rid of me without trial or investigation, after five days' incarceration, without one interrogation, I beg you not to allow this, to intervene immediately, or it will be too late. You have to get in first by telephone." He asked for his case to be investigated by a commission. "Dear comrades, surely executing a member of the Central Committee, and your comrade, in a cellar after five days in prison is not the only correct way of deciding and clarifying a case without a trial. . . . I beg Comrades Malenkov and Khrushchiov not to be stubborn would it really be bad if a comrade was rehabilitated?"

Beria was given no more paper. Khrushchiov chose a new chief prosecutor, the young and eager Roman Rudenko who had shone at Nuremberg, as the previous prosecutor Grigori Safonov had queried Beria's arrest, which had been carried out by army officers with no warrant. On July 2 a plenary Central Committee meeting began. For six days several hundred men and two women, a handful of whom had suffered at Beria's hands and many of whom owed their careers to him, listened, baying like hounds, to denunciations and disavowals. The participants all spoke so basely that the records of the meeting had to be falsified.[42] There had been less moral turpitude in the terrifying plenum of spring 1938 which condemned Bukharin and Iagoda.

Khrushchiov admitted that the doctors' plot and the Mingrelian affair had been fabrications—not that his audience thought that they should be put right. Khrushchiov implied that Beria only reprieved people who then became his agents. His preamble then degenerated into the incoherence that overcame most speakers. Beria, it turned out, had caused shortages of bread and meat; he did not care about the workers, which was why they lived in dugouts. His rehabilitation of the doctors was pure self-publicity; he had amnestied half the GULAG to build up a fief of thieves and murderers loyal to him. He was a man "of Bonaparte spirit ready to cross mountains of corpses and rivers of blood" for power.

Georgian leaders were bitter: rehabilitated Mingrelians, they complained, were now demanding ministerial posts. Beria's crony in Azerbaijan Bagirov was so spiteful—he was to share Beria's fate—that for once the audience turned on a speaker. Molotov and Kaganovich came better prepared. They portrayed Beria as a man who had misled and corrupted Stalin, frustrated economic planning and put the state at risk to please capitalists; he had probably been a fascist plant since 1920. Others thought up new accusations: Beria had engineered the fatal quarrel between Stalin and Orjonikidze and the estrangement between Stalin and Molotov. Beria, said Andrei Andreevich Andreev, who had left his sickbed for the meeting, was a second Tito—this perhaps the most perceptive of all accusations. Beria, complained others, visited them in their nightmares.

Malenkov in his summing-up tacitly conceded that Beria was

right—there had been a personality cult of an elderly dictator who had lost his grip, the doctors and the Jewish antifascists had been unjustly arrested, East Germany's "building of socialism" had been misconceived. But Beria, Malenkov insisted, was right for the wrong reasons.

On July 15 Beria lost all his medals, awards, and titles. The intensive interrogation began of everyone who had had contact, official or private, with him. Several dozen women—wives and daughters of party officials, actresses, opera singers, professional prostitutes—were questioned about his sexual techniques. Witnesses came from Baku and Tbilisi to testify that Beria was a British spy who had begun as an Azeri nationalist.[43]

Six of Beria's men, Dekanozov, Merkulov, Vlodzimirsky, Meshik, Goglidze, and Bogdan Kobulov—all from Tbilisi except Pavel Meshik, a Ukrainian—were included in the indictment. Hoping to escape their master's fate, they were cooperative. Beria's medical records added to the indictment, showing that he frequently had intercourse knowing he was infected with venereal diseases. Fantastic accusations against Beria were made by his servants—that he stuffed women's bodies down the drains or dissolved them in sulfuric acid—but these were not used in court.

Beria held up well, but when Rudenko finally read out an indictment a hundred pages long he held his hands to his ears and went on hunger strike. The trial was held behind closed doors in the second half of September 1953 with no defense lawyers. The chief judge was Marshal Konev, a fighting general with no legal training. Another judge was General Moskalenko, arrested by Beria in 1938. Moskalenko had the buttons cut off Beria's trousers to stop him jumping up and down in the dock.[44]

Just as he refrained from citing Stalin as his accomplice—he had been warned not to—Beria gallantly asked the court to withhold the names of female witnesses testifying to his moral depravity. None expressed any affection for him; the mother of one even demanded Beria's property as compensation for her daughter's lost honor. Beria's own cousin Gerasime Beria gave evidence that he had been a Menshevik spy when in prison in Kutaisi. Even Beria's son Sergo linked him to enemies of the people. Witnesses accused Beria of engineering murder after murder, from the infamous Tbilisi airplane crash of 1925 that killed

Mogilevsky, Atarbekov, and Aleksandr Miasnikian to Solomon Mikhoels's death in Minsk.

Beria's six henchmen denied him all merit and virtue, and gave graphic accounts of prisoners beaten not just on his orders but by his own hand. Beria admitted charges that were self-evidently true—murders of innocent citizens, membership of the Azeri Musavat party, sexual intercourse with minors—but denied everything else: he had not plagiarized his book on Stalin's leading role in the Caucasus; he had not protected foreign spies.

The sentence for Beria and his co-defendants on December 23, 1953, was, as expected, death.[45] All were shot on the same night. For Beria a special execution cell was set up, with a wooden shield to which he was tied so that no ricochet could injure the spectators. Beria was dressed in his best black suit for death. He faced his executioners with courage and tried to speak but Rudenko had his mouth stuffed with a towel. There was a scuffle among the officers over who would fire the first bullet. In the event, General Batitsky, who had been guarding Beria for six months, shot him straight in the forehead, and the body was wrapped in canvas and driven to the crematorium. Only the prison carpenter who had made the shield and brought Beria his food was upset by the spectacle.

Beria's relatives were hounded and deported to the Urals, Kazakhstan, and Siberia. Mirtskhulava wrote from Georgia on August 25, 1953, "His close relatives are busy with baseless vicious conversations, they are sources for the spreading of various provocational rumors. Beria's mother, Marta Beria, a deeply religious woman, visits churches and prays for her son, an enemy of the people."[46] Beria's two female cousins were imprisoned for complaining about his fate.

Khrushchiov and Malenkov were not consistent in punishing Beria's associates and Stalin's other surviving hangmen. Many languished in prison. Bogdan Kobulov's younger brother, Amayak, and Solomon Milshtein were not executed until October 1954. Shalva Tsereteli, the illiterate aristocrat who had specialized in abduction and murder, was flown from retirement to Moscow and shot. Lev Shvartsman again simulated insanity—he claimed to have invented a miraculous loom—but was shot in April 1955. Akvsenti Rapava, the head of the Georgian MVD, was not shot until November 1955. The last to die, in April 1956, was Shvartsman's sadistic partner Boris Rodos.[47]

In April 1957 Aleksandr Langfang was the last, perhaps the vilest, of Beria's henchmen to be tried. He defended himself vigorously: "If you're trying me, why not try Molotov, whose guilt is proven?" When the prosecutor demanded twenty-five years, Langfang asked for shooting on the grounds that he would be murdered in prison. The Soviet supreme court appealed against Langfang's sentence of ten years. He finally got fifteen. Constantly protesting his honor, Langfang served his sentence and then lived a further eighteen years.[48] Others got off more lightly: Leonid Raikhman, described by his interrogator as "a large, terrible beast, experienced, sly, skillful, one of the immediate perpetrators and creators of lawlessness," served one year in prison before the amnesty of 1957, and then lived until 1990.

Those who had served Beria and then Abakumov in foreign intelligence, such as Naum Eitingon and Pavel Sudoplatov, were given tolerable prison conditions. Beria's more intellectual friends were also treated gently. The novelist Konstantine Gamsakhurdia never had to account for his twenty years' friendship with Beria and even acquired moral authority and wealth as Georgia's greatest living writer, living like a feudal lord in Tbilisi and preparing his son to rule their country. Petre Sharia, the editor of Stalin's Georgian works, went back to prison, where he again wrote verse:

> It's hurtful, bitter to perish, not knowing why.
> For I have nothing to repent of, or to struggle with!
> If only I knew what fateful force
> Burns me so slowly on the fire.

Like others in prison for their links to Beria, Sharia spent a decade locked up with polite warders, access to books, and an unshaken belief in Stalin, before retiring to Tbilisi. His dying words, however, were, "I'm choking in blood."[49]

Ivan Serov was well rewarded for his treachery. He headed Khrushchiov's new KGB and died of old age in 1990. Kruglov, however, was pensioned off in 1958, expelled from the party and evicted from his large apartment for "involvement in political repression." He was run over by a train in 1977. Some, like Mikeil Gvishiani, who murdered even more Chechens than Kruglov, were saved from retribution by being sons-in-law of prominent party leaders. Gvishiani merely lost his general's rank in November 1954 for "discrediting himself." The same demotion was suffered by Vasili Mikhailovich Blokhin, the NKVD's chief executioner; a sick man, he died at the age of sixty in 1955. Nadaraia, Beria's executioner and, with Sarkisov, his pimp, spent a short time in prison. Aleksandr Khvat, the torturer of Vavilov, was still receiving a generous pension in the 1990s.

Abakumov knew Beria had fallen when his interrogations began again; they were perfunctory, however, merely selecting material for his indictment. Abakumov was moved to the Lubianka where doctors could keep him alive. Malenkov did not care about Abakumov's arrests of Jews or doctors; it was the framing of the aviation ministers in 1946 and of the Leningrad party in 1949 for which Malenkov wanted revenge. The officers' club in Leningrad where Kuznetsov and Voznesensky had been sentenced to death was therefore chosen for the trial of Abakumov and five of his henchmen. Abakumov had recovered enough to fight back. He blamed Beria and Riumin for his plight; he had only obeyed Stalin's orders in torturing his victims. He and three of his men were sentenced to death. Abakumov had no idea that the sentence would be carried out immediately and was saying, "I shall write to the Politburo—" when the bullet hit him on December 19, 1954.[50]

Lavrenti Tsanava, even though arrested by Beria was kept in prison by Malenkov and Khrushchiov. He hanged himself in October 1955. Ignatiev's deputy, the cautious Ogoltsov, was released by Khrushchiov in August 1953. He was deprived of his general's rank for "discrediting himself while working in the organs" but lived on his pension until 1977. Ignatiev, the minister who had supervised the persecution of the Jews, was sent by Malenkov to the foothills of the Urals as Bashkir party secretary. He enjoyed an early, and long, retirement.

Riumin, who had tortured the Jews and the doctors, had to face the music. Completely isolated, Riumin did not know Beria had fallen when he wrote to him in August 1953:

Dear Lavrenti Pavlovich, in the past, when I went to the Central Committee, my thoughts often turned to you, I always expected valuable advice, help and protection from you. Now I have come to be deeply aware how hard it is to endure the tears of children, wives and mothers. . . . Now I am overwhelmed every minute by the tears of three children, my wife and my mother who is living (if she hasn't died) her last days with heavy grief. Dear Lavrenti Pavlovich, I beg you <u>forgive</u>.[51]

Abakumov's consolation was that his tormentor Mikhail Riumin was executed five months before him, on July 7, 1954.

Rukhadze, the fabricator of the Mingrelian affair against Beria, had expected to be released but remained in prison and was shot in 1955. By contrast, after a short spell in jail, Professor Grigori Mairanovsky, chief poisoner to Iagoda, Ezhov, and Beria, reapplied to the KGB and continued his work in a laboratory in Dagestan.

The party elite—Kaganovich, Khrushchiov, Malenkov, Molotov, and Voroshilov—had as many deaths on their consciences as Beria or Abakumov but died in their beds, surrounded by their families. Except for Khrushchiov, who had glimmers of humanity as well as peasant cunning, they died quite uncontrite.

★ ★ ★ The Soviet Union and its successor states have never achieved what psychiatrists call closure. Khrushchiov's "destalinization" was essentially a series of political maneuvers to achieve sole power at the expense of his co-conspirators Molotov and Malenkov. It was impossible for him, and for the rest of the old guard such as Mikoyan, to entirely renounce Stalin without offering themselves up for trial as murderers. Many victims of Stalin, Trotskyists for instance, had in Khrushchiov's and his successor Brezhnev's eyes deserved their fate. Survivors of the GULAG and relatives of those executed received not justice, not even an act of contrition, but a "rehabilitation" that consisted of an often mendacious certificate and a month's salary. Whenever Soviet historians or novelists dared to take destalinization a step further, the brakes were applied—books were banned, people lost their jobs—and the public was upbraided about the sanctity of Lenin's heritage and the "positive" aspects of Stalin's leadership. Even after perestroika, when historians began to publish archival secrets and mass graves were opened up, the

KGB—soon to be the FSB—took part in the process in order to limit and then stop the revelations.

It is a paradox that Russia's two greatest novelists, Dostoevsky and Leo Tolstoi, in all their work insisted that only by full confession could the crimes of the past be absolved and life become endurable again, yet today's Russian state refuses to abjure Stalin and his hangmen. Denunciations have come either from nongovernmental organizations—Memorial, the Sakharov Center—using whatever material they have been able to compile or extract, or else from men who, like Khrushchiov, were up to their neck in blood. Stalin and his secret services are still lauded in print and in official speeches. The official myth, passively or actively believed by much of the population, is that Stalin's murders and terrorism were aberrations into which he was inveigled by Ezhov and Beria. Today's secret police, the FSB, take pride in their Cheka ancestry. They foster the cult of themselves as Dzierżyński's samurai, this time protecting the Russian nation, rather than the working class, against its enemies. It takes breathtaking ignorance to regard Menzhinsky's and Iagoda's murderers as noble warriors who fell victim to an inferior tribe of butchers under Ezhov and Beria, but the corrupt Russian media and ramshackle educational system do little to dissipate it. The dwindling number of victims receive no recognition of their suffering; their elderly torturers get big pensions and parade their medals with pride.

The Russian state in 2004 is ruled by a man who is, by career and choice, a successor to Iagoda and Beria. And while Russia's political prisoners number hundreds, not hundreds of thousands, the FSB has taken, in alliance with bandits and extortioners, the commanding heights of the country's government and economic riches, and goes on lying to, and when expedient murdering, its citizens. Russia is now locked into a global economy and today's rulers have no reason to murder millions of peasants or terrorize the professional classes. Genocide, however, is carried on by other means, and not only in Chechnya. In the last ten years, for instance, half of the indigenous peoples of Russia's Arctic regions have perished: 240,000 were alive in 1989, 120,000 are alive today. By destroying their pastures and fishing grounds, removing every support for their existence except vodka and tobacco, Russia's present government has proved as lethal as the GULAG. For Chechens, today's war of extermination is even worse than yesterday's repressions and deportations, for there is no effort to conceal the horrors, given the compliance and complacency of the rest of the world.

As the fates of Galina Starovoitova, Sergei Iushenkov, and Dmitri Kholodov have shown, any genuinely democratic politician or journalist in Russia has not much more life expectancy today than under the Bolsheviks. Russian citizens are too preoccupied with making ends meet and surviving to old age to be interested in forcing the state to account for itself, or to insist on electing honest men and women to power. Much of the truth about the past is locked up in closed archives which with every month grow even less accessible. School history textbooks, with few exceptions, pass over in silence the record of Stalinism.[52] Until the story is told in full, and until the world community insists that the legacy of Stalin is fully accounted for and expiated, Russia will remain spiritually sick, haunted by the ghosts of Stalin and his hangmen and, worse, by nightmares of their resurrection.

NOTES

Abbreviations for archives: GASPI = Russian State Archive of Social-Political History; GARF = State Archive of the Russian Federation. The numbers given refer (in order) to the *fond,* the *opis,* the *delo,* and the page(s).

ONE • The Long Road to Power

1. Quoted in Stanislav Kuniaev and Sergei Kuniaev, *Rasterzannye teni,* 1995, 82. Vasiliev was released in 1932 despite these verses being in his dossier. He was shot on August 13, 1937.
2. The Osetians are an Iranian people settled in the central Caucasus. Osetians were until recently integrated with their Georgian neighbors; Stalin's possibly Osetic blood is no more significant to Georgian or Russian history than Henry Tudor's Welshness is to English history.
3. N. Tlashadze, GASPI 8, 2:1, 48, 20.
4. GASPI 71, 1, 275, 23.
5. GASPI 558, 11, 721, 68.
6. GASPI 558, 11, 722, 51.
7. See Iakob Gogebashvili, *Rcheuli tkhzulebani,* 1990, vol. 2, 80–98.
8. *Bezbozhnik,* December 21, 1939, quoted in E. S. Gromov, *Stalin,* 1998, 38.
9. Pasha subsequently married and had a child. Her husband, her child, and her mother all died in the mid-1930s and, shortly before her husband's aunt wrote to Stalin to find her, she herself vanished, no doubt arrested, from the streets of Moscow. See B. S. Ilizarov, *Tainaia zhizn' Stalina,* 2002, 284–6.
10. K. Gamsakhurdia, *Davit Aghmashenebeli,* Tbilisi: 1942, 465.
11. Roman Brackman asserts that Stalin chose the name Koba after his natural father, Prince Koba Egnatashvili.
12. See Ilizarov, 2002, 411–53 for a full analysis of Stalin's reading of Dostoevsky.
13. Stalin took steps to set up an institute of experimental medicine under a certain Professor Bogomoltsev, who promised an elixir of life. When Bogomoltsev himself died aged only sixty-five, Stalin laughed bitterly.
14. GASPI 558, 3, 406.
15. Most of Russia's Esperantists were later shot as cosmopolitans and spies.
16. Stalin appears also to have had a reading knowledge of French. On May 4, 1923, he circulated Fridtjof Nansen's protest (in French) on the impending execution of Patriarch Tikhon to the Politburo, and only Tomsky marked the document, "Did not read, for unfortunately I have not studied French." (*Politburo i tserkov',* 1997, 1, 302–03).
17. *Pravda,* December 21, 1994. Underneath Stalin appended in blue pencil: "Alas, what do we see, what do we see?"
18. Cartoons attributed by Ilizarov in *Tainaia zhizn' Stalina,* 2002, to Stalin, such as a doodle of the finance minister Briukhanov hanging by his genitals, do not tally with the geometric, abstract nature of his doodling.
19. Grigol Eliava died in 1925, but his son, the bacteriologist Gogi Eliava, was arrested by Beria and shot in 1937.
20. Archive documentation neither supports nor fully refutes this suspicion. Much archival material quoted here was first published by Aleksandr Ostrovsky in his monograph, *Kto stoial za spinoi Stalina,* St. Petersburg, 2002.

21. *Zaria Vostoka,* December 23, 1925.
22. In 1944, living enviably uneventfully as a housewife, Polina wrote her memoirs, and was made to surrender these and all her gifts from Stalin to the party archives. GASPI 558, 4, 647.
23. Petrovsky's claim to fame is that he was the only member of this Central Committee Stalin allowed to survive the terror of the 1930s.
24. This dossier is not available; it may be in the Presidential Archive of the Russian Federation.
25. Ozoliņš published his memoir in 1933 when, as director of the Latvian Bank, he was negotiating a trade agreement with the USSR; his critique of Stalin was therefore tactful. He was nevertheless shot on Stalin's orders in 1941. For a Russian translation of Ozoliņš's memoir and Boris Ravdin's article on it, see *Daugava,* Riga, 2002, 4, 126–42.
26. The Bolsheviks had a fashion for "hard" pseudonyms: apart from Stalin (steel) there was Kamenev (stone) and Molotov (hammer), not to mention Fiodor Raskol'nikov who named himself after Dostoevsky's axe-murderer.
27. Kibirov was posted to Turukhansk as a punishment for misdemeanors in the Caucasus, which explains why he sided with Stalin against the gendarme.
28. This son, Aleksandr, was subsequently adopted by a peasant, Davydov, to whom Lidia was later married off. Aleksandr Davydov became a major in the Red Army and died in 1987.
29. GASPI 558, 1, 54, 1–3.
30. Bednyi means "the poor"; his real surname was more appropriate, Pridvorov (of the court). He was probably the illegitimate son of one of the Tsar's cousins.
31. GASPI 558, 11, 701.
32. GASPI 558, 11, 721, 126.
33. *Obshchaia gazeta,* St. Petersburg, No. 9, March 1–7, 2001, 15.
34. The fate of Shapiro, arguably the bravest man in Stalin's entourage, is unknown.
35. Chuev, *100 razgovorov,* as cited by D. V. Koliosov, *I. V. Stalin,* 2000, 200–01.

TWO • Stalin, Dzierżyński, and the Cheka

1. Even in Polish, despite his talent for graphic writing, Dzierżyński was an outsider: he spoke both Polish and Russian with a Lithuanian accent. GASPI 76, 4, 139: circular of October 29, 1920, when Leon Skrzędzienko, a schoolmate of Dzierżyński's, reported seeing him in disguise on the streets of Warsaw. The Red Army was approaching Białystok with a group of proposed ministers for a Soviet Polish republic including Dzierżyński. The *"dyktator czrezvyczajki"* is described as tall, thin, bald, about forty-five.
2. Feliks Dzierżyński, *Listy do siostry Aldony,* 1951, 155–6.
3. P. Filevskii, *Ocherki iz proshlogo Taganrogskoi gimnazii,* Taganrog: 1906.
4. She died in 1966 at the age of ninety-six.
5. It is typical of Feliks's punctiliousness that after Stanisław's murder he confiscated the family estate and assets for the Soviet government, sending Aldona just a few trinkets.
6. See Lev Korneshov, "Liubimaia zhenshchina Dzerzhinskogo," *Rossiiskaia gazeta,* February 17, 1994, 7.
7. She later became the protector of another romantic killer and died curator of the Lermontov museum in Piatigorsk.
8. Rosół was released in 1901 "just skin and bones" and died in Kaunas in 1902, his last words, Dzierżyński claimed, being, "Long live the Polish Social Democrat Workers' Union."
9. See Zofia Dzierżyńska, *Lata wielkich bojów,* Warsaw: 1969.
10. Ironically this prison would be death row for Stalin's political enemies—including the leader of the social revolutionaries, Mariia Spiridonova, and his own

brother-in-law Aliosha Svanidze—whose executions he put off until August 1941 when Beria had all 150 shot.

11. Lenin's secretary Fotieva recounted an episode in which Lenin asked Dzierżyński how many counterrevolutionaries he had under arrest. Dzierżyński passed him a slip of paper with the figure of 1,500. Lenin returned the paper, marking it with a cross to show that he had read it. Dzierżyński, Fotieva claims, interpreted the cross as a death sentence and had all 1,500 shot.

12. A plane crash in 1925 that killed Atarbekov and two other *chekisty* was greeted by many as divine vengeance even though the young and ambitious Georgian chekist Lavrenti Beria was suspected of sabotage.

13. Bruce-Lockhart found Dzierżyński much more intimidating: "his eyes deeply sunk, they blazed with a steady fire of fanaticism. They never twitched. His eyelids seemed to be paralyzed." For Bruce-Lockhart Stalin, who took part with Dzierżyński in these first Anglo-Soviet soundings, was beneath notice: "a strongly-built man with a sallow face, black mustache, heavy eyebrows and black hair worn *en brosse* . . . He did not seem of sufficient importance to include in my gallery of Bolshevik portraits."

14. Peterss never relented. In Russia Maisie became, against her father's wishes, a pupil of Isadora Duncan. In 1938 Peterss, like almost every adult Latvian in the party and the Cheka, was arrested as a fascist spy, tortured, and shot. His son became an NKVD informer. May Freeman died during the Second World War; Maisie, often hungry, found work at the British embassy, but despite contacting the British foreign minister, Ernest Bevin, and an affair with a military attaché, was arrested in 1949 by the KGB and sentenced to ten years in the camps for spying. She died in 1971, still hoping for an exit visa. See Valentin Shteinberg, "Svecha na vetru," *Zemlia* (Riga) January 5–February 2, 1993.

15. See Viktor Fradkin, *Delo Kol'tsova,* Moscow: 2002, 46.

16. Mārtiņš Lācis, *Chrezvychainaia komissiia po bor'be s Kontr-revoliutsiei,* Moscow: Gosiz, 1921.

17. Mārtiņš Lācis, "Dzierżyński i Cheka" in *F. Dzierżyński,* 1931.

18. The first attempt to look the ugly facts in the face without reverting to Russophile anti-Semitism was in the second volume of Solzhenitsyn's *Dvesti let vmeste (Russians and the Jews: Two Hundred Years Together),* Moscow: 2003. Inevitably, the facts feed anti-Semitic propaganda, but ignoring them is to do anti-Semites an even greater service.

19. In 1924 Dzierżyński wrote of Zionism to his deputies Menzhinsky and Iagoda: "We must assimilate only the most insignificant % of Jews, that's enough. The others must be Zionists. . . . Let's meet the Zionists halfway and try to give jobs not to them but to those who consider the USSR, not Palestine, their homeland." But in 1918 Zionists had their funds and archive confiscated; "right-wing" Zionists were arrested in 1920. The Politburo gave Stalin on May 6, 1920, the task of negotiating with Semion Dimanshtein, the Bolshevik commissar for Jewish affairs, to make Jews conform to Soviet nationalities policies.

20. His receipt is printed in V. I. Lenin, *Polnoe Sobranie Sochinenii,* vol. 51, Moscow, 1975.

21. *Krest'ianskoe dvizhenie v Povolzh'e,* Moscow, 2002, 707.

22. Ibid., 462.

23. Valerii Shambarov, *Gosudarstvo i revoliutsii,* 2001, 17.

24. *Chekisty* often took a reciprocal interest in the writing of poetry: when the Armenian poet Ovanes Tumanian died in 1923, a critique of his "creative and social worth" was published in Erevan under the pseudonym Martuni by Aleksandr Miasnikiants, who had, on behalf of the party and the Cheka, just slaughtered Tumanian's closest friends.

25. There is an almost plausible theory that Lenin's shooting was an attempted coup d'etat by Sverdlov. Trotsky was at the front at Kazan, Stalin at Tsaritsyn, Zinoviev and Dzierżyński in Petrograd. Sverdlov took over the reins of power, gave

the order for Kaplan to be killed without a confession, let alone trial, and did all he could to dissuade Lenin from resuming work until late October. Hitherto healthy, Sverdlov died, apparently of flu, the following March, and his post (chairman of the Executive Committee) was given to Stalin and Lenin's puppet, Mikhail Kalinin.

Moscow's first crematorium was opened shortly afterward in the Donskoi monastery. Muscovites objected to firewood being used to burn the dead when the living were freezing for lack of fuel. The Cheka's victims had priority.

26. See Shambarov, 2001, 132. Bokii, after further killings in Turkestan, ran a commune at Kuchino, where his guests and underlings mixed with naked prostitutes and Bokii's daughters during orgies and mock executions.

27. See A. G. Latyshev, *Rassekrechennyi Lenin,* 1996, 57.

28. Dmitrii Volkogonov, *Trotskii I,* 1999, 295.

29. This was too liberal for Aleksandr Beloborodov, who had signed the order for the killing of the Tsar and his family and was now plenipotentiary for suppressing Cossack uprisings: "those who are captured are not to be tried: they are to suffer mass reprisals." See *Bol'shevistskoe rukovodstvo: perepiska 1912–1927,* Moscow, 1996, 95.

30. Kedrov is unique among arrested chekists in that a trial actually acquitted him, in 1941. Beria had him shot nevertheless.

31. Only in Siberia—through migration, deportation, and isolation from fighting—did the population grow.

32. Zofia Dzierżyńska in her memoirs insists that Feliks loved children and that they were drawn to him. Dzierżyński sent his own son Jasiek to a summer camp run by the Cheka.

33. In February 1920 Dzierżyński acquired an even more devoted colleague, his secretary Vladimir (Veniamin) Gerson, who fussed over his health to the day he died. Gerson was later shot by Beria.

34. *Bol'shevistskoe rukovodstvo,* 53.

35. Ibid., 156.

36. *Izvestiia TsK KPSS,* 1989, 11, 174.

37. Feliks Dzierżyński, 1951, 155–6.

38. The irony is that Piłsudski grew up on an estate neighboring Dzierżyński's.

39. *Bol'shevistskoe rukovodstvo,* 156.

40. Latyshev, 1996, 282.

41. GASPI 558, 11, 816, 71, March 7, 1923.

42. Orjonikidze's fiery temperament, his drinking and womanizing, and his readiness to use his fists had annoyed Lenin before.

43. Kamenev had a dacha at Zubalovo. In autumn 1922, once he had constructed a branch line and gotten a neighboring collective farm to provide food, Stalin persuaded Lenin to stay there too.

44. His first break for three years, from suppressing "bandits" and anarchists in the Ukraine, was a course of hydrotherapy in summer 1921 in Kharkov at Lenin's insistence.

45. Lakoba archive, now in Hoover Institute.

46. Ibid.

47. V. I. Lenin, *Neizvestnye dokumenty,* 2000, 439.

48. When, in March 1922, Kamenev's and Stalin's mental states worried Lenin and Dzierżyński was told to find them a dacha for restful weekends, Stalin voted the proposal down.

49. GASPI 558, 11, 816, 75.

50. GASPI 558, 11, 816, 177.

51. See V. Iu. Cherniaev (ed.), *Piterskie rabochie i "diktatura proletariata"—Oktiabr' 1917–29,* 2000, 193.

52. A. Ia. Livshin et al. (eds.) *Pis'ma vo vlast' 1917–1927,* 1998, 463–8.

53. Lenin, 2000, 487.

54. *Bol'shevistskoe rukovodstvo,* 277.
55. Ibid., 278.
56. Ibid., 311.
57. GASPI 76, 3, 231, 2. Only in despair did Dzierżyński confess to Kamenev that the only way to revive the rural economy would be to restore the dispossessed landowners.
58. GASPI 76, 3, 237, 21. Telegram from Belenky to Gerson, November 7, 1922.
59. GASPI 76, 4, 30, 8.
60. GASPI 482, 1, 46, 9. Quoted by Nekrasov, 1995, 62.

TIIREE · The Exquisite Inquisitor

1. A typed copy of Menzhinsky's dissertation is in OR 384, 25, 60.
2. His son, Rudolf, was killed in the First World War. Not until the late 1920s did Menzhinsky, then a sick man, remarry. His second wife was Alla Semionovna, by whom he had a son, another Rudolf (who died in 1951), in 1927.
3. Menzhinsky's unpublished prose was lost in Paris; some lies in the FSB archives.
4. Menzhinsky, like Dzierżyński, visited Gorky on Capri and, like Iagoda, forged a lifelong link with him.
5. Blok had asthma, scurvy, and paranoia; Sologub's wife was going mad and doctors in Germany or Finland were their last hope.
6. Under arrest the previous year, Blok had told a fellow writer that the Bolsheviks "will kill us all and everything else."
7. Agranov, not yet thirty, was a frustrated poet. He eventually became a boon companion of Mayakovsky and mixed with Pilniak and Mandelstam. In 1921 he could break into intellectual circles only with a revolver.
8. See *Zven'ia I,* 1991, 470.
9. It also decreed death for any deportee who returned without permission.
10. G. Latyshev, *Rassekrechennyi Lenin,* Moscow: 1996, 202.
11. GASPI 2, 2, 1338. See Latyshev, 1996, 263–4.
12. Latyshev, 1996, 216–17.
13. See M. V. Zelenov, *Apparat CK RKP (b) VKP (b): Tsenzura i istoricheskaia nauka v 1920-e gody,* Nizhni Novgorod, 2000.
14. Surta became a neuropathologist and rose to become commissar for health in Belorussia. He was shot in 1937.
15. A. Krivova, *Vlast' i tserkov' v 1922–1925 gg.,* Moscow: 1997, 128.
16. N. Pokrovskii and S. G. Petrov, *Politburo i tserkov' 1922–1925 gg.,* Moscow, 1997, I, 9.
17. Ibid., I, 141–2.
18. Ibid., I, 232–8.
19. The Bashkir cavalry fought against the Bolsheviks. On February 17, 1920, Lenin and Dzierżyński ordered all Bashkir leaders to be arrested and the rebellion in the area to be "liquidated with the harshest measures." (Politburo session, GASPI 17, 3, 62, 1).
20. Zinoviev was called Grisha, not always affectionately and not only by Stalin. He reminded his colleagues of Grigori Rasputin and Grisha Otrepiev, the seventeenth-century pretender who claimed to be a son of Ivan the Terrible.
21. GASPI 558, 11, 753.
22. The GPU's statistics are mendacious: in the Solovetsky islands concentration camps alone some 700 prisoners were shot in 1923.
23. *Bol'shevistskoe rukovodstvo,* 297–8.
24. Ibid.
25. Ibid., 298.
26. Ibid., 305. Letter to Mekhlis, editor of *Pravda,* before May 1, 1925.
27. Balitsky's contribution to Soviet security was marked by Vladimir Putin with a commemorative postage stamp in 2002.

28. GASPI 558, 11, 701, 37.
29. Stalin reported to Rykov: "Grisha was saying, 'Everything here is getting worse, collapse is inevitable, etc.' Bukharin gave him an exemplary thrashing. . . . Grisha got a reasonable reception at first, then people began interrupting and booing him. Bukharin was received very well, had an ovation, etc. There were about 2,000 present. I'm told there were about 30–40 on the side of the opposition." GASPI 558, 11, 131, 73: May 10, 1927.
30. Trotsky's energies were dissipated by minor posts: one of his jobs was exporting Russian furs to Germany, where the proceeds were used to fund the Berlin Institute for Psychiatry, in which he had an interest.
31. *Bol'shevistskoe rukovodstvo,* 309–12.
32. GASPI 558, 11, 131, 14 et seq.
33. GASPI 76, 3, 245, 19 & 26.
34. GASPI 2, 2, 380 & 447.
35. When Dzhunkovsky, as head of Moscow's gendarmerie, denounced Rasputin's orgies, he was immediately dismissed on the Tsaritsa's orders.
36. While Menzhinsky was alive, Dzhunkovsky was protected. He was shot in 1937.
37. GASPI 558, 11, 726, 38. Letter to Kamenev, Dzierżyński, Kalinin, August 9, 1924.
38. Leonid Mlechin, *KGB: predsedateli organov bezopasnosti,* Moscow: 2001, 364. Much of Mlechin's account relies on Khrushchiov's uncorroborated memoirs.
39. See Andrew Cook, *On His Majesty's Secret Service—Sidney Reilly,* London: 2002.
40. GASPI 558, 11, 71: June 22, 1926.

FOUR • Stalin Solo

1. See Mikhail Reiman, *"Dokumenty kanuna stalinshchiny"* in *Sintaksis 13,* Paris, 1985, 132–62.
2. *Pis'ma vo vlast' 1917–1927,* Moscow, 1998, 401.
3. Article 107 of the legal code.
4. *Tragediia sovetskoi derevni I,* 1999, 159.
5. Ibid., 212.
6. V. Kvashonkin et al., *Sovetskoe rukovodstvo: perepiska 1928–1941,* Moscow: ROSSPÈN, 1999, 78–9.
7. Vadim Rogovin, *Vlast' i oppozitsiia,* Moscow: 1993, 45.
8. Bazhanov in his *Memoirs* says that a Czech communist who specialized in automatic telephone exchanges was instructed by Stalin to install a system giving Stalin access to all calls made in the Kremlin, and that Stalin then told Iagoda to kill the Czech engineer. A special monitoring telephone certainly existed, but there are no records of any missing Czech telephone engineer.
9. Ibid., 48–54.
10. See Rogovin, 1993, 166–7.
11. Chess was for the Soviet Union an avenue for international contacts. Krylenko declared in 1932, "We must once and for all condemn the formula 'chess for chess's sake,' like the formula 'art for art's sake.' We must organize shock-tactics brigades of chess players and immediately start carrying out a five-year plan for chess."
12. *Kak lomali NÈP,* Moscow: 2000, I, 412.
13. *Pis'ma I. V. Stalina V. M. Molotovu 1925–1936,* Moscow, 1995, 178–81.
14. Part of the evidence against Chaianov was a science fiction novel set in 1984, *My Brother Aleksei's Journey to the Land of Peasant Utopia,* published in 1920.
15. Rogovin, 1993, 198.
16. Ramzin later received the Stalin Order and all his life referred fondly to the "Boss" despite admitting that he had been framed by the Lubianka.

17. *Pis'ma I. V. Stalina V. M. Molotovu 1925–1936 gg.,* Moscow, 1995, 187–8.
18. Demian Bedny wrote for Stalin's delectation a satire, "From the *History of Russia* by Karamzin to Ramzin."
19. Diary of S. A. Piontkovsky, quoted in *Menshevistskii protsess 1931 goda,* Moscow, 1999, 13.
20. Stalin doubtless found Frunze's death convenient, but it is unproven that he ordered an overdose of anesthetic. Dzierżyński had in 1923 requisitioned all the chloroform he could find; much was unfit for anesthesia and patients died.
21. Chertkov's letters to Dzierżyński and Stalin: OR 369, 363, 15 & 22; 369, 364, 2.
22. *Vlast' i intelligentsia,* Moscow: 1999, 86–101.
23. V. Dmitriev, *Sotsiologiia politicheskogo iumora,* Moscow, 1998, 63.
24. Stanislav Kuniaev and Sergei Kuniaev, 1995, 230–31.
25. Stalin, however, found Pavlov hard to stomach: on September 26, 1934, on the eve of Pavlov's eighty-fifth birthday, he reminded Molotov and Kaganovich: "Pavlov is not one of us. . . . He should not be given honors, even if he wanted to have them."
26. Nicholas II found Platonov "dry and undoubtedly unsympathetic to the cult of Russian heroes."
27. It is significant that Platonov's interrogator, Sergei Zhupakhin, a former draftsman and railway engineer, was in 1938 removed from the NKVD and shot for excessive brutality: Zhupakhin had his juniors carry out executions with an ax.
28. Annenkov had given up fighting and become a horse breeder. He was forced to say that he had returned voluntarily to the USSR; he and the general were shot in 1927.
29. Radek never fully renounced Trotsky. When Klim Voroshilov called him Trotsky's stooge ("tail" in Russian) he replied with an epigram: "O Klim, your head's an empty space! / Your thoughts are in a mess. / Better to be the Leo's tail / Than Stalin's prick."
30. *Tragediia sovetskoi derevni I,* Moscow: 1999, 491.
31. A. I. Kokurin and N. V. Petrov (eds.), *GULAG 1918–1960,* Moscow, 2000, 62.
32. Figures from Iu. A. Poliakov, *Naselenie Rossii v XX veke,* Moscow: ROSSPĖN, 2000, I, 316.
33. A. G. Tepliakov, *Personal i povsednevnost' novosibirskogo UNKVD v 1936–1946, Minuvshee 21,* Moscow/St. Petersburg: 1997, 245–6.
34. *Tragediia sovetskoi derevni II,* 2000, 103–04.
35. Ibid., 145.
36. A. K. Sokolov (ed.), *Golos naroda 1918–1932,* Moscow: 1998, 293.
37. *Tragediia sovetskoi derevni II,* Moscow: 2000, 787.
38. Over 200,000 escaped of which a fifth were recaptured: another 80,000 got away by marrying a "free" local citizen, entering an institute of higher education, or by proving themselves invalids.
39. GASPI 667, 1, 16, 8–9.
40. *Stalin i Kaganovich: perepiska 1931–1936 gg.,* Moscow, 2001, 239.
41. *Tragediia sovetskoi derevni III,* 2001, 549.
42. Ibid., 577.
43. As for private property, Stalin wanted it protected only when a peasant stole it from a senior Bolshevik. In 1932 an army officer, Ivan Korneev, shot dead a youth he caught stealing apples from his orchard and a military tribunal sentenced Korneev to six years in prison. Stalin insisted Korneev be freed: "he had a right to shoot at hooligans who had broken in at night. It is bad and ugly for the organs of authority to defend hooligans against a decent dedicated officer." See *Stalin i Kaganovich,* 2001, 279–81.
44. Not until 1938 did the death rate for deported families drop below the birthrate.
45. *Tragediia sovetskoi derevni III,* 649.
46. Ibid., 664.
47. Ibid., 774.

48. Even in 1990 the horrors of 1932 and 1933 were deemed unfit for publication: the writer Aleksei Markov, who had lived through the famine as a child, found it impossible to print his verse memoirs. He recalled his father sending him out of the house before blocking the chimney and suffocating the fourteen remaining members of the family; he saw Young Communists striding over emaciated corpses on their way to their special canteen.
49. *Tragediia sovetskoi derevni III,* 644–5.
50. Ibid., 720.
51. *Stalin i Kaganovich,* 2001, 277.
52. Ibid., 274.

FIVE • Iagoda's Rise

1. Gorky's diary was seized after his death and remains secret. This passage was reported by one of the NKVD officers who took possession of it and is in Gorky's style. See Vadim Baranov, *Gor'kii, bez grima: Taina smerti,* 2001.
2. Stalin's office was issued 6,000 cigarettes a month, while Kaganovich had 500; rations were issued to staff who worked after 11 p.m. See *Stalinskoe politburo v 1930-e gody,* Moscow: 1995, 28–9.
3. Only one commissariat, foreign affairs, needed a less thuggish face, acceptable to the West. Stalin put up with Georgi Chicherin, a refined polyglot and long-standing friend of Menzhinsky and of decadent poets, an alcoholic and a notorious homosexual (thus perpetuating the traditions of the Tsars' Foreign Ministry, which was under Baron Lamsdorf called "a male brothel"). As diabetes and multiple sclerosis disabled Chicherin, he handed over to Litvinov, whose English wife and Anglophilia grated on Stalin.
4. It was small comfort that in his childhood a chunk had been torn out by a dog.
5. See the apologia recorded from Molotov's lips by Feliks Chuev, in *Molotov: poluderzhavnyi vlastelin,* Moscow, 2002. Chuev rarely put a pointed question to Molotov, who admitted even more rarely his supererogatory brutality.
6. Iagoda registered himself as Jewish, and stressed his name the Polish-Jewish way Iagóda (Jehuda) not the Russian way, which Stalin preferred to tease him with: Iágoda (berry).
7. The facts about Iagoda's early life are to be found in Mikhail Il'inskii, *Narkom Iagoda,* 2002.
8. Ibid., 62.
9. Iagoda told Stalin he had refused exit visas to three delegates to the Hague conference in June 1922 because they had counterrevolutionary records.
10. See Robert Urch, *The Rabbit King of Russia,* London, 1939.
11. See A. N. Pirozhkova and N. N. Iurgeneva, *Vospominaniia o Babele,* Moscow: 1989, 271, and *Minuvshee* 10, Moscow, 1992, 70.
12. Il'inskii, 2002, 13–17.
13. It was only mildly embarrassing that the doyen of Soviet realism was living in fascist Italy, for relations between Mussolini and Stalin were amicable.
14. Stalin had no illusions about Gorky's genius. On the last page of the juvenile poem "The Maiden and Death" Stalin scrawled, "This thing is more powerful than Goethe's *Faust.*" In 1951, the editors reproduced this page with Stalin's inscription in Gorky's *Collected Verse,* unaware that Stalin made the remark in drunken mockery. In Stalin's copy of *Collected Verse* the facsimile is angrily crossed out in red pencil.
15. In the end, Stalin canceled Gorky's commission to write his biography. Gorky's American publisher had advertised it as containing revelations in which Stalin would say what he thought about Lenin and Trotsky.
16. *Novyi mir,* 1997, 9, 168–92.
17. O. V. Khlevniuk, *Politburo,* 1996, 98–9.

18. Zinovi Peshkov continued to rebel against his family by joining the French Foreign Legion. By 1927 he was a general attached to the Kuomintang, killing communists in Shanghai, a fact which did not stop his nephew Andrei Sverdlov becoming one of the NKVD's most brutal interrogators.
19. Il'inskii, 2002, 364.
20. The next canal project Iagoda supervised, the Moscow–Volga canal, was designed by free engineers, and the slaves were backed up by proper materials and machinery.
21. Like the GULAG men and Iagoda who built the canal, those who celebrated it mostly perished as counterrevolutionaries. The book on the canal was three years later to be withdrawn from the market and from libraries. See the facsimile edition of *The Stalin White Sea–Baltic Canal,* Moscow: 1998.
22. *Stalin i Kaganovich,* 2001, 224.
23. Two such encounters in autumn 1932 were documented by Korneli Zelinsky. See *Voprosy literatury,* 1990, 1 and *Minuvshee* 10, 1992, 88–120.
24. Viktor Shklovsky's memoir in Benedikt Sarnov, *Nash sovetskii novoiaz,* Moscow, 2002, 28.
25. See Vadim Baranov, *Bezzakonnaia kometa,* Moscow: 2001, 164–5.
26. See *Minuvshee* 10, 1992, 65–88; also G. S. Smith, *Dmitri Sviatopolk-Mirsky,* Cambridge, 2000.
27. Bulgakov, Gorky told Stalin, was "no kith or kin to me, but a talented writer . . . There is no sense making martyrs for an idea out of [such people]. An enemy must be either annihilated or re-educated. In this case I vote for re-education." Gorky advised Stalin to meet Bulgakov personally. (*Novy mir,* 1997, 9, 188–9).
28. Both Gorky and Stalin liked Dostoevsky's *Devils,* with its bloodthirsty, paranoiac, and treacherous revolutionaries: in 1935, *The Devils* came out in a magnificent edition.
29. *Stalin i Kaganovich,* 2001, 436–7.
30. *Vlast' i khudozhestvennaia intelligentsiia,* Moscow, 1999, 227–8. It is conceivable that OGPU fabricated the document just to see who would fail to report it or even dare to circulate it.
31. Extracts from the Gorky–Iagoda correspondence are to be found in Il'inskii, 2002, 361–82.
32. See Aleksandr Afinogenov's diary, quoted in Vadim Baranov, *Bezzakonnaia kometa,* Moscow, 2001, 148.
33. For a full consideration of the evidence that Stalin wanted, and had, Gorky (and other writers) killed, see Vadim Baranov, *Gor'kii bez grima: taina smerti,* Moscow: Agraf, 2001.
34. The "Gorky of the Balkans," the Romanian Panait Istrati, unable to stomach show trials, collectivization, or purges, "turned Trotskyist." In the Soviet Union, Istrati "saw the broken eggs but couldn't see the omelette." He died unexpectedly in Bucharest in 1935. Barbusse, apparently in fine health, died in Moscow in August 1935 after his hagiography of Stalin appeared. "That teaches us to be careful," Rolland wrote to Gorky. Eugène Dabit, a healthy young proletarian accompanying André Gide (and sharing his disquiet) on a tour of the USSR, died, poisoned, at the age of thirty-eight in a Sevastopol hotel in July 1936.
35. Quoted from Roi Medvedev, "Pisateli Evropy na priiome u Stalina," *Moskovskie novosti,* 2002, 28, 17.
36. H. G. Wells, *Experiment in Autobiography,* 1934. The interview took place on July 23, 1934.
37. Terentiev was so intrigued by his interrogators' fantasies that he helped them make the charges even more ludicrous. See *Minuvshee* 18, Moscow, 1995, 533–608.
38. Kuniaev and Kuniaev, 1995, 82.

39. For a full account, based on surviving records in St. Petersburg, see A. V. Blium, *Sovetskaia tsenzura v èpokhu total'nogo terrora 1929–1953,* St. Petersburg, 2000.
40. In 1800 Tsar Paul had forbidden naming cats or goats Masha, to prevent lèse-majesté against the Tsaritsa Mariia Fiodorovna.
41. Khlevniuk, 1996, 36.
42. *Voennye arkhivy Rossii,* 1993, I, 103; Khlevniuk, 1996, 36.
43. A. Afanasiev (ed.) *Oni ne molchali,* Moscow, 1991, 136.
44. See B. A. Starkov, "Pravo-levye fraktsionery" in A. Afanasiev (ed.) *Oni ne molchali,* Moscow: 1991, 125–44; also O. V. Khlevniuk, 1993, 21–9.
45. Lominadze, according to Avdeev's memoir, said the meeting took place just before dawn, and that he was alone with Stalin. See Afanasiev, 1991, 136–7.
46. Afanasiev, 1991, 139.
47. This blew up in OGPU's face, for it was widely rumored that Riutin's Platform had been fabricated by Menzhinsky.
48. From there he continued the struggle in letters to his children. Five years later Riutin was required to incriminate himself and his associates as terrorists. He went on hunger strike and attempted suicide, but this time resisted torture. He was shot on January 10, 1937.
49. Two days before, at a Red Square parade, Nadezhda had marched with other students at her academy and joined party leaders on the tribune. She told Nikita Khrushchiov (a fellow student) she was worried that Stalin was standing in the cold with his coat unbuttoned.
50. Iu. G. Murin, *Iosif Stalin v ob"iatiiakh sem'i,* Moscow, 1993, 29–42.
51. L. Vasil'eva in *Kremliovskie zhiony,* Moscow: 1995, 170, cites hearsay that Nadezhda was driven to despair when she came to believe that Stalin had slept with her mother and was perhaps her father. See also Eremei Parnov, *Skelety v seife,* Moscow, 2000, I, 65–104.
52. The matter could be settled by exhuming the body. Dr. Vladimir Rozanov twice operated on famous revolutionaries who died on the operating table: Nogin in 1924, Frunze in 1925. He removed Stalin's appendix in 1921.
53. Parnov, *Skelety v seife I,* 2000, 97.
54. Feliks Chuev, *Tak govoril Kaganovich,* Moscow, 1992, 154.
55. Probably 1932. See A. Kirilina, *Neizvestnyi Kirov,* St. Petersburg, 2001, 341.
56. Beria and Molotov ensured that Menzhinsky's widow kept her three-room dacha and received special rations, while his sickly young son, Rudolf, his first wife, Iulia Ivanovna (thought by Beria to be his mother), his surviving sister, and his nephew and niece were all on the NKVD's payroll. See GARF 9401, 2, 105 and 206; T. Gladkov et al., *Menzhinskii,* Moscow, 1969, 340–43.

SIX • Murdering the Old Guard

1. Compare Bernard Gui, *Procedures of the Office of the Inquisition for Trying Heretics, c.* 1310, which also dispenses with lawyers, witnesses, and appeals. Stalin and Molotov had in September 1934 authorized Robert Eikhe, the satrap of western Siberia, to set up troikas that sentenced victims to death without formalities, but only for the six weeks of grain procurement.
2. The testimony of some NKVD men including the defector Orlov, Iagoda's ambiguous remarks at his trial in 1938, Trotsky's speculations, and Nikita Khrushchiov's accusations in his destalinization speech in 1956 have persuaded many historians that, on Stalin's orders, Nikolaev was manipulated by Iagoda's men into killing Kirov.
3. The best-documented account of Kirov's murder is Kirilina, 2001.
4. Orjonikidze, as close to Kirov as either was to Stalin but a person who might not have agreed to falsification, was told not to come to Leningrad: Stalin claimed it might be "bad for his heart." See Rogovin, 1994, 83.

5. The suspicious death of the sole eyewitness to Kirov's murder has further fueled conspiracy theories, but the condition of the truck and the shocked reactions of the driver and guard are well attested.

6. *Stalin i Kaganovich,* 2001, 411–12, 425.

7. Ibid., 419.

8. V. V. Sapov (ed.), *Makiavelli: pro i contra,* St. Petersburg: 2002, 502–06.

9. The only justifiable arrests and trials—apart from Nikolaev's—were of the NKVD men answerable for Kirov's safety. Filipp Medved was arrested, on December 7 his deputy and likely successor, Ivan Zaporozhets, was detained, although he had been nursing a broken leg in the Caucasus at the time of the murder and had not worked since summer. Eleven *chekisty* were convicted of "criminal neglect of duty." For the time being, they served short spells of imprisonment. Medved and Ivan Zaporozhets were sent to the farthest part of the USSR, Kolyma. Here, the GULAG chief Jan Berzin treated them as colleagues; they were joined by their wives and children and began redeeming themselves by hard work. They were shot only when Berzin fell from grace.

10. Vadim Rogovin, *Stalinskii nèonèp,* 1994, 89.

11. Enukidze had been a confidant of Stalin's second wife and the second person, after the nanny, to find her dead body. He got on well enough with Stalin to intercede for petitioners. He was notorious for womanizing and for his aristocratic lifestyle.

12. The diary, with Stalin's and Iagoda's annotations, is in GASPI 558, 11, 69. Extracts in B. V. Sokolov, *Narkomy strakha,* Moscow, 2001, 24–37.

13. When in October 1934 a Soviet sailor jumped ship in Poland, Stalin rounded on Iagoda: "Tell me without delay: have the members of this sailor's family been arrested . . . If not, then who is responsible for the inertia of the authorities, and has this new criminal been punished?" GASPI 558, 11, 69. The sailor turned out to have no relatives to punish.

14. Akulov, his friends recalled, loved life, nature, music, family, and friends, and was unfitted for judicial killing: He fell seriously ill in 1936. Akulov's successor, Andrei Vyshinsky, and his former deputy, Grigori Roginsky, both sent their best wishes. A year later, under torture, Akulov confessed he was a Trotskyist. On October 31, 1937, as he was led out to be shot, Akulov turned to Roginsky, now his prosecutor, and said, "You know I'm not guilty." Roginsky responded with virulent abuse. See A. G. Zviagintsev and Iu. G. Orlov, *Raspiatye revoliutsiei: rossiiskie i sovetskie prokurory 1922–1936,* Moscow, 1998, 256.

15. See Il'inskii, 2002, 241.

16. Hitler had them arrested, so Stalin detained several German citizens. Molotov and Kaganovich reported to Stalin on October 21, 1933, that "Hitler has personally given an order to allow our journalists . . . to the trial. He expressed his certainty that our journalists will be objective. . . . The person responsible for arresting them will be punished."

17. *Stalin i Kaganovich,* 397–8.

18. Mikhail Geller and Aleksandr Nekrich, *Utopiia u vlasti,* Moscow: 2000, 270.

19. *Stalin i Kaganovich,* 569–70.

20. Valerii Shambarov, *Gosudarstvo i revoliutsii,* Moscow: 2001, 301.

21. Fascism was no bar to cooperation. In the 1920s the USSR bought minesweepers from Mussolini to rebuild its navy, which had been shrunk badly when the Whites used the Russian Black Sea fleet to evacuate their soldiers to Istanbul.

22. To avoid publicity, handcuffs and rubber truncheons were bought from Germany via third countries.

23. GASPI 558, 11, 85, 26.

24. Sergei Gorlov, *Alians Moskva–Berlin 1920–1933,* Moscow, 2001, 315.

25. In 1934, the Commissariat for Foreign Affairs was the only Soviet ministry allowed two differing opinions. While Commissar Litvinov opted for joining France and Britain against Germany, the ambassador to Berlin, Surits, friendly with Hermann Goering's cousin Herbert, shared Kandelaki's Germanophilia.

26. Dmitrii Volkogonov, *Stalin triumf i tragedia,* 1990, I, 209.
27. Despite Krupskaia's demoralized compliance, Stalin laid into her for encouraging Marinetta Shaginian to write a biography of Lenin revealing that his maternal grandfather was a Jew. The biography was banned.
28. Krupskaia's death in 1939, immediately after tasting a birthday cake sent from the Kremlin, may not have been of natural causes.
29. In 1951 she submitted her diary pages for 1934, wherever Stalin was mentioned, for Stalin's approval. See GASPI 558, 11, 750.
30. GASPI 558, 11, 749, 14, February 3, 1935.
31. GASPI 558, 11, 749, 21, October 10, 1936.
32. Arkadii Vaksberg, *Valkiriia revoliutsii,* Smolensk, 1998, 393.
33. Iurii Druzhnikov, *Russkie mify: Donoschik 001 ili Voznesenie Pavlika Morozova,* Ekaterinburg: 2001.
34. Kartashov virtually confessed to Druzhnikov in the 1960s.
35. GASPI 558, 11, 727, 38–57.
36. Stalin added his comments to Ezhov's text, but the treatise was never published.
37. *Stalin i Kaganovich,* 613–15.
38. Il'inskii, 2002, 236.
39. See V. A. Kovaliov, *Raspiatie dukhom,* Moscow, 1996, 151.
40. A. Orlov, *Tainaia istoriia stalinskikh prestuplenii,* 1953, 133.
41. *Stalin i Kaganovich,* 627.
42. I. Gorelov, *Tsugtzvang Mikhaila Tomskogo,* 2000, 233–4.
43. L. Mlechin, *Ministry inostrannykh del* 2001, 128.
44. Pauker had arrested both Kamenev and Zinoviev on Iagoda's warrant. He ran the NKVD charity The Children's Friend as well as managing the Dinamo soccer team of which Iagoda was patron. Pauker did not outlive Iagoda; he was shot in August 1937.
45. Told to Sidney Hook; see *New Leader,* October 10, 1960, 22–3.
46. *Stalin i Kaganovich,* 665.
47. *Voprosy istorii,* 1995, 1, 8.
48. Khlevniuk, 1996, 203–04.
49. GASPI 17, 2, 575, 1–143; see also *Voprosy istorii* Moscow, 1995, 1.
50. Extracts from Iagoda's statements are to be found in Il'inskii, 2002, 150–54, and Sokolov, 2001, 764–6.
51. Il'inskii, 2002, 404–11.
52. Sokolov, 2001, 76–8.
53. Il'inskii, 2002, 448–9.

SEVEN • The Ezhov Bloodbath

1. But in prerevolution Russia eleven-year-old boys were not employed in major factories, and youths went into the army after their twentieth birthday.
2. An émigré recalled a St. Petersburg concierge's son called Ezhov who tormented cats and bullied smaller children.
3. One of his sponsors was a certain Shifris; like nearly everyone who had recommended Ezhov, he was shot in 1938.
4. Petrov would be charged in 1935 with "hindering Ezhov from carrying out Leninist-Stalinist policies," and on May 10, 1938, after appealing to Ezhov for mercy, he was shot. A small Mari town was named Ezhov.
5. Five years later, Ezhov, at Stalin's behest, took great trouble to have Mayakovsky's works published in an exemplary edition.
6. *Stalin i Kaganovich,* 244.
7. Ibid., 432.
8. Ibid., 572.

9. These talks were minuted by Lakoba and the minutes kept in the Lakoba museum in Sukhum, which was destroyed totally by the Georgian "army" in 1992.
10. Lakoba archive: Stalin to Lakoba and Meladze, October 19, 1929.
11. He begged Lakoba to help a GPU man who'd gone too far: "Do what you have to for his rehabilitation, everything he is charged with is rubbish, he would never have done that and he won't, and if he did do it, it was in the interests of the cause."
12. In 1937 Beria shot Mikhail Lakoba dead in Sukhum NKVD headquarters.
13. There is ironic justice in Lakoba's fate. In 1822 his ancestor Urus Lakoba had poisoned at dinner a Georgian vassal, the hereditary prince of Abkhazia.
14. Trilisser was moved to the Comintern and given the surname Moskvin.
15. See N. V. Petrov and K. V. Skorkin, *Kto rukovodil NKVD 1934–1941*, Moscow: 1999, 492–500.
16. Stalin's authorization of torture was at this point given by encrypted telegram; in 1939 it was stated openly, as a measure to be used against "enemies who refuse to disarm."
17. See A. G. Tepliakov, "Personal i povsednevnost" novosibirskogo NKVD . . ." in *Minuvshee*, Moscow/St. Petersburg, 1997, 240–95.
18. A. A. Papchinskii and M. A. Tumshis, *Shchit, raskolotyi mechom: NKVD protiv VChK*, Moscow, 2001, 188.
19. These figures omit people rounded up and shot in outlying regions without notifying the center.
20. A. Ia. Razumov (ed.) *Leningradskii martirolog*, vols. 1–4 (more to appear), St. Petersburg, 1995–9.
21. *Butovskii poligon 1937–1938 gg.*, Moscow, 1999, III, 344.
22. Il'inskii, 2002, 256–7.
23. Ibid., 258.
24. Bukharin's letters to Stalin are in GASPI 558, 11, 710, 3–184. See also Bukharin's letters in *Istoricheskii arkhiv*, 1999, 1, 48–78.
25. The proceedings are summarized in V. Rogovin, *1937*, Moscow, 1996, 201–11.
26. The 1,000 pages of political history, fiction, and poetry, as well as desperate letters to Stalin, that Bukharin composed in prison all ended up in Stalin's personal archive.
27. See N. I. Bukharin, *Tiuremnye tetradi*, Moscow, 1994; *Istochnik*, Moscow, 1993, 1, 23–5; V. Rogovin, *Partiia rasstreliannykh*, Moscow, 1997, 40–42.
28. Romain Rolland tried once more. In August 1937 he begged Stalin to spare Aleksandr Arosev, formerly Soviet ambassador to Lithuania and one of Molotov's closest friends. Arosev was shot a few months later.
29. Enukidze was notorious as a womanizer with a penchant, like Stalin, for pubescent girls; as an old friend of Stalin, he knew far too much to be trusted with a public appearance.
30. GASPI 558, 3, 231, 302.
31. Orjonikidze's brother was arrested on capital charges and his widow, Zinaida, spent many years in psychiatric wards; her only influential friend was Dzierżyński's widow. She insisted that the NKVD had killed her husband. Officially, he died of a heart attack and towns and railways were named after him; Stalin would not, however, let statues be put up to him.
32. Voroshilov had a collection of silk embroidery given to him by the wives of his commanders. The collection was destroyed along with all Voroshilov's possessions in 1953, when his grandson set fire to a Christmas tree and the Voroshilov dacha burned down.
33. This theory was not touched on when Red Army commanders were interrogated in 1937. In 1945 German officers, questioned by Soviet intelligence, said that they had recruited nobody but one NKVD disinformation officer.
34. Budionny proved his loyalty in summer 1937 by taking his second wife, the opera contralto Olga Mikhailova, in his own car to imprisonment in the Lubianka; she

had refused to bear him children and was friendly to foreigners. Budionny then married his housekeeper. When after Tukhachevsky's execution arrests continued, Voroshilov is said to have calmed Budionny's nerves by saying that Stalin was liquidating "only the clever marshals."

35. Feldman's interrogator, Zinovi Ushakov, was not normally so humane; he was shot a year later.
36. On the contradictory behavior of Voroshilov, see Vadim Rogovin, 1997, 160–69.
37. Kaminsky was doomed after a clash with Stalin, which began with Kaminsky's remark "If we go like this we'll shoot the whole party!" to which Stalin retorted, "You wouldn't by chance be friends of these enemies? . . . Well, then, you're birds of a feather."
38. Vladimir Osipovich Piatnitskii, *Zagovor protiv Stalina,* Moscow: 1998.
39. *Vlast' i intelligentsia,* 1999, 317.
40. Ibid., 348.
41. Ibid., 365–7.
42. Vitali Shentalinskii, *Raby svobody,* Moscow: 1995, 242–3.
43. *Vlast' i intelligentsia,* 365–7.
44. See Iurii Murin, *Pisatel' i vozhd',* Moscow: 1997 for the Sholokhov–Stalin correspondence.
45. See Marc Jansen and Nikita Petrov, *Stalin's Loyal Executioner: Ezhov,* Hoover, 2002.
46. For Russian diaries of the 1930s see Véronique Garros, Natalia Korenevskaya, and Thomas Lahusen, *Intimacy and Terror,* New York: 1995.
47. See B. I. Ilizarov, 2002, 284–6.
48. Stalin had Trotsky's other son, Sergei, killed in the USSR. Both Trotsky's daughters had died, one of suicide, the other of tuberculosis.
49. In 1956 Rodos was the last KGB man shot on Khrushchiov's orders for excessive cruelty.
50. Aleksei Polianskii, *Ezhov,* Moscow, 2001, 304–05.

EIGHT · The Rise of Lavrenti Beria

1. The Berias' first son died in infancy of smallpox and their daughter, Tamara, or Eteri, became deaf-mute after measles. There was no contact with two children from Marta's previous marriage. A cousin, Gerasime Beria, was to be an intelligence officer in the Soviet army which invaded Georgia in 1921.
2. The dossiers (some thirty volumes) of Beria's 1953 interrogation are locked in FSB archives. An unsuccessful attempt to steal them was made in 2003.
3. Anastas Mikoyan probably knew the truth, but he was the only Baku commissar to escape the bullets fired by Azeri nationalist police on British orders in 1918 that killed the other twenty-six, and Baku was a sore point for him. Beria's ally Mir-Jafar Bagirov led the Azeri party, and had likewise worked for the Musavat and therefore kept quiet.
4. At some point Beria also learned French. In the 1930s he impressed Svetlana Allilueva's teacher, Mlle. Lavranche, with his fluency (and his manners).
5. A. Antonov-Ovseenko, *Beria,* 1999, 31.
6. In 1932 Beria had Kaganovich halve grain requisitions from Georgia and divert trucks and buses from Moscow's depots to Tbilisi.
7. Beria got his closest aide, Bogdan Kobulov, to beat Mamia Orakhelashvili to death.
8. V. F. Nekrasov (ed.) *Beria: konets kar'ery,* Moscow, 1991, 354.
9. Lakoba archive, Hoover Institute.
10. Lakoba archive.
11. *Minuvshee 7,* Moscow, 1992, 472.
12. GASPI 558, 11, 722, 63.

13. Khanjian's body was wrapped in a bloodstained carpet and delivered to his hotel in the trunk of Beria's car. He was reported to have committed suicide.

14. Robakidze later won notoriety with his essays "Adolf Hitler, Seen by a Foreign Poet" and "Mussolini: Visions on Capri."

15. Galaktion, despite his Baudelairean poetics, was declared persona grata by Beria in 1935. He kept his distance from other poets and Russian sympathizers and feigned alcoholism. His notebooks include lines declaring himself "too tired to go near the writers' palace / Where Beria's wolves growl." Galaktion's wife was exiled to northern Russia and murdered in 1944. The very popular Grishashvili, now more bibliophile than poet, was indiscreet enough, even in 1937, to mock Lenin in verse.

16. For a full account, see D. Rayfield, "The Death of Paolo Iashvili," *Slavonic & East European Review* 68, London: October 1990, 631–64. For Georgian Union of Writers sessions see *fond* 8, *opis* 1, file 2 in the Georgian Central State Archive for Literature and Art. In 1991 Zviad Gamsakhurdia had some files destroyed.

17. The defiant Geronti Kikodze survived.

18. Under his real name, Janjghava, too difficult for Russians to articulate, he had supervised the draining of Georgia's marshes.

19. Kirill Stoliarov, *Igry v pravosudie,* Moscow, 2000, 289–90.

20. Shvartsman's sexual proclivities appealed to Beria. Shvartsman liked to make love with a female colleague in an office where they could hear tortured prisoners screaming. For details of Ezhov's hangmen whom Beria kept, see Arkadii Vaksberg, *Neraskrytye tainy,* Moscow, 1993, 107–54.

21. Its theme song "Fragrant flower of the prairie, Lavrenti Pavlovich Beria" never got past rehearsal.

22. Bulgakov had written to Stalin asking for Erdman to be forgiven. Erdman was, however, aghast at his new job: "Would you expect to have a Gestapo song and dance ensemble?" he exclaimed. Erdman's plays had to wait until the 1990s to be performed, but Beria saved him physically.

23. This story was filmed by Evgeni Tsymbal in *Zashchitnik Sedov* (1986).

24. See A. G. Zviagintsev and Iu. G. Orlov, *Prigovorennye vremenem: rossiiskie i sovetskie prokurory 1937–1953,* Moscow, 2001, 118–24.

25. Roginsky's legal and personal talents were best shown in his own defense. He resisted two years of interrogation by feigning madness and insisting on better prison conditions. Although he was moved to Sukhanovka, where Ezhov was broken, Roginsky confessed only to lesser crimes and delayed his trial until after war began. He forced the judges to spend not twenty minutes but two hours trying him. He escaped execution but died in the camps. See Zviagintsev and Orlov, 2001, 190–94.

26. See *Voenno istoricheskii arkhiv,* 1997, 107–14.

27. The details of these murders emerged in the interrogation of Beria's subordinates in 1953. See Stoliarov, 2000, 240–48. Kulik himself was shot in 1950.

28. Koltsov's brother Boris Efimov was *Pravda*'s cartoonist and compensated for his conformist ideology with grotesque draftmanship.

29. Stalin sent Babel and Pasternak, both mute with shock, to the congress's last session.

30. Vladimir Stavsky, general secretary of the writers' union, was a hated apparatchik; Fadeev's sanction carried more weight with the intelligentsia.

31. Antonov-Ovseenko, 1999, 251.

32. Eisenstein's tireless enemy Boris Shumiatsky, head of Soviet cinematography, once refused to drink a toast to Stalin; born in Buriat-Mongolia, he was shot as a Japanese agent. Eisenstein then became a favorite of Stalin's.

33. *Vlast' i intelligentsiia,* 1999, 456.

34. Text cited from GARF in *Izvestiia,* June 5, 2002, "Nauka" section, II.

35. In the early 1970s, Lysenko was interviewed by young Soviet geneticists. He suddenly screamed three times, "I didn't kill Vavilov!" In the 1990s the KGB pen-

sioner Aleksandr Khvat proudly told television cameras that he had done his duty by torturing Vavilov.

36. In 1950 it was Stalin himself, not Beria, or even Soviet linguists, who demolished Marrism.

37. Even the few hundred Eskimos on the Soviet side of the Bering Strait were now forbidden from canoeing across to visit their cousins in Alaska.

38. In northern Korea the Japanese deported Koreans as potential Soviet spies.

39. For this and other detailed reminiscences of the deportations, see Svetlana Alieva (ed.) *Tak èto bylo,* 3 vols., Moscow, 1993.

40. Certain categories, including 8,000 prostitutes, were sent to Kazakhstan.

41. These are the best attested figures, based on the NKVD's own unashamed documentation. Other estimates, extrapolated from lists of missing persons or from later censuses, are very much higher. See Pavel Polian, *Ne po svoei vole,* Moscow, 2001, 98–102.

42. The fullest collection of primary materials is in Polish: *Katyń. Dokumenty zbrodni,* 4 vols., Warsaw: 1998. The most important original Russian documents are in *Katyn': plenniki neob''iavlennoi voiny,* Moscow, 1999 and *Katyn': mart 1940 g.—sentiabr' 2000 g.,* Moscow, 2001.

43. It was ironic that Polish officers of the 1920 campaign were rewarded with landholdings in the newly acquired eastern provinces, which ensured that they would be captured by the Soviets in 1939.

44. This was convenient when the crime was later blamed on the Nazis, but Blokhin brought Walther revolvers simply because they did not jam in continuous use.

45. Andrei Artizov and Oleg Naumov (eds.) *Vlast' i khudozhestvennaia intelligentsia,* 1999, 445–6.

46. Naum Eitingon's brother Max dealt with Trotsky and made a fortune out of the Soviet fur trade, then managed by Trotsky. Max Eitingon spent his money subsidizing the Berlin Institute for Psychiatry, another of Trotsky's hobbies. See Aleksandr Ètkind, *Èros nevozmozhnogo,* St. Petersburg, 1993, 269–310.

47. Siqueiros escaped to Chile, helped by the poet Pablo Neruda; years later Siqueiros apologized for his crime. Grigulevich had Sheldon Harte shot dead.

48. The promise was broken in 1951: Eitingon and other Jewish MVD officers were arrested.

49. Artizov and Naumov, 1999, 451.

NINE • Hangmen at War

1. Sorge, under cover as a German businessman in Tokyo, was providing the German ambassador, as well as the NKVD, with information on Japanese intentions, and the NKVD with information on German intentions. His assurances that the Japanese would not attack the Soviet Union in the east were believed; his warnings that Hitler would attack in the west were disregarded.

2. Two months before the invasion, Golikov stopped assuring Stalin of the Germans' peaceful intentions: he noted troop movements toward the border, but desisted from comments that might irritate Stalin.

3. Merkulov often blundered: when the Americans retrieved from the Finns a half-burned book of Soviet codes, he failed to change the ciphers, and as a result, from 1944 all traffic between the NKVD and Soviet missions in the United States was intercepted. Merkulov also failed to assassinate General Vlasov when the latter organized a small army out of millions of Soviet POWs to fight alongside the Germans. By 1946 Merkulov had outlived his usefulness and Stalin attacked him for not pursuing Trotskyists during the war. Merciful or forgetful, Stalin allowed Merkulov life and liberty; he stayed in the Central Committee of the party and became responsible for Soviet property abroad.

4. If he was born in 1908, then he was a child when he joined Dzierżyński's special purpose units. His decrepit health at the end of his life, discounting the effects of torture, also suggests he was much older.
5. See Iakov Aizenshtat, *Zapiski sekretaria voennogo tribunala,* London: 1991.
6. Zemliachka, until her death in 1947, and her sister were among the very few persons whom Mekhlis could call friends.
7. In the skirmishes with the Japanese at Khasan, where Bliukher distinguished himself, Mekhlis countermanded Bliukher's orders. Bliukher said of Mekhlis and Ezhov's deputy Frinovsky, "Sharks have come to gobble me up; I don't know if they'll eat me or I them—the latter is unlikely."
8. Iu. Rubtsov, *Alter ègo Stalina,* Moscow, 1999, 226.
9. Ibid., 262.
10. See V. K. Abarinov, *Katynskii labirint,* Moscow: 1991.
11. The story is widespread but undocumented. The fullest documentation on this deportation is to be found in N. Bugai, *«Ikh nado deportirovat'»,* Moscow: 1992, 36–83; statistics are collated in Pavel Polian, *Ne po svoei vole,* Moscow: 2001, 102–10.
12. When the moment came, the military would denounce Beria for nearly losing them the Caucasus, but in November 1952, when Stalin, paranoiacally jealous, disliked public praise of Beria, General Ivan Maslennikov stuck his neck out by printing in *Military Thinking* a tribute to Beria's leadership on the Caucasian front. Maslennikov had helped Beria tame the military in 1939, instituted the dreaded blocking squads behind the front line, and had commanded an army in the Caucasus.
13. See Alieva, 1993, vol. 2, 42.
14. Gvishiani escaped punishment when Beria's men were arrested as he was the son-in-law of Aleksei Kosygin, future co-ruler with Brezhnev.
15. The German Foreign Ministry was sympathetic to the lobbying of the Turkish ambassador, Nuri Pasha, to establish an autonomous republic of Caucasian peoples and a free Tatar state in the Crimea, but the Germans nevertheless exterminated large numbers of Crimean Tatars, burning villages they suspected of sheltering partisans and sending thousands as forced labor to Germany. See Bugai, 1992, 151.
16. The most convincing demographic statistics are to be found in V. B. Zhiromskaia, *Naselenie Rossii v XX veke,* Moscow, 2001, vol. 2. They are nevertheless conservative, as they are based on extant documentation. It is likely that actual deaths were higher, but few demographers allow more than 10 percent for undocumented mortality.
17. In early 1942, 3,000 died of starvation every day in Leningrad; the NKVD killed another twenty or so daily for such crimes as wishing aloud for the Germans to enter the city and finish the siege. See Nikita Lomagin, *Neizvestnaia blokada,* Moscow: Olma, 2002.
18. Of a total of 3,486,206 prisoners taken by the Soviets on the western front, 2,388,443 were Germans; the other large contingents were Hungarians (half a million), Romanians and Austrians (each over 150,000). Statistics and information come from Stefan Karner, *Arkhipelag GUPVI,* Moscow/Vienna: 2002 (Russian version of 1995 German edition).
19. The NKVD allowed senior German officers better rations and freedom from work. In March 1943 General von Paulus even ordered winter shoes, socks, a sweater, and a new suitcase from the German military attaché in Ankara, the bill to be sent to his wife in Berlin. Ibid., 74.
20. The memoirs of Pavel Sudoplatov (*Spetsoperatsii: Lubianka i Kreml' 1930–1950 gody,* Moscow, 1997, 432–49) are mendacious, but his account of Wallenberg's fate is not contradicted by other evidence.
21. One can be sure that if a writer said anything dissident it would be reported, less sure that it would be reported accurately. See *Vlast' i intelligentsia* 487–99 and 522–33.

TEN • The Gratification of Cruelty

1. Iu. G. Murin, *Iosif Stalin v ob"iatiiakh sem'i,* Moscow, 1993, 95.
2. *Politburo CK VKP(b) i sovet ministrov SSSR 1945–1953,* Moscow: 2002, 195–200.
3. Ibid., 25–6.
4. Ibid., 205–06.
5. Malenkov had reason to fear worse; he knew that he had been named in Ezhov's confessions. In 1954 Malenkov got hold of Ezhov's statements and destroyed them.
6. The exception was the deputy minister of geology Academician Iosif Grigoriev, who was beaten to death in 1949 by Beria's henchman Shvartsman. See Arkadii Vaksberg, *Neraskrytye tainy,* Moscow, 1993, 112.
7. In 1947, however, the Politburo forbade the publication of *The Journal of Physics in the USSR* in Western languages on the grounds that this "makes the work of foreign intelligence much easier."
8. For reports of these proceedings see Artizov and Naumov (eds.) Moscow, 1999, 549–603.
9. But Chaplin's antifascist film *The Great Dictator* remained banned in the USSR.
10. Eisenstein and Cherkasov reconstructed this conversation from memory. See Artizov and Naumov (eds.) 612–19.
11. Aleksei Kuznetsov had temporarily taken over the government of Leningrad when Zhdanov's nerve broke. He rallied the city's population, taking his twelve-year-old son everywhere and sleeping in dugouts, not bunkers.
12. B. Kostyrchenko, *Tainaia politika Stalina,* Moscow: 2001, 229. This is the authoritative work on Stalin and the Jews: for a vivid account of the fate of the Jewish Antifascist Committee, see also Vaksberg, 1993, 222–302.
13. Kostyrchenko, 2001, 234.
14. Ibid., 514.
15. Vaksberg, 1993, 261–5.
16. Grigulevich became ambassador to the Vatican and wrote a history of the Spanish Inquisition.
17. Stalin was intrigued by group sex, to judge by his marginal comments on polygamy in Engels's book on the origin of the family.
18. Once again, Ogoltsov evaded the hot ministerial seat, but he became Ignatiev and Riumin's loyal assistant.
19. For an account of Abakumov's fate, see K. A. Stoliarov, *Palachi i zhertvy,* Moscow, 1997, 11–148.
20. This device, a denunciation from an obscure underling, had last been used by Stalin to unseat Ezhov on a similar accusation of inadequate zeal. Viktor Zhuravliov, a major from Ivanovo, was credited in November 1938 with unmasking Ezhov to the Politburo. Mediocrities like Zhuravliov and Riumin would not have risked, unprompted, such suicidal initiatives. Zhuravliov's fate (he died mysteriously, at age forty-two, in December 1946) should have given Riumin pause for thought. Sukhanov got his comeuppance in 1956, when it was discovered that he had stolen 100,000 rubles from Beria's safe on the date of his arrest. See K. A. Stoliarov, *Igry v pravosudie,* Moscow, 2000, 284–6.
21. *Timewatch,* BBC2, August 9, 2002. Kremlin doctors such as Vinogradov were so overloaded with duties as professors and editors, in addition to having to take care of caseloads of party leaders, many of whom were in bad health, that they were unfit to treat patients. Unlike Lenin and Dzierżyński, Stalin and Beria would not consult foreign doctors.
22. Vinogradov knew the dangers. In 1938 he was summoned by Ezhov as an expert to damn his colleague Dr. Pletniov. Ezhov warned him: "Bear in mind that every third person is my agent and tells me everything. I advise you to talk less."

23. Leonid Mlechin, *KGB: predsedateli organov bezopasnosti,* Moscow, 2001, 364. Mlechin's account relies on Khrushchiov's uncorroborated memoirs. When Ignatiev died in 1983, *Pravda*'s obituary praised his "modesty and sensitive attitude to people."

24. Kostyrchenko, 2001, 649.

25. The letter was never printed. The text is in Vaksberg, 1993, 295–6.

26. Ibid., 276–80.

27. "Politburo TsK" in *Sovet ministrov 1945–1953,* Moscow, 2002, 349–54.

28. Not that Georgians were a favored nation. Fewer survived interrogation in prison, and fewer males survived the war in Georgia than in other republics.

29. Ibid., 358–9.

30. See GARF 9401, 2, 99, 386. Vyshinsky dribbled while listening to his telephone and in September 1945 it stopped working. Beria immediately sent two colonels, a captain, and a major, who diagnosed moisture in the microphone and replaced it. This was reported in detail to Stalin.

31. T. V. Volokitina et al. (eds.) *Moskva i vostochnaia Evropa 1949–53,* Moscow, 2002, 518.

32. Fifteen years later, when his victims were rehabilitated, Rákosi insisted that the torture had been justified.

33. Mlechin, 2001, 562.

34. Kaganovich had had a hand in his brother's suicide in 1941: his telephone call warned Mikhail he was to be arrested.

35. Stoliarov, 2000, 212–13.

36. Mlechin, 2001, 386.

37. Pavel Sudoplatov (see *Spetsoperatsii,* Moscow, 1997, 547) claims that Beria proposed an amnesty for political prisoners too, but that this was rejected by the Presidium.

38. See A. I. Kokurin and N. V. Petrov (eds.) *GULAG 1918–1960,* Moscow, 2000, 367–72. In February 1954 Khrushchiov and Malenkov handed the GULAG and prisons back to the MVD.

39. Beria was annoyed when the Lithuanian minister for internal affairs then sent his report to Moscow in Lithuanian.

40. In May 1953 Beria found that Malenkov had copied for his own speech at the nineteenth party congress a paragraph from a speech by a Tsarist minister of the interior. Beria ignored this damning evidence against Malenkov, but the fact that he knew was brought to Malenkov's attention, a reason for the end of their alliance. See Sudoplatov, 1997, 554–5.

41. V. P. Naumov and Iu. Sigachiov, *Lavrenti Beriia 1953,* Moscow, 1999, 69–70.

42. The first publication of the unedited shorthand transcript is in Naumov and Sigachiov, 1999, 87–218.

43. The investigation dossier in the FSB archives is inaccessible, at least until 2040, when the last woman on whom Beria forced himself will have died. This account is based on the glimpses that previous researchers have had and from accounts by the investigators. See V. F. Nekrasov (ed.) *Beria: konets kar'ery,* 1991, 300–415.

44. Moskalenko suppressed evidence linking Beria's actions to Stalin's, notably the soundings in 1941–2 through the Bulgarian ambassador for peace with the Germans.

45. On May 29, 2000, the Russian supreme court reprieved three of the executed men, Dekanozov, Meshik, and Vlodzimirsky, and substituted twenty-five-year prison sentences so that their heirs could recover confiscated property. See *Izvestiia,* May 30, 2000, 1.

46. Naumov and Sigachiov, 1999, 380.

47. Imre Nagy, the prime minister of Hungary during the 1956 uprising, who was treacherously hanged on June 16, 1958, on Khrushchiov's orders, might be counted as the last of Beria's men to be executed.

48. The fate of Beria's men is recounted in Vaksberg, 1995, 112–54.

49. O. Volin, "S Berievtsami vo Vladimirskoi tiur'me" in *Minuvshee 7,* Moscow, 1992, 357–72. Chichiko Pachulia, Beria's head of the NKVD in Abkhazia, was released in 1970. He lived in Tbilisi and died suddenly outside his house while taking to the KGB a denunciation of his daughter and grandson for listening to Voice of America. See F. Blagoveshchenskii, "V gostiakh u P. A. Sharii" in *Minuvshee 7,* 472.

50. K. A. Stoliarov, 2000: 98–100. In 1994 Abakumov and his co-defendants had their crimes reclassified as not treasonable. The death sentences were not quashed but his heirs, forty years later, could recover his confiscated property.

51. Ibid., 217–18.

52. One exception is the unofficial teachers' handbook of documents on political repression and resistance to totalitarianism, produced by the Sakharov Center in Moscow: *Kniga dlia uchitelia. Istoriia politicheskikh repressii i soprotivleniia nesvobode v SSSR,* Moscow, Mosgorarkhiv, 2002.

SELECT BIBLIOGRAPHY

This is a selection of works that I have found useful. Sources to which I am heavily indebted are marked with an asterisk. A full bibliography would be the size of a monograph, and is best compiled by searching a website such as www.copac.ac.uk by subject, title, and author. Unlike in the text, where Russian names are given in a slightly simplified version of the standard Anglo-American system, here Russian names are presented in an exact transliteration.

LENINIANA

Arutiunov, Akim. *Lenin. Lichostnaia i politicheskaia biografiia.* Moscow: Veche, 2002 (2 vols.).
Latyshev, A. G. *Rassekrechennyi Lenin.* Moscow: Mart, 1996.
Lenin, V. I. *Polnoe sobranie sochinenii,* vol. 51.
*Lenin, V. I. *Neizvestnye dokumenty 1891–1922.* Moscow: ROSSPÈN, 2000.
Volkogonov, Dmitrii. *Lenin.* Moscow: Novosti, 1999 (2 vols.).

STALINIANA

Antonov-Ovseenko, A. *Teatr Iosifa Stalina.* Moscow: AST, 2000.
Brackman, Roman. *The Secret File on Joseph Stalin.* London/Portland, Ore.: Frank Cass, 2001.
Deutscher, Isaac. *Stalin: A Political Biography.* London: Pelican, 1966.
Djilas, Milovan, tr. Michael B. Petrovich. *Conversations with Stalin.* London: Pelican, 1969.
*Gromov, Evgenii Sergeevich. *Stalin: vlast' i iskusstvo.* Moscow: Izdatel'stvo Respublika, 1998.
*Ilizarov, B. S. *Tainaia zhizn' Stalina.* Moscow: Veche, 2002.
Istoricheskii arkhiv, 1994–1999 especially *Arkhiv vozhdei: posetiteli kabineta I. V. Stalina v Kremle 1924–1953.*
Kolesnik, Aleksandr. *Mify i pravda o sem'e Stalina.* Kharkov: Prostor, 1991.
Koliosov, D. V. *I. V. Stalin: pravo na vlas'.* Moscow: Flinta, 2000.
Marie, Jean-Jacques. *Staline.* Paris: Fayard, 2001.
Medvedev, Zh. A. and R. A. *Neizvestnyi Stalin.* Moscow: AST, 2002.
Mlechin, Leonid. *Smert' Stalina. Vozhd' i ego soratniki.* Moscow: Tsentrpoligraf, 2003.
*Ostrovskii, Aleksandr. *Kto stoial za spinoi Stalina.* St. Petersburg: Neva, 2002.
Radzinskii, Edvard. *Stalin.* Moscow: Vagrius, 1997.
Rayfield, D. "Stalin as Poet," *PN Review* 44, Manchester: 1984, 44–7.
Sebag-Montefiore, Simon. *Stalin: The Court of the Red Tsar.* London: Weidenfeld and Nicolson, 2003.
Ulam, Adam B. *Stalin: The Man and His Era.* London: Tauris, 1989.
Veiskopf, Mikhail. *Pisatel' Stalin.* Moscow: Novoe literaturnoe obozrenie, 2001.
Volkogonov, Dmitrii. *Stalin: triumf i tragediia.* Moscow: Novosti, 1990 (2 vols.).
Zakaridze, Nodar. *St'alini da sakartvelo.* Tbilisi: 1997.

BIOGRAPHICAL HANDBOOKS

*Borodai, A. D., Kuz'mina, A. L., Koroliov, A. A. *Politbiuro (Prezidium) TsK partii v 1917–1989 gg.: personalii: spravochnoe posobie.* Moscow: Vysshaia Komsomol'skaia Shkola Pri TsK VLKSM, Kafedra Istorii KPSS, 1990.

Istoriia politicheskikh repressii i soprotivleniia nesvobode v SSSR. Moscow: Mosgorarkhiv, 2002.

*Ivkin, V. I. *Gosudarstvennaia vlast' SSSR . . . istoriko-biograficheskii spravochnik.* Moscow: ROSSPÈN, 1999.

*Petrov, N. V., Skorkin, K. V. *Kto rukovodil NKVD 1934–1941: spravochnik.* Moscow: Zven'ia, 1999.

Torchinov, V. A., Leontiuk, A. M. *Vokrug Stalina: istoriko-biograficheskii spravochnik.* St. Petersburg: Filfak, 2000.

*Zalesskii, K. A. *Imperiia Stalina: biograficheskii èntsiklopedicheskii slovar'.* Moscow: Veche, 2000.

DOCUMENTS AND MATERIALS

Akademicheskoe delo 1929–1931, vypusk 1: delo S. F. Platonova. St. Petersburg: 1993.

*Artizov, Andrei; Naumov, Oleg (eds.). *Vlast' i khudozhestvennaia intelligentsia: dokumenty 1917–1953.* Moscow: MFD, 1999.

Butovskii poligon, 1937–1938 gg. Kniga pamiati zhertv politicheskikh repressii 1–5. Moscow: Panorama, Al'zo, 1997–2001 (5 vols.).

Cherniaev, V. Iu. (ed.). *Piterskie rabochie i «diktatura proletariata» oktiabr' 1917–1929.* St. Petersburg: BLITs, 2000.

*Danilov, V. P., Khlevniuk, O. V., Vatlin, A. Iu. (eds.). *Kak lomali NÈP: stenogrammy plenumov TsK VKP(b) 1928–1929 gg.* Moscow: MFD, 2000 (5 vols.).

Danilov, V. P., Shanin, T. (eds.). *Krest'ianskoe dvizhenie v Povolzh'e 1919–1922: dokumenty i materialy.* Moscow: ROSSPÈN, 2002.

Esakov, V. D. (ed.). *Akademiia nauk v resheniiakh Politbiuro . . . 1922–1952.* Moscow: ROSSPÈN, 2000.

Fel'shtinskii, Iu. G. (ed.). *VChK-GPU dokumenty i materialy.* Moscow: Izdatel'stvo Gumanitarnoi Literatury, 1995.

Garros, Véronique; Korenevskaya, Natalia; Lahusen, Thomas, tr. Carol A. Flath. *Intimacy and Terror: Soviet Diaries of the 1930s.* New York: The New Press, 1995.

Gromova, T. V. (ed.). *Vospominaniia krest'ian-tolstovtsev 1910–1930-e gody.* Moscow: Kniga, 1989.

Khaustov, V. N., et al. (eds.). *Lubianka. Stalin: VChK-GPU-OGPU-NKVD 1922–36.* Moscow: Materik, 2003.

*Khlevniuk, O. V. *Stalinskoe Politbiuro v 30-e gody: sbornik dokumentou.* Moscow: AIR O-XX, 1995.

Khrustaliov, V. M. (ed.). *Skorbnyi put' Romanovykh 1917–1918 gg. Gibel' tsarskoi sem'i. Sbornik dokumentov i materialov.* Moscow: ROSSPÈN, 2001.

Koenker, Diane P., Backman, Ronald D. (eds.). *Revelations from the Russian Archives.* Washington, D.C.: Library of Congress, 1997.

*Kokurin, A. I., Petrov, N. V. (eds.). *Lubianka. VChK-OGPU-NKVD-NKGB-MGB-MVD-KGB 1917–1960 spravochnik.* Moscow: MFD, 1997.

*Kokurin, A. I., Petrov, N. V. (eds.). *GULAG 1918–1960.* Moscow: MFD, 2000.

*Kozlov, V. A., Mironenko, S. V. (eds.). *«Osobaia papka» I. V. Stalina. Iz materialov Sekretariata NKVD-MVD SSSR 1944–1953 gg.* Moscow: GARF, 1994.

Krivosheeva, G. F. (ed.). *Grif sekretnosti sniat: poteri vooruzhionnykh sil SSR . . . .* Moscow: Voennoe Izdatel'stvo, 1993.

*Kvashonkin, A. V., Khlevniuk, O. V., Kosheliova, L. P., Rogovaia, L. A. (eds.). *Bol'shevistskoe rukovodstvo: perepiska, 1912–1927.* Moscow: ROSSPÈN, 1996.

*Livshin, A. Ia., Orlov, I. B., Khlevniuk, O. V. (eds.). *Pis'ma vo vlast' 1917–1927. Zaiavleniia, zhaloby, donosy . . . .* Moscow: ROSSPÈN, 1998.

Livshin, A. Ia., Orlov, I. B., Khlevniuk, O. V. (eds.). *Pis'ma vo vlast' 1928–1939. Zaiavleniia, zhaloby, donosy* . . . . Moscow: ROSSPÈN, 2002.

Menshevistskii protsess 1931 goda: sbornik dokumentov v 2-kh knigakh. Moscow: ROSSPÈN, 1999 (2 vols.).

Naumov, V. P., Kosakovskii, A. A. (eds.). *Kronstadt 1921.* Moscow: MFD, 1997.

Osipov, Iurii Sergeevich (ed.). *Akademiia nauk v resheniiakh Politbiuro TsK RKP(b)-VKP(b)-KPSS, 1922–1991.* Moscow: ROSSPÈN, 2000.

*Pis'ma I. V. Stalina V. M. Molotovu 1925–1936 gg.: sbornik dokumentov. Moscow: Rossiia Molodaia, 1995.

*Razumov, A. Ia. (ed.). Leningradskii martirolog vols. 1 4. St. Petersburg: 1995 9.

Reiman, Mikhail (ed.). "Dokumenty kanuna stalinshchiny" in *Sintaksis 13.* Paris: 1985.

*Rogovaia, L. A., Anderson, K. M., Adibekov, Grant Mkrtychevich (eds.). *TsK RKP(b)-VKP(b): katalog, I 1919–1929, II 1930–1939, III 1940–1952.* Moscow: ROSSPÈN, 2000–01 (3 vols.).

Rupasov, A. I., Ken, Oleg (eds.). *Politbiuro TsK VKP(b) i otnosheniia SSSR s zapadnymi sosednimi gosudarstvami (konets 1920–1930-kh gg.): problemy, opyt kommentarii* St. Petersburg: Evropeiskii Dom, 2000.

Russkaia pravoslavnaia tserkov' i kommunisticheskoe gosudarstvo 1917–1941: dokumenty i fotomaterialy. Moscow: Bibleisko-bogoslovskii Institut Sv. Ap. Andreiia, 1996.

Shelokhaev, V. V. (ed.). *Kniga dlia uchitelia. Istoriia politicheskikh repressii i soprotivleniia nesvobode v SSSR.* Moscow: Mosgorarkhiv, 2002.

Shishkin, V. I. (ed.). *Sibirskaia Vandeiia. Tom I 1919–1920.* Moscow: MFD, 2000.

Smirnov, M. B. (ed.). *Sistema ispravitel'no-trudovykh lagerei v SSSR, 1923 1960. Spravochnik.* Moscow: Zven'ia, 1998.

Sokolov, A. K. (ed.). *Golos naroda: pis'ma i otkliki riadovykh sovetskikh grazhdan o sobytiiakh 1918–1932.* Moscow: ROSSPÈN, 1998.

*Sovetskaia derevnia glazami VChK-OGPU: 1 1918–1922, 2 1923–1929, 3 1930–1931. Moscow: ROSSPÈN, 2000–03.

*Stalin i Kaganovich: perepiska 1931–1936 gg. Moscow: ROSSPÈN, 2001.

*Tragediia kazachestva I, II. Moscow: Terra, 1996.

*Tragediia sovetskoi derevni: dokumenty i materialy 1 1927–1929; 2 1929–1930; 3 1930–1933; 4 1934–1936. Moscow: ROSSPÈN, 1999 2002.

Vilenskii, S. S., Kokurin, A. I., et al. (eds.). *Deti GULAGa 1918–1956.* Moscow: MFD, 2002.

**Volokitina, T. V., et al. (eds.). *Iz Varshavy. Moskva, tovarishchu Beriia . . . dokumenty NKVD SSSR o pol'skom podpol'e 1944–1945 gg.* Moscow/Novosibirsk: Sibirskii Khronograf, 2001.

HISTORICAL MONOGRAPHS

*Conquest, Robert. *The Great Terror.* London: Penguin, 1971.

*Druzhnikov, Iurii. *Russkie mify: donoschik 001 ili Voznesenie Pavlika Morozova.* Ekaterinburg: U-Faktoriia, 2001.

*Geller, Mikhail, Nekrich, Aleksandr. *Utopiia u vlasti.* Moscow: MIK, 2000.

Germann, Leo. *Pravda o velikoi Izhi: 1 Vozhdi; 2 Bol'shaia voina.* St. Petersburg: Lira, 2001 (2 vols.).

Gimpel'son, E. G. *Sovetskie upravlentsy. 20-e gody.* Moscow: RAN, 2001.

Khizhniakov, S. S., Khlevniuk, O. V. *XVIII partkonferentsiia: vremia, problemy, resheniia.* Moscow: Izdatel'stvo Politicheskoi Literatury, 1990.

*Khlevniuk, O. V. *Politbiuro: mekhanizmy politicheskoi vlasti v 1930-e gody.* Moscow: ROSSPÈN, 1996.

Parnov, Eremei. *Skelety v seife.* Moscow: Terra, 2000 (2 vols.).

*Parrish, Michael. *The Lesser Terror: Soviet State Security 1939–1953.* Westport, Conn: Praeger, 1996.

Piatnitskii, Vladimir Osipovich. *Zagovor protiv Stalina.* Moscow, 1998.

*Rogovin, Vadim. *Vlast' i oppozitsiia.* Moscow: Zhurnal «Teatr», 1993.

*Rogovin, Vadim. *Stalinskii nèonèp.* Moscow, 1994.
*Rogovin, Vadim. *1937.* Moscow, 1996.
*Rogovin, Vadim. *Partiia rasstreliannykh.* Moscow: RAN, 1997.
Rogovin, Vadim. *Mirovaia revoliutsiia i mirovaia voina.* Moscow, 1998.
Rogovin, Vadim. *Konets oznachaet nachalo.* Moscow, 2002.
* Shambarov, Valerii. *Gosudarstvo i revoliutsii.* Moscow: Algoritm, 2001.
Solzhenitsyn, A. I. *Dvesti let vmeste: chast' II.* Moscow: Russkii Put', 2002.
Thurston, Robert W. *Life and Terror in Stalin's Russia 1934–1941.* London: Yale University Press, 1996.
Urch, Robert G. *The Rabbit King of Russia.* London: The Right Book Club, 1939.
*Zhiromskaia, V. B. *Naselenie Rossii v XX veke I, II.* Moscow: ROSSPÈN, 2000–01.
Zhuravliov, Sergei. *«Malen'kie liudi» i «bol'shaia istoriia».* *Inostrantsy Moskovskogo Èlektrozavoda v sovetskom obshchestve 1920-kh–1930-kh gg.* Moscow: ROSSPÈN, 2000.

SOVIET LEGAL SYSTEM

Aizenshtat, Iakov. *Zapiski sekretaria voennogo tribunala.* London, 1991.
Beda, A. M. *Sovetskaia politicheskaia kul'tura cherez prizmu MVD 1946–1958.* Moscow: Mosgorarkhiv, 2002.
Berezhkov, V. I. *Piterskie prokuratory.* St. Petersburg: BLITs, 1998.
Panov, S. *Reabilitirovan posmertno.* Moscow: Iuridicheskaia Literatura, 1988 (2 vols.).
Sheinin, L. *Zapiski sledovatelia.* Moscow: Sovetskii Pisatel', 1938.
Smirnov, N. G. *Represirovannoe pravosudie.* Moscow: Gelios ARV, 2001.
Stoliarov, K. A. *Igry v pravosudie.* Moscow: Olma, 2000.
*Vaksberg, Arkadii. *Tsaritsa dokazatel'stv: Vyshinskii i ego zhertvy.* Moscow: AO "Kniga i Biznes," 1992.
*Zviagintsev, A. G., Orlov, Iu. G. *Raspiatye revoliutsiei: rossiiskie i sovetskie prokurory 1922–1936.* Moscow: ROSSPÈN, 1998.
Zviagintsev, A. G., Orlov, Iu. G. *Prokurory dvukh èpokh: Andrei Vyshinskii, Roman Rudenko.* Moscow: Olma, 2001.

MILITARY

Belenkin, Boris. *Avantiuristy velikoi smuty.* Moscow: Olma, 2001.
Burin, Sergei. *Grigorii Kotovskii.* Moscow: Olimp, 1999.
Finkel'shtein, Iurii. *Svideteli obvineniia: Tukhachevskii, Vlasov i drugie . . .* St. Petersburg: Neva, 2001.
*Kolpakidi, Aleksandr; Prokhorov, Dmitrii. *Imperiia GRU: Ocherki istorii rossiiskoi voennoi razvedki.* Moscow: Olma, 2001.
Minakov, S. T. *Za otvorotom marshal'skoi shineli (delo Tukhachevskogo).* Oriol, 1999.
Minakov, S. T. *Sovetskaia voennaia èlita 20-x godov.* Oriol, 2000.
*Rubtsov, Iu. *Alter ègo Stalina (Mekhlis).* Moscow: Zvonnitsa MG, 1999.
Savchenko, V. I. *Avantiuristy grazhdanskoi voiny.* Moscow: Folio, 2000.
Sokolov, B. V. *Istreblionnye marshaly.* Smolensk: Rusich, 2000.
*Sokolov, B. V. *Mikhail Tukhachevskii: Zhizn' i smert' krasnogo marshala.* Smolensk: Rusich, 1998.
Voenno-istoricheskii arkhiv. Moscow: Graal', 1997, 1; 2.
Voennye arkhivy Rossii. 1993, I.

DIPLOMACY, FOREIGN INTELLIGENCE

Baltiiskii arkhiv: Russkaia kul'tura v Pribaltike. Tallinn: Avenarius; Riga: Daugava, 1999 (6 vols).

Bazhanov, Boris. *Mémoires.* Paris, 1928.
Bruce-Lockhart, R. H. *Memoirs of a British Agent.* London: Penguin Books, 1950.
Cook, Andrew. *On His Majesty's Secret Service—Sidney Reilly.* London, 2002.
Costello, J., Tsariov, O. *Deadly Illusions (The Orlov Affair).* New York: Crown, 1993.
Dullin, Sabine. *Des hommes d'influences: les ambassadeurs de Staline en Europe 1930–1939.* Paris: Payot, 2001.
Fesiun, A. G. *Delo Rikharda Zorge: neizvestnye dokumenty.* St. Petersburg: Letnii Sad, 2000.
*Gorlov, Sergei. *Alians Moskva–Berlin 1920–1933.* Moscow: Olma, 2001.
*Karner, Stefan, tr. O. Aapiaova. *Arkhipelag GUPVI.* Moscow: RGGU, 2002
Mlechin, Leonid. *Ministry inostrannykh del.* Moscow: Tsentrpoligraf, 2001.
Pynsent, Robert (ed.). *The Phoney Peace: Power and Culture in Central Europe 1945–49.* London: SSEES, 2000.
Savchenko, V. I. *Otstupnik: drama Fiodor Raskol'nikova.* Moscow: Detektiv-Press, 2001.
Shteinberg, Valentin (De-Straford). *Liubimets sluzhb i zhenshchin: Reilly, Captain Sidney.* Riga: Būdiņa, 2001.
*Vaksberg, Arkadi. *Val'kirIia Revoliutsii (Kollontai).* Smolensk: Rusich, 1998.
*Volokitina, T. V., et al. (eds.). *Moskva i vostochnaia Evropa 1949–53.* Moscow: ROSSPEN, 2002.

CHEKA-GPU-NKVD

Agabekov, G. S. *GPU—zapiski chekista.* Berlin: Strela, 1930.
Agabekov, G. S. *Cheka za robotoi.* Berlin: Strela, 1931.
Berezhkov, Vasilii. *Tainy Gorokhovoi 2. Vnutri i vne «Bol'shogo doma».* St. Petersburg: Bibliopolis, 1995.
Bogdanov, Iu. N. *Strogo sekretno. 30 let v OGPU-NKVD-MVD.* Moscow: Veche, 2002.
Chekisty: sbornik. Moscow: Molodaia Gvardiia, 1987.
Gul', Roman. *Dzerzhinskii, Menzhinskii, Peters, Latsis, Iagoda.* Paris, 1935.
Lācis, M. Ia. (Sūdrabs, J.). *Chrezvychainye komissii po bor'be s Kontr-revoliutsiei.* Moscow: Gosizdat, 1921.
Lācis, M. Ia. (Sūdrabs, J.). *Dva goda bor'by na vnutrennem fronte.* Moscow: Gosizdat, 1920.
*Mlechin, Leonid. *KGB: predsedateli organov bezopasnosti.* Moscow: Tsentrpoligraf, 2001.
*Nekrasov, V. F. *Trinadtsat' «zheleznykh» narkomov.* Moscow: Viorsty, 1995.
Papchinskii, A. A., Tumshis, M. A. *Shchit, raskolotyi mechom: NKVD protiv VChK.* Moscow: Sovremennik, 2001.
Petrov, M. N. *VChK-OGPU: pervoe desiatiletie.* Novgorod, 1995.
Popoff, George. *The Tcheka: The Red Inquisition.* London: Philpot, 1925.
*Sokolov, B. V. *Narkomy strakha.* Moscow: AST, 2001.
*Stoliarov, K. A. *Palachi i zhertvy.* Moscow, 1997.
Sudoplatov, Pavel. *Spetsoperatsii: Lubianka i Kreml' 1930–1950 gody.* Moscow: Olma, 1997.
Sysoev, N. G. *Zhandarmy i chekisty. Ot Benkendorfa do Iagody.* Moscow: Veche, 2002.
Zhukovskii, V. S. *Lubianskaia imperiia NKVD.* Moscow: Veche, 2001.
20 let VChk-OGPU-NKVD. Moscow, 1937.

BIOGRAPHICAL MATERIAL

DZIERŻYŃSKI
Blobaum, Robert. *Feliks Dzierżyński and the SDKPil.* New York: Columbia University Press, 1984.
Dzierżyńska, Zofia. *Lata wielkich bojów.* Warsaw: Książka i Wiedza, 1969.

Dzierżyński, Feliks. *Listy do siostry Aldony.* Warsaw, 1951.
Dzierżyński, Feliks. *Pisma wybrane.* Warsaw: Książka i Wiedza, 1952.
Feliks Dzierżyński: we wspomnieniach i wypowiedziach. Warsaw, 1951.
Ivanov, A. *Neizvestnyi Dzerzhinskii.* Moscow, 1993.
Jaxa-Ronickier, Bogdan. *Dzierżyński, czerwony kat.* Kraków, 1990.
Lācis, M. "Dzierżyńskii Cheka," in *F. Dzierżyński.* Moscow, 1931.
Łątka, Jerzy S. *Krwawy apostol.* Kraków, 1993.
Zarkhii, S. *Narkomput' F. Dzerzhinskii.* Moscow: Transport, 1979.

MENZHINSKY

Gladkov, Teodor; Smirnov, Mikhail. *Menzhinskii.* Moscow: Molodaia Gvardiia, 1969.
O Viacheslave Menzhinskom. Moscow, 1985.

IAGODA

*Il'inskii, Mikhail. *Narkom Iagoda.* Moscow: Veche, 2002.
Kovaliov, V. A. *Dva stalinskikh narkoma.* Moscow: Progress, 1995.

EZHOV

Briukhanov, B. B., Shoshkov, E. N. *Opravdaniiu ne podlezhit: Ezhov i ezhovsh-china 1936–1938 gg.* St. Petersburg, 1998.
*Jansen, Marc; Petrov, Nikita. *Stalin's Loyal Executioner: Ezhov.* Stanford, Calif.: Hoover Press, 2002.
*Polianskii, Aleksei. *Ezhov.* Moscow: Veche, 2001.

BERIA

*Antonov-Ovseenko, A. *Beriia.* Moscow: AST, 1999.
*Naumov, V. P., Sigachiov, Iu. *Lavrentii Beriia, 1953. Stenogramma iiul'skogo plenuma TsK KPSS i drugie dokumenty.* Moscow: MFD, 1999.
*Nekrasov, V. F. (ed.). *Beria: konets kar'ery.* Moscow: Politizdat, 1991.
Rayfield, D. "Beria's Holocaust" in *The Literature of Georgia—A History.* Richmond U.K.: Curzon Press, 2000.
Sigua, Aleksandre. *Mkvleloba berias k'abinet'shi.* Tbilisi: Molodini, 1992.
Sokolov, Boris. *Beriia. Sud'ba vsesil'nogo narkoma.* Moscow: Veche, 2003.
Toptygin, Aleksei. *Neizvestnyi Beriia.* St. Petersburg: Neva, 2002.
*Volin, O. "S Berievtsami vo Vladimirskoi tiur'me" and Blagoveshchenskii, F. "V gosti-akh u P. A. Sharii" in *Minuvshee 7.* Moscow: 1992.

OTHER *CHEKISTY*

Clarke, F. G. *The Will of the Wisp (Peter the Painter).* Melbourne: Oxford University Press, 1983.
Gladkov, Teodor. *Nagrada za vernost'—kazn' (Artuzov).* Moscow: Tsentrpoligraf, 2000.
Gore, I., Niedre, O. *Mārtiņš Lācis—čekists un literāts.* Riga: Avots, 1989.
*Shteinberg, Valentin. *Ekab Peters.* Moscow: Izdatel'stvo Politicheskoi Literatury, 1989.
Shteinberg, Valentin. *Svecha na vetru.* Zemlia (Riga) January 5–February 2, 1993.

POLITBURO MEMBERS

Bukharin, N. I. *Tiuremnye tetradi.* Moscow, 1994.
Ch'eishvili, Rezo. *rk'inis sakhk'omi* (Orjonik'idze). Tbilisi: Merani, 1992.
Chuev, Feliks. *Tak govoril Kaganovich.* Moscow, 1992.
Chuev, Feliks. *Molotov: poluderzhavnyi vlastelin.* Moscow: Olma, 2002.
*Deutscher, Isaac. *The Prophet Armed. Trotsky: 1879–1921; The Prophet Unarmed. Trotsky 1921–1929; The Prophet Outcast. Trotsky 1929–1940.* Oxford: Oxford University Press, 1970 (3 vols.).
*Fel'shtinskii, Iu. G. *Razgovory s Bukharinym.* Moscow: Izdatel'stvo Gumanitarnoi Literatury, 1993.

Gorelov, O. I. *Tsugtsvang Mikhaila Tomskogo.* Moscow: ROSSPÈN, 2000.

*Khlevniuk, O. V. *Stalin i Ordzhonikidze: konflikt v Politbiuro v 30-e gody.* Moscow: Rossiia Molodaia, 1993.

*Kirilina, Alla. *Neizvestnyi Kirov.* St. Petersburg: Neva, 2001.

*Krasnov, V., Daines., V. *Neizvestnyi Trotskii.* Moscow: Olma, 2000.

Rosliakov, Mikhail. *Ubiistvo Kirova.* Leningrad: Leninizdat, 1991.

*Volkogonov, Dmitrii. *Trotskii I, II.* Moscow: Novosti, 1999.

INTELLIGENTSIA: WRITERS, SCIENTISTS, ETC.

Ashnin, F. D., Alpatov, V. M. *«Delo slavistov» 30-e gody.* Moscow: Nasledie, 1994.

*Azadovskii, Konstantin. *Zhizn' Nikolaia Kliueva.* St. Petersburg: Zvezda, 2002.

Babichenko, D. L. *Schast'e literatury: gosudarstvo i pisateli 1925–1938.* Moscow, 1997.

*Baranov, Vadim. *Bezzakonnaia kometa: rokovaia zhenshchina Maksima Gor'kogo.* Moscow: Agraf, 2001.

*Baranov, Vadim. *Gor'kii bez grima: Taina smerti.* Moscow: Agraf, 2001.

Belomorsko-Baltiiskii Kanal imeni Stalina. Moscow: Ogiz, 1934 (1998).

Blium, A. V. *Za kulisami «ministerstva pravdy».* St. Petersburg, 1994.

*Blium, A. V. *Sovetskaia tsenzura v èpokhu total'nogo terrora 1929–1953.* St. Petersburg: Akademicheskii Proekt, 2000.

Chernobaev, A. A. *Professor s pikoi (M. Pokrovskii).* Moscow, 1992.

Dinershtein E. A. *A. K. Voronskii: v poiskakh zhivoi vody.* Moscow: ROSSPÈN, 2001.

Ètkind, Aleksandr. *Èros nevozmozhnogo.* St. Petersburg: Meduza, 1993.

Forsh, Ol'ga. *Sumashedshii korab'.* Washington, D.C.: ILLA, 1964.

*Fradkin, Viktor. *Delo Kol'tsova.* Moscow: Vagrius, 2002.

*Heinemann, Manfred; Kolchinskii, È. I. *Za «zheleznym zanavesom»: mify i realii sovetskoi nauki.* St. Petersburg: IIET RAN, 2002.

Iaroshevskii, M. G. (ed.). *Repressirovannaia nauka.* Leningrad: Nauka, 1991.

Ivanov-Razumnik (Ivanov, Razumnik Vasil'evich). *Tiur'my i ssylki.* New York: Izdatel'stvo Chekhova, 1953.

Kapitsa, Tamm. *Semionov v ocherkakh i pis'makh.* Moscow: Vagrius, 1998.

Koliazin, V. F., Goncharov, V. A. (eds.). *«Vernite mne svobodu» Deiateli literatury i iskusstva Rossii i Germanii—zhertvy stalinskogo terrora.* Moscow: Medium, 1997.

Kumaniov, V. A. *30-e gody v sud'bakh otechestvennoi intelligentsii.* Moscow: Nauka, 1991.

*Kuniaev, S. Iu., Kuniaev S. S. *Rasterzannye teni.* Moscow: Golos, 1995.

Medvedev, Zhorès, A., tr. I. Michael Lerner. *The Rise and Fall of Lysenko.* New York: Columbia University Press, 1969.

*Murin, Iu. G. *Pisatel' i vozhd': perepiska M. A. Sholokhova s. I. V. Stalinym.* Moscow: Raritet, 1997.

Neroznak, V. P. (ed.). *Sumerki lingvistiki: iz istorii otechestvennogo iazykoznaniia.* Moscow: Academia, 2001.

Pavlov I. P.: pro et contra: antologiia. St. Petersburg: RKhGU, 1999.

Rokitianskii, Ia. G., Vavilov, Iu. N., Goncharov, V. A. *Sud palacha. Nikolai Vavilov v zastenkakh NKVD.* Moscow: Academia, 1999.

Sakharov, Vsevolod. *Mikhail Bulgakov: pisatel' i vlast'.* Moscow: Olma, 2000.

*Shentalinskii, Vitalii. *Raby svobody.* Moscow, 1995.

*Shentalinskii, Vitalii. *Donos na Sokrat.* Moscow: Formica-S, 2001.

Shnol, S. È. *Geroi i zlodei rossiiskoi nauki.* Moscow: Kron-Press, 1997.

Smith, G. S. *Dmitri Sviatopolk-Mirsky.* Cambridge, U.K.: Cambridge University Press, 2000.

Vaksberg, Arkadii. *Gibel' Burevestnika: M. Gor'kii—poslednie dvadtsat' let.* Moscow: Terra-Sport, 1999.

Zabolotskii, Nikita. *Zhizn' N. A. Zabolotskogo.* Moscow: Soglasie, 1998.

Zelenov, M. V. *Apparat TsK RKP(b) VKP (b): tsenzura i istoricheskaia nauka v 1920-e gody.* Nizhni Novgorod, 2000.

CHURCH
*Krivova, N. A. *Vlast' i tserkov'v 1922–1925 gg.* Moscow, 1997.
*Pokrovskii, Nikolai Nikolaevich, Petrov, S. G. (eds.). *Politbiuro i tserkov': 1922–1925 gg.* Novosibirsk: Sibirskii Khronograf; Moscow: ROSSPÈN, 1997–8 (2 vols.).

GULAG, DEPORTATIONS, AND MASSACRES
Abarinov, V. K. *Katynskii labirint.* Moscow, 1991.
*Alieva, Svetlana (ed.). *Tak èto bylo: natsional'nye repressii v SSSR 1919–1952 gody.* Moscow: Insan, 1993 (3 vols.).
*Anchabadze, George. *The Vainakhs.* Tbilisi: Caucasian House, 2001.
Applebaum, Anne. *GULAG: A History of the Soviet Camps.* London: Allen Lane, 2003.
Bugai N. *«Ikh nado deportirovat'».* Moscow, 1992.
Katyń: Dokumenty zbrodni. Warsaw, 1998 (4 vols.).
*Kozlov, V. P., Nałęccz, D., et al. (eds.). *Katyn': mart 1940 g.—sentiabr' 2000 g.* Moscow: Ves' Mir, 2001.
Oleskiw, Stephen. *The Agony of a Nation.* London: Ukrainian Publishers, 1983.
*Pikhoia, R. G., Geisztor, A., et al. (eds.). *Katyn': plenniki neob"iavlennoi voiny.* Moscow: MFD, 1999.
*Polian, Pavel. *Ne po svoei vole: Istoriia i geografiia prinuditel'nykh migratsii v SSSR.* Moscow: Memorial, 2001.

JEWISH QUESTION

Arad, Yitzhak. *Unichtozhenie evreev SSSR v gody nemetskoi okkupatsii.* Jerusalem: Yad Vashem, 1992.
Blium, A. V. *Evreiskii vopros pod sovetskoi tsenzuroi.* St. Petersburg, 1996.
Gusarov, Vladimir. *Moi papa ubil Mikhoèlsa.* Frankfurt-am-Main: Posev, 1978.
*Kostyrchenko, G. B. *Tainaia politika Stalina.* Moscow: Mezhdunarodnye otnosheniia, 2001.
Nikolaev, Vladimir. *Stalin, Gitler i my.* Moscow: Prava Cheloveka, 2002.
*Vaksberg, Arkadii. *Neraskrytye tainy.* Moscow: Novosti, 1993.

JOURNALS (MAINLY 1989–2002)

Istochnik
**Istoricheskii arkhiv*
**Minuvshee: Istoricheskii al'manakh, 1–25.* St. Petersburg: Atheneum/Feniks, 1990–99 (25 vols.).
Svobodnaia mysl' 1999–2001
**Voenno-istoricheskii arkhiv*
Voprosy istoriii, esp. 1992, 2–12: records for February–March 1937 plenum.
**Zven'ia: istoricheskii al'manakh I, II.* Moscow: Atheneum, 1991–2 (2 vols.).

MAIN ARCHIVAL RESOURCES (NUMBERS INDICATE *FOND, OPIS, DELO,* AND PAGE NUMBERS)

Georgian Central State Archive for Literature and Art (STsLKhA) 8, 1.
State Archive of the Russian Federation (GARF) FR 9401, 2, 64–269 (Osobaia papka Stalina); FR 9462 (Zinov'ev); FR 9189, 1 (Voroshilov).
Russian State Archive of Social-Political History (GASPI) 2, 2, 380; 17, 3 (literature); 71, 1; 76 (Dzierżyński); 142 (literature); 558, 1–11 (Stalin).
Manuscript department of the Russian State Library (OR) 365 Bonch-Bruevich.
Russian State Archive of Literature and Art (RGALI) 427 (Menzhinsky).

VARIOUS

Filevskii, P. P. *Ocherki iz proshlogo Taganrogskoi gimnazii.* Taganrog, 1906.

Gamsakhurdia, K. *Davit Aghmashenebeli.* Tbilisi, 1942.

Getty, J. Arch. "Excesses are not permitted: mass terror and Stalinist governance in the later 1930s," in *Russian Review* 61, 1. January 2002, 113–38.

Gogebashvili, Iakob. *Rcheuli tkhzulebani* (vol. 2). Tbilisi, 1990.

Hook, Sidney. "A Recollection of Bertholt Brecht" in *The New Leader,* October 10, 1960.

*Jikhashvili, Musto. *Kavkazskoe safari Iosifa Stalina* (forthcoming).

Khronika Rossii. dvadtsatyi vek. Moscow: Slovo, 2002.

Koroliov, S. *Donos v Rossii.* Moscow, 1996.

Kraskova, Valentina. *Kremliovskie deti.* Minsk: Belarest, 1995.

*Lakoba, Stanislav. *Ocherki politicheskoi istorii Abkhazii.* Sukhum: Alashara, 1990.

Maggs, Peter B. *The Mandelstam and "Der Nister" Files.* London/New York: M. E. Sharpe, 1995.

Makarenko, V. P. *Biurokratiia i stalinizm.* Rostov-on-Don: Rostovskii universitet, 1989.

Robakidze, Grigol. *Die gemordete Seele.* Jena: Diderichs, 1933.

Sapov, V. V. (ed.). *Makiavelli: pro i kontra.* St. Petersburg: R GKhI, 2002.

Sarnov, Benedikt. *Nash sovetskii novoiaz.* Moscow: Materik, 2002.

Shalamov, Varlam. *Vospominaniia.* Moscow: Olimp, 2001.

Solzhenitsyn, A. I. (ed.). *Pozhivshi v GULAGe: sbornik vospominanii.* Moscow: Russkii Put', 2001.

*Vasil'eva, Larisa. *Kremliovskie zhiony.* Moscow: AST, 2001.

Wells, H. G. *Experiment in Autobiography,* 1934.

INDEX

This index includes all personal names, all important place-names, and the names of key institutions and events that figure in the text and notes. Wherever ascertainable, dates of birth and death are given, with a very brief annotation on the person's job and death. Figures better known by pseudonyms are listed under these with actual names given in parentheses.

Polish and other east European names are given in the Latin orthography of the language. Georgian names are transliterated directly from Georgian.

Index

Index

About the Author

DONALD RAYFIELD is professor of Russian and Georgian at the University of London and the author of a number of books on Russian writers and intellectuals, including an acclaimed biography of Anton Chekhov.

About the Type

This book was set in Times New Roman, designed by Stanley Morrison specifically for *The Times* of London. The typeface was introduced in the newspaper in 1932. Times New Roman has had its greatest success in the United States as a book and commercial typeface rather than one used in newspapers.